For Reference

Not to be taken from this room

FILM DIRECTORS:
A Guide to Their American Films

by

JAMES ROBERT PARISH

and

MICHAEL R. PITTS

research associate:

William T. Leonard

research assistants:

Pierre Guinle, Norman Miller,

Florence Solomon

75074

The Scarecrow Press, Inc.

Metuchen, N.J.   1974

ACKNOWLEDGMENTS

Richard Bojarski, Michael A. Brown, Bruco Enterprises, Loraine Burdick, Cinemabilia Book Shop (Ernest Burns), John Robert Cocchi, Morris Everett, Jr., Olivier Eyquem, Mrs. R. F. Hastings, Doug McClelland, Albert B. Manski, Jim Meyer, Peter Miglierini, Movie Poster Service (Bob Smith), Connie Staton, Charles K. Stumpf, T. Allan Taylor, Lou Valentino.

Library of Congress Cataloging in Publication Data

Parish, James Robert.
    Film directors: a guide to their American films.

    1. Moving-pictures--Catalogs. 2. Moving-picture producers and directors--United States. I. Pitts, Michael R., joint author. II. Title.
PN1998.P24   791.43'0233'0922   74-17398
ISBN 0-8108-0752-1

for

D. W. GRIFFITH

1875-1948

PREFACE

Only in recent decades has the crucial category of film directors begun to receive its proper aesthetic and scholarly due from cinema writers and researchers. The goal of this volume is to provide a single compendium of domestic and international motion picture directors who have contributed feature-length productions to the American cinema. It is hoped that the following checklists will offer film enthusiasts the needed opportunity to survey a craftsman's output to date and observe the progression and patterns of the subject's career.

Entries include only "full-length" films of over four reels or 40 minutes and only films in which the subject was at least the director. Motion pictures produced in countries other than the United States or England are designated by nation of origin. Those films designated with an asterisk are serials.

We have based our selection of directors on a desire to offer in a manageably sized book a wide spectrum of professionals who have been employed at major or poverty row studios in grade A to Z features, serials, or documentaries, and in the silent and sound eras; obviously this has meant that many directors have been omitted who might have been included--such as, for example, Clarence G. Badger, E. H. Calvert, Charles Giblyn, Burton L. King, Wilfred North, Arthur Rosson, George Terwilliger, Travers Vale, and James Young. Among the newer breed of film directors not included in this initial volume are: George Armitage, Arthur Barron, George Fenady, James Frawley, Bruce Geller, Jack Hill, Charles Jarott, Vincent McEverty, Andy Milligan, Paul Morrissey, Gordon Parks, Jr., Jack Starrett, and Mel Stuart. The prolific output of most underground, sexploitation, and regional directors must be left for a follow-up edition.

We would be most grateful for any suggestions, corrections, or additions that any reader cares to provide.

January 14, 1974

James Robert Parish
2039 Broadway 17F
New York City 10023

Michael R. Pitts
910 West 6th Street #3
Anderson, Indiana 46016

KEY TO ABBREVIATIONS

AA	Allied Artists Pictures Corporation
AIP	American International Pictures
Artcraft	Artcraft-Paramount
Associated FN	Associated First National Pictures, Inc. (later part of Warner Bros., Inc.)
Avco Emb.	Avco Embassy Pictures Corporation
BV	Buena Vista Distribution
Cin.	Cinerama Releasing Corporation
Col.	Columbia Pictures Industries, Inc.
Emb.	Embassy Pictures
ep	episode
FBO	Film Booking Offices
FN	First National Pictures, Inc. (later part of Warner Bros., Inc.)
Fox	Fox Film Corporation
GN	Grand National
Lip.	Lippert Pictures Inc.
Metro-Goldwyn	Metro-Goldwyn Distributing Corporation (later part of Metro-Goldwyn-Mayer, Inc.)
MGM	Metro-Goldwyn-Mayer, Inc.
Mon.	Monogram Pictures Corporation
Par.	Paramount Pictures Corporation
PDC	Producers Distributing Corporation
PRC	Producers Releasing Corporation
Rank	J. Arthur Rank Film Distributors, Ltd.
Rep.	Republic Pictures Corporation
20th	Twentieth Century-Fox Film Corporation
UA	United Artists Corporation
Univ.	Universal Pictures, Inc.
WB	Warner Bros., Inc.
WB-7 Arts	Warner Bros.-Seven Arts, Inc.
*	denotes a serial

ADAMSON, AL.
Two Tickets to Terror (Victor Adamson, 1964)
Blood of Dracula's Castle (Crown-International, 1969) (also co-producer)
Satan's Sadists (Independent-International, 1969) (also producer)
Five Bloody Graves (Independent-International, 1970) (also producer)
Hell's Bloody Devils (Independent-International, 1970) (also producer)
Horror of the Blood Monsters (Independent-International, 1970) (also producer)
Dracula vs. Frankenstein (Independent-International, 1971) (also producer)
The Female Bunch (Dalia, 1971)
Last of the Comancheros (Independent-International, 1971) (also producer)
Blood of Ghastly Horror (Independent-International, 1972) (also producer)
The Brain of Blood (Hemisphere, 1972)

ADAMSON, VICTOR (Denver Dixon), b. 1890, Kansas City, Mo.; d. Nov. 9, 1972.
The White Rider (Independent, 1918)
The Lone Rider (Rollo Sales Corp., 1922) (with Fred Campbell) (also co-script, actor)
Pioneer's Gold (Sanford, 1924)
Ace of the Cactus Ranch (Aywon, 1924) (with Malon Andrus)
Riders of Mystery Range (Aywon, 1924)
Romance of the Wasterland (Aywon, 1924)
Terror of Pueblo (Aywon, 1924)
South of Santa Fe (Aywon, 1924)
Rider of Border Bay (Aywon, 1925)
Compassion (Victor Adamson, 1927) (with Norral McGregor) (also co-producer)
The Old Oregon Trail (Art Mix, 1928) (also producer and actor)
Sweeping Against the Winds (Victor Adamson, 1930)
Desert Vultures (Art Mix, 1930)
Sagebrush Politics (Hollywood Pictures, 1930)
Lightning Bill (Art Mix, 1931)
Rawhide Romance (Art Mix, 1931)
Fighting Romance (Art Mix, 1931)

Ridin' Speed (Art Mix, 1931)
Boss Cowboy (Superior, 1932)
Range Busters (Superior, 1932)
Circle Canyon (Superior, 1932)
Lightning Range (Superior, 1932)
Arizona Trail (Independent, 1934)
Desert Mesa (Security, 1936) (also producer, actor)
Mormon Conquest (Art Mix, 1938) (also producer, actor)
Halfway to Hell (Victor Adamson, 1963)

ADOLFI, JOHN G., b. Feb. 19, 1888, New York City; d. May 10, 1933.
The Man Inside (Reliance, 1915)
A Man and His Mate (Reliance, 1915)
Little Miss Happiness (Fox, 1916)
The Ragged Princess (Fox, 1916)
The Sphinx (Univ., 1916)
The Mischief Maker (Fox, 1916)
The Road to Nowhere (Fox, 1916)
Merely Mary Ann (Fox, 1916)
A Modern Thelma (Fox, 1916)
Patsy (Fox, 1916)
A Small Town Girl (Fox, 1917)
A Child of the Wild (Fox, 1917)
A Modern Cinderella (Fox, 1917)
The Heart of a Girl (World, 1918)
Queen of the Sea (Fox, 1918)
The Cavell Case (Select, 1918)
The Wonder Man (Robertson-Cole, 1919)
Who's Your Brother (Curtiss, 1919)
Keep to the Right (World, 1920)
The Little 'Fraid Lady (Robertson-Cole, 1920)
The Darling of the Rich (Selznick, 1922)
The Little Red Schoolhouse (Arrow, 1923)
What Shall I Do? (W. W. Hodkinson, 1924)
Chalk Marks (PDC, 1924)
The Scarlet West (FN, 1925)
Big Pal (Royal, 1925)
Before Midnight (Henry Ginsberg Distributing, 1925)
The Phantom Express (Henry Ginsberg Distributing, 1925)
The Checkered Flag (Banner, 1926)
Husband Hunters (Tiffany, 1927)
What Happened to Father? (WB, 1927)
The Devil's Skipper (Tiffany-Stahl, 1928)
The Little Snob (WB, 1928)
Prowlers of the Sea (Tiffany-Stahl, 1928)
The Midnight Taxi (WB, 1928)
Sinner's Parade (Col., 1928)
Fancy Baggage (WB, 1929)
In the Headlines (WB, 1929)
Evidence (WB, 1929)
The Show of Shows (WB, 1929)

Recaptured Love (WB, 1930)
Dumbbells in Ermine (WB, 1930)
College Lovers (FN, 1930)
Sinner's Holiday (WB, 1930)
The Millionaire (WB, 1931)
Alexander Hamilton (WB, 1931)
Compromised (FN, 1931)
The Man Who Played God (WB, 1932)
A Successful Calamity (WB, 1932)
Central Park (WB, 1932)
The King's Vacation (WB, 1933)
The Working Man (WB, 1933)
Voltaire (WB, 1933)

ALDRICH, ROBERT, b. Aug. 9, 1918, Cranston, R. I.
The Big Leaguer (MGM, 1953)
World for Ransom (AA, 1954) (also co-producer)
Apache (UA, 1954)
Vera Cruz (UA, 1954)
Kiss Me Deadly (UA, 1955) (also producer)
The Big Knife (UA, 1955) (also producer)
Autumn Leaves (Col., 1956)
Attack (UA, 1956) (also producer)

Joan Crawford and Bette Davis with Robert Aldrich on set of What Ever Happened to Baby Jane? (WB, 1962).

The Garment Jungle (Col., 1957) (uncredited, with Vincent
    Sherman)
The Angry Hills (MGM, 1959)
Ten Seconds to Hell (UA, 1959) (also co-script)
The Last Sunset (Univ., 1961)
Sodom and Gomorrah (Rank, 1962) (with Sergio Leone)
What Ever Happened to Baby Jane? (WB, 1962) (also producer)
Four for Texas (WB, 1963) (also producer, co-script)
Hush ... Hush, Sweet Charlotte (20th, 1965) (also producer)
The Flight of the Phoenix (20th, 1965) (also producer)
The Dirty Dozen (MGM, 1967)
The Legend of Lylah Clare (MGM, 1968) (also producer)
The Killing of Sister George (Cin., 1969) (also producer)
Too Late The Hero (Cin., 1970) (also producer, co-story, co-
    script)
The Grissom Gang (Cin., 1971) (also producer)
Ulzana's Raid (Univ., 1972)
The Emperor of the North Pole (20th, 1973)

ALLEN, IRWIN, b. June 12, 1916, New York City.
The Animal World (WB, 1956) (also producer, script)
The Story of Mankind (WB, 1957) (also producer, co-script)
The Lost World (20th, 1960) (also producer, co-script)
Voyage to the Bottom of the Sea (20th, 1961) (also producer,
    co-story, co-script)
Five Weeks in a Balloon (20th, 1962) (also producer, co-script)
City Beneath the Sea (ABC-TV, 1971)

ALLEN, WOODY (Allen Stewart Konigsberg), b. Dec. 1, 1935,
    Brooklyn, N.Y.
Take the Money and Run (Cin., 1969) (also co-story, co-script,
    actor)
Bananas (UA, 1971) (also co-story, co-script, actor)
Play It Again, Sam (Par., 1972) (also original play, script,
    actor)
Everything You Always Wanted to Know About Sex But Were
    Afraid to Ask (UA, 1972) (also script, actor)
Sleeper (UA, 1973) (also co-script, music, actor)

ALTMAN, Robert, b. Feb. 20, 1925, Kansas City, Mo.
The Delinquents (UA, 1957) (also producer)
The James Dean Story (WB, 1957)
Nightmare in Chicago (Univ., 1967) (also producer)
Countdown (WB-7 Arts, 1968)
That Cold Day in the Park (Commonwealth United, 1969)
M.A.S.H. (20th, 1970)
Brewster McCloud (MGM, 1970)
McCabe & Mrs. Miller (WB, 1971) (also co-script)
Images (Col., 1972) (also script)
The Long Goodbye (UA, 1973)

Julie Christie and Warren Beatty with Robert Altman on set of
McCabe & Mrs. Miller (WB, 1971).

AMATEAU, ROD (Rodney Amateau), b. Dec. 20, 1923, New York
   City.
   The Bushwhackers (Realart, 1951) (also script)
   Monsoon (UA, 1952)
   Pussycat, Pussycat, I Love You (UA, 1970) (also story, script)
   The Statue (Cin., 1971)
   Where Does It Hurt? (Cin., 1972) (also co-producer, script)

ANDERSON, MICHAEL, b. Jan. 20, 1920, London.
   Private Angelo (Associated British-Pathé, 1949) (with Peter
      Ustinov)
   Hell Is Sold Out (Eros, 1951)
   Night Was Our Friend (Monarch, 1951)
   House of the Arrow (Associated British-Pathé, 1952)
   Waterfront Women (Rank, 1952)
   Will Any Gentleman? (Associated British, 1953)
   The Dam Busters (Associated British, 1955)
   1984 (Col., 1956)
   Around the World in 80 Days (UA, 1956)

Yangtse Incident (British Lion, 1957)
Chase a Crooked Shadow (Associated British, 1958)
Shake Hands With the Devil (UA, 1959) (also producer)
The Wreck of the Mary Deare (MGM, 1959)
All the Fine Young Cannibals (MGM, 1960)
The Naked Edge (UA, 1961)
Wild and Wonderful (Univ., 1963)
Flight from Ashiya (UA, 1964)
Operation Crossbow (MGM, 1964)
The Quiller Memorandum (20th, 1967)
The Shoes of the Fisherman (MGM, 1968)
Pope Joan [The Devil's Imposter] (Col., 1972)

ANTHONY, JOSEPH (Joseph Anthony Deuster), b. May 24, 1912,
    Milwaukee.
The Rainmaker (Par., 1956)
The Matchmaker (Par., 1958)
Career (Par., 1959)
All in a Night's Work (Par., 1961)
Conquered City (AIP, 1966)
Tomorrow (Filmgroup, 1972)

APFEL, OSCAR C., b. Cleveland; d. March 21, 1938.
The Man on the Box (Par., 1914) (with Cecil B. DeMille, Wil-
    fred Buckland)
Brewster's Millions (Par., 1914) (with Cecil B. DeMille)
Cameo Kirby (Par., 1914)
The Circus Man (Par., 1914)
The Ghost Breaker (Par., 1914) (with Cecil B. DeMille)
The Last Volunteer (Pathé, 1914)
The Master Mind (Par., 1914) (with Cecil B. DeMille)
The Only Son (Par., 1914) (with Cecil B. DeMille)
Ready Money (Par., 1914)
A Soldier's Oath (Par., 1914)
The Broken Law (Fox, 1915)
Kilmeny (Par., 1915)
Peer Gynt (Par., 1915)
The Wild Olive (Par., 1915)
The Rug Maker's Daughter (Par., 1915)
The Battle of Hearts (Fox, 1916)
The End of the Trail (Fox, 1916)
Fighting Blood (Fox, 1916)
The Fires of Conscience (Fox, 1916)
The Hidden Children (Metro, 1917)
A Man's Man (Par., 1917)
The Price of Her Soul (Variety, 1917)
The Turn of a Card (W.W. Hodkinson, 1918)
The Interloper (World, 1918)
Tinsel (World, 1918)
Merely Players (World, 1918)
To Him That Hath (World, 1918)

The Grouch (World, 1918)
The Roughneck (World, 1919)
Phil-for-Short (World, 1919)
Mandarin's Gold (World, 1919)
The Little Intruder (World, 1919)
Crook of Dreams (World, 1919)
Bringing Up Betty (World, 1919)
The Amateur Widow (World, 1919)
Me and Captain Kidd (World, 1919)
The Oakdale Affair (World, 1919)
The Steel King (World, 1919)
Ten Nights in a Bar Room (Arrow, 1921)
The Man Who Paid (Producers Security, 1922)
Bulldog Drummond (W.W. Hodkinson, 1922)
Auction of Souls (Associated FN, 1922)
The Wolf's Fangs (Producers Security, 1922) (also for own
   production company)
Lion's Mouse (W.W. Hodkinson, 1923)
In Search of a Thrill (Metro, 1923)
A Man's Man (FBO, 1923)
The Social Code (Metro, 1923)
Trail of the Law (Producers Security, 1924)
The Heart Bandit (Metro, 1924)
Trail of the Law (Producers Security, 1924) (also for own pro-
   duction company)
The Sporting Chance (Truart Film, 1925)
The Thoroughbred (Truart Film, 1925)
Borrowed Finery (Tiffany, 1925)
Midnight Limited (Rayart, 1926)
Perils of the Coast Guard (Rayart, 1926)
Somebody's Mother (Rayart, 1926)
Race Wild (Elbee, 1926)
The Last Alarm (Rayart, 1926)
The Call of the Klondike (Rayart, 1926)
Cheaters (Tiffany, 1927)
When Seconds Count (Rayart, 1927)
Code of the Cow Country (Pathé, 1927)

ARCHAINBAUD, GEORGE, b. May 7, 1890, Paris; d. Feb. 20,
   1959.
The Iron Ring (World, 1917)
As Man Made Her (World, 1917)
The Brand of Satan (World, 1917)
Yankee Pluck (World, 1917)
A Maid of Belgium (Peerless-World, 1917)
The Awakening (Peerless-World, 1917)
Diamonds and Pearls (Peerless-World, 1918)
The Divine Sacrifice (Peerless-World, 1918)
The Cross Bearer (Peerless-World, 1918)
The Trap (Peerless-World, 1918)
Love Cheat (Pathé, 1918)
A Damsel in Distress (Pathé, 1919)
In Walked Mary (Pathé, 1920)

The Shadow of Rosalie Byrne (Select, 1920)
One Week of Love (Selznick, 1920)
What Women Want (Pioneer, 1920)
The Wonderful Chance (Selznick, 1920)
Marooned Hearts (Selznick, 1920)
Pleasure Seekers (Selznick, 1921)
The Miracle of Manhattan (Selznick, 1921)
The Girl from Nowhere (Selznick, 1921)
Handcuffs or Kisses (Selznick, 1921)
Clay Dollars (Selznick, 1921)
The Man of Stone (Selznick, 1921)
Evidence (Selznick, 1922)
Under Oath (Selznick, 1922)
Power of a Lie (Univ., 1923)
The Midnight Guest (Univ., 1923)
Cordelia the Magnificent (Metro, 1923)
The Common Law (Selznick, 1923)
The Shadow of the East (Fox, 1924)
For Sale (FN, 1924)
The Plunderer (Fox, 1924)
Single Wives (FN, 1924)
The Storm Daughter (Univ.-Jewel, 1924)
Christine of the Hungry Heart (FN, 1924)
The Mirage (PDC, 1924)
Enticement (FN, 1925)
The Necessary Evil (FN, 1925)
What Fools Men (FN, 1925)
Scarlet Saint (FN, 1925)
Puppets (FN, 1926)
Men of Steel (FN, 1926)
The Silent Lover (FN, 1926)
Easy Pickings (FN, 1927)
Night Life (Tiffany, 1927)
The Man in Hobbles (Tiffany-Stahl, 1928)
Bachelor's Paradise (Tiffany-Stahl, 1928)
The Tragedy of Youth (Tiffany-Stahl, 1928)
Ladies of the Night Club (Tiffany-Stahl, 1928)
A Woman Against the World (Tiffany-Stahl, 1928)
George Washington Cohen (Tiffany-Stahl, 1928)
The Grain of Dust (Tiffany-Stahl, 1928)
The Voice Within (Tiffany-Stahl, 1929)
Three Men and a Maid (Tiffany-Stahl, 1929)
The College Coquette (Col., 1929)
Broadway Scandals (Col., 1929)
The Broadway Hoofer (Col., 1929)
Framed (RKO, 1930)
Alias French Gertie (RKO, 1930)
Shooting Straight (RKO, 1930)
The Silver Horde (RKO, 1930)
Lady Refuses (RKO, 1931)
Three Who Loved (RKO, 1931)
Lost Squadron (RKO, 1932)
Men of Chance (RKO, 1932)

State's Attorney (RKO, 1932)
Thirteen Women (RKO, 1932)
The Penguin Pool Murder (RKO, 1932)
Big Brain (RKO, 1933)
After Tonight (RKO, 1933)
Keep 'Em Rolling (RKO, 1934)
Murder on the Blackboard (RKO, 1934)
Thunder in the Night (Fox, 1935)
My Marriage (Fox, 1935)
Return of Sophie Lang (Par., 1936)
Clarence (Par., 1937)
Hideaway Girl (Par., 1937)
Hotel Haywire (Par., 1937)
Blonde Trouble (Par., 1937)
Thrill of a Lifetime (Par., 1937)
Her Jungle Love (Par., 1938)
Thanks for the Memory (Par., 1938)
Campus Confessions (Par., 1938)
Some Like It Hot (Par., 1939)
Night Work (Par., 1939)
Opened By Mistake (Par., 1940)
Untamed (Par., 1940)
Comin' Round the Mountain (Par., 1940)
Hoppy Serves a Writ (UA, 1943)
The Kansan (UA, 1943)
False Colors (UA, 1943)
The Woman of the Town (UA, 1943)
Texas Masquerade (UA, 1944)
Alaska (Mon., 1944)
Mystery Man (UA, 1944)
The Big Bonanza (Rep., 1945)
Girls of the Big House (Rep., 1945)
The Devil's Playground (UA, 1946)
Fool's Gold (UA, 1946)
Unexpected Guest (UA, 1946)
The Marauders (UA, 1947)
Dangerous Adventure (UA, 1947)
Hoppy's Holiday (UA, 1947)
King of the Wild Horses (Col., 1947)
The Millerson Case (Col., 1947)
Silent Conflict (UA, 1948)
Strange Gamble (UA, 1948)
Border Treasure (RKO, 1950)
Hunt the Man Down (RKO, 1950)
The Old West (Col., 1952)
Night Stage to Galveston (Col., 1952)
Apache Country (Col., 1952)
Barbed Wire (Col., 1952)
The Rough, Tough West (Col., 1952)
Blue Canadian Rockies (Col., 1953)
Winning of the West (Col., 1953)
Goldtown Ghost Riders (Col., 1953)
On Top of Old Smoky (Col., 1953)

Pack Train (Col., 1953)
Saginaw Trail (Col., 1953)
Last of the Pony Riders (Col., 1953)

ARNOLD, JACK, b. Oct. 14, 1916, New Haven, Conn.
Girls in the Night (Univ., 1953)
It Came from Outer Space (Univ., 1953)
The Glass Web (Univ., 1953)
Creature from the Black Lagoon (Univ., 1954)
Revenge of the Creature (Univ., 1955)
Tarantula (Univ., 1955)
The Man from Bitter Ridge (Univ., 1955)
Red Sundown (Univ., 1955)
Outside the Law (Univ., 1957)
The Tattered Dress (Univ., 1957)
The Incredible Shrinking Man (Univ., 1957)
Man in the Shadow (Univ., 1957)
The Lady Takes a Flyer (Univ., 1957)
The Space Children (Univ., 1958)
High School Confidential (MGM, 1958)
Monster on the Campus (Univ., 1958)
No Name on the Bullet (Univ., 1959) (also co-producer)
The Mouse That Roared (Col., 1959)
Bachelor in Paradise (MGM, 1961)
The Lively Set (Univ., 1964)
A Global Affair (MGM, 1964)
Hello Down There (Par., 1968)

ARZNER, DOROTHY, b. Jan. 3, 1900, San Francisco.
Fashions for Women (Par., 1927)
Ten Modern Commandments (Par., 1927)
Get Your Man (Par., 1927)
Manhattan Cocktail (Par., 1928)
The Wild Party (Par., 1929)
Sarah and Son (Par., 1930)
Anybody's Woman (Par., 1930)
Paramount on Parade (Par., 1930) (with Otto Brower, Edmund Goulding, Victor Heerman, Edwin H. Knopf, Rowland V. Lee, Ernst Lubitsch, Lothar Mendes, Victor Schertzinger, A. Edward Sutherland)
Honor Among Lovers (Par., 1931)
Working Girls (Par., 1931)
Merrily We Go to Hell (Par., 1932)
Christopher Strong (RKO, 1933)
Nana (UA, 1934)
Craig's Wife (Col., 1936)
The Bride Wore Red (MGM, 1937)
Dance, Girl, Dance (RKO, 1940)
First Comes Courage (Col., 1943)

ASHER, WILLIAM, b. 1919.
  Beach Party (AIP, 1963)
  Johnny Cool (UA, 1963) (also producer)
  Bikini Beach (AIP, 1964) (also co-script)
  Muscle Beach Party (AIP, 1964) (also co-script)
  Beach Blanket Bingo (AIP, 1965) (also co-script)
  How to Stuff a Wild Bikini (AIP, 1965) (also co-script)
  Fireball 500 (AIP, 1966) (also co-script)

AUER, JOHN H., b. Aug. 3, 1909, Budapest.
  Life for Another (Mexican, 1934)
  The Pervert (Mexican, 1934)
  Rest in Peace (Mexican, 1934)
  His Last Song (Mexican, 1934)
  The Crime of Dr. Crespi (Rep. 1935) (also producer, story)
  Frankie and Johnnie (RKO, 1935)
  A Man Betrayed (Rep., 1937)
  Circus Girl (Rep., 1937)
  Rhythm in the Clouds (Rep., 1937)
  Invisible Enemy (Rep., 1938)
  Outside of Paradise (Rep., 1938)
  A Desperate Adventure (Rep., 1938)
  Orphans of the Street (Rep., 1938)
  I Stand Accused (Rep., 1938) (also co-producer)
  Forged Passport (Rep., 1939) (also co-producer)
  S.O.S. Tidal Wave (Rep., 1939)
  Calling All Marines (Rep., 1939)
  Smuggled Cargo (Rep., 1939) (also co-producer)
  Thou Shalt Not Kill (Rep., 1940)
  Women in War (Rep., 1940)
  The Hit Parade of 1941 (Rep., 1940)
  The Devil Pays Off (Rep., 1941)
  Pardon My Stripes (Rep., 1942)
  Moonlight Masquerade (Rep., 1942) (also co-producer)
  Johnny Doughboy (Rep., 1942) (also co-producer)
  Tahiti Honey (Rep., 1943) (also associate producer)
  Gangway for Tomorrow (RKO, 1943) (also producer)
  Music in Manhattan (RKO, 1944) (also producer)
  Seven Days Ashore (RKO, 1944) (also producer)
  Pan-Americana (RKO, 1945) (also producer)
  Beat the Band (RKO, 1947)
  The Flame (Rep., 1947) (also associate producer)
  I, Jane Doe (Rep., 1948) (also associate producer)
  The Avengers (Rep., 1950) (also associate producer)
  Hit Parade of 1951 (Rep., 1950) (also associate producer)
  Thunderbirds (Rep., 1952) (also associate producer)
  The City That Never Sleeps (Rep., 1953) (also associate producer)
  Hell's Half Acre (Rep., 1954) (also associate producer)
  The Eternal Sea (Rep., 1955) (also associate producer)
  Johnny Trouble (WB, 1957) (also producer)

AVERBACK, HY, b. 1925.
Chamber of Horrors (WB, 1966) (also producer)
Where Were You When the Lights Went Out? (MGM, 1968)
I Love You, Alice B. Toklas! (WB-7 Arts, 1968)
The Great Bank Robbery (WB-7 Arts, 1969)
Suppose They Gave a War and Nobody Came? (Cin., 1970)

AVILDSEN, JOHN G.
Turn on to Love (Haven International, 1969)
Joe (Cannon, 1970) (also camera)
Guess What We Learned in School Today? (Cannon, 1970)
(also camera)
Okay Bill (Four Star Excelsior (also script, camera)
Cry Uncle (Cambist, 1972)
Save the Tiger (Par., 1973)

AXELROD, GEORGE, b. June 9, 1922, New York City.
Lord Love a Duck (UA, 1966) (also producer, co-script)
The Secret Life of an American Wife (20th, 1968) (also pro-
ducer, script)

B

BACON, LLOYD, b. Jan. 16, 1890, San Jose, Calif., d. Nov. 15,
1955.
Broken Hearts of Hollywood (WB, 1926)
Private Izzy Murphy (WB, 1926)
Finger Prints (WB, 1927)
White Flannels (WB, 1927)
The Heart of Maryland (WB, 1927)
A Sailor's Sweetheart (WB, 1927)
Brass Knuckles (WB, 1927)
The Lion and the Mouse (WB, 1928)
Pay as You Enter (WB, 1928)
The Singing Fool (WB, 1928)
Women They Talk About (WB, 1928)
Stark Mad (WB, 1929)
No Defense (WB, 1929)
Honky Tonk (WB, 1929)
Say It With Songs (WB, 1929)
So Long Letty (WB, 1929)
She Couldn't Say No (WB, 1930)
A Notorious Affair (FN, 1930)
The Other Tomorrow (FN, 1930)
Moby Dick (WB, 1930)
The Office Wife (WB, 1930)
Kept Husbands (RKO, 1931)
Sit Tight (WB, 1931)
Fifty Million Frenchmen (WB, 1931)

Gold Dust Gertie (WB, 1931)
Honor of the Family (FN, 1931)
Manhattan Parade (WB, 1932)
Fireman Save My Child (FN, 1932)
The Famous Ferguson Case (FN, 1932)
Miss Pinkerton (FN, 1932)
You Said a Mouthful (FN, 1932)
Crooner (FN, 1932)
Picture Snatcher (WB, 1933)
42nd Street (WB, 1933)
Mary Stevens, M.D. (WB, 1933)
Footlight Parade (WB, 1933)
Son of a Sailor (FN, 1933)
Wonder Bar (FN, 1934)
A Very Honorable Guy (FN, 1934)
He Was Her Man (WB, 1934)
Here Comes the Navy (WB, 1934)
6 Day Bike Rider (FN, 1934)
Devil Dogs of the Air (WB, 1935)
In Caliente (FN, 1935)
The Irish in Us (WB, 1935)
Broadway Gondolier (WB, 1935)
Frisco Kid (WB, 1935)
Sons O'Guns (WB, 1936)
Cain and Mabel (WB, 1936)
Gold Diggers of 1937 (WB, 1936)
Marked Woman (WB, 1937)
Ever Since Eve (WB, 1937)
San Quentin (FN, 1937)
Submarine D-1 (WB, 1937)
A Slight Case of Murder (WB, 1938)
The Cowboy from Brooklyn (WB, 1938)
Boy Meets Girl (WB, 1938)
Racket Busters (WB, 1938)
Wings of the Navy (WB, 1939)
The Oklahoma Kid (WB, 1939)
Indianapolis Speedway (WB, 1939)
Espionage Agent (WB, 1939)
Invisible Stripes (WB, 1940)
A Child Is Born (WB, 1940)
Three Cheers for the Irish (WB, 1940)
Brother Orchid (WB, 1940)
Knute Rockne--All American (WB, 1940)
Honeymoon for Three (WB, 1941)
Footsteps in the Dark (WB, 1941)
Affectionately Yours (WB, 1941)
Navy Blues (WB, 1941)
Larceny, Inc. (WB, 1942)
Wings for the Eagle (WB, 1942)
Silver Queen (UA, 1942)
Action in the North Atlantic (WB, 1943)
Sunday Dinner for a Soldier (20th, 1944)
The Sullivans (20th, 1944)

Captain Eddie (20th, 1945)
Wake Up and Dream (20th, 1946)
Home, Sweet Homicide (20th, 1946)
I Wonder Who's Kissing Her Now? (20th, 1947)
You Were Meant for Me (20th, 1948)
Give My Regards to Broadway (20th, 1948)
Don't Trust Your Husband (UA, 1948)
Mother Is a Freshman (20th, 1949)
It Happens Every Spring (20th, 1949)
Miss Grant Takes Richmond (Col., 1949)
The Good Humor Man (Col., 1950)
Kill the Umpire (Col., 1950)
The Fuller Brush Girl (Col., 1950)
Call Me Mister (20th, 1951) (with choreographer Busby Berkeley)
The Frogmen (20th, 1951)
Golden Girl (20th, 1951)
The I Don't Care Girl (20th, 1953)
The Great Sioux Uprising (Univ., 1953)
Walking My Baby Back Home (Univ., 1953)
The French Line (RKO, 1954)
She Couldn't Say No (RKO, 1954)

BAGGOTT, KING, b. 1880, St. Louis, Mo.; d. July 11, 1948.
Nobody's Fool (Univ., 1921)
Cheated Love (Univ., 1921)
Luring Lips (Univ., 1921)
Moonlight Follies (Univ., 1921)
Kissed (Univ., 1922)
The Kentucky Derby (Univ.-Jewel, 1922)
Human Hearts (Univ.-Jewel, 1922)
A Dangerous Game (Univ., 1922)
The Lavender Bath Lady (Univ., 1922)
Crossed Wires (Univ., 1923) (also co-story)
The Love Letter (Univ., 1923)
Gossip (Univ., 1923)
The Town Scandal (Univ., 1923)
The Darling of New York (Univ.-Jewel, 1923) (also co-story)
The Whispering Name (Univ., 1924)
The Gaiety Girl (Univ.-Jewel, 1924)
The Tornado (Univ.-Jewel, 1924)
Raffles, the Amateur Cracksman (Univ., 1925)
The Home Maker (Univ., 1925)
Tumbleweeds (UA, 1925)
Lovey Mary (MGM, 1926)
The Notorious Lady (FN, 1927)
Down the Stretch (Univ.-Jewel, 1927)
Perch of the Devil (Univ.-Jewel, 1927)
The House of Scandal (Tiffany-Stahl, 1928)
Romance of a Rogue (Quality Distributing, 1928)

BALLIN, HUGO, b. 1880, New York City; d. Nov. 27, 1956.
  Baby Mine (Goldwyn, 1917) (with John S. Robertson)
  Fighting Odds (Goldwyn, 1917) (with Allan Dwan)
  Thais (Goldwyn, 1917) (with Frank Crane)
  The Splendid Sinner (Goldwyn, 1918)
  Pagan Love (W.W. Hodkinson, 1921) (also for own production
    company, script)
  Help Yourself (Goldwyn, 1921)
  East Lynne (W.W. Hodkinson, 1921) (also for own production
    company, script)
  Journey's End (W.W. Hodkinson, 1921) (also for own production
    company, producer, adaptation)
  Jane Eyre (W.W. Hodkinson, 1921) (also for own production
    company, producer, adaptation)
  Other Women's Clothes (W.W. Hodkinson, 1922) (also for own
    production company, producer, script)
  Married People (W.W. Hodkinson, 1922) (also for own produc-
    tion company, co-script)
  Vanity Fair (Goldwyn, 1923) (also for own production company,
    script)
  The Prairie Wife (Metro-Goldwyn, 1925) (also continuity)
  The Shining Adventure (Astor, 1925)

BARE, RICHARD L., b. 1909, Turlock, Calif.
  The Oval Portrait (Univ. of South. California Student Film, 1935)
  Smart Girls Don't Talk (WB, 1948)
  Flaxy Martin (WB, 1949)
  The House Across the Street (WB, 1950)
  Return of the Frontiersman (WB, 1950)
  This Side of the Law (WB, 1950)
  Prisoners of the Casbah (Col., 1953)
  The Outlanders (WB, 1956)
  The Storm Riders (WB, 1956)
  Julesburg (WB, 1956)
  Border Showdown (WB, 1956)
  The Travellers (WB, 1957)
  Shoot Out at Medicine Bend (WB, 1957)
  Girl on the Run (WB, 1958)
  This Rebel Breed (WB, 1960)
  Wicked, Wicked (MGM, 1973) (also producer, script)

BARKER, REGINALD, b. 1886, Bothwell, Scotland; d. Sept. 25,
    1937.
  On the Night Stage (Triangle, 1914)
  The Bargain (Triangle, 1914)
  The Geisha (Triangle, 1914)
  The Typhoon (Triangle, 1914)
  The Wrath of the Gods (Triangle, 1914)
  The Coward (Triangle, 1915)
  The Italian (Triangle, 1915)
  The Golden Claw (Triangle, 1915)

The Conqueror (Triangle, 1915)
The Iron Strain (Triangle, 1915)
The Apostle of Vengeance (Triangle, 1915)
Between Men (Triangle, 1915)
Shell 43 (Triangle, 1916)
Hell's Hinges (Triangle, 1916) (with Clifford Smith)
Civilization (Triangle, 1916) (with Thomas H. Ince, Ra
    B. West, Scott Sidney, J. Parker Read, Jr.)
The Bugle Call (Triangle, 1916)
The Criminal (Triangle, 1916)
Jim Grimsby's Boy (Triangle, 1916)
The Market of Vain Desire (Triangle, 1916)
The Thoroughbred (Triangle, 1916)
Three of Many (Triangle, 1916)
The Stepping Stone (Triangle, 1916)
Happiness (Triangle, 1917)
Back of the Man (Triangle, 1917)
The Iced Bullet (Triangle, 1917)
The Paws of the Bear (Triangle, 1917)
A Strange Transgressor (Triangle, 1917)
Sweetheart of the Doomed (Triangle, 1917)
Golden Rule Kate (Triangle, 1917)
Shackled (Paralta, 1918)
Carmen of the Klondike (Selexart, 1918)
The Branding Iron (Goldwyn, 1918)
Madam Who (Par., 1918)
The Stronger Vow (Goldwyn, 1919)
The Turn of the Wheel (Goldwyn, 1918)
The Hell Cat (Goldwyn, 1918)
The One Woman (Select, 1918)
The Brand (Goldwyn, 1919)
The Crimson Gardenia (Goldwyn, 1919)
Shadows (Goldwyn, 1919)
Girl from the Outside (Goldwyn, 1919)
The Flame of the Desert (Goldwyn, 1919)
The Bonds of Love (Goldwyn, 1919)
Dangerous Days (Goldwyn, 1920)
The Woman and the Puppet (Goldwyn, 1920)
Bunty Pulls the Strings (Goldwyn, 1921) (also supervisor)
Godless Men (Goldwyn, 1921)
Snowblind (Goldwin, 1921)
The Old Nest (Goldwyn, 1921)
The Poverty of Riches (Goldwyn, 1921)
The Storm (Univ.-Jewel, 1922)
Hearts Aflame (Metro, 1923)
Pleasure Mad (Metro, 1923)
The Eternal Struggle (Metro, 1923)
Women Who Give (Metro-Goldwyn, 1924)
Broken Barriers (Metro-Goldwyn, 1924)
The Dixie Handicap (Metro-Goldwyn, 1925)
The Great Divide (Metro-Goldwyn, 1925)
The White Desert (Metro-Goldwyn, 1925)
When the Door Opened (Fox, 1925)

The Flaming Forest (MGM, 1926)
The Frontiersman (MGM, 1927)
Body and Soul (MGM, 1927)
The Toilers (Tiffany-Stahl, 1928)
The Rainbow (Tiffany-Stahl, 1929)
New Orleans (Tiffany-Stahl, 1929)
The Great Divide (FN, 1929)
The Mississippi Gambler (Univ., 1929)
Seven Keys to Baldpate (RKO, 1929)
Hide-Out (Univ., 1930)
The Moonstone (Mon., 1934)
Women Must Dress (Mon., 1935)
The Healer (Mon., 1935)
Forbidden Heaven (Rep., 1936)

BARRYMORE, LIONEL, b. April 28, 1878, Philadelphia; d. Nov. 15, 1954.
Madame X (MGM, 1929)
The Unholy Night (MGM, 1929)
The Green Ghost (MGM, 1929)
His Glorious Night (MGM, 1930) (also producer, musical score)
The Rogue Song (MGM, 1930) (also producer)
Ten Cents a Dance (Col., 1931)

BARTLETT, HALL, b. Nov. 27, 1922, Kansas City, Mo.
Unchained (WB, 1955) (also producer, script)
Drango (UA, 1957) (with Jules Bricken) (also producer, script)
Zero Hour (Par., 1957) (also script)
All the Young Men (Col., 1960) (also for co-production company, producer, script)
The Caretakers (UA, 1963) (also producer, co-story)
Changes (Cin., 1969) (also producer, co-script)
Sandpit General [The Wild Pack] (AIP, 1972) (also producer, script)
Jonathan Livingston Seagull (Par., 1973) (also producer)

BARTON, CHARLES T., b. May 25, 1902, Calif.
Wagon Wheels (Par., 1934)
Car 99 (Par., 1935)
Rocky Mountain Mystery (Par., 1935)
The Last Outpost (Par., 1935)
Timothy's Quest (Par., 1936)
Nevada (Par., 1936)
And Sudden Death (Par., 1936)
Rose Bowl (Par., 1936)
Murder With Pictures (Par., 1936)
The Crime Nobody Saw (Par., 1937)
Forlorn River (Par., 1937)
Thunder Trail (Par., 1937)
Born to the West (Par., 1938)

Titans of the Deep (Grand National, 1938)
Behind Prison Gates (Col., 1939)
Five Little Peppers and How They Grew (Col., 1939)
My Son Is Guilty (Col., 1940)
Five Little Peppers at Home (Col., 1940)
Island of Doomed Men (Col., 1940)
Babies for Sale (Col., 1940)
Out West With the Peppers (Col., 1940)
Five Little Peppers in Trouble (Col., 1940)
Nobody's Children (Col., 1940)
The Phantom Submarine (Col., 1941)
The Big Boss (Col., 1941)
Richest Man in Town (Col., 1941)
Two Latins from Manhattan (Col., 1941)
Harmon of Michigan (Col., 1941)
Tramp, Tramp, Tramp (Col., 1942)
Shut My Big Mouth (Col., 1942)
Hello, Annapolis (Col., 1942)
Sweetheart of the Fleet (Col., 1942)
Parachute Nurse (Col., 1942)
The Spirit of Stanford (Col., 1942)
What's Buzzin' Cousin? (Col., 1943)
Let's Have Fun (Col., 1943)
Lucky Legs (Col., 1943)
Is Everybody Happy? (Col., 1943)
Reveille With Beverly (Col., 1943)
She Has What It Takes (Col., 1943)
Hey, Rookie (Col., 1944)
Jam Session (Col., 1944)
Beautiful But Broke (Col., 1944)
Louisiana Hayride (Col., 1944)
The Beautiful Cheat (Univ., 1945) (also producer)
Men in Her Diary (Univ., 1945) (also associate producer)
Smooth as Silk (Univ., 1946)
The Time of Their Lives (Univ., 1946)
White Tie and Tails (Univ., 1946)
The Ghost Steps Out (Univ., 1946) (also script)
Buck Privates Come Home (Univ., 1947)
The Wistful Widow of Wagon Gap (Univ., 1947)
The Noose Hangs High (Eagle Lion, 1948) (also producer)
Abbott and Costello Meet Frankenstein (Univ., 1948)
Mexican Hayride (Univ., 1948)
Abbott and Costello Meet the Killer, Boris Karloff (Univ., 1949)
Africa Screams (UA, 1949)
Free for All (Univ., 1949)
Double Crossbones (Univ., 1950)
The Milkman (Univ., 1950)
Ma and Pa Kettle at the Fair (Univ., 1952)
Dance With Me Henry (UA, 1956)

BEAUDINE, WILLIAM, b. Jan. 15, 1892, New York City; d. Mar.
     18, 1970.
     Catch My Smoke (US, 1922)

Heroes of the Street (WB, 1922)
Watch Your Step (Goldwyn, 1922)
Boy of Mine (Associated FN, 1923)
The Country Kid (WB, 1923)
Her Fatal Millions (Metro, 1923)
Penrod and Sam (Associated FN, 1923)
The Printer's Devil (WB, 1923)
Cornered (WB, 1924)
Daughters of Pleasure (Principal, 1924)
Lover's Lane (WB, 1924)
The Narrow Street (WB, 1924)
A Self-Made Failure (FN, 1924)
Daring Youth (Principal, 1924)
Wandering Husbands (PDC, 1924)
A Broadway Butterfly (WB, 1925)
How Baxter Butted in (WB, 1925)
Little Annie Rooney (UA, 1925)
The Canadian (Par., 1926)
Hold That Lion (Par., 1926)
The Social Highwayman (Pearless-World, 1926)
Sparrows (UA, 1926)
That's My Baby (Par., 1926)
Frisco Sally Levy (MGM, 1927)
The Irresistible Lover (Univ., 1927)
The Life of Riley (FN, 1927)
The Cohens and the Kellys in Paris (Univ., 1928)
Do Your Duty (FN, 1928)
Give and Take (Univ., 1928)
Heart to Heart (FN, 1928)
Home James (Univ., 1928)
Fugitives (Fox, 1929)
The Girl from Woolworth's (FN, 1929)
Two Weeks Off (FN, 1929)
Wedding Rings (FN, 1930)
Road to Paradise (FN, 1930)
Those Who Dance (WB, 1930)
The Men in Her Life (Col., 1931)
Father's Son (WB, 1931)
Mad Parade (Par., 1931)
The Lady Who Dared (WB, 1931)
Misbehaving Ladies (WB, 1931)
Penrod and Sam (WB, 1931)
The Road to Paradise (WB, 1931)
Make Me a Star (Par., 1932)
Three Wise Girls (Col., 1932)
On Probation (Par., 1932)
Crime of the Century (Par., 1933)
Her Bodyguard (Par., 1933)
The Old Fashioned Way (Par., 1934)
Dandy Dick (BIP, 1934)
So You Won't Talk? (FN, 1935)
Get Off My Foot (FN, 1935)
Boys Will Be Boys (FN, 1935)

Where There's a Will (FN, 1935)
Two Hearts in Harmony (Wardour, 1935)
Windbag the Sailor (Gaumont-British, 1936)
Educated Evans (FN, 1936)
It's in the Bag (WB, 1936)
Take It from Me (FN, 1936)
Mr. Cohen Takes a Wife (WB, 1936)
Feather Your Nest (Associated British Film Distributors, 1937)
Torchy Gets Her Man (WB, 1938)
Sez O'Reilly to McNab (Gaumont-British, 1938)
Torchy Blane in Chinatown (WB, 1939)
Misbehaving Husbands (PRC, 1940)
Desperate Cargo (PRC, 1941)
Emergency Landing (PRC, 1941)
Blonde Comet (PRC, 1941)
The Miracle Kid (PRC, 1941)
Mr. Celebrity (PRC, 1941)
Federal Fugitives (PRC, 1941)
Gallant Lady (PRC, 1942)
One Thrilling Night (Mon., 1942)
Foreign Agent (Mon., 1942)
Professor Creeps (Dixie National, 1942)
The Phantom Killer (Mon., 1942)
Prison Girls (PRC, 1942)
The Living Ghost (Mon., 1942)
The Broadway Big Shot (Mon., 1942)
Duke of the Navy (PRC, 1942)
The Panther's Claw (PRC, 1942)
Men of San Quentin (PRC, 1942)
The Mystery of the 13th Guest (Mon., 1943)
Ghosts on the Loose (Mon., 1943)
Spotlight Scandals (Mon., 1943)
The Clancy Street Boys (Mon., 1943)
Here Comes Kelly (Mon., 1943)
What a Man! (Mon., 1943)
The Ape Man (Mon., 1943)
Voodoo Man (Mon., 1944)
Detective Kitty O'Day (Mon., 1944)
Leave It to the Irish (Mon., 1944)
Hot Rhythm (Mon., 1944)
Follow the Leader (Mon., 1944)
Oh, What a Night (Mon., 1944)
Shadow of Suspicion (Mon., 1944)
Crazy Knights (Mon., 1944)
Bowery Champs (Mon., 1944)
The Adventures of Kitty O'Day (Mon., 1944)
Fashion Model (Mon., 1945)
Swingin' on a Rainbow (Rep., 1945)
Blonde Ransom (Univ., 1945)
Come Out Fighting (Mon., 1945)
Black Market Babies (Mon., 1945)
Girl on the Spot (Univ., 1946)
The Face of Marble (Mon., 1946)

Don't Gamble With Strangers (Mon., 1946)
Below the Deadline (Mon., 1946)
Mr. Hex (Mon., 1946)
Spook Busters (Mon., 1946)
The Red Hornet (Mon., 1947)
Gas House Kids Go West (PRC, 1947)
News Hounds (Mon., 1947)
Hard Boiled Mahoney (Mon., 1947)
Killer at Large (PRC, 1947)
Philo Vance Returns (PRC, 1947)
Too Many Winners (PRC, 1947)
Bowery Buckaroos (Mon., 1947)
The Chinese Ring (Mon., 1947)
Angel's Alley (Mon., 1948)
Jinx Money (Mon., 1948)
The Golden Eye (Mon., 1948)
Jiggs and Maggie in Court (Mon., 1948) (with Edward Cline)
Kidnapped (Mon., 1948)
The Shanghai Chest (Mon., 1948)
Incident (Mon., 1948)
The Feathered Serpent (Mon., 1948)
Forgotten Women (Mon., 1949)
Tuna Clipper (Mon., 1949)
The Lawton Story (Hallmark, 1949)
Jiggs and Maggie in Jackpot Jitters (Mon., 1949)
Tough Assignment (Lip., 1949)
Again Pioneers (Religion-Film Associates, 1950)
Second Chance (RFA, 1950)
Jiggs and Maggie Out West (Mon., 1950)
Lucky Losers (Mon., 1950)
Blonde Dynamite (Mon., 1950)
Blues Busters (Mon., 1950)
County Fair (Mon., 1950)
Blue Grass of Kentucky (Mon., 1950)
Havana Rose (Rep., 1951)
Bowery Battalion (Mon., 1951)
Crazy over Horses (Mon., 1951)
A Wonderful Life (Protestant Film Comm., 1951)
Ghost Chasers (Mon., 1951)
Let's Go Navy (Mon., 1951)
Rodeo (Mon., 1951)
Cuban Fireball (Rep., 1951)
Feudin' Fools (Mon., 1952)
Here Come the Marines (Mon., 1952)
Hold That Line (Mon., 1952)
No Holds Barred (Mon., 1952)
The Rose Bowl Story (Mon., 1952)
Jet Job (Mon., 1952)
Tell It to the Marines (Mon., 1952)
Bela Lugosi Meets a Brooklyn Gorilla [Boys from Brooklyn]
    (Realart, 1952)
Jalopy (AA, 1953)
Roar of the Crowd (AA, 1953)

Murder Without Tears (AA, 1953)
Paris Playboys (AA, 1954)
Yukon Vengeance (AA, 1954)
Pride of the Blue Grass (AA, 1954)
High Society (AA, 1955)
Jail Busters (AA, 1955)
Westward Ho the Wagons! (BV, 1956)
Up in Smoke (AA, 1958)
In the Money (AA, 1958)
Ten Who Dared (BV, 1960
Lassie's Greatest Adventure (20th, 1963)
Billy the Kid vs. Dracula (Emb., 1966)
Jesse James Meets Frankenstein's Daughter (Emb., 1966)

BEAUMONT, HARRY, b. Feb. 10, 1888, Abilene, Kan.; d. 1966.
The Truant Soul (Essanay, 1916)
Skinner's Dress Suit (Essanay, 1917)
Skinner's Bubble (Essanay, 1917)
Skinner's Baby (Essanay, 1917)
Burning the Candle (Essanay, 1917)
Filling His Own Shoes (Essanay, 1917)
Brown of Harvard (Essanay, 1917)
Thirty a Week (Goldwyn, 1918)
Wild Goose Chase (Triangle, 1919)
Little Rowdy (Triangle, 1919)
A Man and His Money (Goldwyn, 1919)
Go West Young Man (Goldwyn, 1919)
One of the Finest (Goldwyn, 1919)
The City of Comrades (Goldwyn, 1919)
Heartsease (Goldwyn, 1919)
Lord and Lady Algy (Goldwyn, 1919)
Toby's Bow (Goldwyn, 1919)
The Gay Lord Quex (Goldwyn, 1919)
The Great Accident (Goldwyn, 1920)
Dollars and Sense (Goldwyn, 1920)
Going Some (Goldwyn, 1920)
Stop Thief (Goldwyn, 1920)
Officer 666 (Goldwyn, 1920
The Fourteenth Lover (Metro, 1922)
The Ragged Heiress (Fox, 1922)
Lights of the Desert (Fox, 1922)
Glass Houses (Metro, 1922)
Very Truly Yours (Fox, 1922)
Seeing's Believing (Metro, 1922)
They Like 'Em Rough (Metro, 1922)
The Five Dollar Baby (Metro, 1922)
Love in the Dark (Metro, 1922)
June Madness (Metro, 1922) (also adaptation, script)
Crinoline and Romance (Metro, 1923)
Main Street (WB, 1923)
A Noise in Newboro (Metro, 1923)
The Gold Diggers (WB, 1923)

Beau Brummel (WB, 1924)
Babbitt (WB, 1924)
Don't Doubt Your Husband (Metro-Goldwyn, 1924)
The Lover of Camille (WB, 1924)
A Lost Lady (WB, 1924)
His Majesty, Bunker Bean (WB, 1925)
Recompense (WB, 1925)
Rose of the World (WB, 1925)
Sandy (Fox, 1926)
Womanpower (Fox, 1926)
One Increasing Purpose (Fox, 1927)
Forbidden Hours (MGM, 1928)
Our Dancing Daughters (MGM, 1928)
A Single Man (MGM, 1929)
The Broadway Melody (MGM, 1929)
Speedway (MGM, 1929)
Children of Pleasure (MGM, 1930)
Lord Byron of Broadway (MGM, 1930) (with William Nigh)
The Floradora Girl (MGM, 1930)
Our Blushing Brides (MGM, 1930)
Those Three French Girls (MGM, 1930)
Dance Fools Dance (MGM, 1931)
Laughing Sinners (MGM, 1931)
The Great Lover (MGM, 1931)
West of Broadway (MGM, 1931)
Are You Listening? (MGM, 1932)
Unashamed (MGM, 1932)
Faithless (MGM, 1932)
Made on Broadway (MGM, 1933)
When Ladies Meet (MGM, 1933)
Should Ladies Behave? (MGM, 1933)
Murder in the Private Car (MGM, 1934)
Enchanted April (RKO, 1935)
The Girl on the Front Page (Univ., 1936)
When's Your Birthday? (RKO, 1937)
Maisie Goes to Reno (MGM, 1944)
Twice Blessed (MGM, 1945)
Up Goes Maisie (MGM, 1946)
The Show-Off (MGM, 1946)
Undercover Maisie (MGM, 1947)
Alias a Gentleman (MGM, 1948)

BEEBE, FORD, b. Nov. 26, 188, Grand Rapids, Mich.
    The Honor of the Range (Univ., 1920) (with Leo Maloney)
    The Shadow of the Eagle* (Macot, 1932) (with B. Reeves Eason)
        (also co-script)
    The Last of the Mohicans* (Mascot, 1932) (with B. Reeves Eason)
        (also co-script)
    The Pride of the Legion* (Mascot, 1932) (also script, dialogue)
    Laughing at Life (Mascot, 1933) (also script)
    Law Beyond the Range (Col., 1934)
    The Adventures of Rex and Rinty* (Mascot, 1935) (with B.
        Reeves Eason)

Man from Guntown (Puritan, 1935) (also script)
Stampede (Col., 1935)
Ace Drummond* (Univ., 1936) (with Cliff Smith)
Jungle Jim* (Univ., 1937) (with Cliff Smith)
Secret Agent X-9* (Univ., 1937) (with Cliff Smith)
Wild West Days* (Univ., 1937) (with Cliff Smith)
Radio Patrol* (Univ., 1937) (with Cliff Smith)
Westbound Limited (Univ., 1937) (also co-script)
Trouble at Midnight (Univ., 1937) (also co-script)
Tim Tyler's Luck* (Univ., 1938) (with Wyndham Gittens, Cliff
    Smith)
Flash Gordon's Trip to Mars* (Univ., 1938) (with Robert F.
    Hill)
Red Barry* (Univ., 1938) (with Allen James)
Buck Rogers* (Univ., 1939) (with Saul A. Goodkind)
The Phantom Creeps* (Univ., 1939) (with Saul A. Goodkind)
The Oregon Trail* (Univ., 1939) (with Saul A. Goodkind)
The Green Hornet* (Univ., 1939) (with Ray Taylor)
Oklahoma Frontier (Univ., 1939) (also script)
Fantasia (RKO, 1940) (sequence director)
Son of Roaring Dan (Univ., 1940)
Flash Gordon Conquers the Universe* (Univ., 1940) (with Ray
    Taylor)
Winners of the West* (Univ., 1940) (with Ray Taylor)
Junior G-Men* (Univ., 1940) (with John Rawlins)
The Green Hornet Strikes Again* (Univ., 1940) (with John Raw-
    lins)
The Masked Rider (Univ., 1941)
Sky Raiders* (Univ., 1941) (with Ray Taylor)
Riders of Death Valley* (Univ., 1941) (with Ray Taylor)
The Reluctant Dragon (RKO, 1941) (with Alfred K. Werker, Jim
    Handley, Hamilton Luke, Jasper Blystone, Erwin Verity)
Sea Raiders* (Univ., 1941) (with John Rawlins)
Don Winslow of the Navy* (Univ., 1941) (with Ray Taylor)
Overland Mail* (Univ., 1942) (with John Rawlins)
Night Monster (Univ., 1942)
Arabian Nights (Univ., 1942) (second unit director only)
Frontier Badmen (Univ., 1943) (also producer)
Son of Dracula (Univ., 1943) (producer and second unit director
    only)
The Invisible Man's Revenge (Univ., 1944) (also producer)
Enter Arsene Lupin (Univ., 1944)
Easy to Look at (Univ., 1945)
Six Gun Serenade (Mon., 1947)
Courtin' Trouble (Mon., 1948) (also script)
My Dog Shep (Screen Guild, 1948) (also script)
Shep Comes Home (Screen Guild, 1948) (also script)
Satan's Cradle (UA, 1949)
Bomba, the Jungle Boy (Mon., 1949)
The Dalton Gang (Lip., 1949) (also script)
Red Desert (Lip., 1949) (also script)
Bomba on Panther Island (Mon., 1950) (also script)
The Lost Volcano (Mon., 1950)

Bomba and the Hidden City (Mon., 1950)
Davy Crockett, Indian Scout (Col., 1950)
The Lion Hunters (Mon., 1951) (also script)
Bomba and the Elephant Stampede (Mon., 1951) (also script)
Bomba and the African Treasure (Mon., 1952)
Bomba and the Jungle Girl (Mon., 1952) (also script)
Bomba and the African Treasure (Mon., 1952)
Wagons West (Mon., 1952)
Bomba and the Safari Drums (AA, 1953)
Safari Drums (AA, 1953) (also producer, script)
The Golden Idol (AA, 1954) (also producer, script)
Killer Leopard (AA, 1954) (also producer, script)
Lord of the Jungle (AA, 1955) (also producer, script)
*Serial

BELL, MONTA, b. Feb. 5, 1891, Washington, D.C.; d. Feb. 4,
    1958.
Broadway After Dark (WB, 1924)
How to Educate a Wife (WB, 1924)
The Snob (MGM, 1924) (also script)
Lady of the Night (MGM, 1925)
Pretty Ladies (MGM, 1925)
Lights of Old Broadway (MGM, 1925)
The King on Main Street (Par., 1925) (also adaptation)
The Torrent (MGM, 1926)
The Boy Friend (MGM, 1926)
Upstage (MGM, 1926)
After Midnight (MGM, 1927) (also story)
Man, Woman, and Sin (MGM, 1927) (also story)
Bellamy Trial (MGM, 1929) (also script)
East Is West (Univ., 1930)
Young Man of Manhattan (Par., 1930)
Fires of Youth (Univ., 1931) (also story)
Up for Murder (Univ., 1931) (also story)
Personal Maid (Par., 1931) (with Lothar Mendes)
Downstairs (MGM, 1932)
The Worst Woman in Paris? (Fox, 1933) (also story)

BELLAMY, EARL, b. March 11, 1917, Minneapolis.
Seminole Uprising (Col., 1955)
Blackjack Ketchum, Desperado (Col., 1956)
Toughest Gun in Tomstone (UA, 1958)
Fluffy (Univ., 1965)
Gunpoint (Univ., 1966)
Incident at Phantom Hill (Univ., 1966)
Munster, Go Home (Univ., 1966)
Three Guns for Texas (Univ., 1968) (with David Lowell Rich,
    Paul Stanley)
Backtrack (NBC-TV, 1968)
The Pigeon (ABC-TV, 1969)
Joaquin Murieta (20th, 1970)

The Desperate Mission (ABC-TV, 1971)
The Trackers (ABC-TV, 1971)

BENEDEK, LASLO, b. March 5, 1907, Budapest.
    The Kissing Bandit (MGM, 1948)
    Port of New York (Eagle Lion, 1949)
    Death of a Salesman (Col., 1951)
    The Wild One (Col., 1953)
    Bengal Brigade (Univ., 1954)
    Kinder, Mütter und Ein General (German, 1955)
    Affair in Havana (AA, 1957)
    Moment of Danger (Associated British, 1960)
    Recourse en Grace (French, 1960)
    Namu the Killer Whale (UA, 1966) (also producer)
    The Daring Game (Par., 1968)
    The Night Visitor (UMC, 1971)

BENNETT, SPENCER GORDON, b. Jan. 5, 1893, Brooklyn, N.Y.
    The Phantom Foe* (Pathé, 1920) (second unit director only)
    Behold the Man (Pathé/Selwyn, 1921)
    Galloping Hoofs* (Pathé, 1924) (with George B. Seitz)
    Play Ball* (Pathé, 1925)
    The Green Archer* (Pathé, 1925)
    The Fighting Marine* (Pathé, 1926)
    House Without a Key* (Pathé, 1926)
    Snowed In* (Pathé, 1926)
    Hawk of the Hills* (Pathé, 1927)
    Melting Millions* (Pathé, 1927)
    The Man Without a Face* (Pathé, 1928)
    The Terrible People* (Pathé, 1928)
    The Yellow Cameo* (Pathé, 1928)
    The Tiger's Shadow* (Pathé, 1928)
    Marked Money (Pathé, 1928)
    The Black Book* (Pathé, 1929) (with Thomas L. Storey)
    Queen of the Northwoods* (Pathé, 1929) (with Thomas L. Storey)
    The Fire Detective* (Pathé, 1929) (with Thomas L. Storey)
    Rogue of the Rio Grande (World Wide, 1930)
    The Last Frontier* (RKO, 1932)
    Justice Takes a Holiday (Golden Arrow, 1933)
    Midnight Warning (Mayfair, 1933)
    Badge of Honor (Mayfair, 1934)
    The Fighting Rookie (Mayfair, 1934)
    The Oil Raider (Mayfair, 1934)
    Night Alarm (Majestic, 1934)
    The Ferocious Pal (Principal, 1934)
    Calling All Cabs (Empire, 1934)
    Rescue Squad (Empire, 1935)
    Get That Man (Empire, 1935)
    Heir to Trouble (Col., 1935)
    Western Courage (Col., 1935)
    Lawless Riders (Col., 1935)

Heroes of the Range (Col., 1936)
Avenging Waters (Col., 1936)
The Cattle Thief (Col., 1936)
The Fugitive Sheriff (Col., 1936)
The Unknown Ranger (Col., 1936)
Ranger Courage (Col., 1936)
Rio Grande Ranger (Col., 1936)
Law of the Ranger (Col., 1937)
Reckless Ranger (Col., 1937)
The Rangers Step In (Col., 1937)
The Mysterious Pilot* (Col., 1937)
Across the Plains (Mon., 1939)
Oklahoma Terror (Mon., 1939)
Riders of the Frontier (Mon., 1939)
Cowboy from Sundown (Mon., 1940)
Westbound Stage (Mon., 1940)
Ridin' the Cherokee Trail (Mon., 1941)
Arizona Bound (Mon., 1941)
Gunman from Bodie (Mon., 1941)
They Raid by Night (PRC, 1942)
The Secred Code* (Col., 1942)
The Valley of Vanishing Men* (Col., 1942)
Calling Wild Bill Elliott (Rep., 1943)
Tucson Raiders (Rep., 1943)
Canyon City (Rep., 1943)
California Joe (Rep., 1943)
Secret Service in Darkest Africa* (Rep., 1943)
The Masked Marvel* (Rep., 1943)
Mojave Firebrand (Rep., 1944)
Beneath the Western Skies (Rep., 1944)
Code of the Prairie (Rep., 1944)
Haunted Harbor* (Rep., 1944)
The Tiger Woman* (Rep., 1944)
Zorro's Black Whip* (Rep., 1944)
Lone Texas Ranger (Rep., 1945)
Manhunt of Mystery Island* (Rep., 1945) (with Wallace Grissell,
    Yakima Canutt)
Federal Operator 99* (Rep., 1945)
The Purple Monster Strikes* (Rep., 1945) (with Fred C. Bran-
    non)
The Phantom Rider* (Rep., 1946) (with Fred C. Brannon)
Daughter of Don Q* (Rep., 1946) (with Fred C. Brannon)
King of the Forest Rangers* (Rep., 1946) (with Fred C. Bran-
    non)
Son of Zorro* (Rep., 1947) (with Fred C. Brannon)
Brick Bradford* (Col., 1947)
The Black Widow* (Rep., 1947) (with Fred C. Brannon)
Superman* (Col., 1948) (with Thomas Carr)
Congo Bill* (Col., 1948) (with Thomas Carr)
Adventures of Sir Galahad* (Col., 1949)
Bruce Gentry--Daredevil of the Skies* (Col., 1949) (with Thom-
    as Carr)
Batman and Robin* (Col., 1949)

Cody of the Pony Express* (Col., 1950)
Atom Man vs. Superman* (Col., 1950)
Pirates of the High Seas* (Col., 1950) (with Thomas Carr)
Roar of the Iron Horse* (Col., 1951) (with Thomas Carr)
Mysterious Island* (Col., 1951)
Captain Video* (Col., 1951) (with Wallace Grissell)
Blackhawk* (Col., 1952)
Brave Warrior (Col., 1952)
Voodoo Tiger (Col., 1952)
Son of Geronimo* (Col., 1952)
King of the Congo* (Col., 1952) (with Wallace Grissell)
The Lost Planet* (Col., 1953)
Savage Mutiny (Col., 1953)
Killer Ape (Col., 1953)
Gunfighters of the Northwest* (Col., 1954)
Riding With Buffalo Bill* (Col., 1954)
Adventures of Captain Africa* (Col., 1955)
The Devil Goddess (Col., 1955)
Perils of the Wilderness* (Col., 1956)
Blazing the Overland Trail* (Col., 1956)
Congo Bill, King of the Jungle* (Col., 1957) (with Thomas
    Carr)
Submarine Attack (AIP, 1958)
Atomic Submarine (AA, 1959)
Son of Geronimo (Col., 1960)
The Bounty Killer (Emb., 1965)
Requiem for a Gunfighter (Emb., 1965)
*Serial

BERGER, LUDWIG (Ludwig Bamberger), b. Jan. 6, 1892, Mainz,
    Germany; d. 1969.
Der Richer Von Zalamea (German, 1920) (also script)
Der Roman der Christine Von Herre (German, 1921) (also
    script)
Ein Glas Wasser (German, 1922) (also co-script)
Das Spiel der Königin (German, 1923) (also co-script)
Ein Waltzertraum (German, 1925)
Der Meister Von Nürnberg (German, 1927) (also co-script)
Liebe, Liebe (German, 1928)
Das Brennende Herz [The Burning Heart] (German, 1928)
The Woman from Moscow (Par., 1928)
Sins of the Father (Par., 1928)
The Vagabond King (Par., 1930)
The Playboy of Paris (Par., 1930)
Le Petit Cafe [French version of The Playboy of Paris]
    (Par., 1930)
Ich Bei Tag und du Bei Nacht (German, 1932)
Moi le Jour, Toi la Nuit [French version of Ich Bei Tag und
    du Bei Nacht] (German, 1932)
Early to Bed [English version of Ich Bei Tag und du Bei Nacht]
    (German, 1932)
Walzerkrieg (German, 1933)

La Guerre des Valses [French version of Walzerkrieg] (German, 1933)
Pygmalion (Dutch, 1937)
Trois Valses (French, 1938)
The Thief of Bagdad (UA, 1940) (with Michael Powell, Tim Whelan)
Ballerina (French, 1950)

BERKE, WILLIAM (Lester William Berke), b. Oct. 3, 1903, Milwaukee; d. Feb. 15, 1958.
Bad Men of the Hills (Col., 1942)
Lawless Plainsmen (Col., 1942)
Down Rio Grande Way (Col., 1942)
Riders of the Northland (Col., 1942)
Overland to Deadwood (Col., 1942)
Riding Through Nevada (Col., 1943)
Pardon My Gun (Col., 1943)
Frontier Fury (Col., 1943)
The Fighting Buckaroo (Col., 1943)
Frontier Badman (Col., 1943)
Hail to the Rangers (Col., 1943)
Law of the Northwest (Col., 1943)
Riders of the Northwest Mounted (Col., 1943)
Robin Hood of the Range (Col., 1943)
Saddles and Sagebrush (Col., 1943)
Silver City Raiders (Col., 1943)
A Tornado in the Saddle (Col., 1943)
Minesweeper (Par., 1943)
Tornado (Par., 1943)
The Girl in the Case (Col., 1944)
Riding West (Col., 1944)
The Vigilantes Ride (Col., 1944)
Wyoming Hurricane (Col., 1944)
Dangerous Passage (Par., 1944)
Dark Mountain (Par., 1944)
Double Exposure (Par., 1944)
The Falcon in Mexico (RKO, 1944)
The Last Horseman (Col., 1944)
The Navy Way (Par., 1944)
Sailor's Holiday (Col., 1944)
That's My Baby (Rep., 1944)
Dick Tracy (RKO, 1945)
Why Girls Leave Home (PRC, 1945)
Betrayal from the East (RKO, 1945)
High Powered (Par., 1945)
Ding Dong Williams (RKO, 1946)
The Falcon's Adventure (RKO, 1946)
Sunset Pass (RKO, 1946)
Code of the West (RKO, 1947) (also producer)
Renegade Girl (UA, 1947) (also producer)
Rolling Home (Screen Guild, 1947) (also producer)
Shoot to Kill (Screen Guild, 1947)

Caged Fury (Par., 1948)
Waterfront at Midnight (Par., 1948)
Speed to Spare (Par., 1948)
Racing Luck (Col., 1948)
Jungle Jim (Col., 1948)
Highway 13 (Screen Guild, 1948)
Arson, Inc. (Screen Guild, 1949)
Sky Liner (Screen Guild, 1949)
The Lost Tribe (Col., 1949)
Zamba (Eagle Lion, 1949)
Treasure of Monte Cristo (Lip., 1949) (also script)
Deputy Marshall (Lip., 1949)
Gunfire (Lip., 1950) (also producer, story, script)
Captive Girl (Col., 1950)
Operation Haylift (Lip., 1950)
Pygmy Island (Col., 1950)
Everybody's Dancing (Lip., 1950) (also producer)
Mark of the Gorilla (Col., 1950)
On the Isle of Samoa (Col., 1950)
Jungle Jim in Pygmy Island (Col., 1950)
Bandit Queen (Lip., 1950) (also producer)
Train to Tombstone (Lip., 1950) (also producer)
Border Rangers (Lip., 1950) (also producer, story, script)
FBI Girl (Lip., 1951)
Danger Zone (Lip., 1951)
Smuggler's Gold (Col., 1951)
Fury of the Congo (Col., 1951)
Pier 23 (Lip., 1951) (also producer)
Roaring City (Lip., 1951) (also producer)
Savage Drums (Lip., 1951) (also producer)
The Jungle (Lip., 1952) (also producer)
Valley of the Headhunters (Col., 1953)
The Marshal's Daughter (UA, 1953)
Four Boys and a Gun (UA, 1957)
Street of Sinners (UA, 1957)
Island Woman (UA, 1958)
Cop Hater (UA, 1958)
The Muggers (UA, 1958)
The Lost Missile (UA, 1958) (also producer)

BERKELEY, BUSBY (William Berkeley Enos), b. Nov. 29, 1895,
    Los Angeles.
As Choreographer:
Whoopie (UA, 1930)
Kiki (UA, 1930)
Palmy Days (UA, 1931)
Flying High (MGM, 1931)
Night World (Univ., 1932)
Bird of Paradise (RKO, 1932)
The Kid from Spain (UA, 1932)
42nd Street (WB, 1933)
Gold Diggers of 1933 (WB, 1933)

Chorus girls Rickey Newell, Diane Bourget, Blanche McDonald, Marie Marks, Marjorie Murphy and Claire Angerot with Busby Berkeley (1933).

Footlight Parade (WB, 1933)
Roman Scandals (UA, 1933)
Fashions of 1934 (FN, 1934)
Wonder Bar (FN, 1934)
Twenty Million Sweethearts (FN, 1934)
Dames (WB, 1934)
Go into Your Dance (FN, 1935)
In Caliente (FN, 1935)
Stars over Broadway (WB, 1935)
Gold Diggers of 1937 (FN, 1936)
The Singing Marine (WB, 1937)
Varsity Show (WB, 1937)
Gold Diggers in Paris (WB, 1938)
Broadway Serenade (MGM, 1939)
Ziegfeld Girl (MGM, 1941)
Lady Be Good (MGM, 1941)
Born to Sing (MGM, 1941)
Girl Crazy (MGM, 1943)
Two Weeks With Love (MGM, 1950)
Call Me Mister (20th, 1951)
Two Tickets to Broadway (RKO, 1951)
Million Dollar Mermaid (MGM, 1952)
Small Town Girl (MGM, 1953)
Easy to Love (MGM, 1953)

Rose-Marie (MGM, 1954)
Billy Rose's Jumbo (MGM, 1962)

As Director:
She Had to Say Yes (FN, 1933) (with George Amy)
Gold Diggers of 1935 (FN, 1935)
Bright Lights (FN, 1935)
I Live for Love (WB, 1935)
Stage Struck (FN, 1936)
The Go Getter (WB, 1937)
Hollywood Hotel (WB, 1937)
Men Are Such Fools (WB, 1938)
Garden of the Moon (WB, 1938)
Comet Over Broadway (WB, 1938)
They Made Me a Criminal (WB, 1939)
Babes in Arms (MGM, 1939)
Fast and Furious (MGM, 1939)
Forty Little Mothers (RKO, 1940)
Strike up the Band (MGM, 1940)
Blonde Inspiration (MGM, 1941)
Babes on Broadway (MGM, 1941)
For Me and My Gal (MGM, 1942)
The Gang's All Here (20th, 1943)
Cinderella Jones (WB, 1946)
Take Me out to the Ball Game (MGM, 1949)

BERNDS, EDWARD
Blondie's Secret (Col., 1948)
Blondie's Big Deal (Col., 1949)
Blondie Hits the Jackpot (Col., 1949)
Feudin' Rhythm (Col., 1949)
Beware of Blondie (Col., 1950)
Blondie's Hero (Col., 1950)
Gasoline Alley (Col., 1951) (also story, script)
Corky of Gasoline Alley (Col., 1951) (also story, script)
Gold Raiders (UA, 1951)
Harem Girl (Col., 1952) (also script)
Ace Lucky (Col., 1952)
White Lightning (AA, 1953)
Private Eyes (AA, 1953) (also co-script)
Loose in London (AA, 1953) (also story, script)
Hot News (AA, 1953)
The Bowery Boys Meet the Monsters (AA, 1954) (also script)
Jungle Gents (AA, 1954) (also script)
Bowery to Bagdad (AA, 1955) (also script)
Spy Chasers (AA, 1955)
World Without End (AA, 1956) (also script)
Navy Wife (AA, 1956)
Dig That Uranium (AA, 1956)
Calling Homicide (AA, 1956) (also script)
The Storm Rider (20th 1957) (also co-script)
Reform School Girl (AIP, 1957) (also script)

Escape from Red Rock (20th, 1958) (also script)
Quantrill's Raiders (20th, 1958)
Space Master X-7 (20th, 1958)
Queen of Outer Space (AA, 1958)
Joy Ride (AA, 1958)
Alaska Passage (20th, 1959) (also script)
The Return of the Fly (20th, 1959) (also script)
Valley of the Dragons (Col., 1961) (also script)
The Three Stooges Meet Hercules (Col., 1962)
The Three Stooges in Orbit (Col., 1962)
Prehistoric Valley (ZRB Productions, 1966) (also script)

BERNHARDT, CURTIS (Kurt Bernhardt), b. April 15, 1899, Worms,
    Germany.
    Qualen der Nacht [Torments of the Night] (German, 1926) (also
        co-script)
    Die Waise von Lowood (German, 1926)
    Kinderseelen Klagen Euch an (German, 1927)
    Das Mädchen mit den Fünf Nullen [Das Grosse Los] (German,
        1927)
    Schinderhannes [The Prince of Rogues] (German, 1928) (also
        co-script)
    Das Letzte Fort (German, 1928)
    Die Frau, Nach der Man Sicht Sehat [Three Loves] (German,
        1929)
    Die Letzte Kompagnie [Thirteen Men and a Girl] (German,
        1930)
    Der Mann, der den Mord Beging [Nachte Am Bosporus] (Ger-
        man, 1931)
    L'Homme Qui Assassina [French version of Der Mann, Der Den
        Mord Beging] (German, 1931)
    Der Rebell (German, 1932) (with Luis Trenker)
    Der Grosse Rausch (German, 1932)
    Der Tunnel (German and French versions, 1933)
    L'Or dans la Rue (French, 1934)
    Le Vagabond Bien-Aimé (French, 1936)
    The Beloved Vagabond [British version of Le Vagabond Bien-
        Aimé) (Col., 1936)
    Carrefour (French, 1938)
    Nuit de Decembre (French, 1939)
    My Love Came Back (WB, 1940)
    The Lady with Red Hair (WB, 1940)
    Million Dollar Baby (WB, 1941)
    Juke Girl (WB, 1942)
    Happy Go Lucky (Par., 1943)
    Conflict (WB, 1945)
    Devotion (WB, 1946)
    My Reputation (WB, 1946)
    A Stolen Life (WB, 1946)
    Possessed (WB, 1947)
    The High Wall (MGM, 1949)
    The Doctor and the Girl (MGM, 1949)

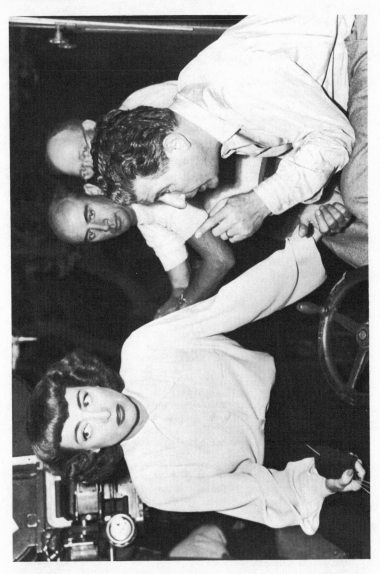

Payment on Demand (RKO, 1951) (also co-script)
Sirocco (Col. , 1951)
The Blue Veil (RKO, 1951)
The Merry Widow (MGM, 1952)
Miss Sadie Thompson (Col. , 1953)
Beau Brummel (MGM, 1954)
Interrupted Melody (MGM, 1955)
Gaby (MGM, 1956)
Damon and Pythias (MGM, 1961)
Stafanie in Rio (Casino, 1963)
Kisses for My President (WB, 1964) (also producer)

BINYON, CLAUDE, b. Oct. 17, 1905, Chicago.
    And the Angels Sing (Par. , 1944) (with George Marshall) (also
        story)
    Family Honeymoon (Univ. , 1948)
    The Saxon Charm (Univ. , 1948) (also script)
    Mother Didn't Tell Me (20th, 1950)
    Stella (20th, 1950) (also script)
    Aaron Slick from Punkin' Crick (Par. , 1952) (also script)
    Dreamboat (20th, 1952) (also script)
    Here Come the Girls (Par. , 1953)

BLACHE, ALICE GUY, b. 1878, Paris.
    The Shadow of the Moulin Rouge (Blache, 1914)
    The Woman of Mystery (State Rights, 1914)
    The Monster and the Girl (State Rights, 1914)
    The Dream Woman (State Rights, 1914) (also story, script)
    My Madonna (Metro, 1915)
    The Heart of a Painted Woman (Metro, 1915)
    What Will People Say? (Metro, 1916)
    Behind the Mask (National Films, 1917)
    The Empress (Pathé, 1917)
    The Adventurer (U.S. Amusement Corp. , 1917)
    When You and I Were Young (Art Dramas, 1917)
    The House of Cards (U.S. Amusement Corp. , 1917)
    A Soul Adrift (Pathé, 1918)
    The Great Adventure (Pathé, 1918)
    Tarnished Reputations (Pathé, 1920)

BLACHE, HERBERT, b. London.
    The Star of India (Blache, 1913)
    Fighting Death (State Rights, 1914)
    Hook and Hand (State Rights, 1914)
    The Chimes (U.S. Amusement Corp. , 1914) (with Tom Terrias)
    The Million Dollar Robbery (Solax, 1914)

Facing page: Joan Crawford with Curtis Bernhardt on the set of
Possessed (WB, 1947).

The Ocean Waif (International, 1915)
The Shooting of Dan McGrew (Metro, 1915)
Greater Love Hath No Man (Metro, 1915)
Her Own Way (Metro, 1915)
Barbara Frietchie (Metro, 1915)
The Song of the Wage Slave (Metro, 1915)
The Girl With Green Eyes (Pathé, 1916)
The Woman's Fight (Pathé, 1916)
Think It Over (Art Dramas, 1917) (also script)
The Auction of Virtue (Art Dramas, 1917)
The Divorce (Vitagraph, 1917)
A Man and a Woman (U.S. Amusement Corp., 1917)
The Silent Woman (Metro, 1918)
Loaded Dice (Pathé, 1918)
A Man's World (Metro, 1918)
The Uplifters (Metro, 1919)
Fools and Their Money (Metro, 1919)
The Man Who Stayed at Home (Metro, 1919)
Jeanne of the Gutter (Metro, 1919)
Satan Junior (Metro, 1919)
The Brat (Metro, 1919)
Stronger Than Death (Metro, 1920)
The Walk-Offs (Metro, 1920)
The Hope (Metro, 1920)
The New York Idea (Realart, 1920)
Saphead (Metro, 1921)
Out of the Chorus (Realart, 1921)
Nobody's Bride (Univ., 1923)
The Wild Party (Univ., 1923)
The Near Lady (Univ., 1923)
Fools and Riches (Univ., 1923)
High Speed (Univ., 1924)
Secrets of the Night (Univ.-Jewel, 1925)
Head Winds (Univ.-Jewel, 1925)
The Calgary Stampede (Univ.-Jewel, 1925)
The Mystery Club (Univ.-Jewel, 1926)
Burning the Wind (Univ., 1929)

BLACKTON, J. STUART (John Stuart Blackton), b. Jan.5, 1875,
    Sheffield, Eng.; d. Aug. 13, 1941.
  Womanhood, or the Glory of a Nation (Vitagraph, 1917) (with
    William P.S. Earle)
  The Message of the Mouse (Vitagraph, 1917)
  The Judgment House (Par., 1917)
  Safe for Democracy (Blackton, 1918) (with Elmer Clifton) (also
    producer)
  World for Sale (Par., 1918)
  Missing (Par., 1918)
  The Common Cause (Vitagraph, 1918)
  Life's Greatest Problem (Film Clearing House, 1919) (also pro-
    ducer)
  A House Divided (Film Clearing House, 1919) (also producer)
  The Littlest Scout (Film Clearing House, 1919) (also producer)

Respectable by Proxy (Vitagraph, 1919)
My Boy (Vitagraph, 1919) (also producer)
Dawn (Pathé, 1919)
The Moonshine Trail (Pathé, 1919)
My Husband's Other Wife (Pathé, 1919)
The Blood Barrier (Pathé, 1920)
The House of the Tolling Bell (Pathé, 1920) (also producer)
The Passer-By (Pathé, 1920)
Forbidden Valley (Pathé, 1920)
The Glorious Adventure (Stoll, 1922) (also producer)
A Gypsy Cavalier (British, 1922)
The Virgin Queen (Rose, 1923) (also producer)
On the Banks of the Wabash (Vitagraph, 1923)
Let Not Man Put Asunder (Vitagraph, 1924)
Between Friends (Vitagraph, 1924)
The Beloved Brute (Vitagraph, 1924)
Behold This Woman (Vitagraph, 1924)
The Clean Heart (Vitagraph, 1924)
The Redeeming Sin (Vitagraph, 1925)
Tides of Passion (Vitagraph, 1925)
The Happy Warrior (Vitagraph, 1925)
Bride of the Storm (WB, 1926)
The Gilded Highway (WB, 1926)
Hell-Bent for Heaven (WB, 1926)
The Passionate Quest (WB, 1926)

BLYSTONE, JOHN G., b. Dec. 2, 1892, Rice Lake, Wisc.; d.
      Aug. 7, 1938.
A Friendly Husband (Fox, 1923) (also story)
Soft Boiled (Fox, 1923) (also co-story, script)
Our Hospitality (Metro, 1923) (with Buster Keaton)
Ladies to Board (Fox, 1924)
Oh, You Tony! (Fox, 1924)
The Last Man on Earth (Fox, 1924)
Teeth (Fox, 1924)
Dick Turpin (Fox, 1925)
The Lucky Horseshoe (Fox, 1925)
The Everlasting Whisper (Fox, 1925)
The Best Bad Man (Fox, 1925)
My Own Pal (Fox, 1926)
Hard Boiled (Fox, 1926)
The Family Upstairs (Fox, 1926)
Wings of the Storm (Fox, 1926)
Ankles Preferred (Fox, 1927)
Slaves of Beauty (Fox, 1927)
Pajamas (Fox, 1927)
Sharp Shooters (Fox, 1928)
Mother Knows Best (Fox, 1928)
Captain Lash (Fox, 1929)
Thru Different Eyes (Fox, 1929)
The Sky Hawk (Fox, 1929)
The Big Party (Fox, 1930)

So This Is London (Fox, 1930)
Tol'able David (Col., 1930)
Mr. Lemon of Orange (Fox, 1931)
Men on Call (Fox, 1931)
Young Sinners (Fox, 1931)
She Wanted a Millionaire (Fox, 1932)
Charlie Chan's Chance (Fox, 1932)
Amateur Daddy (Fox, 1932)
Painted Woman (Fox, 1932)
Too Busy to Work (Fox, 1932)
Hot Pepper (Fox, 1933)
Shanghai Madness (Fox, 1933)
My Lips Betray (Fox, 1933)
Coming Out Party (Fox, 1934)
Change of Heart (Fox, 1934)
Hell in the Heavens (Fox, 1934)
The County Chairman (Fox, 1935)
Bad Boy (Fox, 1935)
Gentle Julia (20th, 1936)
Little Miss Nobody (20th, 1936)
The Magnificent Brute (Univ., 1936)
Great Guy (Grand National, 1936)
23 1/2 Hours Leave (Grand National, 1937)
Woman Chases Man (UA, 1937)
Music for Madame (RKO, 1937)
Swiss Miss (MGM, 1938)
Blockheads (MGM, 1938)

BOETTICHER, BUDD (Oscar Boetticher, Jr.), b. July 29, 1916,
    Chicago.
As Oscar Boetticher:
    One Mysterious Night (Col., 1944)
    The Missing Juror (Col., 1944)
    A Guy, a Gal and a Pal (Col., 1945)
    Escape in the Fog (Col., 1945)
    Youth on Trial (Col., 1945)
    The Fleet That Came to Stay (Par., 1946)
    Assigned to Danger (Eagle Lion, 1948)
    Behind Locked Doors (Eagle Lion, 1948)
    The Wolf Hunters (Mon., 1949)
    Black Midnight (Mon., 1949)
    Killer Shark (Mon., 1950)

As Budd Boetticher:
    The Bullfighter and the Lady (Rep., 1951)
    The Sword of D'Artagnan (Univ., 1951)
    The Cimarron Kid (Univ., 1951)
    Red Ball Express (Univ., 1952)
    Bronco Buster (Univ., 1952)
    Horizons West (Univ., 1952)
    City Beneath the Sea (Univ., 1953)
    Seminole (Univ., 1953)

The Man from the Alamo (Univ., 1953)
East of Sumatra (Univ., 1953)
Wings of the Hawk (Univ., 1953)
The Magnificent Matador (20th, 1955)
The Killer Is Loose (UA, 1956)
Seven Men from Now (WB, 1956)
The Tall T (Col., 1957)
Decision at Sundown (Col.., 1957)
Buchanan Rides Alone (Col., 1958)
Ride Lonesome (Col., 1959) (also producer)
Westbound (WB, 1959)
Comanche Station (Col., 1960) (also producer)
The Rise and Fall of Legs Diamond (WB, 1960)
A Time for Dying (Etoile, 1971) (also producer, script)
Arruza (Avco Emb., 1972) (also producer, script)

BOGART, PAUL, b. Nov. 21, 1919, New York City.
Marlow (MGM, 1969)
Halls of Anger (UA, 1970)
Cancel My Reservation (WB, 1972)
Class of '44 (WB, 1973) (also producer)

BOGDANOVICH, PETER, b. July 30, 1939, Kingston, N.Y.
Voyage to the Planet of Prehistoric Women (AIP, 1966) (also
    narrator) (as Derek Thomas)
Targets (Par., 1968) (also producer, script, actor)
The Last Picture Show (Col., 1971) (also script)
What's Up Doc (WB, 1972) (also producer, story)
Paper Moon (Par., 1973) (also producer)

BOLESLAWSKI (or BOLESLAVSKY), RICHARD (Ryszard Strzed-
    nicki Boleslavsky), b. Feb. 4, 1889, Warsaw; d. Jan. 17,
    1937.
Tri Vstrechi (Russian, 1915)
Ti Yeshye Nye Umeyesh Lyubit [Nina] (Russian, 1915) (also
    actor)
Nye Razum, a Strasti Pravyat Mirom [Otravlennoye Serdtse]
    [Skorbnaya Povest Unikh Dush] (Russian, 1916)
Semya Polenovikh [Sgubila Strast Bezumnaya] (Russian, 1916)
    (also actor)
Khleb [Bread] (Russian, 1918) (with Boris Sushkevich) (also
    script, actor)
Bohaterstwo Polskiego Skauta Poland (Polish, 1919)
Cud Nad Wisla [Miracle on the Vistula] (Polish, 1921)
The Last of the Lone Wolf (Col., 1930)
The Gay Diplomat (RKO, 1931)
Woman Pursued (RKO, 1931)
Rasputin and the Empress (MGM, 1933)
Storm at Daybreak (MGM, 1933)
Beauty for Sale (MGM, 1933)

Operator 13 (MGM, 1934)
Men in White (MGM, 1934)
Fugitive Lovers (MGM, 1934)
The Painted Veil (MGM, 1934)
Hollywood Party (MGM, 1934) (uncredited, with uncredited Allan
    Dwan and Roy Rowland)
Clive of India (20th, 1935)
Les Miserables (20th, 1935)
Metropolitan (20th, 1935)
O'Shaughnessy's Boy (MGM, 1935)
The Garden of Allah (UA, 1936)
Theodora Goes Wild (Col., 1936)
Three Godfathers (MGM, 1936)
The Last of Mrs. Cheyney (MGM, 1937)

BOORMAN, JOHN, b. Jan. 18, 1933, London, Eng.
Catch Us if You Can (Warner-Pathé/Anglo-Amalgamated, 1965)
Point Blank (MGM, 1967)
Hell in the Pacific (Cin., 1968)
Leo the Last (UA, 1970) also co-script)
Deliverance (WB, 1972) (also producer)

BORZAGE, FRANK, b. April 23, 1894, Salt Lake City, Utah; d.
    June 19, 1962.
The Land of Lizards (Mutual, 1916) (also actor)
Silent Shelby (Mutual, 1916) (also actor)
Immediate Lee (Mutual, 1916) (also actor)
Flying Colors (Triangle, 1917)
Until They Get Me (Triangle, 1917)
The Gun Woman (Triangle, 1918)
The Shoes That Danced (Triangle, 1918)
Innocents' Progress (Triangle, 1918)
Society for Sale (Triangle, 1918)
An Honest Man (Triangle, 1918)
Who Is to Blame? (Triangle, 1918)
The Ghost Flower (Triangle, 1918)
The Curse of Iku (Essanay, 1918)
Toton (Triangle, 1919)
Prudence of Broadway (Triangle, 1919)
Whom the Gods Would Destroy (FN, 1919)
Humoresque (Par., 1920)
The Duke of Chimney Butte (Federated, 1921)
Get-Rich-Quick Wallingford (Par., 1921)
Back Pay (Par., 1922)
Billy Jim (FBO, 1922)
The Good Provider (Par., 1922)
The Valley of Silent Men (Par., 1922)
The Pride of Palomar (Par., 1922)
Children of Dust (Associated FN, 1923) (also producer)
The Nth Commandment (Par., 1923)
The Age of Desire (Associated FN, 1923) (also producer)

Marlene Dietrich and Gary Cooper (right) with Frank Borzage on
the set of <u>Desire</u> (Par., 1936).

Secrets (FN, 1924)
The Lady (FN, 1925) (also producer)
Daddy's Gone A'Hunting (Metro-Goldwyn, 1925) (also producer)
The Circle (Metro-Goldwyn, 1925)
Lazybones (Fox, 1925)
Wages for Wives (Fox, 1925)
The First Year (Fox, 1926)
The Dixie Merchant (Fox, 1926)
Early to Wed (Fox, 1926)
Marriage License? (Fox, 1926)
Seventh Heaven (Fox, 1927)
Street Angel (Fox, 1928)
The River (Fox, 1929)
Lucky Star (Fox, 1929)
They Had to See Paris (Fox, 1929)
Song O'My Heart (Fox, 1930)
Liliom (Fox, 1930)
Doctors' Wives (Fox, 1931)
Bad Girl (Fox, 1931)
Young As You Feel (Fox, 1931)
After Tomorrow (Fox, 1932)
Young America (Fox, 1932)

A Farewell to Arms (Par., 1932)
A Man's Castle (Col., 1933)
Secrets (UA, 1933)
No Greater Glory (Col., 1934)
Little Man What Now? (Univ., 1934)
Flirtation Walk (FN, 1934) (also producer)
Living on Velvet (FN, 1935)
Stranded (WB, 1935)
Shipmates Forever (FN, 1935)
Desire (Par., 1936)
Hearts Divided (FN, 1936)
Green Light (WB, 1937)
History Is Made at Night (UA, 1937)
The Big City (MGM, 1937)
Mannequin (MGM, 1937)
Three Comrades (MGM, 1938)
The Shining Hour (MGM, 1938)
I Take This Woman (MGM, 1938) (replaced Josef von Sternberg,
   film completed by W.S. Van Dyke II in 1940)
Disputed Passage (Par., 1939)
The Mortal Storm (MGM, 1940)
Strange Cargo (MGM, 1940)
Flight Command (MGM, 1940)
Smilin' Through (MGM, 1941)
The Vanishing Virginian (MGM, 1941)
Seven Sweethearts (MGM, 1942)
Stage Door Canteen (UA, 1943)
His Butler's Sister (Univ., 1943)
Till We Meet Again (Par., 1944)
The Spanish Main (RKO, 1945)
I've Always Loved You (Rep., 1946)
The Magnificent Doll (Univ., 1946)
That's My Man (Rep., 1947)
Moonrise (Rep., 1948)
China Doll (UA, 1958)
The Big Fisherman (BV, 1959)
L'Atalantide [Journey Beneath the Desert] (AIP, 1960) (uncred-
   ited, with Edgar G. Ulmer and Giuseppe Masini)

BRABIN, CHARLES J., b. April 17, 1883, Liverpool, Eng.; d. Nov.
   3, 1957.
The Man Who Disappeared* (Edison, 1914)
The Raven (Essanay, 1915)
The House of the Lost Court (Edison, 1915)
That Sort (Essanay, 1916)
The Price of Fame (Vitagraph, 1916)
Mary Jane's Pa (Vitagraph, 1917)
The Sixteenth Wife (Vitagraph, 1917)
The Secret Kingdom* (Vitagraph, 1917) (with Theodore Marston)
Babette (Vitagraph, 1917)
Persuasive Peggy (Mayfair Shallenberger & Priest, 1917)
The Adopted Son (Metro, 1917)

Red, White and Blue Blood (Metro, 1917)
Breakers Ahead (Metro, 1918)
Social Quicksands (Metro, 1918)
A Pair of Cupids (Metro, 1918)
The Poor Rich Man (Metro, 1918)
Buchanan's Wife (Fox, 1918)
His Bonded Wife (Metro, 1918)
Thou Shalt Not (Fox, 1919)
La Belle Russe (Fox, 1919)
Kathleen Mavourneen (Fox, 1919)
While New York Sleeps (Fox, 1920)
Blind Wives (Fox, 1921) (also script)
Footfalls (Fox, 1921) (also script)
The Broadway Peacock (Fox, 1922)
The Lights of New York (Fox, 1922) (also story)
Driven (Univ., 1923) (also for production company)
Six Days (Goldwyn, 1923)
So Big (FN, 1924)
Stella Maris (Univ., 1925) (also co-script)
Mismates (FN, 1926)
Twinkletoes (FN, 1926)
Framed (FN, 1927)
Hard-Boiled Haggerty (FN, 1927)
The Valley of the Giants (FN, 1927)
Burning Daylight (FN, 1928)
The Whip (FN, 1928)
The Bridge of San Luis Rey (MGM, 1929)
The Ship from Shanghai (MGM, 1930)
Call of the Flesh (MGM, 1930)
The Great Meadow (MGM, 1931)
Sporting Blood (MGM, 1931)
Beast of the City (MGM, 1932)
New Morals for Old (MGM, 1932)
Washington Masquerade (MGM, 1932)
The Mask of Fu Manchu (MGM, 1932)
The Secret of Madame Blanche (MGM, 1933)
Stage Mother (MGM, 1933)
Day of Reckoning (MGM, 1933)
A Wicked Woman (MGM, 1934)

BRADBURY, ROBERT NORTH
   The Iron Test* (Vitagraph, 1918) (with Paul Hurst)
   The Perils of Thunder Mountain* (Vitagraph, 1919) (with W.J.
       Bauman)
   The Faith of the Strong (Select, 1919)
   The Last of His People (Select, 1919) (with Frank Howard
       Clark) (also co-script)
   The Death Trap (Pathé, 1920) (also script)
   Things Men Do (M.B. Schlesinger, 1921) (also script)
   Riders of the Law (Sunset, 1922) (also script)
   Desert Rider (Sunset, 1923)
   The Forbidden Trail (Sunset, 1923) (also script, titles, editor)

Galloping Thru (Sunset, 1923)
The Red Warning (Univ., 1923)
What Love Will Do (Univ., 1923)
Behind Two Guns (Sunset, 1924) (also script)
Wanted By the Law (Sunset, 1924) (also script)
Yankee Speed (Sunset, 1924) (also script)
The Galloping Ace (Sunset, 1924)
In High Gear (Sunset, 1924) (also story, co-script)
The Man from Wyoming (Univ., 1924)
The Phantom Horseman (Univ., 1924)
The Battler (Bud Barsky, 1925) (also script)
The Speed Demon (Bud Barsky, 1925)
The Danger Zone (Bud Barsky, 1925)
Just Plain Folks (Bud Barsky, 1925)
Hidden Loot (Univ., 1925)
Moccasins (Independent Pictures, 1925)
Riders of Mystery (Independent Pictures, 1925)
Daniel Boone Through the Wilderness (Sunset, 1926)
The Border Sheriff (Univ., 1926) (also continuity)
Davy Crockett at the Fall of the Alamo (Sunset, 1926)
The Fighting Doctor (Hercules, 1926)
Looking for Trouble (Univ., 1926)
The Mojave Kid (FBO, 1927)
Sitting Bull at the Spirit Lake Massacre (Sunset, 1927)
The Bantam Cowboy (FBO, 1928) (also supervisor, story)
Headin' for Danger (FBO, 1928)
Lightning Speed (FBO, 1928) (also story, continuity)
Forbidden Trails (Cosmos, 1929) (also story, titles, editor)
Son of the Plains (Syndicate, 1931) (also story, script)
Dugan of the Bad Lands (Mon., 1931) (also story, script)
Son of Oklahoma (Sono Art-World Wide, 1932)
Texas Buddies (Sono Art-World Wide, 1932)
Riders of the Desert (Sono Art-World Wide, 1932)
Man from Hell's Hinges (Sono Art-World Wide, 1932) (also
     story, script)
Law of the West (Sono Art-World Wide, 1932) (also story,
     script)
Hidden Valley (Sono Art-World Wide, 1933)
The Gallant Fool (Mon., 1933)
Breed of the Border (Mon., 1933)
Galloping Romeo (Mon., 1933) (also story)
The Ranger's Code (Mon., 1933)
Riders of Destiny (Mon., 1933) (also story, script)
Western Justice (Supreme, 1934)
West of the Divide (Mon., 1934) (also story, script)
Lucky Texan (Mon., 1934) (also story, script)
Blue Steel (Mon., 1934 (also story, script)
The Man from Utah (Mon., 1934)
Happy Landing (Mon., 1934)
The Star Packer (Mon., 1934) (also story, script)
The Trail Beyond (Mon., 1934)
Lawless Frontier (Mon., 1935) (also script)
Smokey Smith (Supreme, 1935)

Rainbow Valley (Mon., 1935)
Courageous Avenger (Supreme, 1935) (also story)
Kid Courageous (Supreme, 1935)
The Dawn Rider (Mon., 1935) (also script)
Rider of the Law (Supreme, 1935)
Westward Ho (Rep., 1935)
Between Men (Supreme, 1935) (also story)
Lawless Range (Rep., 1935)
The Last of the Warrens (Supreme, 1936) (also story)
Cavalry (Rep., 1936)
Sundown Saunders (Supreme, 1936) (also story, script)
Headin' for Rio Grande (Grand National, 1936)
The Gun Ranger (Rep., 1937)
Riders of the Dawn (Mon., 1937) (also producer)
Stars over Arizona (Mon., 1937) (also producer)
The Trusted Outlaw (Rep., 1937)
Where Trails Divide (Mon., 1937)
Danger Valley (Mon., 1937) (also producer)
Hittin' the Trail (Grand National, 1937)
Riders of the Rockies (Grand National, 1937)
Sing, Cowboy, Sing (Grand National, 1937)
Trouble in Texas (Grand National, 1937)

BRADLEY, DAVID, b. 1920, Winnetka, Ill.
Oliver Twist (Brandon, 1940) (also producer, adaptation, music,
    co-camera, editor, actor)
Peer Gynt (Brandon, 1941) (also producer, co-adaptation, co-
    camera, editor, actor)
Julius Caesar (Brandon, 1949) (also producer, adaptation, actor)
Talk About a Stranger (MGM, 1952)
Dragstrip Riot (AIP, 1958)
Twelve to the Moon (Col., 1960)

BRAHM, JOHN (Hans Brahm), b. Aug. 17, 1893, Hamburg, Ger-
    many.
Broken Blossoms (Twickenham, 1936)
Counsel for Crime (Col., 1937)
Penitentiary (Col., 1938)
Girls' School (Col., 1938)
Let Us Live (Col., 1939)
Rio (Univ., 1939)
Escape to Glory (Col., 1940)
Wild Geese Calling (20th, 1941)
The Undying Monster (20th, 1942)
Tonight We Raid Calais (20th, 1943)
Wintertime (20th, 1943)
The Lodger (Univ., 1944)
Guest in the House (UA, 1944) (replaced by Milestone)
Hangover Square (20th, 1945)
Three Little Girls in Blue (20th, 1945) (replaced by H. Bruce
    Humberstone)

The Locket (RKO, 1946)
The Brasher Doubloon (20th, 1947)
Singapore (Univ., 1947)
Il Ladro Di Venezia (20th, 1951)
The Miracle of Our Lady of Fatima (WB, 1952)
Face to Face (ep: "The Secret Sharer") (RKO, 1952) (with
    Bretaigne Windust)
The Diamond Queen (WB, 1953)
The Mad Magician (Col., 1954)
Die Goldene Pest (German, 1954)
Von Himmel Gefallen (German, 1955)
Bengazi (RKO, 1955)
Hot Rods to Hell (MGM, 1967)

BRANNON, FRED C., b. April 26, 1901, New Orleans.
The Purple Monster Strikes* (Rep., 1945) (with Spencer Gordon
    Bennett)
The Crimson Ghost* (Rep., 1946) (with William Witney)
Daughter of Don Q* (Rep., 1946) (with Spencer Gordon Bennett)
King of the Forest Rangers* (Rep., 1946) (with Spencer Gordon
    Bennett)
The Phantom Rider* (Rep., 1946) (with Spencer Gordon Ben-
    nett)
The Black Widow* (Rep., 1947) (with Spencer Gordon Bennett)
Jesse James Rides Again* (Rep., 1947) (with Thomas Carr)
Son of Zorro* (Rep., 1947) (with Spencer Gordon Bennett)
Adventures of Frank and Jesse James* (Rep., 1948) (with
    Yakima Canutt)
Dangers of the Canadian Mounted* (Rep., 1948) (with Yakima
    Canutt)
G-Men Never Forget* (Rep., 1948) (with Yakima Canutt)
Federal Agents vs. Underworld Inc.* (Rep., 1949)
Ghost of Zorro* (Rep., 1949)
King of the Rocket Men* (Rep., 1949)
Frontier Investigator (Rep., 1949)
Bandit King of Texas (Rep., 1949)
Desperadoes of the West* (Rep., 1950)
The Invisible Monster* (Rep., 1950)
The James Brothers of Missouri* (Rep., 1950)
Radar Patrol vs. Spy King* (Rep., 1950)
Gunmen of Abilene (Rep., 1950)
Salt Lake Raiders (Rep., 1950)
Vigilante Hideout (Rep., 1950)
Code of the Silver Sage (Rep., 1950)
Rustlers on Horseback (Rep., 1950)
Don Daredevil Rides Again* (Rep., 1951)
Flying Disc Man from Mars* (Rep., 1951)
Government Agents vs. Phantom Legion* (Rep., 1951)
Arizona Manhunt (Rep., 1951)
Night Riders of Montana (Rep., 1951)
Rough Riders of Durango (Rep., 1951)
Night Raiders (Mon., 1952)

Radar Men from the Moon* (Rep. , 1952)
Wild Horse Ambush (Rep. , 1952)
Zombies of the Stratosphere* (Rep. , 1952)
Captive of Billy the Kid (Rep. , 1952)
Jungle Drums of Africa* (Rep. , 1953)

BRETHERTON, HOWARD, b. Feb. 13, 1896, Tacoma, Wash.; d.
        April 12, 1969.
While London Sleeps (WB, 1926)
The Black Diamond Express (WB, 1927)
The Bush Leaguer (WB, 1927)
Hills of Kentucky (WB, 1927)
One-Round Hogan (WB, 1927)
The Silver Slave (WB, 1927)
Across the Atlantic (WB, 1928)
Caught in the Fog (WB, 1928)
The Chorus Kid (Lumas, 1928)
Turn Back the Hours (Lumas, 1928)
The Argyle Case (WB, 1929)
From Headquarters (WB, 1929)
The Greyhound Limited (WB, 1929)
The Time, the Place and the Girl (WB, 1929)
Isle of Escape (WB, 1930)
Second Choice (WB, 1930)
The Match King (WB, 1932)
Ladies They Talk About (WB, 1933) (with William Keighley)
Return of the Terror (WB, 1934)
El Cantante de Napoles (WB, 1934)
Dinky (WB, 1935) (with D. Ross Lederman)
Hop-Along Cassidy (Par. , 1935)
The Eagle's Brood (Par. , 1935)
Bar 20 Rides Again (Par. , 1935)
Call of the Prairie (Par. , 1935)
Three on the Trail (Par. , 1936)
Heart of the West (Par. , 1936)
Secret Valley (20th, 1936)
The Leathernecks Have Landed (Rep. , 1936)
Girl from Mandalay (Rep. , 1936)
Wild Brian Kent (RKO, 1936)
King of the Royal Mounted (20th, 1936)
It Happened Out West (20th, 1937)
Western Gold (20th, 1937)
County Fair (Mon. , 1937)
Wanted by the Police (Mon. , 1938)
Tough Kid (Mon. , 1938)
Boy's Reformatory (Mon. , 1938)
Irish Luck (Mon. , 1938)
Undercover Agent (Mon. , 1939)
Sky Patrol (Mon. , 1939)
Danger Flight (Mon. , 1939)
Navy Secrets (Mon. , 1939)

Midnight Limited (Mon. , 1940)
On the Spot (Mon. , 1940)
Chasing Trouble (Mon. , 1940)
Up in the Air (Mon. , 1940)
Laughing at Danger (Mon. , 1940)
The Showdown (Par. , 1940)
In Old Colorado (Par. , 1941)
Outlaws of the Desert (Par. , 1941)
Twilight on the Trail (Par. , 1941)
You're Out of Luck (Mon. , 1941)
Sign of the Wolf (Mon. , 1941)
West of Tombstone (Col. , 1942)
Rhythm Parade (Mon. , 1942)
Pirates of the Prairie (RKO, 1942)
Ghost Town Law (Mon. , 1942)
Down Texas Way (Mon. , 1942)
Below the Border (Mon. , 1942)
Riders of the West (Mon. , 1942)
West of the Law (Mon. , 1942)
Dawn on the Great Divide (Mon. , 1943)
Beyond the Last Frontier (Rep. , 1943)
Wagon Wheels West (Rep. , 1943)
Whispering Footsteps (Rep. , 1943)
Crimson City Cyclone (Rep. , 1943)
Fugitive from Sonora (Rep. , 1943)
Bordertown Gun Fighters (Rep. , 1943)
Riders of the Rio Grande (Rep. , 1943)
Outlaws of Sante Fe (Rep. , 1944)
Hidden Valley Outlaws (Rep. , 1944)
Law of Death Valley (Univ. , 1944)
The San Antonio Kid (Rep. , 1944)
Law of the Valley (Mon. , 1944)
The Girl Who Dared (Rep. , 1944)
Gunsmoke (Mon. , 1945)
The Navajo Trail (Univ. , 1945)
The Topeka Terror (Rep. , 1945)
Renegades of the Rio Grande (Univ. , 1945)
The Big Show-Off (Rep. , 1945)
Identity Unknown (Rep. , 1945) (also associate producer)
The Monster and the Ape (Col. , 1945)
Who's Guilty* (Col. , 1945) (with Wallace Grissell)
The Trap (Mon. , 1947
Ridin' Down the Trail (Mon. , 1947)
The Prince of Thieves (Col. , 1948)
Where the North Begins (Screen Guild, 1948)
The Story of Life (Crusade, 1948)
Triggerman (Mon. , 1948)
Whip Law (Mon. , 1950)
Night Raiders (Mon. , 1952)

BROOKS, RICHARD, b. May 18, 1912, Philadelphia.
   Crisis (MGM, 1950) (also script)
   The Light Touch (MGM, 1951) (also script)
   Deadline U.S.A. (20th, 1952) (also script)
   Battle Circus (MGM, 1952) (also script)
   Take the High Ground (MGM, 1953)
   The Flame and the Flesh (MGM, 1954)
   The Last Time I Saw Paris (MGM, 1954)
   The Blackboard Jungle (MGM, 1955) (also script)
   The Last Hunt (MGM, 1956) (also script)
   The Catered Affair (MGM, 1956)
   Something of Value (MGM, 1957) (also script)
   The Brothers Karamazov (MGM, 1958) (also script)
   Cat on a Hot Tin Roof (MGM, 1958) (also script)
   Elmer Gantry (UA, 1960) (also script)
   Sweet Bird of Youth (MGM, 1962) (also script)
   Lord Jim (Col., 1965) (also script)
   The Professionals (Col., 1966) (also script)
   In Cold Blood (Col., 1967) (also script)
   The Happy Ending (UA, 1969) (also producer, script)
   $ [i.e., "Dollars"] (Col., 1971) (also script)

BROWN, CLARENCE, b. May 10, 1890, Clinton, Mass.
   The Last of the Mohicans (Associated Producers, 1920) (with
     Maurice Tourneur)
   The Great Redeemer (Metro, 1920) (with Maurice Tourneur)
   The Foolish Matrons (Associated Producers, 1921)
   The Light in the Dark (Associated FN, 1922) (also co-script)
   Robin Hood, Jr. (East Coast, 1923) (uncredited, with Clarence
     Bricker)
   Don't Marry for Money (Webster, 1923)
   The Acquittal (Univ., 1923)
   The Signal Tower (Univ., 1924)
   Butterfly (Univ., 1924)
   Smouldering Fires (Univ., 1924)
   The Goose Woman (Univ., 1925)
   The Eagle (Unov., 1925)
   Kiki (FN, 1926)
   Flesh and the Devil (MGM, 1927)
   Trail of '98 (MGM, 1928)
   A Woman of Affairs (MGM, 1928)
   Wonder of Women (MGM, 1929)
   Navy Blues (MGM, 1930)
   Anna Christie (MGM, 1930)
   Romance (MGM, 1930)
   Inspiration (MGM, 1931)
   A Free Soul (MGM, 1931)
   Possessed (MGM, 1931)

Emma (MGM, 1932)
Letty Lynton (MGM, 1932)
The Son-Daughter (MGM, 1932)
Looking Forward (MGM, 1933)
Night Flight (MGM, 1933)
Sadie McKee (MGM, 1934)
Chained (MGM, 1934)
Anna Karenina (MGM, 1935)
Ah, Wilderness! (MGM, 1935)
Wife vs. Secretary (MGM, 1936)
The Gorgeous Hussy (MGM, 1936)
Conquest (MGM, 1937)
Of Human Hearts (MGM, 1938)
Idiot's Delight (MGM, 1939)
The Rains Came (20th, 1939)
Edison, the Man (MGM, 1940)
Come Live With Me (MGM, 1941) (also producer)
They Met in Bombay (MGM, 1941)
The Human Comedy (MGM, 1943) (also producer)
The White Cliffs of Dover (MGM, 1944)
National Velvet (MGM, 1944)
The Yearling (MGM, 1946) (also producer)
Song of Love (MGM, 1947) (also producer)
Intruder in the Dust (MGM, 1949) (also producer)
To Please a Lady (MGM, 1950)
It's a Big Country (MGM, 1951) (with Charles Vidor, Richard
    Thorpe, John Sturges, Don Hartman, Don Weis, William
    Wellman)
Angels in the Outfield (MGM, 1951) (also producer)
When in Rome (MGM, 1952) (also producer)
Plymouth Adventure (MGM, 1952) (also producer)

BROWN, HARRY JOE, b. Sept. 22, 1893, Pittsburgh.
Bashful Buccaneer (Rayart, 1925) (also producer)
Broadway Billy (Rayart, 1926) (also producer)
Danger Quest (Rayart, 1926) (also producer)
The Dangerous Dude (Rayart, 1926) (also producer)
Fighting Thorobreds (Rayart, 1926) (also producer)
The High Flyer (Rayart, 1926) (also producer)
Kentucky Handicap (Rayart, 1926) (also producer)
Moran of the Mounted (Rayart, 1926) (also producer)
The Night Owl (Rayart, 1926) (also producer)
One Punch O'Day (Rayart, 1926) (also producer)
Racing Romance (Rayart, 1926) (also producer)
Rapid Fire Romance (Rayart, 1926) (also producer)
The Self Starter (Rayart, 1926) (also producer)
Stick to Your Story (Rayart, 1926) (also producer)
The Windjammer (Rayart, 1926) (also producer)
The Winner (Rayart, 1926) (also producer)
The Land Beyond the Law (FN, 1927)
Gun Gospel (FN, 1927)
The Racing Fool (Rayart, 1927) (also producer)

Romantic Rogue (Rayart, 1927) (also producer)
The Royal American (Rayart, 1927) (also producer)
The Scorcher (Rayart. 1927) (also producer)
The Wagon Show (FN, 1928)
Code of the Scarlet (FN, 1928)
The Lawless Legion (FN, 1929)
The Royal Rider (FN, 1929)
The Fighting Legion (Univ., 1930)
Lucky Larkin (Univ., 1930)
Mountain Justice (Univ., 1930)
Parade of the West (Univ., 1930)
Song of the Caballero (Univ., 1930)
Sons of the Saddle (Univ., 1930)
The Squealer (Col., 1930)
A Woman of Experience (Pathé, 1931)
Madison Square Garden (Par., 1932)
The Billion Dollar Scandal (Par., 1933)
I Love That Man (Par., 1933)
Sitting Pretty (Par., 1933)
Knickerbocker Holiday (UA, 1944) (also producer)

BROWN, KARL, b. Pennsylvania.
Prince of Diamonds (Col., 1930)
Flames (Mon., 1932)
The White Legion (Grand National, 1936)
In His Steps (Grand National, 1936)
Michael O'Halloran (Rep., 1937)
Port of Missing Girls (Mon., 1938)
Numbered Woman (Mon., 1938)
Barefoot Boy (Mon., 1938)
Under the Big Top (Mon., 1938)

BROWN, ROWLAND C., b. Nov. 6, 1900, Akron, Ohio; d. May 6,
    1963.
Quick Millions (Fox, 1931) (also co-script)
Hell's Highway (RKO, 1932) (also co-script)
Blood Money (UA, 1933) (also co-script)
The Devil Is a Sissy (MGM, 1936) (replaced by W.S. Van Dyke
    II) (also story)

BROWNING, TOD, b. July 12, 1882, Louisville, Ky.; d. Oct. 6,
    1962.
Jim Bludso (Fine Arts-Triangle, 1917) (with Wilfred Lucas)
A Love Sublime (Fine Arts-Triangle, 1917) (with Wilfred Lucas)
Hands Up! (Fine Arts-Triangle, 1917) (with Wilfred Lucas
Peggy, the Will O' the Wisp (Metro, 1917)
The Jury of Fate (Metro, 1917)
The Eyes of Mystery (Metro, 1918)
The Brazen Beauty (Univ., 1918)
The Legion of Death (Metro, 1918)

Revenge (Metro, 1918)
Which Woman? (Bluebird-Univ., 1918) (also co-continuity)
The Deciding Kiss (Bluebird-Univ., 1918) (also co-script)
Set Free (Bluebird-Univ., 1918) (also co-script)
The Wicked Darling (Univ., 1919)
The Exquisite Thief (Univ., 1919)
The Unpainted Woman (Univ., 1919)
The Petal on the Current (Univ., 1919)
Bonnie, Bonnie Lassie (Univ., 1919) (also co-script)
The Virgin of Stamboul (Univ.-Jewel, 1920) (also co-script)
Outside the Law (Univ.-Jewel, 1921) (also producer, co-story,
    co-script)
No Woman Knows (Univ.-Jewel, 1921) (also co-script)
The Wise Kid (Univ., 1922)
The Man Under Cover (Univ., 1922)
Under Two Flags (Univ.-Jewel, 1922) (also adaptation)
Drifting (Univ.-Jewel, 1923) (also co-script)
White Tiger (Univ.-Jewel, 1923) (also story, co-script)
The Day of Faith (Goldwyn, 1923)
The Dangerous Flirt (FBO, 1924)
Silk Stocking Sal (FBO, 1924)
The Unholy Three (MGM, 1925)
Dollar Down (Truart, 1925)
The Mystic (MGM, 1925) (also story)
The Blackbird (MGM, 1926) (also story)
The Road to Mandalay (MGM, 1926) (also co-story)
The Show (MGM, 1927)
The Unknown (MGM, 1927) (also story)
London After Midnight (MGM, 1927) (also producer, story, co-
    script)
The Big City (MGM, 1928) (also story)
West of Zanzibar (MGM, 1928)
Where East Is East (MGM, 1929) (also producer, co-story)
The Thirteenth Chair (MGM, 1929)
Outside the Law (Univ., 1930) (also story, co-script)
Dracula (Univ., 1931)
The Iron Man (Univ., 1931)
Freaks (MGM, 1932)
Fast Workers (MGM, 1933)
Mark of the Vampire (MGM, 1935) (also story)
The Devil-Doll (MGM, 1936) (also story)
Miracles for Sale (MGM, 1939)

BRUCKMAN, CLYDE, b. 1894, San Bernardino, Calif.; d. 1955.
    The General (UA, 1927) (also co-story, co-adaptation)
    Horse Shoes (Pathé, 1927)
    A Perfect Gentleman (Pathé, 1928)
    Welcome Danger (Par., 1929) (also co-script)
    Feet First (Par., 1930)

Facing page: The cast of Freaks (MGM, 1932) with Tod Browning.

Everything's Rosie (RKO, 1931)
Movie Crazy (Par., 1932)
Spring Tonic (Fox, 1935)
Man on the Flying Trapeze (Par., 1935)

BUCHOWETSKI (BUCHOWETZKI), DIMITRI, b. 1895, Russia; d. 1932.
Anita Jo (German, 1919)
Die Letzte Stunde (German, 1920)
Danton [All for a Woman] (German, 1920)
Sappho [Mad Love] (German, 1921) (also script)
Der Galilaer (German, 1921)
Othello [The Moor] (German, 1922) (also co-script)
Peter der Grosse (German, 1922)
Das Laster des Spiels (German, 1923)
Das Karussel des Lebens (German, 1923) (also co-script)
Men (Par., 1924) (also story)
Lily of the Dust (Par., 1924)
The Swan (Par., 1925) (also script)
Graustark (FN, 1925)
The Crown of Lies (Par., 1926)
The Midnight Sun (Univ.-Jewel, 1926)
Valencia (MGM, 1926) (also co-story)
Love (MGM, 1927) (replaced by Edmund Goulding)
Weib im Dschungel [German version of The Letter] (Par., 1930)
Le Requisitoire [French version of Manslaughter] (Par., 1930)
Die Nacht der Entscheindung [German version of The Virtuous Sin] (Par., 1931)
Stamboul (Par., 1931)

BUCQUET, HAROLD S., b. April 10, 1891, London, Eng.; d. Feb. 13, 1946.
Young Dr. Kildare (MGM, 1938)
Calling Dr. Kildare (MGM, 1939)
On Borrowed Time (MGM, 1939)
Secret of Dr. Kildare (MGM, 1939)
Dr. Kildare's Strange Case (MGM, 1940)
We Who Are Young (MGM, 1940)
Dr. Kildare Goes Home (MGM, 1940)
Dr. Kildare's Crisis (MGM, 1940)
The Penalty (MGM, 1941)
The People vs. Dr. Kildare (MGM, 1941)
Dr. Kildare's Wedding Day (MGM, 1941)
Kathleen (MGM, 1941)
Calling Dr. Gillespie (MGM, 1942)
The War Against Mrs. Hadley (MGM, 1942)
Tartu (The Adventures of Tartu) (MGM, 1943)
Dragon Seed (MGM, 1944) (with Jack Conway)
Without Love (MGM, 1945) (with Jack Conway

Shirley Temple with Harold S. Bucquet on <u>Kathleen</u> set (MGM, 1941).

BUTLER, DAVID, b. Dec. 17, 1894, San Francisco.
 High School Hero (Fox, 1927) (also co-story)
 Win That Girl (Fox, 1927)
 The News Parade (Fox, 1928) (also co-story)
 Prep and Pep (Fox, 1928)
 Masked Emotions (Fox, 1929) (with Kenneth Hawks)
 Fox Movietone Follies of 1929 (Fox, 1929) (also story)
 Chasing Through Europe (Fox, 1929) (with Alfred E. Werker)
 Sunny Side Up (Fox, 1929) (also script)
 Just Imagine (Fox, 1930) (also script)
 High Society Blues (Fox, 1930)
 Delicious (Fox, 1931)
 A Connecticut Yankee (Fox, 1931)
 Business and Pleasure (Fox, 1931)
 Down to Earth (Fox, 1932)
 Handle With Care (Fox, 1932)
 Hold Me Tight (Fox, 1933)
 My Weakness (Fox, 1933) (also co-script)
 Bottoms Up (Fox, 1934) (also co-story, co-script)
 Handy Andy (Fox, 1934)
 Have a Heart (MGM, 1934) (also co-script)
 Bright Eyes (Fox, 1934) (also co-story)
 The Little Colonel (Fox, 1935)
 The Littlest Rebel (20th, 1935)
 Doubting Thomas (20th, 1935)
 Captain January (20th, 1936)
 White Fang (20th, 1936)
 Pigskin Parade (20th, 1936)

You're a Sweetheart (20th, 1937)
Ali Baba Goes to Town (20th, 1937)
Kentucky (20th, 1938)
Kentucky Moonshine (20th, 1938)
Straight, Place and Show (20th, 1938)
East Side of Heaven (Univ., 1939) (also co-story)
That's Right--You're Wrong (RKO, 1939)
If I Had My Way (Univ., 1940) (also producer, co-story)
You'll Find Out (RKO, 1940) (also producer, co-story)
Caught in the Draft (Par., 1941)
Playmates (RKO, 1941)
Road to Morocco (Par., 1942)
They Got Me Covered (RKO, 1942)
Thank Your Lucky Stars (WB, 1943)
Shine on Harvest Moon (WB, 1944)
The Princess and the Pirate (RKO, 1944)
San Antonio (WB, 1946) (uncredited, with Raoul Walsh)
The Time, the Place and the Girl (WB, 1946)
Two Guys from Milwaukee (WB, 1946)
My Wild Irish Rose (WB, 1947)
Two Guys from Texas (WB, 1948)
Look for the Silver Lining (WB, 1949)
It's a Great Feeling (WB, 1949)
John Loves Mary (WB, 1949)
Tea for Two (WB, 1950)
The Daughter of Rosie O'Grady (WB, 1950)
Painting the Clouds With Sunshine (WB, 1951)
Lullaby of Broadway (WB, 1951)
Where's Charley? (WB, 1952)
April in Paris (WB, 1952)
By the Light of the Silvery Moon (WB, 1953)
Calamity Jane (WB, 1953)
The Command (WB, 1954)
King Richard and the Crusaders (WB, 1954)
Jump into Hell (WB, 1955)
Glory (RKO, 1955) (also producer)
The Girl He Left Behind (WB, 1956)
The Right Approach (20th, 1961)
C'mon Let's Live a Little (Par., 1967)

BUZZELL, EDWARD, b. Nov. 13, 1897, Brooklyn, N.Y.
Big Timer (Col., 1932)
Hollywood Speaks (Col., 1932)
Virtue (Col., 1932)
Child of Manhattan (Col., 1933)
Ann Carver's Profession (Col., 1933)
Love Honor and Oh, Baby (Univ., 1933)
Cross Country Cruise (Univ., 1934)
The Human Side (Univ., 1934)
The Girl Friend (Col., 1935)
Transient Lady (Univ., 1936)
Three Married Men (Par., 1936)

The Luckiest Girl in the World (Univ., 1936)
As Good as Married (Univ., 1937)
Paradise for Three (MGM, 1938)
Fast Company (MGM, 1938)
Honolulu (MGM, 1939)
At the Circus (MGM, 1939)
Go West (MGM, 1940)
The Get-Away (MGM, 1941)
Married Bachelor (MGM, 1941)
Ship Ahoy (MGM, 1942)
The Omaha Trail (MGM, 1942)
The Youngest Profession (MGM, 1943)
Best Foot Forward (MGM, 1943)
Keep Your Powder Dry (MGM, 1945)
Easy to Wed (MGM, 1946)
Three Wise Fools (MGM, 1946)
Song of the Thin Man (MGM, 1947)
Neptune's Daughter (MGM, 1949)
A Woman of Distinction (Col., 1950)
Emergency Wedding (Col., 1950)
Confidentially Connie (MGM, 1953)
Ain't Misbehavin' (Univ., 1955)
Mary Had a Little (UA, 1961)

C

CABANNE, CHRISTY (William Christy Cabanne), b. April 16, 1888,
    St. Louis, Mo.; d. Oct. 15, 1950.
    The Dishonored Medal (Continental, 1914)
    The Outlaw's Revenge (Majestic, 1914)
    The Great Leap (Mutual, 1914)
    The Absentee (Majestic, 1915) (with Frank E. Woods)
    The Martyrs of the Alamo (Triangle, 1915)
    The Lost House (Majestic, 1915)
    The Lamb (Triangle, 1915)
    The Failure (Mutual, 1915)
    Enoch Arden (Triangle, 1915)
    Sold for Marriage (Triangle, 1916)
    The Flying Torpedo (Triangle, 1916)
    Diane of the Follies (Triangle, 1916)
    Daphne and the Pirates (Triangle, 1916)
    Reggie Mixes In (Triangle, 1916)
    Flirting With Fate (Triangle, 1916)
    Miss Robinson Crusoe (Metro, 1917)
    God's Outlaw (Metro, 1917)
    One of Many (Metro, 1917)
    The Slacker (Metro, 1917)
    The Great Secret* (Metro, 1917)
    Draft 258 (Metro, 1918)
    Cyclone Higgins M.D. (Metro, 1918)
    The Pest (Goldwyn, 1919)
    A Regular Fellow (Triangle, 1919)

The Mayor of Filbert (Triangle, 1919)
Fighting Through (W.W. Hodkinson, 1919)
The Triflers (Univ., 1920)
Burnt Wings (Univ., 1920)
The Notorious Mrs. Sands (Robertson-Cole, 1920)
The Beloved Cheater (Robertson-Cole, 1920)
Life's Twist (Robertson-Cole, 1920)
At the Stage Door (Robertson-Cole, 1921) (also script)
The Barricade (Robertson-Cole, 1921)
Live and Let Live (Robertson-Cole, 1921) (also script)
What's a Wife Worth? (Robertson-Cole, 1921) (also script)
Beyond the Rainbow (Robertson-Cole, 1922)
Till We Meet Again (Associated Exhibitors, 1922) (also script)
The Average Woman (C.C. Burr, 1924)
Is Love Everything? (Associated Exhibitors, 1924)
Lend Me Your Husband (C.C. Burr, 1924)
The Sixth Commandment (Associated Exhibitors, 1924) (also
    producer)
The Spitfire (Associated Exhibitors, 1924)
Youth for Sale (C.C. Burr, 1924)
The Masked Bride (MGM, 1925)
The Midshipman (MGM, 1925)
Monte Carlo (MGM, 1926)
Altars of Desire (MGM, 1927)
Annapolis (Pathé, 1928)
Driftwood (Col., 1928)
Nameless Men (Tiffany, 1928)
Restless Youth (Col., 1928)
Conspiracy (RKO, 1930)
The Dawn Trail (Col., 1930)
Sky Raiders (Col., 1931)
Carne de Cabaret [Spanish version of Ten Cents a Dance] (Col.,
    1931)
Convicted (Artclass, 1931)
Graft (Univ., 1931)
Hotel Continental (Tiffany, 1932)
Midnight Patrol (Mon., 1932)
Hearts of Humanity (Majestic, 1932)
Western Limited (Mon., 1932)
Red Haired Alibi (Tower, 1932)
The Unwritten Law (Majestic, 1932)
The Eleventh Commandment (Alliance, 1933)
World Gone Mad (Majestic, 1933)
Midshipman Jack (RKO, 1933)
Money Means Nothing (Mon., 1934)
Jane Eyre (Mon., 1934)
The Girl of the Limberlost (Mon., 1934)
When Strangers Meet (Liberty, 1934)
Behind the Green Lights (Mascot, 1935)
Rendezvous at Midnight (Univ., 1935)
One Frightened Night (Mon., 1935)
Keeper of the Bees (Mon., 1935)
Storm over the Andes (Univ., 1935)

Asalto Sobre El Chaco [Spanish version of Storm over the Andes]
    (Univ. , 1935)
Another Face (RKO, 1935)
The Last Outlaw (RKO, 1936)
We Who Are About to Die (RKO, 1936)
Criminal Lawyer (RKO, 1937)
The Outcasts of Poker Flats (RKO, 1937)
Don't Tell the Wife (RKO, 1937)
You Can't Beat Love (RKO, 1937)
Annapolis Salute (RKO, 1937)
The Westland Case (Univ. , 1937)
Night Spot (RKO, 1938)
Everybody's Doing It (RKO, 1938)
This Marriage Business (RKO, 1938)
Smashing the Spy Ring (Col. , 1938)
Mutiny on the Blackhawk (Univ. , 1939)
Tropic Fury (Univ. , 1939)
Legion of Lost Flyers (Univ. , 1939)
Man from Montreal (Univ. , 1940)
Danger on Wheels (Univ. , 1940)
Alias the Deacon (Univ. , 1940)
Hot Steel (Univ. , 1940)
Black Diamonds (Univ. , 1940)
Melody and Moonlight (Univ. , 1940)
The Mummy's Hand (Univ. , 1940)
The Devil's Pipeline (Univ. , 1940)
Scattergood Baines (RKO, 1941)
Scattergood Pulls the Strings (RKO, 1941)
Scattergood Meets Broadway (RKO, 1941)
Drums of the Congo (Univ. , 1942)
Scattergood Baines Rides High (RKO, 1942)
Timber (Univ. , 1942)
Scattergood Survives a Murder (RKO, 1942)
Top Sergeant (Univ. , 1942)
Cinderella Swings It (RKO, 1943)
Keep 'Em Slugging (Univ. , 1943)
Dixie Jamboree (PRC, 1944)
The Man Who Walked Alone (PRC, 1945) (also associate pro-
    ducer, story)
Sensation Hunters (Mon. , 1946)
Robin Hood of Monterey (Mon. , 1947) (also story)
King of the Bandits (Mon. , 1947)
Back Trail (Mon. , 1948)
Silver Trails (Mon. , 1948)

CAHN, EDWARD L. , b. Feb. 2, 1907, Brooklyn, N.Y.; d. Aug.
    25, 1963.
Radio Patrol (Univ. , 1932)
Laughter in Hell (Univ. , 1932)
Afraid to Talk (Univ. , 1932)
Law and Order (Univ. , 1932)
Homicide Squad (Univ. , 1932)

Emergency Call (RKO, 1933)
Confidential (Univ., 1935)
Bad Guy (MGM, 1937)
Red Head (Mon., 1941)
Main Street After Dark (MGM, 1944)
Dangerous Partners (MGM, 1945)
Born to Speed (PRC, 1947)
Gas House Kids in Hollywood (PRC, 1947)
The Checkered Coat (20th, 1948)
Bungalow 13 (20th, 1948)
I Cheated the Law (20th, 1949)
Prejudice (M. P. Sales Corp., 1949)
You Can't Beat the A-Bomb (RKO, 1950)
The Great Plane Robbery (UA, 1950)
Experiment Alcatraz (RKO, 1950) (also producer)
Two Dollar Bettor (Realart, 1951)
Creature With the Atom Brain (Col., 1954)
Betrayed Women (AA, 1955)
Runaway Daughters (AIP, 1956)
The She Creature (AIP, 1956)
Girls in Prison (AIP, 1956)
Flesh and the Spur (AIP, 1956)
Shake, Rattle and Rock (AIP, 1956)
Zombies of Mora-Tau (AIP, 1957)
Voodoo Woman (AIP, 1957)
Dragstrip Girl (AIP, 1957)
Invasion of the Saucer Men (AIP, 1957)
Motorcycle Gang (AIP, 1957)
Guns, Girls and Gangsters (UA, 1958)
Suicide Battalion (AIP, 1958)
Jet Attack (AIP, 1958)
Curse of the Faceless Man (UA, 1958
It! The Terror from Beyond Space (UA, 1958)
Hong Kong Confidential (UA, 1958)
The Four Skulls of Jonathan Drake (UA, 1959)
Inside the Mafia (UA, 1959)
Invisible Invaders (UA, 1959)
Pier 5, Havana (UA, 1959)
Three Came to Kill (UA, 1960)
Twelve Hours to Kill (20th, 1960)
Cage of Evil (UA, 1960)
Vice Raid (UA, 1960)
Oklahoma Territory (UA, 1960)
Noose for a Gunman (UA, 1960)
The Music Box Kid (UA, 1960)
A Dog's Best Friend (UA, 1960)
Gunfighters of Abilene (UA, 1960)
The Gambler Wore a Gun (UA, 1961)
The Police Dog Story (UA, 1961)
Gun Fight (UA, 1961)
Frontier Uprising (UA, 1961)
Gun Street (UA, 1961)
When the Clock Strikes (UA, 1961)

Riot in Juvenile Prison (UA, 1961)
The Boy Who Caught a Crook (UA, 1961)
Five Guns to Tombstone (UA, 1961)
Secret of Deep Harbor (UA, 1961)
Beauty and the Beast (UA, 1962)
The Clown and the Kid (UA, 1962)
Incident in an Alley (UA, 1963)

CAMBELL, COLIN, b. 1893, Falkirk, Scotland; d. March 25, 1966.
The Spoilers (Selig, 1914)
In the Days of the Thundering Herd (Selig, 1914)
Sweet Alyssum (Selig, 1915)
The Rosary (Selig, 1915)
The Carpet from Bagdad (Selig, 1915)
The Smouldering Flame (Selig, 1916)
The Crisis (Selig, 1916)
The Ne'er Do Well (Selig, 1916)
Thou Shalt Not Covet (Selig, 1916)
Beware of Strangers (Selig, 1917)
The Love of Madge O'Mara (Selig, 1917)
The Railroader (Selig, 1917)
The Law North of '65 (Selig, 1917)
The Garden of Allah (Selig, 1917)
The Yellow Dog (Univ., 1918)
A Hoosier Romance (Selig, 1918)
The Still Alarm (Select, 1918)
Who Shall Take My Life (Film Market, 1918)
Sea Flower (Univ., 1918)
Beware of Strangers (Film Market, 1918)
City of Purple Dreams (Film Market, 1918)
Railroaders (Triangle, 1919)
Little Orphan Annie (Pioneer, 1919)
The Beauty Market (FN, 1919)
The Corsican Brothers (United Pictures, 1919)
The Thunderbolt (FN, 1919)
Moon Madness (Robertson-Cole, 1920)
Big Happiness (Robertson-Cole, 1920)
When Dawn Came (Producers Security, 1920)
The First Born (Robertson-Cole, 1921)
Black Roses (Robertson-Cole, 1921)
The Lure of Jade (Robertson-Cole, 1921)
Where Lights Are Low (Robertson-Cole, 1921)
The Swamp (Robertson-Cole, 1921)
The Girl from Nowhere (Robertson-Cole, 1921)
Two Kinds of Women (Robertson-Cole, 1922)
The World's a Stage (Principal, 1922) (also co-script)
The Buster (Fox, 1923)
Bucking the Barrier (Fox, 1923)
Three Who Paid (Fox, 1923)
The Grail (Fox, 1923)
Pagan Passions (Selznick, 1924)

The Bowery Bishop (Selznick, 1924)

CAPELLANI, ALBERT, b. 1871, Paris; d. 1931.
Le Courrier de Lyon (French, 1911)
Notre Dame de Paris (French, 1911)
Les Mystères de Paris (French, 1911)
Les Misérables (French, 1911)
Le Roman d'un Jeune Homme Pauvre (French, 1913)
Germinal (French, 1913)
La Glu (French, 1913)
Patrie I (French, 1913)
Quatre-Vingt-Treize (French, 1914)
Les Espaves de l'Amour (French, 1915)
Le Rêve Interdit (French, 1915)
The Flash of an Emerald (World, 1915)
The Face in the Moonlight (World, 1915)
Camille (World, 1916)
The Common Law (World, 1916)
The Dark Silence (World, 1916)
The Feast of Life (World, 1916)
The Foolish Virgin (World, 1916)
La Vie de Bohème (World, 1916)
The Easiest Way (Selig, 1917)
American Maid (Mutual, 1917)
Daybreak (Metro, 1918)
The Richest Girl (Empire Mutual, 1918)
Social Hypocrites (Metro, 1918)
The House of Mirth (Metro, 1918)
Eye for Eye (Metro, 1918)
Out of the Fog (Metro, 1919)
The Red Lantern (Metro, 1919)
Oh Boy (Pathé, 1919)
The Virtuous Model (Pathé, 1919)
The Fortune Teller (Robertson-Cole, 1920)
The Inside of the Cup (Par., 1921) (also co-script)
The Wild Goose (Par., 1921)
Sisters (American Releasing, 1922)
The Young Diana (Par., 1922)

CAPRA, FRANK, b. May 19, 1897, Palermo, Sicily.
The Strong Man (FN, 1926)
Long Pants (FN, 1927)
For the Love of Mike (FN, 1927)
That Certain Thing (Col., 1928)
So This Is Love (Col., 1928)
The Matinee Idol (Col., 1928)
The Way of the Strong (Col., 1928)
Say It With Sables (Col., 1928) (also co-script)
Submarine (Col., 1928)
The Power of the Press (Col., 1928)
The Younger Generation (Col., 1929)

The Donovan Affair (Col., 1929)
Flight (Col., 1929) (also dialog)
Ladies of Leisure (Col., 1930)
Rain or Shine (Col., 1930)
Dirigible (Col., 1931)
The Miracle Woman (Col., 1931)
Platinum Blonde (Col., 1931)
Forbidden (Col., 1932) (also story)
American Madness (Col., 1932)
The Bitter Tea of General Yen (Col., 1932)
Lady for a Day (Col., 1933)
It Happened One Night (Col., 1934)
Broadway Bill (Col., 1934)
Mr. Deeds Goes to Town (Col., 1936) (also producer)
Lost Horizon (Col., 1937) (also producer)
You Can't Take It With You (Col., 1938) (also producer)
Mr. Smith Goes to Washington (Col., 1939) (also producer)
Meet John Doe (WB, 1941) (also producer)
Prelude to War (U.S. Government, 1942)
The Nazis Strike (U.S. Government, 1942) (with Anatole Litvak)
Divide and Conquer (U.S. Government, 1942) (with Anatole Litvak)
The Battle of China (U.S. Government, 1944) (with Anatole Litvak)
Arsenic and Old Lace (WB, 1944)
It's a Wonderful Life (RKO, 1947) (also producer, co-script)
State of the Union (MGM, 1948) (also co-producer)
Riding High (Par., 1950) (also producer)
Here Comes the Groom (Par., 1951) (also producer)
A Hole in the Head (UA, 1959) (also producer)
A Pocketful of Miracles (UA, 1961) (also co-producer)

CAREWE, EDWIN, b. 1883, Gainesville, Tex.; d. Jan. 22, 1940.
The Final Judgment (Metro, 1915)
Their Compact (Metro, 1917)
The Voice of Conscience (Metro, 1917)
The Splendid Sinner (Goldwyn, 1918)
The Trail to Yesterday (Metro, 1918)
The House of Gold (Metro, 1918)
Pals First (Metro, 1918)
False Evidence (Metro, 1919)
Way of the Strong (Metro, 1919)
Shadows of Suspicion (Metro, 1919)
Easy to Make Money (Metro, 1919)
The Right to Lie (Pathé, 1919)
Isobel (David Distributing, 1920)
The Web of Deceit (Pathé, 1920)
Rio Grande (Pathé, 1920)
My Lady's Latch Key (Associated FN, 1921)
Habit (Associated FN, 1921)
Playthings of Destiny (Associated FN, 1921)
The Invisible Fear (Associated FN, 1921)

Her Mad Bargain (Associated FN, 1921)
A Question of Honor (Associated FN, 1922)
I Am the Law (Affiliated, 1922) (also for production company)
Silver Wings (Fox, 1922)
Mighty Lak' a Rose (Associated FN, 1923) (also for production company, presenter, personal supervisor)
The Girl of the Golden West (Associated FN, 1923) (also presenter)
The Bad Man (Associated FN, 1923) (also for production company)
A Son of the Sahara (FN, 1924) (also for production company, presenter)
Madonna of the Streets (FN, 1924) (also for production company, presenter)
My Son (FN, 1925) (also presenter)
The Lady Who Lied (FN, 1925) (also presenter)
Joanna (FN, 1925) (also for production company, presenter)
Why Women Love (FN, 1925) (also for production company, presenter)
High Steppers (FN, 1926) (also for production company, presenter)
Pals First (FN, 1926) (also for production company, presenter)
Resurrection (UA, 1927) (also for co-production company, also producer, co-adaptation)
Ramona (UA, 1928)
Revenge (UA, 1928) (also for production company)
Evangeline (UA, 1929) (also for co-production company)
The Spoilers (Par., 1930)
Resurrection (Univ., 1931)
Are We Civilized? (Raspin, 1934)

CASSAVETES, JOHN, b. Dec. 9, 1929, New York City.
Shadows (Lion International, 1961)
Too Late Blues (Par., 1962) (also producer, co-script)
A Child Is Waiting (UA, 1962)
Faces (Continental, 1968) (also script)
Husbands (Col., 1970) (also script, actor)
Minnie and Moscowitz (UA, 1972) (also script, actor)

CASTLE, WILLIAM, b. April 24, 1914, New York City.
The Chance of a Lifetime (Col., 1944)
The Whistler (Col., 1944)
She's a Soldier Too (Col., 1944)
Mark of the Whistler (Col., 1944)
When Strangers Marry (Betrayed) (Mon., 1944)
Voice of the Whistler (Col., 1945) (also co-script)
The Crime Doctor's Warning (Col., 1945)
Just Before Dawn (Col., 1946)
The Mysterious Intruder (Col., 1946)
The Crime Doctor's Manhunt (Col., 1946)
The Return of Rusty (Col., 1946)

Sarah Lane with William Castle on I Saw What You Did (Univ.,
1965).

The Crime Doctor's Gamble (Col., 1947)
Texas, Brooklyn and Heaven (UA, 1948)
The Gentleman from Nowhere (Col., 1948)
Johnny Stool Pigeon (Univ., 1949)
Undertow (Univ., 1949)
It's a Small World (Eagle Lion, 1950) (also co-script)
The Fat Man (Univ., 1951)
The Hollywood Story (Univ., 1951)
Cave of the Outlaws (Univ., 1951)
Fort Ti (Col., 1953)
Conquest of Cochise (Col., 1953)
Serpent of the Nile (Col., 1953)
Slaves of Babylon (Col., 1953)
Drums of Tahiti (Col., 1954)
Battle of Rogue River (Col., 1954)
The Iron Glove (Col., 1954)
The Law vs. Billy the Kid (Col., 1954)
Jesse James vs. the Daltons (Col., 1954)
The Saracen Blade (Col., 1954)

Charge of the Lancers (Col., 1954)
Masterson of Kansas (Col., 1955)
The Americano (RKO, 1955)
New Orleans Uncensored (Col., 1955)
The Gun That Won the West (Col., 1955)
Duel on the Mississippi (Col., 1955)
The Houston Story (Col., 1956)
Uranium Boom (Col., 1956)
The Decks Ran Red (MGM, 1958) (also producer, script)
Macabre (AA, 1958) (also producer)
Cry Terror (MGM, 1958) (also producer, script)
The House on Haunted Hill (AA, 1959) (also producer)
The Tingler (Col., 1959) (also producer)
13 Ghosts (Col., 1960) (also producer)
Homicidal (Col., 1961) (also producer, narrator)
Mr. Sardonicus (Col., 1961) (also producer)
Zotz! (Col., 1962) (also producer)
The Old Dark House (Col., 1963) (also producer)
13 Frightened Girls (Col., 1963) (also producer)
Straight-Jacket (Col., 1964) (also producer)
The Night Walker (Univ., 1965) (also producer)
I Saw What You Did (Univ., 1966) (also producer)
Let's Kill Uncle (Univ., 1966) (also producer)
The Spirit Is Willing (Par., 1967) (also producer)
The Busy Body (Par., 1967) (also producer)
Project X (Par., 1968) (also producer)

CHAPLIN, CHARLES, b. April 16, 1889, London.
The Kid (UA, 1921) (also producer, script, actor)
The Pilgrim (UA, 1923) (also producer, script, actor)
A Woman of Paris (UA, 1923) (also producer, script, actor)
The Gold Rush (UA, 1925) (also producer, script, actor)
The Circus (UA, 1928) (also producer, script, actor)
City Lights (UA, 1931) (also producer, script, music, actor)
Modern Times (UA, 1936) (also producer, script, music, actor)
The Great Dictator (UA, 1940) (also producer, script, music, actor)
Monsieur Verdoux (UA, 1947) (also producer, script, music, actor) (with assoc. dir. Robert Florey)
Limelight (UA, 1952) (also producer, script, music, actor)
A King in New York (Archway, 1957) (also producer, script, music, actor)
A Countess from Hong Kong (Univ., 1967) (also producer, script, music, actor)

CHAUDET, LOUIS W., b. March 20, 1884, Manhattan, Kan.
Follow the Girl (Univ., 1917)
Merry Andrews (Rhodes, 1917)
The Finger of Justice (Arrow, 1918)
The Edge of the Law (Univ., 1917)
Society's Driftwood (Univ., 1917)

The Long Lane's Turning (Exclusive International, 1919)
The Love Call (Exclusive International, 1919)
The Girl of My Dreams (Exclusive International, 1918)
The Blue Bonnet (W.W. Hodkinson, 1919)
The Kingfisher's Roost (Pinnacle, 1922) (with Paul Hurst) (also
    co-story, co-script)
Fools of Fortune (American Releasing, 1922)
Defying Destiny (Selznick, 1923)
A Man of Nerve (FBO, 1925)
Fighting Jack (Goodwill, 1926)
Eyes Right! (Goodwill, 1926)
Lightning Bill (Goodwill, 1926)
A Captain's Courage (Rayart, 1926)
Tentacles of the North (Rayart, 1926)
Speeding Hoofs (Rayart, 1927)
Outcast Souls (Sterling, 1928)

CHAUTARD, EMILE, b. 1865, Paris; d. April 24, 1934.
    The Dancer and the King (World, 1914)
    The Arrival of Perpetua (World, 1915)
    The Little Dutch Girl (World, 1915)
    The Boss (World, 1915)
    Human Driftwood (World, 1915)
    The Heart of a Hero (World, 1916)
    Friday the 13th (Brady-World, 1916)
    All Man (Peerless-Brady-World, 1916)
    The Hungry Heart (Peerless-Brady-World, 1917)
    The Web of Desire (Peerless-Brady-World, 1917)
    Heart of Ezra Greer (Pathé, 1917)
    The Fires of Youth (Pathé, 1917)
    The Family Honor (World, 1917)
    The Man Who Forgot (World, 1917)
    Forget-Me-Not (Peerless-Brady-World, 1917)
    Magda (Selig, 1917)
    Under False Colors (Pathé, 1917)
    The Eternal Temptress (Par., 1917)
    The Marionettes (Selznick, 1918)
    The House of Glass (Selznick, 1918)
    The Ordeal of Rosetta (Selznick, 1918)
    Her Final Reckoning (Par., 1918)
    Under the Greenwood Tree (Artcraft, 1918)
    A Daughter of the Old South (Par., 1918)
    The Marriage Price (Artcraft, 1919)
    Eyes of the Soul (Artcraft, 1919)
    His Parisian Wife (Par., 1919)
    Paid in Full (Par., 1919)
    Out of the Shadows (Par., 1919)
    The Mystery of the Yellow Room (Realart, 1919)
    The Black Panther's Cub (Equity, 1921)
    Forsaking All Others (Univ., 1922)
    The Glory of Clementina (Robertson-Cole, 1922)
    Living Lies (Mayflower, 1922)

Youth to Youth (Metro, 1922) (also producer)
Daytime Wives (FBO, 1923)
Untamed Youth (FBO, 1924)

CHRISTENSEN, BENJAMIN, b. 1879, Viborg, Denmark; d. 1959.
Det Hemmelighedsfulde X (Danish, 1913) (also co-script, editor,
    actor)
Haevens Nat (Danish, 1915) (also script, actor)
Häxan [Witchcraft Through the Ages] (Swedish, 1918) (also
    script, actor)
Seine Frau die Unbekannte (German, 1923) (also script)
Die Frau mit dem Schlechten Ruf (German, 1925)
The Devil's Circus (MGM, 1926) (also story, script)
Mockery (MGM, 1927) (also producer, story)
The Hawk's House (FN, 1928)
The Haunted House (FN, 1928)
The House of Horror (FN, 1929)
The Mysterious Island (FN, 1929) (with Lucien Hubbard, Maur-
    ice Tourneur)
Seven Footprints to Satan (FN, 1929)
Skilsmissens Born (Danish, 1939) (also script)
Barnet (Danish, 1939) (also co-script)
Gaa med Mig Hjem (Danish, 1941)
Damen med de Lyse Handsker (Danish, 1942) (also script)

CLAIR, RENÉ (René Chomette), b. Nov. 11, 1898, Paris.
Paris Qui Dort (French, 1924) (also script)
Entr'acte (French, 1924) (also editor)
Le Fantôme du Moulin Rouge (French, 1925) (also script)
Le Voyage Imaginaire (French, 1925) (also script)
La Proie du Vent (French, 1926) (also script)
Un Chapeau de Paille d'Italie (French, 1927) (also script)
Les Deux Timides (French, 1928) (also script)
La Tour (French, 1928) (also script)
Sous les Toits de Paris (French, 1930) (also script)
Le Million (French, 1931) (also script)
A Nous la Liberté (French, 1932) (also script)
Quatorze Juillet (French, 1933) (also script)
Le Dernier Milliardaire (French, 1934) (also script)
The Ghost Goes West (UA, 1935) (also co-script)
Break the News (General Film Distributors, 1938) (also co-
    producer, co-script)
Air Pur (unfinished, 1939) (also co-script)
The Flame of New Orleans (Univ., 1941) (also co-script)
I Married a Witch (Par., 1942) (also co-producer)
Forever and a Day (RKO, 1943) (with Edmund Goulding, Cedric
    Hardwicke, Frank Lloyd, Victor Saville, Robert Stevenson)
    (also co-producer)
It Happened Tomorrow (UA, 1944) (also co-script)
And Then There Were None (20th, 1945) (also producer, co-
    script)

Le Silence Est d'Or (French, 1947) (also co-producer, script)
La Beauté du Diable (French, 1950) (also co-script)
Les Belles de Nuit (French, 1952) (also script)
Les Grandes Manoeuvres (French, 1955) (also script)
Porte des Lilas (French, 1957) (also script)
La Française et l'Amour (eg: "Marriage") (French, 1960) (also
   script)
Tout l'Or du Monde (French, 1961) (also co-script)
Les Quatre Vérités (ep: "Les Deux Pigeons") (French, 1962)
   (also script)
Les Fêtes Galantes (French, 1965)

CLARKE, SHIRLEY, b. 1925.
   The Connection (Films Around the World, 1962) (also co-pro-
      ducer)
   The Cool World (Cinema V, 1964) (also co-script)
   Portrait of Jason (Film-Makers, 1967)

CLAVELL, JAMES, b. 1924, Sydney, Australia.
   Five Gates to Hell (20th, 1959) (also producer, script)
   Walk Like a Dragon (Par., 1960) (also producer, co-script)
   To Sir, With Love (Col., 1967) (also producer, script)
   Where's Jack (Par., 1969)
   The Last Valley (Cin., 1971) (also producer, script)

CLAXTON, WILLIAM F.
   Half Past Midnight (20th, 1948)
   Tucson (20th, 1949)
   All That I Have (Family Films, 1951)
   Stagecoach to Fury (20th, 1956)
   The Quiet Gun (20th, 1957)
   Young and Dangerous (20th, 1957) (also producer)
   Rockabilly Baby (20th, 1957) (also producer)
   God Is My Partner (20th, 1957)
   Desire in the Dust (20th, 1960) (also producer)
   Young Jesse James (20th, 1960)
   Law of the Lawless (Par., 1963)
   Stage to Thunder Rock (Par., 1964)
   Night of the Lepus (MGM, 1972)

CLEMENS, WILLIAM, b. Sept. 10, 1905, Saginaw, Mich.
   Man Hunt (WB, 1936)
   The Case of the Velvet Claws (FN, 1936)
   Here Comes Carter (FN, 1936)
   The Law in Her Hands (FN, 1936)
   The Case of the Stuttering Bishop (WB, 1937)
   Footloose Heiress (WB, 1937)
   Missing Witness (WB, 1937)
   Once a Doctor (WB, 1937)

Talent Scout (WB, 1937)
Accidents Will Happen (WB, 1938)
Mr. Chump (WB, 1938)
Nancy Drew--Detective (WB, 1938)
Torchy Blane in Panama (WB, 1938)
Nancy Drew and the Hidden Staircase (WB, 1939)
Nancy Drew--Trouble Shooter (WB, 1939)
Nancy Drew, Reporter (WB, 1939)
On Dress Parade (WB, 1939)
Devil's Island (WB, 1940)
Calling Philo Vance (WB, 1940)
King of the Lumberjacks (WB, 1940)
Knockout (WB, 1941)
She Couldn't Say No (WB, 1941)
The Night of January 16th (Par., 1941)
Sweater Girl (Par., 1941)
A Night in New Orleans (Par., 1942)
The Falcon and the Coeds (RKO, 1943)
Lady Bodyguard (Par., 1943)
The Falcon in Danger (RKO, 1943)
The Falcon Out West (RKO, 1943)
Crime by Night (WB, 1944)

CLIFT, DENISON, b. May 3, 1892, San Francisco; d. Dec. 17, 1961.
The Iron Heart (Peerless-World, 1917) (also story, script)
What Would You Do? (Fox, 1920)
The Last Straw (Fox, 1920) (also script)
Why Men Forget (FBO, 1921)
The Diamond Necklace (Ideal, 1921) (also producer, script)
Demos (Ideal, 1921) (also producer, script)
A Woman of No Importance (Deal, 1921) (also producer, script)
Sonia (Ideal, 1921) (also producer, script)
The Old Wives' Tale (Ideal, 1921) (also producer, script)
A Woman of No Importance (Selznick, 1922) (also producer, script)
A Bill of Divorcement (Associated Exhibitors, 1922) (also producer, script)
Bentley's Conscience (Ideal, 1922) (also producer, script)
Diana of the Crossways (Ideal, 1922) (also producer, script)
The Woman Who Came Back (Playgoers, 1922)
Out to Win (Ideal, 1923) (also producers, script)
The Loves of Mary Queen of Scots (Ideal, 1923) (also producer, script)
This Freedom (Fox, 1923)
There's Millions in It (FBO, 1924)
The Great Diamond Mystery (Fox, 1924)
Honor Among Men (Fox, 1924) (also script)
Flames of Desire (Fox, 1924) (also co-script)
Ports of Call (Fox, 1925)
Paradise (Wardour, 1928)
City of Play (Woolf and Freedman, 1929)

Taxi for Two (Woolf and Freedman, 1929)
High Seas (First National-Pathé, 1929)
The Mystery of The Mary Celeste [Phantom Ship] (General
    Films, 1935)

CLIFTON, ELMER, b. 1890, Chicago; d. Oct. 15, 1949.
    Th High Sign (Univ., 1917)
    The Midnight Man (Univ., 1917)
    High Speed (Univ., 1917)
    Her Official Fathers (Triangle, 1917) (with Joseph Henaberry)
    The Love Claim (Univ., 1917)
    A Stormy Knight (Bluebird, 1917)
    Flirting With Death (Bluebird, 1917)
    The Man Trap (Bluebird, 1917)
    The Flash of Fate (Univ., 1918)
    The Two Soul Woman (Univ., 1918)
    Safe for Democracy (Blackton, 1918) (with J. Stuart Blackton)
    Brace Up (Bluebird, 1918)
    The Guilt of Silence (Bluebird, 1918)
    The Eagle (Bluebird, 1918)
    Smashing Through (Bluebird, 1918)
    Winner Takes All (Univ., 1918)
    Battling Jane (Par., 1918)
    Kiss or Kill (Univ., 1918)
    The Hope Chest (Par., 1918)
    Boots (Par., 1919)
    Peppy Polly (Par., 1919)
    I'll Get Him Yet (Par., 1919)
    Nugget Nell (Par., 1919)
    Out of Luck (Par., 1919)
    Turning the Tables (Par., 1919)
    Mary Ellen Comes to Town (Par., 1920)
    Down to the Sea in Ships (W.W. Hodkinson, 1922) (also pre-
        senter)
    Six Cylinder Love (Fox, 1923)
    The Warrens of Virginia (Fox, 1923)
    Daughters of the Night (Fox, 1924)
    Truth About Men (Macfadden True Story, 1926)
    Wives at Auction (Macfadden True Story, 1926) (also story)
    The Wreck of the Hesperus (Pathé, 1927)
    Let 'Er Go Gallegher (Pathé, 1928)
    Virgin Lips (Col., 1928)
    Beautiful But Dumb (Tiffany-Stahl, 1928)
    Tropical Nights (Tiffany-Stahl, 1928)
    The Bride of the Colorado (Pathé, 1928)
    The Devil's Apple Tree (Tiffany-Stahl, 1929)
    Maid to Order (Weil, 1930)
    Captured in Chinatown (Superior, 1935) (also co-script)
    Rip Roaring Riley (Puritan, 1935)
    Skull and Crown (Reliable, 1935)
    Pals of the Range (First Division, 1935)
    Cyclone of the Saddle (First Division, 1935)

Rough Riding Rangers (First Division, 1935)
Fighting Caballero (First Division, 1935)
Gambling With Souls (Kay Dee Kay, 1936)
Wildcat Trooper (Ambassador, 1936)
Custer's Last Stand* (Mascot, 1936)
Death in the Air (Puritan, 1937)
Mile a Minute Love (Ace, 1937)
The Secret of Treasure Island* (Col., 1938)
Wolves of the Sea (Guaranteed, 1938) (also script)
Paroled from the Big House (Syndicate, 1938)
Law of the Texan (Col., 1938)
California Frontier (Col., 1938)
Crime Afloat (Treo, 1938)
The Stranger from Arizona (Col., 1938)
Crashing Thru (Mon., 1939)
Isle of Destiny (RKO, 1940)
The City of Missing Girls (Select, 1941)
I'll Set My Life (Select, 1941)
Hard Guy (PRC, 1941)
Swamp Woman (PRC, 1942)
Deep in the Heart of Texas (Univ., 1942)
The Sundown Kid (Rep., 1942)
The Old Chisholm Trail (Univ., 1943) (also script)
Captain America* (Rep., 1944) (with John English)
The Return of the Rangers (PRC, 1944) (also script)
Seven Doors to Death (PRC, 1944) (also script)
Boss of Rawhide (PRC, 1944) (also script)
Guns of the Law (PRC, 1944) (also script)
The Pinto Bandit (PRC, 1944) (also script)
Spook Town (PRC, 1944) (also script)
Dead or Alive (PRC, 1944)
The Whispering Skull (PRC, 1944)
Gangsters of the Frontier (PRC, 1944) (also script)
Marked for Murder (PRC, 1945) (also script)
Not Wanted (Film Classics, 1949)
The Judge (Film Classics, 1949)

CLINE, EDWARD, b. Nov. 7, 1892, Kenosha, Wisc.; d. May 22, 1948.
Three Ages (Metro, 1923) (with Buster Keaton)
Circus Days (Associated FN, 1923) (also co-script)
The Meanest Man in the World (Associated FN, 1923)
When a Man's a Man (Associated FN, 1924)
Captain January (Principal, 1924)
Good Bad Boy (Principal, 1924)
Little Robinson Crusoe (Metro-Goldwyn, 1924)
Along Came Ruth (Metro-Goldwyn, 1924)
The Rag Man (Metro-Goldwyn, 1925)
Old Clothes (Metro-Goldwyn, 1925)
Let It Rain (Par., 1927)
Vamping Venus (FN, 1928)
The Head Man (FN, 1928)

The Crash (FN, 1928)
Broadway Fever (Tiffany-Stahl, 1929)
His Lucky Day (Univ., 1929)
The Forward Pass (FN, 1929)
In the Next Room (FN, 1930)
Sweet Mama (FN, 1930)
Leathernecking (RKO, 1930)
The Widow from Chicago (FN, 1930)
The Girl Habit (Par., 1931)
The Naughty Flirt (FN, 1931)
Million Dollar Legs (Par., 1932)
So This Is Africa (Col., 1933)
Peck's Bad Boy (Fox, 1934)
The Dude Ranger (Fox, 1934)
The Cowboy Millionaire (Fox, 1935)
When a Man's a Man (British Lion, 1935)
It's a Great Life! (Par., 1935)
F-Man (Par., 1936)
On Again--Off Again (RKO, 1937)
Forty Naughty Girls (RKO, 1937)
High Flyers (RKO, 1937)
Hawaii Calls (RKO, 1938)
Breaking the Ice (RKO, 1938)
Peck's Bad Boy With the Circus (RKO, 1938)
Go Chase Yourself (RKO, 1938)
My Little Chickadee (Univ., 1939)
The Villain Still Pursued Her (RKO, 1940)
The Bank Dick (Univ., 1940)
Never Give a Sucker an Even Break (Univ., 1941)
Meet the Chump (Univ., 1941)
Hello Sucker (Univ., 1941)
What's Cookin? (Univ., 1942)
Give Out, Sisters (Univ., 1942)
Snuffy Smith, Yard Bird (Mon., 1942)
Behind the Eight Ball (Univ., 1942)
Private Buckaroo (Univ., 1942)
Crazy House (Univ., 1943)
He's My Guy (Univ., 1943)
The Ghost Chasers (Univ., 1943)
Night Club Girl (Univ., 1944)
Slightly Terrific (Univ., 1944)
Swingtime Johnny (Univ., 1944)
Penthouse Rhythm (Univ., 1945)
See My Lawyer (Univ., 1945)
Bringing Up Father (Mon., 1946) (also co-script)
Jiggs and Maggie in Society (Mon., 1948) (also co-story, co-
    script)
Jiggs and Maggie in Court (Mon., 1948) (with William Beaudine)
    (also co-story, co-script)

COE, FRED, b. Dec. 23, 1914, Alligator, Miss.
    A Thousand Clowns (UA, 1965) (also producer)
    Me, Natalie (National General, 1970)

COLLINS, LEWIS D., b. Jan. 12, 1897, Baltimore, Md.
　　The Devil's Pit (Univ., 1930) (also script)
　　Young Desire (Univ., 1930)
　　Law of the Tongs (Syndicate, 1931)
　　Via Pony Express (Majestic, 1933)
　　Gun Law (Majestic, 1933)
　　Trouble Busters (Majestic, 1933)
　　Skyway (Mon., 1933)
　　Ship of Wanted Men (Showmen's Pictures, 1933)
　　Public Stenographer (Marcy Exchange, 1934)
　　Man from Hell (Willis Kent, 1934)
　　Sing Sing Nights (Mon., 1934)
　　Brand of Hate (William Steiner, 1934)
　　Ticket to a Crime (Beacon, 1934)
　　Hoosier Schoolmaster (Mon., 1935)
　　Make a Million (Mon., 1935)
　　The Spanish Cape Mystery (Rep., 1935)
　　Manhattan Butterfly (Imperial, 1935)
　　Desert Trail (Mon., 1935)
　　The Return of Jimmy Valentine (Rep., 1936)
　　The Leavenworth Case (Rep., 1936)
　　Doughnuts and Society (Mascot, 1936)
　　Down to the Sea (Rep., 1936)
　　The Mighty Treve (Univ., 1937)
　　Fury and the Woman (Rialto, 1937)
　　The Wildcatter (Univ., 1937)
　　River of Missing Men (Col., 1937)
　　Under Suspicion (Col., 1937)
　　The House of Mystery (Col., 1938)
　　Making the Headlines (Col., 1938)
　　Crime Takes a Holiday (Col., 1938)
　　Flight into Nowhere (Col., 1938)
　　Reformatory (Col., 1938)
　　Outside the Law (Col., 1938)
　　Trapped in the Sky (Col., 1939)
　　Whispering Enemies (Col., 1939)
　　Hidden Power (Col., 1939)
　　Fugitive at Large (Col., 1939)
　　Outside the 3-Mile Limit (Col., 1940)
　　Fugitive from a Prison Camp (Col., 1940)
　　Passport to Alcatraz (Col., 1940)
　　The Great Plane Robbery (Col., 1940)
　　The Great Swindle (Col., 1941)
　　Borrowed Hero (Mon., 1941)
　　Danger in the Pacific (Univ., 1942)
　　Little Joe, the Wrangler (Univ., 1942)
　　Tenting on the Old Camp Grounds (Univ., 1943)
　　Raiders of San Joaquin (Univ., 1943)
　　Trigger Trail (Univ., 1944)
　　Oklahoma Raiders (Univ., 1944)
　　The Old Texas Trail (Univ., 1944)
　　Sweethearts of the U.S.A. (Mon., 1944)
　　Danger Woman (Univ., 1946)

Killer Dill (Screen Guild, 1947)
Heading for Heaven (PRC, 1947) (also script)
Jungle Goddess (Screen Guild, 1948)
Ride, Ryder, Ride! (Eagle Lion, 1949)
Roll Thunder Roll (Eagle Lion, 1949)
The Fighting Redhead (Eagle Lion, 1949)
Cowboy and the Prizefighter (Eagle Lion, 1950)
Hot Rod (Mon. , 1950)
Cherokee Uprising (Mon. , 1950)
Law of the Panhandle (Mon. , 1950)
Colorado Ambush (Mon. , 1951)
Oklahoma Justice (AA, 1951)
Man from Sonora (Mon. , 1951)
Nevada Badman (Mon. , 1951)
Canyon Raiders (Mon. , 1951)
Abilene Trail (Mon. , 1951)
Stage from Blue River (Mon. , 1951)
Lawless Cowboys (Mon. , 1951)
Texas Lawmen (Mon. , 1951)
Wild Stallion (Mon. , 1952)
The Gunman (Mon. , 1952)
Kansas Territory (Mon. , 1952)
The Longhorn (Mon. , 1952)
Texas City (Mon. , 1952)
Canyon Ambush (Mon. , 1952)
Dead Man's Trail (Mon. , 1952)
Fargo (Mon. , 1952)
Montana Incident (Mon. , 1952)
Texas Marshal (Mon. , 1952)
The Marksman (AA, 1953)
The Homesteader (AA, 1953)
Two Guns and a Badge (AA, 1954)

CONWAY, JACK (Hugh Ryan Conway), b. July 17, 1887, Graceville,
    Minn. ; d. Oct. 11, 1952.
    The Penitents (Triangle, 1915)
    The Beckoning Trail (Red Films, 1916)
    The Social Buccaneers (Bluebird, 1916)
    The Silent Battle (Bluebird, 1916)
    The Measure of a Man (Bluebird, 1916)
    Judgment of the Guilty (Univ. , 1916)
    The Mainspring (R. F. , 1916)
    Bitter Sweet (Univ. , 1916)
    A Jewel in the Pawn (Bluebird, 1917)
    Polly Redhead (Bluebird, 1917)
    Her Soul's Inspiration (Bluebird, 1917)
    The Little Orphan (Pathé, 1917)
    Come Through (Univ. , 1917)
    The Charmer (Bluebird, 1917)
    The Bond of Fear (Triangle, 1917)
    Because of a Woman (Triangle, 1917)
    Her Decision (Triangle, 1918)

You Can't Believe Everything (Triangle, 1918)
Little Red Decides (Triangle, 1918)
Desert Law (Triangle, 1918)
Restless Souls (Triangle, 1918) (also actor)
A Diplomatic Mission (Vitagraph, 1919)
Lombardi Ltd. (Metro, 1919)
The Servant in the House (FBO, 1920)
Riders of the Dawn (Desert of Wheat) (W.W. Hodkinson, 1920)
The Dwelling Place of Light (W.W. Hodkinson, 1920)
The Money Changers (Pathé, 1920)
The U.P. Trail (W.W. Hodkinson, 1920)
A Daughter of the Law (Univ., 1921)
The Kiss (Univ., 1921)
The Millionaire (Univ., 1921)
The Rage of Paris (Univ., 1921)
The Spenders (W.W. Hodkinson, 1921)
Across the Deadline (Univ., 1922)
Another Man's Shoes (Univ., 1922)
Don't Shoot (Univ., 1922)
The Long Chance (Univ., 1922)

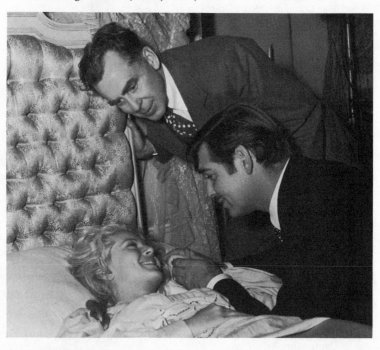

Lana Turner and Clark Gable with Jack Conway on the set of Honky Tonk (MGM, 1941).

Step On It! (Univ., 1922)
Lucretia Lombard (WB, 1923)
The Prisoner (Univ., 1923)
Quicksands (Selznick, 1923)
Sawdust (Univ., 1923)
Trimmed in Scarlet (Univ., 1923)
What Wives Want (Univ., 1923)
The Trouble Shooter (Fox, 1924)
The Heart Buster (Fox, 1924)
The Roughneck (Fox, 1924)
The Hunted Woman (Fox, 1925)
The Only Thing (MGM, 1925)
Brown of Harvard (MGM, 1926)
Soul Mates (MGM, 1926)
The Understanding Heart (MGM, 1927)
Twelve Miles Out (MGM, 1927)
The Smart Set (MGM, 1928)
Bringing up Father (MGM, 1928)
While the City Sleeps (MGM, 1928)
Alias Jimmy Valentine (MGM, 1928)
Our Modern Maidens (MGM, 1929)
Untamed (MGM, 1930)
They Learned About Women (MGM, 1930) (with Sam Wood)
The Unholy Three (MGM, 1930)
New Moon (MGM, 1930)
The Easiest Way (MGM, 1931)
Just a Gigolo (MGM, 1931)
Arsene Lupin (MGM, 1932)
But the Flesh Is Weak (MGM, 1932)
Red Headed Woman (MGM, 1932)
Hell Below (MGM, 1933)
The Nuisance (MGM, 1933)
Solitaire Man (MGM, 1933)
Viva Villa! (MGM, 1934)
The Girl from Missouri (MGM, 1934)
The Gay Bride (MGM, 1934)
One New York Night (MGM, 1935)
A Tale of Two Cities (MGM, 1935)
Libeled Lady (MGM, 1936)
Saratoga (MGM, 1937)
A Yank at Oxford (MGM, 1938)
Too Hot to Handle (MGM, 1938)
Let Freedom Ring (MGM, 1939)
Lady of the Tropics (MGM, 1939)
Boom Town (MGM, 1940)
Love Crazy (MGM, 1941)
Honky Tonk (MGM, 1941)
Crossroads (MGM, 1942)
Assignment in Brittany (MGM, 1943)
Dragon Seed (MGM, 1944) (with Harold S. Bucquet)
Without Love (MGM, 1945) (with Harold S. Bucquet)
High Barbaree (MGM, 1947)
The Hucksters (MGM, 1947)
Julia Misbehaves (MGM, 1948)

COOPER, MERIAN C., b. Oct. 5, 1893, Jacksonville, Fla.; d.
     April 21, 1973.
   Grass: A Nation's Battle for Life (Par., 1925) (with Ernest
     B. Schoedsack, Marguerite Harrison) (also co-producer, co-
     camera)
   Chang (Par., 1927) (with Ernest B. Schoedsack) (also co-pro-
     ducer)
   The Four Feathers (Par., 1929) (with Ernest B. Schoedsack,
     Lothar Mendes) (also co-camera)
   King Kong (RKO, 1933) (with Ernest B. Schoedsack) (also co-
     producer, co-story)

COPPOLA, FRANCIS FORD, b. April 7, 1939, Detroit.
   Tonight for Sure [The Wide Open Spaces] (Premier, 1961) (also
     producer, script)
   Battle Beyond the Sun [Dementia 13] (Filmgroup/AIP, 1963)
   You're a Big Boy Now (7 Arts, 1967) (also script)
   Finian's Rainbow (WB-7 Arts, 1968)
   The Rain People (WB-7 Arts, 1969) (also script)
   The Godfather (Par., 1972) (also co-script)

Petula Clark, Don Francks, Fred Astaire, producer Joseph Landon,
and Tommy Steele with Francis Ford Coppola (left) on the set of
Finian's Rainbow (WB-7 Arts, 1968).

CORMAN, ROGER (Roger (William Corman), b. April 5, 1926, Los
     Angeles.
   Five Guns West (AIP, 1955) (also producer)
   The Apache Woman (AIP, 1955) (also producer)
   The Day the World Ended (AIP, 1955) (also producer)
   It Conquered the World (AIP, 1956) (also producer)
   The Oklahoma Woman (AIP, 1956) (also producer)
   Swamp Women (AIP, 1956)

Gunslinger (AIP, 1956) (also producer)
The Undead (AIP, 1956) (also producer)
Not of This Earth (AA, 1956) (also producer)
Reception (unfinished, 1957)
The Little Guy (unfinished, 1957)
Naked Paradise (AIP, 1957) (also producer)
Attack of the Crab Monsters (AA, 1957) (also producer)
Rock All Night (AA, 1957) (also producer)
The She-Gods of Shark Reef (AIP, 1957)
The Viking Women and the Sea Serpent (AIP, 1957) (also pro-
    ducer)
Teenage Doll (AIP, 1957) (also producer)
Sorority Girl (AIP, 1957) (also producer)
Carnival Rock (Howco, 1957) (also producer)
War of the Satellites (AA, 1958)
Machine Gun Kelly (AIP, 1958) (also producer)
Teenage Caveman (AIP, 1958) (also producer)
I, Mobster (20th, 1959) (also co-producer)
A Bucket of Blood (AIP, 1959) (also producer)
The Wasp Woman (AIP, 1959) (also producer)
Ski Troop Attack (Filmgroup, 1960) (also producer)
House of Usher (AIP, 1960) (also producer)
The Little Shop of Horrors (AIP, 1960) (also producer)
The Last Woman on Earth (Filmgroup, 1960) (also producer)
Creature from the Haunted Sea (Filmgroup, 1960) (also pro-
    ducer)
Atlas (Filmgroup, 1960) (also producer)
The Intruder (Filmgroup, 1961) (also producer)
The Pit and the Pendulum (AIP, 1961) (also producer)
Tower of London (UA, 1962)
The Premature Burial (AIP, 1962) (also producer)
Tales of Terror (AIP, 1962) (also producer)
The Young Racers (AIP, 1962) (also producer)
The Raven (AIP, 1963) (also producer)
The Terror (AIP, 1963) (also producer)
X, the Man With the X-Ray Eyes (AIP, 1963) (also producer)
The Haunted Palace (AIP, 1964) (also producer)
The Secret Invasion (20th, 1964)
The Masque of the Red Death (AIP, 1965) (also producer)
The Tomb of Ligeia (AIP, 1965)
The Wild Angels (AIP, 1966) (also producer)
The St. Valentine's Day Massacre (20th, 1967) (also producer)
The Trip (AIP, 1967) (also producer)
How to Make It [What's In It for Harry?] (unreleased, 1968)
A Time for Killing [The Long Ride Home] (Col., 1968) (un-
    credited, with Phil Karlson)
Bloody Mama (AIP, 1970) (also producer
Gas-s-s! (AIP, 1970) (also producer)
Von Richthofen and Brown [The Red Baron] (UA, 1971)

CORNFIELD, HUBERT, b. 1929, Istanbul, Turkey.
    Angel Baby (AA, 1961) (replaced by Paul Wendkos)

Sudden Danger (AA, 1955)
Lure of the Swamp (20th, 1957)
Plunder Road (20th, 1957)
The Third Voice (20th, 1959) (also co-script)
Pressure Point (UA, 1962) (also co-script)
The Night of the Following Day (Univ., 1969) (also co-script)

CORRIGAN, LLOYD, b. Oct. 16, 1900, San Francisco; d. Nov. 5, 1969.
Along Came Youth (Par., 1930) (with Norman McLeod)
Daughter of the Dragon (Par., 1931)
Beloved Bachelor (Par., 1931)
No One Man (Par., 1932)
The Broken Wing (Par., 1932)
He Learned About Women (Par., 1933) (also story)
By Your Leave (RKO, 1934)
Murder on a Honeymoon (RKO, 1935)
Dancing Pirate (RKO, 1936)
Night Key (Univ., 1937)
Lady Behave (Rep., 1937)

CORTEZ, RICARDO (Jake Krantz), b. Sept. 19, 1899, Brooklyn, N.Y.
The Inside Story (20th, 1938)
Chasing Danger (20th, 1939)
The Escape (20th, 1939)
Heaven With a Barbed Wire Fence (20th, 1940)
Free, Blonde and 21 (20th, 1940)
The Girl in 313 (20th, 1940)
City of Chance (20th, 1940)

CRISP, DONALD, b. 1880, Aberfeldy, Eng; d. May 26, 1974.
Ramona (Cline, 1916)
The Cook of Canyon Camp (Par., 1917)
His Sweetheart (Par., 1917)
The Bond Between (Par., 1917)
Lost in Transit (Par., 1917)
The Countess Charming (Par., 1917)
The Clever Mrs. Carfax (Par., 1917)
Jules of the Strong Heart (Par., 1918)
Rimrock Jones (Par., 1918)
The House of Silence (Par., 1918)
Believe Me, Xantippe (Par., 1918)
The Firefly of France (Par., 1918)
The Eyes of the World (Clune, 1918)
Less Than Kin (Par., 1918)
The Goat (Metro, 1918)
The Way of a Man With a Maid (Par., 1919)
Something to Do (Par., 1919)
Venus in the East (Par., 1919)

Love Insurance (Par., 1919)
Poor Boob (Par., 1919)
A Very Good Young Man (Par., 1919)
Johnny Get Your Gun (Artclass, 1919)
Under the Top (Artclass, 1919)
It Pays to Advertise (Par., 1919)
Why Smith Left Home (Par., 1919)
The Six Best Cellars (Par., 1920)
Too Much Johnson (Par., 1920)
Miss Hobbs (Realart, 1920)
Held by the Enemy (Par., 1920)
The Barbarian (Pioneer, 1921)
Appearances (Par., 1921)
The Princess of New York (Par., 1921)
The Bonnie Briar Bush (Par., 1921) (also actor)
Ponjola (Associated FN, 1923) (Possibly directed instead by
    James Young)
The Navigator (Metro-Goldwyn, 1924) (with Buster Keaton)
Don Q, Son of Zorro (UA, 1925) (also actor)
Sunny Side Up (PDC, 1926)
Young April (PDC, 1926)
Man Bait (PDC, 1926)
Nobody's Widow (PDC, 1927)
Vanity (PDC, 1927) (also producer)
The Fighting Eagle (Pathé, 1927) (also producer)
Dress Parade (Pathé, 1927) (also producer)
Stand and Deliver (Pathé, 1928) (also producer)
The Cop (Pathé, 1928) (also producer)
The Runaway Bride (RKO, 1930)

CROMWELL, JOHN, b. Dec. 23, 1888, Toledo, Ohio.
    Close Harmony (Par., 1929) (with A. Edward Sutherland)
    The Dance of Life (Par., 1929) (with A. Edward Sutherland)
    The Mighty (Par., 1930)
    Street of Chance (Par., 1930) (also actor)
    Tom Sawyer (Par., 1930)
    The Texan (Par., 1930)
    For the Defense (Par., 1930)
    Scandal Sheet (Par., 1931)
    Rich Man's Folly (Par., 1931)
    The Vice Squad (Par., 1931)
    Unfaithful (Par., 1931)
    The World and the Flesh (Par., 1932)
    Sweepings (RKO, 1933)
    The Silver Cord (RKO, 1933)
    Double Harness (RKO, 1933)
    Ann Vickers (RKO, 1933)
    Spitfire (RKO, 1934)
    This Man Is Mine (RKO, 1934)
    Of Human Bondage (RKO, 1934)
    The Fountain (RKO, 1934)
    Jaina (RKO, 1935)

James Bush and Margaret Sullavan with John Cromwell (left) on the set of <u>So Ends Our Night</u> (UA, 1941).

Village Tale (RKO, 1935)
I Dream Too Much (RKO, 1935)
Little Lord Fauntleroy (UA, 1936)
To Mary--With Love (20th, 1936)
Banjo on My Knee (20th, 1936)
The Prisoner of Zenda (UA, 1937)
Algiers (UA, 1938)
Made for Each Other (UA, 1939)
In Name Only (RKO, 1939)
Abe Lincoln in Illinois (RKO, 1940)
Victory (Par., 1940)
So Ends Our Night (UA, 1941)
Son of Fury (20th, 1942)
Since You Went Away (UA, 1944) (with credited André
    De Toth)
The Enchanted Cottage (RKO, 1945)
Anna and the King of Siam (20th, 1946)
Dead Reckoning (Col., 1947)
Night Song (RKO, 1947)
Caged (WB, 1950)
The Company She Keeps (RKO, 1950)
The Racket (RKO, 1951)
The Goddess (Col., 1958)
The Scavengers (Par., 1959)
A Matter of Morals (German, 1960)

CROSLAND, ALAN, b. Aug. 10, 1894, New York City; d. July 16,
    1936.
    The Light in Darkness (Edison, 1917)
    Apple-Tree Girl (Edison Perfection, 1917)
    Kidnapped (Forum, 1917)
    The Whirlpool (Select, 1918)
    The Unbeliever (Edison-Kleine, 1918)
    Country Cousin (Select, 1919)
    Broadway and Home (Select, 1920)
    The Flapper (Select, 1920)
    Youthful Folly (Select, 1920)
    Greater Than Fame (Select, 1920)
    A Point of View (Select, 1920)
    Worlds Apart (Select, 1921)
    Is Life Worth Living? (Select, 1921)
    Room and Board (Par., 1921)
    Why Announce Your Marriage? (Select, 1922) (also co-story,
        co-script)
    Shadows of the Sea (Select, 1922)
    The Prophet's Paradise (Select, 1922)
    Slim Shoulders (W.W. Hodkinson, 1922)
    The Snitching Hour (Clark-Cornelius Corp., 1922)
    The Face in the Fog (Par., 1922)
    The Enemies of Women (Goldwyn, 1923)
    Under the Red Robe (Goldwyn, 1924)
    Three Weeks (Goldwyn, 1924)
    Miami (W.W. Hodkinson, 1924) (also producer)
    Sinners in Heaven (Par., 1924)
    Unguarded Women (Par., 1924)
    Bobbed Hair (WB, 1925)
    Contraband (Par., 1925)
    Compromise (WB, 1925)
    Don Juan (WB, 1926)
    When a Man Loves (WB, 1926)
    The Beloved Rogue (UA, 1927)
    Old San Francisco (WB, 1927)
    The Jazz Singer (WB, 1927)
    Glorious Betsy (WB, 1928)
    The Scarlet Lady (Col., 1928)
    On With the Show (WB, 1929)
    General Crack (WB, 1929)
    Big Boy (WB, 1930)
    The Furies (FN, 1930)
    Song of the Flame (FN, 1930)
    Viennese Nights (WB, 1930)
    Captain Thunder (WB, 1931)
    Children of Dreams (WB, 1931)
    The Silver Lining (UA, 1932) (also producer)
    Week-Ends Only (Fox, 1932)
    Massacre (FN, 1934)
    Midnight Alibi (FN, 1934)
    The Personality Kid (WB, 1934)
    The Case of the Howling Dog (WB, 1934)

The White Cockatoo (WB, 1935)
It Happened in New York (Univ., 1935)
Mister Dynamite (Univ., 1935)
Lady Tubbs (Univ., 1935)
King Solomon of Broadway (Univ., 1935)
The Great Impersonation (Univ., 1935)

CRUZE, JAMES (Jens Cruz Bosen), b. March 27, 1884, Ogden,
       Utah; d. Aug. 4, 1942.
Too Many Millions (Par., 1918)
The Dub (Par., 1919)
The Roaring Roads (Par., 1919)
Alias Mike Moran (Par., 1919)
You're Fired (Par., 1919)
The Love Burglar (Par., 1919)
The Lottery Man (Par., 1919)
Hawthorne of the U.S.A. (Par., 1919)
An Adventure in Hearts (Par., 1919)
Terror Island (Par., 1920)
Mrs. Temple's Telegram (Par., 1920)
A Full House (Par., 1920)
Always Audacious (Par., 1920)
What Happened to Jones (Par., 1920)
Food for Scandal (Realart, 1920)
The Sins of St. Anthony (Par., 1920)
Charm School (Par., 1921)
The Dollar a Year Man (Par., 1921)
Crazy to Marry (Par., 1921)
Gasoline Gus (Par., 1921)
Leap Year (Par., 1921--unreleased)
Fast Freight (Par., 1921--unreleased)
One Glorious Day (Par., 1922)
Is Matrimony a Failure? (Par., 1922)
The Dictator (Par., 1922)
The Old Homestead (Par., 1922)
Thirty Days (Par., 1922)
The Covered Wagon (Par., 1923)
Hollywood (Par., 1923)
Ruggles of Red Gap (Par., 1923) (also producer)
To the Ladies (Par., 1923) (also producer)
The Garden of Weeds (Par., 1924) (also producer)
The Fighting Coward (Par., 1924) (also producer)
The City That Never Sleeps (Par., 1924) (also producer)
The Enemy Sex (Par., 1924) (also producer)
Merton of the Movies (Par., 1924) (also producer)
The Goose Hangs High (Par., 1925) (also producer)
Beggar on Horseback (Par., 1925) (also producer)
Waking Up the Town (UA, 1925) (also co-script)
Welcome Home (Par., 1925) (also producer)
Marry Me (Par., 1925) (also producer)
The Pony Express (Par., 1925) (also producer)
Mannequin (Par., 1926) (also producer)

Old Ironsides (Par., 1926) (also producer)
We're All Gamblers (Par., 1927) (also producer)
The City Gone Wild (Par., 1927) (also producer)
On to Reno (Pathé, 1928)
Red Mark (Pathé, 1928)
Excess Baggage (MGM, 1928) (also producer)
Mating Call (Par., 1928)
The Duke Steps Out (MGM, 1929) (also producer)
A Man's Man (MGM, 1929) (also producer)
The Great Gabbo (Sono Art-World Wide, 1929)
Once a Gentleman (Sono Art-World Wide, 1930)
She Got What She Wanted (Tiffany, 1930) (also co-producer, for
    production company)
Salvation Nell (Tiffany, 1931) (also for production company)
Washington Merry-Go-Round (Col., 1932) (also for production
    Company
If I Had a Million (eps: "The Streetwalker," "The Old Ladies'
    Home") (Par., 1932)
Sailor Be Good (RKO, 1933)
Racetrack (World Wide, 1933) (also for production company)
I Cover the Waterfront (UA, 1933)
Mr. Skitch (Fox, 1933)
David Harum (Fox, 1934)
Their Big Moment (RKO, 1934)
Helldorado (Fox, 1935)
Two-Fisted (Par., 1935)
Sutter's Gold (Univ., 1936)
The Wrong Road (Rep., 1937)
Prison Nurse (Rep., 1938)
The Gangs of New York (Rep., 1938)
Come on Leathernecks (Rep., 1938)

CUKOR, GEORGE, b. July 7, 1899, New York City.
    Grumpy (Par., 1930) (with Cyril Gardner)
    The Virtuous Sin (Par., 1930) (with Louis Gasnier)
    The Royal Family of Broadway (Par., 1930) (with Cyril Gard-
        ner)
    Tarnished Lady (Par., 1931)
    Girls About Town (Par., 1931)
    One Hour With You (Par., 1932) (uncredited, with Ernst Lub-
        itsch)
    What Price Hollywood? (RKO, 1932)
    A Bill of Divorcement (RKO, 1932)
    Rockabye (RKO, 1932)
    Our Betters (RKO, 1933)
    Dinner at Eight (MGM, 1933)
    Little Women (RKO, 1933)
    David Copperfield (MGM, 1935)
    Sylvia Scarlett (RKO, 1935)
    Romeo and Juliet (MGM, 1936)
    Camille (MGM, 1937)
    Holiday (Col., 1938)

Katharine Hepburn and author Hugh Walpole with George Cukor (left) on the set of <u>Sylvia Scarlett</u> (RKO, 1935).

Zaza (Par., 1939)
Gone With the Wind (MGM, 1939) (uncredited, with Victor
    Fleming and uncredited Sam Wood)
The Women (MGM, 1939)
The Philadelphia Story (MGM, 1940)
Susan and God (MGM, 1940)
A Woman's Face (MGM, 1941)
Two-Faced Woman (MGM, 1941)
Her Cardboard Lover (MGM, 1942)
Keeper of the Flame (MGM, 1943)
Gaslight (MGM, 1944)
Winged Victory (20th, 1944)
Desire Me (MGM, 1947) (uncredited, with Jack Conway)
A Double Life (Univ., 1947)
Edward, My Son (MGM, 1949)
Adam's Rib (MGM, 1949)
A Life of Her Own (MGM, 1950)
Born Yesterday (Col., 1950)
The Model and the Marriage Broker (20th, 1951)
The Marrying Kind (Col., 1952)
Pat and Mike (MGM, 1952)
The Actress (MGM, 1953)

A Star Is Born (WB, 1954)
It Should Happen to You (Col., 1954)
Bhowani Junction (MGM, 1956)
Les Girls (MGM, 1957)
Wild Is the Wind (Par., 1957)
Heller in Pink Tights (Par., 1960)
Song Without End (Col., 1960) (uncredited, with Charles Vidor)
Let's Make Love (20th, 1960)
The Chapman Report (WB, 1962)
Something's Got to Give (20th, 1962--unfinished)
My Fair Lady (WB, 1964)
Justine (20th, 1969) (replaced Joseph Strick)
Travels With My Aunt (MGM, 1972)

CUMMINGS, IRVING, b. Oct. 9, 1888, New York City; d. April
    18, 1959.
    The Man from Hell's River (Western Pictures, 1922) (also pro-
        ducer, script, actor)
    Paid Back (Univ., 1922)
    The Jilt (Univ., 1922)
    Flesh and Blood (Western Pictures, 1922) (also producer)
    Environment (Principal, 1922) (also producer)
    Broad Daylight (Univ., 1922)
    Broken Hearts of Broadway (Lesser, 1923) (also producer)
    The Drug Traffic (Lesser, 1923) (also producer)
    East Side, West Side (Principal, 1923) (also producer)
    The Dancing Cheat (Univ., 1924)
    Fool's Highway (Univ., 1924)
    In Every Woman's Life (FN, 1924)
    Riders Up (Univ., 1924)
    The Rose of Paris (Univ., 1924)
    Stolen Secrets (Univ., 1924)
    One Year to Live (FN, 1925)
    Just a Woman (FN, 1925)
    As Man Desires (FN, 1925)
    The Desert Flower (FN, 1925)
    Infatuation (FN, 1925)
    Rustling for Cupid (Fox, 1926)
    The Country Beyond (Fox, 1926) (also co-script)
    The Midnight Kiss (Fox, 1926)
    The Johnstown Flood (Fox, 1926)
    Bertha the Sewing Machine Girl (Fox, 1926)
    The Brute (WB, 1927)
    Dressed to Kill (Fox, 1928) (also co-story)
    The Port of Missing Girls (Brenda, 1928)
    Romance of the Underworld (Fox, 1928)
    In Old Arizona (Fox, 1929) (with Raoul Walsh)
    Not Quite Decent (Fox, 1929)
    Behind That Curtain (Fox, 1929)
    Cameo Kirby (Fox, 1930)
    A Devil With Women (Fox, 1930)
    On the Level (Fox, 1930)

Holy Terror (Fox, 1931)
The Cisco Kid (Fox, 1931)
Attorney for the Defense (Col., 1932)
The Night Club Lady (Col., 1932)
Man Against Woman (Col., 1932)
Man Hunt (RKO, 1933)
The Woman I Stole (Col., 1933)
Mad Game (Fox, 1933)
I Believed in You (Fox, 1934)
Grand Canary (Fox, 1934)
The White Parade (Fox, 1934)
It's a Small World (Fox, 1935)
Curly Top (Fox, 1935)
Nobody's Fool (Univ., 1936)
The Poor Little Rich Girl (20th, 1936)
Girls' Dormitory (20th, 1936)
White Hunter (20th, 1936)
Vogues of 1938 (UA, 1937)
Merry-Go-Round of 1938 (Univ., 1937)
Little Miss Broadway (20th, 1938)
Just Around the Corner (20th, 1938)
The Story of Alexander Graham Bell (20th, 1939)
Hollywood Cavalcade (20th, 1939)
Everything Happens at Night (20th, 1939)
Lillian Russell (20th, 1940)
Down Argentine Way (20th, 1940)
That Night in Rio (20th, 1941)
Belle Starr (20th, 1941)
Louisiana Purchase (Par., 1941)
My Gal Sal (20th, 1942)
Springtime in the Rockies (20th, 1942)
Sweet Rosie O'Grady (20th, 1943)
What a Woman (Col., 1943) (also producer)
The Impatient Years (Col., 1944) (also producer)
The Dolly Sisters (20th, 1945)

CURTIZ, MICHAEL (Mihaly Kertesz), b. Dec. 24, 1888, Budapest;
    d. April 11, 1962.
    Az Utolsó Bohém (Hungarian, 1912)
    Ma es Holnap (Hungarian, 1912) (also co-script, actor)
    Rablelek (Hungarian, 1913)
    Házasokik Az Uram (Hungarian, 1913)
    Az Eiszaka Rabja (Hungarian, 1914) (also actor)
    Aranyásó (Hungarian, 1914)
    Bánk Bán (Hungarian, 1914)
    A Tolonc (Hungarian, 1914)
    A Kolesonkert Csecsemok (Hungarian, 1914)
    A Hercegnő Pongyolában (Hungarian, 1914)
    Akit Ketten Szeretnek (Hungarian, 1915) (also actor)
    A Karthauzi (Hungarian, 1916)
    Makkhetes (Hungarian, 1916)
    A Fekete Szivárvány (Hungarian, 1916)

Doktor Ur (Hungarian, 1916)
A Magyar Föld Ereje (Hungarian, 1916)
A Medikus (Hungarian, 1916)
Zoárd Mester (Hungarian, 1917)
A Vörös Sámson (Hungarian, 1917)
Az Utolsó Hajnal (Hungarian, 1917)
A Senki Fia (Hungarian, 1917)
A Szentjóbi Erdó Titka (Hungarian, 1917)
A Kuruzsló (Hungarian, 1917)
A Halázcsengö (Hungarian, 1917)
A Föld Embre (Hungarian, 1917)
Az Ezredes (Hungarian, 1917)
Egy Drajcár Törénete (Hungarian, 1917)
A Beke Utja (Hungarian, 1917)
Az Árdendá Zsidó (Hungarian, 1917)
Tatárjárás (Hungarian, 1917) (also script)
Az Orvos (Hungarian, 1918)
Tavasz a Télben (Hungarian, 1917)
A Napraforgos Holgy (Hungarian, 1918)
Lulu (Hungarian, 1918)
Kilencven Kilenc (Hungarian, 1918)
Az Ordog (Hungarian, 1918)
Judas (Hungarian, 1918)
A Csunya Fiju (Hungarian, 1918)
Alraune (Hungarian, 1918)
A Vig Özvegy (Hungarian, 1918)
Varázskeringö (Hungarian, 1918)
Lu, a Kokott (Hungarian, 1918)
Liliom (Hungarian, 1918--unfinished)
Jön Az Öcsem (Hungarian, 1919)
Wellington Rejtély (Swedish, 1919)
Odette et l'Histoire des Femmes Illustrés (Swedish, 1919)
Die Dame mit dem Schwarzen Handschuh (Austrian, 1919)
Der Stern von Damaskus (Austrian, 1919)
Die Gottesgeissel (Austrian, 1920)
Die Dame mit den Sonnenblumen (Austrian, 1920)
Labyrinth des Grauvens (Austrian, 1920)
Wege des Schrecken (Austrian, 1921)
Frau Dorothys Bekenntnis (Austrian, 1921)
Miss Tutti Frutti (Austrian, 1921)
Herzogin Satanella (Austrian, 1921)
Sodom und Gomorrha (Austrian, part one 1922; part two, 1923)
    (also co-script)
Die Lasvine (Austrian, 1923)
Der Junge Medardus (Austrian, 1923) (with Sascha Kolowrat)
Samson und Dalila (Austrian, 1923)
Namenlos (Austrian, 1923)
Ein Spiel Ums Leben (Austrian, 1924)
General Babka (Austrian, 1924)
The Uncle from Sumatra (Austrian, 1924)
Avalanche (Austrian, 1924)
Harun Al Raschid (Austrian, 1924)

Die Slavenkönigin [Moon of Israel] (Austrian, 1924)
Das Spielzeug Von Paris [Red Heels] (German-Austrian, 1925)
Der Goldene Schmetterling [The Road to Happiness] (German-
  Austrian, 1926)
Flaker Nr. 13 (Austrian-German, 1926)
The Third Degree (WB, 1926
The Million Bid (WB, 1927)
The Desired Woman (WB, 1927)
Good Time Charley (WB, 1927)
Tenderloin (WB, 1928)
Noah's Ark (WB, 1928)
Hearts in Exile (WB, 1929)
Glad Rag Doll (WB, 1929)
Madonna of Avenue A (WB, 1929)
The Gamblers (WB, 1929)
Mammy (WB, 1930)
Under a Texas Moon (WB, 1930)
The Matrimonial Bed (WB, 1930)
Bright Lights (FN, 1930)
A Soldier's Plaything (WB, 1930)
River's End (WB, 1930)
Dämon des Meeres (WB, 1931)
God's Gift to Women (WB, 1931)
The Mad Genius (WB, 1931)
The Woman from Monte Carlo (FN, 1932)
Alias the Doctor (FN, 1932)
The Strange Love of Molly Louvain (FN, 1932)
Doctor X (FN, 1932)
The Cabin in the Cotton (FN, 1932) (with William Keighley)
20,000 Years in Sing Sing (FN, 1933)
The Mystery of the Wax Museum (FN, 1933)
The Keyhole (WB, 1933)
Private Detective 62 (WB, 1933)
Goodbye Again (FN, 1933)
The Kennel Murder Case (WB, 1933)
Female (FN, 1933)
Mandalay (FN, 1934)
British Agent (FN, 1934)
Jimmy the Gent (WB, 1934)
The Key (WB, 1934)
Black Fury (WB, 1935)
The Case of the Curious Bride (WB, 1935)
Front Page Woman (WB, 1935)
Little Big Shot (WB, 1935)
Captain Blood (WB, 1935)
The Walking Dead (WB, 1936)
The Charge of the Light Brigade (WB, 1936)
Mountain Justice (WB, 1937)
Stolen Holiday (WB, 1937)
Kid Galahad (WB, 1937)
The Perfect Specimen (WB, 1937)
Gold Is Where You Find It (WB, 1938)
The Adventures of Robin Hood (WB, 1938) (with William Keigh-
  ley)

Four Daughters (WB, 1938)
Four's a Crowd (WB, 1938)
Angels With Dirty Faces (WB, 1938)
Dodge City (WB, 1939)
Daughters Courageous (WB, 1939)
Four Wives (WB, 1939)
The Private Lives of Elizabeth and Essex (WB, 1939)
Virginia City (WB, 1940)
The Sea Hawk (WB, 1940)
The Santa Fe Trail (WB, 1940)
The Sea Wolf (WB, 1941)
Dive Bomber (WB, 1941)
Captains of the Clouds (WB, 1941)
Yankee Doodle Dandy (WB, 1942)
Casablanca (WB, 1943)
Mission to Moscow (WB, 1943)
This Is the Army (WB, 1943)
Passage to Marseille (WB, 1944)
Janie (WB, 1944)
Roughly Speaking (WB, 1945)
Mildred Pierce (WB, 1945)
Night and Day (WB, 1946)
Life With Father (WB, 1947)
The Unsuspected (WB, 1947)
Romance on the High Seas (WB, 1948)
My Dream Is Yours (WB, 1949) (also producer)
Flamingo Road (WB, 1949)
The Lady Takes a Sailor (WB, 1949)
Young Man With a Horn (WB, 1950)
Bright Leaf (WB, 1950)
The Breaking Point (WB, 1950)
Jim Thorpe--All American (WB, 1951)
Force of Arms (WB, 1951)
I'll See You in My Dreams (WB, 1952)
The Story of Will Rogers (WB, 1952)
The Jazz Singer (WB, 1953)
Trouble Along the Way (WB, 1953)
The Boy from Oklahoma (WB, 1954)
The Egyptian (20th, 1954)
White Christmas (Par., 1954)
We're No Angels (Par., 1955)
The Scarlet Hour (Par., 1956) (also producer)
The Vagabond King (Par., 1956)
The Best Things in Life Are Free (20th, 1956)
The Helen Morgan Story (WB, 1957)
The Proud Rebel (BV, 1958)
King Creole (Par., 1958)
The Hangman (Par., 1959)
The Man in the Net (UA, 1959)
The Adventures of Huckleberry Finn (MGM, 1960)
A Breath of Scandal (Par., 1960)
Francis of Assisi (20th, 1961)
The Comancheros (20th, 1961)

D

DA COSTA, MORTON (Morton Tecosky), b. March 7, 1918, Phila-
delphia.
Auntie Mame (WB, 1958)
The Music Man (WB, 1962) (also producer)
Island of Love (WB, 1963) (also producer)

D'ARRAST, HARRY d'ABBADIE, b. 1897, Argentina; d. March 17,
1968.
Service for Ladies (Par., 1927)
A Gentleman of Paris (Par., 1927)
Serenade (Par., 1927)
The Magnificent Flirt (Par., 1928) (also co-script)
Dry Martini (Fox, 1928)
Raffles (UA, 1930) (uncredited, with George Fitzmaurice)
Laughter (Par., 1930) (also co-story)
Topaze (RKO, 1933)
The Three Cornered Hat (1935)
La Meunière Débauchée (French, 1935) (also script)
La Traviesa Molierna [Spanish version of La Meunière Dé-
bauchée] (French, 1935) (with Ricardo Soriano)
It Happened in Spain [English version of La Meunière Débau-
chee] (French, 1935)

DASSIN, JULES, b. Dec. 18, 1911, Middletown, Conn.
Nazi Agent (MGM, 1942)
The Affairs of Martha (MGM, 1942)
Reunion in France (MGM, 1942)
Young Ideas (MGM, 1943)
The Canterville Ghost (MGM, 1944)
A Letter for Evie (MGM, 1945)
Two Smart People (MGM, 1946)
Brute Force (Univ., 1947)
The Naked City (Univ., 1948)
Thieves' Highway (20th, 1949) (also actor
Night and the City (20th, 1950)
Du Rififi Chez les Hommes (Pathé, 1954) (also co-script, actor)
Celui Qui Doit Mourir (French-Italian, 1957) (also co-script)
La Loi (French-Italian, 1958) (also co-script)
Never on Sunday (Loppert, 1960) (also producer, script, actor)
Phaedra (Loppert, 1962) (also producer, co-script, actor)
Topkapi (UA, 1964) (also producer)
10:30 P.M. Summer (Loppert, 1966) (also producer, co-script)
Uptight (Par., 1968) (also co-script)
Promise at Dawn (Avco-Emb., 1970) (also script)

DAVES, DELMER, b. July 24, 1904, San Francisco.
Destination Tokyo (WB, 1943) (also co-script)

Mary Astor with Delmer Daves on <u>Youngblood Hawke</u> (WB, 1964).

The Very Thought of You (WB, 1944) (also co-script)
Hollywood Canteen (WB, 1944) (also script)
Pride of the Marines (WB, 1945) (also co-script)
The Red House (UA, 1947) (also script)
Dark Passage (WB, 1947) (also script)
To the Victor (WB, 1948)
A Kiss in the Dark (WB, 1949)
Task Force (WB, 1949) (also script)
Broken Arrow (20th, 1950
Bird of Paradise (20th, 1951) (also script)
Return of the Texan (20th, 1952)
Treasure of the Golden Condor (20th, 1953)
Never Let Me Go (MGM, 1953)
Demetrius and the Gladiators (20th, 1954)
Drum Beat (WB, 1954) (also script)
Jubal (Col., 1956)
The Last Wagon (20th, 1956) (also co-script)
3:10 to Yuma (Col., 1957)

Cowboy (Col., 1958)
Kings Go Forth (UA, 1958)
The Badlanders (MGM, 1958)
The Hanging Tree (WB, 1959)
A Summer Place (WB, 1960) (also producer, script)
Parrish (WB, 1961) (also producer, script)
Susan Slade (WB, 1961) (also producer, script)
Rome Adventure (WB, 1962) (also producer, script)
Spencer's Mountain (WB, 1963) (also producer)
Youngblood Hawke (WB, 1964) (also script)
The Battle of the Villa Fiorita (WB, 1965) (also producer,
   script)

DAVIS, OSSIE, b. Dec. 18, 1917, Cogdell, Ga.
Cotton Comes to Harlem (UA, 1970)
Black Girl (Cin., 1972)
Gordon's War (20th, 1973)

DAY, ROBERT, b. Sept. 11, 1922, Sheen, Eng.
The Green Man (British Lion, 1956)
Stranger's Meeting (Rank, 1957)
Corridors of Blood (MGM, 1958)
Grip of the Strangler [The Haunted Strangler] (MGM, 1958)
First Man in Space (MGM, 1959)
Life in Emergency Ward 10 (Eros, 1959)
Bobbikins (20th, 1959)
Two Way Stretch (British Lion, 1960)
Tarzan the Magnificent (Par., 1960)
The Rebel [Call Me Genius] (Continental, 1961)
Operation Snatch (Continental, 1962)
Corridors of Blood (MGM, 1962)
Tarzan's Three Challenges (MGM, 1963)
She (MGM, 1965)
Tarzan and the Valley of Gold (AIP, 1966)
Tarzan and the Great River (Par., 1967)
I Think We're Being Followed (1967)
The House on Green Apple Road (ABC-TV, 1970)
Ritual of Evil (ABC-TV, 1970)
Banyon (NBC-TV, 1971)
In Broad Daylight (ABC-TV, 1971)
Mr. and Mrs. Bo Jo Jones (ABC-TV, 1971)
The Reluctant Heroes (ABC-TV, 1971)
The Great American Beauty Contest (ABC-TV, 1972)

DE CORDOVA, FREDERICK, b. Oct. 27, 1910, New York City.
Too Young to Know (WB, 1945)
Her Kind of Man (WB, 1946)
Always Together (WB, 1947)
Love and Learn (WB, 1947)
That Way With Women (WB, 1947)

Wallflower (WB, 1948)
The Countess of Monte Cristo (Univ., 1948)
For the Love of Mary (Univ., 1948)
Illegal Entry (Univ., 1949)
The Gal Who Took the West (Univ., 1949)
Peggy (Univ., 1950)
The Desert Hawk (Univ., 1950)
Buccaneer's Girl (Univ., 1950) *
Katie Did It (Univ., 1951)
Bedtime for Bonzo (Univ., 1951)
Finders Keepers (Univ., 1951)
Little Egypt (Univ., 1951)
Here Come the Nelsons (Univ., 1952)
Yankee Buccaneer (Univ., 1952)
Bonzo Goes to College (Univ., 1952)
Column South (Univ., 1953)
I'll Take Sweden (UA, 1965)
Frankie and Johnny (UA, 1966)

DE LIMUR, JEAN
The Letter (Par., 1929) (also co-dialog, co-editor)
Jealousy (Par., 1929)
Mon Gosse de Père (French, 1930)
The Parisian [English version of Mon Gosse de Père] (French,
    1931)
Circulez! (French, 1931)
Monsieur le Duc (French, 1932)
Paprika (French, 1933)
Mariage à Responsabilité Limitée (French, 1933)
Les Millions de ma Tante (French, 1933)
L'Amour en Cage [French version of Das Verliebte Hotel]
    (French, 1933) (with Carl Lamac)
Le Voyage Imprévu [The Slipper Episode] (Swiss-French, 1934)
Runaway Ladies [English version of Le Voyage Imprévu] (French,
    1935)
L'Auberge du Petit Dragon (French, 1935)
Le Petite Sauvage (French, 1935)
La Rosière des Halles (French, 1935)
La Garçonne (French, 1937)
La Brigade en Jupons (French, 1937)
La Bête aux Sept Manteaux [L'Homme à la Cagoule Noire]
    (French, 1937)
La Cité des Lumieres (French, 1938)
Petite Peste (French, 1938)
Papá Lebonnard [Le Père Lebonnard] (Italian-French, 1939)
L'Age d'Or (French, 1940)
L'Homme Qui Joue avec le Feu (French, 1942)
Apparizione (Italian, 1943)
Le Grande Meute (French, 1944)

DeMILLE, CECIL B. (Cecil Blount DeMille), b. Aug. 12, 1881,
    Ashfield, Mass.; d. Jan. 21, 1959.
  The Squaw Man (Jesse L. Lasky Feature Play, 1913) (with Os-
    car Apfel) (also producer, co-script)
  The Call of the North (Jesse L. Lasky Feature Play, 1914) (al-
    so producer, script)
  The Virginian (Jesse L. Lasky Feature Play, 1914) (also pro-
    ducer, script, co-editor)
  What's His Name (Jesse L. Lasky Feature Play, 1914) (also
    producer, script, editor)
  The Man from Home (Jesse L. Lasky Feature Play, 1914) (al-
    so producer, script, editor)
  Rose of the Rancho (Jesse L. Lasky Feature Play, 1914) (also
    producer, script, editor)
  The Girl of the Golden West (Par., 1915) (also producer, script,
    editor)
  The Warrens of Virginia (Par., 1915) (also producer, editor)
  The Unafraid (Par., 1915) (also producer, script, editor)
  The Captive (Par., 1915) (also producer, co-script, editor)
  The Wild Goose Chase (Par., 1915) (also producer, editor)
  The Arab (Par., 1915) (also producer, co-script, editor)
  Chimmie Fadden (Par., 1915) (also producer, script, editor)
  Kindling (Par., 1915) (also producer, script, editor)
  Carmen (Par., 1915) (also producer, editor)
  Chimmie Fadden Out West (Par., 1915) (also producer, co-
    script, editor)
  The Cheat (Par., 1915) (also producer, editor)
  The Golden Chance (Par., 1915) (also producer, co-script, edi-
    tor)
  Temptation (Par., 1916) (also producer, editor)
  The Trail of the Lonesome Pine (Par., 1916) (also producer,
    editor)
  The Heart of Nora Flynn (Par., 1916) (also producer, editor)
  Maria Rosa (Par., 1916) (also producer, editor)
  The Dream Girl (Par., 1916) (also producer, editor)
  Joan the Woman (Par., 1917) (also producer, editor)
  Romance of the Redwoods (Artcraft-Par., 1917) (also producer,
    editor)
  The Little American (Artcraft-Par., 1917) (also producer, edi-
    tor)
  The Woman God Forgot (Artcraft-Par., 1917) (also producer,
    editor)
  The Devil Stone (Artcraft-Par., 1917) (also producer, editor)
  The Whispering Chorus (Artcraft-Par., 1918) (also producer,
    editor)
  Old Wives for New (Artcraft-Par., 1918) (also producer, editor)
  We Can't Have Everything (Artcraft-Par., 1918) (also producer,
    co-editor)
  Till I Come Back to You (Artcraft-Par., 1918) (also producer)
  The Squaw Man (Artcraft-Par., 1918) (also producer)
  Don't Change Your Husband (Artcraft-Par., 1919)
  For Better, for Worse (Artcraft-Par., 1919) (also producer)
  Male and Female (Par., 1919) (also producer)

Mary Pickford and Darryl F. Zanuck with Cecil B. DeMille (left) at 1953 Academy Awards Ceremonies.

Why Change Your Wife? (Artcraft-Par., 1920) (also producer)
Something to Think About (Artcraft-Par., 1920) (also producer)
Forbidden Fruit (Par., 1921) (also producer, co-script)
The Affairs of Anatol (Par., 1921) (also producer)
Fool's Paradise (Par., 1921) (also producer)
Saturday Night (Par., 1922) (also producer)
Manslaughter (Par., 1922) (also producer)
Adam's Rib (Par., 1923 (also producer)
The Ten Commandments (Par., 1923) (also producer)
Triumph (Par., 1924) (also producer)
Feet of Clay (Par., 1924) (also producer)
The Golden Bed (Par., 1925) (also producer)
The Road to Yesterday (PDC, 1925) (also producer)
The Volga Boatman (PDC, 1926) (also producer)
The King of Kings (Pathé, 1927) (also producer)
The Godless Girl (Pathé, 1929) (also producer)
Dynamite (MGM, 1929) (also producer)
Madam Satan (MGM, 1930) (also producer)
The Squaw Man (MGM, 1931) (also producer)

The Sign of the Cross (Par., 1932) (also producer)
This Day and Age (Par., 1933) (also producer)
Four Frightened People (Par., 1934) (also producer)
Cleopatra (Par., 1934) (also producer)
The Crusades (Par., 1935) (also producer)
The Plainsman (Par., 1937) (also producer)
The Buccaneer (Par., 1938) (also producer)
Union Pacific (Par., 1939) (also producer)
Northwest Mounted Police (Par., 1940) (also producer)
Reap the Wild Wind (Par., 1942) (also producer)
The Story of Dr. Wassell (Par., 1944) (also producer)
Unconquered (Par., 1947) (also producer)
Samson and Delilah (Par., 1949) (also producer)
The Greatest Show on Earth (Par., 1952) (also producer)
The Ten Commandments (Par., 1956) (also producer)

DE MILLE, WILLIAM C. (William Churchill De Mille), b. June 25,
    1878, Washington, D.C.; d. March 18, 1955.
Anton, the Terrible (Par., 1916)
The Blacklist (Par., 1916)
The Heir to the Horrah (Par., 1916)
The Ragamuffin (Par., 1916)
The Sowers (Par., 1916)
Hashimura Togo (Par., 1917)
The Ghost House (Par., 1917)
The Secret Game (Premiere, 1917)
The Widow's Might (Par., 1918)
One More American (Par., 1918)
The Honor of His House (Par., 1918)
Mirandy Smiles (Par., 1918)
The Mystery Girl (Par., 1918)
Peg O' My Heart (Par., 1919--unreleased)
The Tree of Knowledge (Par., 1920)
Jack Straw (Par., 1920)
The Prince Chap (Par., 1920)
Conrad in Quest of His Youth (Par., 1920)
Midsummer Madness (Par., 1920)
What Every Woman Knows (Par., 1921)
After the Show (Par, 1921)
The Lost Romance (Par., 1921)
Miss Lulu Bett (Par., 1921)
Bought and Paid For (Par., 1922)
Nice People (Par., 1922)
Clarence (Par., 1922)
The World's Applause (Par., 1923)
Grumpy (Par., 1923)
Only 38 (Par., 1923)
The Marriage Maker (Par., 1923)
Don't Call It Love (Par., 1924)
Icebound (Par., 1924)
The Bedroom Widow (Par., 1924)
The Fast Set (Par., 1924)

Locked Doors (Par., 1925)
Men and Women (Par., 1925)
Lost--A Wife (Par., 1925)
New Brooms (Par., 1925)
The Splendid Crime (Par., 1926) (also story)
The Runaway (Par., 1926)
For Alimony Only (PDC, 1926)
The Little Adventuress (PDC, 1927)
Craig's Wife (Pathé, 1928)
Tenth Avenue (Pathé, 1928)
The Doctor's Secret (Pathé, 1929) (also adaptation)
The Idle Rich (MGM, 1929)
This Mad World (MGM, 1930)
Passion Flower (MGM, 1930)
Two Kinds of Women (Par., 1932)
His Double Life (Par., 1933) (with Arthur Hopkins)

De TOTH, ANDRE (Endre Toth), b. 1910, Mako, Hungary.

Veronica Lake with Andre De Toth in Hollywood (1944).

Toprini Nasz (Hungarian, 1939) (also co-script)
Öt Óra 40 (Hungarian, 1939)
Ket Lány az Utcán (Hungarian, 1939) (also script)
Semmelweis (Hungarian, 1939)

Hat Het Boldogság (Hungarian, 1939)
Passport to Suez (Col., 1943)
None Shall Escape (Col., 1944)
Dark Waters (UA, 1944)
Since You Went Away (UA, 1944) (uncredited, with John Cromwell)
Ramrod (UA, 1947)
The Other Love (UA, 1947)
Pitfall (UA, 1948)
Slattery's Hurricane (20th, 1949)
Guest in the House (UA, 1944) (uncredited, with Lewis Milestone)
Man in the Saddle (Col., 1951)
Carson City (WB, 1952)
Springfield Rifle (WB, 1952)
Last of the Comanches (Col., 1952)
House of Wax (WB, 1953)
The Stranger Wore a Gun (Col., 1953)
Thunder Over the Plains (WB, 1953)
Riding Shotgun (WB, 1954)
The City Is Dark (WB, 1954)
The Bounty Hunter (WB, 1954)
Tanganyika (Univ., 1954)
The Indian Fighter (UA, 1955)
Monkey on My Back (UA, 1957)
Hidden Fear (UA, 1957) (also co-script)
The Two-Headed Spy (Col., 1959)
Day of the Outlaw (UA, 1959)
Man on a String (Col., 1960)
Morgan the Pirate (MGM, 1960) (also script)
The Mongols (Colorama, 1961) (with Riccardo Freda, Leopold Savona)
Gold for the Caesars (Colorama, 1962) (with Riccardo Freda, Sabatino Ciuffini)
Play Dirty (UA, 1968)

DEL RUTH, ROY, b. Oct. 18, 1895, Philadelphia; d. April 27, 1961.
Eve's Lover (WB, 1925)
Hogan's Alley (WB, 1925)
Three Weeks in Paris (WB, 1926)
The Man Upstairs (WB, 1926)
The Little Irish Girl (WB, 1926)
Footloose Widows (WB, 1926)
Across the Pacific (WB, 1926)
Wolf's Clothing (WB, 1927)
The First Auto (WB, 1927)
Ham and Eggs at the Front (WB, 1927)
If I Were Single (WB, 1928)
Five and Ten Cent Annie (WB, 1928)
Powder My Back (WB, 1928)
The Terror (WB, 1928)
Beware of Bachelors (WB, 1929)

Conquest (WB, 1929)
The Desert Song (WB, 1929)
The Hottentot (WB, 1929)
Gold Diggers of Broadway (WB, 1939)
The Aviator (WB, 1929)
Hold Everything (WB, 1930)
The Second Floor Mystery (WB, 1930)
Three Faces East (WB, 1930)
The Life of the Party (WB, 1930)
My Past (WB, 1931)
Divorce Among Friends (WB, 1931)
The Maltese Falcon (WB, 1931)
Larceny Lane (WB, 1931)
Side Show (WB, 1931)
Blonde Crazy (WB, 1931)
Taxi! (WB, 1932)
Beauty and the Boss (WB, 1932)
Winner Take All (WB, 1932)
Blessed Event (WB, 1932)
Employees' Entrance (FN, 1933)
Mind Reader (FN, 1933)
Little Giant (FN, 1933)
Bureau of Missing Persons (FN, 1933)
Captured! (WB, 1933)
Lady Killer (WB, 1933)
Bulldog Drummond Strikes Back (UA, 1934)
Upper World (WB, 1934)
Kid Millions (UA, 1934)
Folies Bergere (UA, 1935)
Broadway Melody of 1936 (MGM, 1935)
Thanks a Million (20th, 1935)
It Had to Happen (20th, 1936)
Private Number (20th, 1936)
Born to Dance (MGM, 1936)
On the Avenue (20th, 1937)
Broadway Melody of 1938 (MGM, 1937)
Happy Landing (20th, 1938)
My Lucky Star (20th, 1938)
Tail Spin (20th, 1939)
The Star Maker (Par., 1939)
Here I Am Stranger (20th, 1939)
He Married His Wife (20th, 1940)
Topper Returns (UA, 1941)
The Chocolate Soldier (MGM, 1941)
Maisie Gets Her Man (MGM, 1942)
Dubarry Was a Lady (MGM, 1943)
Broadway Rhythm (MGM, 1944)
Barbary Coast Gent (MGM, 1944)
It Happened on Fifth Avenue (AA, 1947) (also producer)
The Babe Ruth Story (AA, 1948)
Red Light (UA, 1949) (also producer)
Always Leave Them Laughing (WB, 1949)
The West Point Story (WB, 1950)

On Moonlight Bay (WB, 1951)
Starlift (WB, 1951)
About Face (WB, 1951)
Stop, You're Killing Me (WB, 1952)
Three Sailors and a Girl (WB, 1953)
Phantom of the Rue Morgue (WB, 1954)
The Alligator People (20th, 1959)
Why Must I Die? (AIP, 1960)

DIETERLE, WILLIAM (Wilhelm Dieterle), b. July 15, 1893, Lud-
wigshafen, Germany; d. Dec. 16, 1972.
Der Menschen am Wege (German, 1923) (also script, actor)
Das Geheimnis des Abbe X (German, 1927) (also script, actor)
Die Heilige und Ihr Narr (German, 1928) (also actor)
Geschlecht in Fesseln (German, 1928) (also actor)
Frühlingsrauschen (German, 1929) (also actor)
Ich Lebe für Dich (German, 1929) (also actor)
Ludwig der Zweite König von Bayern (German, 1929) (also ac-
tor)
Eine Stunde Glücke (German, 1930) (also actor)
Der Tanz Geht Weiter [German version of Those Who Dance]
(FN, 1930) (also actor)
Die Maske Fallt [German version of The Way of All Men] (FN,
1930)
Kismet [German version of American picture] (FN, 1931)
The Last Flight (FN, 1931)
Her Majesty Love (FN, 1931)
Man Wanted (WB, 1932)
Jewel Robbery (WB, 1932)
The Crash (FN, 1932)
Scarlet Dawn (WB, 1932)
Six Hours to Live (Fox, 1932)
Lawyer Man (WB, 1932)
Grand Slam (WB, 1933)
Adorable (Fox, 1933)
The Devil's in Love (Fox, 1933)
From Headquarters (WB, 1933)
The Fashion Follies of 1934 (WB, 1934)
Fog Over Frisco (FN, 1934)
Madame Dubarry (WB, 1934)
The Firebird (WB, 1934)
The Secret Bride (WB, 1934)
Dr. Socrates (WB, 1935)
A Midsummer Night's Dream (WB, 1935) (with Max Reinhardt)
The Story of Louis Pasteur (WB, 1936)
The White Angel (WB, 1936)
Satan Met a Lady (WB, 1936)
The Great O'Malley (WB, 1937)
Another Dawn (WB, 1937)
The Life of Emile Zola (WB, 1937)
Blockade (UA, 1938)
Juarez (WB, 1939)

The Hunchback of Notre Dame (RKO, 1939)
Dr. Ehrlich's Magic Bullet (MGM, 1940)
A Dispatch from Reuter's (WB, 1940)
All That Money Can Buy (RKO, 1941) (also producer)
Syncopation (RKO, 1942) (also producer)
Tennessee Johnson (MGM, 1942)
Kismet (MGM, 1944)
I'll Be Seeing You (UA, 1944)
Love Letters (Par., 1945)
This Love of Ours (Univ., 1945)
The Searching Wind (Par., 1946)
Duel in the Sun (Selznick Releasing, 1946) (uncredited, with
    King Vidor, and uncredited Josef von Sternberg, William
    Cameron Menzies, Otto Brower, Sidney Franklin)
Portrait of Jenny (Selznick Releasing, 1949)
The Accused (Par., 1949)
Volcano (UA, 1949) (also producer)
Rope of Sand (Par., 1949)
Paid in Full (Par., 1950)
Dark City (Par., 1950)
September Affair (Par., 1951)
Peking Express (Par., 1951)
Boots Malone (Col., 1952)
Red Mountain (Par., 1952)
The Turning Point (Par., 1952)
Salome (Col., 1953)
Elephant Walk (Par., 1954)
Magic Fire (Rep., 1956) (also producer)
Omar Khayyam (Par., 1957)
Herrin der Welt (European co-production, 1959) (released in
    two parts)
Il Vendicator (European co-production, 1959) (also actor)
Die Fastnachtsbeichte (German, 1960)
The Confession (Golden Eagle, 1965)

DILLON, JOHN FRANCIS (Jack Dillon), b. July 13, 1887, New York
    City; d. 1934.
    Indiscreet Corrine (Triangle, 1917)
    Betty Takes a Hand (Triangle, 1918)
    Limousine Life (Triangle, 1918)
    An Heiress for a Day (Triangle, 1918)
    Nancy Comes Home (Triangle, 1918)
    The Love Swindle (Univ., 1918)
    She Hired a Husband (Univ., 1918)
    Beans (Univ., 1918)
    The Silk-Lined Burglar (Univ., 1919)
    Taste of Life (Univ., 1919)
    Love's Prisoner (Triangle, 1919)
    The Follies Girl (Triangle, 1919)
    The Winning Stroke (Fox, 1919)
    Burglar By Proxy (Associated FN, 1919)
    The Right of Way (Metro, 1920)

Suds (UA, 1920)
Blackbirds (Realart, 1920)
The Plaything of Broadway (Realart, 1921)
Children of the Night (Fox, 1921)
The Roof Tree (Fox, 1921)
Gleam O'Dawn (Fox, 1922)
The Yellow Stain (Fox, 1922)
The Cub Reporter (Goldstone, 1922)
Calvert's Valley (Fox, 1922)
Man Wanted (Clark-Cornelius, 1922)
The Broken Violin (Arrow Film, 1923)
The Self-Made Wife (Univ., 1923)
Flaming Youth (Associated FN, 1923)
Lilies of the Field (FN, 1924)
The Perfect Flapper (FN, 1924)
If I Marry Again (FN, 1925)
Flirting With Love (FN, 1924)
Chickie (FN, 1925)
One Way Street (FN, 1925)
The Half-Way Girl (FN, 1925)
We Moderns (FN, 1925)
Too Much Money (FN, 1926)
Don Juan's Three Nights (FN, 1926)
Midnight Lovers (FN, 1926)
Love's Blindness (MGM, 1926)
The Sea Tiger (FN, 1927)
The Prince of Headwaiters (FN, 1927)
Man Crazy (FN, 1927)
Smile, Brother, Smile (FN, 1927) (also actor)
The Crystal Cup (FN, 1927)
The Noose (FN, 1928)
The Heart of a Follies Girl (FN, 1928)
Out of the Ruins (FN, 1928)
Scarlet Seas (FN, 1929)
Children of the Ritz (FN, 1929)
Fast Life (FN, 1929)
Careers (FN, 1929)
Sally (FN, 1929)
Spring Is Here (FN, 1930)
Bride of the Regiment (FN, 1930)
The Girl of the Golden West (FN, 1930)
Kismet (FN, 1930)
One Night at Susie's (FN, 1930)
Millie (RKO, 1931)
The Finger Points (FN, 1931)
The Reckless Hour (FN, 1931)
Pagan Lady (Col., 1931)
Cohens and Kellys in Hollywood (Univ., 1932)
Man About Town (Fox, 1932)
Behind the Mask (Col., 1932)
Call Her Savage (Fox, 1932)
Humanity (Fox, 1933)
The Big Shakedown (FN, 1934)

DIXON, IVAN.
  Trouble Man (20th, 1972)
  The Spook Who Sat By the Door (UA, 1972) (also co-producer)

DMYTRYK, EDWARD, b. Aug. 4, 1908, Grand Forks, British
    Columbia.
  The Hawk (Herman Wohl, 1935)
  Million Dollar Legs (Par., 1939) (uncredited, with Nick Grinde)
    (also editor)
  Television Spy (Par., 1939)
  Emergency Squad (Par., 1940)
  Mystery Sea Raiders (Par., 1940)
  Golden Gloves (Par., 1940)
  Her First Romance (Mon., 1940)
  The Devil Commands (Col., 1941)
  Under Age (Col., 1941)
  Sweetheart of the Campus (Col., 1941)
  The Blonde from Singapore (Col., 1941)
  Confessions of Boston Blackie (Col., 1941)
  Secrets of the Lone Wolf (Col., 1941)
  Counter Espionage (Col., 1942)
  Seven Miles from Alcatraz (RKO, 1942)
  The Falcon Strikes Back (RKO, 1943)
  Hitler's Children (RKO, 1943)
  Captive Wild Woman (Univ., 1943)
  Behind the Rising Sun (RKO, 1943)
  Tender Comrade (RKO, 1943)
  Murder My Sweet (RKO, 1945)
  Back to Bataan (RKO, 1945)
  Til the End of Time (RKO, 1945)
  Cross-Fire (RKO, 1947)
  So Well Remembered (RKO, 1947)
  Give Us This Day (Eagle Lion, 1949)
  Obsession [The Hidden Room] (British Lion, 1949)
  Mutiny (Univ., 1952)
  The Sniper (Col., 1952)
  Eight Iron Men (Col., 1952)
  The Juggler (Col., 1953)
  The Caine Mutiny (Col., 1954)
  Broken Lance (20th, 1954)
  The End of the Affair (Col., 1954)
  Soldier of Fortune (20th, 1955)
  The Left Hand of God (20th, 1955)
  The Mountain (Par., 1956) (also producer)
  Raintree County (MGM, 1957)
  The Young Lions (20th, 1958)
  Warlock (20th, 1959) (also producer)
  The Blue Angel (20th, 1959)
  Walk on the Wild Side (Col., 1962)
  The Reluctant Saint (Davis Royal, 1962) (also producer)
  The Carpetbaggers (Par., 1963)
  Where Love Has Gone (Par., 1964)

Mirage (Univ., 1965)
Alvarez Kelly (Col., 1966)
Anzio (Col., 1968)
Shalako (Cin., 1968)
Bluebeard (Cin., 1973) (also co-story, co-script)

DONEN, STANLEY, b. April 13, 1924, Columbia, S.C.
On the Town (MGM, 1949) (with Gene Kelly)
Royal Wedding (MGM, 1951)
Love Is Better Than Ever (MGM, 1952)
Singin' in the Rain (MGM, 1952) (with Gene Kelly) (also co-choreography)
Fearless Fagan (MGM, 1952)
Give a Girl a Break (MGM, 1953) (also co-choreography)
Seven Brides for Seven Brothers (MGM, 1954)
Deep in My Heart (MGM, 1954) (also co-choreography)
It's Always Fair Weather (MGM, 1955) (with Gene Kelly)
Funny Face (Par., 1957) (also co-choreography)
The Pajama Game (WB, 1957) (with George Abbott (also co-producer)
Kiss Them for Me (20th, 1957)
Indiscreet (WB, 1958) (also co-producer)
Damn Yankees (WB, 1958) (with George Abbott) (also co-producer)
Once More With Feeling (Col., 1960) (also co-producer)
Surprise Package (Col., 1960) (also producer)
The Grass Is Greener (Univ., 1960) (also co-producer)
Charade (Univ., 1963) (also producer)
Arabesque (Univ., 1966) (also producer, for production company)
Two for the Road (20th, 1967) (also producer, for production company)
Bedazzled (20th, 1967) (also producer, for production company)
Staircase (20th, 1969) (also producer, for production company)

DOUGLAS, GORDON, b. Dec. 15, 1909, New York City.
General Spanky (MGM, 1936) (with Fred Newmeyer)
Zenobia (UA, 1939)
Saps at Sea (UA, 1940)
Niagara Falls (UA, 1941)
Broadway Limited (UA, 1941)
The Great Gildersleeve (RKO, 1943)
Gildersleeve's Bad Day (RKO, 1943)
Gildersleeve on Broadway (RKO, 1943)
A Night of Adventure (RKO, 1944)
Gildersleeve's Ghost (RKO, 1944)
Girl Rush (RKO, 1944)
The Devil With Hitler (RKO, 1944)
The Falcon in Hollywood (RKO, 1944)
First Yank in Tokyo (RKO, 1945)
Zombies on Broadway (RKO, 1945)
San Quentin (RKO, 1946)

Viveca Lindfors and George Maharis with Gordon Douglas (left) on the set of <u>Sylvia</u> (Par., 1965).

Dick Tracy vs. Cueball (RKO, 1946)
The Black Arrow (Col., 1948)
If You Knew Susie (RKO, 1948)
Walk a Crooked Mile (Col., 1948)
The Doolins of Oklahoma (Col., 1949)
Mr. Soft Touch (Col., 1949) (with Henry Levin)
The Nevadan (Col., 1950)
Fortunes of Captain Blood (Col., 1950)
Rogues of Sherwood Forest (Col., 1950)
Between Midnight and Dawn (Col., 1950)
Kiss Tomorrow Goodbye (UA, 1950)
The Great Missouri Raid (Par., 1951)
Only the Valiant (WB, 1951)
Come Fill the Cup (WB, 1951)
I Was a Communist for the FBI (WB, 1952)
Mara Maru (WB, 1952)
The Iron Mistress (WB, 1952)
She's Back on Broadway (WB, 1953)
The Charge at Feather River (WB, 1953)
So This Is Love (WB, 1953)
Them (WB, 1955)
Young at Heart (WB, 1955)
The McConnell Story (WB, 1955)

Sincerely Yours (WB, 1955)
Santiago (WB, 1956)
The Big Land (WB, 1957)
Bombers B-52 (WB, 1957)
Fort Dobbs (WB, 1958)
The Fiend Who Walked the West (20th, 1958)
Up Periscope (WB, 1958)
Yellowstone Kelly (WB, 1959)
The Sins of Rachel Cade (WB, 1961)
Gold of the Seven Saints (WB, 1961)
Claudette Inglish (WB, 1961)
Follow That Dream (UA, 1962)
Call Me Bwana (UA, 1963)
Rio Conchos (20th, 1964)
Robin and the Seven Hoods (WB, 1964)
Sylvia (Par., 1965)
Harlow (Par., 1965)
Way ... Way Out (20th, 1966)
Stagecoach (20th, 1966)
Chuka (Par., 1967)
In Like Flint (20th, 1967)
Tony Rome (20th, 1967)
The Detective (20th, 1968)
Lady in Cement (20th, 1968)
Barquero (UA, 1969)
They Call Me MISTER Tibbs (UA, 1970)
Skullduggery (Univ., 1970)
The Skin Game (WB, 1971) (with Paul Bogart)
Slaughter's Big Rip-Off (AIP, 1973)

DREIFUSS, ARTHUR, b. March 25, 1908, Frankfurt am Main, Germany.
    Double Deal (International Road Shows, 1939)
    Mystery in Swing (International Road Shows, 1940) (also producer)
    Reg'lar Fellers (PRC, 1941)
    Baby Face Morgan (PRC, 1942)
    Boss of Big Town (PRC, 1942)
    The Pay-Off (PRC, 1942)
    Melody Parade (Mon., 1943)
    Nearly Eighteen (Mon., 1943)
    The Sultan's Daugher (Mon., 1943)
    Campus Rhythm (Mon., 1943)
    Sarong Girl (Mon., 1943)
    Ever Since Venus (Col., 1944) (also co-script)
    Boston Blackie Booked on Suspicion (Col., 1945)
    Boston Blackie's Rendezvous (Col., 1945)
    Eadie Was a Lady (Col., 1945)
    The Gay Senorita (Col., 1945)
    Prison Ship (Col., 1945)
    Freddie Steps Out (Mon., 1946)
    High School Hero (Mon., 1946) (also script)

Junior Prom (Mon., 1946)
Betty Co-ed (Col., 1947) (also script)
Vacation Days (Mon., 1947)
Little Miss Broadway (Col., 1947) (also script)
Sweet Genevieve (Col. 1947) (also script)
Two Blondes and a Redhead (Col., 1947)
Glamour Girl (Col., 1948)
Mary Lou (Col., 1948)
I Surrender Dear (Col., 1948)
An Old Fashioned Girl (Eagle Lion, 1948) (also producer, co-
   adaptation, co-script)
Manhattan Angel (Col., 1948)
All American Pro (Col., 1948)
There's a Girl in My Heart (AA, 1949) (also producer, songs)
Shamrock Hill (Eagle Lion, 1949) (also producer)
Secret File (Triangle, 1955) (also producer)
Assignment Abroad (Triangle, 1956) (also producer)
Life Begins at 17 (Col., 1958)
The Last Blitzkrieg (Col., 1958)
Juke Box Rhythm (Col., 1959)
The Quare Fellow (Astor, 1962) (also script, co-adaptation)
Riot on Sunset Strip (AIP, 1967)
The Love-Ins (Col., 1967) (also co-script)
For Singles Only (Col., 1968) (also co-script)
A Time to Sing (MGM, 1968)
The Young Runaways (MGM, 1968)

DUNLAP, SCOTT R., b. June 20, 1892, Chicago; d. Mar. 30, 1970.
   Words and Music (Fox, 1919)
   Be a Little Sport (Fox, 1919)
   Love Is Love (Fox, 1919)
   The Lost Princess (Fox, 1919)
   Vagabond Luck (Fox, 1919)
   Her Elephant Man (Fox, 1920)
   Would You Forgive? (Fox, 1920)
   The Hell Ship (Fox, 1920)
   Forbidden Trails (Fox, 1920
   The Twins of Suffering Creek (Fox, 1920)
   The Challenge of the Law (Fox, 1920)
   The Iron Rider (Fox, 1920)
   The Cheater Reformed (Fox, 1921)
   Too Much Married (Associated Photoplays, 1921)
   Bluebeard, Jr. (American Releasing, 1922)
   Western Speed (Fox, 1922)
   Trooper O'Neil (Fox, 1922)
   West of Chicago (Fox, 1922)
   Pawn Ticket 210 (Fox, 1922)
   Bells of San Juan (Fox, 1922)
   The Footlight Ranger (Fox, 1923)
   Boston Blackie (Fox, 1923)
   Snowdrift (Fox, 1923)
   Skid Proof (Fox, 1923)

Traffic in Hearts (Col., 1924)
One Glorious Night (Col., 1924)
The Fatal Mistake (Perfection, 1924)
Beyond the Border (PDC, 1925)
Blue Blood (Chadwick, 1925)
Silent Sanderson (PDC, 1925)
The Texas Trail (PDC, 1925)
Wreckage (Henry Ginsburg, 1925)
Blue Blood (Chadwick, 1925)
Winning the Futurity (Chadwick, 1926)
Driftin' Thru (Pathé, 1926)
The Better Man (FBO, 1926)
Doubling With Danger (FBO, 1926)
The Seventh Bandit (Pathé, 1926)
The Frontier Trail (Pathé, 1926)
Desert Valley (Fox, 1926)
Whispering Sage (Fox, 1927)
Good as Gold (Fox, 1927)
Midnight Life (Lumas, 1928)
Object--Alimony (Col., 1928)
Smoke Bellew (First Division, 1929)
One Stolen Night (WB, 1929)

DUNNE, PHILIP, b. Feb. 11, 1908, New York City.
Prince of Players (20th, 1955) (also producer)
The View from Pompey's Head (20th, 1955) (also producer,
    script)
Hilda Crane (20th, 1956) (also script)
Three Brave Men (20th, 1957) (also script)
Ten North Frederick (20th, 1958) (also script)
In Love and War (20th, 1958)
Blue Denim (20th, 1959) (also co-script)
Wild in the Country (20th, 1961)
Lisa (20th, 1961)
Blindfold (Univ., 1966) (also co-script)

DUPONT, E.A. (Ewald André Dupont), b. Dec. 25, 1891, Leitz,
    Germany; d. Dec. 12, 1956.
Europa Postlagernd (German, 1918) (also script)
Mitternacht (German, 1918) (also script)
Der Schatten (German, 1918)
Der Teufel (German, 1918)
Die Japanerin (German, 1918) (also script)
Das Geheimnis der Amerika--Docks (German, 1918) (also script)
Die Apachen (German, 1919)
Die Maske (German, 1919)
Die Spione (German, 1919)
Das Derby (German, 1919)
Der Würger der Welt (German, 1919)
Das Grand Hotel Babylon (German, 1919)
Der Weisse Fan [Tragödie einer Tänzerin] (German, 1920) (also
    co-script)

Whitechapel [Eine Kette von Perlen und Abenteuern] (German,
    1920)
Herztrumpf (German, 1920)
Der Mord Ohne Tater (German, 1920) (also co-script)
Die Geier-Wally (German, 1921) (also script)
Kinder der Finsternis [Part I: Der Mann aus Neapal; Part II:
    Kämpfende Welten] (German, 1921) (also co-script)
Sie und Die Drei (German, 1922)
Das Alte Gesetz (Baruch) (German, 1923)
Die Grune Manuela (German, 1923)
Der Demütige und Die Sängern (German, 1925) (also co-script)
Varieté (German, 1925) (also script)
Love Me and the World Is Mine (Univ., 1927) (also co-script)
Moulin-Rouge (BIP, 1928) (also producer, script)
Piccadilly (BIP, 1928) (also producer)
Atlantic (BIP, 1929) (also producer)
Atlantik [German version of Atlantic] (German, 1929)
Atlantique [French version of Atlantic] (with Jean Kemm) (French,
    1929)
Two Worlds (BIP, 1930) (also producer, co-story)
Zwei Welten [German version of Two Worlds] (German, 1930)
Cape Forlorn [Love Storm] (BIP, 1930)
Menschen in Käfig [German version of Cape Forlorn] (German,
    1930)
Salto Mortale [Trapeze] (German, 1931)
Saltonmortale [French version of Salto Mortale] (French, 1931)
Peter Voss der Millionendieb (German, 1932) (also co-script)
Der Läufer von Marathon (German, 1933)
Ladies Must Love (Univ., 1933)
The Bishop Misbehaves (MGM, 1935)
A Son Comes Home (Par., 1936)
Forgotten Faces (Par., 1936)
A Night of Mystery (Par., 1936)
On Such a Night (Par., 1937)
Love on Toast (Par., 1937)
Hell's Kitchen (WB, 1939) (with Lewis Seiler)
The Scarf (UA, 1951) (also script)
Problem Girls (Col., 1953)
The Neanderthal Man (UA, 1953)
The Steel Lady (UA, 1953)
Return to Treasure Island (UA, 1954)

DUVIVIER, JULIEN, b. Oct. 8, 1896, Lille, France; d. Oct. 31,
    1967.
    Haceldama (French, 1919) (also script)
    La Reincarnation de Serge Renaudier (French, 1920) (also script)
    L'Agonie des Aigles (French, 1921) (with Bernard Deschamps)
        (also script)
    Les Roquevillard (French, 1922) (also script)
    L'Ouragan sur la Montagne (French, 1922) (also story, script)
    Der Unheimliche Gast (German, 1922)
    Le Reflet de Claude Mercoeur (French, 1923) (also script)

Credo (French, 1923) (also script)
L'Oeuvre Immortelle (Belgian, 1923)
La Nuit de la Revanche (French, 1924) (also story, script)
Coeurs Farouches (French, 1924) (also script)
La Machine à Refaire la Vie (French, 1924) (with Henri Lepage)
L'Abbé Constantin (French, 1925) (also story)
Poil de Carotte (French, 1925) (also co-script)
Le Mariage de Mlle. Beulemans (French, 1926) (also script)
L'Agonie de Jerusalem (French, 1927) (also script)
Le Mystère de la Tour Eiffel (French, 1927)
L'Homme à l'Hispano (French, 1927)
Le Tourbillon de Paris (French, 1928)
La Divine Croisière (French, 1928) (also script)
Maman Colibri (French, 1929) (also co-script)
La Vie Miraculeuse de Thérèse Martin (French, 1929) (also
    script)
Au Bonheur des Dames (French, 1929) (also co-script)
David Golder (French, 1930)
Les Cinq Gentlemen Maudits (French, 1931) (also script)
Die Fünf Verfluchten Gentlemen [German version of the pre-
    ceding] (French, 1931) (also script)
Allo Berlin! Ici Paris! (French, 1932) (also script)
Poil de Carotte (French, 1932) (also script)
La Venus du College (French, 1932)
La Tête d'un Homme (French, 1933) (also co-script)
La Machine à Refaire la Vie (French, 1933)
Le Petit Roi (French, 1933) (also script)
Le Paquebot Tenacity (French, 1934) (also co-script)
Maria Chapdelaine (French, 1934) (also script)
Golgotha (French, 1935) (also script)
L'Homme du Jour (French, 1935) (also co-script)
La Bandera (French, 1936) (also co-script)
La Belle Equipe (French, 1936) (also story, co-script)
Le Golem (Czechoslovakian, 1936) (also co-script)
Pépé le Moko (French, 1937) (also co-script)
Un Carnet de Bal (French, 1937) (also co-adaptation, script)
The Great Waltz (MGM, 1938)
La Fin du Jour (French, 1939) (also co-adaptation, script)
La Charrette Fantôme (French, 1939)
Untel Père et Fils (French, 1940) (also story, script)
Lydia (UA, 1941) (also co-script)
Tales of Manhattan (20th, 1942) (also story, co-script)
Flesh and Fantasy (Univ., 1943) (also producer)
The Imposter (Univ., 1944) (also story, script)
Panique (French, 1946) (also co-script)
Anna Karenina (20th, 1948) (also co-script)
Au Royaume des Cieux (French, 1949) (also co-adaptation,
    script)
Black Jack (French, 1950) (also co-script)
Sous le Ciel de Paris (French, 1950) (also co-adaptation,
    script)
Le Petit Monde de Don Camillo (Italian, 1951) (also co-script)
La Fête à Henriette (French, 1953) (also story, co-script)

Le Retour de Don Camillo (Italian, 1953) (also co-adaptation,
   co-script)
L'Affaire Maurizius (French, 1954) (also script)
Marianne de Ma Jeunesse (French, 1954) (also script)
Voici le Temps des Assassins (French, 1956) (also co-script)
L'Homme à l'Impermeable (French, 1957) (also co-script, co-
   dialogue)
Pot-Bouille (French, 1957) (also adaptation, co-script)
Marie-Octobre (French, 1958) (also co-adaptation)
La Femme et le Pantin (French, 1958) (also co-adaptation)
Das Kunstseidene Mädchen (German, 1959)
Boulevard (French, 1960) also adaptation)
La Grande Vie (French, 1960)
La Chambre Ardente (French, 1961) (also co-adaptation)
Le Diable et les Dix Commandments (French, 1963) (also co-
   script)
Chair de Poule (French, 1964) (also co-adaptation)
Diaboliquement Votre (French, 1967) (also co-adaptation)

DWAN, ALLAN (Joseph Aloysius Dwan), b. April 3, 1885, Toronto.
   Richelieu (Univ., 101 Bison, 1914) (also script)
   Wildflower (Par., 1914) (also co-script)
   The County Chairman (Par., 1914) (also co-script)
   The Straight Road (Par., 1914)
   The Conspiracy (Par., 1914)
   The Unwelcome Mrs. Hatch (Par., 1914)
   The Foundling (Par., 1915) (film destroyed, re-directed by
      John B. O'Brien in 1916)
   The Dancing Girl (Par., 1915)
   David Harum (Par., 1915)
   The Love Route (Par., 1915)
   The Commanding Officer (Par., 1915)
   The Pretty Sister of Jose (Par., 1915)
   A Girl of Yesterday (Par., 1915)
   May Blossom (Pathé, 1915)
   Jordan Is a Hard Road (Fine Arts-Triangle, 1915) (also script)
   Betty of Greystone (Fine Arts-Triangle, 1916)
   The Habit of Happiness (Fine Arts-Triangle, 1916) (also script)
   The Good Bad Man (Fine Arts-Triangle, 1916)
   An Innocent Magdalene (Fine Arts-Triangle, 1916)
   The Half-Breed (Fine Arts-Triangle, 1916)
   Manhattan Madness (Fine Arts-Triangle, 1916)
   Fifty-Fifty (Fine Arts-Triangle, 1916) (also script)
   Panthea (Selznick, 1917) (also script)
   The Fighting Odds (Goldwyn, 1917) (with Hugo Ballin)
   A Modern Musketeer (Artcraft, 1917) (also script)
   Mr. Fix-It (Artcraft, 1918) (also script)
   Bound in Morocco (Artcraft, 1918) (also script)
   He Comes Up Smiling (Artcraft, 1918)
   Cheating Cheaters (Select, 1918)
   Getting Mary Married (Select, 1919)
   The Dark Star (Artcraft, 1919)

Soldiers of Fortune (Realart, 1919)
The Luck of the Irish (Realart, 1920)
The Forbidden Thing (Associated Producers, 1920) (also producer, co-script)
The Scoffer (Realart, 1920) (also producer)
A Perfect Crime (Associated Producers, 1921) (also producer, script)
A Broken Doll (Associated Producers, 1921) (also producer, script)
The Sin of Martha Queed (Associated Exhibitors, 1921) (also producer, script)
In the Heart of a Fool (Associated FN, 1921) (also producer)
The Hidden Woman (Nanuet Amusement/American Releasing, 1922) (also producer)
Superstition (Artlee, 1922) (also producer)
Robin Hood (UA, 1922)
The Glimpses of the Moon (Par., 1923) (also producer)
Lawful Larceny (Par., 1923) (also producer)
Zaza (Par., 1923) (also producer)
Big Brother (Par., 1923) (also producer)
A Society Scandal (Par., 1924) (also producer)
Manhandled (Par., 1924) (also producer)
Her Love Story (Par., 1924) (also producer)
Wages of Virtue (Par., 1924)
Argentine Love (Par., 1924) (also producer)
Night Life of New York (Par., 1925) (also producer)
Coast of Folly (Par., 1925) (also producer)
Stage Struck (Par., 1925) (also producer)
Sea Horses (Par., 1926) (also producer)
Padlocked (Par., 1926) (also producer)
Tin Gods (Par., 1926) (also producer)
Summer Bachelors (Fox, 1926) (also producer)
The Music Master (Fox, 1927) (also producer)
The Joy Girl (Fox, 1927) (also producer)
East Side, West Side (Fox, 1927) (also script)
French Dressing (FN, 1927) (also producer)
The Big Noise (FN, 1928) (also producer)
The Iron Mask (UA, 1929)
Tide of the Empire (MGM, 1929)
The Far Call (Fox, 1929)
Frozen Justice (Fox, 1929)
South Sea Rose (Fox, 1929)
What a Widow! (UA, 1930) (also producer)
Man to Man (FN, 1930)
Chances (FN, 1931)
Wicked (Fox, 1931)
While Paris Sleeps (Fox, 1932)
Her First Affaire (Associated British, 1933)
Counsel's Opinion (London Films-Par., 1933)
The Morning After [I Spy] (Wardour-Majestic, 1934)
Hollywood Party (MGM, 1934) (uncredited, with Richard Boleslaw-ski and Roy Rowland)
Black Sheep (Fox, 1935) (also script)

Navy Wife (20th, 1935)
The Song and Dance Man (20th, 1936)
Human Cargo (20th, 1936)
High Tension (20th, 1936)
15 Maiden Lane (20th, 1936)
Woman-Wise (20th, 1937)
That I May Live (20th, 1937)
One Mile from Heaven (20th, 1937)
Heidi (20th, 1937)
Rebecca of Sunnybrook Farm (20th, 1938)
Josette (20th, 1938)
Suez (20th, 1938)
The Three Musketeers (20th, 1939)
The Gorilla (20th, 1939)
Frontier Marshal (20th, 1939)
Sailor's Lady (20th, 1940)
Young People (20th, 1940)
Trail of the Vigilantes (Univ., 1940)
Look Who's Laughing (RKO, 1941) (also producer)
Rise and Shine (20th, 1941)
Friendly Enemies (UA, 1942)
Here We Go Again (RKO, 1942) (also producer)
Around the World (RKO, 1943) (also producer)
Up in Mabel's Room (UA, 1944)
Abroad With Two Yanks (UA, 1944)
Brewster's Millions (UA, 1945)
Getting Gertie's Garter (UA, 1945)
Rendezvous With Annie (Rep., 1946) (also associate producer)
Calendar Girl (Rep., 1947) (also associate producer)
Northwest Outpost (Rep., 1947) (also associate producer)
Driftwood (Rep., 1947)
The Inside Story (Rep., 1948) (also producer)
Angel in Exile (Rep., 1948) (with Philip Ford)
Sands of Iwo Jima (Rep., 1949)
Surrender (Rep., 1950) (also associate producer)
Belle Le Grande (Rep., 1951)
The Wild Blue Yonder (Rep., 1951)
I Dream of Jeanie (Rep., 1952)
Montana Belle (RKO, 1952)
The Woman They Almost Lynched (Rep., 1953)
Sweethearts on Parade (Rep., 1953) (also associate producer)
Flight Nurse (Rep., 1954)
Silver Lode (RKO, 1954)
Passion (RKO, 1954)
Cattle Queen of Montana (RKO, 1954)
Escape to Burma (RKO, 1955)
Pearl of the South Pacific (RKO, 1955)
Tennessee's Partner (RKO, 1955) (also co-script)
Slightly Scarlet (RKO, 1956)
Hold Back the Night (AA, 1956)
The River's Edge (20th, 1957)
The Restless Breed (20th, 1957)
Enchanted Island (WB, 1958)
The Most Dangerous Man Alive (Col., 1961)

E

EASON, B. REEVES (Breezy Eason), b. Oct. 2, 1886, Pryore
Point, Miss.; d. June 10, 1956.
Nine-Tenths of the Law (Atlantic, 1918)
The Moon Riders* (Univ., 1920) (with Albert Russell)
Pink Tights (Univ., 1920)
Human Stuff (Univ., 1920)
Blue Streak McCoy (Univ., 1920)
Two Kinds of Love (Univ., 1920)
The Big Adventure (Univ., 19210
Colorado (Univ., 1921)
The Fire Eater (Univ., 1921)
Red Courage (Univ., 1921)
When East Comes West (Phil Goldstone, 1922)
Pardon My Nerve! (Fox, 1922)
Rough Shod (Fox, 1922)
The Lone Hand (Univ., 1922)
Around the World in 18 Days* (Univ., 1923) (with Robert F.
Hill)
His Last Race (Phil Goldstone, 1923) (with Howard Mitchell)
Tiger Thompson (W.W. Hodkinson, 1924)
Trigger Finger (FBO, 1924)
Flashing Spurs (FBO, 1924)
Women First Col., 1924)
The Texas Bearcat (FBO, 1925)
Ben-Hur (MGM, 1925) (second unit director only)
The New Champion (Perfection-Col., 1925)
Border Justice (Independent Pictures, 1925)
A Fight to the Finish (Col., 1925)
Fighting the Flames (Col., 1925)
Fighting Youth (Col., 1925)
The Shadow on the Wall (Lumas, 1925)
Lone Hand Saunders (FBO, 1926)
The Test of Donald Horton (Chadwick, 1926)
The Sign of the Claw (Lumas, 1926)
The Denver Dude (Univ., 1927)
Johnny Get Your Hair Cut (MGM, 1927) (with Archie Mayo)
Through Thick and Thin (Lumas, 1927) (with Jack Nelson)
Galloping Fury (Univ., 1927)
Painted Ponies (Univ., 1927)
The Prairie King (Univ., 1927)
Clearing the Trail (Univ., 1928)
The Flyin' Cowboy (Univ.-Jewell, 1928) (also continuity)
Riding for Fame (Univ., 1928) (also script)
A Trick of Hearts (Univ., 1928)
The Lariat Kid (Univ., 1929)
The Winged Horseman (Univ., 1929) (with Arthur Rosson)
Roaring Ranch (Univ., 1930) (also story, dialog)
Spurs (Univ., 1930) (also story, dialog)
Trigger Tricks (Univ., 1930) (also story, dialog)

Troopers Three (Tiffany, 1930) (with Norman Taurog)
The Galloping Ghost* (Mascot, 1931)
The Vanishing Legion* (Mascot, 1931)
The Last of the Mohicans* (Mascot, 1932) (with Ford Beebe)
Heart Punch (Mayfair, 1932)
Sunset Trail (Tiffany, 1932)
Honor of the Press (Mayfair, 1932)
Behind Jury Doors (Mayfair, 1933)
Alimony Madness (Mayfair, 1933)
Her Resale Value (Mayfair, 1933)
Revenge at Monte Carlo (Mayfair, 1933)
Dance Hall Hostess (Mayfair, 1933)
Neighbor's Wives (Royer, 1933)
Cornered (Col., 1933)
The Law of the Wild* (Mascot, 1934) (with Armand L. Schaefer)
Mystery Mountain* (Mascot, 1934) (with Otto Brower)
The Phantom Empire* (Mascot, 1935) (with Otto Brower)
The Adventures of Rex and Rinty* (Mascot, 1935) (with Ford
    Beebe)
Fighting Marines* (Mascot, 1935) (with Joseph Kane)
The Miracle Rider* (Mascot, 1935) (with Armand L. Schaefer)
Red River Valley (Rep., 1936)
Darkest Africa* (Rep., 1936) (with Joseph Kane)
The Undersea Kingdom* (Rep., 1936) (with Joseph Kane)
Empty Holsters (WB, 1937)
Prairie Thunder (WB, 1937)
The Daredevil Drivers (WB, 1938)
Call of the Yukon (Rep., 1938) (with John T. Coyle)
The Kid Comes Back (WB, 1938)
Sergeant Murphy (WB, 1938)
Man of Conquest (Rep., 1939) (uncredited, with George Nicholls,
    Jr.)
Blue Montana Skies (Rep., 1939)
Mountain Rhythm (Rep., 1939)
Men With Steel Faces (Times Pictures, 1940) (with Otto Brower)
Spy Ship (WB, 1942)
Murder in the Big House (WB, 1942)
The Phantom* (Col., 1943)
Murder on the Waterfront (WB, 1943)
Truck Busters (WB, 1943)
Black Arrow* (Col., 1944)
The Desert Hawk* (Col., 1947)
Duel in the Sun (Selznick, 1947) (second unit director only)
Northern Stampede (Eagle Lion, 1948) (second unit director only)
Rimfire (Screen Guild, 1949)
Dallas (WB, 1950) (second unit director only)

EASTWOOD, CLINT, b. May 31, 1930, San Francisco.
    Play Misty for Me (Univ., 1971) (also actor)
    High Plains Drifter (Univ., 1973) (also actor)
    Breezy (Univ., 1973)

EDWARDS, BLAKE, b. July 26, 1922, Tulsa, Okla.

Julie Andrews with Blake Edwards on the set for Darling Lili (1970).

Bring Your Smile Along (Col., 1955) (also co-story, script)
He Laughed Last (Col., 1956) (also co-story, script)
Mister Cory (Univ., 1957) (also script)
This Happy Feeling (Univ., 1958) (also script)
The Perfect Furlough (Univ., 1958)
Operation Petticoat (Univ., 1959)
High Time (20th, 1960)
Breakfast at Tiffany's (Par., 1961)
Experiment in Terror (Col., 1962) (also producer)
Days of Wine and Roses (WB, 1962)
The Pink Panther (UA, 1964) (also co-script)
A Shot in the Dark (UA, 1964) (replaced Anatole Litvak) (also
co-script)

The Great Race (WB, 1965) (also co-story)
What Did You Do in the War, Daddy? (UA, 1966) (also co-story)
Gunn (Par., 1967) (also story, co-script)
The Party (UA, 1968) (also story, co-script)
Darling Lili (Par., 1970) (also co-script)
Wild Rovers (MGM, 1971) (also co-producer, script)
The Carey Treatment (MGM 1972)

EMERSON, JOHN, b. May 29, 1878, Sandusky, Ohio; d. March 8, 1956.
Macbeth (Triangle, 1914)
Old Heidelberg (Fine Arts-Triangle, 1915) (also adaptation)
Ghosts (Triangle, 1915)
His Picture in the Papers (Fine Arts-Triangle, 1916) (also co-script)
The Social Secretary (Triangle, 1916)
Wild and Woolly (Artcraft, 1917) (also co-script)
Less Than the Dust (Par., 1917)
Down to Earth (Artcraft, 1917) (also co-script)
The Americano (Par., 1917) (also co-script)
In Again, Out Again (Artcraft, 1918) (also co-script)
Reaching for the Moon (Artcraft, 1917) (also co-script)
Come On In (Par., 1918) (also co-producer, co-script)
Goodbye Bill (Par., 1918) (also co-producer, co-story)
Oh, You Women! (Par., 1919) (also co-story, co-script)
Polly of the Follies (Associated FN, 1922) (also co-script)

ENDFIELD, CY (Cyril Raker), b. Nov., 1914.
Gentleman Joe Palooka (Mon., 1946) (also script)
Stork Bites Man (UA, 1947)
The Argyle Secrets (Film Classics, 1948)
Joe Palooka in the Big Fight (Mon., 1949)
The Underworld Story (UA, 1950)
The Sound of Fury (UA, 1950)
Tarzan's Savage Fury (RKO, 1952)
The Limping Man (Lip., 1953) (uncredited, with Charles de Lautour)
Colonel March Investigates (Criterion, 1953)
The Master Plan (Astor, 1955) (also script)
Impulse (Tempean, 1955) (uncredited, with Charles de Lautour)
The Secret (Eros, 1955) (also script)
Child in the House (Eros, 1956) (uncredited, with Charles de Lautour) (also script)
Hell Drivers (Rank, 1957) (also script)
Sea Fury (Lopert, 1958) (also co-script)
Jet Storm (British-Lion, 1959) (also co-script)
The Mysterious Island (Col., 1961)
Hide and Seek (Univ., 1964)
Zulu (Emb., 1964) (also co-producer, co-script)
Sands of the Kalahari (Emb., 1965) (also co-producer, script)
De Sade (AIP, 1969) (with uncredited Roger Corman)

ENGLISH, JOHN W. (Jack English), b. 1903, Cumberland, Eng.;
    d. Oct. 11, 1969.
    His Fighting Blood (Ambassador, 1935)
    Red Blood of Courage (Ambassador, 1935)
    Arizona Days (Grand National, 1937)
    Whistling Bullets (Ambassador, 1937)
    Zorro Rides Again* (Rep., 1937) (with William Witney)
    Call the Mesquiteers (Rep., 1938)
    Dick Tracy Returns* (Rep., 1938) (with William Witney)
    Fighting Devil Dogs* (Rep., 1938) (with William Witney, Robert
        Becher)
    Hawk of the Wilderness* (Rep., 1938) (with William Witney)
    The Lone Ranger* (Rep., 1938) (with William Witney)
    Daredevils of the Red Circle* (Rep., 1939) (with William Wit-
        ney)
    Dick Tracy's G-Men* (Rep., 1939) (with William Witney)
    The Lone Ranger Rides Again* (Rep., 1939) (with William Wit-
        ney)
    Zorro's Fighting Legion* (Rep., 1939) (with William Witney)
    Adventures of Red Ryder* (Rep., 1940) (with William Witney)
    Hi-Yo Silver (Rep., 1940) (with William Witney)
    Drums of Fu Manchu* (Rep., 1940) (with William Witney)
    King of the Royal Mounted* (Rep., 1940) (with William Witney)
    Mysterious Dr. Satan* (Rep., 1940) (with William Witney)
    Gangs of Sonora (Rep., 1941)
    Adventures of Captain Marvel* (Rep., 1941) (with William Wit-
        ney)
    Dick Tracy vs. Crime, Inc.* (Rep., 1941) (with William Wit-
        ney)
    Raiders of the Range (Rep., 1941)
    Jungle Girl* (Rep., 1941) (with William Witney)
    King of the Texas Rangers* (Rep., 1941) (with William Witney)
    Code of the Outlaw (Rep., 1942)
    Westward Ho (Rep., 1942)
    The Yukon Patrol (Rep., 1942)
    The Phantom Plainsmen (Rep., 1942)
    Shadows on the Range (Rep., 1942)
    Valley of the Hunted Men (Rep., 1942)
    Dead Man's Gulch (Rep., 1943)
    Death Valley Manhunt (Rep., 1943)
    Drums of Fu Manchu* (Rep., 1943) (with William Witney)
    The Man from Thunder River (Rep., 1943)
    Thundering Trails (Rep., 1943)
    Overland Mail Robbery (Rep., 1943)
    Daredevils of the West* (Rep., 1943)
    The Black Hills Express (Rep., 1943)
    Captain America* (Rep., 1944) (with Elmer Clifton)
    The Port of Forty Thieves (Rep., 1944)
    Faces in the Fog (Rep., 1944)
    The Laramie Trail (Rep., 1944)
    Call of the South Seas (Rep., 1944)
    Silver City Kid (Rep., 1944)
    Grissley's Millions (Rep., 1945)

Don't Fence Me In (Rep., 1945)
Utah (Rep., 1945)
The Phantom Speaks (Rep., 1945)
Murder in the Music Hall (Rep., 1946)
Trail to San Antone (Rep., 1947)
The Last Round-Up (Col., 1947)
Thundering Trails (Rep., 1947)
The Strawberry Roan (Col., 1948)
Loaded Pistols (Col., 1949)
Riders of the Whistling Pines (Col., 1949)
Rim of the Canyon (Col., 1949)
The Cowboy and the Indians (Col., 1949)
Riders of the Sky (Col., 1949)
Sons of New Mexico (Col., 1950)
The Blazing Sun (Col., 1950)
Mule Train (Col., 1950)
Cow Town (Col., 1950)
Beyond the Purple Hills (Col., 1950)
Indian Territory (Col., 1950)
Blazing Sun (Col., 1950)
Gene Autry and the Mounties (Col., 1951)
Whirlwind (Col., 1951)
Silver Canyon (Col., 1951)
Hills of Utah (Col., 1951)
Valley of Fire (Col., 1951)

ENRIGHT, RAY (Raymond Enright), b. March 25, 1896, Anderson,
    Ind.; d. April 3, 1965.
    Tracked by the Police (WB, 1927)
    Jaws of Steel (WB, 1927)
    Girl from Chicago (WB, 1927)
    Domestic Troubles (WB, 1928)
    Land of the Silver Fox (WB, 1928)
    Little Wildcat (WB, 1929)
    Stolen Kisses (WB, 1929)
    Kid Gloves (WB, 1929)
    Skin Deep (WB, 1929)
    Song of the West (WB, 1930)
    Golden Dawn (WB, 1930)
    Dancing Sweeties (WB, 1930)
    Scarlet Pages (WB, 1930)
    Play Girl (WB, 1932)
    The Tenderfoot (FN, 1932)
    Blondie Johnson (FN, 1933)
    Silk Express (WB, 1933)
    Tomorrow at 7 (RKO, 1933)
    Havana Widows (FN, 1933)
    I've Got Your Number (WB, 1934)
    20 Million Sweethearts (FN, 1934)
    Circus Clown (FN, 1934)
    Dames (WB, 1934) (with choreographer Busby Berkeley)
    St. Louis Kid (WB, 1934)

Traveling Saleslady (FN, 1935)
While the Patient Slept (FN, 1935)
Alibi Ike (FN, 1935)
We're in the Money (WB, 1935)
Miss Pacific Fleet (WB, 1935)
Snowed Under (FN, 1936)
Earthworm Tractors (FN, 1936)
China Clipper (FN, 1936)
Sing Me a Love Song (FN, 1936)
Ready, Willing and Able (WB, 1937)
Slim (WB, 1937)
Back in Circulation (WB, 1937)
The Singing Marine (WB, 1937)
Swing Your Lady (WB, 1938)
Gold Diggers in Paris (WB, 1938)
Hard to Get (WB, 1938)
Going Places (WB, 1938)
Naughty But Nice (WB, 1939)
On Your Toes (WB, 1939)
Angels Wash Their Faces (WB, 1939)
An Angel from Texas (WB, 1940)
Brother Rat and a Baby (WB, 1940)
River's End (WB, 1940)
The Wagons Roll at Night (WB, 1941)
Thieves Fall Out (WB, 1941)
Bad Men of Missouri (WB, 1941)
Law of the Tropics (WB, 1941)
Wild Bill Hickock Rides (WB, 1941)
The Spoilers (Univ., 1942)
Men of Texas (Univ., 1942)
Sin Town (Univ., 1942)
The Iron Major (RKO, 1943)
Gung Ho! (Univ., 1943)
Good Luck, Mr. Yates (Col., 1943)
China Sky (RKO, 1945)
Man Alive (RKO, 1945)
One Way to Love (Col., 1946)
Trail Street (RKO, 1947)
Albuquerque (Par., 1948)
Return of the Bad Men (RKO, 1948)
Coroner Creek (Col., 1948)
South of St. Louis (WB, 1949)
Montana (WB, 1950) (with Raoul Walsh, uncredited)
Kansas Raiders (Univ., 1950)
Flaming Feather (Par., 1951)
The Man from Cairo (Lip., 1953)

ERSKINE, CHESTER, b. Nov. 29, 1905, Hudson, N.Y.
Midnight (Univ., 1934)
The Egg and I (Univ., 1947) (also producer, script)
Take One False Step (Univ., 1949) (also producer, co-script)
A Girl in Every Port (RKO, 1951) (also script)
Androcles and the Lion (RKO, 1952) (also co-adaptation)

F

FARROW, JOHN (John Villiers Farrow), b. Feb. 10, 1904, Sydney,
    Australia; d. Jan. 27, 1963.
Warlord (WB, 1937)
Men in Exile (WB, 1937)
West of Shanghai (WB, 1937)
The Invisible Menace (WB, 1938)
She Loved a Fireman (WB, 1938)
Little Miss Thoroughbred (WB, 1938)
My Bill (WB, 1938)
Broadway Musketeers (WB, 1938)
Women in the Wind (RKO, 1939)
Sorority House (RKO, 1939)
The Saint Strikes Back (RKO, 1939)
Five Came Back (RKO, 1939)
Full Confession (RKO, 1939)
Reno (RKO, 1939)
Married and in Love (RKO, 1940)
A Bill of Divorcement (RKO, 1940)
Wake Island (Par., 1942)
China (Par., 1943)
Commandos Strike at Dawn (Col., 1943)
The Hitler Gang (Par., 1944)
You Came Along (Par., 1945)
Two Years Before the Mast (Par., 1946)
California (Par., 1947)
Easy Come, Easy Go (Par., 1947)
Blaze of Noon (Par., 1947)
Calcutta (Par., 1947)
The Big Clock (Par., 1948)
Beyond Glory (Par., 1948)
The Night Has a Thousand Eyes (Par., 1948)
Alias Nick Beal (Par., 1949)
Red, Hot and Blue (Par., 1949) (also co-script)
Where Danger Lives (RKO, 1950)
Copper Canyon (MGM, 1950)
His Kind of Woman (RKO, 1951) (with uncredited Richard Fleis-
    cher)
Submarine Command (Par., 1951)
Ride, Vaquero! (MGM, 1953)
Plunder of the Sun (WB, 1953)
Hondo (WB, 1953)
Botany Bay (Par., 1953)
A Bullet Is Waiting (Col., 1954)
The Sea Chase (WB, , 1955) (also producer)
Back from Eternity (RKO, 1956) (also producer)
The Unholy Wife (RKO, 1957)
John Paul Jones (WB, 1959) (also co-script)

FEIST, FELIX E., b. Feb. 28, 1906, New York City; d. Sept. 3, 1965.
  The Deluge (RKO, 1933)
  All By Myself (Univ., 1943)
  You're a Lucky Fellow, Mr. Smith (Univ., 1943)
  Pardon My Rhythm (Univ., 1944)
  Reckless Age (Univ., 1944) (also producer)
  This Is the Life (Univ., 1944)
  George White's Scandals (RKO, 1945)
  The Devil Thumbs a Ride (RKO, 1947)
  The Winner's Circle (20th, 1948)
  Guilty of Treason (Eagle Lion, 1949)
  The Threat (RKO, 1949)
  The Golden Gloves Story (Eagle Lion, 1950)
  The Man Who Cheated Himself (20th, 1950)
  Tomorrow Is Another Day (WB, 1951)
  The Basketball Fix (Realart, 1951)
  This Woman Is Dangerous (WB, 1952)
  The Big Trees (WB, 1952)
  The Man Behind the Gun (WB, 1952)
  Donovan's Brain (UA, 1953) (also script)
  Pirates of Tripoli (Col., 1955)

FEJOS, PAUL, b. Jan. 24, 1897, Budapest; d. April 24, 1963.
  Fekete Kapitány (Hungarian, 1920)
  Lidercynomas (Hungarian, 1920) (also co-script)
  Pán (Hungarian, 1920) (also script)
  Joslat (Hungarian, 1920)
  Ujraélok (Hungarian, 1920)
  Arsen Lupin Utolso Kalandja (Hungarian, 1921)
  Szenzacio (Hungarian, 1922)
  Egri Csillagok (Hungarian, 1923--unfinished) (also script)
  The Last Moment (Zakaro, 1928) (also story, script, editor)
  Lonesome (Univ., 1928)
  Broadway (Univ., 1929)
  The Last Performance [Eric the Great] (Univ., 1929)
  Captain of the Guard (Univ., 1930) (uncredited, with John S. Robertson)
  Menschen Hinter Gittern [German version of The Big House] (MGM, 1930)
  Fantômas (French, 1931) (also co-script)
  Tavaszi Zapor (Hungarian, 1932) (also co-script)
  Itel a Balaton (French-Hungarian, 1932)
  Sonnenstrahl [Gardez le Sourire] (Austrian-French, 1933) (also co-story)
  Fruhlingsstimmen (Austrian, 1933)
  Flugten fra Millionerne (Danish, 1934) (also script)
  Menschen im Sturm (Austrian, 1934)
  Fange Nr 1 (Danish, 1935) (also story)
  Fredlös (Swedish, 1935)
  Den Gyldne Smil (Danish, 1935) (also script)

En Handfull Ris (Siamese, 1938) (with Gunnar Skodund)
Tambora (East Indian, 1938)
Man Och Kvinna (Swedish, 1939)
Yagua (Peruvian, 1941)

FERRER, JOSE (José Vicente Ferrer y Cintrón), b. Jan. 8, 1912,
    Santurce, Puerto Rico.
The Shrike (Univ., 1955) (also actor)
Cockleshell Heroes (Col., 1956) (also actor)
The Great Man (Univ., 1956) (also co-script, actor)
The High Cost of Loving (MGM, 1958) (also actor)
I Accuse (MGM, 1958) (also actor)
Return to Peyton Place (20th, 1961)
State Fair (20th, 1962)

FERRER, MEL (Melchor Gaston Ferrer), b. Aug. 25, 1917, El-
    beron, N. J.
The Girl of the Limberlost (Col., 1945)
Vendetta (RKO, 1950) (with uncredited Stuart Heisler, Howard
    Hughes, Max Ophüls, Preston Sturges)
The Secret Fury (RKO, 1950)
Green Mansions (MGM, 1959)
Cabriola (Col., 1966) (also producer, story, co-script, actor)

FEYDER, JACQUES, b. July 21, 1885, Ixelles, Belgium; d. May
    25, 1948.
M. Pinson, Policier (French, 1915) (with Gaston Ravel)
Tetes de Femmes, Femmes de Tête (French, 1916)
L'Homme de Compaignie (French, 1916)
Le Pied Qui Etreint (French, 1916) (also script)
Tiens, Vous Êtes à Poitiers (French, 1916)
L'Instinct est Maître (French, 1916)
Les Vieilles Dames de l'Hospice (French, 1917)
Le Ravin Sans Fond (French, 1917) (with Raymond Bernard)
La Faute d'Othographie (French, 1919) (also script)
L'Atlantide [Missing Husbands] (French, 1921) (also script)
Crainquebille (French, 1923) (also script, production design)
Visages d'Enfants (French, 1923) (with Françoise Rosay) (also
    script, production design)
L'Image (French, 1925) (also co-story, script)
Gribiche (French, 1925) (also script)
Carmen (French, 1926) (with Françoise Rosay) (also script,
    co-editor)
Au Pays du Roi Lepreux (French, 1927) (also script)
Thérèse Raquin [Shadows of Fear] (French, 1928) (also adapta-
    tion)
Les Nouveaux Messieurs (French, 1929) (also co-script)
The Kiss (MGM, 1929) (also co-script)

Anna Christie [German version] (MGM, 1930)
Le Spectre Vert [French version of The Unholy Night] (MGM, 1930)
Si l'Empereur Savait Ça! [French version of His Glorious Night] (MGM, 1930)
Son of India (MGM, 1931)
Daybreak (MGM, 1931)
Le Grand Jeu (French, 1934) (also co-script)
Pension Mimosas (French, 1935) (also co-script)
La Kermesse Heroique (French, 1935) (also co-script)
Die Klugen Frauen [German version of La Kermesse Heroique] (French, 1936)
Les Gens du Voyage (French, 1937)
Knight Without Armour (UA, 1937)
Fahrendes Volk [German version of Les Gens du Voyage] (German, 1937) (also script)
La Loi du Nord (French, 1939) (also co-script)
Une Femme Disparaît (Swiss, 1942) (also co-producer, script, actor)

FITZMAURICE, GEORGE, b. Feb. 13, 1885, Paris; d. June 13, 1940.
The Quest of the Sacred Gem (Pathé, 1914)
Stop Thief! (Kleine, 1915)
Via Wireless (Pathé, 1915)
Who's Who in Society (Kleine, 1915)
The Money Master (Kleine, 1915)
The Commuters (Kleine, 1915)
At Bay (Pathé, 1915)
The Test (Astra, 1916)
Big Jim Garrity (Pathé, 1916)
Arms and the Woman (Pathé, 1916)
New York (Pathé, 1916)
The Romantic Journey (Pathé, 1916)
Blind Man's Luck (Pathé, 1917)
The Iron Heart (Pathé, 1917)
The Mark of Cain (Pathé, 1917)
The Recoil (Pathé, 1917)
The On-the-Square Girl (World, 1917)
The Hunting of the Hawk (Pathé, 1917)
Sylvia of the Secret Service (Pathé, 1917)
Innocence (Pathé, 1918)
The Naulahka (Pathé, 1918)
The Hillcrest Mystery (Pathé, 1918)
The Narrow Path (Pathé, 1918)
Japanese Nightingale (Pathé, 1918)
The Cry of the Weak (Pathé, 1919)
Our Better Selves (Pathé, 1919)
Common Clay (Pathé, 1919)
The Witness for the Defense (Par., 1919)
The Avalanche (Artclass-Par., 1919)
Profiteer (Pathé, 1919)

A Society Exile (Par., 1919)
Counterfeit (Par., 1919)
On With the Dance (Par., 1920)
The Right to Love (Par., 1920)
Idols of Clay (Par., 1920)
Paying the Piper (Par., 1921) (also producer)
Experience (Par., 1921)
Forever (Par., 1921)
Three Live Ghosts (Par., 1922)
To Have and to Hold (Par., 1922)
The Man from Home (Par., 1922)
Kick In (Par., 1922)
Bella Donna (Par., 1923)
The Cheat (Par., 1923) (also producer)
The Eternal City (Associated FN, 1923)
Cytherea (Associated FN, 1924)
Tarnish (Associated FN, 1924)
A Thief in Paradise (FN, 1925) (also for production company)
The Dark Angel (FN, 1925)
His Supreme Moment (FN, 1925)
The Son of the Sheik (UA, 1926)
The Night of Love (UA, 1927)
The Tender Hour (FN, 1927)
Rose of the Golden West (FN, 1927)
The Love Mart (FN, 1927)
Lilac Time (FN, 1928)
The Barker (FN, 1928)
His Captive Woman (FN, 1929)
The Man and the Moment (FN, 1929)
The Locked Door (UA, 1929)
Tiger Rose (WB, 1929)
The Devil to Pay (UA, 1930)
One Heavenly Night (UA, 1930)
The Bad One (UA, 1930)
Raffles (UA, 1930) (with Harry D'Abbadie D'Arrast)
Strangers May Kiss (MGM, 1931)
The Unholy Garden (UA, 1931)
Mata Hari (MGM, 1932)
As You Desire Me (MGM, 1932)
All Men Are Enemies (Fox, 1934)
Petticoat Fever (MGM, 1936)
Suzy (MGM, 1936)
The Emperor's Candlesticks (MGM, 1937)
Live, Love and Learn (MGM, 1937)
Arsene Lupin Returns (MGM, 1938)
Vacation from Love (MGM, 1938)
Adventure in Diamonds (Par., 1940)

FLAHERTY, ROBERT, b. Feb. 16, 1884, Iron Mountain, Mich.;
    d. July 23, 1951.
    Nanook of the North (Pathé, 1922) (also script, co-titles,
    camera)

Moana: A Romance of the Golden Age (Par., 1926) (also
script, camera, editor)
White Shadows of the South Seas (MGM, 1928) (replaced by
W.S. Van Dyke II) (also co-story)
Acoma, the Sky City (Fox, 1928--unreleased) (also script)
Tabu (Par., 1931) (with F.W. Murnau) (also story, co-script,
co-camera)
Man of Aran (Gaumont-British, 1934) (also script, camera)
Elephant Boy (UA, 1937) (with Zoltan Korda)
Louisiana Story (Loppert, 1948) (also script)

FLEISCHER, RICHARD O., b. Dec. 8, 1916, New York City.
Child of Divorce (RKO, 1946)
Banjo (RKO, 1947)
Design for Death (RKO, 1948)
So This Is New York (UA, 1948)
Bodyguard (RKO, 1948)
The Clay Pigeon (RKO, 1949)
Follow Me Quietly (RKO, 1949) (with uncredited Anthony Mann)
Make Mine Laughs (RKO, 1949)
Trapped (Eagle Lion, 1949)
Armored Car Robbery (RKO, 1950)
His Kind of Woman (RKO 1951) (uncredited with John Farrow)
The Happy Time (Col., 1952)
Arena (MGM, 1953)
20,000 Leagues under the Sea (BV, 1954)
Violent Saturday (20th, 1955)
The Girl in the Red Velvet Swing (20th, 1955)
Bandido (UA, 1956)
Between Heaven and Hell (20th, 1956)
The Vikings (UA, 1958)
These Thousand Hills (20th, 1958)
Compulsion (20th, 1959)
Crack in the Mirror (20th, 1960)
The Big Gamble (20th, 1961)
Barabbas (Col., 1962)
Fantastic Voyage (20th, 1966)
Doctor Dolittle (20th, 1967)
The Boston Strangler (20th, 1968)
Che! (20th, 1969)
Tora! Tora! Tora! (20th, 1970) (with Toshio Masuda, Kinji
Fukasaki)
10 Rillington Place (20th, 1971)
The Last Run (MGM, 1971) (replaced John Huston)
The New Centurions (Col., 1972)
Solyent Green (MGM, 1973)
The Don Is Dead (Univ., 1973)

FLEMING, VICTOR, b. Feb. 23, 1883, Pasadena, Calif.; d. Jan.
6, 1949.
When the Clouds Roll By (UA, 1920) (with Ted Reed)

The Mollycoddle (UA, 1920)
Mama's Affair (Associated FN, 1921)
Woman's Place (FN, 1921)
Anna Ascends (Par., 1922)
Red Hot Romance (FN, 1922)
The Lane That Had No Turning (Par., 1922)
Dark Secrets (Par., 1923)
The Law of the Lawless (Par., 1923)
To the Last Man (Par., 1923)
The Call of the Canyon (Par., 1923)
Empty Hands (Par., 1924) (also producer)
Code of the Sea (Par., 1924)
Adventure (Par., 1925)
The Devil's Cargo (Par., 1925)
A Son of His Father (Par., 1925)

Clark Gable and Vivien Leigh, with cameraman Ernest Haller (rear, center) and Victor Fleming, on the set of Gone With the Wind (MGM, 1939).

Lord Jim (Par., 1925)
The Blind Goddess (Par., 1926)
Mantrap (Par., 1926)
The Rough Riders (Par., 1927)
The Way of All Flesh (Par., 1927)
Hula (Par., 1927)
The Awakening (Par., 1928)
Abie's Irish Rose (Par., 1929) (also producer)
Wolf Song (Par., 1929)
The Virginian (Par., 1929)
Common Clay (Fox, 1930)
Renegades (Fox, 1930)

Around the World in 80 Minutes With Douglas Fairbanks (UA, 1931) (with Douglas Fairbanks)
The Wet Parade (MGM, 1932)
Red Dust (MGM, 1932)
The White Sister (MGM, 1933)
Bombshell (MGM, 1933)
Treasure Island (MGM, 1934)
Reckless (MGM, 1935)
The Farmer Takes a Wife (Fox, 1935)
The Good Earth (MGM, 1937) (uncredited, with George Hill, Gustav Machaty, Sidney Franklin)
Captains Courageous (MGM, 1937)
Test Pilot (MGM, 1938)
The Wizard of Oz (MGM, 1939)
Gone With the Wind (MGM, 1939) (with uncredited George Cukor, Sam Wood)
Dr. Jekyll and Mr. Hyde (MGM, 1941) (also producer)
The Yearling (MGM, 1941--abandoned, reshot in 1946 by Clarence Brown)
Tortilla Flat (MGM, 1942)
A Guy Named Joe (MGM, 1944)
Adventure (MGM, 1945)
Joan of Arc (RKO, 1948)

FLICKER, THEODORE J., b. June 6, 1930, Freehold, N.J.
The Troublemaker (Janus, 1964) (also producer, co-story, co-script, actor)
The President's Analyst (Par., 1967) (also story, script)

FLOREY, ROBERT, b. Sept. 14, 1900, Paris.
One Hour of Love (Tiffany, 1927)
The Romantic Age (Col., 1927)
Face Value (Sterling, 1927)
Night Club (Par., 1928)
The Hole in the Wall (Par., 1929)
The Cocoanuts (Par., 1929) (with Joseph Santley)
The Battle of Paris (Par., 1929)
La Route est Belle (French, 1930)
L'Amour Chante (French, 1930)
Kommzu Mir Zum Rendezvous (German, 1930)
El Professor de Mi Senora (Spanish, 1930)
Le Blanc et le Noir (French, 1930) (with Marc Allegret)
Murders in the Rue Morgue (Univ., 1932)
The Man Called Back (World Wide, 1932)
Those We Love (World Wide, 1932)
Girl Missing (WB, 1933)
Ex-Lady (WB, 1933)
House on 56th Street (WB, 1933)
Bedside (FN, 1934)
Smarty (WB, 1934)
I Sell Anything (FN, 1934)
Registered Nurse (FN, 1934)

I Am a Thief (WB, 1935)
The Woman in Red (FN, 1935)
The Florentine Dagger (WB, 1935)
Going Highbrow (WB, 1935)
Don't Bet on Blondes (WB, 1935)
The Pay-Off (WB, 1935)
Ship Cafe (Par., 1935)
The Preview Murder Mystery (Par., 1936)
'Til We Meet Again (Par., 1936)
Hollywood Boulevard (Par., 1936)
Outcast (Par., 1937)
King of the Gamblers (Par., 1937)
Mountain Music (Par., 1937)
This Way Please (Par., 1937)
Daughter of Shanghai (Par., 1937)
Dangerous to Know (Par., 1938)
King of Alcatraz (Par., 1938)
Disbarred (Par., 1939)
Hotel Imperial (Par., 1939)
The Magnificent Fraud (Par., 1939)
Death of a Champion (Par., 1939)
Women Without Names (Par., 1940)
Parole Fixer (Par., 1940)
The Face Behind the Mask (Col., 1941)
Meet Boston Blackie (Col., 1941)
Two in a Taxi (Col., 1941)
Dangerously They Live (WB, 1941)
Lady Gangster (WB, 1942) (as Florian Roberts)
The Desert Song (WB, 1943)
Roger Touhy, Gangster (20th, 1944)
Man from Frisco (Rep., 1944)
God Is My Co-Pilot (WB, 1945)
Danger Signal (WB, 1945)
The Beast With Five Fingers (WB, 1946)
Monsieur Verdon (UA, 1946) (assoc. director, with Charles Chaplin)
Tarzan and the Mermaids (RKO, 1948)
Rogue's Regiment (Univ., 1948)
Outpost in Morocco (UA, 1948)
The Crooked Way (UA, 1949)
Johnny One-Eye (UA, 1950)
The Vicious Years (Film Classics, 1950)

FORD, FRANCIS, b. Aug. 15, 1882, Portland, Me.; d. Sept. 6,
    1953.
    Lucille Love, Girl of Mystery* (Univ., 1914) (also actor)
    The Mysterious Rose (Univ.;Gold Seal, 1914) (also actor)
    Three Bad Men and a Girl (Univ.-101 Bison, 1915) (also actor)
    The Hidden City (Univ.-101 Bison, 1915) (also actor)
    The Doorway of Destruction (Univ.-101 Bison, 1915) (also actor)
    The Broken Coin* (Univ., 1915) (also actor)
    The Campbells Are Coming (Univ., 1915) (also actor)
    The Adventures of Peg O' the Ring* (Univ., 1916) (with Jacques
        Jaccard; also actor)

The Purple Mask* (Univ., 1916) (also actor)
The Lumber Yard Gang (Univ.-101 Bison, 1916) (also actor)
Chicken-Hearted Jim (Univ.-101 Bison, 1916) (also actor)
The Bandit's Wager (Univ.-101 Bison, 1916) (also actor)
John Ermine of Yellowstone (Univ., 1917) (also actor)
The Silent Mystery* (Burston, 1918) (also actor)
Berlin Via America (Fordart Films, 1918) (also actor)
Who Was the Other Man? (Univ., 1918)
The Craving (M.H. Hoffman, 1918)
The Mystery of Thirteen* (Burston, 1919) (also actor)
Riders of Vengeance (Univ., 1919)
The Crimson Shoals (Monopol, 1920)
Thunderbolt Jack* (Arrow, 1920) (with Murdock MacQuarrie)
Cyclone Bliss (Arrow, 1921)
The Great Reward* (Burston, 1921) (also actor)
I Am the Woman (Victor Kremer, 1921)
The Stampede (Victor Kremer, 1921) (also actor)
They're Off (Anchor, 1922) (also script)
Angel Citizens (Merit, 1922)
Cross Roads (Merit, 1922)
Gold Grabbers (Merit, 1922)
The Heart of Lincoln (Anchor, 1922) (also producer, actor)
So This Is Arizona (Merit, 1922) (also actor)
Storm Girl (Anchor, 1922) (also actor)
Thundering Hoofs (Anchor, 1922) (also actor)
Trail's End (Merit, 1922)
The Fighting Skipper* (Arrow, 1923)
The Cowboy Prince (Arrow, 1924)
Cupid's Rustler (Arrow, 1924) (also script)
The Diamond Bandit (Arrow, 1924) (also script)
In the Days of the Covered Wagons (Independent, 1924)
The Last of Pinto Pete (Arrow, 1924)
Lash of the Whip (Arrow, 1924) (also script)
Midnight Shadows (Arrow, 1924) (also script)
Range Blood (Arrow, 1924) (also script)
A Rodeo Mixup (Arrow, 1924) (also script, actor)
Western Feuds (Arrow, 1924) (also actor)
Western Yesterdays (Arrow, 1924) (also adaptation, actor)
Perils of the Wild* (Univ., 1925)
The Four from Nowhere (Goodwill, 1925) (also producer,
    script, actor)
False Friends (Goodwill, 1926)
The Ghetto Shamrock (Goodwill, 1926)
Her Own Story (Goodwill, 1926)
Melodies (Goodwill, 1926)
The Winking Idol* (Univ., 1926)
Wolf's Trail (Univ., 1927)
Wolves of the Air (Sterling, 1927) (also script as Francis
    O'Fearna)
Call of the Heart (Univ., 1928)

FORD, JOHN (Sean Aloysius O'Feeney), b. Feb. 1, 1895, Cape
    Elizabeth, Me.; d. Aug. 31, 1973.
As Jack Ford:
    Lucille, the Waitress (Univ., 1914)
    Straight Shooting (Butterfly-Univ., 1917)
    The Secret Man (Butterfly-Univ., 1917
    A Marked Man (Butterfly-Univ., 1917)
    Bucking Broadway (Butterfly-Univ., 1917)
    The Phantom Riders (Univ.-Special, 1918)
    Wild Women (Univ.-Special, 1918)
    Thieves' Gold (Univ.-Special, 1918)
    The Scarlet Drop (Univ.-Special, 1918) (also story)
    Hell Bent (Univ.-Special, 1918) (also co-story)
    A Woman's Fool (Univ.-Special, 1918)
    Three Mounted Men (Univ.-Special, 1918)
    Roped (Univ.-Special, 1919)
    A Fight for Love (Univ.-Special, 1919)
    Bare Fists (Univ.-Special, 1919)
    Riders of Vengeance (Univ.-Special, 1919) (also co-story)
    The Outcasts of Poker Flat (Univ.-Special, 1919)
    The Ace of the Saddle (Univ.-Special, 1919)
    The Rider of the Law (Univ.-Special, 1919)
    A Gun Fightin' Gentleman (Univ.-Special, 1919) (also co-story)
    Marked Men (Univ.-Special, 1919)
    The Prince of Avenue A (Univ.-Special, 1920)
    The Girl in No. 29 (Univ.-Special, 1920)
    Hitchin' Posts (Univ.-Special, 1920
    Under Sentence (Univ., 1920) (story)
    Just Pals (Fox-20th Century Brand, 1920)
    The Big Punch (Fox-20th Century Brand, 1921)
    The Freeze-Out (Univ.-Special, 1921)
    The Wallop (Univ.-Special, 1921)
    Desperate Trails (Univ.-Special, 1921)
    Action (Univ.-Special, 1921)
    Sure Fire (Univ.-Special, 1921)
    Jackie (Fox, 1921)
    Little Miss Smiles (Fox, 1922)
    Silver Wings (Fox, 1922) (with Edwin Carewe)
    The Village Blacksmith (Fox, 1922)
    The Face on the Barroom Floor (Fox, 1923)
    Three Jumps Ahead (Fox, 1923)

As John Ford:
    Cameo Kirby (Fox, 1923)
    North of Hudson Bay (Fox, 1923)
    Hoodman Blind (Fox, 1923)
    The Iron Horse (Fox, 1924)
    Hearts of Oak (Fox, 1924)
    Lightnin' (Fox, 1925)
    Kentucky Pride (Fox, 1925)
    The Fighting Heart (Fox, 1925)
    Thank You (Fox, 1925)
    The Shamrock Handicap (Fox, 1926)

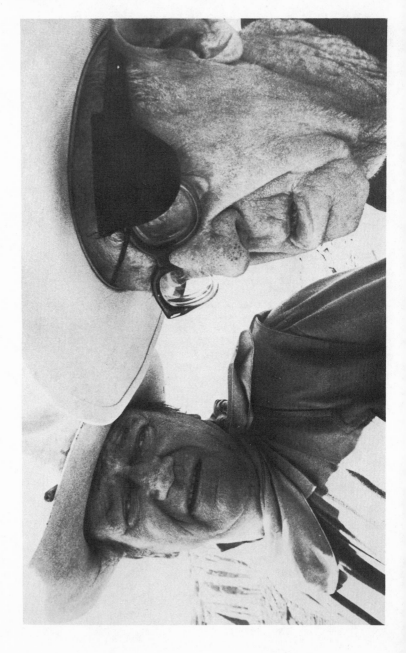

Three Bad Men (Fox, 1926) (also co-story)
The Blue Eagle (Fox, 1926)
Upstream (Fox, 1927)
Mother Machree (Fox, 1928)
Four Sons (Fox, 1928)
Hangman's House (Fox, 1928)
Napoleon's Barber (Fox-Movietone, 1928)
Riley The Cop (Fox, 1928)
Strong Boy (Fox, 1929)
The Black Watch (Fox, 1929)
Salute (Fox, 1929)
Men Without Women (Fox, 1929) (also co-story)
Born Reckless (Fox, 1930) (with Andrew Bennison)
Up the River (Fox, 1930) (also co-script)
Seas Beneath (Fox, 1931)
The Brat (Fox, 1931)
Arrowsmith (UA, 1931)
Air Mail (Univ., 1932)
Flesh (MGM, 1932)
Pilgrimage (Fox, 1933)
Dr. Bull (Fox, 1933)
The Lost Patrol (RKO, 1934)
The World Moves On (Fox, 1934)
Judge Priest (Fox, 1934)
The Whole Town's Talking (Col., 1935)
The Informer (RKO, 1935)
Steamboat 'Round the Bend (20th, 1935)
The Prisoner of Shark Island (20th, 1936)
The Last Outlaw (RKO, 1936) (also co-story)
Mary of Scotland (RKO, 1936)
The Plough and the Stars (RKO, 1936)
Wee Willie Winkie (20th, 1937)
The Hurricane (UA, 1937)
The Adventures of Marco Polo (UA, 1938) (uncredited, with
    Archie Mayo)
Four Men and a Prayer (20th, 1938)
Submarine Patrol (20th, 1938)
Stagecoach (UA, 1939) (also producer)
Young Mr. Lincoln (20th, 1939)
Drums Along the Mohawk (20th, 1939)
The Grapes of Wrath (20th, 1940)
The Long Voyage Home (UA, 1940)
Tobacco Road (20th, 1941)
How Green Was My Valley (20th, 1941)
They Were Expendable (MGM, 1945) (also producer)
My Darling Clementine (20th, 1946)
The Fugitive (RKO, 1947) (also co-producer)
Fort Apache (RKO, 1948) (also co-producer)
Three Godfathers (MGM, 1948) (also co-producer)

Facing page: John Wayne with John Ford on The Man Who Shot
Liberty Valence (Par., 1962).

She Wore a Yellow Ribbon (RKO, 1949) (also co-producer)
Pinky (20th, 1949) (uncredited, with Elia Kazan)
When Willie Comes Marching Home (20th, 1950)
Wagon Master (RKO, 1950) (also co-producer)
Rio Grande (Rep., 1950) (also co-producer)
This Is Korea! (Rep./U.S. Navy, 1951)
What Price Glory? (20th, 1952)
The Quiet Man (Rep., 1952) (also co-producer)
The Sun Shines Bright (Rep., 1953) (also co-producer)
Mogambo (MGM, 1953)
Hondo (WB, 1953) (second unit direction only)
The Long Grey Line (Col., 1955)
Mister Roberts (WB, 1955) (with Mervyn LeRoy)
The Searchers (WB, 1956)
The Wings of Eagles (MGM, 1957)
The Rising of the Moon (WB, 1957)
The Last Hurrah (Col., 1958) (also producer)
Gideon of Scotland Yard (Col., 1959)
The Horse Soldiers (UA, 1959)
Sergeant Rutledge (WB, 1960)
Two Rode Together (Col., 1961)
The Man Who Shot Liberty Valance (Par., 1962)
How the West Was Won (ep: "The Civil War") (MGM, 1962)
    (with George Marshall, Henry Hathaway)
Donovan's Reef (Par., 1963) (also producer)
Cheyenne Autumn (WB, 1964)
Young Cassidy (MGM, 1965) (with Jack Cardiff)
Seven Women (MGM, 1966)

FORDE, EUGENE (Gene Forde), b. Nov. 8, 1898.
Primavera en Otono (Fox, 1932)
Smoky (Fox, 1933)
Charlie Chan in London (Fox, 1934)
Mystery Woman (Fox, 1935)
Great Hotel Murder (Fox, 1935)
Your Uncle Dudley (20th, 1935)
The Country Beyond (20th, 1936)
36 Hours to Kill (20th, 1936)
Step Lively Jeeves! (20th, 1937)
Midnight Taxi (20th, 1937)
Charlie Chan at Monte Carlo (20th, 1937)
Charlie Chan on Broadway (20th, 1937)
International Settlement (20th, 1938)
One Wild Night (20th, 1938)
Meet the Girls (20th, 1938)
Inspector Hornleigh (20th, 1939)
The Honeymoon's Over (20th, 1939)
Charlie Chan's Murder Cruise (20th, 1940)
Pier 13 (20th, 1940)
Michael Shayne, Private Detective (20th, 1940)
Charter Pilot (20th, 1941)
Sleepers West (20th, 1941)

Dressed to Kill (20th, 1941)
Buy Me That Town (20th, 1941)
Man at Large (20th, 1941)
Right to the Heart (20th, 1942)
Berlin Correspondent (20th, 1942)
The Crime Doctor's Strangest Case (Col., 1944)
Shadows in the Night (Col., 1944)
The Crimson Key (20th, 1947)
Backlash (20th, 1947)
Jewels of Brandenburg (20th, 1947)
The Invisible Wall (20th, 1947)

FOSTER, LEWIS R., b. Aug. 5, 1900, Brookfield, Mo.; d. June 10, 1974.
Love Letters of a Star (Univ., 1936)
She's Dangerous (Univ., 1937) (with Milton Carruth) (also co-script)
Armored Car (Univ., 1937) (also co-script)
The Man Who Cried Wolf (Univ., 1937)
Manhandled (Par., 1949) (also co-script)
Captain China (Par., 1949) (also co-script)
The Lucky Stiff (UA, 1949) (also script)
El Paso (Par., 1949) (also script)
The Eagle and the Hawk (Par., 1950) (also co-script)
The Last Outpost (Par., 1951)
Crosswind (Par., 1951) (also script)
Passage West (Par., 1951) (also script)
Hong Kong (Par., 1951) (also story)
Jamaica Run (Par., 1953) (also script)
Those Redheads from Seattle (Par., 1953) (also script)
Top of the World (UA, 1955) (also co-producer)
Crashout (Filmakers, 1955) (also co-script)
The Bold and the Brave (RKO, 1956)
Dakota Incident (Rep., 1956)
Tonka (BV, 1958) (also co-script)

FOSTER, NORMAN, b. Dec. 13, 1900, Richmond, Ind.
I Cover Chinatown (20th, 1936) (also actor)
Fair Warning (20th, 1937) (also script)
Think Fast, Mr. Moto (20th, 1937) (also co-script)
Thank You, Mr. Moto (20th, 1937) (also co-script)
Walking Down Broadway (20th, 1938)
Mr. Moto Takes a Chance (20th, 1938) (also co-story)
Mysterious Mr. Moto (20th, 1938) (also co-script)
Charlie Chan in Reno (20th, 1939)
Mr. Moto Takes a Vacation (20th, 1939) (also co-script)
Charlie Chan at Treasure Island (20th, 1939)
Charlie Chan in Panama (20th, 1940)
Viva Cisco Kid (20th, 1940)
Ride Kelly Ride (20th, 1941)
Scotland Yard (20th, 1941)
Journey into Fear (RKO, 1943) (with uncredited Orson Welles)

Santa (Mexican, 1943)
Hora de la Verdad (Mexican, 1945)
Rachel and the Stranger (RKO, 1948)
Kiss the Blood off My Hands (Univ., 1948)
Tell It to the Judge (Col., 1949)
Father Is a Bachelor (Col., 1950) (with Abby Berlin)
Woman on the Run (Univ., 1950) (also co-script)
Navajo (Mexican, 1951) (also script)
Sky Full of Moon (MGM, 1952) (also script)
Sombrero (MGM, 1954) (also script)
Davy Crockett, King of the Wild Frontier (BV, 1955) (also co-script)
Davy Crockett and the River Pirates (BV, 1956) (also co-script)
The Nine Lives of Elfego Baca (BV, 1959) (also script)
The Sign of Zorro (BV, 1960) (also script)
Hans Brinker, or The Silver Skates (BV, 1962)
Von Drake in Spain (BV, 1962) (with Hamilton Luske)
Indian Paint (Col., 1966) (also script)
Brighty of Grand Canyon (Feature Film Corp. of America, 1967) (also script)
Deathbed (Wargay, 1973)

FOX, WALLACE W., b. March 9, 1896, Purcell, Indian Territory, Okla.; d. June 30, 1958.
The Bandit's Son (FBO, 1927)
Driftin' Sands (FBO, 1928)
The Riding Renegade (FBO, 1928)
Man in the Rough (FBO, 1928)
Breed of the Sunsets (FBO, 1928)
The Trail of Courage (FBO, 1928)
The Avenging Rider (FBO, 1928)
The Amazing Vagabond (FBO, 1929)
Come and Get It (FBO, 1929)
Laughing at Death (FBO, 1929)
Partners of the Trail (Mon., 1931)
Cannonball Express (Sono Art-World Wide, 1932)
Devil on Deck (Sono Art-World Wide, 1932)
Red Morning (RKO, 1935)
Powdersmoke Range (RKO, 1935)
Yellow Dust (RKO, 1936)
The Last of the Mohicans (UA, 1936)
Racing Lady (RKO, 1937)
The Mexicali Kid (Mon., 1938)
Gun Packer (Mon., 1938)
The Lone Star Vigilantes (Col., 1941)
Bowery Blitzkrieg (Mon., 1941)
The Corpse Vanishes (Mon., 1942)
Let's Get Tough! (Mon., 1942)
Smart Alecks (Mon., 1942)
Bowery at Midnight (Mon., 1942)
'Neath Brooklyn Bridge (Mon., 1942)

Kid Dynamite (Mon., 1943)
The Ghost Riders (Mon., 1943)
Outlaws of Stampede Pass (Mon., 1943)
The Girl from Monterey (PRC, 1943)
Career Girl (PRC, 1943)
Riders of the Santa Fe (Univ., 1944)
Block Busters (Mon., 1944)
Pride of the Plains (Rep., 1944)
Song of the Range (Mon., 1944)
The Great Mike (PRC, 1944)
Men on Her Mind (PRC, 1944)
Million Dollar Kid (Mon., 1944)
Docks of New York (Mon., 1945)
Mr. Muggs Rides Again (Mon., 1945)
Pillow of Death (Univ., 1945)
Bad Men of the Border (Univ., 1946) (also producer)
Code of the Lawless (Univ., 1946) (also producer)
Gunman's Code (Univ., 1946) (also producer)
Gun Town (Univ., 1946) (also producer)
Lawless Breed (Univ., 1946) (also producer)
Wild Beauty (Univ., 1946) (also producer)
Trail to Vengeance (Univ., 1946) (also producer)
Rustler's Round-Up (Univ., 1947) (also producer)
The Valiant Hombre (UA, 1948)
The Daring Caballero (UA, 1949)
The Gay Amigo (UA, 1949)
Gunslingers (Mon., 1950) (also producer)
West of Wyoming (Mon., 1950)
Fence Riders (Mon., 1950) (also producer)
Over the Border (Mon., 1950) (also producer)
Arizona Territory (Mon., 1950)
Six Gun Mesa (Mon., 1950) (also producer)
Outlaw Gold (Mon., 1950)
Montana Desperado (Mon., 1951)
Blazing Bullets (Mon., 1951)

FRANK, MELVIN, b. 1913, Chicago.
   The Reformer and the Redhead (MGM, 1950) (with Norman
      Panama) (also co-producer, co-script)
   Strictly Dishonorable (MGM, 1951) (with Norman Panama) (also
      co-producer, co-script)
   Callaway Went Thataway (MGM, 1951) (with Norman Panama)
      (also co-producer, co-script)
   Above and Beyond (MGM, 1952) (with Norman Panama (also
      co-producer, co-story, co-script)
   Knock on Wood (Par., 1954) (with Norman Panama (also co-
      producer, co-script)
   The Court Jester (Par., 1956) (with Norman Panama (also co-
      producer, co-story, co-script)
   That Certain Feeling (Par., 1956) (with Norman Panama) (also
      co-producer, co-story, co-script)
   The Jayhawkers (Par., 1959) (also co-producer, co-script)

Li'l Abner (Par., 1959) (also co-story, co-script)
The Facts of Life (UA, 1960) (also co-script)
Strange Bedfellows (Univ., 1965) (also producer, co-story, co-script)
Buona Sera, Mrs. Campbell (UA, 1968) (also co-producer, co-script)

FRANKENHEIMER, JOHN, b. Feb. 19, 1930, Malba, L.I., N.Y.
The Young Stranger (RKO, 1957)
The Young Savages (UA, 1961)
All Fall Down (MGM, 1962)
Birdman of Alcatraz (UA, 1962)
The Manchurian Candidate (UA, 1962) (also co-producer)
Seven Days in May (Par., 1964)
The Train (UA, 1965) (replaced Arthur Penn)
Seconds (Par., 1966)
Grand Prix (MGM, 1966)

John Frankenheimer shooting The Train (UA, 1965).

The Fixer (MGM, 1968)
The Extraordinary Seaman (MGM, 1969)
The Gypsy Moths (MGM, 1969)
I Walk the Line (Col., 1970) (also co-producer)
The Horsemen (Col., 1971) (also co-producer)
The Iceman Cometh (American Film Theatre, 1973)

FRANKLIN, CHESTER M., b. Sept. 1, 1890, San Francisco.
  Let Katy Do It (Triangle, 1915) (with Sidney A. Franklin)
  Martha's Vindication (Triangle, 1915) (with Sidney A. Franklin)
  The Children in the House (Fine Arts-Triangle, 1916) (with Sid-
    ney A. Franklin)
  Going Straight (Fine Arts-Triangle, 1916) (with Sidney A. Frank-
    lin)
  The Little Schoolma'am (Fine Arts-Triangle, 1916) (with Sid-
    ney A. Franklin)
  Gretchen the Greenhorn (Fine Arts-Triangle, 1916) (with Sidney
    A. Franklin)
  A Sister of Six (Fine Arts- Triangle, 1916) (with Sidney A.
    Franklin)
  Jack and the Beanstalk (Fox, 1917) (with Sidney A. Franklin)
  Aladdin and the Wonderful Lamp (Fox, 1917) (with Sidney A.
    Franklin)
  Babes in the Wood (Fox, 1917) (with Sidney A. Franklin)
  Ali-Baba and the Forty Thieves (Fox, 1917) (with Sidney A.
    Franklin)
  Treasure Island (Fox, 1918) (with Sidney A. Franklin)
  Fan Fan (Fox, 1918) (with Sidney A. Franklin)
  The Girl With the Champagne Eyes (Fox, 1918)
  You Never Can Tell (Realart, 1920)
  All Souls' Eve (Realart, 1921)
  A Private Scandal (Realart, 1921)
  The Case of Becky (Par., 1921)
  Nancy from Nowhere (Par., 1922)
  A Game Chicken (Par., 1922)
  The Toll of the Sea (Metro, 1922)
  Where the North Begins (WB, 1923) (also co-script)
  The Song of Love (Associated FN, 1923) (with Frances Marion)
  Behind the Curtain (Univ., 1924)
  The Silent Accuser (MGM, 1924)
  Wild Justice (UA, 1925)
  The Thirteenth Hour (MGM, 1927) (also co-story, co-script)
  Detectives (MGM, 1928) (also co-story, co-continuity)
  Si el Emperador lo Supiera [Spanish version of His Glorious
    Night] (MGM, 1930)
  Su Ultima Noche [Spanish version of The Gay Deceiver] (MGM,
    1931)
  File 113 (Hollywood, 1932)
  Vanity Fair (Hollywood, 1932)
  The Stoker (Allied Pictures, 1932)
  A Parisian Romance (Allied Pictures, 1932)
  The Iron Master (Aliance, 1933)

Sequoia (MGM, 1934)
Tough Guy (MGM, 1936)

FRANKLIN, SIDNEY A., b. March 21, 1893, San Francisco; d.
     May 18, 1972.
Let Katy Do It (Triangle, 1915) (with Chester Franklin)
Martha's Vindication (Triangle, 1915) (with Chester Franklin)
The Children in the House (Fine Arts-Triangle, 1916) (with
     Chester Franklin)
Going Straight (Fine Arts-Triangle, 1916) (with Chester Frank-
     lin)
The Little Schoolma'am (Fine Arts-Triangle, 1916) (with Ches-
     ter Franklin)
Gretchen the Greenhorn (Fine Arts-Triangle, 1916) (with Ches-
     ter Franklin)
A Sister of Six (Fine Arts-Triangle, 1916) (with Chester Frank-
     lin)
Jack and the Beanstalk (Fox, 1917) (with Chester Franklin)
Aladdin and the Wonderful Lamp (Fox, 1917) (with Chester
     Franklin)
Babes in the Wood (Fox, 1917)
Ali Baba and the Forty Thieves (Fox, 1918) (with Chester
     Franklin)
Six Shooter Andy (Fox, 1918)
Confession (Fox, 1918)
The Bride of Fear (Fox, 1918)
The Safety Curtain (Select, 1918)
Treasure Island (Fox, 1918) (with Chester M. Franklin)
Her Only Way (Select, 1918)
Fan-Fan (Fox, 1918) (with Chester M. Franklin)
The Heart of Wetona (Select, 1918)
The Forbidden City (Select, 1918)
The Probation Wife (Select, 1919)
Heart O' the Hills (FN, 1919)
The Hoodlum (FN, 1919)
Two Weeks (FN, 1920)
Unseen Forces (FN, 1920)
Not Guilty (Associated FN, 1921)
Courage (Associated FN, 1921) (also producer)
Smilin' Through (Associated FN, 1922) (also co-script)
The Primitive Lover (Associated FN, 1922)
East Is West (Associated FN, 1922)
Brass (WB, 1923)
Ducly (Associated FN, 1923)
Tiger Rose (WB, 1923) (also producer)
Her Night of Romance (FN, 1924)
Her Sister from Paris (FN, 1925)
Learning of Love (FN, 1925)
The Duchess of Buffalo (FN, 1926)
Beverly of Graustark (MGM, 1926)
Quality Street (MGM, 1927)
The Actress (MGM, 1928)

Wild Orchids (MGM, 1929)
The Last of Mrs. Cheyney (MGM, 1929)
Devil-May-Care (MGM, 1929)
The Lady of Scandal (MGM, 1930)
A Lady's Morals (MGM, 1930)
The Guardsman (MGM, 1931)
Private Lives (MGM, 1931)
Smilin' Through (MGM, 1932)
Reunion in Vienna (MGM, 1933) (also producer)
The Barretts of Wimpole Street (MGM, 1934)
The Dark Angel (UA, 1935)
The Good Earth (MGM, 1937) (with Sam Wood, George Hill,
   Fred Niblo, Andrew Marton)
Duel in the Sun (Selznick Releasing, 1946) (uncredited) with King
   Vidor, and uncredited William Dieterle, William Cameron
   Menzies, Josef von Sternberg, Otto Brower)
The Barretts of Wimpole Street (MGM, 1957) (also producer)

FRASER, HARRY L.
Oil and Romance (Aywon, 1925)
Queen of Spades (Aywon, 1925)
Sky's the Limit (Aywon, 1925)
West of Mojave (Aywon, 1925)
The Fighting Gob (Aywon, 1926)
General Custer at Little Big Horn (Sunset, 1926)
Sheep Trail (Aywon, 1926)
The Wildcat (Aywon, 1926)
Montana Kid (Mon., 1931) (also story)
Oklahoma Jim (Mon., 1931) (also story)
Land of Wanted Men (Mon., 1932) (also story, script)
Ghost City (Mon., 1932) (also story, script)
The Reckoning (Mon., 1932)
Texas Pioneers (Mon., 1932) (also story)
Mason of the Mounted (Mon., 1932) (also story, script)
Law of the North (Mon., 1932) (also story)
From Broadway to Cheyenne (Mon., 1932)
Honor of the Mounted (Mon., 1932) (also story, dialog)
The Savage Girl (Mon., 1933)
Diamond Trail (Mon., 1933)
Fighting Parson (Mon., 1933)
Rainbow Ranch (Mon., 1933) (also co-story)
The Fugitive (Mon., 1933)
Randy Rides Again (Mon., 1934)
Fighting Through (Mon., 1934)
'Neath Arizona Skies (Mon., 1934)
Wagon Trail (Ajax, 1935)
Fighting Pioneers (Resolute, 1935) (also co-story, co-script)
Rustlers' Paradise (Ajax, 1935)
Saddle Aces (Resolute, 1935)
Last of the Clintons (Ajax, 1935)
The Pecos Kid (Commodore, 1935)
Wild Mustang (William Berke, 1935)

Hair-Trigger Casey (Atlantic, 1936)
Feud of the West (Diversion, 1936)
The Riding Avenger (Diversion, 1936)
Cavalcade of the West (Diversion, 1936)
Romance Rides the Range (Spectrum, 1936)
Aces Wild (Commodore, 1937)
Jungle Menace* (Col., 1937) (with George Melford)
Heroes of the Alamo (Col., 1937)
Galloping Dynamite (Ambassador, 1937)
Spirit of Youth (Grand National, 1937)
Fury Below (Treo Productions, 1938)
Six Shooting' Sheriff (Grand National, 1938)
Songs and Saddles (Road Shows, 1938)
Jungle Man (PRC, 1941)
Brand of the Devil (PRC, 1944)
Gunsmoke Mesa (PRC, 1944)
Enemy of the Law (PRC, 1945) (also script)
Outlaw Roundup (PRC, 1945)
Three in the Saddle (PRC, 1945)
Ambush Trail (PRC, 1946)
Frontier Fugitives (PRC, 1946)
Flaming Bullets (PRC, 1945) (also script)
Navajo Kid (PRC, 1945)
Six Gun Man (PRC, 1946) (also script)
Thunder Town (PRC, 1946)
Six Gun for Hire (PRC, 1946) (also script)
The White Gorilla (Special Attractions, 1947)
Stallion Canyon (Astor, 1949)

FREELAND, THORNTON, b. Feb. 10, 1898, Hope, N.D.
Three Live Ghosts (UA, 1929)
Be Yourself! (UA, 1930)
Whoopee! (UA, 1930) (with choreographer Busby Berkeley)
Six Cylinder Love (Fox, 1931)
Terror by Night (Famous Attractions, 1931)
The Secret Witness (Col., 1931)
The Unexpected Father (Univ., 1932)
Love Affair (Col., 1932)
Week-End Marriage (FN, 1932)
They Call It Sin (FN, 1932)
Flying Down to Rio (RKO, 1933)
George White's Scandals (Fox, 1934)
Skylarks (UA, 1935)
Brewster's Millions (UA, 1935)
Accused (UA, 1936)
The Amateur Gentleman (UA, 1936)
Jericho [Dark Sands] (General Film Distributors, 1937)
Over the Moon (UA, 1937) (with William K. Howard)
Paradise for Two [The Gaiety Girls] (UA, 1937)
Dark Sands (Record, 1938)
So This Is London (20th, 1940)
The Gang's All Here (Mon., 1941)

Too Many Blondes (Univ., 1941)
Marry the Boss's Daughter (20th, 1941)
The Brass Monkey [Lucky Mascot] (Alliance, 1947)
Meet Me at Dawn (20th, 1948)
Dear Mr. Prohack (General Film Distributors, 1949)

FREGONESE, HUGO, b. April 8, 1908, Buenos Aires, Argentina.
Pampa Barbara (Argentinian, 1945) (with Lucas Demare)
Donde Mueren Las Palabras (Argentinian, 1946)
Apenas un Delincuente [Live in Fear] (Argentinian, 1949) (also
  producer, co-story)
De Hombre a Hombre (Argentinian, 1949)
Saddle Tramp (Univ., 1950)
One Way Street (Univ., 1950)
Apache Drums (Univ., 1951)
Mark of the Renegade (Univ., 1951)
My Six Convicts (Col., 1952)
Untamed Frontier (Univ., 1952)
DeCameron Nights (RKO, 1953)
Blowing Wild (WB, 1953)
Man in the Attic (20th, 1954) (uncredited, with R. L. Jacks)
The Raid (20th, 1954)
Black Tuesday (UA, 1954)
I Girovaghi (Italian, 1956)
Seven Thunders [Beast of Marseilles] (Rank, 1957)
Harry Black and the Tiger (20th, 1958)
Marco Polo (AIP, 1962)
Les Cavaliers Rouges [Old Shatterhand] (European co-production,
  1964)
Un Aero per Baalbeck [Dernier Avion pour Ballbeck] (European
  co-production, 1964)
Die Todesstrahlen der Dr. Mabuse [Mission Speciale au Deux-
  ième Bureau] (European co-production, 1964)
Pampa Salvaje [Savage Pampas] (Spanish, 1965) (also co-script)
Operazione Ballabeck [F.B.I. Mission Ballbeck] (European co-
  production, 1965) (with Giuliano Carnimeo)

FREUND, KARL, b. Jan. 16, 1890, Königshof, Bohemia; d. May
  3, 1969.
The Mummy (Univ., 1932)
Moonlight and Pretzels (Univ., 1932)
Madame Spy (Univ., 1934)
The Countess of Monte Cristo (Univ., 1934)
Uncertain Lady (Univ., 1934)
Gift of Gab (Univ., 1934)
I Give My Love (Univ., 1934)
Mad Love (MGM, 1935)

FRIEDKIN, WILLIAM, b. 1939, Chicago.
Good Times (Col., 1967)

The Night They Raided Minsky's (UA, 1968)
The Birthday Party (Continental, 1968)
The Boys in the Band (National General, 1970)
The French Connection (20th, 1971)
The Exorcist (WB, 1973)

FULLER, SAMUEL, b. Aug. 12, 1911, Worcester, Mass.
I Shot Jesse James (Screen Guild, 1949) (also script)
The Baron of Arizona (Lip., 1950) (also script)
The Steel Helmet (Lip., 1951) (also co-producer, script)
Fixed Bayonets (20th, 1951) (also script)
Park Row (UA, 1952) (also producer, script)
Pickup on South Street (20th, 1953) (also script)
Hell and High Water (20th, 1954) (also co-script)
House of Bamboo (20th, 1955) (also additional dialog, actor)
Run of the Arrow (Univ., 1956) (also producer, script)
China Gate (20th, 1957) (also producer, script)
Forty Guns (20th, 1957) (also producer, script)
Verboten! (Col., 1958) (also producer, script)
The Crimson Kimono (Col., 1959) (also producer, script)
Underworld USA (Col., 1961) (also producer, script)
Merrill's Marauders (WB, 1962) (also co-script)
Shock Corridor (AA, 1963) (also producer, story, script)
The Naked Kiss (AA, 1964) (also producer, script)
Shark (Heritage, 1969) (also script)
Tote Taube in der Beethovenstrasse (German-TV, 1972)
Fiata (Spanish, 1972) (replaced)
Dead Pigeon on Beethoven Street (Emerson, 1973) (also script)

FURIE, SIDNEY J., b. 1933, Toronto.
A Dangerous Age (Ajay, 1959) (also script)
A Cool Sound from Hell (Canadian, 1959) (also script)
The Snake Woman (UA, 1961)
Dr. Blood's Coffin (UA, 1961)
During One Night (Gala, 1961) (also co-producer, script)
Three on a Spree (UA, 1961)
The Young Ones (Williams and Pritchard, 1962)
The Leather Boys (Garrick, 1963)
Wonderful Life (Elstree, 1964)
The Ipcress File (Univ., 1965)
The Appaloosa (Univ., 1966)
The Naked Runner (WB-7 Arts, 1967)
The Lawyer (Par., 1969) (also co-script)
Little Fauss and Big Halsy (Par., 1970)
Lady Sings the Blues (Par., 1972)
Hit! (Par., 1973)

FURTHMAN, JULES (Jules Grinnel Furthmann), b. March 5, 1888,
    Chicago; d. Sept. 22, 1966.
The Land of Jazz (Fox, 1921) (also co-story, script)

The Blushing Bride (Fox, 1921) (also story-script)
Colorado Pluck (Fox, 1921) (also script)
Jet Pilot (Univ., 1957) (uncredited, with Josef von Sternberg)
    (also producer, script)

G

GADE, SVEN, b. Feb. 9, 1879, Copenhagen; d. June 25, 1952.
    Die Liebe der Bajadere (German, 1918) (also script)
    Hamlet (German, 1920) (with Heinz Schall (also set sketches)
    Das Geheimnis von Brinkenhof (German, 1923) (also set
        sketches)
    Fifth Avenue Models (Univ.-Jewel, 1925)
    Siege (Univ.-Jewel, 1925)
    Peacock Feathers (Univ.-Jewel, 1925)
    Watch Your Wife (Univ.-Jewel, 1926) (also co-script)
    Into Her Kingdom (FN, 1926)
    The Blonde Saint (FN, 1926)
    Aase Clausen (German Test Film, 1932)
    Balletten Danser (German, 1938) (also co-script)

GARFEIN, JACK, b. July 2, 1930, Mukacevo, Czech.
    The Strange One (Col., 1957)
    Something Wild (UA, 1961)

GARNETT, TAY (William Taylor Garnett), b. June 13, 1905, Los
    Angeles.
    Celebrity (Pathé, 1928) (also script)
    The Spieler (Pathé, 1929) (also script)
    The Flying Fool (Pathé, 1929) (also script)
    Oh, Yeah! (Pathé, 1929) (also co-script)
    Her Man (Pathé, 1930) (also co-production, co-script)
    Officer O'Brien (Pathé, 1930) (also co-script)
    Bad Company (Pathé, 1931) (also co-script)
    Prestige (RKO, 1932) (also co-production, script)
    One Way Passage (WB, 1932) (also co-script)
    Okay, America (Univ., 1932)
    Destination Unknown (Univ., 1932)
    S.O.S. Iceberg (Univ., 1933)
    China Seas (MGM, 1935)
    She Couldn't Take It (Col., 1935)
    Professional Soldier (20th, 1936)
    Slave Ship (20th, 1937)
    Love Is News (20th, 1937)
    Stand-In (WB, 1937)
    The Joy of Living (RKO, 1938)
    Trade Winds (UA, 1939) (also co-script)
    Eternally Yours (UA, 1939)
    Slightly Honorable (UA, 1940)
    Seven Sinners (Univ., 1940)

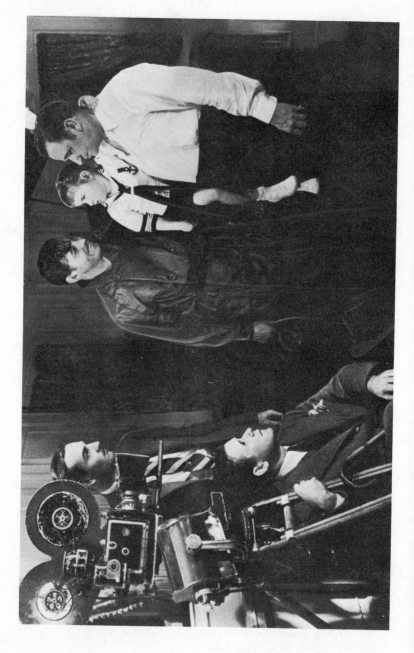

Cheers for Miss Bishop (UA, 1941)
My Favorite Spy (RKO, 1942)
Bataan (MGM, 1943)
The Cross of Lorraine (MGM, 1943)
Mrs. Parkington (MGM, 1944)
Valley of Decision (MGM, 1945)
The Postman Always Rings Twice (MGM, 1946)
Wild Harvest (Par., 1947)
A Connecticut Yankee in King Arthur's Court (Par., 1949)
Fireball (20th, 1950) (also co-script)
Cause for Alarm (MGM, 1951)
Soldiers Three (MGM, 1951)
One Minute to Zero (RKO, 1952)
Main Street to Broadway (MGM, 1953)
The Black Knight (Col., 1954)
Seven Wonders of the World (Cin., 1956) (with Paul Mantz,
    Andrew Marton, Ted Tetzlaff, Walter Thompson)
The Night Fighers (UA, 1960)
Cattle King (MGM, 1963)
The Delta Factor (Continental, 1970) (also co-script)
The Mad Trapper (Alaska Pictures, 1972) (also co-script)
Timber Tramp (Alaska Pictures, 1973)

GASNIER, LOUIS J., b. Sept. 15, 1882, Paris; d. 1948.
    The Perils of Pauline* (Pathé, 1914) (with Donald MacKenzie)
    Detective Swift (Pathé, 1914) (With Donald MacKenzie)
    Ticket-of-Leave Man (Pathé, 1914) (with Donald MacKenzie)
    The Stolen Birthright (Pathé, 1914)
    The Warning (Pathé, 1914)
    The Exploits of Elaine (Pathé, 1915) (with George B. Seitz)
    The King's Game (Pathé, 1916)
    Annabel's Romance (Pathé, 1916)
    Hazel Kirke (Pathé, 1916)
    The Shielding Shadow* (Pathé, 1916) (with Donald MacKenzie)
    The Beloved Cheater (Robertson-Cole, 1919)
    The Corsican Brothers (Robertson-Cole, 1920)
    The Butterfly Man (Robertson-Cole, 1920)
    Kismet (Robertson-Cole, 1920)
    Good Women (Robertson-Cole, 1921)
    A Wife's Awakening (Robertson-Cole, 1921)
    Silent Years (Robertson-Cole, 1921)
    The Call of Home (Robertson-Cole, 1922)
    Rich Men's Wives (Preferred, 1922)
    Thorns and Orange Blossoms (Preferred, 1922)
    The Hero (Preferred, 1923)
    Poor Men's Wives (Preferred, 1923)
    Daughters of the Rich (B.P. Schulberg, 1923)

Facing page: Clark Gable, Carol Ann Beery, and Wallace Beery
with producer Irving Thalberg (standing) and Tay Garnett on the set
of China Seas (MGM, 1935).

Mothers-In-Law (Preferred, 1923)
Maytime (Preferred, 1923)
Poisoned Paradise: The Forbidden Story of Monte Carlo (Preferred, 1924)
The Breath of Scandal (B. P. Schulberg, 1924)
Wine (Univ., 1924)
White Man (B. P. Schulberg, 1924)
The Triflers (B. P. Schulberg, 1924)
The Parasite (B. P. Schulberg, 1925)
The Boomerang (B. P. Schulberg, 1925)
Faint Perfume (B. P. Schulberg, 1925)
Parisian Love (B. P. Schulberg, 1925)
Pleasures of the Rich (Renown, 1926)
Out of the Storm (Tiffany, 1926)
Sin Cargo (Tiffany, 1926)
Lost at Sea (Tiffany, 1926)
That Model from Paris (Tiffany, 1926)
Beauty Shoppers (Tiffany, 1927)
Streets of Shanghai (Tiffany-Stahl, 1927)
Fashion Madness (Col., 1928)
Darkened Rooms (Par., 1929)
Slightly Scarlet (Par., 1930) (with Edwin H. Knopf)
Shadow of the Law (Par., 1930)
The Virtuous Sin (Par., 1930) (with George Cukor)
Amor Audaz [Spanish version of Slightly Scarlet] (Par., 1930) (with A. Washington Pezet)
L'Enigmatique Monsieur Parkes [French version of Slightly Scarlet] (Par., 1930)
The Lawyer's Secret (Par., 1931) (with Max Marcin)
Silence (Par., 1931) (with Max Marcin)
The Strange Case of Clara Deane (Par., 1932) (with Max Marcin)
Forgotten Commandments (Par., 1932) (with William Schorr)
Gambling Ship (Par., 1933) (with Max Marcin)
Espérame (French, 1932)
Melodia de Arrabal (French, 1933)
Irish, Perdue et Retrouvée (Par., 1933)
Topaza (Par., 1933)
Cuesta Abajo (Par., 1934)
Fedora (Par., 1934)
El Tango en Broadway (Par., 1934)
The Last Outpost (Par., 1935) (with Charles Barton)
The Old Racket (Grand National, 1937)
Bank Alarm (Grand National, 1937)
The Sunset Strip Case [High Explosive] (Grand National, 1938)
Juan Palido (Mexican, 1938)
La Immaculada (UA, 1939)
Tell Your Children [The Burning Question] [Reefer Madness] (1939)
Murder on the Yukon (Mon., 1940)
Stolen Paradise (Mon., 1941)

GERING, MARION, b. June 9, 1901, Rostoff on Don, Russia.
I Take This Woman (Par., 1931)
Ladies of the Big House (Par., 1932)
The Devil and the Deep (Par., 1932)
Madame Butterfly (Par., 1932)
Pick-Up (Par., 1933)
Jennie Gerhardt (Par., 1933)
A Good Dame (Par., 1934) •
Thirty Day Princess (Par., 1934)
Ready for Love (Par., 1934)
Rumba (Par., 1935)
Rose of the Rancho (Par., 1936)
Lady of Secrets (Col., 1936)
Thunder in the City (Col., 1937)
She Married an Artist (Col., 1938)
Sarumba (Eagle Lion, 1950) (also co-producer)

GIRARD, BERNARD.
The Green-Eyed Blonde (WB, 1957)
Ride Out for Revenge (UA, 1958)
As Young as We Are (Par., 1958)
The Party Crashers (Par., 1958) (also script)
Dead Heat on a Merry-Go-Round (Col., 1966) (also script)
The Mad Room (Col., 1967)
Hunters Are for Killing (CBS-TV, 1970)
The Happiness Cage (Cin., 1972)
Gone With the West [Man Without Mercy] (Cine Globe, 1973)

GODFREY, PETER, b. Oct. 16, 1899, London.
The Lone Wolf Spy Hunt (Col., 1939)
Unexpected Uncle (RKO, 1941)
Highway by Night (RKO, 1942)
Make Your Own Bed (WB, 1944)
Christmas in Connecticut (WB, 1945)
Hotel Berlin (WB, 1945)
One More Tomorrow (WB, 1946)
Cry Wolf (WB, 1947)
The Two Mrs. Carrolls (WB, 1947)
Escape Me Never (WB, 1947)
That Hagen Girl (WB, 1947)
The Woman in White (WB, 1948)
The Decision of Christopher Blake (WB, 1948)
The Girl from Jones Beach (WB, 1949)
One Last Fling (WB, 1949)
Barricade (WB, 1950)
The Great Jewel Robbery (WB, 1950)
He's a Cockeyed Wonder (Col., 1950)
One Big Affair (UA, 1952)
One Life (20th, 1955)
Please Murder Me (Distributors Corp. of America, 1956)

GOLDBECK, WILLIS, b. 1900, New York City.
  Dr. Gillespie's New Assistant (MGM, 1942)
  Dr. Gillespie's Criminal Case (MGM, 1943)
  Rationing (MGM, 1944)
  Three Men in White (MGM, 1944)
  Between Two Women (MGM, 1944)
  She Went to the Races (MGM, 1945)
  Love Laughs at Andy Hardy (MGM, 1946)
  Dark Delusion (MGM, 1947)
  Johnny Holiday (UA, 1949)
  Ten Tall Men (Col., 1951) (also co-story)

GOLDSTONE, JAMES, b. June 8, 1931, Los Angeles.
  Jigsaw (Univ., 1968)
  A Man Called Gannon (Univ., 1969)
  Winning (Univ., 1969)
  Brother John (Col., 1971)
  Red Sky at Morning (Univ., 1971)
  The Gang That Couldn't Shoot Straight (MGM, 1971)
  They Only Kill Their Masters (MGM, 1972)

GOODWINS, LESLIE, b. Sept. 17, 1889, London; d. Jan. 8, 1970.
  With Love and Kisses (Conn, 1936)
  Headline Crasher (Conn, 1937)
  Anything for a Thrill (Conn, 1937)
  Young Dynamite (Conn, 1937)
  Mr. Doodle Kicks Off (RKO, 1938)
  Crime Ring (RKO, 1938)
  Fugitives for a Night (RKO, 1938)
  Almost a Gentleman (RKO, 1938)
  The Day the Bookies Wept (RKO, 1939)
  Sued for Libel (RKO, 1938)
  Tarnished Angels (RKO, 1938)
  Glamor Boy (RKO, 1938)
  The Girl from Mexico (RKO, 1939)
  Mexican Spitfire (RKO, 1939)
  Mexican Spitfire Out West (RKO, 1940)
  Pop Always Pays (RKO, 1940)
  They Met in Argentina (RKO, 1941)
  Parachute Battalion (RKO, 1941)
  Mexican Spitfire's Baby (RKO, 1942)
  Mexican Spitfire at Sea (RKO, 1942)
  Mexican Spitfire Sees a Ghost (RKO, 1942)
  Mexican Spitfire's Elephant (RKO, 1942)
  Silver Skates (RKO, 1943)
  Ladies' Day (RKO, 1943)
  Mexican Spitfire's Blessed Event (RKO, 1943)
  The Adventures of a Rookie (RKO, 1943)
  Rookies in Burma (RKO, 1943)
  Casanova in Burlesque (Rep., 1944)
  The Singing Sheriff (Univ., 1944)

Goin' to Town (RKO, 1944)
Hi, Beautiful (Univ., 1944)
Murder in the Blue Room (Univ., 1944)
The Mummy's Curse (Univ., 1945)
An Angel Comes to Brooklyn (Rep., 1945)
I'll Tell the World (Univ., 1945)
What a Blonde (RKO, 1945)
Radio Stars on the Air (RKO, 1945)
Vacation in Reno (RKO, 1946)
Riverboat Rhythm (RKO, 1946)
Genius at Work (RKO, 1946)
The Lone Wolf in London (Col., 1947)
Dragnet (Screen Guild, 1947)
Gold Fever (Mon., 1952)
Fireman Save My Child (Univ., 1954)
Paris Follies of 1956 (AA, 1955)
The Go-Getter (Pacific-Globe, 1955) (with Leigh Jason)
Tammy and the Millionaire (Univ., 1967) (with Sidney Miller, Ezra Stone)

GORDON, BERT I., b. Sept. 24, 1922, Kenosha, Wisc.
King Dinosaur (Lip., 1955) (also co-producer)
Beginning of the End (Rep., 1957) (also producer)
The Amazing Colossal Man (AIP, 1957) (also producer, co-script, special effects)
The Cyclops (AA, 1957) (also producer, script)
Attack of the Puppet People (AIP, 1958) (also producer, story, special effects)
War of the Colossal Beast (AIP, 1958) (also producer, story, special effects)
The Spider (AIP, 1958) (also producer, story, special effects)
Tormented (AA, 1960) (also producer, story, co-special effects)
The Magic Sword (UA, 1962) (also producer)
Village of the Giants (Emb., 1965) (also producer)
Picture Mommy Dead (Emb., 1966) (also producer)
How to Succeed With Sex (Medford, 1970) (also script)
Necromancy (Zenith International, 1971) (also producer, script)
The Mad Bomber (Cinemation, 1973)

GORDON, MICHAEL, b. Sept. 6, 1909, Baltimore, Md.
Crime Doctor (Col., 1943)
One Dangerous Night (Col., 1943)
The Web (Univ., 1947)
Another Part of the Forest (Univ., 1948)
An Act of Murder (Univ., 1948)
The Lady Gambles (Univ., 1949)
Woman in Hiding (Univ., 1949)
Cyrano de Bergerac (UA, 1950)
I Can Get It for You Wholesale (20th, 1951)
The Secret of Convict Lake (20th, 1951)

Wherever She Goes (Mayer-Kingsley, 1953) (also script)
Pillow Talk (Univ., 1959)
Portrait in Black (Univ., 1960)
Boys' Night Out (MGM, 1962)
For Love or Money (Univ., 1963)
Move Over, Darling (20th, 1963)
A Very Special Favor (Univ., 1965)
Texas Across the River (Univ., 1966)
The Impossible Years (MGM, 1968)
How Do I Love Thee? (Cin., 1970)

GOULDING, EDMUND, b. March 30, 1891, London; d. Dec. 24,
    1959.
Sun Up (MGM, 1925) (also producer, script)
Sally, Irene and Mary (MGM, 1925) (also producer, script)
Paris (MGM, 1926) (also script)
Women Love Diamonds (MGM, 1927) (also producer, story)
Love (MGM, 1928) (also producer)
The Trespasser (UA, 1929) (also producer, script, song)
The Devil's Holiday (Par., 1930) (also story, script, music)
Paramount on Parade (Par., 1930) (with Dorothy Arzner, Otto
    Brower, Victor Heerman, Edwin Knopf, Rowland V. Lee,
    Ernst Lubitsch, Lothar Mendes, Victor Schertzinger, A. Ed-
    ward Sutherland)
Reaching for the Moon (UA, 1931) (also co-script)
The Night Angel (Par., 1931) (also script)
Blondie of the Follies (MGM, 1932)
Grand Hotel (MGM, 1932)
Riptide (MGM, 1934) (also script)
The Flame Within (MGM, 1935) (also script)
That Certain Woman (WB, 1937) (also script)
The Dawn Patrol (WB, 1938)
White Banners (WB, 1938)
Dark Victory (WB, 1939)
The Old Maid (WB, 1939)
We Are Not Alone (WB, 1939)
'Til We Meet Again (WB, 1940)
The Great Lie (WB, 1941)
The Constant Nymph (WB, 1943)
Claudia (20th, 1943)
Forever and a Day (RKO, 1943) (with Rene Clair, Cedric Hard-
    wicke, Frank Lloyd, Victor Saville, Robert Stevenson, Her-
    bert Wilcox) (also co-producer)
Of Human Bondage (WB, 1946)
The Razor's Edge (20th, 1946)
Nightmare Alley (20th, 1947)
Everybody Does It (20th, 1949)
Mister 880 (20th, 1950)

Facing page: Charles Coburn with Edmund Goulding (right) on the
set of The Constant Nymph (WB, 1943).

We're Not Married (20th, 1952)
Down Among the Sheltering Palms (20th, 1952)
Teenage Rebel (20th, 1956)
Mardi Gras (20th, 1958)

GRAUMAN, WALTER E., b. 1922.
Lady in a Cage (Par., 1964)
633 Squadron (UA, 1964)
A Rage to Live (UA, 1965)
I Deal in Danger (20th, 1966)
Daughter of the Mind (ABC-TV, 1969) (also producer)
The Last Escape (UA, 1970)
The Old Man Who Cried Wolf (ABC-TV, 1970) (also producer)
Crowhaven Farm (ABC-TV, 1970) (also producer)
The Forgotten Man (ABC-TV, 1971) (also executive producer)
Paper Man (CBS-TV, 1971) (also executive producer)
They Called it Murder (NBC-TV, 1971) (also producer)
Dead Men Tell No Tales (CBS-TV, 1971) (also executive producer)

Olivia de Havilland and dress designer Edith Head with Walter Grauman discussing <u>Lady in a Cage</u> (Par., 1964).

GREEN, ALFRED E. , b. 1889, Perris, Calif.; d. Sept. 4, 1960.
   The Lad and the Lion (Selig, 1917)
   The Princess of Patches (Selig, 1917)
   Lost and Found (Selig, 1917)
   Little Lost Sister (Selig, 1917)
   The Web of Chance (Fox, 1919)
   A Double-Dyed Deceiver (Goldwyn, 1920)
   Silk Husbands and Calico Wives (Equity, 1920)
   Just Out of College (Goldwyn, 1921)
   The Man Who Had Everything (Goldwyn, 1921)
   Through the Back Door (UA, 1921) (with Jack Pickford)
   Little Lord Fauntleroy (UA, 1921) (with Jack Pickford)
   The Ghost Breaker (Par. , 1922)
   The Bachelor Daddy (Par. , 1922)
   Come on Over (Goldwyn, 1922)
   Our Leading Citizen (Par. , 1922)
   The Man Who Saw Tomorrow (Par. , 1922)
   Back Home and Broke (Par. , 1922)
   The Ne'er-Do-Well (Par. , 1923)
   Woman-Proof (Par. , 1923)
   Pied Piper Malone (Par. , 1924)
   In Hollywood With Potash and Perlmutter (FN, 1924)
   Inez from Hollywood (FN, 1924)
   Sally (FN, 1925)
   The Man Who Found Himself (Par. , 1925)
   The Talker
   The Girl from Montmartre (FN, 1926)
   Irene (FN, 1926)
   Ella Cinders (FN, 1926)
   It Must Be Love (FN, 1926)
   Ladies at Play (FN, 1926)
   The Auctioneer (Fox, 1927)
   Is Zat So? (Fox, 1927)
   2 Girls Wanted (Fox, 1927)
   Come to My House (Fox, 1927)
   Honor Bound (Fox, 1928)
   Making the Grade (Fox, 1929)
   Disraeli (WB, 1929)
   The Green Goddess (WB, 1930)
   The Man from Blankley's (WB, 1930)
   Old English (WB, 1930)
   Sweet Kitty Bellairs (WB, 1930)
   Smart Money (WB, 1931)
   Men of the Sky (FN, 1931)
   The Road to Singapore (WB, 1931)
   Union Depot (FN, 1932)
   It's Tough to Be Famous (FN, 1932)
   The Rich are Always With Us (FN, 1932)
   The Dark Horse (FN, 1932)
   Silver Dollar (FN, 1932)
   Parachute Jumper (WB, 1933)
   The Narrow Corner (WB, 1933)
   Baby Face (WB, 1933)

I Loved a Woman (FN, 1933)
As the Earth Turns (WB, 1934)
Dark Hazard (FN, 1934)
Side Streets (FN, 1934)
Housewife (WB, 1934)
The Merry Frinks (FN, 1934)
Gentlemen Are Born (FN, 1934)
A Lost Lady (FN, 1935)
Sweet Music (WB, 1935)
The Girl from Tenth Avenue (FN, 1935)
Here's to Romance (Fox, 1935)
The Goose and the Gander (WB, 1935)
Dangerous (WB, 1935)
Colleen (WB, 1936)
The Golden Arrow (FN, 1936)
They Met in a Taxi (Col., 1936)
Two in a Crowd (Univ., 1936)
More Than a Secretary (Col., 1936)
Let's Get Married (Col., 1937)
The League of Frightened Men (Col., 1937)
Mr. Dodd Takes the Air (WB, 1937)
Thoroughbreds Don't Cry (MGM, 1937)
The Duke of West Point (UA, 1938)
Ride a Crooked Mile (Par., 1938)
King of the Turf (UA, 1939)
The Gracie Allen Murder Case (Par., 1939)
20,000 Men a Year (20th, 1939)
Shooting High (20th, 1940)
Flowing Gold (WB, 1940)
East of the River (WB, 1940)
Adventure in Washington (Col., 1941)
Badlands of Dakota (Univ., 1941)
The Mayor of 44th Street (RKO, 1942)
Meet the Stewarts (Col., 1942)
Appointment in Berlin (Col., 1943)
There's Something About a Soldier (Col., 1943)
Mr. Winkle Goes to War (Col., 1944)
Strange Affair (Col., 1944)
A Thousand and One Nights (Col., 1945)
The Jolson Story (Col., 1946)
Tars and Spars (Col., 1946)
Copacabana (UA, 1947)
The Fabulous Dorseys (UA, 1947)
Four Faces West (UA, 1948)
The Girl from Manhattan (UA, 1948)
Cover-Up (UA, 1949)
Sierra (Univ., 1950)
The Jackie Robinson Story (Eagle Lion, 1951)
Two Gals and a Guy (UA, 1951
Invasion U.S.A. (Col., 1952)
The Eddie Cantor Story (WB, 1953)
Paris Model (Col., 1953)
Top Banana (UA, 1954)

GREEN, GUY, b. 1913, Somerset, Eng.
  River Beat (Lip. , 1954)
  Portrait of Alison (Rank, 1955)
  Lost (Rank, 1956)
  House of Secrets (Rank, 1956)
  The Snorkel (Col. , 1957)
  Sea of Sand (Rank, 1958)
  S.O.S. Pacific (Rank, 1959)
  The Angry Silence (Valiant, 1960)
  The Mark (Continental, 1961)
  Light in the Piazza (MGM, 1962)
  Diamond Head (Col. , 1963)
  A Patch of Blue (MGM, 1965) (also script)
  Pretty Polly (Rank, 1967)
  The Magus (20th, 1969)
  A Walk in the Spring Rain (Col. , 1970)

GRIES, THOMAS S. , b. Dec. 20, 1922, Chicago.
  Will Penny (Par. , 1969) (also script)
  100 Rifles (20th, 1969) (also co-script)
  Number One (UA, 1969)
  The Hawaiians (UA, 1970)
  Fools (Cin. , 1970)
  Journey Through Rosebud (GSF, 1971)
  Lady Ice (National General, 1973)

GRIFFITH, D.W. (David Wark Griffith), b. Jan. 22, 1875, Crest-
    wood, Ky.; d. July 23, 1948.
  Judith of Bethulia (Artcraft, 1913)
  The Battle of the Sexes (Mutual, 1914)
  The Escape (Mutual, 1914)
  Home, Sweet, Home (Mutual, 1914)
  The Avenging Conscience (Mutual, 1914)
  The Birth of a Nation (Mutual, 1915) (also co-script)
  Intolerance (Triangle, 1916) (also co-script)
  Hearts of the World (Artcraft, 1918) (also producer, script)
  The Great Love (Artcraft, 1918) (also producer, script)
  A Romance of Happy Valley (Artcraft, 1919) (also producer,
    script)
  The Greatest Thing in Life (Artcraft, 1919 (also producer,
    script)
  The Girl Who Stayed at Home (Artcraft, 1919) (also producer)
  Broken Blossoms (UA, 1919) (also producer, script, co-music)
  True Heart Susie (Artcraft, 1919) (also producer)
  Scarlet Days (Artcraft, 1919) (also producer)
  The Greatest Question (Associated FN, 1919) (also producer)
  The Idol Dancer (Associated FN, 1920) (also producer)
  The Love Flower (Associated FN, 1920) (also producer)
  Way Down East (UA, 1920) (also producer)
  Dream Street (UA, 1921) (also producer, script)
  Orphans of the Storm (UA, 1922) (also script)

One Exciting Night (UA, 1922) (also script)
The White Rose (UA, 1923) (also script)
America (UA, 1924) (also from play)
Isn't Life Wonderful (UA, 1924)
Sally of the Sawdust (UA, 1925)
That Royale Girl (Par., 1926)
The Sorrows of Satan (Par., 1926)
Drums of Love (UA, 1928)
The Battle of the Sexes (UA, 1928)
Lady of the Pavements (UA, 1929)
Abraham Lincoln (UA, 1930)
The Struggle (UA, 1931) (also producer, co-music)
One Million B.C. (UA, 1940) (uncredited, with Hal Roach, Hal
  Roach, Jr.)

GRIFFITH, EDWARD H., b. Aug. 23, 1894, Lynchburg, Va.
The Awakening of Ruth (Edison Perfection, 1917)
The Law of the North (Edison, 1917)
Fit to Win (U.S. Public Service, 1919)
The End of the Road (Edison, 1919)
The Garter Girl (Vitagraph, 1920)
Bab's Candidate (Vitagraph, 1920)
The Vice of Fools (Vitagraph, 1920)
Scrambled Wives (Associated FN, 1921)
The Land of Hope (Realart, 1921)
If Women Only Knew (Robertson-Cole, 1921)
Dawn of the East (Par., 1921)
Free Air (W.W. Hodkinson, 1922)
The Go-Getter (Par., 1923)
Sea Raiders (Maritime, 1923)
Unseeing Eyes (Goldwyn, 1923)
Week-End Husbands (Equity, 1924)
Another Scandal (W.W. Hodkinson, 1924)
Bad Company (Associated Exhibitors, 1925)
Headlines (Associated Exhibitors, 1925)
White Mice (Associated Exhibitors, 1926)
Atta Boy (Pathé, 1926)
The Price of Honor (Col., 1927)
Afraid to Love (Par., 1927)
Alias the Lone Wolf (Col., 1927)
The Opening Night (Col., 1927)
Hold 'Em Yale! (Pathé, 1928)
Captain Swagger (Pathé, 1928)
Love Overnight (Pathé, 1928)
The Shady Lady (Pathé, 1929)
Paris Pound (Pathé, 1929)
Rich People (Pathé, 1929)
Holiday (Pathé, 1930)
Rebound (Pathé, 1931)
Lady With a Past (RKO, 1932)
The Animal Kingdom (RKO, 1933)
Another Language (RKO, 1933)

Susan Hayward with Edward H. Griffith (left) and makeup man between scenes of <u>Young and Willing</u> (UA, 1943).

Biography of a Bachelor Girl (MGM, 1935)
No More Ladies (MGM, 1935)
Next Time We Love (Univ. , 1936)
Ladies in Love (20th, 1936)
Cafe Metropole (20th, 1937)
I'll Take Romance (Col. , 1937)
Cafe Society (Par. , 1939)

Honeymoon in Bali (Par., 1939)
Safari (Par., 1940)
Virginia (Par., 1941)
One Night in Lisbon (Par., 1941)
Bahama Passage (Par., 1941)
Young and Willing (UA, 1943) (also producer)
The Sky's the Limit (RKO, 1943)
Perilous Holiday (Col., 1946)

GRINDE, NICK [NICHOLAS] (Harry A. Grinde), b. Jan. 12, 1894,
    Madison, Wis.
Beyond the Sierras (MGM, 1928)
Riders of the Dark (MGM, 1928)
The Desert Rider (MGM, 1929)
Morgan's Last Raid (MGM, 1929)
The Bishop Murder Case (MGM, 1930)
Good News (MGM, 1930)
Remote Control (MGM, 1930) (with Malcolm St. Clair)
Wu-Li-Chang [Spanish version of Mr. Wu] (MGM, 1930)
This Modern Age (MGM, 1931)
Shopworn (Col., 1932)
Vanity Street (Col., 1932)
Border Brigands (Univ., 1935)
Stone of Silver Creek (Univ., 1935)
Ladies Crave Excitement (Mascot, 1935)
Jailbreak (WB, 1936)
Public Enemy's Wife (WB, 1936)
Fugitive in the Sky (WB, 1937)
The Captain's Kid (WB, 1937)
Public Wedding (WB, 1937)
White Bondage (WB, 1937)
Love Is on the Air (FN, 1937)
Exiled to Shanghai (Rep., 1937)
Down in Arkansaw (Rep., 1938)
Federal Man-Hunt (Rep., 1939)
King of Chinatown (Par., 1939)
Million Dollar Legs (Par., 1939)
The Man They Could Not Hang (Col., 1939)
A Woman Is the Judge (Col., 1939)
Scandal Sheet (Col., 1939)
Convicted Woman (Col., 1940)
The Man With Nine Lives (Col., 1940)
Men Without Souls (Col., 1940)
Girls of the Road (Col., 1940)
Before I Hang (Col., 1940)
Friendly Neighbors (Rep., 1940)
Mountain Moonlight (Rep., 1941)
The Girl from Alaska (Rep., 1942)
Hitler--Dead or Alive (PRC, 1943)
Road to Alcatraz (Rep., 1945)

GRISSEL, WALLACE A., b. Sept. 3, 1904, Hounslow, Eng.
  Haunted Harbor* (Rep., 1944) (with Spencer Gordon Bennet)
  The Tiger Woman* (Rep., 1944) (with Spencer Gordon Bennet)
  Zorro's Black Whip* (Rep., 1944) (with Spencer Gordon Ben-
     net)
  Marshal of Reno (Rep., 1944)
  Vigilantes of Dodge City (Rep., 1944)
  Wanderer of the Wasteland (RKO, 1945) (with Edward Killy)
  Corpus Christi Bandits (Rep., 1945)
  Federal Operator 99* (Rep., 1945) (with Spencer Gordon Ben-
     net)
  Manhunt of Mystery Island* (Rep., 1945) (with Spencer Gordon
     Bennet, Yakima Canutt)
  Who's Guilty?* (Col., 1945) (with Howard Bretherton)
  Wild Horse Mesa (RKO, 1947)
  Western Heritage (RKO, 1948)
  Captain Video* (Col., 1951) (with Spencer Gordon Bennet)
  King of the Congo* (Col., 1952) (with Spencer Gordon Bennet)
  A Yank in Indo-China (Col., 1952)

                              H

HAAS, CHARLES, b. 1913, Chicago.
  Star in the Dust (Univ., 1955)
  Showdown at Abilene (Univ., 1955)
  Screaming Eagles (Univ., 1955)
  Summer Love (Univ., 1957)
  Wild Heritage (Univ., 1958)
  The Beat Generation (MGM, 1959)
  The Big Operator (MGM, 1959)
  Girl's Town (MGM, 1959)
  Platinum High School (MGM, 1960)

HAAS, HUGO, b. Feb. 19, 1901, Brno, Czech.; d. Dec., 1968.
  Velbloud Uchem Jehly (Hungarian, 1937) (with Otakar Vavra)
     (also co-script, actor)
  Devcata, Nedejts Se! (Hungarian, 1937) (also co-story, co-
     script, actor)
  Kvocna (Hungarian, 1937) (also co-script, co-songs)
  Bila Nemoc (Hungarian, 1937) (also script, actor)
  Co Se Septa (Hungarian, 1938) (also story, script, actor)
  Pickup (Col., 1951) (also producer, co-script, actor)
  Girl on the Bridge (20th, 1951) (also producer, script, actor)
  Strange Fascination (Col., 1952) (also producer, actor)
  One Girl's Confession (Col., 1953) (also producer, actor)
  Bait (Col., 1954) (also producer, actor)
  The Other Woman (20th, 1954) (also producer, actor)
  Thy Neighbor's Daughter [Thy Neighbor's Wife] (20th, 1955)
     (also producer, actor)
  Hold Back Tomorrow (Univ., 1955) (also producer, script,
     actor)

Edge of Hell (Univ., 1956) (also producer, actor)
Hit and Run (UA, 1957) (also producer, script, actor)
Lizzie (MGM, 1957) (also actor)
Born to Be Loved (Univ., 1959) (also producer, actor)
Night of the Quarter Moon (MGM, 1959) (also actor)
Paradise Alley [Stars in Your Backyard] (Astor, 1962) (also
    producer, script, actor)

HALL, ALEXANDER, b. 1894, Boston; d. July 30, 1968.
Sinners in the Sun (Par., 1932)
Madame Racketeer (Par., 1932) (with Harry Wagstaff Gribble)
The Girl in 419 (Par., 1933) (with George Sommes)
Midnight Club (Par., 1933) (with George Sommes)
Torch Singer (Par., 1933) (with George Sommes)
Miss Fane's Baby Is Stolen (Par., 1934)
Little Miss Marker (Par., 1934)
Pursuit of Happiness (Par., 1934)
Limehouse Blues (Par., 1934)
Goin' to Town (Par., 1935)
Annapolis Farewell (Par., 1935)
Give Us This Night (Par., 1936)
Yours for the Asking (Par., 1936)
Exclusive (Par., 1937)
There's Always a Woman (Col., 1938)
I Am the Law (Col., 1938)
There's That Woman Again (Col., 1938)
The Lady's from Kentucky (Par., 1939)
Good Girls Go to Paris (Col., 1939)
The Amazing Mr. Williams (Col., 1939)
He Stayed for Breakfast (Col., 1940)
The Doctor Takes a Wife (Col., 1940)
This Thing Called Love (Col., 1941)
Here Comes Mr. Jordan (Col., 1941)
Bedtime Story (Col., 1941)
They All Kissed the Bride (Col., 1942)
My Sister Eileen (Col., 1942)
The Heavenly Body (MGM, 1943)
Once Upon a Time (Col., 1944)
She Wouldn't Say Yes (Col., 1945)
Down to Earth (Col., 1947)
The Great Lover (Par., 1949)
Love That Brute (20th, 1950)
Louisa (Univ., 1950)
Up Front (Univ., 1951)
Because You're Mine (MGM, 1952)

HALLER, DANIEL, b. 1929, Los Angeles.
Die, Monster, Die (AIP, 1965)
Devil's Angels (AIP, 1967)
The Wild Racers (AIP, 1968)
Paddy (AA, 1970)
Pieces of Dreams (UA, 1970)

HALPERIN, VICTOR H. (Victor Hugo Halperin), b. Aug. 24, 1895,
    Chicago.
    Greater Than Marriage (Vitagraph, 1924) (also script)
    When a Girl Loves (Associated Exhibitors, 1924) (also pro-
        ducer, script)
    The Unknown Lover (Vitagraph, 1925) (also script)
    School for Wives (Vitagraph, 1925) (also script)
    In Borrowed Plumes (Arrow, 1926)
    Dance Magic (FN, 1927)
    Party Girl (Tiffany, 1930)
    Ex-Flame (Tiffany, 1930)
    White Zombie (UA, 1932)
    Supernatural (Par., 1933)
    I Conquer the Sea (Academy, 1936)
    Revolt of the Zombies (Academy, 1936)
    Nation Aflame (Treasure, 1937) (also co-producer)
    Torture Ship (PRC, 1939)
    Buried Alive (PRC, 1940)
    Girl's Town (PRC, 1942)

HARRINGTON, CURTIS, b. Sept. 17, 1928, Los Angeles.
    Night Tide (AIP, 1963) (also script)
    Queen of Blood [Planet of Blood] [Cosmonauts on Venus] (AIP,
        1966) (also script)
    Games (Univ., 1967) (also co-story)
    How Awful About Allan (ABC-TV, 1970)
    What's the Matter With Helen? (UA, 1971)
    Who Slew Auntie Roo? (AIP, 1971)
    The Killing Kind (Media Cinema, 1973)

HART, HARVEY, b. 1928, Toronto.
    Bus Riley's Back in Town (Univ., 1964)
    The Dark Intruder (Univ., 1965)
    Sullivan's Empire (Univ., 1967) (with Thomas Carr)
    The Sweet Ride (20th, 1968)
    The Young Lawyers (ABC-TV, 1969)
    Fortune and Men's Eyes (MGM, 1971)
    Mahoney's Estate (NBC-TV, 1972)
    The Pyx (Cin., 1973)

HARTMAN, DON (Samuel Donald Hartman), b. Nov. 18, 1900,
    Brooklyn, N.Y.; d. March 23, 1958.
    It Had to Be You (Col., 1947) (with Rudolph Mate) (also pro-
        ducer, script)
    Every Girl Should Be Married (RKO, 1948) (also producer, co-
        script)
    Holiday Affair (RKO, 1949) (also producer)
    Mr. Imperium (MGM, 1951) (also co-script)
    It's a Big Country (MGM, 1951) (with Clarence Brown, John
        Sturges, Richard Thorpe, Charles Vidor, Don Weis, William
        Wellman)

HASKIN, BYRON, b. 1899, Portland, Ore.
  Ginsberg the Great (WB, 1927)
  The Siren (Col., 1927)
  I Walk Alone (Par., 1947)
  Man-Eater of Kumaon (Univ., 1948)
  Too Late for Tears (UA, 1949)
  Treasure Island (RKO, 1950)
  Tarzan's Peril (RKO, 1951)
  Silver City (Univ., 1951)
  Warpath (Par., 1951)
  Denver & Rio Grande (Par., 1952)
  His Majesty O'Keefe (WB, 1953)
  The War of the Worlds (Par., 1953)
  The Naked Jungle (Par., 1954)
  Long John Silver (Distributors Corp. of America, 1954)
  Conquest of Space (Par., 1955)
  The First Texan (AA, 1956)
  The Boss (UA, 1956)
  From the Earth to the Moon (WB, 1958)
  The Little Savage (20th, 1959)
  Jet Over the Atlantic (Intercontinent Releasing, 1959)
  September Storm (20th, 1960)
  Armored Command (AA, 1961)
  Captain Sinbad (MGM, 1963)
  Robinson Crusoe on Mars (Par., 1964)
  The Power (MGM, 1968) (with George Pal)

HATHAWAY, HENRY, b. March 13, 1898, Sacramento, Calif.
  Wild Horse Mesa (Par., 1933)
  Heritage of the Desert (Par., 1933)
  Under the Tonto Rim (Par., 1933)
  Sunset Pass (Par., 1933)
  Man of the Forest (Par., 1933)
  To the Last Man (Par., 1933)
  The Thundering Herd (Par., 1934)
  Come on Marines! (Par., 1934)
  The Witching Hour (Par., 1934)
  The Last Round-Up (Par., 1934)
  Now and Forever (Par., 1934)
  The Lives of a Bengal Lancer (Par., 1935)
  Peter Ibbetson (Par., 1935)
  The Trail of the Lonesome Pine (Par., 1936)
  Go West, Young Man (Par., 1936)
  I Loved a Soldier (Par., 1936--unfinished)
  Souls at Sea (Par., 1937)
  Spawn of the North (Par., 1938)
  The Real Glory (UA, 1939)
  Johnny Apollo (20th, 1940)
  Brigham Young--Frontiersman (20th, 1940)
  The Shepherd of the Hills (Par., 1941)
  Sundown (UA, 1941)
  Ten Gentlemen from West Point (20th, 1942)

China Girl (20th, 1942)
Home in Indiana (20th, 1944)
Wing and a Prayer (20th, 1944)
Nob Hill (20th, 1945)
The House on 92nd Street (20th, 1945)
The Dark Corner (20th, 1946)
13 Rue Madeleine (20th, 1947)
Kiss of Death (20th, 1947)
Call Northside 777 (20th, 1948)
Down to the Sea in Ships (20th, 1949)
The Black Rose (20th, 1950)
Rawhide (20th, 1951)
Fourteen Hours (20th, 1951)
The Desert Fox (20th, 1951)
You're in the Navy Now (20th, 1951)
Diplomatic Courier (20th, 1952)
O'Henry's Full House (ep: "The Clarion Call") (20th, 1952)
Niagara (20th, 1953)
White Witch Doctor (20th, 1953)
Prince Valiant (20th, 1954)
Garden of Evil (20th, 1954)
The Racers (20th, 1955)
The Bottom of the Bottle (20th, 1956)
23 Paces to Baker Street (20th, 1956)
Legend of the Lost (UA, 1957) (also producer)
From Hell to Texas (20th, 1958)
Woman Obsessed (20th, 1959)
Seven Thieves (20th, 1960)
North to Alaska (20th, 1960) (also producer)
How the West Was Won (ep: "The Rivers," "The Plains,"
    "The Outlaws") (MGM, 1962)
Rampage (WB, 1963) (uncredited, with Phil Karlson)
Of Human Bondage (MGM, 1964) (with Ken Hughes)
Circus World (Par., 1964)
The Sons of Katie Elder (Par., 1965) (also producer)
Nevada Smith (Par., 1966) (also producer)
The Last Safari (Par., 1967) (also producer)
Five Card Stud (Par., 1968)
True Grit (Par., 1969)
Airport (Univ., 1970) (uncredited, with George Seaton)
Raid on Rommel (Univ., 1971)
Shootout (Univ., 1971)

HAWKS, HOWARD, b. May 30, 1896, Goshen, Ind.
    The Little Princess (Par., 1917 (uncredited, with Marshall
        Neilan)
    The Road to Glory (Fox, 1926) (also story)
    Fig Leaves (Fox, 1926) (also story)
    The Cradle Snatchers (Fox, 1927)
    Paid to Love (Fox, 1927)
    A Girl in Every Port (Fox, 1928) (also story)
    Fazil (Fox, 1928)

The Air Circus (Fox, 1928) (with Lewis Seiler)
Trent's Last Case (Fox, 1929)
The Dawn Patrol (FN, 1930) (also co-script)
The Criminal Code (Col., 1931)
The Crowd Roars (WB, 1932) (also story)
Scarface: Shame of a Nation (UA, 1932) (also co-producer)
Tiger Shark (FN, 1932)
Today We Live (MGM, 1933) (also producer)
The Prizefighter and the Lady (MGM, 1933) (uncredicted, with
   W.S. Van Dyke)
Viva Villa! (MGM, 1934) (uncredited, with Jack Conway)
Twentieth Century (Col., 1934) (also producer)
Barbary Coast (UA, 1935)
Ceiling Zero (FN, 1935)
The Road to Glory (20th, 1936)
Come and Get It (UA, 1936) (with William Wyler)
Bringing Up Baby (RKO, 1938) (also producer)
Only Angels Have Wings (Col., 1939) (also producer, story)
His Girl Friday (Col., 1940) (also producer)
Sergeant York (WB, 1941)
Ball of Fire (RKO, 1941)
Air Force (WB, 1943)
The Outlaw (RKO, 1943) (uncredited, with Howard Hughes)
   (made in 1940)
To Have and Have Not (WB, 1945) (also producer)
The Big Sleep (WB, 1946) (also producer)
Red River (UA, 1948) (also producer)
A Song Is Born (RKO, 1948)
I Was a Male War Bride (20th, 1949)
The Thing (RKO, 1951) (uncredited, with Christian Nyby)
The Big Sky (RKO, 1952) (also producer)
O. Henry's Full House (ep: "The Ransom of Red Chief") (20th,
   1952)
Monkey Business (20th, 1952)
Gentlemen Prefer Blondes (20th, 1953)
Land of the Pharaohs (WB, 1955) (also producer)
Rio Bravo (WB, 1959) (also producer)
Hatari! (Par., 1962) (also producer)
Man's Favorite Sport? (Univ., 1964) (also producer)
Red Line 7000 (Par., 1965) (also producer, co-script)
El Dorado (Par., 1966) (also producer)
Rio Lobo (National General, 1970) (also producer)

HECHT, BEN, b. Feb. 28, 1894, New York City; d. April 18, 1964.
   Crime Without Passion (Par., 1934) (with Charles MacArthur)
      (also co-producer, co-story, co-script)
   The Scoundrel (Par., 1935) (with Charles MacArthur) (also
      co-producer, co-story, co-script)

Facing page: Howard Hawks (seated, shirted) shooting Land of the
Pharaohs (WB, 1955).

Once in a Blue Moon (Par., 1936) (with Charles MacArthur)
(also co-producer, co-script)
Soak the Rich (Par., 1936) (with Charles MacArthur) (also co-
producer, co-story, co-script)
Angels over Broadway (Col., 1940) (with Lee Garmes) (also
producer, story, script)
Specter of the Rose (Rep., 1946) (also producer, story, script)

HEERMAN, VICTOR, b. Aug. 27, 1893, Surrey, Eng.
The Poor Simp (Selznick, 1920)
The Chicken in the Case (Select, 1921) (also story)
A Divorce of Convenience (Select, 1921) (also story)
My Boy (Associated FN, 1921)
John Smith (Select, 1922) (also story)
Love Is an Awful Thing (Selznick, 1922) (also story)
Rupert of Hentzau (Selznick, 1923)
Modern Matrimony (Selznick, 1923) (also story)
The Dangerous Maid (Associated FN, 1923)
The Confidence Man (Par., 1924)
Old Home Week (Par., 1925)
Irish Luck (Par., 1925)
For Wives Only (PDC, 1926)
Rubber Heels (Par., 1927)
Ladies Must Dress (Fox, 1927) (also story)
Love Hungry (Fox, 1928) (also co-story)
Personality (Col., 1930)
Paramount on Parade (Par., 1930) (with Dorothy Arzner, Otto
Brower, Edmund Goulding, Edwin Knopf, Rowland V. Lee,
Ernst Lubitsch, Lothar Mendes, Victor Schertzinger, A. Ed-
ward Sutherland, Frank Tuttle)
Animal Crackers (Par., 1930)
Sea Legs (Par., 1930)

HEISLER, STUART, b. 1894, Los Angeles.
Straight from the Shoulder (Par., 1936)
The Hurricane (UA, 1937) (uncredited, with John Ford)
The Biscuit Eater (Par., 1940)
The Monster and the Girl (Par., 1941)
Among the Living (Par., 1941)
The Remarkable Andrew (Par., 1942)
The Glass Key (Par., 1942)
Along Came Jones (RKO, 1945)
Blue Skies (Par., 1946)
Smash Up--the Story of a Woman (Univ., 1947)
Tulsa (Eagle Lion, 1949)
Tokyo Joe (Col., 1949)
Vendetta (RKO, 1950) (uncredited, with Mel Ferrer and uncred-
ited Howard Hughes, Max Ophuls, Preston Sturges)
Chain Lightning (WB, 1950)
Dallas (WB, 1950)
Storm Warning (WB, 1951)

Journey into Light (20th, 1951)
Island of Desire (UA, 1952)
The Star (20th, 1953)
Beachhead (UA, 1954)
This Is My Love (RKO, 1954)
I Died a Thousand Times (WB, 1955)
The Lone Ranger (WB, 1956)
The Burning Hills (WB, 1956)
Hitler (AA, 1962)

HENABERY, JOSEPH E., b. Omaha, Neb.
    Her Official Fathers (Triangle, 1917) (with Elmer Clifton)
    Say! Young Fellow (Artcraft, 1917)
    The Man from Painted Post (Artcraft, 1917)
    His Majesty, the American (UA, 1919)
    The Inferior Sex (Associated FN, 1920)
    Love Madness (W.W. Hodkinson, 1920)
    The Life of the Party (Par., 1920)
    The Fourteenth Man (Par., 1920)
    Brewster's Millions (Par., 1921)
    The Traveling Salesman (Par., 1921)
    Don't Call Me Little Girl (Par., 1921)
    Her Winning Way (Par., 1921)
    Moonlight and Honeysuckle (Realart, 1921)
    The Call of the North (Par., 1921)
    Her Own Money (Par., 1922)
    The Man Unconquerable (Par., 1922)
    While Satan Sleeps (Par., 1922)
    Missing Millions (Par., 1922)
    North of the Rio Grande (Par., 1922)
    Making a Man (Par., 1922)
    Sixty Cents an Hour (Par., 1923)
    The Tiger's Claw (Par., 1923)
    Stephen Steps Out (Par., 1923)
    A Gentleman of Leisure (Par., 1923)
    The Stranger (Par., 1924)
    The Guilty One (Par., 1924)
    A Sainted Evil (Par., 1924)
    Tongues of Flame (Par., 1924)
    Cobra (Par., 1925)
    The Pinch Hitter (Associated Exhibitors, 1925)
    The Broadway Boob (Associated Exhibitors, 1926)
    Meet the Prince (PDC, 1926)
    Shipwrecked (PDC, 1926)
    Play Safe (Pathé, 1927
    See You in Jail (FN, 1927)
    Lonesome Ladies (FN, 1927)
    Hellship Bronson (Lumas, 1928)
    Sailor's Wives (FN, 1928)
    United States Smith (Lumas, 1928)
    The River Woman (Lumas, 1928)
    The Quitter (Col., 1929)

Light Fingers (Col., 1929)
Clear the Decks (Univ.-Jewel, 1929)
Red Hot Speed (Univ.-Jewel, 1929)
The Love Trader (Tiffany, 1930) (also co-producer)
The Leather Burners (UA, 1943)

HENDERSON, DEL[L] (George Delbert Henderson), b. July 5, 1883,
    St. Thomas, Ontario; d. Dec. 4, 1956.
Divorcons (Biograph, 1915)
A Coney Island Princess (Par., 1916)
Rolling Stones (Par., 1916)
The Kiss (Par., 1916)
A Girl Like That (Par., 1917)
The Outcast (Empire Mutual, 1917)
The Runaway (Empire Mutual, 1917)
The Beautiful Adventure (Empire Mutual, 1917)
Please Help Emily (Empire Mutual, 1917)
Hitting the Trail (World, 1918)
The Golden Wall (World, 1918)
The Beloved Blackmailer (World, 1918)
Her Second Husband (Empire Mutual, 1918)
The Imposter (Empire Mutual, 1918)
By Hook or Crook (World, 1918)
The Road to France (World, 1918)
Courage for Two (World, 1919)
Hit or Miss (World, 1919)
Love in a Hurry (World, 1919)
The Social Pirate (World, 1919)
Three Green Eyes (World, 1919)
The Dead Line (Exclusive International, 1919)
The Shark (Fox, 1920)
The Servant Question (Select, 1920)
The Plunger (Fox, 1920)
Dynamite Allen (Fox, 1921)
Dead or Alive (Arrow, 1921)
The Girl from Porcupine (Arrow, 1921)
The Broken Silence (Arrow, 1922)
Sure Fire Flint (Mastodon, 1922)
Jacqueline, or Blazing Barriers (Arrow, 1923)
The Love Bandit (Vitagraph, 1924)
Gambling Wives (Arrow, 1924) (also for production company)
One Law for the Woman (Vitagraph, 1924)
Battling Brewster* (Rayart, 1924)
Defend Yourself (Ellbee, 1925)
Quick Change (Rayart, 1925) (also for production company)
Pursued (Ellbee, 1925)
Rough Stuff (Rayart, 1925) (also for production company)
The Bad Lands (Hunt Stromberg, 1925)
Accused (Independent, 1925)
The Pay Off (Ellbee, 1926)
The Rambling Ranger (Univ., 1927)

HENREID, PAUL (Paul George Julius von Henreid), b. Jan. 10,
     1908, Trieste, Italy.
     For Men Only (Lip., 1952) (also producer, actor)
     A Woman's Devotion (Rep., 1956) (also actor)
     Live Fast, Die Young (Univ., 1958)
     Girls on the Loose (Univ., 1958)
     Dead Ringer (WB-7 Arts, 1964)
     Ballad in Blue (Alsa, 1965)
     Blues for Lovers (20th, 1966) (also co-script)

HILL, GEORGE ROY, b. Dec. 20, 1922, Minneapolis, Minn.
     Period of Adjustment (MGM, 1962)
     Toys in the Attic (UA, 1963)
     The World of Henry Orient (UA, 1964)
     Hawaii (UA, 1966)
     Thoroughly Modern Millie (Univ., 1967)
     Butch Cassidy and the Sundance Kid (20th, 1969)
     Slaughterhouse Five (Univ., 1972)
     The Sting (Univ., 1973)

HILL, ROBERT F. (Bob Hill), b. April 14, 1886, Port Rohen,
     Ontario.
     The Great Radium Mystery* (Univ., 1919) (with Robert Road-
         well)
     The Flaming Disc* (Univ., 1920)
     The Adventures of Tarzan* (Weiss Bros., 1921)
     The Adventures of Robinson Crusoe* (Univ., 1922)
     The Radio King* (Univ., 1922)
     Around the World in 18 Days* (Univ., 1923) (with B. Reeves
         Eason)
     The Phantom Fortune* (Univ., 1923)
     The Social Buccaneer* (Univ., 1923)
     Crooked Alley (Univ., 1923) (also adaptation)
     His Mystery Girl (Univ., 1923)
     Shadows of the North (Univ., 1923)
     The Breathless Moment (Univ., 1924)
     The Dangerous Blonde (Univ., 1924)
     Dark Stairways (Univ., 1924)
     Excitement (Univ., 1924)
     Jack O'Clubs (Univ., 1924)
     Young Ideas (Univ., 1924)
     Idaho* (Pathé, 1925)
     Wild West* (Pathé, 1925)
     The Bar-C Mystery* (Pathé, 1926)
     The Stolen Ranch (Univ., 1926) (also story)
     Blazing Days (Univ., 1927) (also co-script)
     Hands Off (Univ., 1927) (also adaptation)
     Range Courage (Univ., 1927) (also adaptation)
     Blake of Scotland Yard* (Univ., 1927)
     The Return of the Riddle Rider* (Univ., 1927)
     Haunted Island* (Univ., 1928)

Life's Mockery (Chadwick, 1928)
A Million for Love (Sterling, 1928)
Melody Lane (Univ., 1929) (also co-adaptation)
Silks and Saddles (Univ., 1929)
Spell of the Circus* (Univ., 1931)
Cheyenne Kid (RKO, 1933)
Tarzan the Fearless (Principal, 1933)
Cowboy Holiday (Beacon, 1934)
Frontier Days (Spectrum, 1934)
Inside Information (Stage & Screen Productions, 1934)
A Demon for Trouble (Supreme, 1934)
Cyclone Ranger (Spectrum, 1935)
Texas Rambler (Spectrum, 1935)
Vanishing Riders (Spectrum, 1935)
The Rogue's Tavern (Puritan, 1936)
Too Much Beef (Grand National, 1936)
Prison Shadows (Victory, 1936)
Idaho Kid (Grand National, 1936)
Kelly of the Secret Service (Principal, 1936)
Shadow of Chinatown* (Victory, 1936)
West of Nevada (Colony, 1936)
Face in the Fog (Victory, 1936)
Rio Grande Romance (Victory, 1936)
Taming the Wild (Victory, 1936)
Blake of Scotland Yard* (Victory, 1937)
Million Dollar Racket (Victory, 1937)
Two Minutes to Play (Victory, 1937)
Whirlwind Horseman (Grand National, 1938)
Flash Gordon's Trip to Mars* (Univ., 1938)
Man's Country (Mon., 1938)
Flying Fists (Treo., 1938)
The Painted Trail (Mon., 1938)
Wild Horse Canyon (Mon., 1939)
Drifting Westward (Mon., 1939)
Overland Mail (Mon., 1939)
East Side Kids (Mon., 1940)
Wanderers of the West (Mon., 1941)

HILLER, ARTHUR, b. Nov. 22, 1923, Edmonton, Alberta, Canada.
The Careless Years (UA, 1957)
Miracle of the White Stallions (BV, 1963)
The Wheeler Dealers (MGM, 1963)
The Americanization of Emily (MGM, 1964)
Promise Her Anything (Par., 1966)
Penelope (MGM, 1966)
Tobruk (Univ., 1967)
The Tiger Makes Out (Col., 1967)
Popi (UA, 1968)
The Out-of-Towners (Par., 1970)
Love Story (Par., 1970)
Plaza Suite (Par., 1971)
Man of La Mancha (UA, 1972) (also producer)

Natalie Wood with Arthur Hiller discussing <u>Penelope</u> (MGM, 1966).

HILLYER, LAMBERT, b. July 8, 1895, Plymouth, Ind.
   An Even Break (Triangle, 1917) (also script)
   The Narrow Trail (Artcraft, 1917)
   Branding Broadway (Artcraft, 1918)
   Riddle Gawne (Artcraft, 1918)
   Breed of Men (Artcraft, 1919)
   John Petticoats (Artcraft, 1919)
   The Money Corral (Artcraft, 1919) (also co-script)
   The Poppy Girl's Husband (Artcraft, 1919)
   Wagon Tracks (Artcraft, 1919)
   Sand (Artcraft, 1919) (also script)
   The Toll Gate (Artcraft, 1920) (also co-script)
   The Testing Block (Artcraft, 1920)
   O'Malley of the Mounted (Artcraft, 1921) (also co-script)
   White Oak (Artcraft, 1921)
   Three Word Brand (Artcraft, 1921)
   The Man from Lost River (Goldwyn, 1921)
   The Whistle (Par., 1921)
   The Altar Stairs (Univ., 1922)
   Caught Bluffing (Univ., 1922)
   Travelin' On (Artcraft, 1922)
   Skin Deep (Associated FN, 1922)

The Super-Sex (American Releasing, 1922)
White Hands (FBO, 1922)
Eyes of the Forest (Fox, 1923)
The Lone Star Ranger (Fox, 1923) (also script)
Mile-A-Minute Romeo (Fox, 1923)
Scars of Jealousy (Associated FN, 1923)
The Shock (Univ., 1923)
The Spoilers (Goldwyn, 1923)
Temporary Marriage (Principal, 1923)
Barbara Frietchie (PDC, 1924)
Idle Tongues (FN, 1924)
Those Who Dance (FN, 1924)
I Want My Man (FN, 1925)
The Knockout (FN, 1925)
The Making of O'Malley (FN, 1925)
The Unguarded Hour (FN, 1925)
Her Second Chance (FN, 1926)
Miss Nobody (FN, 1926)
30 Below Zero (Fox, 1926)
Chain Lightning (Fox, 1927)
Hills of Peril (Fox, 1927)
The War Horse (Fox, 1927)
The Branded Sombrero (Fox, 1928)
Fleetwing (Fox, 1928)
Beau Bandit (RKO, 1930)
Hide-Out (Univ., 1930)
One Man's Law (Col., 1931) (also story, script)
South of the Rio Grande (Col., 1932)
The Fighting Fool (Col., 1932)
Born to Trouble (Col., 1932)
White Eagle (Col., 1932)
The Deadline (Col., 1932) (also story, script)
Hello Trouble (Col., 1932) (also producer, script)
The Forbidden Trail (Col., 1932)
The Sundown Rider (Col., 1932)
The California Trail (Col., 1933)
Police Car 17 (Col., 1933)
Unknown Valley (Col., 1933)
Before Midnight (Col., 1933)
Master of Men (Col., 1933)
The Fighting Code (Col., 1934)
Once to Every Woman (Col., 1934)
Most Precious Thing in Life (Col., 1934)
One Is Guilty (Col., 1934)
The Defense Rests (Col., 1934)
Against the Law (Col., 1934)
The Man Trailer (Col., 1934) (also story, script)
Men of the Night (Col., 1935) (also story, script)
Behind the Evidence (Col., 1935)
In Spite of Danger (Col., 1935)
Men of the Hour (Col., 1935)
The Awakening of Jim Burke (Col., 1935)
Superseed (Col., 1935)

Guard That Girl (Col., 1935) (also story, script)
Dangerous Waters (Univ., 1936)
The Invisible Ray (Univ., 1936)
Dracula's Daughter (Univ., 1936)
Girls Can Play (Col., 1937)
Speed to Spare (Col., 1937)
Gang Bullets (Mon., 1938)
My Old Kentucky Home (Mon., 1938)
All American Sweetheart (Col., 1938)
Women in Prison (Col., 1938)
Extortion (Col., 1938)
Should a Girl Marry? (Mon., 1939)
The Girl from Rio (Mon., 1939)
The Durango Kid (Col., 1940)
The Wildcat of Tucson (Rep., 1940)
Beyond the Sacramento (Rep., 1941)
The Medico of Painted Springs (Col., 1941)
The Pinto Kid (Col., 1941)
Thunder over the Prairie (Col., 1941)
The Son of Davy Crockett (Rep., 1941) (also script)
The Return of Daniel Boone (Rep., 1941)
North from the Lone Star (Rep., 1941)
King of Dodge City (Rep., 1941)
Roaring Frontiers (Rep., 1941)
Hands Across the Rockies (Rep., 1941)
Prairie Stranger (Col., 1941)
Royal Mounted Patrol (Col., 1941)
North of the Rockies (Col., 1942)
Devil's Trail (Col., 1942)
Prairie Gunsmoke (Col., 1942)
Vengeance of the West (Rep., 1942)
Fighting Frontier (RKO, 1943)
Batman* (Col., 1943)
Smart Guy (Mon., 1944)
Range Law (Mon., 1944)
West of the Rio Grande (Mon., 1944)
Land of the Outlaws (Mon., 1944)
Ghost Guns (Mon., 1944)
Partners of the Trail (Mon., 1944)
Law Men (Mon., 1944)
Beyond the Pecos (Univ., 1945)
Flame of the West (Mon., 1945)
Frontier Feud (Mon., 1945)
South of the Rio Grande (Mon., 1945)
Border Bandits (Mon., 1946)
Under Arizona Skies (Mon., 1946)
Shadows on the Range (Mon., 1946)
Raiders of the South (Mon., 1946)
Silver Range (Mon., 1946)
The Gentleman from Texas (Mon., 1946)
Valley of Fear (Mon., 1947)
Trailin' Danger (Mon., 1947)
Land of the Lawless (Mon., 1947)

The Case of the Baby Sitter (Screen Guild, 1947)
The Hat Box Mystery (Screen Guild, 1947)
The Law Comes to Gunsight (Mon., 1947)
Flashing Guns (Mon., 1947)
Prairie Express (Mon., 1947)
Gun Talk (Mon., 1947)
Overland Trails (Mon., 1947)
Frontier Agent (Mon., 1948)
Range Renegades (Mon., 1948)
Partners of the Sunset (Mon., 1948)
Oklahoma Blues (Mon., 1948)
Song of the Drifter (Mon., 1948)
Outlaw Brand (Mon., 1948)
The Fighting Ranger (Mon., 1948)
The Sheriff of Medicine Bow (Mon., 1948)
Gun Runner (Mon., 1949)
Gun Law Justice (Mon., 1949)
Haunted Trails (Mon., 1949)
Riders of the Dusk (Mon., 1949)
Trail's End (Mon., 1949)

HITCHCOCK, ALFRED, b. Aug. 13, 1899, London.
Number Thirteen (unfinished, 1922)
Always Tell Your Wife (unfinished, 1922) (with Seymour Hicks)
The Pleasure Garden (Gainsborough-Emelka, 1925)
The Mountain Eagle (Gainsborough-Emelka, 1926)
The Lodger (Gainsborough, 1926) (also co-script)
Downhill (Gainsborough, 1927)
Easy Virtue (Gainsborough, 1927)
The Ring (BIP, 1927) (also script)
The Farmer's Wife (BIP, 1928) (also script)
Champagne (BIP, 1928) (also adaption)
The Manxman (BIP, 1929)
Blackmail (BIP, 1929) (also co-script)
Elstree Calling (BIP, 1930) (with Adrian Brunel)
Juno and the Paycock (BIP, 1930)
Murder (BIP, 1930)
The Skin Game (BIP, 1931) (also co-script)
Rich and Strange (BIP, 1932)
Number Seventeen (BIP, 1932) (also script)
Waltzes from Vienna (Gaumont-British, 1933)
The Man Who Knew Too Much (Gaumont-British, 1934)
The 39 Steps (Gaumont-British, 1935)
The Secret Agent (Gaumont-British, 1936)
Sabotage (Gaumont-British, 1936)
Young and Innocent (Gaumont-British, 1937)
The Lady Vanishes (Gainsborough, 1938)
Jamaica Inn (Mayflower, 1939)
Rebecca (UA, 1940)
Foreign Correspondent (UA, 1940)
Mr. and Mrs. Smith (RKO, 1941)
Suspicion (RKO, 1941)

Saboteur (Univ., 1942)
Shadow of a Doubt (Univ., 1943)
Lifeboat (20th, 1944)
Bon Voyage (Associated British, 1944)
Adventure Malgache (Associated British, 1944)
Spellbound (UA, 1945)
Notorious (RKO, 1946) (also producer)
The Paradine Case (Selznick Releasing, 1948)
Rope (Transatlantic, 1948)
Under Capricorn (Transatlantic, 1949)
Stage Fright (WB, 1950) (also producer)
Strangers on a Train (WB, 1951) (also producer)
I Confess (WB, 1953) (also producer)
Dial M for Murder (WB,
    1954) (also producer)
Rear Window (Par.,
    1954) (also producer)
To Catch a Thief (Par.,
    1955) (also producer)
The Trouble With Harry
    (Par., 1966) (also prod.)
The Man Who Knew Too
    Much (Par., 1956) (also
    producer)
The Wrong Man (WB, 1957)
    (also producer)
Vertigo (Par., 1958) (also
    producer)
North by Northwest (MGM,
    1959) (also producer)
Psycho (Par., 1960) (also
    producer)
The Birds (Univ., 1963)
    (also producer)
Marnie (Univ., 1964) (also
    producer)
Torn Curtain (Univ., 1966)
    (also producer)
Topaz (Univ., 1969) (also
    producer)
Frenzy (Univ., 1972) (al-
    so producer)

David O. Selznick with Alfred
Hitchcock on the set of Rebecca
(UA, 1940).

HOGAN, JAMES P., b. c.1891, Lowell, Mass.; d. Nov. 4, 1943.
    Bare Knuckles (Fox, 1921) (also script)
    Where Is My Wandering Boy Tonight? (Equity, 1922)
    Unmarried Wives (Lumas, 1924)
    Black Lightning (Lumas, 1924)
    Women and Gold (Lumas, 1925)
    Capital Punishment (Preferred, 1925)
    The Mansion of Aching Hearts (B.P. Schulberg, 1925)
    Jimmie's Millions (FBO, 1925)

My Lady's Lips (B. P. Schulberg, 1925)
S. O. S. Perils of the Sea (Col., 1925)
The Bandit's Baby (FBO, 1925)
Steel Preferred (FBO, 1926)
The Isle of Retribution (FBO, 1926)
The King of the Turf (FBO, 1926)
Flaming Fury (FBO, 1926)
The Final Extra (Lumas, 1927)
Finnegan's Ball (First Division, 1927)
The Silent Avenger (Lumas, 1927)
Mountains of Manhattan (Lumas, 1927)
Top Sergeant Mulligan (Anchor, 1928)
The Broken Mask (Anchor, 1928)
Hearts of Men (Anchor, 1928)
Burning Bridges (Pathé, 1928)
Code of the Air (Bischoff, 1928)
The Border Patrol (Pathé, 1928)
The Sheriff's Secret (Cosmos, 1931) (also story, script)
Desert Gold (Par., 1936)
The Arizona Raiders (Par., 1936)
The Accusing Finger (Par., 1936)
Arizona Mahoney (Par., 1937)
Bulldog Drummond Escapes (Par., 1937)
Last Train from Madrid (Par., 1937)
Ebb Tide (Par., 1937)
Scandal Street (Par., 1938)
Bulldog Drummond's Peril (Par., 1938)
The Texans (Par., 1938)
Sons of the Legion (Par., 1938)
Arrest Bulldog Drummond (Par., 1939)
Bulldog Drummond's Secret Police (Par., 1939)
Grand Jury Secrets (Par., 1939)
Bulldog Drummond's Bride (Par., 1939)
$1000 a Touchdown (Par., 1939)
The Farmer's Daughter (Par., 1940)
Queen of the Mob (Par., 1940)
Ellery Queen's Penthouse Mystery (Col., 1941)
Texas Rangers Ride Again (Par., 1941)
Power Dive (Par., 1941)
Ellery Queen and the Perfect Crime (Col., 1941)
Ellery Queen and the Murder Ring (Col., 1941)
Enemy Agents Meet Ellery Queen (Col., 1942)
The Strange Death of Adolph Hitler (Univ., 1943)
The Mad Ghoul (Univ., 1943)
No Place for a Lady (Col., 1943)

HOPKINS, ARTHUR, b. Oct. 4, 1878, Cleveland, O.; d. March 22, 1950.
His Double Life (Par., 1933) (with William C. DeMille) (also co-script)

HORNE, JAMES W., b. Dec. 14, 1881, San Francisco; d. June 30, 1942.
Stingaree (Kalem Series, 1915)
The Girl Detective (Kalem Series, 1915)
Mysteries of the Grand Hotel (Kalem Series, 1915)
The Social Pirates (Kalem Series, 1915)
The Pitfall (Kalem, 1915)
The Barn Stormers (Kalem, 1915)
The Girl from Friscoe (Kalem Series, 1915)
Bull's Eye* (Univ., 1918)
Hands Up* (Univ., 1918)
The Midnight Man* (Univ., 1919)
The Third Eye* (Pathé, 1920)
Occasionally Yours (Robertson-Cole, 1920)
The Bronze Bell (Par., 1921)
A Dangerous Pastime (Louis J. Gasnier, 1922)
Don't Doubt Your Wife (Associated Exhibitors, 1922)
The Forgotten Law (Metro, 1922)
The Hottentot (Associated FN, 1922)
Can a Woman Love Twice? (FBO, 1923)
The Sunshine Trail (Associated FN, 1923)
Itching Palms (FBO, 1923)
A Man of Action (Associated FN, 1923)
Blow Your Own Horn (FBO, 1923)
Alimony (FBO, 1924)
American Manners (FBO, 1924)
The Yankee Consul (Associated Exhibitors, 1924)
In Fast Company (Truart, 1924)
Hail the Hero (FBO, 1924)
Laughing at Danger (FBO, 1924)
Stepping Lively (FBO, 1924)
Youth and Adventure (FBO, 1925)
Kosher Kitty Kelly (FBO, 1926)
The Cruise of the Jasper B (PDC, 1926)
College (UA, 1927)
The Big Hop (Buck Jones, 1928)
Black Butterflies (Quality, 1928)
The Ace of Scotland Yard* (Univ., 1929) (with Ray Taylor)
Bonnie Scotland (MGM, 1935)
The Bohemian Girl (MGM, 1936) (with Charles Rogers)
Way Out West (MGM, 1936)
All Over Town (Rep., 1937)
The Spider's Web* (Col., 1938) (with Ray Taylor)
Flying G-Men* (Col., 1938) (with Ray Taylor)
Deadwood Dick* (Col., 1940)
The Green Archer* (Col., 1940)
The Shadow* (Col., 1940)
Terry and the Pirates* (Col., 1940)
Holt of the Secret Service* (Col., 1941)
The Iron Claw* (Col., 1941)
The Spider Returns* (Col., 1941)
White Eagle* (Col., 1941)
Captain Midnight* (Col., 1942)
Perils of the Royal Mounted* (Col., 1942)

HOWARD, DAVID (David Paget Davis III), b. Oct. 6, 1896, Philadelphia; d. Dec. 21, 1941.

Del Mismo Barro [Spanish version of The Common Clay] (Fox,
1930)

El Ultimo de los Vargas [Spanish version of Last of the Du-
anes] (Fox, 1930)

Ladrón de Amor [Spanish version of Love Gambler] (Fox, 1930)
(with William Scully)

Esclavas de la Moda [Spanish version of On Your Back] (Fox,
1930

Horizontes Nuevos [Spanish version of The Big Trail] (Fox,
1931)

Conocesa Yu Mujer [Spanish version of Don't Bet on Women]
(Fox, 1931)

Eran Trece [Spanish version of Charlie Chan Carries on] (Fox,
1932)

Marido y Mujer [Spanish version of Bad Girl] (Fox, 1932)

The Rainbow Trail (Fox, 1932)

Mystery Ranch (Fox, 1932)

The Golden West (Fox, 1932)

Smoke Lightning (Fox, 1933)

Mystery Squadron* (Mascot, 1933) (with Colbert Clark)

The Lost Jungle* (Mascot, 1934) (with Armand Schaefer)

Crimson Romance (Mascot, 1934)

In Old Santa Fe (Mascot, 1934)

The Marines Are Coming (Mascot, 1934)

Thunder Mountain (Fox, 1935)

Hard-Rock Harrigan (Fox, 1935)

Whispering Smith Speaks (Fox, 1935)

O'Malley of the Mounted (20th, 1936)

The Mine With the Iron Door (Col., 1936)

The Border Patrolman (20th, 1936)

Daniel Boone (RKO, 1936)

Conflict (Univ., 1936)

Park Avenue Logger (RKO, 1937)

Hollywood Stadium Mystery (Rep., 1938)

Gun Law (RKO, 1938)

Painted Desert (RKO, 1938)

Arizona Legion (RKO, 1938)

Border G-Men (RKO, 1938)

Lawless Valley (RKO, 1938)

Trouble in Sundown (RKO, 1939)

Renegade Rangers (RKO, 1939)

The Fighting Gringo (RKO, 1939)

Legion of the Lawless (RKO, 1940)

The Marshal of Mesa City (RKO, 1940)

Bullet Code (RKO, 1940)

Prairie Law (RKO, 1940)

Triple Justice (RKO, 1940)

Dude Cowboy (RKO, 1941)

Six Gun Gold (RKO, 1941)

HOWARD, WILLIAM K., b. June 16, 1899, St. Mary's, O.; d.
    Feb. 21, 1954.
  Get Your Man (Fox, 1921) (with George W. Hill)
  Play Square (Fox, 1921)
  What Love Will Do (Fox, 1921)
  Extra! Extra! (Fox, 1922)
  Deserted at the Altar (Goldstone, 1922)
  Captain Fly-By-Night (FBO, 1922)
  Lucky Dan (Goldstone, 1922)
  The Fourth Musketeer (FBO, 1923)
  Danger Ahead (Goldstone, 1923)
  Let's Go (Truart, 1923)
  The Border Legion (Par., 1924)
  East of Broadway (Encore, 1924)
  The Thundering Herd (Par., 1925)
  Code of the West (Par., 1925)
  The Light of Western Stars (Par., 1925)
  Red Dice (PDC, 1926)
  Bachelor Brides (PDC, 1926)
  Volcano (Par., 1926)
  Gigolo (PDC, 1926)
  White Gold (PDC, 1927)
  The Main Event (Pathé, 1927)
  A Ship Comes in (Pathé, 1928)
  The River Pirate (Fox, 1928)
  Christina (Fox, 1929)
  The Valiant (Fox, 1929)
  Love, Live and Laugh (Fox, 1929)
  Good Intentions (Fox, 1930)
  Scotland Yard (Fox, 1930)
  Don't Bet on Women (Fox, 1931)
  Transatlantic (Fox, 1931)
  Surrender (Fox, 1931)
  The Trial of Vivienne Ware (Fox, 1932)
  The First Year (Fox, 1932)
  Sherlock Holmes (Fox, 1932)
  The Power and the Glory (Fox, 1933)
  This Side of Heaven (MGM, 1934)
  The Cat and the Fiddle (MGM, 1934)
  Evelyn Prentice (MGM, 1934)
  Vanesa, Her Love Story (MGM, 1935)
  Rendezvous (MGM, 1935)
  Mary Burns--Fugitive (Par., 1935)
  The Princess Comes Across (Par., 1936)
  Fire over England (UA, 1937)
  Murder on Diamond Row [The Squeaker] (UA, 1937)
  Back Door to Heaven (Par., 1939) (also producer, script)
  Money and the Woman (WB, 1940)
  Bullets for O'Hara (WB, 1941)
  Klondike Fury (Mon., 1942)
  Johnny Come Lately (UA, 1943)
  When the Lights Go on Again (PRC, 1944)
  A Guy Could Change (Rep., 1945) (also associate producer)

HUGHES, HOWARD, b. Dec. 24, 1905, Houston, Tex.
Hell's Angels (UA, 1930) (uncredited, with Howard Hawks) (also co-producer)
The Outlaw (RKO, 1943) (replaced Howard Hawks) (also producer)
Vendetta (RKO, 1950) (uncredited, with Mel Ferrer and uncredited Stuart Heisler, Max Ophüls, Preston Sturges) (also producer)
Jet Pilot (Univ., 1957) (uncredited, with Josef von Sternberg) (also executive producer)

HUMBERSTONE, H. BRUCE, b. Nov. 18, 1903, Buffalo, N.Y.
Strangers of the Evening (Tiffany, 1932)
The Crooked Circle (Sono Art-World Wide, 1932)
If I Had a Million (Par., 1932) (with James Cruze, Ernst Lubitsch, Stephen Roberts, William A. Seiter, Norman Taurog)
King of the Jungle (Par., 1933) (with Max Marcin)
Goodbye Love (RKO, 1934)
Merry Wives of Reno (WB, 1934)
The Dragon Murder Case (FN, 1934)
Ladies Love Danger (Fox, 1935)
Silk Hat Kid (Fox, 1935)
Three Live Ghosts (MGM, 1935)
Charlie Chan at the Race Track (20th, 1936)
Charlie Chan at the Opera (20th, 1936)
Charlie Chan at the Olympics (20th, 1937)
Checkers (20th, 1937)
Rascals (20th, 1938)
Charlie Chan in Honolulu (20th, 1938)
Time Out for Murder (20th, 1938)
Pack Up Your Troubles (20th, 1939)
Lucky Cisco Kid (20th, 1940)
The Quarterback (20th, 1940)
Tall, Dark and Handsome (20th, 1941)
Sun Valley Serenade (20th, 1941)
I Wake Up Screaming (20th, 1941)
To the Shores of Tripoli (20th, 1942)
Iceland (20th, 1942)
Hello, Frisco, Hello (20th, 1943)
Pin-Up Girl (20th, 1944)
Wonder Man (RKO, 1945)
Within These Walls (20th, 1945)
Three Little Girls in Blue (20th, 1945) (replaced John Brahm)
The Homestretch (20th, 1947)
Fury at Furnace Creek (20th, 1948)
South Sea Sinner (Univ., 1950)
Happy Go Lovely (RKO, 1951)
She's Working Her Way Through College (WB, 1952)
The Desert Song (WB, 1953)
Ten Wanted Men (Col., 1955)
The Purple Mask (Univ., 1955)
Tarzan and the Lost Safari (MGM, 1957)

Tarzan's Fight for Life (MGM, 1958)
Tarzan and the Trappers (Sol Lesser, 1958)
Madison Avenue (20th, 1962) (also producer)

HURST, PAUL C., b. 1889, Traver, Calif.; d. Feb. 27, 1953.
    Lass of the Limberlands* (Signal, 1916) (with J. P. McGowan)
    The Iron Test* (Vitagraph, 1918) (with Robert North Bradbury)
    A Woman in the Web* (Vitagraph, 1918) (with David Smith)
    Lightning Bryce* (Arrow, 1919) (also actor)
    The Tiger's Trail (Pathé, 1919) (with Robert Ellis)
    Shadows of the West (National Players, 1921)
    Black Sheep (Pinnacle, 1921)
    The Crow's Nest (Aywon, 1922)
    The Heart of a Texan (William Steiner, 1922) (also script)
    The Kingfisher's Roost (Pinnacle, 1922) (with Louis Chaudet)
      (also script with Chaudet)
    Table Top Ranch (William Steiner, 1922) (also script)
    Golden Silence (Kipling Enterprises, 1923)
    Branded a Bandit (Arrow, 1924) (also script)
    The Courageous Coward (Usla, 1924)
    The Passing of Wolf Maclean (Usla, 1924)
    Battling Bunyon (Associated Exhibitors, 1925)
    The Demon Rider (Davis Distributing, 1925)
    The Fighting Cub (Truart, 1925)
    The Gold Hunters (Davis Distributing, 1925)
    The Rattler (Ermine, 1925)
    The Son of Sontag (Goodwill, 1925)
    A Western Engagement (Arrow, 1925)
    Battling Kid (Bud Barsky, 1926)
    Blue Streak O'Neill (Bud Barsky, 1926)
    Fighting Ranger (Bud Barsky, 1926)
    The Haunted Range (Davis Distributing, 1926)
    Law of the Snow Country (Bud Barsky, 1926)
    The Midnight Message (Goodwill, 1926)
    Roaring Road (Bud Barsky, 1926)
    Shadows of Chinatown (Bud Barsky, 1926)
    Sun of a Gun (Bud Barsky, 1926)
    The Range Raiders (Bud Barsky, 1927)
    Rider of the Law (Bud Barsky, 1927)

HUSTON, JOHN, b. Aug. 5, 1906, Nevada, Mo.
    The Maltese Falcon (WB, 1941) (also script)
    In This Our Life (WB, 1942) (also co-script)
    Across the Pacific (WB, 1942)
    The Treasure of Sierra Madre (WB, 1948) (also script, actor)
    Key Largo (WB, 1948) (also co-script)
    We Were Strangers (Col., 1949) (also co-script)
    The Asphalt Jungle (MGM, 1950) (also co-script)
    The Red Badge of Courage (MGM, 1951) (also script)
    The African Queen (UA, 1951) (also co-script)
    Moulin Rouge (UA, 1952) (also producer, script)

Lauren Bacall with John Huston (ca. 1968).

Beat the Devil (UA, 1954) (also co-script)
Moby Dick (WB, 1956) (also co-producer, co-script)
Heaven Knows, Mr. Allison (20th, 1957) (also co-script)
The Barbarian and the Geisha (20th, 1958)
The Roots of Heaven (20th, 1958
The Unforgiven (UA, 1960
The Misfits (UA, 1961)
Freud (Univ., 1962) (also co-script)
The List of Adrian Messenger (Univ., 1963)
The Night of the Iguana (MGM, 1964) (also producer, co-script)
The Bible (20th, 1966) (also narrator, actor)
Casino Royale (Col., 1967) (with Val Guest, Ken Hughes, Joe
    McGrath, Robert Parish) (also actor)
Reflections in a Golden Eye (WB-7 Arts, 1967)
Sinful Davey (UA, 1969)
The Madwoman of Chaillot (WB-7 Arts, 1969) (replaced by
    Bryan Forbes)
A Walk With Love and Death (20th, 1969) (also co-producer)
The Kremlin Letter (20th, 1970) (also co-script)
The Last Run (RMG, 1971) (replaced by Richard Fleischer)
Fat City (Col., 1972) (also for co-production company)
The Life and Times of Judge Roy Bean (National General, 1973)
    (also actor)
The Mackintosh Man (WB, 1973)

I

INCE, RALPH W., b. Jan. 16, 1887, Boston; d. April 11, 1937.
    A Million Bid (Vitagraph, 1914)
    The Goddess* (Vitagraph, 1915)
    The Juggernaut (Vitagraph, 1915)
    Sins of the Mother (Vitagraph, 1915)
    The Combat (Vitagraph, 1916)
    The Conflict (Vitagraph, 1916)
    The Destroyers (Vitagraph, 1916)
    His Wife's Good Name (Vitagraph, 1916)

My Lady's Slippers (Vitagraph, 1916)
The Ninety and Nine (Vitagraph, 1916)
The Argyle Case (Selznick, 1917)
Today (State Rights, 1917)
The Co-Respondent (Univ., 1917)
Tempered Steel (Associated FN, 1918)
Fields of Honor (Goldwyn, 1918)
The Eleventh Commandment (Advanced, 1918)
Her Man (Pathé, 1918)
Our Mrs. McChesney (Metro, 1918)
The Panther Woman (Associated FN, 1918)
Stitch in Time (Vitagraph, 1919)
Too Many Crooks (Vitagraph, 1919)
Two Women (Vitagraph, 1919)
The Perfect Lover (Selznick, 1919)
Out Yonder (Selznick, 1919)
Sealed Hearts (Selznick, 1919)
His Wife's Money (Selznick, 1920
Out of the Snow (Selznick, 1920)
The Law Bringers (Selznick, 1920) (also actor)
Red Foam (Selznick, 1920)
The Highest Law (Selznick, 1921) (also actor)
A Man's Home (Selznick, 1921)
Remorseless Love (Select, 1921)
Wet Gold (Goldwyn, 1921) (also actor)
Tropical Love (Associated Exhibitors, 1921)
After Midnight (Selznick, 1921)
The Last Door (Select, 1921)
Channing of the Northwest (Select, 1922)
Reckless Youth (Select, 1922)
A Wide-Open Town (Select, 1922)
The Referee (Select, 1922)
Counterfeit Love (Playgoers, 1923) (with Roy Sheldon)
Success (Metro, 1923)
Homeward Bound (Par., 1923)
The Uninvited Guest (Metro, 1924)
The Moral Sinner (Par., 1924)
The House of Youth (PDC, 1924)
Dynamite Smith (Pathé, 1924)
The Chorus Lady (PDC, 1924)
Alias Mary Flynn (FBO, 1925)
Lady Robinhood (FBO, 1925)
Playing With Souls (FN, 1925)
Smooth as Satin (FBO, 1925)
Yellow Fingers (Fox, 1926) (also actor)
The Lone Wolf Returns (Col., 1926)
Bigger Than Barnum's (FBO, 1926) (also actor)
Breed of the Sea (FBO, 1926) (also actor)
The Sea Wolf (PDC, 1926) (also actor)
The Better Way (Col., 1926) (also actor)
Wandering Girls (Col., 1927)
Home Struck (FBO, 1927)
Moulders of Men (FBO, 1927)
Not for Publication (FBO, 1927) (also for production company,

producer, actor)
Shanghaied (FBO, 1927) (also for production company, actor)
South Sea Love (FBO, 1927)
Coney Island (FBO, 1928
Chicago After Midnight (FBO, 1928) (also actor)
Danger Street (FBO, 1928)
Hit of the Show (FBO, 1928)
The Singapore Mutiny (FBO, 1928) (also co-titles, actor)
Hardboiled (FBO, 1929) (also titles)
Hurricane (Col. , 1930)
La Fuerza del Querer [Spanish version of The Big Fight]
    (Sono Art-World Wide, 1930)
Men of America (RKO, 1933) (also actor)
Lucky Devils (RKO, 1933)
Flaming Gold (RKO, 1934)
No Escape (British FN, 1934)
What's a Name (British FN, 1934)
Murder at Monte Carlo (British FN, 1935)
Mr. What's His Name (British FN, 1935)
Unlimited (British FN, 1935)
Black Mask (British FN, 1935)
Blue Smoke (British FN, 1935)
Rolling House (British FN, 1935)
Jury's Evidence (British FN, 1936)
It's You I Want (British FN, 1936)
Jail Break (British FN, 1936)
Twelve Good Men (British FN, 1936)
Fair Exchange (British FN, 1936)
Hail and Farewell (British FN, 1936)
The Vulture (British FN, 1937)
Side Street Angel (British FN, 1937)
It's Not Cricket (British FN, 1937)
The Perfect Crime (British FN, 1937)
The Man Who Made Diamonds (British FN, 1937)

INCE, THOMAS HARPER, b. Nov. 6, 1882, Newport, R.I.; d.
    Nov. 19, 1924.
    The Battle of Gettysburg (Ince, 1913) (with Charles Giblyn,
        Raymond B. West)
    Civilization (Ince, 1916) (with Raymond B. West, Reginald
        Barker, Scott Sidney, J. Parker Read, Jr.)

INGRAHAM, LLOYD, b. Rochelle, Ill.; d. April 4, 1956.
    The Sable Lorcha (Par., 1915)
    The Fox Woman (Majestic, 1915)
    American Aristocracy (Triangle, 1916)
    Casey at the Bat (Triangle, 1916)
    A Child of Paris Streets (Triangle, 1916)
    The Children Pay (Triangle, 1916)
    The Little Liar (Triangle, 1916)
    Nina, the Flower Girl (Triangle, 1917)
    An Old Fashioned Young Man (Triangle, 1917)
    Charity Castle (American Mutual, 1917)
    Her Country's Call (Mutual, 1917)

Peggy Leads the Way (American Mutual, 1917)
Miss Jackie of the Army (American Mutual, 1917)
Molly Go Get 'Em (American Mutual, 1918)
Jilted Janet (American Mutual, 1918)
Ann's Finish (American Mutual, 1918)
The Primitive Woman (Mutual, 1918)
A Square Deal (American Mutual, 1918)
Impossible Susan (American Mutual, 1918)
The Eyes of Julia Deep (American Mutual, 1918)
Wives and Other Wives (Pathé, 1918)
The Amazing Imposter (Pathé, 1919)
The Intrusion of Isabel (Pathé, 1919)
Rosemary Climbs the Heights (Pathé, 1919)
Man's Desire (Exclusive International, 1919)
The House of Intrigue (Exclusive International, 1919)
Mary's Ankle (Par., 1920)
What's Your Husband Doing (Par., 1920)
Let's Be Fashionable (Par., 1920)
Twin Beds (Associated FN, 1920)
The Jailbird (Par., 1920)
Old Dad (Associated FN, 1920)
Keeping Up With Lizzie (W.W. Hodkinson, 1921)
The Girl in the Taxi (Associated FN, 1921)
Lavender and Old Lace (W.W. Hodkinson, 1921)
Marry the Poor Girl (Associated Exhibitors, 1921)
My Lady Friends (Associated FN, 1921)
At the Sign of the Jack O'Lantern (W.W. Hodkinson, 1922)
Second Hand Rose (Univ., 1922)
The Veiled Woman (W.W. Hodkinson, 1922)
The Danger Point (American Releasing, 1922)
Going Up (Associated Exhibitors, 1923)
The Lightning Rider (W.W. Hodkinson, 1924)
No More Women (Allied Producers & Distributors, 1924)
The Wise Virgin (PDC, 1924)
The Beauty Prize (Metro-Goldwyn, 1924)
Soft Shoes (PDC, 1925)
Midnight Molly (FBO, 1925)
The Nut-Cracker (Associated Exhibitors, 1926)
Hearts and Fists (Associated Exhibitors, 1926)
Oh, What a Night! (Sterling, 1926)
Don Mike (FBO, 1927) (also continuity)
Arizona Nights (FBO, 1927)
Silver Comes Through (FBO, 1927) (also adaptation, continuity)
Jesse James (Par., 1927)
The Pioneer Scout (Par., 1928)
Kit Carson (Par., 1928) (with Alfred L. Werker)
The Sunset Legion (Par., 1928)
Take the Heir (Screenstory, 1930)

INGRAM, REX (Reginald Ingram Montgomery Hitchcock), b. 1892,
      Dublin, Ireland; d. July 21, 1950.
    The Great Problem (Bluebird, 1916) (also producer, script)

Broken Fetters (Bluebird, 1916) (also producer, script)
The Chalice of Sorrow (Bluebird, 1916) (also adaptation)
Black Orchids (Univ., 1971) (also script)
The Reward of the Faithless (Bluebird, 1917) (also producer, script)
The Pulse of Life (Bluebird, 1917) (also script)
The Flower of Doom (Red Films, 1917) (also script)
His Robe of Honor (W.W. Hodkinson, 1918)
Humdrum Brown (W.W. Hodkinson, 1918)
The Day She Paid (Univ., 1919)
Under Crimson Skies (Univ., 1920)
Shore Acres (Metro, 1920)
Hearts Are Trumps (Metro, 1920)
The Four Horsemen of the Apocalypse (Metro, 1921)
The Conquering Power (Metro, 1921) (also producer)
Turn to the Right (Metro, 1922)
The Prisoner of Zenda (Metro, 1922) (also producer)
Trifling Women (Metro, 1922) (also producer, story)
Where the Pavement Ends (Metro, 1923) (also producer, adaptation)
Scaramouche (Metro, 1923) (also producer)
The Arab (Metro-Goldwyn, 1924)
Mare Nostrum (MGM, 1926)
The Magician (MGM, 1926) (also adaptation)
The Garden of Allah (MGM, 1927) (also producer)
The Three Passions (UA, 1929) (also producer, script)
Love in Morocco [Baroud] (Gaumont-British, 1933) (also producer, co-story, co-script, actor)

INGSTER, BORIS, b. ca.1913.
Stranger on the Third Floor (RKO, 1940)
The Judge Steps Out (RKO, 1949) (also co-script)
Southside 1-1000 (AA, 1950) (also co-script)

J

JEWISON, NORMAN, b. July 21, 1926, Toronto.
40 Pounds of Trouble (Univ., 1962)
The Thrill of It All (Univ., 1963)
Send Me No Flowers (Univ., 1964)
The Art of Love (Univ., 1965)
The Cincinnati Kid (Univ., 1965)
The Russians Are Coming, The Russians Are Coming (UA, 1966) (also producer)
In the Heat of the Night (UA, 1967)
The Thomas Crown Affair (UA, 1968) (also producer)
Gaily Gaily (UA, 1969) (also producer)
Fiddler on the Roof (UA, 1971) (also producer)
Jesus Christ Superstar (Univ., 1973) (also co-producer, co-script)

Topol with Norman Jewison on the set for <u>Fiddler on the Roof</u> (UA, 1971).

JOHNSON, LAMONT, b. Stockton, Calif.
Thin Ice (20th, 1961)
A Covenant With Death (WB-7 Arts, 1966)
Kona Coast (WB-7 Arts, 1968)
Deadlock (NBC-TV, 1969)
My Sweet Charlie (Univ., 1970)
The McKenzie Break (UA, 1970)
A Gunfright (Par., 1971)
The Groundstar Conspiracy (Univ., 1972)
You'll Like My Mother (Univ., 1972)
That Certain Summer (ABC-TV, 1973)

JOHNSON, NUNNALLY, b. Dec. 5, 1897, Columbus, Ga.
Night People (20th, 1954) (also producer, script)
Black Widow (20th, 1954) (also producer, script)

How to Be Very, Very Popular (20th, 1955) (also producer, script)
The Man in the Gray Flannel Suit (20th, 1956) (also script)
The Three Faces of Eve (also producer, script)
Oh, Men! Oh, Women! (20th, 1957) (also producer, script)
The Man Who Understood Women (20th, 1959) (also producer, script)
The Angel Wore Red (MGM, 1960) (also script)

JOSE, EDWARD, b. Antwerp, Belgium.
The Beloved Vagabond (Pathé, 1915)
Simon the Jester (Pathé, 1915)
The Closing Net (Pathé, 1915)
Nedra (Pathé, 1915)
The Light That Failed (Pathé, 1916)
The Iron Claw* (Pathé, 1916)
Pearl of the Army* (Pathé, 1916)
Poppy (Select, 1917)
May Blossom (Pathé, 1917)
The Moth (Select, 1917)
Her Silent Sacrifice (Select, 1918)
Woman and Wife (Select, 1918)
La Tosca (Par., 1918)
Resurrection (Par., 1918)
Love's Conquest (Par., 1918)
Fedora (Par., 1918)
My Cousin (Artclass, 1918)
Private Peat (Artclass, 1918)
Woman of Impulse (Par., 1918)
Two Brides (Par., 1919)
Fires of Fate (Par., 1919)
The Isle of Conquest (Select, 1919)
The Fighting Shepherdess (Associated FN, 1920)
The Riddle: Woman (Pathé, 1920)
The Yellow Typhoon (Associated FN, 1920)
The Isle of Conquest (Selznick, 1919)
Mothers of Men (Rep., 1920)
Her Lord and Master (Vitagraph, 1921)
What Women Will Do (Pathé, 1922)
The Scarab Ring (Vitagraph, 1921)
The Inner Chamber (Vitagraph, 1921)
The Matrimonial Web (Vitagraph, 1921)
Rainbow (Vitagraph, 1921)
The Girl in His Room (Vitagraph, 1922)
The Prodigal Judge (Vitagraph, 1922)
The Man from Downing Street (Vitagraph, 1922)

JULIAN, RUPERT, b. Jan. 25, 1889, Auckland, N.Z.; d. Dec. 30, 1943.
Jewel (Univ., 1915) (also actor)
The Turn of the Wheel (Univ., 1916) (also actor)

Naked Hearts (Univ., 1916) (also actor)
Bettina Loved a Soldier (Univ., 1916) (also actor)
The Bugler of Algiers (Univ., 1916) (also actor)
The Evil Women Do (Univ., 1916) (also actor)
The Right to Be Happy (Univ., 1917) (also actor)
The Gift Girl (Univ., 1917) (also actor)
The Circus of Life (Univ., 1917) (also actor)
The Mysterious Mr. Tiller (Bluebird, 1917) (also actor)
The Desire of the Moth (Bluebird, 1917) (also actor)
Mother O' Mine (Univ., 1917) (also actor, script)
A Kentucky Cinderella (Univ., 1917) (also actor)
The Door Between (Bluebird, 1917)
The Savage (Bluebird, 1917)
Hands Down (Bluebird, 1918)
Hungry Eyes (Bluebird, 1918) (also actor)
The Kaiser, the Beast of Berlin (Univ., 1918) (also actor)
Midnight Madness (Bluebird, 1918)
Creaking Stairs (Univ., 1919)
The Sleeping Lion (Univ., 1919)
The Fire Flingers (Univ., 1919) (also actor)
Millionaire Pirate (Bluebird, 1919)
The Honey Bee (Pathé, 1920)
The Girl Who Ran Wild (Univ., 1922) (also co-script)
Merry-Go-Round (Univ.-Jewel, 1923) (replaced Erich von Stro-
    heim)
Love and Glory (Univ.-Jewel, 1924) (also co-script)
Hell's Highroad (PDC, 1925)
The Phantom of the Opera (Univ.-Jewel, 1925) (with Edward
    Sedgwick)
Three Faces East (PDC, 1926)
Silence (PDC, 1926)
The Yankee Clipper (PDC, 1927)
The Country Doctor (Pathé, 1927)
The Leopard Lady (Pathé, 1928)
Walking Back (Pathe, 1928)
Love Comes Along (RKO, 1930)
The Cat Creeps (Univ., 1930)

JURAN, NATHAN (Nathan Hertz Juran), b. Sept. 1, 1907, Austin,
    Tex.
The Black Castle (Univ., 1952)
Gunsmoke (Univ., 1953)
Law and Order (Univ., 1953)
Tumbleweed (Univ., 1953)
The Golden Blade (Univ., 1953)
Drums Along the River (Univ., 1954)
Highway Dragnet (AA, 1954)
The Crooked Web (Col., 1955)
The Deadly Mantis (Univ., 1957)
Hellcats of the Navy (Col., 1957)
20 Million Miles to Earth (Col., 1957)
Good Day for a Hanging (Col., 1958)
Flight of the Lost Balloon (Anglo-Amalgamated, 1961) (also co-
    producer, story, script)

Jack the Giant Killer (Zenith, 1961) (also co-script)
Siege of the Saxons (Col., 1963)
East of Sudan (Col., 1964)
First Men in the Moon (Col., 1964)
Boy Who Cried Werewolf (Univ., 1973)

K

KANE, JOSEPH (Joseph Inman Kane), b. Mar. 19, 1897, San Diego.
    In Old Santa Fe (Mascot, 1934)
    Fighting Marines* (Mascot, 1935) (with B. Reeves Eason)
    Tumbling Tumbleweeds (Rep., 1935)
    Melody Trail (Rep., 1935)
    The Sagebrush Troubadour (Rep., 1935)
    The Lawless Nineties (Rep., 1936)
    King of the Pecos (Rep., 1936)
    The Lonely Trail (Rep., 1936)
    Darkest Africa* (Rep., 1936) (with B. Reeves Eason)
    The Undersea Kingdom* (Rep., 1936) (with B. Reeves Eason)
    Guns and Guitars (Rep., 1936)
    Oh Susannah! (Rep., 1936)
    Ride, Ranger, Ride (Rep., 1936)
    Fighting Marines (Rep., 1936)
    The Old Corral (Rep., 1936)
    Paradise Express, (Rep., 1937)
    Ghost Town Gold (Rep., 1937)
    Gunsmoke Ranch (Rep., 1937)
    Come on Cowboys (Rep., 1937)
    Heart of the Rockies (Rep., 1937)
    Round-Up Time in Texas (Rep., 1937)
    Git Along, Little Dogies (Rep., 1937)
    Yodelin' Kid from Pine Ridge (Rep., 1937)
    Public Cowboy No. 1 (Rep., 1937)
    Boots and Saddles (Rep., 1937)
    Springtime in the Rockies (Rep., 1937)
    Born to Be Wild (Rep., 1938)
    Arson Racket Squad (Rep., 1938)
    The Old Barn Dance (Rep., 1938)
    Gold Mine in the Sky (Rep., 1938)
    Man from Music Mountain (Rep., 1938)
    Under Western Skies (Rep., 1938)
    Billy the Kid Returns (Rep., 1938)
    Come on Rangers (Rep., 1938)
    Shine on Harvest Moon (Rep., 1938)
    In Old Monterey (Rep., 1939)
    Rough Riders Roundup (Rep., 1939) (also co-producer)
    Frontier Pony Express (Rep., 1939) (also co-producer)
    Southward Ho! (Rep., 1939) (also co-producer)
    In Old Caliente (Rep., 1939)
    Wall Street Cowboy (Rep., 1939) (also co-producer)
    The Arizona Kid (Rep., 1939) (also co-producer)
    Saga of Death Valley (Rep., 1939) (also co-producer)
    Days of Jesse James (Rep., 1939) (also co-producer)

Young Buffalo Bill (Rep. , 1940) (also co-producer)
The Carson City Kid (Rep. , 1940) (also co-producer)
The Ranger and the Lady (Rep. , 1940) (also co-producer)
Colorado (Rep. , 1940) (also co-producer)
Young Bill Hickock (Rep. , 1940) (also co-producer)
The Border Legion (Rep. , 1940) (also co-producer)
Robin Hood of the Pecos (Rep. , 1941) (also co-producer)
In Old Cheyenne (Rep. , 1941) (also co-producer)
Nevada City (Rep. , 1941) (also co-producer)
Sheriff of Tombstone (Rep. , 1941) (also co-producer)
Bad Man of Deadwood (Rep. , 1941) (also co-producer)
Jesse James at Bay (Rep. , 1941) (also co-producer)
Red River Valley (Rep. , 1941) (also co-producer)
The Great Train Robbery (Rep. , 1941) (also co-producer)
Rags to Riches (Rep. , 1941) (also co-producer)
South of Santa Fe (Rep. , 1942) (also co-producer)
The Man from Cheyenne (Rep. , 1942) (also co-producer)
Sunset on the Desert (Rep. , 1942) (also co-producer)
Romance on the Range (Rep. , 1942) (also co-producer)
Sons of the Pioneers (Rep. , 1942) (also co-producer)
Sunset Serenade (Rep. , 1942) (also co-producer)
Heart of the Golden West (Rep. , 1942) (also co-producer)
Ridin' Down the Canyon (Rep. , 1942)
Idaho (Rep. , 1943) (also co-producer)
King of the Cowboys (Rep. , 1943)
Song of Texas (Rep. , 1943)
Silver Spurs (Rep. , 1943)
The Man from Music Mountain (Rep. , 1943)
Hands Across the Border (Rep. , 1943)
The Cowboy and the Senorita (Rep. , 1944)
The Yellow Rose of Texas (Rep. , 1944)
Song of Nevada (Rep. , 1944)
South of Santa Fe (Rep. , 1944)
The Cheaters (Rep. , 1945) (also co-producer)
Flame of the Barbary Coast (Rep. , 1945) (also associate pro-
    ducer)
Dakota (Rep. , 1945) (also associate producer)
In Old Sacramento (Rep. , 1946) (also associate producer)
The Plainsman and the Lady (Rep. , 1946) (also associate pro-
    ducer)
Wyoming (Rep. , 1947) (also associate producer)
The Gallant Legion (Rep. , 1948) (also associate producer)
Old Los Angeles (Rep. , 1948) (also associate producer)
The Plunderers (Rep. , 1948) (also associate producer)
The Last Bandit (Rep. , 1949) (also associate producer)
Brimstone (Rep. , 1949) (also associate producer)
Rock Island Trail (Rep. , 1950) (also associate producer)
The Savage Horde (Rep. , 1950) (also associate producer)
California Passage (Rep. , 1950) (also associate producer)
Fighting Coast Guard (Rep. , 1951) (also associate producer)
Oh Susanna (Rep. , 1951) (also associate producer)
The Sea Hornet (Rep. , 1951) (also associate producer)
Woman of the North Country (Rep. , 1952) (also associate producer)

Ride the Man Down (Rep., 1952) (also associate producer)
Hoodlum Empire (Rep., 1953) (also associate producer)
San Antone (Rep., 1953) (also associate producer)
Fair Wind to Java (Rep., 1953) (also associate producer)
Sea of Lost Ships (Rep., 1953) (also associate producer)
Jubilee Trail (Rep., 1954) (also associate producer)
Timberjack (Rep., 1955) (also associate producer)
The Road to Denver (Rep., 1955) (also associate producer)
Hell's Outpost (Rep., 1955) (also associate producer)
The Vanishing American (Rep., 1955) (also associate producer)
The Maverick Queen (Rep., 1956) (also associate producer)
Accused of Murder (Rep., 1956) (also producer)
Thunder Over Arizona (Rep., 1956) (also associate producer)
Duel at Apache Wells (Rep., 1957) (also associate producer)
Spoilers of the Forest (Rep., 1957) (also associate producer)
Last Stagecoach West (Rep., 1957)
The Crooked Circle (Rep., 1957)
The Lawless Eighties (Rep., 1957) (also associate producer)
Gunfire at Indian Gap (Rep., 1957) (also associate producer)
The Notorious Mr. Monks (Rep., 1958)
The Man Who Died Twice (Rep., 1958)
Track of Thunder (UA, 1968)
Country Boy (Howco, 1968)

KANIN, GARSON, b. Nov. 24, 1912, Rochester, N.Y.
A Man to Remember (RKO, 1938)
Next Time I Marry (RKO, 1938)
The Great Man Votes (RKO, 1939)
Bachelor Mother (RKO, 1939)
My Favorite Wife (RKO, 1940)
They Knew What They Wanted (Col., 1940)
Tom, Dick and Harry (RKO, 1941)
Fellow Americans (Office of Emergency Management, 1942)
Ring of Steel (Office of Emergency Management, 1942)
German Manpower (Office of Emergency Management, 1943)
The True Glory (Col., 1945) (with Carol Reed)
Where It's At (UA, 1969) (also script)
Some Kind of a Nut (UA, 1969)

KANTER, HAL, b. Dec. 18, 1918, Savannah, Ga.
Loving You (Par., 1957) (also co-script)
I Married a Woman (Univ., 1958)
Once Upon a Horse (Univ., 1958) (also story, script)

KARLSON, PHIL (Phil Karlstein), b. July 2, 1908, Chicago.
A Wave, a Wac and a Marine (Mon., 1944)
There Goes Kelly (Mon., 1945)
G.I. Honeymoon (Mon., 1945)
The Shanghai Cobra (Mon., 1945)
Dark Alibi (Mon., 1946)

Live Wives (Mon., 1946)
The Missing Lady (Mon., 1946)
Swing Parade of 1946 (Mon., 1946)
Behind the Mask (Mon., 1946)
Bowery Bombshell (Mon., 1946)
Wife Wanted (Mon., 1946)
Black Gold (AA, 1947)
Kilroy Was Here (Mon., 1947)
Louisiana (Mon., 1947)
Adventures in Silverado (Col., 1948)
Rocky (Mon., 1948)
Thunderhoof (Col., 1948)
Ladies of the Chorus (Col., 1948)
Down Memory Lane (Eagle Lion, 1949)
The Big Cat (Eagle Lion, 1949)
The Iroquois Trail (UA, 1950)
Lorna Doone (Col., 1951)
The Texas Rangers (Col., 1951)
Mask of the Avenger (Col., 1951)
Scandal Sheet (Col., 1952)
Kansas City Confidential (UA, 1952)
The Brigand (Col., 1952)
99 River Street (UA, 1953)
They Rode West (Col., 1954)
Hell's Island (Par., 1955)
Tight Spot (Col., 1955)
Five Against the House (Col., 1955)
The Phenix City Story (AA, 1955)
The Brothers Rico (Col., 1957)
Gunman's Walk (Col., 1958)
The Scarface Mob (WB-TV, 1958)
Hell to Eternity (Col., 1960)
Key Witness (MGM, 1960)
The Secret Ways (Univ., 1961) (with uncredited Richard Wid-
    mark)
The Young Doctors (UA, 1961)
Kid Galahad (UA, 1962)
Rampage (WB, 1963) (with uncredited Henry Hathaway)
The Silencers (Col., 1966)
A Time for Killing (Col., 1967) (with uncredited Roger Corman)
The Wrecking Crew (Col., 1968)
Hornet's Nest (UA, 1970)
Ben (Cin., 1972)
Walking Tall (Cin., 1973)

KATZIN, LEE H.
    Hondo and the Apaches (MGM, 1967)
    Heaven With a Gun (MGM, 1969)
    Whatever Happened to Aunt Alice? (Cin., 1969)
    The Phynx (WB, 1970)
    Along Came a Spider (ABC-TV, 1970)
    Le Mans (National General, 1971)

The Saltzburg Connection (20th, 1972)
The Voyage of the Yes (CBS-TV, 1973)

KÄUTNER, HELMUT, b. March 25, 1908, Düsseldorf, Germany.
Kitty und die Weltkonferenz (German, 1939) (also script)
Die Act Entfesselten (German, 1939)
Frau nach Mass (German, 1940) (also script)
Kleider Machen Leute (German, 1940) (also script)
Auf Wiedersehen, Franziska (German, 1941) (also script)
Anuschka (German, 1942) (also co-script)
Wir Machen Musik (German, 1942) (also script)
Romanze in Moll (German, 1942) (also co-script, actor)
Grosse Freiheit Nr 7 (German, 1944) (also co-script, actor)
Unter den Brücken (German, 1945) (also co-script)
In Jenen Tagen (German, 1947) (also co-script)
Der Apfel Ist Ab (also from own play, co-dialogue, co-script,
    co-lyrics, actor)
Königskinder (German, 1949) (also co-script, actor)
Epilog (German, 1950) (also co-script, actor)
Käpt'n Bay-Bay (Austrian, 1952) (also co-script)
Die Letzte Brücke (German, 1953) (also co-script)
Bildnis einer Unbekannten (German, 1954) (also co-script)
Glanz und Ende eines Kongis [Ludwig II] (German, 1955)
Des Teufels General (German, 1955) (also co-script)
Himmel Ohne Sterne (German, 1955) (also from own play, co-
    script)
Ein Mädchen aus Flandern (German, 1956) (also co-script)
Der Hauptmann von Köpenick (German, 1956) (also co-script)
Die Zürcher Verlobung [The Affairs of Julie] (German, 1957)
    (also co-script, actor)
Monpti (German, 1957) (also co-script)
The Restless Years (Univ., 1958)
A Stranger in My Arms (Univ., 1958)
Der Schinderhannes (German, 1958)
Der Rest Ist Schweigen (German, 1959) (also script)
Die Gans von Sedan (German, 1959) (also co-script)
Das Glas Wasser (German, 1960) (also script)
Schwarzer Kies (German, 1961) (also co-script)
Der Traum von Lieschen Muller (German, 1961)
Die Rote (German, 1962)
Das Haus in Montevideo (German, 1963)
Lausbubengeschichten (German, 1964)
Die Feuerzangenbowle (German, 1970)

KAZAN, ELIA (Elia Kazanijoglou), b. Sept. 7, 1909, Istanbul, Tur-
    key.
It's Up to You (U.S. Dept. of Agriculture, 1941)
A Tree Grows in Brooklyn (20th, 1945)
The Sea of Grass (MGM, 1946)
Boomerang! (20th, 1947)
Gentleman's Agreement (20th, 1947)
Pinky (20th, 1949) (with uncredited John Ford)

Stathis Ghialdis with Elia Kazan at the time of <u>America, America</u> (WB, 1963).

Panic in the Streets (20th, 1950)
A Streetcar Named Desire (WB, 1951)
Viva Zapata! (20th, 1952)
Man on a Tightrope (20th, 1953)
On the Waterfront (Co., 1954)
East of Eden (WB, 1955) (also producer)
Baby Doll (WB, 1956) (also producer)
A Face in the Crowd (WB, 1957) (also producer)
Wild River (20th, 1960) (also producer)
Splendor in the Grass (WB, 1961) (also producer)
America, America (WB, 1963) (also producer, script)
The Arrangement (WB, 1969) (also producer, script)
The Visitors (UA, 1972)

KEATON, BUSTER (Joseph Francis Keaton), b. Oct. 4, 1895,
    Piqua, Kans.; d. Feb. 1, 1966.
    The Three Ages (Metro, 1923) (with Edward Cline) (also actor)
    Our Hospitality (Metro, 1923) (with Jack Blystone) (also co-
        script, actor)
    Sherlock Junior (Metro, 1924) (also actor)
    The Navigator (Metro, 1924) (with Donald Crips) (also co-script,
        actor)

Seven Chances (Metro, 1925) (also script, actor)
Go West (Metro, 1925) (also idea, actor)
Battling Butler (Metro, 1926) (also actor)
The General (UA, 1926) (also co-original idea, actor)

KEIGHLEY, WILLIAM, b. Aug. 4, 1893, Philadelphia.
The Match King (FN, 1932) (with Howard Bretherton)
Ladies They Talk About (WB, 1933) (with Howard Bretherton)
Easy to Love (WB, 1934)
Journal of a Crime (FN, 1934)
Dr. Monica (WB, 1934)
Big-Hearted Herbert (WB, 1934)
Kansas City Princess (WB, 1934)
Babbitt (FN, 1934)
The Right to Live (WB, 1935)
The G-Men (WB, 1935)
Mary Jane's Pa (FN, 1935)
Special Agent (WB, 1935)
Stars over Broadway (WB, 1935) (with co-choreographer Busby
    Berkeley)
The Singing Kid (FN, 1936)
The Green Pastures (WB, 1936) (with Marc Connelly)
Bullets or Ballots (FN, 1936)
God's Country and the Woman (WB, 1936)
The Prince and the Pauper (WB, 1937)
Varsity Show (WB, 1937) (with choreographer Busby Berkeley)
The Adventures of Robin Hood (WB, 1938) (with Michael Curtiz)
Valley of the Giants (WB, 1938)
The Secrets of an Actress (WB, 1938)
Brother Rat (WB, 1938)
Yes, My Darling Daughter (WB, 1939)
Each Dawn I Die (WB, 1939)
The Fighting 69th (WB, 1940)
Torrid Zone (WB, 1940)
No Time for Comedy (WB, 1940)
Four Mothers (WB, 1941)
The Bride Came C.O.D. (WB, 1941)
The Man Who Came to Dinner (WB, 1942)
George Washington Slept Here (WB, 1942)
Honeymoon (RKO, 1947)
The Street With No Name (20th, 1948)
Rocky Mountain (WB, 1950)
Close to My Heart (WB, 1951) (also script)
The Master of Ballantrae (WB, 1953)

KELLER, HARRY, b. Feb. 22, 1913, Los Angeles.
Blonde Bandit (Rep., 1949)
Tarnished (Rep., 1950)
Fort Dodge Stampede (Repl, 1951)
Desert of Lost Men (Rep., 1951)
Rose of Cimarron (20th, 1952)
Leadville Gunslinger (Rep., 1952)

Black Hills (Rep. , 1952)
Thundering Caravans (Rep. , 1952)
Marshal of Cedar Rock (Rep. , 1953)
Bandits of the West (Rep. , 1953)
Savage Frontier (Rep. , 1953)
El Paso Stampede (Rep. , 1953)
Red River Shore (Rep. , 1954)
The Unguarded Moment (Univ. , 1956)
Man Afraid (Univ. , 1957)
Day of the Bad Man (Univ. , 1958)
The Female Animal (Univ. , 1958)
Voice in the Mirror (Univ. , 1958)
Step Down to Terror (Univ. , 1958)
Seven Ways from Sundown (Univ. , 1960)
Tammy, Tell Me True (Univ. , 1961)
Six Black Horses (Univ. , 1962)
Tammy and the Doctor (Univ. , 1963)
The Brass Bottle (Univ. , 1964)
Geronimo's Revenge (BV, 1965) (with James Neilson)
Stampede at Bitter Creek (BV, 1966)
In Enemy Country (Univ. , 1968) (also producer)

KELLY, GENE (Eugene Curran Kelly), b. Aug. 23, 1912, Pitts-
    burgh.
    On the Town (MGM, 1949) (with Stanley Donen) (also choreog-
        raphy, actor)
    Singin' in the Rain (MGM, 1952) (with Stanley Donen) (also co-
        choreography, actor)
    It's Always Fair Weather (MGM, 1955) (with Stanley Donen)
        (also choreography, actor)
    Invitation to the Dance (MGM, 1956) (also script, choreography,
        actor)
    The Happy Road (MGM, 1957) (also producer, actor)
    The Tunnel of Love (MGM, 1958)
    Gigot (20th, 1962)
    A Guide for the Married Man (20th, 1967)
    Hello, Dolly! (20th, 1969)
    The Cheyenne Social Club (National General, 1970) (also pro-
        ducer)

KENNEDY, BURT, b. 1923, Muskegon, Mich.
    The Canadians (20th, 1961) (also script)
    Mail Order Bride (MGM, 1963)
    The Rounders (MGM, 1965) (also script)
    The Money Trap (MGM, 1966)
    Return of the Seven (UA, 1966)
    Welcome to Hard Times (MGM, 1967) (also script)
    The War Wagon (Univ. , 1967)
    Support Your Local Sheriff (UA, 1969)
    Young Billy Young (UA, 1969) (also script)
    The Good Guys and the Bad Guys (WB, 1969)

Dirty Dingus Magee (MGM, 1970)
Support Your Local Gunfighter (UA, 1971) (also executive pro-
    ducer)
Hannie Caulder (Tigon British, 1971) (also script, as Z.X.
    Jones)
The Deserter (Par., 1971)
The Train Robbers (WB, 1973) (also script)

KENTON, ERLE C., b. Aug. 1, 1896, Norboro, Mo.
A Small Town Idol (Associated Producers, 1921)
Tea With a Kick (Associated Producers, 1922)
The Danger Signal (Col., 1925)
A Fool and His Money (Col., 1925)
Red Hot Tires (WB, 1925)
The Palm Beach Girl (Par., 1926)
The Sap (WB, 1926)
The Love Toy (WB, 1926)
Other Women's Husbands (WB, 1926)
The Girl in the Pullman (Pathé, 1927)
Wedding Bills (Par., 1927)
The Rejuvenation of Aunt Mary (PDC, 1927)
Bare Knees (Lumas, 1928)
The Companionate Marriage (FN, 1928)
Golf Widows (Col., 1928)
Name the Woman (Col., 1928)
Nothing to Wear (Col., 1928)
The Sideshow (Col., 1928)
The Sporting Age (Col., 1928)
The Street of Illusion (Col., 1928)
Father and Son (Col., 1929)
Mexicali Rose (Col., 1929)
The Song of Love (Col., 1929)
Trial Marriage (Col., 1929)
A Royal Romance (Col., 1931)
The Last Parade (Col., 1931)
Lover Come Back (Col., 1931)
Leftover Ladies (Tiffany, 1931)
X Marks the Spot (Tiffany, 1932)
Guilty as Hell (Par., 1932)
Island of Lost Souls (Par., 1932)
Stranger in Town (WB, 1932)
From Hell to Heaven (Par., 1933)
Disgraced! (Par., 1933)
The Big Executive (Par., 1933)
You're Telling Me (Par., 1934)
Search for Beauty (Par., 1934)
The Best Man Wins (Col., 1935)
Party Wire (Col., 1935)
Grand Exit (Col., 1935)
Public Menace (Col., 1935)
End of the Trail (Col., 1936) (also actor)
Counterfeit (Col., 1936)

The Devil's Squadron (Col., 1936)
The Devil's Playground (Col., 1937)
Racketeers in Exile (Col., 1937)
Little Tough Guys in Society (Univ., 1938)
Everything's on Ice (RKO, 1939)
Remedy for Riches (RKO, 1940)
Melody for Three (RKO, 1941)
They Meet Again (RKO, 1941)
Naval Academy (Col., 1941)
Flying Cadets (Univ., 1941)
Petticoat Politics (Rep., 1941)
Pardon My Sarong (Univ., 1942)
The Ghost of Frankenstein (Univ., 1942)
Who Done It? (Univ., 1942)
North to the Klondike (Univ., 1942)
Frisco Lil (Univ., 1942)
How's About It? (Univ., 1943)
It Ain't Hay (Univ., 1943)
Always a Bridesmaid (Univ., 1943)
She Gets Her Man (Univ., 1945)
House of Frankenstein (Univ., 1945)
House of Dracula (Univ., 1945)
The Cat Creeps (Univ., 1946)
Little Miss Big (Univ., 1946)
Bob and Sally (Social Guidance, 1948)
One too Many (Hallmark, 1950)

KERSHNER, IRVIN (Irvin Kerschner), b. April 29, 1923, Philadel-
    phia.
    Stakeout on Dope Street (WB, 1958) (also co-script)
    The Young Captives (Par., 1959)
    The Hoodlum Priest (UA, 1961)
    A Face in the Rain (Emb., 1963)
    The Luck of Ginger Coffey (Con., 1964)
    A Fine Madness (WB, 1966)
    The Flim Flam Man (20th, 1967)
    Loving (Col., 1970)
    Up the Sandbox (National General, 1972)

KING, HENRY, b. Jan. 24, 1888, Lafayette, Va.
    Who Pays? (Pathé, 1915)
    Pay Dirt (Pathé, 1916)
    The Stained Pearl (Pathé, 1916)
    Little Mary Sunshine (Pathé, 1916)
    Once Upon a Time (Pathé, 1916)
    Joy and the Dragon (Pathé, 1916) (also actor)
    Shadows and Sunshine (Pathé, 1916)
    Twin Kiddies (Pathé, 1917)
    Told at Twilight (Pathé, 1917) (also actor)
    Sunshine and Gold (Pathé, 1917)
    The Bride's Silence (American Mutual, 1917)

Sands of Sacrifice (American Mutual, 1917)
The Spector of Suspicion (Mutual, 1917)
Souls in Pawn (American Mutual, 1917)
The Mainspring (Mutual, 1917) (also actor)
Southern Pride (Mutual, 1917)
A Game of Wits (American Mutual, 1917)
The Mate of the Sally Ann (American Mutual, 1917)
Beauty and the Rogue (American Mutual, 1918)
Powers That Prey (American Mutual, 1918)
Hearts or Diamonds? (Mutual, 1918)
The Locked Heart (General, 1918) (also actor)
When a Man Rides Alone (Pathé, 1918)
Hobbs in a Hurry (Pathé, 1918)
Cupid by Proxy (Pathé, 1918)
All the World to Nothing (Pathé, 1918)
The Child of M'sieu (Triangle, 1919)
Where the West Begins (Pathé, 1919)
Some Liar (Pathé, 1919)
Brass Buttons (Pathé, 1919)
A Sporting Chance (Pathé, 1919)
This Hero Stuff (Pathé, 1919)
Six Feet Four (Pathé, 1919)
A Fugitive from Matrimony (R.C., 1919)
23 and 1/2 Hours Leave (F.P.L., 1919)
Haunting Shadows (R.C., 1920)
The White Dove (Robertson-Cole, 1920)
Uncharted Channels (Robertson-Cole, 1920)
One Hour Before Dawn (Pathé, 1920)
Dice of Destiny (Pathé, 1920)
Help Wanted--Male (Pathé, 1920) (also actor)
When We Were 21 (Pathé, 1921)
Mistress of Shenstone (R.C., 1921)
Salvage (R.C., 1921)
The Sting of the Lash (R.C., 1921)
Tol'able David (FN, 1921)
Seventh Day (FN, 1922)
Sonny (FN, 1922)
Bond Boy (FN, 1922)
Fury (FN, 1923)
The White Sister (Metro, 1924)
Romola (Metro-Goldwyn, 1925)
Any Woman (Par., 1925) (also producer)
Sackcloth and Scarlet (Par., 1925) (also producer)
Stella Dallas (UA, 1925)
Partners Again (UA, 1926)
The Winning of Barbara Worth (UA, 1926)
The Magic Flame (UA, 1927) (also producer)
The Woman Disputed (UA, 1928) (with Sam Taylor, also pro-
    ducer)
She Goes to War (UA, 1929) (also producer)
Hell Harbor (UA, 1930) (also producer)
Lightnin' (Fox, 1930)
The Eyes of the World (Fox 1930) (also producer)

Merely Mary Ann (Fox, 1931)
Over the Hill (Fox, 1931)
The Woman in Room 13 (Fox, 1932)
State Fair (Fox, 1933)
I Loved You Wednesday (Fox, 1933) (with William Cameron
    Menzies)
Carolina (Fox, 1934)
Marie Galante (Fox, 1934)
One More Spring (Fox, 1935)
Way Down East (Fox, 1935)
The Country Doctor (20th, 1936)
Lloyds of London (20th, 1936)
Ramona (20th, 1936)
Seventh Heaven (20th, 1937)
In Old Chicago (20th, 1938)
Alexander's Ragtime Band (20th, 1938)
Jesse James (20th, 1939)
Stanley and Livingstone (20th, 1939)
Little Old New York (20th, 1940)
Maryland (20th, 1940)
Chad Hanna (20th, 1940)
A Yank in the RAF (20th, 1941)
Remember the Day (20th, 1941)
The Black Swan (20th, 1942)
The Song of Bernadette (20th, 1943)
Wilson (20th, 1944)
A Bell for Adano (20th, 1945)
Margie (20th, 1946)
Captain from Castile (20th, 1947)
Deep Waters (20th, 1948)
Twelve O'Clock High (20th, 1949)
Prince of Foxes (20th, 1949)
The Gunfighter (20th, 1950)
I'd Climb the Highest Mountain (20th, 1951)
David and Bathsheba (20th, 1951)
Wait Till the Sun Shines, Nellie (20th, 1952)
O. Henry's Full House (ep: "The Gift of the Magi") (20th,
    1952)
The Snows of Kilimanjaro (20th, 1952)
King of the Khyber Rifles (20th, 1953)
Untamed (20th, 1955)
Love Is a Many-Splendored Thing (20th, 1955)
Carousel (20th, 1956)
The Sun Also Rises (20th, 1957)
The Bravados (20th, 1958)
The Old Man and the Seas (WB, 1958) (uncredited, with Fred
    Zinneman and uncredited John Sturges)
This Earth Is Mine (Univ., 1959)
Beloved Infidel (20th, 1959)
Tender Is the Night (20th, 1961)

KLEIN, CHARLES (Charles Frederick Klein), b. Jan. 28, 1898, Andernach, Germany.
Blindfold (Fox, 1928)
The Sin Sister (Fox, 1929)
Pleasure Crazed (Fox, 1929) (with Donald Gallaher)
Wenn am Sonntagabend die Dorfinusik Spielt (German, 1933)
Zigeunerblut [Ungarmädel] (German, 1934)
Ihr Privatsekretär (German, 1940)

KOCH, HOWARD W., b. April 11, 1916, New York City.
Shield for Murder (UA, 1954) (with Edmond O'Brien)
Big House USA (UA, 1955)
Untamed Youth (WB, 1957)
Bop Girl (UA, 1957)
Jungle Heat (UA, 1957)
The Girl in Black Stockings (UA, 1957)
Fort Bowie (UA, 1958)
Violent Road (WB, 1958)
Frankenstein--1970 (AA, 1958)
Andy Hardy Comes Home (MGM, 1958)
The Last Mile (UA, 1959)
Born Reckless (WB, 1959)
Badge 373 (Par., 1973) (also producer)

KORDA, ALEXANDER (SIR), b. Sept. 16, 1893, Turkeye, Hungary; d. Jan. 23, 1956.
A Becsapot Ujsagiro (Hungarian, 1914) (with Gyula Zilahi)
Lyon Lea (Hungarian, 1915) (with Miklos M. Pasztory)
A Tiszti Kardbojt (Hungarian, 1915)
Tutyu es Totyo (Hungarian, 1915) (with Gyula Zilahi)
Vergödö Szivek (Hungarian, 1916) (also script)
Feher Éjszakak [Fedora] (Hungarian, 1916) (also script)
Nagymama (Hungarian, 1916) (also script)
A Dolovai Nabob Leánya (Hungarian, 1916) (with Jeno Janovics)
Ciklamen (Hungarian, 1916)
A Kétziyü Férfi (Hungarian, 1916) (also script)
A Neveto Szaszkia (Hungarian, 1916)
Magnas Miska (Hungarian, 1917) (also script)
Mesek az Ivogeprol (Hungarian, 1917) (also script)
As Egymillio Fontos Banko (Hungarian, 1917) (also script)
A Gölyakalifa (Hungarian, 1917) (also script)
Harrison es Harrison (Hungarian, 1917)
Magia (Hungarian, 1917)
Szent Peter Esernyöje (Hungarian, 1917)
Faun (Hungarian, 1917)
A Ketlelku Asszony (Hungarian, 1917)
Mary Ann (Hungarian, 1918)
Az Aranyember (Hungarian, 1918)
Se Ki Se Be (Hungarian, 1918)
Ave Caesar! (Hungarian, 1919)
Feher Rozsa (Hungarian (1919)

A 111-Es (Hungarian, 1919)
Yamata (Hungarian, 1919)
Prinz und Bettelknabe [Seine Majestat das Bettelkind] [The
    Prince and the Pauper] (Austrian, 1920)
Dietro la Maschera (Italian, 1921)
Heeren der Meere (Austrian, 1933)
Eine Versunkeme Welt (Austrian, 1933)
Samson und Delila (Austrian, 1922) (also co-script)
Das Unbekannte Morgen (German, 1923) (also producer, script)
Jedermanns Weib [Jedermanns Frau] (Austrian, 1924)
Tragödie im Hause Habsbourg (German, 1924) (also producer)
Der Tänzer Meiner Frau [Dance Fever] (German, 1925) (also
    script)
Eine du Barry von Heute [A Modern DuBarry] (German, 1926)
Madame Wünscht Keine Kinder [Madame Wants No Children]
    (German, 1926)
The Stolen Bride (FN, 1926)
The Private Life of Helen of Troy (FN, 1927)
The Night Watch (FN, 1928)
The Yellow Lily (FN, 1928)
Love and the Devil (FN, 1929)
The Squall (FN, 1929)
Her Private Life (FN, 1929)
Lilies of the Field (FN, 1930)
Women Everywhere (Fox, 1930)
The Princess and the Plumber (Fox, 1930)
Rive Gauche [French version of Laughter] (Par., 1931)
Die Manner um Lucie [German version of Laughter] (Par.,
    1931)
Marius (French, 1931)
Zum Goldenen Auker [German version of Marius] (Par., 1931)
Service for Ladies [Reserved for Ladies] (Par., 1932) (also
    producer)
Wedding Rehearsal (Ideal, 1932) (also producer)
La Dame de Chez Maxim's (French, 1932) (also co-producer)
The Girl from Maxim's [English version of La Dame de Chez
    Maxim's] (UA, 1932)
The Private Life of Henry VIII (UA, 1933) (also producer)
The Private Life of Don Juan (UA, 1934) (also producer)
Rembrandt (UA, 1936) (also producer)
That Hamilton Woman (UA, 1941) (also producer)
Perfect Strangers [Vacation from Marriage] (MGM, 1945) (also
    co-producer)
An Ideal Husband (20th, 1947) (also producer)

KOSTER, HENRY (Hermann Kosterlitz), b. May 1, 1905, Berlin.
    Das Abenteuer der Thea Roland [Das Abenteur einer Schönen
        Frau] [Der Storch Hat Uns Getraut] (German, 1932)
    Das Hässliche Mädchen (German, 1933) (also co-script)
    Peter (Hungarian-Austrian, 1934)
    Kleine Mutti [Kismama] (Hungarian-Austrian, 1935)
    Das Tagebuch der Geliebten [Maria Baschkirtzeff] [The Affairs
        of Maupassant] (Austrian-Italian, 1935)

Il Diario di una Amata [Italian version of Das Tagebuch Der Geliebten] (Italian, 1936)
Katharina, die Letzte (Austrian, 1935)
Three Smart Girls (Univ., 1936)
One Hundred Men and a Girl (Univ., 1937)
The Rage of Paris (Univ., 1938)
First Love (Univ., 1939)
Three Smart Girls Grow Up (Univ., 1939)
Spring Parade (Univ., 1940)
It Started With Eve (Univ., 1941)
Between Us Girls (Univ., 1942) (also producer)
Music for Millions (MGM, 1944)
Two Sisters from Boston (MGM, 1946)
The Unfinished Dance (MGM, 1947)
The Luck of the Irish (20th, 1948)
The Bishop's Wife (RKO, 1948)
Come to the Stable (20th, 1949)
The Inspector General (WB, 1949)
Wabash Avenue (20th, 1950)
My Blue Heaven (20th, 1950)
Harvey (Univ., 1950)
Mr. Belvedere Rings the Bell (20th, 1951)
No Highway in the Sky (20th, 1951)
Elopement (20th, 1951)
O'Henry's Full House (ep: "The Cop and the Anthem") (20th, 1952)
Stars and Stripes Forever (20th, 1952)
My Cousin Rachel (20th, 1952)
The Robe (20th, 1953)
Desiree (20th, 1954)
A Man Called Peter (20th, 1955)
The Virgin Queen (20th, 1955)
Good Morning, Miss Dove (20th, 1955)
D-Day the Sixth of June (20th, 1956)
The Power and the Prize (MGM, 1956)
My Man Godfrey (Univ., 1957)
Fraulein (20th, 1958)
The Naked Maja (UA, 1959)
The Story of Ruth (20th, 1960)
Flower Drum Song (Univ., 1961)
Mr. Hobbs Takes a Vacation (20th, 1962)
Take Her, She's Mine (20th, 1963)
Dear Brigitte (20th, 1965)
The Singing Nun (MGM, 1965)

KRAMER, STANLEY E., b. Sept. 29, 1913, New York City.
Not as a Stranger (UA, 1955) (also producer)
The Pride and the Passion (UA, 1957) (also producer)
The Defiant Ones (UA, 1958) (also producer)
On the Beach (UA, 1959) (also producer)
Inherit the Wind (UA, 1960) (also producer)
Judgment at Nuremberg (UA, 1961) (also producer)

Vivien Leigh with Stanley Kramer on the <u>Ship of Fools</u> (Col., 1965).

It's a Mad, Mad, Mad, Mad, World (UA, 1963) (also producer)
Ship of Fools (Col., 1965) (also producer)
Guess Who's Coming to Dinner (Col., 1967) (also producer)
The Secret of Santa Vittoria (UA, 1969) (also producer)
R. P. M. (Col., 1970) (also producer)
Bless the Beasts and Children (Col., 1971) (also producer)
Oklahoma Crude (Col., 1973) (also producer)

KRASNA, NORMAN, b. Nov. 7, 1909, Corona, L. I., N. Y.
Princess O'Rourke (WB, 1943)
The Big Hangover (MGM, 1950) (also producer, script)
The Ambassador's Daughter (UA, 1956) (also producer, script)

KUBRICK, STANLEY, b. July 26, 1928, New York City.
Fear and Desire (Joseph Burstyn, Inc., 1953) (also producer,
    camera, editor)
Killer's Kiss (UA, 1955) (also co-producer, story, script,
    camera, editor)

The Killing (UA, 1956) (also script)
Paths of Glory (UA, 1957) (also co-script)
Spartacus (Univ., 1960) (replaced Anthony Mann)
Lolita (Col., 1962)
Dr. Strangelove, or How I Learned to Stopy Worrying and Love
    the Bomb (Col., 1964) (also producer, co-script)
2001: A Space Odyssey (MGM, 1968) (also producer, co-script)
A Clockwork Orange (WB, 1971) (also producer, script)

KULIK, BUZZ (Seymour Kulik), b. 1922, New York City.
The Explosive Generation (UA, 1961)
The Yellow Canary (20th, 1963)
Ready for the People (WB, 1965)
Warning Shot (Par., 1967) (also producer)
Sergeant Ryker (Univ., 1968)
Villa Rides (Par., 1968)
Riot (Par., 1968)
Vanished (NBC-TV, 1971)
Owen Marshall, Counselor at Law (ABC-TV, 1971)
Brian's Song (ABC-TV, 1971)
To Find a Man (Col., 1972)
Shamus (Col., 1973)

L

LA CAVA, GREGORY, b. March 10, 1892, Towanda, Pa.; d.
    March 1, 1952.
His Nibs (Exceptional Pictures, 1921)
Restless Wives (C.C. Burr, 1924)
The New School Teacher (C.C. Burr, 1924)
Womanhandled (Par., 1925)
Let's Get Married (Par., 1926)
So's Your Old Man (Par., 1926)
Say It Again (Par., 1926)
The Gay Defender (Par., 1927)
Paradise for Two (Par., 1927) (also producer
Running Wild (Par., 1927)
Tell It to Sweeney (Par., 1927) (also producer)
Feel My Pulse (Par., 1928) (also producer)
Half a Bride (Par., 1928)
Saturday's Children (FN, 1929)
Big News (Pathé, 1929)
His First Comman (Pathé, 1930)
Laugh and Get Rich (RKO, 1931) (also script)
Smart Woman (RKO, 1931)
Symphony of Six Million (RKO, 1932)
Age of Consent (RKO, 1932)
The Half-Naked Truth (RKO, 1932) (also co-script)
Gabriel over the White House (MGM, 1933)
Bed of Roses (RKO, 1933) (also co-dialog)
Gallant Lady (UA, 1933)

Patric Knowles (second from left) and Irene Dunne on location with Gregory La Cava for Lady in a Jam (Univ., 1942).

The Affairs of Cellini (UA, 1934)
What Every Woman Knows (MGM, 1934)
Private Worlds (Par., 1935) (also co-script)
She Married Her Boss (Col., 1935)
My Man Godfrey (Univ., 1936) (also producer)
Stage Door (RKO, 1937)
Fifth Avenue Girl (RKO, 1939) (also producer)
Primrose Path (RKO, 1940) (also producer, co-script)
Unfinished Business (Univ., 1941) (also producer)
Lady in a Jam (Univ., 1942) (also producer)
Living in a Big Way (MGM, 1947) (also story, co-scrip)

LACHMAN, HARRY, b. June 29, 1886, La Salle, Ill.
Week-End Wives (British International, 1928)
The Compulsory Husband (British International, 1928)
Under the Greenwood Tree (British International, 1929)
The Yellow Mask (British International, 1929)
Song of Soho (British International, 1929)
The Love Habit (British International, 1931)
La Couturière de Luneville (French, 1931)
La Belle Marinière (French, 1931)
The Outsider (MGM, 1931) (also script)

Down Our Street (Par., 1932)
Insult (Par., 1932)
Face in the Sky (Fox, 1933)
Paddy the Next Best Thing (Fox, 1933)
George White's Scandals (Fox, 1934) (with George White, Thornton Freeland)
I Like It That Way (Fox, 1934)
Nada Mas Que Una Mujer [Spanish version of Pursued] (Fox, 1934)
Baby Take a Bow (Fox, 1934)
Dressed to Thrill (Fox, 1935)
Dante's Inferno (Fox, 1935)
Charlie Chan at the Circus (20th, 1936)
Our Relations (MGM, 1936)
The Man Who Lived Twice (Col., 1936)
The Devil Is Driving (Col., 1937)
It Happened in Hollywood (Col., 1937)
No Time to Marry (Col., 1938)
They Came By Night (20th, 1940)
Murder over New York (20th, 1940)
Dead Men Tell (20th, 1941)
Charlie Chan in Rio (20th, 1941)
Castle in the Desert (20th, 1942)
The Loves of Edgar Allan Poe (20th, 1942)
Dr. Renault's Secret (20th, 1942)

LAMONT, CHARLES, b. May 5, 1898, San Francisco.
The Curtain Fall (Chesterfield, 1934)
The Last Trap (Chesterfield, 1935)
Tomorrow's Youth (Mon., 1935)
Gigolette (RKO, 1935)
The World Accuses (Chesterfield, 1935)
Sons of Steel (Chesterfield, 1935)
A Shot in the Dark (Chesterfield, 1935)
Circumstantial Evidence (Chesterfield, 1935)
The Girl Who Came Back (Chesterfield, 1935)
False Pretenses (Chesterfield, 1935)
Happiness C.O.D. (Chesterfield, 1935)
The Lady in Scarlet (Chesterfield, 1935)
The Dark Hour (Chesterfield, 1936)
August Week-End (Chesterfield, 1936)
Ring Around the Moon (Chesterfield, 1936)
The Little Red School House (Chesterfield, 1936)
Below the Deadline (Chesterfield, 1936)
Bulldug Edition (Rep., 1936)
Wallaby Jim of the Islands (Grand National, 1937)
International Crime (Grand National, 1938)
Shadows over Shanghai (Grand National, 1938)
Slander House (Progressive, 1938)
Long Shot (Grand National, 1938)
Cipher Bureau (Grand National, 1938)
Panama Patrol (Grand National, 1939)

Pride of the Navy (Rep., 1939)
Inside Information (Univ., 1939)
Unexpected Father (Univ., 1939)
Little Accident (Univ., 1939)
Oh Johnny, How You Can Love (Univ., 1940)
Sandy Is a Lady (Univ., 1940)
Give Us Wings (Univ., 1940)
Love, Honor and Oh, Baby! (Univ., 1940)
San Antonio Rose (Univ., 1941)
Moonlight in Hawaii (Univ., 1941)
Road Agent (Univ., 1941)
Melody Lane (Univ., 1941)
Almost Married (Univ., 1942)
Hi, Neighbor (Univ., 1942)
Get Hep to Love (Univ., 1942)
When Johnny Comes Marching Home (Univ., 1942)
You're Telling Me (Univ., 1942)
Don't Get Personal (Univ., 1942)
It Comes Up Love (Univ., 1943)
Mister Big (Univ., 1943)
Hit the Ice (Univ., 1943)
Fired Wife (Univ., 1943)
Top Man (Univ., 1943)
Bowery to Broadway (Univ., 1944)
Her Primitive Man (Univ., 1944)
The Merry Monahans (Univ., 1944)
Chip off the Old Block (Univ., 1944)
Salome, Where She Danced (Univ., 1945)
Frontier Gal (Univ., 1945)
That's the Spirit (Univ., 1945)
The Runaround (Univ., 1946)
She Wrote the Book (Univ., 1946)
Slave Girl (Univ., 1947)
The Untamed Breed (Col., 1948)
Ma and Pa Kettle (Univ., 1949)
Bagdad (Univ., 1949)
Ma and Pa Kettle Go to Town (Univ., 1950)
I Was a Shoplifter (Univ., 1950)
Curtain Call at Cactus Creek (Univ., 1950)
Abbott and Costello in the Foreign Legion (1950)
Abbott and Costello Meet the Invisible Man (Univ., 1951)
Comin' Round the Mountain (Univ., 1951)
Flame of Araby (Univ., 1951)
Abbott and Costello Meet Captain Kidd (Univ., 1952)
Abbott and Costello Go to Mars (Univ., 1953)
Ma and Pa Kettle on Vacation (Univ., 1953)
Abbott and Costello Meet Dr. Jekyll and Mr. Hyde (Univ., 1953)
Ma and Pa Kettle at Home (Univ., 1954)
Ricochet Romance (Univ., 1954)
Untamed Heiress (Rep., 1954)
Abbott and Costello Meet the Keystone Kops (Univ., 1955)
Abbott and Costello Meet the Mummy (Univ., 1956)

Carolina Cannonball (Rep., 1956)
Lay That Rifle Down (Rep., 1955)
The Kettles in the Ozarks (Univ., 1956)
Francis in the Haunted House (Univ., 1956)

LANDERS, LEW (Louis Friedlander), b. Jan. 2, 1901, New York
    City; d. Dec. 16, 1962.
As Louis Friedlander:
    The Red Rider* (Univ., 1934)
    Tailspin Tommy* (Univ., 1934)
    The Vanishing Shadow* (Univ., 1934)
    The Call of the Savage* (Univ., 1935)
    Rustlers of Red Dog* (Univ., 1935)
    The Raven (Univ., 1935)
    Stormy (Univ., 1935)
    Parole! (Univ., 1936)

As Lew Landers:
    Without Orders (RKO, 1936)
    Night Waitress (RKO, 1936)
    They Wanted to Marry (RKO, 1937)
    The Man Who Found Himself (RKO, 1937)
    You Can't Buy Luck (RKO, 1937)
    Border Cafe (RKO, 1937)
    Flight from Glory (RKO, 1937)
    Danger Patrol (RKO, 1937)
    Living on Love (RKO, 1937)
    Double Danger (RKO, 1938)
    Condemned Women (RKO, 1938)
    Crashing Hollywood (RKO, 1938)
    Law of the Underworld (RKO, 1938)
    Blind Alibi (RKO, 1938)
    Sky Giant (RKO, 1938)
    Smashing the Rackets (RKO, 1938)
    Annabel Takes a Tour (RKO, 1938)
    Twelve Crowded Hours (RKO, 1939)
    Pacific Liner (RKO, 1939)
    Fixer Dugan (RKO, 1939)
    Bad Lands (RKO, 1939)
    Honeymoon Deferred (Univ., 1940)
    Enemy Agent (Univ., 1940)
    Ski Patrol (Univ., 1940)
    La Conga Nights (Univ., 1940)
    Wagons Westward (Rep., 1940)
    Sing, Dance, Plenty Hot (Rep., 1940)
    Girl from Havana (Rep., 1940)
    Slightly Tempted (Rep., 1940)
    Back in the Saddle (Rep., 1941)
    Ridin' in a Rainbow (Rep., 1941)
    Lucky Devils (Univ., 1941)
    The Singing Hill (Rep., 1941)
    I Was a Prisoner on Devil's Island (Col., 1941)

Mystery Ship (Col., 1941)
The Stork Pays Off (Col., 1941)
Not a Ladies Man (Col., 1942)
Smith of Minnesota (Col., 1942)
The Boogie Man Will Get You (Col., 1942)
Last of the Buccaneers (Col., 1942)
Submarine Raiders (Col., 1942)
Atlantic Convoy (Col., 1942)
The Man Who Returned to Life (Col., 1942)
Sabotage Squad (Col., 1942)
Cadets on Parade (Col., 1942)
Stand By All Networks (Col., 1942)
Junior Army (Col., 1942)
Harvard, Here I Come (Col., 1942)
Return of the Vampire (Col., 1943)
Murder in Times Square (Col., 1943)
The Deerslayer (Rep., 1943)
Doughboys in Ireland (Col., 1943)
After Midnight With Boston Blackie (Col., 1943)
Power of the Press (Col., 1943)
Redhead from Manhattan (Col., 1943)
Stars on Parade (Col., 1944)
U-Boat Prisoner (Col., 1944)
Two-Man Submarine (Col., 1944)
I'm from Arkansas (PRC, 1944)
The Black Parachute (Col., 1944)
The Ghost That Walks Alone (Col., 1944)
Cowboy Canteen (Col., 1944)
Swing in the Saddle (Col., 1944)
The Power of the Whistler (Col., 1945)
Follow That Woman (Par., 1945)
Tokyo Rose (Par., 1945)
Arson Squad (PRC, 1945)
Crime Inc. (PRC, 1945)
Shadow of Terror (PRC, 1945)
The Enchanted Forest (PRC, 1945)
The Mask of Dijon (PRC, 1946)
A Close Call for Boston Blackie (Col., 1946)
The Truth About Murder (RKO, 1946)
Hot Cargo (Par., 1946)
Secrets of a Sorority Girl (PRC, 1946)
Devil Ship (Col., 1947)
Under the Tonto Rim (RKO, 1947)
Thunder Mountain (RKO, 1947)
Seven Keys to Baldpate (RKO, 1947)
Danger Street (RKO, 1947)
Death Valley (Screen Guild, 1947)
The Son of Rusty (Col., 1947)
My Dog Rusty (Col., 1948)
Inner Sanctum (Film Classics, 1948)
Adventures of Gallant Bess (Eagle Lion, 1948)
The Stagecoach Kid (RKO, 1949)
Air Hostess (Col., 1949)

Law of the Barbary Coast (Col., 1949)
Barbary Pirate (Col., 1949)
Girl's School (Col., 1950)
Chain Gang (Col., 1950)
Revenue Agent (Col., 1950)
Beauty on Parade (Col., 1950)
State Penitentiary (Col., 1959)
Tyrant of the Sea (Col., 1950)
Dynamite Pass (RKO, 1950)
Davy Crockett, Indian Scout (UA, 1950)
Last of the Buccaneers (Col., 1950)
When the Redskins Rode (Col., 1951)
A Yank in Korea (Ool., 1951)
Hurricane Island (Col., 1951)
Jungle Manhunt (Col., 1951)
The Magic Carpet (Col., 1951)
Blue Blood (Col., 1951)
The Big Gusher (Col., 1951)
Jungle Jim in the Forbidden Land (Col., 1952)
Aladdin and His Lamp (Col., 1952)
California Conquest (Col., 1952)
Arctic Flight (Mon., 1952)
Riders of Capistrano (Revue-Exclusive, 1952)
Bad Men of Marysville (Revue-Exclusive, 1952)
The Range Masters (Revue-Exclusive, 1952)
Run for the Hills (Broder, 1953)
Torpedo Alley (AA, 1953)
The Neon Tornado (Revue-Exclusive, 1953)
Tangier Incident (AA, 1953)
The Return of Trigger Dawson (Revue-Exclusive, 1953)
Captain John Smith and Pocahontas (UA, 1953)
Roaring Challenge (Revue-Exclusive, 1953)
Man in the Dark (Col., 1953)
Captain Kidd and the Slave Girl (UA, 1954)
The Cruel Tower (AA, 1956)
Hot Rod Gang (AIP, 1958)
The Challenge of Rin-Tin-Tin (Col., 1958)
Terrified (Crown-International, 1964)

LANDRES, PAUL, b. Aug. 21, 1912, New York City.
Grand Canyon (Screen Guild, 1949)
Square Dance Jubilee (Lip., 1949)
Hollywood Varieties (Lip., 1950)
A Modern Marriage (Mon., 1950)
Navy Bound (Mon., 1951)
Rhythm Inn (Mon., 1951)
Army Bound (Mon., 1952)
Eyes of the Jungle (Lip., 1953)
Tangier Incident (AA, 1953)
Hell Canyon Outlaws (Rep., 1957)
Last of the Redmen (AA, 1957)
The Vampire (UA, 1957)

The Return of Dracula (UA, 1957)
Chain of Evidence (AA, 1957)
New Day at Sundown (AA, 1957)
Oregon Passage (AA, 1957)
Johnny Rocco (AA, 1958)
The Flame Barrier (UA, 1958)
Frontier Gun (20th, 1958)
Man from God's Country (AA, 1958)
The Miracle of the Hills (20th, 1959)
Lone Texan (20th, 1959)
Son of a Gunfighter (MGM, 1966)

LANFIELD, SIDNEY, b. April 20, 1899, Chicago.
Cheer Up and Smile (Fox, 1930)
El Barbero de Napoleon [Spanish version of Napoleon's Barber]
  (Fox, 1930)
Three Girls Lost (Fox, 1931)
Hush Money (Fox, 1931)
Dance Team (Fox, 1931)
Hat Check Girl (Fox, 1931)
Broadway Bad (Fox, 1933)
Moulin Rouge (UA, 1934)
The Last Gentleman (UA, 1934)
Hold 'Em Yale (Par., 1935)
Red Salute (UA, 1935)
King of Burlesque (20th, 1935)
Half Angel (20th, 1936)
Sing Baby Sing (20th, 1936)
One in a Million (20th, 1936)
Wake Up and Live (20th, 1937)
Thin Ice (20th, 1937)
Love and Hisses (20th, 1937)
Always Goodbye (20th, 1938)
The Hound of the Baskervilles (20th, 1939)
Second Fiddle (20th, 1939)
Swanee River (20th, 1939)
You'll Never Get Rich (Col., 1941)
The Lady Has Plans (Par., 1942)
My Favorite Blonde (Par., 1942)
Let's Face It (Par., 1943)
The Meanest Man in the World (20th, 1943)
Standing Room Only (Par., 1944)
Bring on the Girls (Par., 1945)
The Well Groomed Bride (Par., 1946)
The Trouble With Women (Par., 1947)
Where There's Life (Par., 1947)
Station West (RKO, 1948)
Sorrowful Jones (Par., 1949)
Follow the Sun (20th, 1951)
The Lemon Drop Kid (Par., 1951)
Skirts Ahoy (MGM, 1952)

Kathleen Case and Glenn Ford (right) with Fritz Lang on a break on the set of <u>Human Desire</u> (Col., 1954).

LANG, FRITZ, b. Dec. 5, 1890, Vienna.
  Halbblut (German, 1919) (also script)
  Der Herr der Liebe (German, 1919)
  Die Spinnen (German, 1919) (also script)
  Harakiri (German, 1919)
  Vier um die Frau (German, 1920) (also co-script)
  Das Wandernde Bild (German, 1920) (also co-script)
  Der Mude Tod (German, 1921) (also script)
  Dr. Mabuse, der Spieler (German, 1922) (also co-script)
  Die Nibelungen (German, 1924) (also co-script)
  Metropolis (German, 1926) (also co-script)
  Spione (German, 1928) (also producer, co-script)
  Die Frau im Mond (German, 1929) (also producer, co-script)
  M (German, 1931) (also co-script)
  Das Testament Des Mr. Mabuse (German, 1933) (also co-script)
  Liliom (Fox Europa, 1934)
  Fury (MGM, 1936) (also co-script)
  You Only Live Once (UA, 1937)
  You and Me (Par., 1938) (also producer)
  The Return of Frank James (20th, 1940)
  Western Union (20th, 1941)
  Confirm or Deny (20th, 1941) (uncredited, with Archie Mayo)
  Moontide (20th, 1942) (replaced by Archie Mayo)
  Man Hunt (20th, 1941)
  Hangmen Also Die (UA, 1943) (co-producer, co-story)
  The Ministry of Fear (Par., 1944)
  The Woman in the Window (RKO, 1944)
  Scarlet Street (Univ., 1945) (also producer)
  Cloak and Dagger (WB, 1946)
  Secret Beyond the Door (Univ., 1948) (also producer)
  House by the River (Rep., 1950)
  American Guerrilla in the Philippines (20th, 1950)
  Rancho Notorious (RKO, 1952)
  Clash by Night (RKO, 1952)
  The Blue Gardenia (WB, 1953)
  The Big Heat (Col., 1953)
  Human Desire (Col., 1954)
  Moonfleet (MGM, 1955)
  While the City Sleeps (RKO, 1956)
  Beyond a Reasonable Doubt (RKO, 1956)
  Der Tiger Von Eschnapur (German, 1958)
  Das Indische Grabmal (German, 1958)
  Die 1000 Augen des Dr. Mabuse (German, 1960) (also co-
    script)

LANG, WALTER, b. Aug. 10, 1898, Memphis, Tenn.; d. Feb. 7,
    1972.
  Red Kimono (Vital Exchange, 1925)
  The Carnival Girl (Vitagraph, 1926)
  The Earth Woman (Associated Exhibitors, 1926)
  The Golden Web (Lumas, 1926)
  Money to Burn (Lumas, 1926)

By Whose Hand? (Col., 1927)
The College Hero (Col., 1927)
The Ladybird (Chadwick, 1927)
Sally in Our Alley (Col., 1927)
The Satin Woman (Lumas, 1927)
The Desert Bride (Col., 1928)
The Night Flyer (Pathé, 1928)
The Spirit of Youth (Tiffany, 1929)
The Big Fight (World Wide, 1930)
Brothers (Col., 1930)
Cock O' the Walk (World Wide, 1930) (with Roy William Neill)
The Costello Case (World Wide, 1930)
Hello Sister (World Wide, 1930)
Hell Bound (Tiffany, 1931)
No More Orchids (Col., 1932)
The Warrior's Husband (Fox, 1933)
The Mighty Barnum (UA, 1934)
Carnival (Col., 1935)
Love Before Breakfast (Univ., 1936)
Wife, Doctor and Nurse (20th, 1937)
Second Honeymoon (20th, 1937)
The Baroness and the Butler (20th, 1938)
I'll Give a Million (20th, 1938)
The Little Princess (20th, 1939)
The Blue Bird (20th, 1940)
Star Dust (20th, 1940)
The Great Profile (20th, 1940)
Tin Pan Alley (20th, 1940)
Moon Over Miami (20th, 1941)
Weekend in Havana (20th, 1941)
Song of the Islands (20th, 1942)
The Magnificent Dope (20th, 1942)
Coney Island (20th, 1943)
Greenwich Village (20th, 1944)
State Fair (20th, 1945)
Sentimental Journey (20th, 1946)
Claudia and David (20th, 1946)
Mother Wore Tights (20th, 1947)
Sitting Pretty (20th, 1948)
When My Baby Smiles at Me (20th, 1948)
You're My Everything (20th, 1949)
Cheaper by the Dozen (20th, 1950)
The Jackpot (20th, 1950)
On the Riviera (20th, 1951)
With a Song in My Heart (20th, 1952)
Call Me Madam (20th, 1953)
There's No Business Like Show Business (20th, 1954)
The King and I (20th, 1956)
The Desk Set (20th, 1957)
But Not for Me (20th, 1959)
Can-Can (20th, 1960)
The Marriage-Go-Round (20th, 1960)
Snow White and the Three Stooges (20th, 1961)

LAUGHTON, CHARLES, b. July 1, 1899, Scarborough, Eng.; d.
    Dec. 15, 1962.
    Night of the Hunter (UA, 1955)

LAVEN, ARNOLD, b. Feb. 23, 1922, Chicago.
    Without Warning (UA, 1952)
    Vice Squad (UA, 1953)
    The Rack (MGM, 1956)
    The Monster That Challenged the World (UA, 1957)
    Slaughter on Tenth Avenue (Univ., 1957)
    Anna Lucasta (UA, 1958)
    Geronimo (UA, 1962) (also producer, co-story)
    The Glory Guys (UA, 1965) (also co-producer)
    Rought Night in Jericho (Univ., 1967)
    Sam Whiskey (UA, 1969) (also co-producer)

LE BORG, REGINALD, b. Dec. 11, 1902, Vienna.
    She's for Me (Univ., 1943)
    Calling Dr. Death (Univ., 1943)
    Adventure in Music (AFE, 1944) (with S. K. Winston, Ernest
        Matray)
    Dead Man's Eyes (Univ., 1944)
    Weird Woman (Univ., 1944)
    Destiny (Univ., 1944)
    San Diego, I Love You (Univ., 1944) (also producer)
    Jungle Woman (Univ., 1944)
    The Mummy's Ghost (Univ., 1944)
    Honeymoon Ahead (Univ., 1945)
    Susie Steps Out (UA, 1946)
    Joe Palooka, Champ (Mon., 1946)
    Little Iodine (UA, 1946)
    Fall Guy (Mon., 1947)
    Adventures of Don Coyote (UA, 1947)
    Joe Palooka in the Knockout (Mon., 1947)
    Philo Vance's Secret Mission (PRC, 1947)
    Port Said (Col., 1948)
    Fighting Mad (Mon., 1948)
    Joe Palooka in Winner Take All (Mon., 1948)
    Trouble Makers (Mon., 1948)
    Fighting Fools (Mon., 1949)
    Hold That Baby (Mon., 1949)
    Joe Palooka in Counterpunch (Mon., 1949)
    Wyoming Mail (Univ., 1950) (also script)
    Young Daniel Boone (Mon., 1950)
    The Squared Circle (Mon., 1950)
    Joe Palooka in Triple Cross (Mon., 1951)
    G. I. Jane (Lip., 1951)
    Models, Inc. (Mutual, 1952)
    Bad Blonde (Lip., 1953)
    Sins of Jezebel (Lip., 1953)
    The Great Jesse James Raid (Lip., 1953)

Lon Chaney, Jr. (right) with Reginald Le Borg on a break from shooting <u>The Mummy's Ghost</u> (Univ., 1944).

The Flanagan Boy (Exclusive, 1953)
The White Orchid (UA, 1954) (also producer, co-script)
The Black Sleep (UA, 1956)
Voodoo Island (UA, 1957)
War Drums (UA, 1957)
The Dalton Girls (UA, 1957)

The Flight That Disappeared (UA, 1961)
Deadly Duo (UA, 1962)
Diary of a Madman (UA, 1962)
The Eyes of Annie Jones (20th, 1964)
So Evil, My Sister (Zenith International, 1973)

LEACOCK, PHILIP, b. 1917, London.
　　Riders of the New Forest (Crown, 1947)
　　The Brave Don't Cry (Rank, 1952)
　　Appointment in London (Rank, 1953)
　　The Kidnappers (Rank, 1953)
　　Escapade (Rank, 1955)
　　The Spanish Gardener (Rank, 1956)
　　High Tide at Noon (Rank, 1957)
　　Innocent Sinners (Rank, 1958)
　　The Rabbit Trap (UA, 1958)
　　Take a Giant Step (UA, 1959)
　　Let No Man Write My Epitaph (Col., 1959)
　　Hand in Hand (Williams and Pritchard, 1960)
　　13 West Street (Col., 1961)
　　Reach for Glory (Gala, 1962)
　　The War Lover (Col., 1962)
　　Tamahine (MGM, 1961)
　　The Birdmen (ABC-TV, 1971
　　The Daughters of Joshua Cabe (ABC-TV, 1972)
　　When Michael Calls (ABC-TV, 1972)
　　Adam's Woman (WB, 1972)
　　The Great Man's Whiskers (NBC-TV, 1973)
　　Key West (NBC-TV, 1973)
　　Dying Room Only (ABC-TV, 1973)

LEDERMAN, D. ROSS (David Ross Lederman), b. Dec. 11, 1895,
　　　　Lancaster, Pa.
　　A Dog of the Regiment (WB, 1927)
　　A Race for Life (WB, 1928)
　　Rinty of the Desert (WB, 1928)
　　Shadows of the Night (MGM, 1928) (also script)
　　The Million Dollar Collar (WB, 1929)
　　The Man Hunter (WB, 1929)
　　The Phantom of the West* (Mascot, 1931)
　　The Texas Ranger (Col., 1931)
　　Branded (Col., 1931)
　　Range Feud (Col., 1931)
　　Ridin' for Justice (Col., 1931)
　　McKenna of the Mounted (Col., 1932)
　　The Fighting Marshal (Col., 1932)
　　Two Fisted Law (Col., 1932)
　　Texas Cyclone (Col., 1932)
　　Daring Danger (Col., 1932)
　　The Riding Tornado (Col., 1932)
　　The End of the Trail (Col., 1932)

High Speed (Col., 1932)
Speed Demon (Col., 1933)
State Trooper (Col., 1933)
Soldiers of the Storm (Col., 1933)
The Whirlwind (Col., 1933)
Rusty Rides Alone (Col., 1933)
Silent Men (Col., 1933)
Hell Bent for Love (Col., 1934)
Beyond the Law (Col., 1934)
The Crime of Helen Stanley (Col., 1934)
Girl in Danger (Col., 1934)
Texas Ranger (Col., 1934)
Man's Game (Col., 1934)
Murder in the Clouds (WB, 1934)
Dinky (WB, 1935) (with Howard Bretherton)
Red Hot Tires (WB, 1935)
Alibi for Murder (Col., 1936)
Come Closer Folks (Col., 1936)
Moonlight on the Prairie (WB, 1936)
Counterfeit Lady (Col., 1937)
I Promise to Pay (Col., 1937)
Adventure in Sahara (Col., 1938)
Juvenile Court (Col., 1938)
The Little Adventuress (Col., 1938)
Tarzan's Revenge (MGM, 1938)
Racketeers of the Range (RKO, 1939)
Glamour for Sale (Col., 1940)
Military Academy (Col., 1940)
Thundering Frontier (Col., 1940)
Father's Son (WB, 1941)
Passage from Hong Kong (WB, 1941)
Shadows on the Stairs (WB, 1941)
Strange Alibi (WB, 1941)
Across the Sierra (Col. 1941)
A Bullet Scars (WB, 1942)
Buses Roar (WB, 1942)
Escape from Crime (WB, 1942)
I Was Framed (WB, 1942)
The Body Disappears (WB, 1942)
The Gorilla Man (WB, 1943)
Find the Blackmailer (WB, 1943)
Adventure in Iraq (WB, 1943)
Three of a Kind (Mon., 1944)
The Racket Man (Col., 1944)
The Last Ride (WB, 1944)
Out of the Depths (Col., 1945)
The Phantom Thief (Col., 1946)
Sing While You Dance (Col., 1946)
Boston Blackie and the Law (Col., 1946)
Dangerous Business (Col., 1946)
The Notorious Lone Wolf (Col., 1946)
The Lone Wolf in Mexico (Col., 1947)
Key Witness (Col., 1947)

The Return of the Whistler (Col., 1948)
The Babe Ruth Story (AA, 1948)
Military Academy With That 10th Avenue Gang (Col., 1950)

LEE, ROWLAND V., b. Sept. 6, 1891, Findlay, O.
Blind Hearts (Associated Producers, 1921)
The Cup of Life (Associated Producers, 1921)
Cupid's Brand (Arrow, 1921)
The Sea Lion (Associated Producers, 1931)
Whims of the Gods (Goldwyn, 1922)
The Dust Flower (Goldwyn, 1922)
His Back Against the Wall (Goldwyn, 1922)
The Men of Zanzibar (Fox, 1922)
Mixed Faces (Fox, 1922)
Money to Burn (Fox, 1922)
A Self-Made Man (Fox, 1922) (also co-script)
Shirley of the Circus (Fox, 1922)
Alice Adams (Associated Exhibitors, 1923) (also adaptation)
Desire (Metro, 1923)
Gentle Julia (Fox, 1923)
You Can't Get Away With It (Fox, 1923)
In Love With Love (Fox, 1924)
Havoc (Fox, 1925)
The Man Without a Country (Fox, 1925)
The Outsider (Fox, 1926)
The Silver Treasure (Fox, 1926)
The Whirlwind of Youth (Fox, 1927)
Doomsday (Par., 1928)
The First Kiss (Par., 1928)
Loves of an Actress (Par., 1928) (also script)
The Secret Hour (Par., 1928) (also script)
Three Sinners (Par., 1928)
A Dangerous Woman (Par., 1929)
The Mysterious Dr. Fu Manchu (Par., 1929)
The Wolf of Wall Street (Par., 1929)
Derelict (Par., 1930)
Ladies Love Brutes (Par., 1930)
The Man from Wyoming (Par., 1930)
Paramount on Parade (Par., 1930) (with Dorothy Arzner, Otto
    Brower, Edmund Goulding, Victor Heerman, Edwin H. Knopf,
    Ernst Lubitsch, Lothar Mendes, Victor Schertzinger, A. Ed-
    ward Sutherland)
The Return of Dr. Fu Manchu (Par., 1930)
The Guilty Generation (Par., 1931)
The Ruling Voice (FN, 1931)
Upper Underworld (FN, 1931)
That Night in London [Overnight (Par., 1932)
Zoo in Budapest (Fox, 1933)
I Am Suzanne (Fox, 1934)
The Count of Monte Cristo (Univ., 1934)
Gambling (Fox, 1934)
Cardinal Richelieu (UA, 1935)

Cary Grant (left) with Rowland V. Lee on the set for The Toast of New York (RKO, 1937)

The Three Musketeers (RKO, 1935) (also co-script)
One Rainy Afternoon (UA, 1936)
Love from a Stranger (UA, 1937)
The Toast of New York (RKO, 1937)
Mother Carey's Chicken (RKO, 1938)
Service de Luxe (Univ., 1938)
The Son of Frankenstein (Univ., 1939) (also producer)
The Sun Never Sets (Univ., 1939) (also producer)
Tower of London (Univ., 1939) (also producer)
The Son of Monte Cristo (UA, 1940)
Powder Town (RKO, 1942)
The Bridge of San Luis Rey (UA, 1944)
Captain Kidd (UA, 1945)

LEEDS, HERBERT I. (Herbert I. Levy), b. New York City.
Love on a Budget (20th, 1938)
Island in the Sky (20th, 1938)
Keep Smiling (20th, 1938)
The Arizona Wildcat (20th, 1938)
Five of a Kind (20th, 1938)
Mr. Moto in Danger Island (20th, 1939)

The Return of the Cisco Kid (20th, 1939)
Chicken Wagon Family (20th, 1939)
Charlie Chan in the City in Darkness (20th, 1939)
The Cisco Kid and the Lady (20th, 1940)
Yesterday's Heroes (20th, 1940)
Ride on Vaquero (20th, 1941)
Romance of the Rio Grande (20th, 1941)
Blue, White and Perfect (20th, 1941)
The Man Who Wouldn't Die (20th, 1942)
Just Off Broadway (20th, 1942)
Manila Calling (20th, 1942)
Time to Kill (20th, 1942)
It Shouldn't Happen to a Dog (20th, 1946)
Let's Live Again (20th, 1948)
Bunco Squad (RKO, 1950)
Father's Wild Game (Mon., 1950)

LEISEN, MITCHELL, b. Oct. 6, 1899, Menominee, Mich.; d. Oct.
        28, 1972.
Cradle Song (Par., 1933)
Death Takes a Holiday (Par., 1934)
Murder at the Vanities (Par., 1934)
Behold My Wife (Par., 1935)
Four Hours to Kill (Par., 1935)
Hands Across the Table (Par., 1935)
Thirteen Hours By Air (Par., 1935)
The Big Broadcast of 1937 (Par., 1936)
Swing High, Swing Low (Par., 1937)
Easy Living (Par., 1937)
The Big Broadcast of 1938 (Par., 1938)
Artists and Model Abroad (Par., 1938)
Midnight (Par., 1939)
Remember the Night (Par., 1940) (also producer)
Arise My Love (Par., 1940)
I Wanted Wings (Par., 1941)
Hold Back the Dawn (Par., 1941) (also actor)
The Lady Is Willing (Par., 1942) (also producer)
Take a Letter, Darling (Par., 1942)
No Time for Love (Par., 1943) (also producer)
Lady in the Dark (Par., 1944)
Frenchman's Creek (Par., 1944)
Practically Yours (Par., 1944)
Kitty (Par., 1945)
Masquerade in Mexico (Par., 1945)
To Each His Own (Par., 1946)
Suddenly It's Spring (Par., 1947)
Golden Earrings (Par., 1947)
Dream Girl (Par., 1948)
Song of Surrender (Par., 1949)
Bride of Vengeance (Par., 1949)
Captain Carey U.S.A. (Par., 1950)
No Man of Her Own (Par., 1950)

Susan Hayward with Mitchell Leisen in Hollywood (ca.1939).

The Mating Season (Par., 1951)
Darling, How Could You! (Par., 1951)
Young Man With Ideas (MGM, 1952)
Tonight We Sing (20th, 1953)
Bedevilled (MGM, 1955)
The Girl Most Likely (Univ., 1957)
Spree (Trans America, 1967) (with Walon Green)

LENI, PAUL A., b. July 8, 1885, Stuttgart, Germany; d. Sept. 2,
    1929.
    Dornröschen (German, 1917) (also script, set designer, cos-
        tumes, camera)
    Das Rätsel von Bangalore (German, 1917) (with Alexander An-
        talffy) (also set decorator)
    Primavera (German, 1917) (also set decorator)
    Die Platonische Ehe (German, 1919) (also co-set designer)
    Prinz Kuckuck (German, 1919) (also script, co-set designer)

Die Verschworung zu Genua [Fiesko] (German, 1920) (also co-
    set designer)
Patience (German, 1920) (also set designer)
Die Hintertreppe (German, 1921) (with Leopold Jessner)(also
    set designer)
Das Gespensterschiff (German, 1921) (also set designer)
Komödie der Leidenschaften (German, 1921) (also set designer)
Das Tagebuch des Dr. Hartl (German, 1921) (also set designer)
Das Wachsfigurenkabinett (German, 1924) (also decorator)
The Cat and the Canary (Univ., 1927)
The Chinese Parrot (Univ., 1928)
The Man Who Laughs (Univ., 1928)
The Last Warning (Univ., 1929)

LEONARD, ROBERT Z[IGLER], b. Oct. 7, 1889, Denver, Colo.;
    d. Aug. 27, 1968.
The Master Key* (Univ., 1914) (also actor)
The Silent Command (Univ., 1915) (also actor)
Heritage (Univ., 1915) (also script, actor)
Judge Not, or The Woman of Mona Diggings (Univ., 1915)
The Crippled Hand (Univ., 1916) (with David Kirkland) (also
    actor)
The Plow Girl (Par., 1916)
The Love Girl (Univ., 1916)
The Eagle's Wings (Univ., 1916)
Little Eve Edgarton (Univ., 1916)
Secret Love (Univ., 1916)
The Little Orphan (Univ., 1917)
At First Sight (Univ., 1917)
The Primrose Ring (Par., 1917)
A Mormon Maid (Par., 1917)
Princess Virtue (Bluebird, 1917)
Face Value (Bluebird, 1918) (also co-story)
The Bride's Awakening (Univ., 1918)
Her Body in Bond (Murray, 1918)
Danger--Go Slow (Univ., 1918) (also co-script)
Modern Love (Univ., 1918)
The Delicious Little Devil (Univ., 1919)
The Big Little Person (Univ., 1919)
What Am I Bid? (Univ., 1919)
The Scarlet Shadow (Univ., 1919)
The Way of a Woman (Selznick, 1919)
The Miracle of Love (Par., 1919)
April Folly (Par., 1920)
Restless Sex (Par., 1920)
The Gilded Lily (Par., 1921) (also producer)
Heedless Moths (Equity, 1921)
Peacock Alley (Metro, 1921) (for production company)
Fascination (Metro, 1922) (for production company)
Broadway Rose (Metro, 1922) (for production company)
Jazzmania (Metro, 1923) (for production company)
The French Doll (Metro, 1923) for production company)

Fashion Row (Metro, 1923) (also producer, for production com-
pany)
Circe, the Enchantress (Metro, 1924) (for production company)
Mademoiselle Midnight (Metro-Goldwyn, 1924) (for production
company)
Love's Wilderness (FN, 1924)
Cheaper to Marry (Metro-Goldwyn, 1925)
Bright Lights (Metro-Goldwyn, 1925) (also producer)
Time, the Comedian (Metro-Goldwyn, 1925)
Dance Madness (MGM, 1926)
The Waning Sex (MGM, 1926)
Mademoiselle Modiste (MGM, 1926)
The Demi-Bride (MGM, 1927) (also producer)
A Little Journey (MGM, 1927) (also producer)
Adam and Evil (MGM, 1927)
Tea for Three (MGM, 1927) (also producer)
Baby Mine (MGM, 1928) (also producer)
The Cardboard Lover (MGM, 1928)
A Lady of Chance (MGM, 1928) (also producer)
Marianne (MGM, 1929)
In Gay Madrid (MGM, 1930) (also producer)
The Divorcée (MGM, 1930) (also producer)
Let Us Be Gay (MGM, 1930) (also producer)
The Bachelor Father (MGM, 1931) (also co-producer)
It's a Wise Child (MGM, 1931) (also co-producer)
Five and Ten (MGM, 1931) (also co-producer)
Susan Lenox--Her Fall and Rise (MGM, 1931) (also producer)
Lovers Courageous (MGM, 1932) (also producer)
Strange Interlude (MGM, 1932) (also producer)
Peg O' My Heart (MGM, 1933) (also producer)
Dancing Lady (MGM, 1933)
Outcast Lady (MGM, 1934) (also producer)
After Office Hours (MGM, 1935) (also co-producer)
Escapade (MGM, 1935) (also co-producer)
The Great Ziegfeld (MGM, 1936) (also co-producer)
Piccadilly Jim (MGM, 1936) (also co-producer)
Maytime (MGM, 1937) (also co-producer)
The Firefly (MGM, 1937) (also co-producer)
The Girl of the Golden West (MGM, 1938)
Broadway Serenade (MGM, 1939) (also producer)
New Moon (MGM, 1940) (also producer)
Pride and Prejudice (MGM, 1940)
Third Finger, Left Hand (MGM, 1940)
Ziegfeld Girl (MGM, 1941)
When Ladies Meet (MGM, 1941) (also co-producer)
We Were Dancing (MGM, 1942) (also co-producer)
Stand By for Action (MGM, 1942) (also co-producer)
The Man from Down Under (MGM, 1943) (also co-producer)
Marriage Is a Private Affair (MGM, 1944)
Weekend at the Waldorf (MGM, 1945) (also co-producer)
The Secret Heart (MGM, 1946)
Cynthia (MGM, 1947)
B. F. 's Daughter (MGM, 1948)

The Bribe (MGM, 1949)
In the Good Old Summertime (MGM, 1949)
Nancy Goes to Rio (MGM, 1950)
Duchess of Idaho (MGM, 1950)
Grounds for Marriage (MGM, 1950)
Too Young to Kiss (MGM, 1951)
Everything I Have Is Yours (MGM, 1952)
The Clown (MGM, 1953)
The Great Diamond Robberty (MGM, 1953)
Her Twelve Men (MGM, 1954)
The King's Thief (MGM, 1955)
La Donna Più Bella del Mondo (Italian, 1955)
Kelly and Me (Univ., 1956)

LERNER, IRVING, b. March 7, 1909, New York City.
C-Man (Four Continents, 1949) (also producer)
Man Crazy (20th, 1953)
Edge of Fury (UA, 1958) (with Robert Gurney, Jr.)
Murder by Contract (Col., 1958)
City of Fear (Col., 1959)
Studs Lonigan (UA, 1960)
Cry of Battle (AA, 1963)
Royal Hunt of the Sun (National General, 1969)

LeROY, MERVYN, b. Oct. 15, 1900, San Francisco.
No Place to Go (FN, 1927)
Harold Teen (FN, 1928)
Flying Romeos (FN, 1928)
Oh Kay! (FN, 1928)
Naughty Baby (FN, 1929)
Hot Stuff (FN, 1929)
Little Johnny Jones (FN, 1929)
Broadway Babies (FN, 1929)
Playing Around (FN, 1930)
Numbered Men (FN, 1930)
Little Caesar (FN, 1930)
Showgirl in Hollywood (FN, 1930)
Top Speed (FN, 1930)
Gentleman's Fate (FN, 1931)
Too Young to Marry (WB, 1931)
Broad-Minded (FN, 1931)
Local Boy Makes Good (FN, 1931)
Five Star Final (FN, 1931)
Tonight or Never (UA, 1931)
High Pressure (WB, 1932)
Two Seconds (FN, 1932)
Heart of New York (WB, 1932)
Big City Blues (WB, 1932)
Three on a Match (FN, 1932)
I am a Fugitive from a Chain Gang (WB, 1932)
Gold Diggers of 1933 (WB, 1933) (with choreographer Busby
    Berkeley)

Robert Taylor with Mervyn LeRoy on the set of <u>Quo Vadis</u> (MGM, 1951).

Tugboat Annie (MGM, 1933)
Hard to Handle (WB, 1933)
Elmer the Great (FN, 1933)
The World Changes (FN, 1933)
Hi! Nellie (WB, 1934)
Heat Lightning (WB, 1934)
Happiness Ahead (FN, 1934)
Sweet Adeline (WB, 1935)
Oil for the Lamps of China (WB, 1935)
Page Miss Glory (WB, 1935)
I Found Stella Parish (FN, 1935)
Three Men on a Horse (FN, 1936)
The King and the Chorus Girl (WB, 1937)
They Won't Forget (WB, 1937)
Fools for Scandal (WB, 1938)
Waterloo Bridge (MGM, 1940)
Escape (MGM, 1940)
Blossoms in the Dust (MGM, 1941)
Johnny Eager (MGM, 1941)
Unholy Partners (MGM, 1941)
Random Harvest (MGM, 1942)

Madame Curie (MGM, 1943)
Thirty Seconds over Tokyo (MGM, 1945)
Without Reservations (RKO, 1946)
Homecoming (MGM, 1948)
Little Women (MGM, 1949) (also producer)
Any Number Can Play (MGM, 1949)
East Side, West Side (MGM, 1949)
Quo Vadis   (MGM, 1951) (with Anthony Mann)
Lovely to Look at (MGM, 1952)
Million Dollar Mermaid (MGM, 1952)
Latin Lovers (MGM, 1952)
Rose-Marie (MGM, 1954) (also producer)
Mister Roberts (WB, 1955) (with John Ford)
Strange Lady in Town (WB, 1955) (also producer)
The Bad Seed (WB, 1956) (also producer)
Toward the Unknown (WB, 1956)
No Time for Sergeants (WB, 1957) (also producer)
Home Before Dark (WB, 1958) (also producer)
The FBI Story (WB, 1959) (also producer)
Wake Me When It's Over (20th, 1960)
The Devil at Four O'Clock (Col., 1961) (also co-producer)
A Majority of One (WB, 1961) (also producer)
Gypsy (WB, 1962) (also producer)
Mary, Mary (WB, 1963) (also producer)
Moment to Moment (Univ., 1965)
The Green Berets (WB-7 Arts, 1968) (uncredited, with John
    Wayne, Ray Kellogg)

LEVIN, HENRY, b. June 5, 1909, Trenton, N.J.
Sergeant Mike (Col. 1944)
Cry of the Werewolf (Col., 1944)
Dancing in Manhattan (Col., 1945)
I Love a Mystery (Col., 1945)
The Fighting Guardsman (Col., 1946)
The Bandit of Sherwood Forest (Col., 1946)
Night Editor (Col., 1946)
The Return of Monte Cristo (Col., 1946)
The Devil's Mask (Col., 1946)
The Unknown (Col., 1946)
The Corpse Came C.O.D. (Col., 1947)
The Guilt of Janet Ames (Col., 1947)
The Mating of Millie (Col., 1948)
The Gallant Blade (Col., 1948)
The Man from Colorado (Col., 1948)
Mr. Soft Touch (Col., 1949) (with Gordon Douglas)
Jolson Sings Again (Col., 1949)
And Baby Makes Three (Col., 1950)
The Flying Missile (Col., 1950)
Convicted (Col., 1950)
The Petty Girl (Col., 1950)
The Family Secret (Col., 1951)
Two of a Kind (Col., 1951)

Belles on Their Toes (20th, 1952)
Mister Scoutmaster (20th, 1953)
The President's Lady (20th, 1953) (also associate producer)
The Farmer Takes a Wife (20th, 1953)
The Warriers (AA, 1955)
Dark Avenger (AA, 1955)
The Lonely Man (Par., 1957)
Bernardine (20th, 1957)
April Love (20th, 1957)
Let's Be Happy (AA, 1957)
A Nice Little Bank That Should Be Robbed (20th, 1958)
The Remarkable Mr. Pennypacker (20th, 1959)
Journey to the Center of the Earth (20th, 1959)
Holiday for Lovers (20th, 1959)
The Wonders of Aladdin (MGM, 1961)
The Wonderful World of the Brothers Grimm (MGM, 1962)
   (with George Pal)
Come Fly With Me (MGM, 1963)
Honeymoon Hotel (MGM, 1964)
Genghis Khan (Col., 1965)
Murderer's Row (Col., 1966)
Kiss the Girls and Make Them Die (Col., 1967)
The Ambushers (Col., 1967)
The Desperados (Col., 1969)
That Man Bolt (Univ., 1973) (with David Lowell Rich)

LEWIN, ALBERT, b. Sept. 23, 1894, Brooklyn, N.Y.; d. May 9,
   1968.
   The Moon and Sixpence (UA, 1942) (also for co-production com-
      pany, script)
   The Picture of Dorian Gray (MGM, 1945) (also script)
   The Private Affairs of Bel Ami (UA, 1947) (also for co-produc-
      tion company, script)
   Pandora and the Flying Dutchman (MGM, 1951) (also co-pro-
      ducer, script)
   Saadia (MGM, 1953) (also producer, script)
   The Living Idol (MGM, 1957) (also co-producer, story, script)

LEWIS, JERRY, b. March 16, 1926, Newark, N.J.
   The Bellboy (Par., 1960) (also producer, script, actor)
   The Ladies' Man (Par., 1961) (also producer, co-script, actor)
   The Errand Boy (Par., 1962) (also co-script, actor)
   The Nutty Professor (Par., 1963) (also co-script, actor)
   The Patsy (Par., 1964) (also co-script, actor)
   The Family Jewels (Par., 1965) (also producer, co-script, ac-
      tor)
   Three on a Couch (Col., 1966) (also producer, actor)
   The Big Mouth (Col., 1967) (also producer, co-script, actor)
   One More Time (UA, 1970)
   Which Way to the Front? (WB, 1970) (also producer, actor)

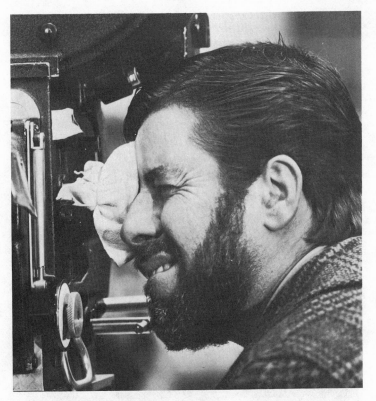

Jerry Lewis shooting <u>One More Time</u> (UA, 1970).

LEWIS, JOSEPH H., b. April 6, 1900, New York City.
    Navy Spy (Univ., 1937) (with Crane Wilbur)
    Courage of the West (Univ., 1937)
    Singing Outlaw (Univ., 1937)
    The Spy Ring (Univ., 1938)
    Border Wolves (Univ., 1938)
    The Last Stand (Univ., 1938)
    Two-Fisted Rangers (Col., 1939)
    Blazing Six Shooters (Col., 1940)
    Texas Stagecoach (Col., 1940)
    The Man from Tumbleweeds (Col., 1940)
    Boys of the City (Mon., 1940)
    The Return of Wild Bill (Col., 1940)
    That Gang of Mine (Mon., 1940)
    Pride of the Bowery (Mon., 1940)
    Criminals Within (Mon., 1941)

The Invisible Ghost (Mon., 1941)
The Mad Doctor of Market Street (Univ., 1941)
Bombs over Burma (PRC, 1942) (also co-script)
The Silver Bullet (Univ., 1942)
The Boss of Hangtown Mesa (Univ., 1942)
Secrets of a Coed (Univ., 1943)
Minstrel Man (Univ., 1944)
The Falcon in San Francisco (RKO, 1945)
My Name Is Julia Ross (Col. 1946)
So Dark the Night (Col., 1946)
The Jolson Story (Col., 1946) (with Alfred E. Green)
The Swordsman (Col., 1947)
The Return of October (Col., 1948)
Undercover Man (Col., 1949)
Deadly Is the Female [Gun Crazy] (UA, 1949)
A Lady Without Passport (MGM, 1950)
Retreat--Hell! (WB, 1952)
Desperate Search (MGM, 1952)
Cry of the Hunted (MGM, 1953)
The Big Combo (AA, 1954)
A Lawless Street (Col., 1955)
The Seventh Cavalry (Col., 1956)
The Halliday Brand (UA, 1957)
Terror in a Texas Town (UA, 1958)

LITVAK, ANATOLE (Michael Anatole Lutwak), b. May 10, 1902,
    Kiev, Russia.
Dolly Macht Karriere (German, 1930)
Nie Wieder Liebe (German, 1931) (also co-script) (also French
    version of same)
Coeur de Lilas (German, 1932)
Das Lied einer Nacht (German, 1932)
La Chanson d'une Nuit [French version of Das Lied Einer Nacht]
    (German, 1932)
Tell Me Tonight [Be Mine Tonight] [British version of Das Lied
    Einer Nacht] (German, 1932)
Sleeping Car (Gaumont-British, 1933)
Cette Vieille Canaille (French, 1933)
Mademoiselle Docteur (French, 1934) (with G.W. Pabst)
L'Equipage [Flight into Darkness] (French, 1935) (also co-script)
Mayerling (French, 1936)
The Woman I Love (RKO, 1937)
Tovarich (WB, 1937)
The Amazing Dr. Clitterhouse (WB, 1938) (also co-producer)
The Sisters (WB, 1938)
Confessions of a Nazi Spy (WB, 1939)
The Roaring Twenties (WB, 1939) (replaced by Raoul Walsh)
Castle on the Hudson (WB, 1940)

Facing page: Tony Perkins, Ingrid Bergman, and Yves Montand
with Anatole Litvak (left) on the set of Goodbye Again (UA, 1961).

City for Conquest (WB, 1940)
All This and Heaven Too (WB, 1940)
One Foot in Heaven (WB, 1941) (replaced by Irving Rapper)
Out of the Fog (WB, 1941)
Blues in the Night (WB, 1941)
This Above All (20th, 1942)
The Nazis Strike (U.S. Government, 1942) (with Frank Capra)
Divide and Conquer (U.S. Government, 1942) (with Frank Capra)
The Battle of Russia (20th, 1943)
The Battle of China (U.S. Government, 1944) (with Frank Capra)
War Comes to America (RKO, 1945) (also co-script)
The Long Night (RKO, 1947) (also co-producer)
Sorry, Wrong Number (Par., 1948) (also co-producer)
The Snake Pit (20th, 1948) (also co-producer)
Decision Before Dawn (20th, 1951) (also producer)
Act of Love (UA, 1953) (also producer, co-script)
The Deep, Blue Sea (20th, 1955) (also producer)
Anastasia (20th, 1956)
Mayerling (NBC-TV, 1957)
The Journey (MGM, 1959) (also producer)
Goodbye Again (UA, 1961) (also producer)
Le Cocteau dans la Plaie [Five Miles to Midnight] (UA, 1963)
A Shot in the Dark (UA, 1964) (replaced by Blake Edwards)
The Night of the Generals (Col., 1967)
The Lady in the Car With Glasses and a Gun (Col., 1971) (also co-producer)

LLOYD, FRANK, b. Feb. 2, 1887, Glasgow, Scotland; d. Aug. 9, 1960.
Jane (Par., 1915)
The Gentleman from Indiana (Par., 1915)
The Intrigue (Par., 1915)
The Reform Candidate (Par., 1915)
The Call of the Cumberlands (Par., 1915)
Madame La President (Par., 1916)
David Garrick (Par., 1916)
The Making of Maddalena (Par., 1916)
An International Marriage (Par., 1916)
The Tongues of Men (Par., 1916)
The Stronger Love (Par., 1916)
The Code of Marcia Gray (Par., 1916)
Sins of Her Parent (Fox, 1916)
The Price of Silence (Fox, 1917 (also script)
A Tale of Two Cities (Fox, 1917) (also script)
American Methods (Fox, 1917) (also script)
When a Man Sees Red (Fox, 1917) (also script)
The Heart of a Lion (Fox, 1917) (also script)
The Kingdom of Love (Fox, 1918) (also script)
The Plunderer (Fox, 1918)
Les Miserables (Fox, 1918) (also co-script)

The Blindness of Divorce (Fox, 1918) (also script)
True Blue (Fox, 1918) (also script)
The Rainbow Trail (Fox, 1918) (also co-script)
The Riders of the Purple Sage (Fox, 1918) (also script)
For Freedom (Fox, 1918)
The Man Hunter (Fox, 1919) (also story, script)
Pitfalls of a Big City (Fox, 1919)
The Loves of Letty (Fox, 1919
The World and Its Women (Goldwyn, 1919)
The Silver Horde (Goldwyn, 1920)
The Woman in Room 13 (Goldwyn, 1920)
Madame X (Goldwyn, 1920) (also co-script)
The Great Lover (Goldwyn, 1920)
A Tale of Two Worlds (Goldwyn, 1921)
A Voice in the Dark (Goldwyn, 1921)
Roads of Destiny (Goldwyn, 1921)
The Invisible Power (Goldwyn, 1921) (also producer)
The Man from Lost River (Goldwyn, 1921)
The Grim Comedian (Goldwyn, 1921)
The Sin Flood (Goldwyn, 1922)
The Eternal Flame (Associated FN, 1922)
Oliver Twist (Associated FN, 1922) (also co-script)
Within the Law (Associated FN, 1923)
Ashes of Vengeance (Associated FN, 1923) (also script)
The Voice from the Minaret (Associated FN, 1923)
Black Oxen (FN, 1924) (also producer)
The Silent Watcher (FN, 1924)
The Sea Hawk (FN, 1924)
Winds of Chance (FN, 1925) (also producer)
Her Husband's Secret (FN, 1925) (also producer)
The Splendid Road (FN, 1925) (also producer)
The Wise Guy (FN, 1926) (also producer)
The Eagle of the Sea (Par., 1926)
Children of Divorce (Par., 1927) (also producer)
Adoration (FN, 1928) (also producer)
The Divine Lady (FN, 1929) (also producer)
Weary River (FN, 1929)
Drag (FN, 1929)
Dark Streets (FN, 1929) (also producer)
Young Nowheres (FN, 1929) (also producer)
Son of the Gods (FN, 1930) (also producer)
The Way of All Men (FN, 1930) (also producer)
The Lash (FN, 1930) (also producer)
The Right of Way (FN, 1931) (also producer)
The Age for Love (UA, 1931)
East Lynne (Fox, 1931)
A Passport to Hell (Fox, 1932)
Cavalcade (Fox, 1933)
Berkeley Square (Fox, 1933)
Hoopla (Fox, 1933)
Servants' Entrance (Fox, 1934)
Mutiny on the Bounty (MGM, 1935) (also producer)
Under Two Flags (20th, 1936)

Maid of Salem (Par., 1937) (also producer)
Wells Fargo (Par., 1937) (also producer)
If I Were King (Par., 1938) (also producer)
Rulers of the Sea (Par., 1939) (also producer)
The Howards of Virginia (Col., 1940) (also producer)
The Lady from Cheyenne (Col., 1941)
This Woman Is Mine (Univ., 1941)
Forever and a Day (RKO, 1943) (with Rene Clair, Edmund
    Goulding, Cedric Hardwicke, Victor Saville, Robert Steven-
    son, Herbert Wilcox) (also co-producer)
Blood on the Sun (UA, 1945)
The Shanghai Story (Rep., 1954)
The Last Command (Rep., 1955)

LOGAN, JOSHUA, b. Oct. 5, 1908, Texarkana, Tex.

Joshua Logan (left) and composer Alan Jay Lerner on <u>Paint Your Wagon</u> (Par., 1969).

I Met My Love Again (UA, 1938) (with Arthur Ripley)
Picnic (Col., 1956)
Bus Stop (20th, 1956)
Sayonara (WB, 1957)
South Pacific (Magna, 1958) (collaborator on source play)
Tall Story (WB, 1960) (also producer)

Fanny (WB, 1961) (also producer, collaboratory on source play)
Ensign Pulver (WB, 1964) (also producer, co-script)
Camelot (WB-7 Arts, 1967)
Paint Your Wagon (Par., 1969)

LOSEY, JOSEPH, b. Jan. 14, 1909, La Crosse, Wis.
   The Boy With Green Hair (RKO, 1948)
   The Lawless (Par., 1950)
   The Prowler (UA, 1951)
   M (Col., 1951)
   The Big Night (UA, 1951) (also co-script)
   Stranger on the Prowl (UA, 1952) (as Andrea Forzano)
   The Sleeping Tiger (Anglo-Amalgamated, 1954) (as Victor Han-
      bury)
   The Intimate Stranger (Anglo-Amalgamated, 1955) (as Joseph
      Walton)
   Time Without Pity (Eros, 1956)
   The Gypsy and the Gentleman (Rank, 1957)
   Blind Date [Chance Meeting] (Rank, 1958)
   The Criminal [The Concrete Jungle] (Anglo-Amalgamated, 1960)
   The Damned [These Are the Damned] (Col., 1961)
   Eve (Italian, 1962)
   The Servant (Warner-Pathé, 1963) (also co-producer)
   King and Country (Warner-Pathé, 1964) (also co-producer)
   Modesty Blaise (20th, 1966)
   Accident (London Independent Producers, 1967) (also co-pro-
      ducer)
   Boom! (Univ., 1968)
   Secret Ceremony (Univ., 1968)
   Figures in a Landscape (20th, 1970)
   The Go-Between (MGM, 1971)
   The Assassination of Trotsky (Cin., 1972) (also co-producer)
   A Doll's House (Tomorrow Entertainment, 1973) (also pro-
      ducer)

LUBIN, ARTHUR, b. July 25, 1901, Los Angeles.
   A Successful Failure (Mon., 1934)
   Great God Gold (Mon., 1935)
   Two Sinners (Rep., 1935)
   Frisco Waterfront (Rep., 1935)
   Yellowstone (Univ., 1936)
   The House of a Thousand Candles (Rep., 1936)
   California Straight Ahead (Univ., 1937)
   I Cover the War (Univ., 1937)
   Mysterious Crossing (Univ., 1937)
   Idol of the Crowds (Univ., 1937)
   Adventure's End (Univ., 1937)
   The Beloved Brat (WB, 1938)
   Midnight Intruder (Univ., 1938)
   Prison Break (Univ., 1938)
   Secrets of a Nurse (Univ., 1938)

Big Town Czar (Univ., 1939)
Mickey the Kid (Rep., 1939)
Call a Messenger (Univ., 1939)
Risky Business (Univ., 1939)
The Big Guy (Univ., 1940)
Black Friday (Univ., 1940)
Gangs of Chicago (Rep., 1940)
I'm Nobody's Sweetheart Now (Univ., 1940)
Meet the Wildcat (Univ., 1940)
Hold That Ghost (Univ., 1940)
Where Did You Get That Girl? (Univ., 1941)
In the Navy (Univ., 1941)
San Francisco Docks (Univ., 1941)
Buck Privates (Univ., 1941)
Keep 'Em Flying (Univ., 1941)
Ride 'Em Cowboy (Univ., 1942)
Eagle Squadron (Univ., 1942)
The Phantom of the Opera (Univ., 1943)
White Savage (Univ., 1943)
Ali Baba and the 40 Thieves (Univ., 1944)
Delightfully Dangerous (UA, 1945)
The Spider Woman Strikes Back (Univ., 1946)
A Night in Paradise (Univ., 1946)
New Orleans (UA, 1947)
Impact (UA, 1949)
Francis (Univ., 1949)
Francis Goes to the Races (Univ., 1951)
Queen for a Day (UA, 1951)
Rhubarb (UA, 1951)
Francis Goes to West Point (Univ., 1951)
It Grows on Trees (Univ., 1952)
South Sea Woman (WB, 1953)
Francis Covers the Big Town (Univ., 1953)
Francis Joins the Wacs (Univ., 1954)
Footsteps in the Fog (Col., 1955)
Lady Godiva (Univ., 1955)
Francis in the Navy (Univ., 1955)
Star of India (UA, 1956)
The First Traveling Saleslady (Univ., 1956)
Escapade in Japan (Univ., 1957)
The Thief of Baghdad (MGM, 1961)
The Incredible Mr. Limpet (WB, 1963)
Hold On! (MGM, 1966)
Rain for a Dusty Summer (Do-Bar, 1970)

LUBITSCH, ERNST, b. Jan. 28, 1892, Berlin, Germany; d. Nov.
    30, 1947.
    Blindekuh (German, 1914) (also actor)
    Fräulein Seifenschaum (German, 1914) (also actor)
    Auf Eisgefuhrt (German, 1915) (also actor)
    Zucker und Zimt (German, 1915 (with Ernst Matray) (also co-
        script, co-titles, actor)

Wo Ist Mein Schatz? (German, 1916) (also actor)
Das Schönste Geschenk (German, 1916) (also actor)
Der Kraftmeier (German, 1916) (also actor)
Der Schwarze Moritz (German, 1916) (also actor)
Schuhpalast Pinkus (German, 1916) (also actor)
Der Gemischte Frauenchor (German, 1916) (also actor)
Leutnant auf Befchl (German, 1916) (also actor)
Der G. M. G. H. Tenor (German, 1916) (also actor)
Seine Neue Nase (German, 1917) (also actor)
Der Blusenkönig (German, 1917) (also actor)
Ein Fideles Gefängnis (German, 1917) (also actor)
Ossis Tagebuch (German, 1917)
Wenn Vier Dasselbe Tun (German, 1917) (also co-script, actor)
Prinz Sami (German, 1917) (also actor)
Der Rodelkavalier (German, 1918) (also actor)
Der Fall Rosentopf (German, 1918) (also actor)
Die Augen der Mumie Ma (German, 1918) (also actor)
Das Model von Ballett (German, 1918)
Carmen [Gypsy Blood] (German, 1918)
Meine Frau, die Filmschauspielerin (German, 1918) (also co-
   script)
Meyer aus Berlin (German, 1918) (also actor)
Das Schwabemädle (German, 1919)
Die Austernprinzessin (German, 1919)
Rausch (German, 1919)
Madame DuBarry [Passion] (German, 1919)
Die Puppe (German, 1919) (also co-script)
Ich Mächte Kein Mann Sein (German, 1919) (also script)
Kohlhiesels Tochter (German, 1920) (also co-script)
Romeo und Julia im Schnee (German, 1920) (also co-script)
Sumurun [One Arabian Night] (German, 1920) (also co-script,
   actor)
Anna Boleyn [Deception] (German, 1920)
Die Bergkatze (German, 1921) (also co-script)
Das Weib des Pharao [The Loves of Pharaoh] (German, 1921)
   (also for own production company)
Die Flamme [Montmartre] (German, 1922) (also for own pro-
   duction company)
Rosita (UA, 1923)
The Marriage Circle (WB, 1924)
Three Women (WB, 1924) (also co-story)
Forbidden Paradise (Par., 1924)
Kiss Me Again (WB, 1925)
Lady Windermere's Fan (WB, 1925)
So This Is Paris? (WB, 1926)
The Student Prince (MGM, 1927)
The Patriot (Par., 1928)
Eternal Love (UA, 1929)
The Love Parade (Par., 1929)
Paramount on Parade (Par., 1930) (with Dorothy Arzner, Otto
   Brower, Edmund Goulding, Victor Heerman, Edwin H. Knopf,
   Rowland V. Lee, Lothar Mendes, Victor Schertzinger, A.
   Edward Sutherland, Frank Tuttle)

Monte Carlo (Par. , 1930)
The Smiling Lieutenant (Par. , 1931) (also co-script)
The Man I Killed [Broken Lullaby] (Par. , 1932)
One Hour With You (Par. , 1932) (with uncredited George Cukor)
Trouble in Paradise (Par. , 1932) (also producer)
If I Had a Million (ep: "The Clerk") (Par. , 1932) (also script)
Design for Living (Par. , 1933)
The Merry Widow (MGM, 1934)
Angel (Par. , 1937) (also producer)
Bluebeard's Eighth Wife (Par. , 1938)
Ninotchka (MGM, 1939)
The Shop Around the Corner (MGM, 1940)
That Uncertain Feeling (UA, 1941)
To Be or Not to Be (UA, 1942) (also co-producer, co-story)
Heaven Can Wait (20th, 1943)
Cluny Brown (20th, 1946)
That Lady in Ermine (20th, 1948) (with uncredited Otto Prem-
    inger)

LUDWIG, EDWARD, b. c.1900.
Steady Company (Univ. , 1932)
They Just Had to Get Married (Univ. , 1933)
A Woman's Man (Mon. , 1934)
Let's Be Ritzy (Univ. , 1934)
Friends of Mr. Sweeney (Par. , 1934)
The Man Who Reclaimed His Head (Univ. , 1935)
Age of Indiscretion (MGM, 1935)
Old Man Rhythm (RKO, 1935)
Three Kids and a Queen (Univ. , 1935)
Fatal Lady (Par. , 1936)
Adventure in Manhattan (Col. , 1936)
Her Husband Lies (Par. , 1937)
The Barrier (Par. , 1937)
The Last Gangster (MGM, 1937)
That Certain Age (Univ. , 1938)
Coast Guard (Col. , 1939)
Swiss Family Robinson (RKO, 1940)
The Man Who Lost Himself (Univ. , 1941)
Born to Sing (MGM, 1942) (with choreographer Busby Berkeley)
They Came to Blow Up America (20th, 1943)
Three Is a Family (UA, 1944)
The Fighting Seebees (Rep. , 1944)
The Fabulous Texan (Rep. , 1947)
Wake of the Red Witch (Rep. , 1948)
The Big Wheel (UA, 1949)
Smuggler's Island (Univ. , 1951)
Big Jim McLain (WB, 1952)
Caribbean (Par. , 1952)
The Blazing Forest (Par. , 1952)
The Vanquished (Par. , 1953)
Sangaree (Par. , 1953)
Jivaro (Par. , 1954)

Flame of the Islands (Rep., 1955)
The Black Scorpion (WB, 1957)
The Gun Hawk (AA, 1963)

LUMET, SIDNEY, b. June 25, 1924, Philadelphia.
Twelve Angry Men (UA, 1956)
Stage Struck (RKO, 1958)
That Kind of Woman (Par., 1959)
The Fugitive Kind (UA, 1959)
A View from the Bridge (Par., 1961)
Long Day's Journey into Night (20th, 1962)
Fail Safe (Col., 1963)
The Pawnbroker (AA, 1965)
The Hill (MGM, 1965)
The Group (UA, 1966)
The Deadly Affair (Col., 1967) (also producer)
Bye Bye Braverman (WB-7 Arts, 1968) (also producer)
The Sea Gull (WB-7 Arts, 1968) (also producer, for own production company)
Last of the Mobile Hot-Shots (WB, 1970)
King: A Filmed Record...Montgomery to Memphis (Maron, 1970) (with Joseph L. Mankiewicz)
The Anderson Tapes (Col., 1971)
Child's Play (Par., 1972)
The Offense (UA, 1973)
Serpico (Par., 1973)

Ida Lupino and producer Collier Young (1947).

LUPINO, IDA, b. Feb. 4, 1918, London.
  Never Fear [The Young Lovers] (Eagle Lion, 1950) (also co-
    script)
  Outrage (RKO, 1950) (also co-script)
  Hard, Fast and Beautiful (RKO, 1951)
  The Hitch Hiker (RKO, 1953) (also co-script)
  The Bigamist (Filmakers, 1953) (also actress)
  The Trouble With Angels (Col., 1966)

LYON, FRANCIS D., b. July 29, 1905, Bowbelle, N.Y.
  Crazylegs (Rep., 1953)
  The Bob Mathias Story (Rep., 1954)
  Cult of the Cobra (Univ., 1955)
  The Great Locomotive Chase (BV, 1956)
  The Oklahoman (AA, 1957)
  Gunsight Ridge (UA, 1957)
  Bailout at 43000 (UA, 1957)
  South Seas Adventure (S-W Cinerama, 1958) (with Walter Thomp-
    son)
  Escort West (UA, 1959)
  The Tomboy and the Champ (Univ., 1961)
  The Young and the Brave (MGM, 1963)
  Destination Inner Space (Magna, 1966)
  Castle of Evil (Commonwealth United, 1966)
  The Destructors (Feature Film Corp. of America, 1968)
  The Money Jungle (Commonwealth United, 1968)
  The Girl Who Knew Too Much (Commonwealth United, 1970)

M

MacARTHUR, CHARLES, b. Nov. 5, 1895, Scranton, Pa.; d. April
    21, 1956.
  Crime Without Passion (Par., 1934) (with Ben Hecht) (also co-
    producer, co-story, co-script)
  The Scoundrel (Par., 1935) (with Ben Hecht) (also co-producer,
    co-story, co-script)
  Once in a Blue Moon (Par., 1936) (with Ben Hecht) (also co-
    producer, co-script)
  Soak the Rich (Par., 1936) (with Ben Hecht) (also co-producer,
    co-story, co-script)

McCAREY, LEO, b. Oct. 3, 1898, Los Angeles.
  Society Secrets (Univ., 1921)
  Red Hot Rhythm (Pathé, 1929) (also co-script)
  The Sophomore (Pathé, 1929)
  Let's Go Native (Par., 1930)
  Wild Company (Fox, 1930)
  Part-Time Wife (Fox, 1930) (also co-script)
  Indiscreet (UA, 1931)
  The Kid from Spain (UA, 1933) (with choreographer Busby Ber-
    keley)

Ingrid Bergman and Bing Crosby (right) with Leo McCarey on the set of The Bells of St. Mary's (RKO, 1945).

Duck Soup (Par., 1933)
Six of a Kind (Par., 1934)
Belle of the Nineties (Par., 1934)
Ruggles of Red Gap (Par., 1935)
The Milky Way (Par., 1936)
Make Way for Tomorrow (Par., 1937) (also producer)
The Awful Truth (Col., 1937) (also producer)
Love Affair (RKO, 1939) (also co-story)
Once Upon a Honeymoon (RKO, 1942) (also producer, co-story)
Going My Way (Par., 1944) (also producer, story)
The Bells of St. Mary's (also producer, story)
Good Sam (RKO, 1948) (also producer, co-story)
My Son John (Par., 1952) (also producer, story, co-script)
Rally 'Round the Flag, Boys! (20th, 1958) (also producer, co-script)
An Affair to Remember (20th, 1957) (also co-story, co-script, co-songs)
Satan Never Sleeps (20th, 1961) (also producer, co-script)

McCARTHY, JOHN P., b. March 17, 1885, San Francisco.
  Out of Dust (McCarthy -St. Regent, 1920)
  Shadows of Conscience (Russell, 1921) (also co-story, co-script)
  Brand of Cowardice (Truart, 1925)
  Pals (Truart, 1925)
  Vanishing Hoofs (Weiss Bros. -Artclass, 1926)
  The Border Whirlwind (FBO, 1926)
  The Devil's Masterpiece (Sanford F. Arnold, 1927)
  His Foreign Wife (Pathé, 1927) (also story)
  The Lovelorn (MGM, 1927)
  Becky (MGM, 1927)
  Diamond Handcuffs (MGM, 1928)
  The Eternal Woman (Col., 1929)
  Oklahoma Cyclone (Tiffany, 1930) (also story, script)
  The Land of Missing Men (Tiffany, 1930) (also story, co-script)
  Headin' North (Tiffany, 1930) (also script)
  Ridin' Fool (Tiffany, 1931)
  Rider of the Plains (Syndicate, 1931)
  Sunrise Trail (Tiffany, 1931)
  Rose of the Rio Grande (Mon., 1931) (also co-script)
  God's Country and the Man (Syndicate, 1931)
  Ships of Hate (Mon., 1931)
  Mother and Son (Mon., 1931)
  Nevada Buckaroo (Tiffany, 1931)
  Cavalier of the West (Artclass, 1931) (also story, co-script)
  The Fighting Champ (Mon., 1932)
  The Forty-Niners (Freuler Film Associates, 1932)
  The Western Code (Col., 1933)
  Lucky Larrigan (Mon., 1933)
  Trailing North (Mon., 1933)
  The Return of Casey Jones (Mon., 1933)
  The Lawless Border (Spectrum, 1935)
  The Song of the Gringo (Grand National, 1936) (also co-story, co-script)
  Raiders of the Border (Mon., 1944)
  Marked Trails (Mon., 1944) (also co-script)
  The Cisco Kid Returns (Mon., 1945)

McDONALD, FRANK, b. Nov. 9, 1899, Baltimore.
  Broadway Hostess (WB, 1935)
  The Murder of Doctor Harrigan (WB, 1936)
  The Big Noise (WB, 1936)
  Boulder Dam (WB, 1936)
  Isle of Fury (WB, 1936)
  Love Begins at 20 (WB, 1936)
  Murder By an Aristocrat (WB, 1936)
  The Murder of Dr. Harrigan (WB, 1936)
  Treachery Rides the Range (WB, 1936)
  Adventurous Blonde (WB, 1937)
  Dance Charlie Dance (WB, 1937)

Fly-Away Baby (WB, 1937)
Her Husband's Secretary (WB, 1937)
Midnight Court (WB, 1937)
Smart Blonde (WB, 1937)
Reckless Living (Univ., 1938)
Freshman Year (Univ., 1938)
Flirting With Fate (MGM, 1938)
First Offenders (Univ., 1938)
Blondes at Work (WB, 1938)
Over the Wall (WB, 1938)
They Asked for It (Univ., 1939)
Jeepers Creepers (Rep., 1939)
Death Goes North (Warwick, 1939)
Village Barn Dance (Rep., 1940)
In Old Missouri (Rep., 1940)
Grand Old Opry (Rep., 1940)
Barnyard Follies (Rep., 1940)
Rancho Grande (Rep., 1940)
Gaucho Serenade (Rep., 1940)
Carolina Moon (Rep., 1940)
Ride, Tenderfoot, Ride (Rep., 1940)
Under Fiesta Skies (Rep., 1941)
No Hands on the Clock (Par., 1941)
Flying Blind (Par., 1941)
Arkansas Judge (Rep., 1941)
Country Fair (Rep., 1941)
Under Fiesta Stars (Rep., 1941)
Tuxedo Junction (Rep., 1941)
Shepherd of the Ozarks (Rep., 1942)
The Old Homestead (Rep., 1942)
Mountain Rhythm (Rep., 1942)
Wildcat (Par., 1942)
The Traitor Within (Rep., 1942)
Oh, My Darling Clementine (Rep., 1943)
Wrecking Crew (Par., 1943)
Swing Your Partner (Rep., 1943)
Alaska Highway (Par., 1943)
Submarine Alert (Par., 1943)
Hoosier Holiday (Rep., 1943)
High Explosive (Par., 1943)
Timber Queen (Par., 1944)
Gambler's Choice (Par., 1944)
Take It Big (Par., 1944)
Sing, Neighbor, Sing (Rep., 1944)
One Body Too Many (Par., 1944)
Lights of Santa Fe (Rep., 1944)
The Chicago Kid (Rep., 1945)
Scared Stiff (Par., 1945)
Tell It to a Star (Rep., 1945)
Along the Navajo Trail (Rep., 1945)
Bells of Rosarita (Rep., 1945)
The Man from Oklahoma (Rep., 1945)
Sunset in Eldorado (Rep., 1945)

Song of Arizona (Rep. , 1946)
Rainbow over Texas (Rep. , 1946)
My Pal Trigger (Rep. , 1946)
Under Nevada Skies (Rep. , 1946)
Sioux City Sue (Rep. , 1946)
Twilight on the Rio Grande (Rep. , 1947)
Hit Parade of 1947 (Rep. , 1947) (also associate producer)
Bulldog Drummond Strikes Back (Col. , 1947)
Linda Be Good (PRC, 1947)
When a Girl's Beautiful (Col. , 1947)
French Leave (Screen Guild, 1948)
Mr. Reckless (Par. , 1948)
13 Lead Soldiers (20th, 1948)
Gun Smugglers (20th, 1948)
Ringside (Screen Guild, 1949)
The Big Sombrero (Col. , 1949)
Apache Kid (Lip. , 1949)
Call of the Klondike (Mon. , 1950)
Snow Dog (Mon. , 1950)
Texans Never Cry (Mon. , 1951)
Father Takes the Air (Mon. , 1951)
Yellow Fin (Mon. , 1951)
Yukon Manhunt (Mon. , 1951)
Sierra Passage (Mon. , 1951)
Northwest Territory (Mon. , 1951)
Yukon Gold (Mon. , 1952)
Sea Tiger (Mon. , 1952)
Son of Belle Starr (AA, 1953)
Border City Rustlers (AA, 1953)
Six Gun Decision (AA, 1953)
Two Gun Marshal (AA, 1953)
Thunder Pass (Lip. , 1954)
Treasure of Ruby Hills (AA, 1955)
The Big Tip-Off (AA, 1955)
Raymie (AA, 1960)
The Purple Gang (AA, 1960)
The Underwater City (Col. , 1962)
Gunfight at Comanche Creek (AA, 1963)
Mara of the Wilderness (AA, 1965)

MacFADDEN, HAMILTON, b. April 26, 1901, Chelsea, Mass.
Are You There? (Fox, 1930)
Crazy That Way (Fox, 1930) (also script, dialog)
Harmony at Home (Fox, 1930)
Oh, for a Man! (Fox, 1930)
The Black Camel (Fox, 1931)
Charlie Chan Carries On (Fox, 1931)
Riders of the Purple Sage (Fox, 1931)
Their Mad Moment (Fox, 1931) (with Chandler Sprague)
Cheaters at Play (Fox, 1932)
Second Hand Wife (Fox, 1933) (also adaptation)
Trick for Trick (Fox, 1933)

Charlie Chan's Greatest Case (Fox, 1933)
The Fourth Horseman (Univ., 1933)
The Man Who Dared (RKO, 1933)
As Husbands Go (Fox, 1934)
Hold That Girl (Fox, 1934)
Stand Up and Cheer (Fox, 1934)
She Was a Lady (Fox, 1934)
Elinor Norton (Fox, 1934)
Fighting Youth (Univ., 1935)
Legion of Missing Men (Mon., 1937)
The Three Legionaires (General, 1937)
It Can't Last Forever (Col., 1937)
Sea Racketeers (Rep., 1937)
Escape By Night (Rep., 1937)
Inside the Law (PRC, 1942)

McGANN, WILLIAM H., b. April 5, 1898, Pittsburgh, Pa.
On the Border (WB, 1930)
El Hombre Malo [Spanish version of The Bad Man] (FN, 1930)
La Llama Segrada [Spanish version of The Sacred Flame]
    (FN, 1930)
Amour Contra Amour (FN, 1930)
La Dama Atrevida [Spanish version of The Lady Who Dared]
    (FN, 1930)
Los Que Danzen [Spanish version of Those Who Dance] (FN,
    1930)
On the Border (WB, 1930)
I Like Your Nerve (FN, 1931)
Illegal (WB, 1932)
Murder on the Second Floor (WB, 1932)
Illegal (WB, 1932)
The Silver Greyhound (WB, 1932)
Her Night Out (WB, 1932)
Little Fella (WB, 1932)
Long Live the King (WB, 1933)
La Buen Aventura (WB, 1934)
Night at the Ritz (WB, 1935)
Maybe It's Love (FN, 1935)
Man of Iron (WB, 1935)
Freshman Love (WB, 1936)
Brides Are Like That (FN, 1936)
Times Square Playboy (WB, 1936)
Two Against the World (FN, 1936)
Hot Money (WB, 1936)
Polo Joe (WB, 1936)
The Case of the Black Cat (FN, 1936)
Penrod and Sam (WB, 1937)
Marry the Girl (WB, 1937)
Sh! the Octopus (WB, 1937)
Alcatraz Island (WB, 1938)
Penrod and His Twin Brother (WB, 1938)
When Were You Born? (WB, 1938)

Girls on Probation (WB, 1939)
Blackwell's Island (WB, 1939)
Sweepstakes Winner (WB, 1939)
Everybody's Hobby (WB, 1939)
Pride of Bluegrass (WB, 1939)
Wolf of New York (Rep., 1940)
Dr. Christian Meets the Women (RKO, 1940)
A Shot in the Dark (WB, 1941)
The Parson of Panamint (Par., 1941)
Highway West (WB, 1941)
We Go Fast (20th, 1941)
In Old California (Rep., 1942)
Tombstone, the Town Too Tough to Die (Par., 1942)
American Empire (UA, 1942)

McGOWAN, J. P. (John P. McGowan), b. Feb. 1880, Terowie,
    South Australia; d. March 26, 1952.
The Hazards of Helen* (Kalem, 1914)
Blackbirds (Par., 1915)
The Girl and the Game* (Signal, 1915) (also actor)
The Voice in the Fog (Par., 1915)
Lass of the Lumberlands* (Signal, 1916) (with Paul C. Hurst)
Whispering Smith (Mutual, 1916) (also actor)
Medicine Bend (Mutual, 1916) (also actor)
The Lost Express* (Signal, 1917)
The Railroad Raiders* (Signal, 1917) (also actor)
Lure of the Circus* (Univ., 1918)
The Red Glove* (Univ., 1919)
Elmo, the Fearless* (Univ., 1920)
King of the Circus* (Univ., 1920)
Do or Die* (Univ., 1921) (also actor)
Below the Deadline (Anchor, 1921)
A Crook's Romance (American, 1921) (also actor)
Discontented Wives (Playgoers, 1921) (also actor)
The Moonshine Menace (American, 1921)
The Ruse of the Rattler (Playgoers, 1921) (also actor)
Tiger True (Univ., 1921)
Hills of Missing Men (Associated Exhibitors, 1922) (also script)
Captain Kid* (Star Serial Corp., 1922)
Reckless Chances (Playgoers, 1922) (also actor)
Perils of the Yukon* (Univ., 1922) (with Perry Vekroff, Jay
    Marchant)
One Million in Jewels (American Releasing, 1923) (also script,
    actor)
Stormy Seas (Associated Exhibitors, 1923) (also actor)
Baffled (Independent Pictures, 1924)
Calibre 45 (Independent Pictures, 1924)
Courage (Independent Pictures, 1924)
Crossed Trails (Independent Pictures, 1924) (also actor)
A Desperate Adventure (Independent Pictures, 1924)
A Two Fisted Tenderfoot (Independent Pictures, 1924)
The Whipping Boss (Mon., 1924) (also actor)

Western Vengeance (Independent Pictures, 1924)
Barriers of the Law (Mon., 1925) (also actor)
Blood and Steel (Mon., 1925)
Border Intrigue (Mon., 1925)
Cold Nerve (Mon., 1925)
Duped (Mon., 1925) (also actor)
The Fighting Sheriff (Mon., 1925)
The Gambling Fool (Mon., 1925)
Outwitted (Mon., 1925) (also script and actor)
Peggy of the Secret Service (Davis Distributing, 1925)
The Train Wreckers (Anchor, 1925)
Webs of Steel (Anchor, 1925)
The Ace of Clubs (Rayart, 1926)
Buried Gold (Rayart, 1926)
Crossed Signals (Rayart, 1926)
Cyclone Bob (Anchor, 1926)
Desperate Chance (Rayart, 1926)
Fighting Luck (Rayart, 1926) (also producer)
Iron Fist (Rayart, 1926)
The Lost Express (Rayart, 1926)
The Lost Trail (Rayart, 1926)
Mistaken Orders (Rayart, 1926)
The Open Switch (Rayart, 1926)
Peril of the Rail (Anchor, 1926)
Red Blood (Rayart, 1926) (also actor)
Riding for Life (Rayart, 1926)
Riding Romance (Anchor, 1926)
Road Agent (Rayart, 1926)
Silver Fingers (Capitol, 1926)
Unseen Enemies (Anchor, 1926)
Aflame in the Sky (FBO, 1927)
The Lost Limited (Rayart, 1927 (also actor)
The Outlaw Dog (FBO, 1927)
Red Signals (Sterling, 1927) (also actor)
Tarzan and the Golden Lion (FBO, 1927)
Thunderbolt's Tracks (Rayart, 1927)
When a Dog Loves (FBO, 1927)
The Chinatown Mystery* (Syndicate, 1928)
Arizona Days (Syndicate, 1928) (also co-script, actor)
Headin' Westward (Syndicate, 1928) (also actor)
Law of the Mounted (Syndicate, 1928) (also actor)
Lightnin' Shot (Rayart, 1928) (also script, actor)
Manhattan Cowboy (Syndicate, 1928)
Devil's Tower (Rayart, 1928) (also actor)
Mystery Valley (Rayart, 1928) (also script)
On the Divide (Syndicate, 1928) (also actor)
Painted Trail (Rayart, 1928)
Silent Trail (Syndicate, 1928) (also actor)
Texas Tommy (Syndicate, 1928) (also actor)
Trail Riders (Rayart, 1928) (also script)
Trailin' Back (Rayart, 1928) (also script)
West of Santa Fe (Syndicate, 1928) (also actor)
Bad Man's Money (Bell, 1929) (also actor)

Below the Deadline (Chesterfield, 1929) (also actor)
Captain Cowboy (J. Charles Davis, 1929) (also script, editor)
Code of the West (Syndicate, 1929)
The Cowboy and the Outlaw (Syndicate, 1929) (also actor)
The Fighting Terror (Syndicate, 1929) (also producer, actor)
The Invaders (Syndicate, 1929) (also actor)
The Last Roundup (Syndicate, 1929) (also producer)
The Lone Horseman (Syndicate, 1929) (also producer)
The Man from Nevada (Syndicate, 1929)
The Oklahoma Kid (Syndicate, 1929) (also producer)
The Phantom Rider (Syndicate, 1929) (also actor)
Riders of the Rio Grande (Syndicate, 1929) (also producer)
Riders of the Storm (J. Charles Davis, 1929) (also script)
Beyond the Law (Syndicate, 1930)
Breezy Bill (Syndicate, 1930) (also actor)
Call of the Desert (Syndicate, 1930)
The Canyon of Missing Men (Syndicate, 1930) (also actor)
Code of Honor (Syndicate, 1930)
Covered Wagon Trails (Syndicate, 1930) (also actor)
Hunted Men (Syndicate, 1930)
The Man from Nowhere (Syndicate, 1930)
Near the Rainbow's End (Tiffany, 1930)
The Oklahoma Sheriff (Syndicate, 1930)
O'Malley Rides Alone (Syndicate, 1930) (also actor)
The Parting of the Trails (Syndicate, 1930)
Under Texas Skies (Syndicate, 1930)
Pioneers of the West (Syndicate, 1930) (also script, actor)
Western Honor (Syndicate, 1930)
'Neath Western Skies (Syndicate, 1930) (also actor)
Code of the West (Syndicate, 1930)
Riders of the North (Syndicate, 1931)
Headin' for Trouble (Big 4, 1931)
Quick Trigger Lee (Big 4, 1931)
Cyclone Kid (Big 4, 1931)
The Hurricane Express* (Mascot, 1932) (with Armand L. Schaefer)
Human Target (Big 4, 1932)
Mark of the Spur (Big 4, 1932)
Tangled Fortunes (Big 4, 1932)
Scarlet Brand (Big 4, 1932)
Man from New Mexico (Mon., 1932)
When a Man Rides Alone (Freuler Film Associates, 1933)
Deadwood Pass (Freuler Film Associates, 1933)
War of the Range (Freuler Film Associates, 1933)
Rough Riding Rhythm (Ambassador, 1937) (also actor)
Roaring Six Guns (Ambassador, 1938)

MACHATY, GUSTAV, b. May 9, 1901, Prague, Czech.; d. Dec. 14, 1963.
Sonata Kreutzerova (Czechoslovakian, 1926) (also script)
Svejk v Civilu (Czechoslovakian, 1927)
Erotikon (Czechoslovakian, 1929) (also script)

Nacera Dec, Kral Kibicu (Czechoslovakian, 1931) (also co-
    script)
Ze Soboty Na Nedel I (Czechoslovakian, 1931) (also co-script)
Extase (Czechoslovakian, 1932) (also script)
Nocturno (Austrian, 1934) (also co-script)
Ballerine (Italian, 1936)
Within the Law (MGM, 1939)
Jealousy (Rep., 1945) (also associate producer, co-script)
Suchkind 312 (German, 1956) (also co-script)

MacKENDRICK, ALEXANDER, b. 1912, Boston.
    Whiskey Galore (Rank, 1948) (also co-script)
    The Man in the White Suit (Rank, 1951) (also co-script)
    Mandy (Rank, 1952)
    The Maggie (Rank, 1954)
    The Ladykillers (Rank, 1955)
    Sweet Smell of Success (UA, 1957)
    The Devil's Disciple (UA, 1959) (replaced by Guy Hamilton)
    The Guns of Navarone (Col., 1961) (replaced by J. Lee Thomp-
        son)
    Sammy Going South (Par., 1965)
    A High Wind in Jamaica (BV, 1965)
    Don't Make Waves (MGM, 1967)

McLAGLEN, ANDREW V., b. July 23, 1920, London.
    Gun the Man Down (UA, 1956)
    Man in the Vault (Univ., 1956)
    The Abductors (20th, 1957)
    Freckles (20th, 1960)
    The Little Shepherd of Kingdom Come (20th, 1961)
    McLintock (UA, 1963)
    Shenandoah (Univ., 1965)
    The Rare Breed (Univ., 1966)
    Monkeys Go Home! (BV, 1966)
    The Way West (UA, 1967)
    The Ballad of Josie (Univ., 1968)
    The Devil's Brigade (UA, 1968)
    Bandolero! (20th, 1968)
    Hellfighters (Univ., 1969)
    The Undefeated (20th, 1969)
    Chisum (WB, 1970)
    One More Train to Rob (Univ., 1971)
    Something Big (20th, 1971)
    Fools' Parade (Col., 1971)

McLEOD, NORMAN Z., b. Sept. 20, 1898, Grayling, Mich.; d.
        Jan. 26, 1964.
    Taking a Chance (Fox, 1928)
    Along Came Youth (Par., 1930) (with Lloyd Corrigan)
    Monkey Business (Par., 1931)

Finn and Hattie (Par., 1931) (with Norman Taourog) (also co-script)
Touchdown (Par., 1931)
Skippy (Par., 1931) (also co-script)
The Miracle Man (Par., 1932)
Horse Feathers (Par., 1932)
If I Had a Million (ep: "The Forger") (Par., 1932)
Mama Loves Papa (Par., 1933)
Alice in Wonderland (Par., 1933) (also co-script)
A Lady's Profession (Par., 1933)
Many Happy Returns (Par., 1934)
A Melody in Spring (Par., 1934)
Here Comes Cookie (Par., 1935)
Redheads on Parade (Fox, 1935)
Pennies from Heaven (Col., 1936)
Early to Bed (Par., 1936)
Mind Your Own Business (Par., 1936)
Topper (UA, 1937)
Merrily We Live (MGM, 1938)
There Goes My Heart (UA, 1938)
Topper Takes a Trip (UA, 1939)
Remember? (MGM, 1939) (also co-story, co-script)
Little Men (RKO, 1940)
The Trial of Mary Dugan (MGM, 1940)
Lady Be Good (MGM, 1941)
Jackass Mail (MGM, 1941)
Panama Hattie (MGM, 1942)
The Powers Girl (UA, 1942)
Swing Shift Maisie (MGM, 1943)
The Kid from Brooklyn (RKO, 1946)
The Secret Life of Walter Mitty (RKO, 1947)
Road to Rio (Par., 1947)
The Paleface (Par., 1948)
Isn't It Romantic (Par., 1948)
Let's Dance (Par., 1950)
My Favorite Spy (Par., 1951)
Never Wave at a Wac (RKO, 1952)
Casanova's Big Night (Par., 1954)
Public Pigeon No. 1 (Univ., 1957)
Alias Jesse James (UA, 1959)

McRAE, HENRY (Henry Alexander McRae), b. 188, Staynor, Ont.
Liberty, a Daughter of the U.S.A.* (Univ., 1916) (with Jacques Jaccard)
Behind the Lines (Univ., 1916)
The Mystery Ship* (Univ., 1917) (with Harry Harvey)
Elmo, the Mighty* (Univ., 1919)
The Dragon's Net* (Univ., 1920)
God's Crucible (W.W. Hodkinson, 1921)
Cameron of the Royal Mounted (W.W. Hodkinson, 1922)
The Critical Age (W.W. Hodkinson, 1923)
The Man from Glengarry (W.W. Hodkinson, 1923)

A Fight for Honor (C.B.C. Film Sales, 1924)
The Price She Paid (C.B.C. Film Sales, 1924)
Racing for Life (C.B.C. Film Sales, 1924)
Tainted Money (C.B.C. Film Sales, 1924)
The Fearless Lover (Perfection, 1925)
Ace of Spades* (Univ., 1925)
The Scarlet Streak* (Univ., 1926)
Strings of Steel* (Univ., 1927)
Wild Beauty (Univ.-Jewel, 1927)
Trail of the Tiger* (Univ., 1927)
Guardians of the Wild (Univ., 1928)
The Danger Rider (Univ.-Jewel, 1928)
The Two Outlaws (Univ., 1928) (also story)
Tarzan, the Tiger* (Univ., 1929)
King of the Rodeo (Univ., 1929)
Burning the Wind (Univ., 1929)
Wild Blood (Univ., 1929)
Plunging Hoofs (Univ., 1929)
Smilin' Guns (Univ.-Jewel, 1929)
Hoofbeats of Vengeance (Univ., 1929)
The Harvest of Hate (Univ., 1929)
The Indians Are Coming* (Univ., 1930)
The Lightning Express* (Univ., 1930)
Terry of the Times* (Univ., 1930)
Detective Lloyd* (Univ., 1932)
The Lost Special* (Univ., 1932)
Rustler's Roundup (Univ., 1933)

MAMOULIAN, ROUBEN, b. Oct. 8, 1898, Tiflis, Russia.
Applause (Par., 1930)
City Streets (Par., 1931)
Dr. Jekyll and Mr. Hyde (Par., 1932) (also producer)
Love Me Tonight (Par., 1932) (also producer)
The Song of Songs (Par., 1933) (also producer)
Queen Christina (MGM, 1933)
We Live Again (UA, 1933) (also producer)
Becky Sharp (RKO, 1935) (also co-producer) (replaced Lowell
    Sherman)
The Gay Desperado (UA, 1936)
High, Wide and Handsome (Par., 1938)
Golden Boy (Col., 1939)
The Mark of Zorro (20th, 1940)
Blood and Sand (20th, 1941)
Rings on Her Fingers (20th, 1942)
Laura (20th, 1944) (replaced by Otto Preminger)
Summer Holiday (MGM, 1948)
The Wild Heart (RKO, 1952) (uncredited, with Michael Powell)
Silk Stockings (MGM, 1957)
Porgy and Bess (Col., 1959) (replaced by Otto Preminger)
Cleopatra (20th, 1963) (replaced by Joseph L. Mankiewicz)

Joseph L. Mankiewicz and Peggy Cummins aboard the "Queen Elizabeth" (1948).

MANKIEWICZ, JOSEPH L. (Leo), b. Feb. 11, 1909, Wilkes Barre, Pa.
Dragonwyck (20th, 1946) (also script)
Somewhere in the Night (20th, 1946) (also co-script)
The Late George Apley (20th, 1947)
The Ghost and Mrs. Muir (20th, 1947)
Escape (20th, 1948)
A Letter to Three Wives (20th, 1949) (also script)
House of Strangers (20th, 1949)
No Way Out (20th, 1950) (also co-script)
All About Eve (20th, 1950) (also script)
People Will Talk (20th, 1951) (also script)
Five Fingers (20th, 1952)
Julius Caesar (MGM, 1953) (also script)
The Barefoot Contessa (UA, 1954) (also producer, script)
Guys and Dolls (MGM, 1955) (also script)
The Quiet American (UA, 1958) (also producer, script)
Suddenly Last Summer (Col., 1959) (also producer)
Cleopatra (20th, 1963) (replaced Rouben Mamoulian et al) (also co-script)
Carol for Another Christmas (ABC-TV, 1964)
The Honey Pot (UA, 1967) (also co-producer, script)
There Was a Crooked Man (WB, 1970) (also producer)
King: A Filmed Record...Montgomery to Memphis (Maron, 1970) (with Sidney Lumet)
Sleuth (20th, 1972)

MANN, ANTHONY, (Anton Bundsmann; Anton Mann), b. June 30, 1906, San Diego; d. April 29, 1967.
Dr. Broadway (Par., 1942)
Moonlight in Havana (Univ., 1942)
Nobody's Darling (Rep., 1943)
My Best Gal (Rep., 1944)
Strangers in the Night (Rep., 1944)
The Great Flamarion (Rep., 1945)
Two O'Clock Courage (RKO, 1945)
Sing Your Way Home (RKO, 1945)
Strange Impersonation (Rep., 1946)
The Bamboo Blonde (RKO, 1946)
Desperate (RKO, 1947) (also co-story)
Railroaded (Eagle Lion, 1947)
T-Men (Eagle Lion, 1947) (also uncredited co-story)
Raw Deal (Eagle Lion, 1948)
He Walked By Night (Eagle Lion, 1948) (uncredited, with Alfred Werker)
Reign of Terror (Eagle Lion, 1949)
Follow Me Quietly (RKO, 1949) (uncredited, with Richard Fleischer)
Border Incident (MGM, 1949)
Side Street (MGM, 1949)
Devil's Doorway (MGM, 1950)
The Furies (Par., 1950)

Winchester '73 (Univ., 1950)
The Tall Target (MGM, 1951)
Quo Vadis (MGM, 1951) (uncredited for fire sequences, with
    Mervyn LeRoy)
Bend of the River (Univ. 1952)
The Naked Spur (MGM, 1953)
Thunder Bay (Univ., 1953)
The Glenn Miller Story (Univ., 1954)
The Far Country (Univ., 1955)
Strategic Air Command (Par., 1955)
The Man from Laramie (Col., 1955)
The Last Frontier (Col., 1955)
Serenade (WB, 1956)
Men in War (UA, 1957)
Night Passage (Univ., 1957) (uncredited, with James Neilson)
The Tin Star (Par., 1957)
God's Little Acre (UA, 1958) (also co-producer)
Man of the West (UA, 1958)
Spartacus (Univ., 1960) (uncredited, with Stanley Kubrick)
Cimarron (MGM, 1960) (completed by Charles Walters)
El Cid (AA, 1961)
The Fall of the Roman Empire (Par., 1964)
The Heroes of Telemark (Col., 1955)
A Dandy in Aspic (Col., 1968) (died during production, with
    uncredited Laurence Harvey)

MANN, DANIEL, b. Aug. 8, 1912, New York City.
Come Back Little Sheba (Par., 1952)
About Mrs. Leslie (Par., 1954)
The Rose Tattoo (Par., 1955)
I'll Cry Tomorrow (MGM, 1956)
The Teahouse of the August Moon (MGM, 1956)
Hot Spell (Par., 1958)
The Last Angry Man (Col., 1959)
The Mountain Road (Col., 1960)
Butterfield 8 (MGM, 1960)
Ada (MGM, 1961)
Five Finger Exercise (Col., 1962)
Who's Got the Action? (Par., 1962)
Who's Been Sleeping in My Bed (Par., 1963)
Judith (Par., 1965)
Our Man Flint (20th, 1965)
For Love of Ivy (Cin., 1968)
A Dream of Kings (National General, 1970)
Willard (Cin., 1971)
The Revengers (20th, 1972)
Maurie (National General, 1973)

MANN, DELBERT, b. Jan. 30, 1920, Lawrence, Kan.
Marty (UA, 1955)
The Bachelor Party (UA, 1957)

Desire Under the Elms (Par., 1958)
Separate Tables (UA, 1958)
Middle of the Night (Col., 1959)
The Dark at the Top of the Stairs (WB, 1960)
Lover Come Back (Univ., 1961)
The Outsider (Univ., 1961)
That Touch of Mink (Univ., 1962)
A Gathering of Eagles (Univ., 1963) (with Robert R. Webb,
    Paul Mantz)
Dear Heart (MGM, 1964)
Quick Before It Melts (MGM, 1964) (also co-producer)
Mister Buddwing (MGM, 1965)
Fitzwilly (UA, 1967)
Heidi (NBC-TV, 1968)
The Pink Jungle (Univ., 1968)
David Copperfield (NBC-TV, 1970)
Jane Eyre (NBC-TV, 1971)
Kidnapped (AIP, 1971)

MARIN, EDWIN L., b. Feb. 21, 1899, Jersey City, N.J.; d. May
    2, 1951.
The Death Kiss (World Wide, 1932)
A Study in Scarlet (World Wide, 1933)
The Avenger (Mon., 1933)
Sweetheart of Sigma Chi (Mon., 1933)
Bombay Mail (Univ., 1934)
The Crosby Case (Univ., 1934)
Affairs of a Gentleman (Univ., 1934)
Paris Interlude (MGM, 1934)
The Casino Murder Case (MGM, 1935)
Pursuit (MGM, 1935)
Moonlight Murder (MGM, 1936)
The Garden Murder Case (MGM, 1936)
Speed (MGM, 1936)
I'd Give My Life (Par., 1936)
Sworn Enemy (MGM, 1936)
All American Chump (MGM, 1936)
Man of the People (MGM, 1937)
Married Before Breakfast (MGM, 1937)
Everybody Sing (MGM, 1938)
Hold That Kiss (MGM, 1938)
The Chaser (MGM, 1938)
A Christmas Carol (MGM, 1938)
Listen, Darling (MGM, 1938)
Fast and Loose (MGM, 1939)
Society Lawyer (MGM, 1939)
Maisie (MGM, 1939)
Florian (MGM, 1940)
Henry Goes Arizona (MGM, 1940)
Gold Rush Maisie (MGM, 1940
Hulabaloo (MGM, 1940)
Maisie Was a Lady (MGM, 1941)

George Raft (left) with Edwin L. Marin discussing <u>Mr. Ace</u> (UA, 1946).

Ringside Maisie (MGM, 1941)
Paris Calling (Univ. , 1941)
A Gentleman After Dark (UA, 1942)
Miss Annie Rooney (UA, 1942)
Invisible Agent '(Univ. , 1942)
Two Tickets to London (Univ. , 1943) (also producer)
Show Business (RKO, 1944)
Tall in the Saddle (RKO, 1944)
Johnny Angel (RKO, 1945)
Abilene Town (UA, 1946)
Lady Luck (RKO, 1946)
Mr. Ace (UA, 1946)
Nocturne (RKO, 1946)
Young Widow (UA, 1946)
Christmas Eve (UA, 1947)
Intrigue (UA, 1947)
Race Street (RKO, 1948)
The Younger Brothers (WB, 1949)
Canadian Pacific (20th, 1949)
Fighting Man of the Plains (20th, 1949)
Colt .45 (WB, 1950)
The Cariboo Trail (20th, 1950)
Sugarfoot (WB, 1941)
Raton Pass (WB, 1951)
Fort Worth (WB, 1951)

MARION, FRANCES, b. Nov. 18, 1888, San Francisco; d. May 12,
    1973.
    The Love Light (UA, 1921) (also script)
    Just Around the Corner (Par. , 1922) (also script)
    The Song of Love (FN, 1924) (with Chester M. Franklin) (also
        script)

MARSHALL, GEORGE, b. Dec. 29, 1891, Chicago.
    Love's Lariat (Bluebird, 1916)
    The Man from Montana (Butterfly, 1917)
    The Embarrassment of Riches (W.W. Hodkinson, 1918)
    The Adventures of Ruth* (Pathé, 1919)
    Ruth of the Rockies* (Pathé, 1920)
    Prairie Trails (Fox, 1920)
    After Your Own Heart (Fox, 1921)
    Hands Off (Fox, 1921)
    The Jolt (Fox, 1921)
    A Ridin' Romeo (Fox, 1921)
    Why Trust Your Husband? (Fox, 1921)
    The Lady from Longacre (Fox, 1922)
    Smiles Are Trumps (Fox, 1922)
    Haunted Valley* (Pathé, 1923)
    Don Quickshot of the Rio Grande (Univ. , 1923)
    Men in the Raw (Univ. , 1923)
    Where Is This West? (Univ. , 1923)

A Trip to Chinatown (Fox,
    1926)
The Gay Retreat (Fox, 1927)
The Adventures of Ruth*
    (Pathé, 1929)
Pack Up Your Troubles
    (MGM, 1932) (with Ray-
    mond McCarey)
Ever Since Eve (Fox, 1934)
Wild Gold (Fox, 1934)
She Learned About Sailors
    (Fox, 1934)
365 Nights in Hollywood
    (Fox, 1934)
Life Begins at Forty (Fox,
    1935)
$10 Raise (Fox, 1935)
In Old Kentucky (Fox, 1935)
Show Them No Mercy (Fox,
    1935)
Music Is Magic (Fox, 1935)
A Message to Garcia (20th,
    1936)
The Crime of Dr. Forbes
    (20th, 1937)
Can This Be Dixie (20th,
    1937) (also co-story)
Nancy Steele Is Missing
    (20th, 1937
Love Under Fire (20th,
    1937)

George Marshall (drawing by Sam
Patrick, ca. 1962).

The Goldwyn Follies (UA, 1938)
Battle of Broadway (20th, 1938)
Hold That Coed (20th, 1938)
You Can't Cheat an Honest Man (Univ., 1939)
Estry Rides Again (Univ., 1939)
The Ghost Breakers (Par., 1940)
When the Daltons Rode (Univ., 1940)
Pot O' Gold (UA, 1941)
Texas (Col., 1941)
Valley of the Sun (RKO, 1942)
The Forest Rangers (Par., 1942)
Star Spangled Rhythm (Par., 1942)
True to Life (Par., 1943)
Riding High (Par., 1943)
And the Angels Sing (Par., 1944) (with Claude Binyon)
Murder He Says (Par., 1945)
Incendiary Blonde (Par., 1945)
The Blue Dahlia (Par., 1946)
Monsieur Beaucaire (Par., 1946)
The Perils of Pauline (Par., 1947)
Variety Girl (Par., 1947)
Hazard (Par., 1948)

Tap Roots (Par., 1948)
My Friend Irma (Par., 1949)
Fancy Pants (Par., 1950)
Never a Dull Moment (RKO, 1950)
A Millionaire for Christy (20th, 1951)
The Savage (Par., 1952)
Off Limits (Par., 1953)
Scared Stiff (Par., 1953)
Houdini (Par., 1953)
Money from Home (Par., 1953)
Red Garters (Par., 1954)
Duel in the Jungle (WB, 1954)
Destry (Univ., 1954)
The Second Greatest Sex (Univ., 1955)
Pillars of the Sky (Univ., 1956)
The Guns of Fort Petticoat (Col., 1957)
Beyond Mombasa (Col., 1957)
The Sad Sack (Par., 1957)
The Sheepman (MGM, 1958)
Imitation General (MGM, 1958)
The Mating Game (MGM, 1959)
It Started With a Kiss (MGM, 1959)
The Gazebo (MGM, 1959)
Cry for Happy (Col., 1961)
The Happy Thieves (UA, 1962)
How the West Was Won (ep: "The Railroad") (MGM, 1962)
Papa's Delicate Condition (Par., 1963)
Dark Purpose (Univ., 1964)
Advance to the Rear (MGM, 1964)
Boy, Did I Get a Wrong Number? (UA, 1966)
Eight on the Lam (UA, 1967)
The Wicked Dreams of Paula Schultz (UA, 1968)
Hook, Line and Sinker (Col., 1969)
Hec Ramsey (NBC-TV, 1972)

MATE, RUDOLPH (Rudolf Mathéh), b. 1898, Cracow, Poland; d.
    Oct. 26, 1964.
    It Had to Be You (Col., 1947) (with Don Hartman) (also cam-
    era)
    The Dark Past (Col., 1948)
    D.O.A. (UA, 1949)
    No Sad Songs for Me (Col., 1950)
    Union Station (Par., 1950)
    Branded (Par., 1950)
    The Prince Who Was a Thief (Univ., 1951)
    When Worlds Collide (Par., 1951)
    The Green Glove (UA, 1952)
    Paula (Col., 1952)
    Sally and Saint Anne (Univ., 1952)
    The Mississippi Gambler (Univ., 1953)
    Second Chance (RKO, 1953)
    Forbidden (Univ., 1953)

The Siege at Red River (20th, 1954)
The Black Shield of Falworth (Univ., 1954)
The Violent Men (Col., 1955)
The Far Horizons (Par., 1955)
Miracle in the Rain (WB, 1956)
The Rawhide Years (Univ., 1956)
Port Afrique (Col., 1956)
Three Violent People (Par., 1956)
The Deep Six (WB, 1958)
Serenade einer Grossen Liebe (German, 1958)
For the First Time (MGM, 1959)
Revak, lo Schiavo di Cartagine (Italian, 1960)
The Immaculate Road (20th, 1960)
The 300 Spartans (20th, 1962) (also co-producer)
Aliki (Funos-Aquarius, 1962)
Seven Seas to Calais (MGM, 1963) (also co-producer)

MAY, JOE (Joseph Mandel), b. Nov. 7, 1880, Vienna; d. May 5,
   1954.
   In der Tiefe des Schactes (German, 1912) (also script)
   Vorghiten des Balkanbrandes (German, 1912)
   Ein Ausgestossener (Part I) (German, 1913)
   Heimat und Fremde (German, 1913) (also script)
   Der Verschlierte Bild von Grozs-Kleindorf (German, 1913)
   Entsagungen (German, 1913)
   Die Unheilbringende Perle (German, 1913)
   Der Mann im Kellar (German, 1914)
   Der Spuk in Hause des Professors (German, 1914)
   Das Panzergewölhe (German, 1914)
   Die Geheimnisvolle Villa (German, 1914)
   Charley, der Wunderaffe (German, 1915)
   In der Nacht (German, 1915)**
   Das Gesetz der Mine (German, 1915)** (also script)
   Sein Schwierigster Fall (German, 1915)** (also co-script)
   Dev Geheimsekretär (German, 1915)** (also co-script)
   Die Sunde der Helga Arndt (German, 1915) (German, 1915)**
       (also co-script)
   Die Gespenteruhr (German, 1915)** (also co-script)
   Nebel und Sonne (German, 1916)**
   Ein Blatt Papier (German, 1916)** (also co-script)
   Arme Eva Maria (German, 1916)**
   Wie Ich Detektiv Wurde (German, 1916)**
   Das Rätselhafte Inserat (German, 1916)**
   Die Silhouette des Teufels (German, 1917)**
   Das Geheimnis der Leeren Wasserflasche (German, 1917)**
   Der Schwarze Chauffeur (German, 1917)** (also script)
   Der Onyxknopf (German, 1917)
   Des Vaters Letzter Wille (German, 1917)**
   Die Hochzeit im Excentricclub (German, 1917)**
   Die Liebe der Hetty Raymond (German, 1917)**

**For own production company.

Ein Lichtstrahl im Dunkel (German, 1917)**
Hide Warren und Dertod (German, 1917)**
Krähen Fliegen um den Turm (German, 1917)**
Das Klima von Vancourt (German, 1918)**
Das Opfer (German, 1918)**
Ihr Grosses Geheimnis (German, 1918)**
Die Bettelgräfin (German, 1918)** (also co-script)
Wogen des Schicksals (German, 1918)**
Sein Bester Freund (German, 1918)**
Veritas Vincit (German, 1919)**
Die Herrin der Welt* (German, 1919) (with Jens Krafft, Karl
    Gerhardt)
Fraülein Zahnarzt (German, 1919)** (also co-script)
Die Legende von der Heiligen Simplicia (German, 1920)**
Die Schuld der Lavinia Morland [The Wife Trap] (German,
    1920)** (also co-script)
Das Indische Grabmal (Part I and II) German, 1921)**
Tragodie der Liebe (Parts I-IV) (German, 1923)**
Der Farmer aus Texas (German, 1925)** (also co-script)
Dagfin (German, 1926)** (also co-script)
Heimkehr [The Homecoming] (German, 1929)
Asphalt (German, 1929)
Ihre Majestät die Liebe (German, 1930)**
Und Das Ist die Haupstsache (German, 1931)**
Zwei in Einem Auto (German, 1932)**
Voyage de Nose [French version of Hochzeitreise zu Dritt]
    (German, 1933)
Ein Lied für Dich (German, 1933)
Tout pour l'Amour [French version of Ein Lied für Dich] (Ger-
    man, 1933)
Two Hears in Waltztime (Gaumont-British, 1934) (with Carmine
    Gallone)
Music in the Air (Fox, 1934)
Confession (WB, 1937)
Society Smugglers (Univ., 1939)
The House of Fear (Univ., 1939)
The Invisible Man Returns (Univ., 1940) (also co-script)
The House of Seven Gables (Univ., 1940)
You're Not So Tough (Univ., 1940)
Hit the Road (Univ., 1941)
Johnny Doesn't Live Here Anymore (Mon., 1944)

MAYO, ARCHIE L. (Archibald L. Mayo), b. 1891, New York City;
    d. Dec. 4, 1968.
    Money Talks (MGM, 1926)
    Unknown Treasures (Sterling, 1926)
    Christine of the Big Tops (Sterling, 1926)
    Johnny Get Your Hair Cut (MGM, 1927) (with B. Reaves Eason)
    Quarantined Rivals (Lumas, 1927)
    Dearie (WB, 1927)
    Slightly Used (WB, 1927)
    The College Widow (WB, 1927)

Beware of Married Men (WB, 1928)
Crimson City (WB, 1928)
State Street Sadie (WB, 1928)
On Trial (WB, 1928)
My Man (WB, 1928)
Sonny Boy (WB, 1929)
The Sap (WB, 1929)
Is Everybody Happy? (WB, 1929)
The Sacred Flame (WB, 1929)
Vengeance (Col., 1930)
Wide Open (WB, 1930)
Courage (WB, 1930)
Oh! Sailor Behave! (WB, 1930)
The Doorway to Hell (WB, 1930)
Illicit (WB, 1931)
Svengali (WB, 1931)
Bought (WB, 1931)
Under 18 (WB, 1932)
The Expert (WB, 1932)
Two Against the World (WB, 1932)
Night After Night (Par., 1932)
The Life of Jimmy Dolan (WB, 1933)
Mayor of Hell (WB, 1933)
Ever in My Heart (WB, 1933)
Convention City (WB, 1933)
Gambling Lady (WB, 1934)
Desirable (WB, 1934)
The Man With Two Faces (WB, 1934)
Go into Your Dance (WB, 1935)
Bordertown (WB, 1935)
The Case of the Lucky Legs (WB, 1935)
The Petrified Forest (WB, 1936)
I Married a Doctor (FN, 1936)
Give Me Your Heart (WB, 1936)
Black Legion (WB, 1936)
Call It a Day (WB, 1937)
It's Love I'm After (WB, 1937)
The Adventures of Marco Polo (UA, 1938)
Youth Takes a Fling (Univ., 1938)
They Shall Have Music (UA, 1939)
The House Across the Bay (UA, 1940)
Four Sons (20th, 1940)
The Great American Broadcast (20th, 1941)
Charley's Aunt (20th, 1941)
Confirm or Deny (20th, 1941) (replaced uncredited Fritz Lang)
Moontide (20th, 1942) (replaced uncredited Fritz Lang)
Orchestra Wives (20th, 1942)
Crash Dive (20th, 1943)
Sweet and Low Down (20th, 1944)
A Night in Casablanca (UA, 1946)
Angel on My Shoulder (UA, 1946)

MAZURSKY, PAUL
    Bob & Carol & Ted & Alice (Col., 1969) (also co-script)
    Alex in Wonderland (MGM, 1970) (also co-script, actor)
    Blume in Love (WB, 1973) (also producer, co-script, actor)

MELFORD, GEORGE, b. c.1877, Rochester, N.Y.; d. April 25,
    1961.
    The Invisible Power (Kalem, 1914)
    The Boer War (Kalem, 1914)
    Shannon of the Sixth (Kalem, 1914)
    The Unknown (Par., 1915)
    Armstrong's Wife (Par., 1915)
    The Fighting Hope (Par., 1915)
    The Immigrant (Par., 1915)
    The Marriage of Kitty (Par., 1915)
    Out of the Darkness (Par., 1915)
    The Puppet Crown (Par., 1915)
    Stolen Goods (Par., 1915)
    The Woman (Par., 1915)
    Young Romance (Par., 1915)
    The House of Golden Windows (Par., 1916)
    To Have and to Hold (Par., 1916)
    The Years of the Locust (Par., 1916)
    The Yellow Pawn (Par., 1916)
    The Evil Eye (Par., 1917)
    Her Strange Wedding (Par., 1917)
    A School for Husbands (Par., 1917)
    The Winning of Sally Temple (Par., 1917)
    The Cost of Hatred (Par., 1917)
    The Crystal Gazer (Par., 1917)
    On the Level (Par., 1917)
    The Sunset Trail (Par., 1917)
    The Call of the East (Par., 1917)
    Nan of Music Mountain (Par., 1917)
    Sandy (Par., 1917)
    The Hidden Pearls (Par., 1918)
    Wild Youth (Par., 1918)
    Such a Little Pirate (Par., 1918)
    The Bravest Way (Par., 1918)
    The Source (Par., 1918)
    The Cruise of the Make-Believes (Par., 1918)
    The City of Dim Faces (Par., 1919)
    Good Gracious Annabelle (Par., 1919)
    Jane Goes A-Wooing (Par., 1919)
    Men, Women and Money (Par., 1919)
    Pettigrew's Girl (Par., 1919)
    Sporting Chance (Par., 1919)
    Told in the Hills (Par., 1919)
    Everywoman (Par., 1919)
    The Sea Wolf (Par., 1920)
    The Round Up (Par., 1920)
    The Jucklins (Par., 1920)

Behold My Wife (Par., 1920)
The Faith Healer (Par., 1921)
The Great Impersonation (Par., 1921)
A Wise Fool (Par., 1921)
The Sheik (Par., 1921)
Moran of the Lady Letty (Par., 1922)
The Woman Who Walked Alone (Par., 1922)
Burning Sands (Par., 1922)
Ebb Tide (Par., 1922)
Java Head (Par., 1923)
The Light That Failed (Par., 1923)
Salomy Jane (Par., 1923)
You Can't Fool Your Wife (Par., 1923)
Flaming Barriers (Par., 1924)
The Dawn of a Tomorrow (Par., 1924)
Tiger Love (Par., 1924)
Big Timber (Par., 1924)
Friendly Enemies (PDC, 1925)
The Top of the World (Par., 1925)
Simon the Jester (PDC, 1925)
Without Mercy (PDC, 1925)
Rocking Moon (PDC, 1926)
The Flame of the Yukon (PDC, 1926)
Whispering Smith (PDC, 1926)
Going Crooked (Fox, 1926)
A Man's Past (Univ.-Jewel, 1927)
Lingerie (Tiffany-Stahl, 1928)
Sinners in Love (FBO, 1928)
Freedom of the Press (Univ.-Jewel, 1928)
The Charlatan (Univ.-Jewel, 1929)
Love in the Desert (FBO, 1929)
The Woman I Love (FBO, 1929)
Sea Fury (H.H. Rosenfield, 1929) (also co-story)
The Poor Millionaire (Biltmore, 1930)
La Voluntad del Muerto [Spanish version of The Cat Creeps]
   (Univ., 1930)
Oriente y Occidente [Spanish version of East Is West] (Univ., 1930)
Don Juan Diplomatico [Spanish version of The Boudoir Diplomat]
   (Univ., 1931)
Dracula [Spanish version of same] (Univ., 1931)
The Viking (J.D. Williams, 1931)
East of Borneo (Univ., 1931)
Homicide Squad (Univ., 1931)
A Scarlet Week-End (Maxim, 1932)
The Boiling Point (Allied, 1932)
The Penal Code (Freuler Film Associates, 1933)
Officer 13 (First Division, 1933)
Man of Action (Col., 1933)
The Cowboy Counsellor (Alliance, 1933)
The Eleventh Commandment (Alliance, 1933)
Dude Bandit (Alliance, 1933)
Hired Wife (Pinnacle, 1934)
East of Java (Univ., 1935)
Jungle Menace* (Col., 1937) (with Harry Fraser)

MENDES, LOTHAR, b. May 19, 1894, Berlin; d. Feb. 25, 1974.
Das Geheimnis der Santa Maria (German, 1921)
Der Abenteuer (German, 1921) (also co-script)
Deportiert (German, 1922)
Scheine des Todes (German, 1922) (also co-script)
S.O.S. die Insel der Tränen (German, 1923)
Der Mönch von Santarem (German, 1924)
Liebe Macht Blind (German,•1925)
Die Drei Kuckucksuhren (German, 1926)
The Prince of Tempters (FN, 1926)
Convoy (FN, 1927) (completed by Joseph C. Boyle)
A Night of Mystery (Par., 1928)
Interference (Par., 1928)
Dangerous Curves (Par., 1929)
Illusion (Par., 1929)
The Marriage Playground (Par., 1929)
The Four Feathers (Par., 1929) (with Merian C. Cooper,
Ernest B. Schoedsack)
Paramount on Parade (Par., 1930) (with Dorothy Arzner, Otto
Brower, Edmund Goulding, Victor Heerman, Edwin H. Knopf,
Rowland V. Lee, Ernst Lubitsch, Victor Schertzinger, A. Ed-
ward Sutherland, Frank Tuttle)
Ladies' Man (Par., 1931)
I Take This Woman (Par., 1931)
Personal Maid (Par., 1931) (with Monta Bell)
Strangers in Love (Par., 1932)
Payment Deferred (Par., 1932)
Luxury Liner (Par., 1932)
Jew Suss [Power] (Gaumont-British, 1934)
The Man Who Could Work Miracles (UA, 1937)
Moonlight Sonata (UA, 1937) (also producer)
International Squadron (WB, 1941) (with uncredited Louis Seiler)
Flight for a Freedom (RKO, 1943)
Tampico (20th, 1944)
The Walls Came Tumbling Down (Col., 1946)

MENZIES, WILLIAM CAMERON, b. July 29, 1896, New Haven,
Conn.; d. March 5, 1957.
The Spider (Fox, 1931) (with Kenneth McKenna)
Always Goodbye (Fox, 1931) (with Kenneth McKenna) (also art
director)
Chandu, the Magician (Fox, 1932) (with Marcel Varnel)
I Love You Wednesday (Fox, 1933) (with Henry King)
The Wharf Angel (Par., 1934) (with George Somnes)
Things to Come (UA, 1936) (also art director)
The Green Cockatoo [Four Dark Hours] (20th, 1937)
Address Unknown (Col., 1944) (also producer)
Duel in the Sun (Selznick Releasing, 1946) (uncredited, with
King Vidor, and uncredited William Dieterle, Josef von
Sternberg, Otto Brower, Sidney Franklin)
Drums in the Deep South (RKO, 1951) (also art director)
The Whip Hand (RKO, 1951) (also art director)

Invaders from Mars (20th, 1953) (also production designer)
The Maze (AA, 1953)

MEYER, RUSS, b. 1923, Oakland, Calif.
  The Immoral Mr. Teas (Padram, 1959)
  Eve and the Handyman (Eve, 1961)
  Lorna (Eve, 1964) (also producer, story, camera, editor)
  Motor Psycho (Eve, 1965) (also producer, co-story, camera)
  Fanny Hill (Pan World, 1965)
  Faster, Pussycat, Kill Kill (Eve, 1966)
  Mondo Topless (Eve, 1966)
  Good Morning--and Goodbye (Eve, 1967)
  Common Law Cabin [How Much Loving Does a Normal Couple
    Need?] (Eve, 1967)
  Vixen (Eve, 1968) (also producer, story, camera editor)
  Finders Keepers, Lovers Weepers (Eve, 1968) (also producer,
    story, camera, co-editor)
  Cherry, Harry and Raquel (Eve, 1969) (also producer, co-
    script, camera, co-editor)
  Rope of Flesh [Mud Honey] (Delta, 1969) (also co-producer)
  Beyond the Valley of the Dolls (20th, 1970)
  The Seven Minutes (20th, 1971)
  Sweet Suzy (Trident, 1973) (also producer, co-script)

MICHEAUX, OSCAR, d. 1951.
  The Gunsaulus Mystery (**, 1921)
  The Hypocrite (**, 1921)
  Symbol of the Unconquered (**, 1921)
  The Shadow (**, 1921)
  The Dungeon (**, 1922)
  The Homesteader (**, 1922) (also story)
  Uncle Jasper's Will (**, 1922)
  Deceit (**, 1923)
  The Ghost of Tolston's Manor (**, 1923)
  The Virgin of Seminole (**, 1923)
  Birthright (**, 1924)
  A Son of Satan (**, 1924)
  Body and Soul (**, 1925)
  The Brute (**, 1925)
  Marcus Garland (**, 1925)
  The Conjure Woman (**, 1926)
  The Devil's Disciple (**, 1926)
  The Broken Violin (**, 1927)
  The House Behind the Cedars (**, 1927)
  The Millionaire (**, 1927)
  The Spider's Web (**, 1927)

**All of his films were made for his own production company, Mi-
cheaux; he was also producer and script writer for all the films
listed.

Thirty Years Later (**, 1928)
When Men Betray (**, 1928)
Wages of Sin (**, 1929)
Daughter of the Congo (**, 1930)
Easy Street (**, 1930)
Darktown Revue (**, 1931)
The Exile (**, 1931)
Veiled Aristocrats (**, 1932)
Black Magic (**, 1932)
Ten Minutes to Live (**, 1932)
The Girl from Chicago (**, 1933)
Ten Minutes to Kill (**, 1933)
Harlem After Midnight (**, 1934)
Lem Hawkin's Confession (**, 1935)
Temptation (**, 1936)
Underworld (**, 1936)
God's Stepchildren (**, 1937)
Betrayal (**, 1948)

MILESTONE, LEWIS, b. Sept. 30, 1895, Odessa, Ukraine, Russia.
Seven Sinners (WB, 1925) (also co-story, co-adaptation)
The Cave Man (WB, 1926)
The New Klondike (Par., 1926)
Two Arabian Nights (UA, 1927)
The Garden of Eden (UA, 1928) (also producer)
The Racket (Par., 1928)
Betrayal (Par., 1929)
New York Nights (UA, 1929)
All Quiet on the Western Front (Univ., 1930)
The Front Page (UA, 1931)
Rain (WA, 1932) (also producer)
Hallelujah, I'm a Bum (UA, 1933)
The Captain Hates the Sea (Col., 1934)
Paris in Spring (Par., 1935)
Anything Goes (Par., 1936)
The General Died at Dawn (Par., 1936)
Of Mice and Men (UA, 1939) (also producer)
The Night of Nights (American Releasing, 1940)
Lucky Partners (RKO, 1940)
My Life With Caroline (RKO, 1941) (also producer)
Our Russian Front (Harry Rathner, 1942)
Edge of Darkness (WB, 1943)
The North Star (RKO, 1943)
The Purple Heart (20th, 1944)
Guest in the House (UA, 1944) (uncredited, replaced John
    Brahm, with uncredited André De Toth)
A Walk in the Sun (20th, 1945) (also producer)
The Strange Love of Martha Ivers (Par., 1946)
The Arch of Triumph (UA, 1948) (also co-script)
No Minor Vices (MGM, 1948) (also producer)
The Red Pony (Rep., 1949) (also producer)
Halls of Montezuma (20th, 1951)

Kangaroo (20th, 1952)
Les Miserables (20th, 1952)
Melba (UA, 1953)
They Who Dare (Associated Artists, 1954)
La Vedova (Italian, 1955)
Pork Chop Hill (UA, 1959)
Ocean's 11 (WB, 1960) (also producer)
Mutiny on the Bounty (MGM, 1962)
PT-109 (WB, 1963) (uncredited, with Leslie H. Martinson)
The Dirty Game (AIP, 1966) (uncredited, replaced Terence
    Young)

MILLAND, RAY (Reginald Truscott-Jones, b. Jan. 3, 1907, Neath,
    Glmorganshire, Wales, Eng.
    A Man Alone (Rep., 1955) (also actor)
    Lisbon (Rep., 1956) (also associate producer, actor)
    The Safecracker (MGM, 1957) (also actor)
    Panic in Year Zero (AIP, 1962) (also actor)
    Hostile Witness (UA, 1970) (also actor)

MILLER, DAVID, b. Nov. 28, 1909.
    Billy the Kid (MGM, 1941)
    Sunday Punch (MGM, 1942)
    Flying Tigers (Rep., 1942)
    Top O' the Morning (Par., 1949)
    Our Very Own (RKO, 1950)
    Love Happy (UA, 1950)
    Saturday's Hero (Col., 1951)
    Sudden Fear (RKO, 1952)
    Twist of Fate (UA, 1954) (also story)
    Diane (MGM, 1955)
    The Opposite Sex (MGM, 1956)
    The Story of Esther Costello (Col., 1957)
    Happy Anniversary (UA, 1959)
    Midnight Lace (Univ., 1960)
    Back Street (Univ., 1961)
    Lonely Are the Brave (Univ., 1962)
    Captain Newman, M.D. (Univ., 1963)
    Hammerhead (Col., 1968)
    Hail Hero! (National General, 1969)
    Executive Action (National General, 1973)

MILTON, ROBERT, b. Jan. 24, 18??, Dinaburgh, Russia.
    Charming Sinners (Par., 1929)
    The Dummy (Par., 1929)
    Behind the Make-Up (Par., 1930)
    Outward Bound (WB, 1930)
    Sin Takes a Holiday (Pathé, 1930)
    The Bargain (FN, 1931)
    Devotion (Pathé, 1931)

Husband's Holiday (Par., 1932)
Westward Passage (RKO, 1932)
Dance of Witches (London, 1933)
Bella Donna (Gaumont-British, 1934)

MINNELLI, VINCENTE, b. Feb. 28, 1906, Chicago.
Cabin in the Sky (MGM, 1943)
I Dood It (MGM, 1943)
Meet Me in St. Louis (MGM, 1944)
The Clock (MGM, 1945)
Yolanda and the Thief (MGM, 1945)
Ziegfeld Follies (MGM, 1946)
Undercurrent (MGM, 1946)
Till the Clouds Roll By (MGM, 1946) (directed Judy Garland
    numbers, with Richard Whorf)
The Pirate (MGM, 1948)
Madame Bovary (MGM, 1949)
Father of the Bride (MGM, 1950)
An American in Paris (MGM, 1951)
Father's Little Dividend (MGM, 1951)
The Bad and the Beautiful (MGM, 1952)
The Band Wagon (MGM, 1953)
The Story of Three Loves (ep: "Mademoiselle") (MGM, 1953)
The Long, Long Trailer (MGM, 1954)
Brigadoon (MGM, 1954)
The Cobweb (MGM, 1955)
Kismet (MGM, 1955)
Lust for Life (MGM, 1956)
Tea and Sympathy (MGM, 1956)
Designing Woman (MGM, 1957)
The Seventh Sin (MGM, 1957) (uncredited, with Ronald Neame)
Gigi (MGM, 1958)
The Reluctant Debutante (MGM, 1958)
Some Came Running (MGM, 1958)
Home from the Hill (MGM, 1960)
Bells Are Ringing (MGM, 1960)
The Four Horsemen of the Apocalypse (MGM, 1961)
Two Weeks in Another Town (MGM, 1962)
The Courtship of Eddie's Father (MGM, 1963)
Goodbye Charlie (20th, 1964)
The Sandpiper (MGM, 1965)
On a Clear Day You Can See Forever (Par., 1970)

MONTGOMERY, ROBERT, b. May 21, 1904.
They Were Expendable (MGM, 1945) (uncredited, with John
    Ford) (also actor)
Lady in the Lake (MGM, 1946) (also actor)
Ride the Pink Horse (Univ., 1947) (also actor)
Once More, My Darling (Univ., 1949) (also actor)
Eye Witness (Eagle Lion, 1950) (also actor)
The Gallant Hours (UA, 1960) (also producer)

MORSE, TERRY O., b. Jan. 30, 1906, St. Louis, Mo.
Adventures of Jane Arden (WB, 1939)
No Place to Go (WB, 1939)
On Trial (WB, 1939)
Smashing the Money Ring (WB, 1939)
Waterfront (WB, 1939)
Tear Gas Squad (WB, 1940)
A Fugitive from Justice (WB, 1940)
British Intelligence (WB, 1940)
Fog Island (PRC, 1945)
Danny Boy (PRC, 1946)
Don Ricardo Returns (PRC, 1946)
Shadows over Chinatown (Mon., 1946)
Dangerous Money (Mon., 1946)
Bells of San Fernando (Screen Guild, 1947)
Unknown World (Lip., 1951)
Godzilla, King of the Monsters (Emb., 1956) (with Inoshiro
    Honda)
Young Dillinger (AA, 1965)

MOXEY, JOHN LLEWELLYN, b. 1920, Hurlingham, Eng.
Foxhole in Cairo (British Lion-Britannia, 1960)
City of the Dead [Horror Hotel] (British Lion, 1961)
Death Trap (Anglo, 1962) (also script)
Ricochet (Warner-Pathé, 1963)
The £20,000 Kiss (Anglo, 1963)
Downfall (Warner-Pathé, 1964)
Face of a Stranger (Warner-Pathé, 1966)
Strangler's Web (Anglo, 1966)
The Tormentor (ITC, 1967)
Circus of Fear [Psycho-Circus] (Anglo, 1967)
SFX--San Francisco International Airport (NBC-TV, 1970)
The House That Would Not Die (ABC-TV, 1970)
The Last Child (ABC-TV, 1971)
Taste of Evil (ABC-TV, 1971)
The Death of Me Yet! (ABC-TV, 1971)
Escape (ABC-TV, 1971)
The Bounty Man (ABC-TV, 1972)
The Night Stalker (ABC-TV, 1972)
Hard Case (ABC-TV, 1972)
Genesis II (CBS-TV, 1973)

MULLIGAN, ROBERT, b. 1925, New York City.
Fear Strikes Out (Par., 1957)
The Rat Race (Par., 1960)
The Great Imposter (Univ., 1960)
Come September (Univ., 1961)
The Spiral Road (Univ., 1962)
To Kill a Mockingbird (Univ., 1962)
Love With the Proper Stranger (Par., 1964)
Baby, the Rain Must Fall (Col., 1965)

Inside Daisy Clover (WB, 1966)
Up the Down Staircase (WB-7 Arts, 1967)
The Stalking Moon (National General, 1969)
The Pursuit of Happiness (Col., 1971) (also co-producer)
Summer of '42 (WB, 1971)
The Other (20th, 1972) (also producer)

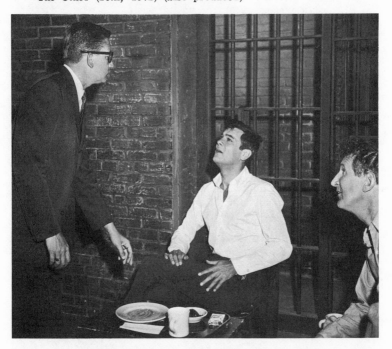

Tony Curtis and Doodles Weaver with Robert Mulligan (left) on the
set for The Great Imposter (Univ., 1961)

MURNAU, F.W. (Friedrich Wilhelm Murnau or F.W. Plumpe), b.
    Dec. 28, 1888, Bielefeld, Westphalia, Germany; d. March
    11, 1931.
    Der Knabe in Blau (German, 1919)
    Satanas (German, 1919)
    Abend... Nacht... Morgen (German, 1920)
    Der Bucklige und die Tänzerin (German, 1920)
    Der Gang in die Nacht (German, 1920)
    Der Januskopf (German, 1920)
    Sehnsucht (German, 1920)
    Marizza, Genannt die Schmugglermadonna (German, 1921)
    Schloss Vogelod (German, 1921)
    Der Brennende Acker (German, 1922)

Nosferatu, eine Symphonie des Grauens (German, 1922)
Phantom (German, 1922)
Die Austreibung (German, 1923)
Die Finanzen des Grossherzogs (German, 1923)
Der Letze Mann (German, 1924)
Tartuff (German, 1924)
Faust (German, 1926)
Sunrise (Fox, 1927)
Four Devils (Fox, 1928)
Tabu (Par., 1931) (with Robert Flaherty) (also co-producer, co-script)

MURPHY, DUDLEY, b. July 10, 1897, Winchester, Mass.
High Speed Lee (Arrow, 1923) (also adaptation, 1923)
Alex the Great (FBO, 1928) (also script)
Stocks and Blondes (FBO, 1928) (also story, script)
Confessions of a Co-Ed (Par., 1931) (with David Burton)
The Sport Parade (RKO, 1932)
The Emperor Jones (UA, 1933)
The Night Is Young (MGM, 1935)
Don't Gamble With Love (Col., 1936)
One Third of a Nation (Par., 1939)
Main Street Lawyer (Rep., 1939)
Yolanda (Mexican, 1942) (with Manuel Reachi)
Alma del Bronce (Mexican, 1944) (also script)

MURPHY, RICHARD, b. 1912, Boston.
Three Stripes in the Sun (Col., 1955) (also script)
The Wackiest Ship in the Army (Col., 1960) (also script)

N

NAZARRO, RAY (Raymond Nazarro), b. Sept. 25, 1902, Boston.
Outlaws of the Rockies (Col., 1945)
Song of the Prairie (Col., 1945)
Cowboy Blues (Col., 1946)
The Desert Horseman (Col., 1946)
Galloping Thunder (Col., 1946)
Gunning for Vengeance (Col., 1946)
Roaring Rangers (Col., 1946)
Singing on the Trail (Col., 1946)
Throw a Saddle on a Star (Col., 1946)
Two-Fisted Stranger (Col., 1946)
Heading West (Col., 1946)
Texas Panhandle (Col., 1946)
That Texas Jamboree (Col., 1946)
Lone Star Moonlight (Col., 1946)
Over the Santa Fe Trail (Col., 1947)
Rose of Santa Rosa (Col., 1947)
Law of the Canyon (Col., 1947)

The Lone Hand Texan (Col., 1947)
Terror Trail (Col., 1947)
West of Dodge City (Col., 1947)
Buckaroo from Powder River (Col., 1947)
Last Days of Boot Hill (Col., 1947)
Phantom Valley (Col., 1948)
Six-Gun Law (Col., 1948)
Song of Idaho (Col., 1948)
West of Sonora (Col., 1948)
Trail to Laredo (Col., 1948)
Laramie (Col., 1949)
Bandits of El Dorado (Col., 1949)
Frontier Outpost (Col., 1949)
Renegades of the Sage (Col., 1949)
Blazing Trail (Col., 1949)
Quick on the Trigger (Col., 1949)
Challenge of the Range (Col., 1949)
South of Death Valley (Col., 1949)
El Dorado Pass (Col., 1949)
The Palomino (Col., 1950)
Outcast of Black Mesa (Col., 1950)
David Harding, Counterspy (Col., 1950)
Texas Dynamo (Col., 1950)
Hoedown (Col., 1950)
Trail of the Rustler (Col., 1950)
Streets of Ghost Town (Col., 1950)
Smoky Mountain Melody (Col., 1950)
The Tougher They Come (Col., 1950)
Al Jennings of Oklahoma (Col., 1951)
Flame of Stamboul (Col., 1951)
China Corsair (Col., 1951)
Fort Savage Raiders (Col., 1951)
Cyclone Fury (Col., 1951)
The Kid from Amarillo (Col., 1951)
War Cry (Col., 1951)
The Rough, Tough West (Col., 1952)
Indian Uprising (Col., 1952)
Laramie Mountains (Col., 1952)
Montana Territory (Col., 1952)
Cripple Creek (Col., 1952)
Junction City (Col., 1952)
Gun Belt (UA, 1953)
The Bandits of Corsica (UA, 1953)
Kansas Pacific (AA, 1953)
The Lone Gun (UA, 1954)
The Black Dakotas (Col., 1954)
Southwest Passage (UA, 1954)
Top Gun (UA, 1955)
The White Squaw (Col., 1956)
The Phantom Stagecoach (Col., 1957)
Domino Kid (Col., 1957)
The Hired Gun (MGM, 1957)
Return to Warbow (Col., 1958)

Apache Territory (Col., 1958)
Einer Frisst den Andern (Neubach, 1964)

NEGULESCO, JEAN, b. Feb. 29, 1900, Craiova, Rumania.
Singapore Woman (WB, 1941)
The Mask of Dimitrios (WB, 1944)
The Conspirators (WB, 1944)
Nobody Lives Forever (WB, 1946)
Three Strangers (WB, 1946)
Humoresque (WB, 1947)
Deep Valley (20th, 1947)
Road House (20th, 1948)
Johnny Belinda (WB, 1948)
The Forbidden Street (20th, 1949)
The Mudlark (20th, 1950)
Under My Skin (20th, 1950)
Three Came Home (20th, 1950)
Take Care of My Little Girl (20th, 1951)
Phone Call from a Stranger (20th, 1952)
Lydia Bailey (20th, 1952)
Lure of the Wilderness (20th, 1952)
O. Henry's Full House (ep: "The Last Leaf") (20th, 1952)
Scandal at Scourie (MGM, 1953)
Titanic (20th, 1953)
How to Marry a Millionaire (20th, 1953)
Three Coins in the Fountain (20th, 1954)
Woman's World (20th, 1954)
Daddy Long Legs (20th, 1955)
The Rains of Ranchipur (20th, 1955)
Boy on a Dolphin (20th, 1957)
The Gift of Life (20th, 1958)
A Certain Smile (20th, 1958)
Count Your Blessings (MGM, 1959)
The Best of Everything (20th, 1959)
Jessica (UA, 1962)
The Pleasure Seekers (20th, 1964)
Hello--Goodbye (20th, 1970)
The Invincible Six (Continental, 1970)

NEILAN, MARSHALL A., b. April 11, 1891, San Bernardino,
    Calif.; d. Oct. 27, 1958.
The Chronicles of Bloom Center (Selig, 1915) (series of two-
    reelers)
The Cycle of Fate (Selig, 1916) (also script)
The Prince Chap (Selig, 1916)
The Country That God Forgot (Selig, 1916) (also script)
Those Without Sin (Par., 1917)
The Bottle Imp (Par., 1917)
The Tides of Barnegat (Par., 1917)
The Girl at Home (Par., 1917)
The Silent Partner (Par., 1917)

Freckles (Par., 1917)
The Jaguar's Claws (Par., 1917)
Rebecca of Sunnybrook Farm (Artcraft-Par., 1917)
The Little Princess (Artcraft-Par., 1917)
Stella Maris (Artcraft-Par., 1918)
Amarilly of Clothes Line Alley (Artcraft-Par., 1918)
M'Liss (Artcraft-Par., 1918)
Hit-the-Trail Holliday (Artcraft-Par., 1918)
The Heart of the Wilds (Par., 1918)
Out of a Clear Sky (Par., 1918)
Three Men and a Girl (Par., 1919)
Daddy Long Legs (Associated FN, 1919)
The Unpardonable Sin (Garson-Neilan, 1919)
Her Kingdom of Dreams (Associated FN, 1920)
In Old Kentucky (Associated FN, 1920)
The River's End (Associated FN, 1920)
Don't Ever Marry (Associated FN, 1920) (with Victor Heerman)
Go and Get It (Associated FN, 1920) (with Henry Symonds) (al-
   so producer**)
Dinty (Associated FN, 1921) (with John W. McDermott) (also
   producer**, script)
Bob Hampton of Placer (Associated FN, 1921) (also producer**)
Bits of Life (Associated FN, 1921) (also producer**, additional
   story)
The Lotus Eater (Associated FN, 1922) (also producer**)
Fools First (Associated FN, 1922) (also producer**)
Minnie (Associated FN, 1922) (with Frank Urson) (also pro-
   ducer**, script)
Penrod (Associated FN, 1922) (also producer**)
The Stranger's Banquet (Goldwyn, 1922) (also producer**, co-
   script)
The Eternal Three (Goldwyn, 1923) (with Frank Urson) (also
   story)
The Rendezvous (Goldwyn, 1923)
Dorothy Vernon of Haddon Hall (UA, 1924)
Tess of the D'Urbervilles (Metro-Goldwyn, 1925)
The Sporting Venus (Metro-Goldwyn, 1925)
The Great Love (MGM, 1925)
Mike (MGM, 1926) (also story)
The Skyrocket (Associated Exhibitors, 1926)
Wild Oats Lane (PDC, 1926) (also producer)
Diplomacy (Par., 1926)
Everybody's Acting (Par., 1926) (also story)
Venus of Venus (FN, 1927)
Her Wild Oat (FN, 1927)
Three-Ring Marriage (FN, 1928)
Take Me Home (Par., 1928)
Taxi 13 (FBO, 1928)
His Last Haul (FBO, 1928)
The Awful Truth (Pathé, 1929)
Tanned Legs (RKO, 1929)

**For own production company.

The Vagabond Lover (RKO, 1929)
Sweethearts on Parade (Col., 1930)
Chloe (Pinnacle, 1934)
Social Register (Col., 1934)
The Lemon Drop Kid (Par., 1934)
This Is the Life (20th, 1935)
Sing While You're Able (Ambassador, 1937)
Swing It, Professor (Ambassador, 1937)

NEILL, ROY WILLIAM (Roland de Gostrie), b. 1890, Dublin, Ireland; d. Dec. 14, 1946.
A Corner in Colleens (Triangle, 1916) (also actor)
The Girl Glory (Triangle, 1917)
The Mother Instinct (Triangle, 1917)
They're Off (Triangle, 1917)
The Price Mark (Par., 1917)
Love Letter (Par., 1917)
Vive La France (Par., 1918)
The Kaiser's Shadow (Par., 1918)
Flare Up Sal (Par., 1918)
Love Me (Par., 1918)
Tyrant Fear (Par., 1918)
The Mating of Marcella (Par., 1918)
Green Eyes (Par., 1918)
Charge It to Me (Pathé, 1919)
Puppy Love (Par., 1919)
Trixie from Broadway (Pathé, 1919)
Career of Katherine Bush (Par., 1919)
The Bandbox (W.W. Hodkinson, 1919)
The Inner Voice (American, 1920)
The Woman Gives (Associated FN, 1920)
Yes or No (Associated FN, 1920)
Dangerous Business (Associated FN, 1920)
Good References (Associated FN, 1920)
Something Different (Realart, 1921)
The Conquest of Canaan (Par., 1921)
The Idol of the North (Par., 1921)
The Iron Trail (Par., 1921)
What's Wrong With Women? (Equity, 1922)
Radio-Mania (W.W. Hodkinson, 1923)
Toilers of the Sea (Selznick, 1923) (also producer)
Broken Laws (FBO, 1924)
By Divine Right (FBO, 1924)
Vanity's Price (FBO, 1924)
Greater Than a Crown (Fox, 1925)
The Kiss Barrier (Fox, 1925)
Marriage in Transit (Fox, 1925)
Percy (Pathé, 1925)
Black Paradise (Fox, 1926)
The City (Fox, 1926)
The Cowboy and the Countess (Fox, 1926)
The Fighting Buckaroo (Fox, 1926)

A Man Four Square (Fox, 1926)
The Arizona Wildcat (Fox, 1927)
Marriage (Fox, 1927)
Lady Raffles (Col., 1928)
The Olympic Hero (Supreme-Zakoro, 1928)
San Francisco Nights (Lumas, 1928)
Behind Closed Doors (Col., 1929)
The Viking (MGM, 1929)
Wall Street (Col., 1929)
Cock O' the Walk (Sono-Art World Wide, 1930) (with Walter
    Lang)
Just Like Heaven (Tiffany, 1930)
The Melody Man (Col., 1930)
The Good Bad Girl (Col., 1931)
The Avenger (Col., 1931)
Fifty Fathoms Deep (Col., 1931)
The Menace (Col., 1932)
That's My Boy (Col., 1932)
The Circus Queen Murder (Col., 1933)
As the Devil Commands (Col., 1933)
Above the Clouds (Col., 1933)
Black Moon (Col., 1934)
Fury of the Jungle (Col., 1934)
9th Guest (Col., 1934)
The Whirlpool (Col., 1934)
Blind Date (Col., 1934)
Jealousy (Col., 1934)
I'll Fix It (Col., 1934)
The Black Room (Col., 1935)
Eight Bells (Col., 1935)
Mills of the Gods (Col., 1935)
Black Room Mystery (Col., 1935)
The Lone Wolf Returns (Col., 1936)
Dr. Syn (General Film Distributors, 1937)
Simply Terrific (WB, 1938)
Thank Evans (FN, 1938)
The Viper (FN, 1938)
The Good Old Days (FN, 1938)
Everything Happens to Me (FN, 1938)
Many Tanks Mr. Atkins (FN, 1938)
Murder Will Out (WB, 1939) (also co-script)
Hoots Mon (WB, 1939) (also co-script)
His Brothers Keeper (FN, 1939) (also co-script)
Sherlock Holmes and the Secret Weapon (Univ., 1942) (also
    producer)
Madame Spy (Univ., 1942)
Sherlock Holmes Fights Back (Univ., 1942)
Eyes of the Underworld (Univ., 1943)
Frankenstein Meets the Wolfman (Univ., 1943)
Rhythm of the Islands (Univ., 1943)
Sherlock Holmes in Washington (Univ., 1943) (also producer)
Sherlock Holmes Faces Death (Univ., 1944) (also producer)
Sherlock Homes and the Spider Woman (Univ., 1944) (also pro-
    ducer)

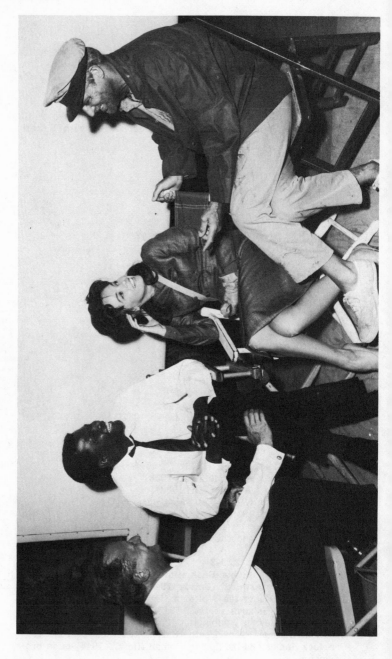

The Scarlet Claw (Univ., 1944) (also producer)
The Pearl of Death (Univ., 1944) (also producer)
Gypsy Wildcat (Univ., 1944)
The House of Fear (Univ., 1945) (also producer)
The Woman in Green (Univ., 1945) (also producer)
Pursuit to Algiers (Univ., 1945) (also producer)
Terror By Night (Univ., 1946) (also producer)
Dressed to Kill (Univ., 1946) (also producer)
Black Angel (Univ., 1946) (also co-producer)

NELSON, RALPH, b. Aug. 12, 1916, New York City.
Requiem for a Heavyweight (Col., 1962)
Lilies of the Field (UA, 1963) (also producer)
Soldier in the Rain (AA, 1963)
Fate is the Hunter (20th, 1964)
Father Goose (Univ., 1964)
Once a Thief (MGM, 1965)
Duel at Diablo (UA, 1966) (also co-producer)
Counterpoint (Univ., 1968)
Charly (Cin., 1968) (also producer)
tick...tick...tick (MGM, 1970) (also co-producer)
Soldier Blue (Avco-Emb., 1970)
Flight of the Doves (Col., 1971) (also producer)
The Wrath of God (MGM, 1972) (also script)

NEUMANN, KURT, b. April 5, 1908, Nuremburg, Germany; d.
    Aug. 21, 1958.
The King of Jazz [Spanish and German versions] (Univ., 1930)
Information Kid (Univ., 1932)
Fast Companions (Univ., 1932)
My Pal, the King (Univ., 1932)
The Big Cage (Univ., 1933)
Secrets of the Blue Room (Univ., 1933)
King for a Night (Univ., 1933)
Let's Talk It Over (Univ., 1934)
Half a Sinner (Univ., 1934)
Alias Mary Dow (Univ., 1935)
The Affair of Susan (Univ., 1935)
Let's Sing Again (RKO, 1936)
Rainbow on the River (RKO, 1936)
Espionage (MGM, 1937)
Make a Wish (RKO, 1937)
Hold 'Em Navy (Par., 1937)
Wide Open Faces (Col., 1938)
Touchdown Army (Par., 1938)
Ambush (Par., 1939)
Unmarried (Par., 1939)

Facing page: (from right) Cary Grant, Leslie Caron, and Sidney
Poitier with director Ralph Nelson (left) on the set of Father Goose
(Universal, 1965).

Island of Lost Men (Par., 1939)
All Women Have Secrets (Par., 1939)
A Night at Earl Carroll's (Par., 1940)
Ellery Queen, Master Detective (Col., 1940)
About Face (UA, 1942)
Brooklyn Orchid (UA, 1942)
Taxi, Mister (UA, 1942)
Yanks Ahoy (UA, 1943)
Fall In (UA, 1943)
The Unknown Guest (Mon., 1943)
The McGuerins from Brooklyn (UA, 1943)
Tarzan and the Amazons (RKO, 1945) (also associate producer)
Tarzan and the Leopard Woman (RKO, 1946) (also associate
    producer)
Tarzan and the Huntress (RKO, 1947) (also associate producer)
The Dude Goes West (AA, 1948)
Badmen of Tombstone (AA, 1948)
Bad Boy (AA, 1949)
The Kid from Texas (Univ., 1950)
Rocket Ship X-M (Lip., 1950) (also producer, story, script)
Cattle Drive (Univ., 1951)
Reunion in Reno (Univ., 1951)
Son of Ali Baba (Univ., 1952)
The Ring (UA, 1952)
Hiawatha (AA, 1952)
Tarzan and the She-Devil (RKO, 1953)
Carnival Story (RKO, 1954) (also co-script) (also German ver-
    sion)
They Were So Young (Lip., 1955) (also producer, co-script)
Mohawk (20th, 1956)
The Desperadoes Are in Town (20th, 1956) (also producer, co-
    script)
She Devil (20th, 1957) (also producer, co-script)
Kronos (20th, 1957) (also producer)
The Deerslayers (20th, 1957) (also producer, co-script)
The Fly (20th, 1958) (also producer)
Machete (UA, 1958) (also producer, co-script)
Watusi (MGM, 1959)
Counterplot (UA, 1959) (also producer)

NEWFIELD, SAM (Samuel Newfield), b. Dec. 6, 1899, New York
    City; d. Nov. 10, 1964.
    Reform Girl (Tower, 1933)
    Important Witness (Tower, 1933)
    Under Secret Orders (Progressive, 1933)
    Big Time or Bust (Tower, 1934)
    Marrying Widows (Tower, 1934)
    Beggar's Holiday (Tower, 1934)
    Code of the Mounted (Ambassador, 1935)
    Northern Frontier (Ambassador, 1935)
    Trails of the Wild (Ambassador, 1935)
    Racing Luck (Rep., 1935)

Bulldog Courage (Puritan, 1935)
Timber War (Ambassador, 1936)
Federal Agent (Rep., 1936)
Burning Gold (Rep., 1936)
Border Caballero (Puritan, 1936)
Lightnin' Bill Carson (Puritan, 1936)
Roarin' Guns (Puritan, 1936)
The Lion's Den (Puritan, 1936)
Ghost Patrol (Puritan, 1936)
Aces and Eights (Puritan, 1936)
Go-Get-'Em Haines (Rep., 1936)
The Traitor (Puritan, 1936)
Stormy Trails (Grand National, 1936)
Melody of the Plains (Spectrum, 1937)
Doomed at Sundown (Rep., 1937)
Bar Z Bad Man (Rep., 1937)
Roarin' Lead (Rep., 1937) (with Mack V. Wright)
Guns in the Dark (Rep., 1937)
Gun Lords of Stirrup Basin (Rep., 1937)
A Lawman Is Born (Rep., 1937)
Boothill Brigade (Rep., 1937)
Arizona Gunfighter (Rep., 1937)
Ridin' the Lone Trail (Rep., 1937)
The Colorado Kid (Rep., 1937)
Paroled--To Die (Rep., 1938)
Rangers Roundup (Spectrum, 1938)
Harlem on the Prairie (Associated Features, 1938)
Code of the Rangers (Mon., 1938)
Six Gun Trail (Victory, 1938)
Thunder in the Desert (Rep., 1938)
Songs and Bullets (Rep., 1938)
Desert Patrol (Rep., 1938)
The Phantom Ranger (Mon., 1938)
Terror of Tiny Town (Col., 1938)
Frontier Scout (Grand National, 1938)
Lightning Carson Rides Again (Victory, 1938)
Crashin' Thru Danger (Excelsior, 1938)
Lightnin' Crandall (Rep., 1938)
Durango Valley Raiders (Rep., 1938)
The Feud Maker (Rep., 1938)
Six Gun Rhythm (Grand National, 1939)
Trigger Fingers (Victory, 1939)
Trigger Pals (Grand National, 1939)
Code of the Cactus (Victory, 1939)
Texas Wildcats (Victory, 1939)
Outlaws Paradise (Victory, 1939)
The Fighting Renegade (Victory, 1939)
Fighting Mad (Mon., 1939)
Flaming Lead (Colony, 1939)
The Sagebrush Family Trail West (PDC, 1939) (as Peter Stew-
    art)
The Invisible Killer (PDC, 1939) (as Sherman Scott)
Beasts of Berlin [Goose Step, Hell's Devils] (PRC, 1940)

Straight Shooter (Victory, 1940)
Secrets of a Model (Continental, 1940)
Hold That Woman! (PRC, 1940) (as Sherman Scott)
I Take This Oath (PRC, 1940) (as Sherman Scott)
A Fugitive from Justice (PRC, 1940) (as Sherman Scott)
Marked Men (PRC, 1940) (as Sherman Scott)
Arizona Gang Busters (PRC, 1940) (as Peter Stewart)
Billy the Kid in Texas (PRC, 1940) (as Peter Stewart)
Billy the Kid Outlawed (PRC, 1940) (as Peter Stewart)
Billy the Kid's Gun Justice (PRC, 1940) (as Peter Stewart)
Frontier Crusaders (PRC, 1940) (as Peter Stewart)
Gun Code (PRC, 1940) (as Peter Stewart)
Riders of Black Mountain (PRC, 1940) (as Peter Stewart)
Texas Renegades (PRC, 1940) (as Peter Stewart)
The Lone Rider Ambushed (PRC, 1941)
The Lone Rider and the Bandit (PRC, 1941)
The Lone Rider Crosses the Rio (PRC, 1941)
The Lone Rider Fights Back (PRC, 1941)
The Lone Rider in Frontier Fury (PRC, 1941)
The Lone Rider in Ghost Town (PRC, 1941)
The Lone Rider Rides on (PRC, 1941)
Billy the Kid Is Wanted (PRC, 1941) (as Sherman Scott)
Billy the Kid's Fighting Pals (PRC, 1941) (as Sherman Scott)
Billy the Kid's Roundup (PRC, 1941) (as Sherman Scott)
Billy the Kid in Santa Fe (PRC, 1941) (as Sherman Scott)
Billy the Kid's Range War (PRC, 1941) (as Peter Stewart)
Outlaws of the Rio Grande (PRC, 1941) (as Peter Stewart)
The Texas Marshal (PRC, 1941) (as Peter Stewart)
Along the Sunset Trail (PRC, 1942) (as Peter Stewart)
Billy the Kid Trapped (PRC, 1942) (as Sherman Scott)
Billy the Kid's Smoking Guns (PRC, 1942) (as Sherman Scott)
Law and Order (PRC, 1942) (as Sherman Scott)
Raiders of the West (PRC, 1942) (as Peter Stewart)
Rolling Down the Great Divide (PRC, 1942) (as Peter Stewart)
Jungle Siren (PRC, 1942)
The Lone Rider in Border Roundup (PRC, 1942)
The Lone Rider in Cheyenne (PRC, 1942)
The Lone Rider in Texas Justice (PRC, 1942)
The Mad Monster (PRC, 1942)
Outlaws of Boulder Pass (PRC, 1943)
Overland Stagecoach (PRC, 1943)
Queen of Broadway (PRC, 1943)
Western Cyclone (PRC, 1943)
Wild Horse Hustlers (PRC, 1943)
Along the Sundown Trail (PRC, 1943) (as Peter Stewart)
Prairie Pals (PRC, 1943) (as Peter Stewart)
The Mysterious Rider (PRC, 1943) (as Sherman Scott)
The Kid Rides Again (PRC, 1943) (as Sherman Scott)
Sheriff of Sage Valley (PRC, 1943) (as Sherman Scott)
Danger! Women at Work (PRC, 1943)
Harvest Melody (PRC, 1943)
The Renegades (PRC, 1943)
Tiger Fangs (PRC, 1943)

The Black Raven (PRC, 1943)
Blazing Frontier (PRC, 1943)
Border Roundup (PRC, 1943)
Dead Men Walk (PRC, 1943)
Death Rides the Plains (PRC, 1943)
Fugitive of the Plains (PRC, 1943)
Cattle Stampede (PRC, 1943)
Wolves of the Range (PRC, 1944)
The Contender (PRC, 1944)
The Drifter (PRC, 1944)
Frontier Outlaws (PRC, 1944)
I Accuse My Parents (PRC, 1944)
Fuzzy Settles Down (PRC, 1944)
The Monster Maker (PRC, 1944)
Nabonga (PRC, 1944)
Oath of Vengeance (PRC, 1944)
Rustler's Hideout (PRC, 1944)
Swing Hostess (PRC, 1944)
Thundering Gun Slingers (PRC, 1944)
Valley of Vengeance (PRC, 1944)
Wild Horse Phantom (PRC, 1944)
Apology for Murder (PRC, 1945)
Border Badmen (PRC, 1945)
Fighting Bill Carson (PRC, 1945)
The Lady Confesses (PRC, 1945)
Gangster's Den (PRC, 1945)
His Brother's Ghost (PRC, 1945)
The Kid Sister (PRC, 1945)
Texas Manhunt (PRC, 1945) (as Peter Stewart)
Prairie Rustlers (PRC, 1945)
Raiders of Red Gap (PRC, 1945)
Stagecoach Outlaws (PRC, 1945)
Lightning Raiders (PRC, 1945)
White Pongo (PRC, 1945)
Outlaw of the Plains (PRC, 1945)
Blonde for a Day (PRC, 1946)
Gashouse Kids (PRC, 1946)
Ghost of Hidden City (PRC, 1946)
Lady Chasers (PRC, 1946)
Larceny in Her Heart (PRC, 1946)
Murder Is My Business (PRC, 1946)
Overland Raiders (PRC, 1946)
Queen of Burlesque (PRC, 1946)
Terrors on Horseback (PRC, 1946)
The Flying Serpent (PRC, 1946) (as Sherman Scott)
Prairie Badmen (PRC, 1946)
Raiders of Red Rock (Eagle Lion, 1947)
Three on a Ticket (PRC, 1947)
Frontier Fighters (Eagle Lion, 1947)
Code of the Plains (Eagle Lion, 1947)
Ghost of Hidden Valley (PRC, 1947)
Adventure Island (Par., 1947) (as Peter Stewart)
The Counterfeiters (20th, 1948) (as Peter Stewart)

Money Madness (Film Classics, 1948) (as Peter Stewart)
Lady at Midnight (Eagle Lion, 1948) (as Sherman Scott)
The Strange Mrs. Crane (Eagle Lion, 1948) (as Sherman Scott)
State Department File 649 (Film Classics, 1949) (as Peter Stewart)
The Devil's Weed [Wild Weed] (PRC, 1949) (as Sherman Scott)
Motor Patrol (Lip., 1950)
Radar Secret Service (Lip., 1950)
Western Pacific Agent (Lip., 1950)
Hi-Jacked (Lip., 1950)
The Lost Continent (Lip., 1951)
Skip Along Rosenbloom (UA, 1951)
Sky High (Lip., 1951)
Fingerprints Don't Lie (Lip., 1951)
Mask of the Dragon (Lip., 1951)
Leave It to the Marines (Lip., 1951)
Three Desperate Men (Lip., 1951)
Outlaw Women (Lip., 1952) (with Ron Ormond)
The Gambler and the Lady (Lip., 1952)
Lady in the Fog (Lip., 1952)
Thunder over Sangoland (Lip., 1954)
Last of the Desperados (Associated, 1955)
Frontier Gambler (Associated, 1956)
The Three Outlaws (Associated, 1956)
The Wild Dakotas (Associated, 1956) (with Sig Neufield) (also co-producer)
Along the Mohawk Trail (ITC, 1956)
The Long Rifle and the Tomahawk (ITC, 1956) (with Sidney Salkow)
The Pathfinder and the Mohican (ITC, 1956)
The Redmen and the Renegades (ITC, 1956)
Flaming Frontier (20th, 1958)
Wolf Dog (20th, 1958) (also producer)

NEWMAN, JOSEPH M. (Joe Newman), b. Aug. 7, 1909, Logan, Utah.
Northwest Rangers (MGM, 1942)
Jungle Patrol (20th, 1948)
The Great Dan Patch (UA, 1949)
Abandoned (Univ., 1949)
711 Ocean Drive (Col., 1950)
Lucky Nick Cain (20th, 1951)
The Guy Who Came Back (20th, 1951)
Love Nest (20th, 1951)
Red Skies of Montana (20th, 1952)
The Outcasts of Poker Flat (20th, 1952)
Pony Soldier (20th, 1952)
Dangerous Crossing (20th, 1953)
The Human Jungle (AA, 1954)
Kiss of Fire (Univ., 1955)
This Island Earth (Univ., 1955)
Flight to Hong Kong (UA, 1956) (also producer, co-script)

Death in Small Doses (AA, 1957)
Fort Massacre (UA, 1958)
The Gunfight at Dodge City (UA, 1959)
The Big Circus (AA, 1959)
Tarzan, the Ape Man (MGM, 1959)
The Lawbreakers (MGM-TV, 1960)
King of the Roaring 20's--The Story of Arnold Rothstein (AA, 1961)
A Thunder of Drums (MGM, 1961)
The George Raft Story (AA, 1961)
Twenty Plus Two (AA, 1961)

NEWMAN, PAUL, b. Jan. 26, 1925, Shaker Heights, Ohio.
Rachel, Rachel (WB-7 Arts, 1968) (also producer)
Sometimes a Great Notion (Univ., 1971) (with uncredited Richard Colla)
The Effect of Gamma Rays on Man-in-the-Moon Marigolds (20th, 1972) (also producer)

NEWMEYER, FRED, b. Aug. 9, 1888, Denver, Colo.
A Sailor-Made Man (Associated Exhibitors, 1921)
Grandma's Boy (Associated Exhibitors, 1922)
Doctor Jack (Pathé, 1922)
Safety Last (Pathé, 1923)
Why Worry? (Pathé, 1923)
Girl Shy (Pathé, 1924) (with Sam Taylor)
Hot Water (Pathé, 1924) (with Sam Taylor)
The Freshman (Pathé, 1925)
Seven Keys to Baldpate (Par., 1925)
The Perfect Clown (Chadwick, 1925)
The Savage (FN, 1926)
The Quarterback (Par., 1926)
Too Many Crooks (Par., 1927)
The Potters (Par., 1927)
The Lunatic at Large (FN, 1927)
That's My Daddy (Univ., 1928)
Warming Up (Par., 1928)
The Night Bird (Univ., 1928)
It Can Be Done (Univ., 1929)
The Rainbow Man (Par., 1929)
Sailor's Holiday (Pathé, 1929)
The Grand Parade (Pathé, 1930)
Queen High (Par., 1930)
Fast and Loose (Par., 1930)
Subway Express (Col., 1931)
Discarded Lovers (Tower, 1932)
They Never Came Back (Artclass, 1932)
The Fighting Gentleman (Freuler Film Associates, 1932)
The Gambling Sex (Freuler Film Associates, 1932)
Easy Millions (Freuler Film Associates, 1933)
The Big Race (Showmen's Pictures, 1934)

The Moth (Marcy Exchange, 1934)
No Ransom (Liberty, 1935)
Secrets of Chinatown (Northern Films, 1935)
General Spanky (MGM, 1936) (with Gordon Douglas)

NIBLO, FRED, b. Jan. 6, 1874, York, Neb.; d. Nov. 11, 1948.
A Desert Wooing (Par., 1918)
The Marriage Ring (Par., 1918)
When Do We Eat? (Par., 1918)
Fuss and Feathers (Par., 1918)
Happy Though Married (Par., 1919)
The Haunted Bedroom (Par., 1919)
The Law of Men (Par., 1919)
Partners Three (Par., 1919)
The Virtuous Thief (Par., 1919)
Stepping Out (Par., 1919)
What Every Woman Learns (Par., 1919)
The Woman in the Suitcase (Par., 1920)
Dangerous Hours (Par., 1920)
Sex (W.W. Hodkinson, 1920)
The False Road (Par., 1920)
Hairpins (Par., 1920)
Her Husband's Friend (Par., 1920)
The Mark of Zorro (UA, 1920)
Silk Hosiery (Par., 1921)
Mother O' Mine (Associated Producers, 1921)
Greater Than Love (Associated Producers, 1921)
The Three Musketeers (UA, 1921)
The Woman He Married (FN, 1922)
Rose O' the Sea (FN, 1922)
Blood and Sand (Par., 1922)
The Famous Mrs. Fair (Metro, 1923)
Strangers of the Night (Metro, 1923) (also producer)
Thy Name Is Woman (Metro-Goldwyn, 1924)
The Red Lily (Metro-Goldwyn, 1924) (also script)
Ben-Hur (MGM, 1925)
The Temptress (MGM, 1926)
Camille (FN, 1927) (also producer)
The Devil Dancer (UA, 1927) (also producer)
The Enemy (MGM, 1928) (also producer)
Two Lovers (UA, 1928) (also producer)
The Mysterious Lady (MGM, 1928)
Dream of Love (MGM, 1928)
Redemption (MGM, 1930) (also producer)
Way Out West (MGM, 1930)
Young Donovan's Kid (MGM, 1931)
The Big Gamble (Pathé, 1931)

NICHOLS, DUDLEY, b. April 6, 1895, Wapakoneta, Ohio; d. Jan.
4, 1960.
Government Girl (RKO, 1943) (also producer, script)

Sister Kenny (RKO, 1946) (also producer, co-script)
Mourning Becomes Electra (RKO, 1947) (also co-producer)

NICHOLS, MIKE (Michael Igor Peschkowsky), b. Nov. 6, 1931,
      Berlin.
Who's Afraid of Virginia Woolf (WB, 1966)
The Graduate (Embassy, 1967)
Catch 22 (Par., 1970)
Carnal Knowledge (Avco Embassy, 1971) (also producer)
The Day of the Dolphin (Avco Embassy, 1973)

NIGH, WILLIAM, b. Oct. 12, 1881, Berlin, Wisc.
Salomy Jane (California Motion Picture Co., 1914)
A Royal Family (Metro, 1915)
A Yellow Streak (Metro, 1915) (also script)
Emmy of Stork's Nest (Metro, 1915)
Life's Shadows (Metro, 1916)
Her Debt of Honor (Col.-Metro, 1916) (also actor)
The Kiss of Hate (Metro, 1916)
Notorious Gallagher or His Great Triumph (Metro, 1916)
The Slave (Fox, 1917)
Thou Shalt Not Steal (Fox, 1918)
My Four Years in Germany (State Rights, 1918)
Sunshine Alley (Goldwyn, 1918)
The Fighting Roosevelts (Associated FN, 1919)
Our Teddy (Associated FN, 1919)
Democracy, the Vision Restored (Democracy Photoplays, 1920)
School Days (WB, 1921) (also script)
Skinning Skinners (Tyrad, 1921)
The Soul of Man (Producers Security, 1921)
Why Girls Leave Home (WB, 1921) (also script)
Notoriety (Apollo, 1922) (also script)
Your Best Friend (WB, 1922) (also script)
Marriage Morals (Weber & North, 1923) (also script)
Born Rich (FN, 1924) (also producer)
Fear-Bound (Vitagraph, 1925) (also script)
The Fire Brigade (MGM, 1926)
The Little Giant (Univ., 1926) (also adaptation)
Casey of the Coast Guard* (Pathé, 1926)
Mr. Wu (MGM, 1927)
The Nest (Excellent, 1927)
Across to Singapore (MGM, 1928)
Four Walls (MGM, 1928)
The Law of the Range (MGM, 1928)
Desert Nights (MGM, 1929)
Thunder (MGM, 1929)
Fighting Thru: or California in 1878 (Tiffany, 1930)
Lord Byron of Broadway (MGM, 1930) (with Harry Beaumont)
Today (Majestic, 1930)
Lightning Flyer (Col., 1931)
Single Sin (Tiffany, 1931)

The Sea Ghost (Peerless, 1931) (also script)
Border Devils (Artclass, 1932)
Night Rider (Artclass, 1932)
Without Honors (Artclass, 1932)
House of Mystery (A. Hull Shirk, 1934)
School for Girls (Liberty, 1934)
Dizzy Dames (Liberty, 1935)
The Mysterious Mr. Wong (Mon., 1935)
Sweepstake Annie (Liberty, 1935)
The Headline Woman (Mascot, 1935)
The Old Homestead (Liberty, 1935)
She Gets Her Man (Univ., 1935)
His Night Out (Univ., 1935)
Penthouse Party (Liberty, 1936)
North of Nome (Col., 1936)
Don't Get Personal (Univ., 1936)
Crash Donovan (Univ., 1936)
Bill Cracks Down (Rep., 1937)
The Thirteenth Man (Mon., 1937)
A Bride for Henry (Mon., 1937)
Atlantic Flight (Mon., 1937)
The Hoosier Schoolboy (Mon., 1937)
Boy of the Streets (Mon., 1937)
Female Fugitive (Mon., 1938)
Rose of the Rio Grande (Mon., 1938)
I Am a Criminal (Mon., 1938)
Romance of the Limberlost (Mon., 1938)
Gangster's Boy (Mon., 1938)
Mr. Wong, Detective (Mon., 1938)
Streets of New York (Mon., 1939)
The Mystery of Mr. Wong (Mon., 1939)
Mr. Wong in Chinatown (Mon., 1939)
Mutiny in the Big House (Mon., 1939)
The Fatal Hour (Mon., 1940)
Son of the Navy (Mon., 1940)
Doomed to Die (Mon., 1940)
The Ape (Mon., 1940)
The Underdog (PRC, 1940)
Zis Boom Bah (Univ., 1941)
The Kid from Kansas (Univ., 1941)
Secret Evidence (PRC, 1941)
No Greater Sin (Univ., 1941)
The Strange Case of Dr. RX (Univ., 1942)
The Lady from Chunking (PRC, 1942)
City of Silent Men (PRC, 1942)
Mr. Wise Guy (Mon., 1942)
Black Dragons (Mon., 1942)
Tough as They Come (Univ., 1942)
Escape from Hong Kong (Univ., 1942)
Where Are Your Children? (Mon., 1943)
The Underdog (PRC, 1943)
Corregidor (PRC, 1943)
The Ghost and the Guest (PRC, 1943)

Are These Our Parents? (Mon., 1944)
They Shall Have Faith [Forever Yours] (Mon., 1944)
Trocadero (Rep., 1944)
Allotment Wives (Mon., 1945)
Divorce (Mon., 1945)
The Right to Live (Mon., 1945)
Beauty and the Bandit (Mon., 1946)
Partners in Time (RKO, 1946)
The Gay Cavalier (Mon., 1946)
South of Monterey (Mon., 1946)
Riding the California Trail (Mon., 1947)
I Wouldn't Be in Your Shoes (Mon., 1948)
Stage Struck (Mon., 1948)

NUGENT, ELLIOTT (Elliott John Nugent), b. Sept. 20, 1899, Dover,
    Ohio.
The Mouthpiece (WB, 1932) (with James Flood)
Life Begins (FN, 1932) (with James Flood)
Whistling in the Dark (MGM, 1933) (also script)
Three Cornered Moon (Par., 1933)
If I Were Free (RKO, 1933)
She Loves Me Not (Par., 1934)
Strictly Dynamite (RKO, 1934)
Two Alone (RKO, 1934)
Love in Bloom (Par., 1935)
Enter Madame (Par., 1935)
College Scandal (Par., 1935)
Splendor (UA, 1935)
And So They Were Married (Col., 1936)
Wives Never Know (Par., 1936)
It's All Yours (Col., 1937)
Professor Beware (Par., 1938)
Give Me a Sailor (Par., 1938)
Never Say Die (Par., 1939)
The Cat and the Canary (Par., 1939)
Nothing But the Truth (Par., 1941)
The Male Animal (WB, 1942)
The Crystal Ball (UA, 1943)
Up in Arms (RKO, 1944)
My Favorite Brunette (Par., 1947)
Welcome Stranger (Par., 1947)
My Girl Tisa (WB, 1948)
Mr. Belvedere Goes to College (20th, 1949)
The Great Gatsby (Par., 1949)
The Skipper Surprised His Wife (MGM, 1950)
My Outlaw Brother (Eagle Lion, 1951)
Just For You (Par., 1952)

NYBY, CHRISTIAN,
    The Thing [...From Another World] (RKO, 1951) (with uncred-
    ited Howard Hawks)

Hell on Devil's Island (20th, 1957)
Six Gun Law (BV, 1962)
Young Fury (Par., 1964)
Operation CIA (AA, 1965)
First to Fight (WB, 1967)

O

OBOLER, ARCH, b. Dec. 7, 1909, Chicago.
  Strange Holiday (PRC, 1946) (also script)
  Bewitched (MGM, 1946) (also script)
  The Arnelo Affair (MGM, 1947) (also script)
  Five (Col., 1951) (also producer, script)
  Bwana Devil (UA, 1952) (also producer, script)
  The Twonkey (UA, 1953) (also producer, script)
  1 + 1: Exploring the Kinsey Reports (Selected, 1961)
  The Bubble (Arch Oboler, 1967) (also producer, script)

OLCOTT, SIDNEY (John S. Alcott), b. Sept. 20, 1873, Toronto,
    Canada; d. Dec. 16, 1949.
  From the Manger to the Cross (Kalem, 1913)
  All for Ireland (Lubin, 1915)
  Seven Sisters (Par., 1915)
  The Daughter of MacGregor (Par., 1916)
  Diplomacy (Par., 1916)
  The Innocent Lie (Par., 1916)
  My Lady Incognito (Par., 1916)
  Poor Little Peppina (Par., 1916)
  The Smugglers (Par., 1916)
  The Moth and the Flame (Par., 1916)
  The Belgian (World, 1917) (also for production company)
  Marriage for Convenience (Sherry, 1919)
  Scratch My Back (Goldwyn, 1920)
  The Right Way (Producers Security Corp., 1921)
  God's Country and the Law (Arrow, 1921)
  Pardon My French (Goldwyn, 1921)
  Timothy's Quest (American Releasing, 1922)
  The Green Goddess (Goldwyn, 1923)
  Little Old New York (Goldwyn, 1923)
  The Humming Bird (Par., 1924)
  Monsieur Beaucaire (Par., 1924)
  The Only Woman (FN, 1924)
  The Charmer (Par., 1925)
  Salome of the Tenements (Par., 1925)
  Not So Long Ago (Par., 1925)
  The Best People (Par., 1925)
  Ranson's Folly (FN, 1926)
  The Amateur Gentleman (FN, 1926)
  The White Black Sheep (FN, 1926)
  The Claw (Univ.-Jewel, 1927)

OPHULS, MAX (Max Oppenheimer), b. May 6, 1902, Saarbrücken,
    Saare; d. March 26, 1957.
    Dann Schon Lieber Lebertran (German, 1930) (also co-script)
    Die Verliebte Firma (German, 1931)
    Die Verkaufte Braut (German, 1932)
    Lachenden Erben (German, 1932)
    Liebelei (German, 1932)
    Une Histoire d'Amour [French version of Liebelei] (German,
        1933)
    On a Volé un Homme (French 1933)
    La Signora di Tutti (Italian, 1934) (also co-script)
    Divine (French, 1935) (also co-script)
    Komedie Om Geld (Dutch, 1936) (also co-script)
    La Tendre Ennemie (French, 1936) (also co-script)
    Yoshiwara (French, 1937) (also co-script)
    Werther (French, 1938) (also co-script)
    Sans Lendemain (French, 1939)
    De Mayerling à Sarajevo (French, 1939) (also co-script)
    L'Ecole des Femmes (French, 1940--unfinished)
    The Exile (Univ. , 1947)
    Letter from an Unknown Woman (Univ. , 1948)
    Caught (MGM, 1949)
    The Reckless Moment (Col. , 1949)
    Vendetta (RKO, 1950) (uncredited, with credited Mel Ferrer,
        and uncredited Stuart Heisler, Howard Hughes, Preston
        Sturges)
    La Ronde (French, 1950) (also co-script)
    Le Plaisir (French, 1952) (also co-script)
    Madame de (French, 1953) (also co-script)
    Lola Montés (French, 1955) (also co-script)

OSWALD, GERD, b. 1916, Berlin.
    The Ox-Bow Incident (CBS-TV, 1955)
    A Kiss Before Dying (UA, 1956)
    The Brass Legend (UA, 1956)
    Crime of Passion (UA, 1957)
    Fury at Showdown (UA, 1957)
    Valerie (UA, 1957)
    Paris Holiday (UA, 1958)
    Screaming Mimi (Col. , 1958)
    Am Tag als der Regen Kam (German, 1959)
    Schachnovelle (German, 1960) (also co-script)
    Brainwashed (AA, 1961)
    The Longest Day (20th, 1962) (uncredited, with Ken Annakin,
        Andrew Marton, Barnhard Wicki)
    Tempestà Su Ceylon (Italian, 1963)
    Agent for H. A. R. M. (Univ. , 1966)
    80 Steps to Jonah (WB, 1969)
    Bunny O'Hare (AIP, 1971) (also producer, co-script)

P

PAKLULA, ALAN J., b. April 7, 1928, New York City.
   The Sterile Cuckoo (Par., 1969) (also co-producer)
   Klute (WB, 1971) (also producer)
   Love and Pain and the Whole Damn Thing (Col., 1973) (also
      producer)

PAL, GEORGE, b. Feb. 1, 1908, Cegled, Hungary.
   Tom Thumb (MGM, 1958) (also producer)
   The Time Machine (MGM, 1960) (also producer)
   Atlantis, the Lost Continent (MGM, 1960) (also producer)
   The Wonderful World of the Brothers Grimm (MGM, 1962)
      (with Henry Levin) (also producer)
   The Seven Faces of Dr. Lao (MGM, 1964)
   The Power (MGM, 1968) (with Byror Haskin)

PANAMA, NORMAN, b. April 21, 1914, Chicago.
   The Reformer and the Redhead (MGM, 1950) (with Melvin
      Frank) (also co-producer, co-script)
   Strictly Dishonorable (MGM, 1951) (with Melvin Frank) (also
      co-producer, co-script)
   Callaway Went Thataway (MGM, 1951) (with Melvin Frank) (al-
      so co-producer, co-script)
   Above and Beyond (MGM, 1952) (with Melvin Frank) (also co-
      producer, co-story, co-script)
   Knock on Wood (Par., 1954) (with Melvin Frank) (also co-pro-
      ducer, co-script)
   The Court Jester (Par., 1956) (with Melvin Frank) (also co-
      producer, co-story, co-script)
   That Certain Feeling (Par., 1956) (with Melvin Frank) (also
      co-producer, co-story, co-script)
   The Trap (Par., 1959) (also co-producer, co-script)
   Not With My Wife You Don't (WB, 1966) (also producer, co-
      story, co-script)
   How to Commit Marriage (Cin., 1969)
   The Maltese Bippy (MGM, 1969)
   Coffee, Tea or Me? (CBS-TV, 1973)

PARIS, JERRY, b. c.1926.
   Never a Dull Moment (BV, 1968)
   How Sweet It Is (National General, 1968)
   Don't Raise the Bridge, Lower the River (Col., 1968)
   Viva Max! (Commonwealth United, 1969)
   The Grasshopper (National General, 1970)
   But I Don't Want to Be Married (ABC-TV, 1970)
   Star Spangled Girl (Par., 1971)
   The Feminist and the Fuzz (ABC-TV, 1971)
   What's a Nice Girl Like You? (ABC-TV, 1971)
   Evil Roy Slade (CBS-TV, 1972)

PARK, IDA MAY (Mrs. Joseph De Grasse), b. Los Angeles.
    The Grip of Jealousy (Univ., 1916)
    The Rescue (Univ., 1917)
    The Flashlight (Univ., 1917)
    The Fires of Rebellion (Univ., 1917)
    Bondage (Bluebird, 1917)
    Her Fling (Univ., 1918)
    The Grand Passion (Univ., 1918)
    The Model's Confession (Univ., 1918)
    Broadway Love (Bluebird, 1918)
    The Risky Road (Bluebird, 1918)
    Bread (Univ., 1918)
    The Vanity Pool (Univ., 1918)
    The Amazing Wife (Univ., 1919)
    The Butterfly Man (Robertson-Cole, 1920)
    Bonnie May (Federated, 1920) (with Joseph De Grasse)
    The Midlanders (Federated, 1920) (with Joseph De Grasse)

PARKS, GORDON, b. Fort Scott, Kans.
    The Learning Tree (WB, 1969)
    Shaft (MGM, 1971)
    Shaft's Big Score (MGM, 1972)

PARRISH, ROBERT, b. Jan. 4, 1916, Columbus, Ga.
    The Mob (Col., 1951)
    Cry Danger (RKO, 1951)
    The San Francisco Story (WB, 1952)
    Assignment--Paris (Col., 1952)
    My Pal Gus (20th, 1952)
    Shoot First (UA, 1953)
    The Purple Plain (UA, 1955)
    Lucy Gallant (Par., 1955)
    Fire Down Below (Col., 1957)
    Saddle the Wind (MGM, 1958)
    The Wonderful Country (UA, 1959)
    In the French Style (Col., 1963)
    Up from the Beach (20th, 1965)
    Casino Royale (Col., 1967) (with John Huston, Ken Hughes,
      Val Guest, Joe McGrath)
    The Bobo (WB, 1967)
    Duffy (Col., 1968)
    Journey to the Far Side of the Sun (Univ., 1970)
    A Town Called Hell (Scotia International, 1971)

PARROTT, JAMES, b. 1892, Baltimore; d. May 11, 1939.
    Pardon Us (MGM, 1931)

PECKINPAH, SAM, b. Feb. 21, 1925, Fresno, Calif.
    The Deadly Companions (Pathé-American, 1961)

Ride the High Country (MGM, 1962)
The Cincinnati Kid (MGM, 1965) (replaced by Norman Jewison)
Major Dundee (Col., 1965) (also co-script)
The Wild Bunch (WB, 1969) (also co-script)
The Ballad of Cable Hogue (WB, 1970)
Straw Dogs (Cin., 1971) (also co-script)
The Getaway (National General, 1972)
Junior Bonner (Par., 1973)
Pat Garett and Billy the Kid (MGM, 1973)

PEERCE, LARRY, b. Bronx, N.Y.
One Potato, Two Potato (Cinema V, 1964)
The Big T.N.T. Show (AIP, 1966)
The Incident (20th, 1967)
Goodbye, Columbus (Par., 1969)
The Sporting Club (Avco-Emb., 1971)
A Separate Peace (Par., 1972)
Ash Wednesday (Par., 1973)

PENN, ARTHUR, b. Sept. 27, 1922, Philadelphia.
The Left-Handed Gun (WB, 1958)
The Miracle Worker (UA, 1962)
Mickey One (Col., 1965) (also producer)
The Train (UA, 1965) (replaced by John Frankenheimer)
The Chase (Col., 1966)
Bonnie and Clyde (WB-7 Arts, 1967)
Alice's Restaurant (UA, 1969) (also co-script)
Little Big Man (National General, 1970)
Visions of Eight (Cinema V, 1973) (with Milos Forman, Kom
    Schikawa, Claude Lelouch, Juri Ozerov, Michael Pfeghar,
    John Schlesinger, Mai Zetterling)

PERRET, LEONCE, b. May 13, 1880, Niort, France; d. Aug. 15,
    1936.
L'Enfant de Paris (French, 1913) (also script)
Le Roi de la Montagne (French, 1914)
Les Mystères de l'Ombre (French, 1914)
Le Poilus de la Rivanche (French, 1915)
L'Voix de la Patrie (French, 1915)
The Life of Moliere (French, 1917)
The Ransom of Happiness (French, 1917)
The Romance of a Middy (French, 1917)
The Child of Paris (French, 1917)
Stand Up Dead Soldiers (French, 1917)
The Angelus of Victory (French, 1917)
The Slave of Phydias (French, 1917)
Godmothers of France (French, 1917)
The Last Love (French, 1917)
The Silent Master (Pathé, 1917) (also script)
The Mad Lover (Pathé, 1917) (also script)

The Accidental Honeymoon (Metro, 1918) (also script)
Lest We Forget (Metro, 1918) (also script)
The Million Dollar Dollies (Metro, 1918)
Lafayette We Come (Affiliated, 1918)
The Unknown Love (Pathé, 1919) (also for production company)
The Thirteenth Chair (Pathé, 1919) (also for production company)
The A.B.C. of Love (Pathé, 1919) (also for production company)
The Twin Pawns (Pathé, 1919) (also for production company)
Lifting Shadows (Pathé, 1920) (also for production company)
A Modern Salome (Metro, 1920)
The Empire of Diamonds (Pathé, 1920) (also for production company)
The Money Maniac (Pathé, 1921) (also for production company, script)
Koenigsmark (French, 1923)
Madame Sans-Gêne (Par., 1925)
La Femme Hué (French, 1926)
Margane la Sirene (French, 1928)
La Danseuse Orchidée (French, 1928)
La Possession (French, 1928) (with Jean Cassagne)
Quand Nous Etions Deux (French, 1928)
Arthur (French, 1930)
Aprés l'Amour (French, 1931)
Enlevez-Moi (French, 1932)
Il Etait une Fois (French, 1933)
Sapho (French, 1934)
Les Précieuses Ridicules (French, 1935)

PERRY, FRANK, b. 1933, New York City.
David and Lisa (Continental, 1962)
Ladybug, Ladybug (UA, 1963) (also producer)
The Swimmer (Col., 1968) (with uncredited Sidney Pollack) (also co-producer)
Trilogy (AA, 1969) (also producer)
Last Summer (AA, 1969)
Diary of a Mad Housewife (Univ., 1970) (also producer)
Doc (UA, 1971) (also producer)
Play It as It Lays (Univ., 1972) (also producer)

PETRIE, DANIEL M., b. 1920.
The Bramble Bush (WB, 1960)
A Raisin in the Sun (Col., 1961)
The Main Attraction (MGM, 1962)
Stolen Hours (UA, 1963)
The Idol (Emb., 1966)
The Spy With a Cold Nose (Emb., 1966)
The City (ABC-TV, 1971)
The Neptune Factor (20th, 1973)

PEVNEY, JOSEPH, b. 1920, New York City.
    Shakedown (Univ., 1950)
    Undercover Girl (Univ., 1950)
    Iron Man (Univ., 1951)
    Air Cadet (Univ., 1951)
    The Lady from Texas (Univ., 1951)
    The Strange Door (Univ., 1951)
    Meet Danny Wilson (Univ., 1952)
    Flesh and Fury (Univ., 1952)
    Just Across the Street (Univ., 1952)
    Because of You (Univ., 1952)
    Desert Legion (Univ., 1953)
    It Happens Every Thursday (Uni., 1953)
    Back to God's Country (Univ., 1953)
    Yankee Pasha (Univ., 1954)
    Playgirl (Univ., 1954)
    Three Ring Circus (Par., 1954)
    Six Bridges to Cross (Univ., 1955)
    Foxfire (Univ., 1955)
    Female on the Beach (Univ., 1955)
    Away All Boats (Univ., 1956)
    Congo Crossing (Univ., 1956)
    Istanbul (Univ., 1956)
    Man of a Thousand Faces (Univ., 1957)
    The Midnight Story (Univ., 1957)
    Tammy and the Bachelor (Univ., 1957)
    Torpedo Run (MGM, 1958)
    Twilight for the Gods (Univ., 1959)
    Cash McCall (WB, 1960)
    The Crowded Sky (WB, 1960)
    The Plunderers (AA, 1960) (also producer)
    Portrait of a Mobster (WB, 1961)
    The Night of the Grizzly (Par., 1966)

PICHEL, IRVING, b. June 24, 1891, Pittsburgh, Pa.; d. July 13,
    1954.
    The Most Dangerous Game (RKO, 1932) (with Ernest B. Schoed-
        sack) (also co-producer)
    Before Dawn (RKO, 1933)
    She (RKO, 1935) (with Lansing C. Holden)
    The Gentleman from Louisiana (Rep., 1936)
    Ladies Beware (Rep., 1936)
    Larceny on the Air (Rep., 1937)
    The Duke Comes Back (Rep., 1937)
    The Sheik Steps Out (Rep., 1937)
    The Great Commandment (20th, 1939)
    Earthbound (20th, 1940)
    The Man I Married (20th, 1940)
    Hudson's Bay (20th, 1941)
    Dance Hall (20th, 1941)
    Secret Agent of Japan (20th, 1942)
    The Pied Piper (20th, 1942)

Life Begins at 8:30 (20th, 1942)
The Moon Is Down (20th, 1943)
Happy Land (20th, 1943)
And Now Tomorrow (Par., 1944)
A Medal for Benny (Par., 1945)
Colonel Effingham's Raid (20th, 1945)
Tomorrow Is Forever (Rep., 1945)
The Bride Wore Boots (Par., 1946)
O.S.S. (Par., 1946)
Temptation (Univ., 1946)
They Won't Believe Me (RKO, 1947)
Something in the Wind (Univ., 1947)
The Miracle of the Bells (RKO, 1948)
Mr. Peabody and the Mermaid (Univ., 1948)
Without Honor (Univ., 1949)
The Great Rupert (Eagle Lion, 1950)
Quicksand (UA, 1950)
Destination Moon (Eagle Lion, 1950)
Santa Fe (Col., 1951) (also script, actor)
Martin Luther (De Rochemont, 1953) (also script, actor)
Day of Triumph (George J. Schaefer, 1953)

POITIER, SIDNEY, b. Feb. 24, 1924, Miami, Fla.
    Buck and the Preacher (Col., 1972) (also actor)
    A Warm December (National General, 1973) (also actor)

POLANSKI, ROMAN, b. Aug. 18, 1933, Paris.
    Noz w Wodzie [Knife in the Water] [The Young Lover] [The
        Long Sunday] (Polish, 1962) (also script)
    Repulsion (Compton-Cameo, 1965) (also script, actor)
    Cul-de-Sac (Compton-Cameo, 1966) (also co-script)
    The Vampire Killers [The Fearless Vampire Killers] [Dance of
        the Vampires] (MGM, 1967) (also co-script, actor)
    Rosemary's Baby (Par., 1968) (also script)
    MacBeth (Col., 1971) (also co-script)
    What? (Avco Emb., 1973) (also co-script, actor)

POLLACK, SYDNEY, b. July 1, 1934, South Bend, Ind.
    The Slender Thread (Par., 1965)
    This Property Is Condemened (Par., 1966)
    The Swimmer (Col., 1968) (uncredited, with Frank Perry)
    The Scalphunters (UA, 1968)
    Castle Keep (Col., 1969)
    They Shoot Horses, Don't They? (Cin., 1969)
    Jeremiah Johnson (WB, 1972)
    The Way We Were (Col., 1973)

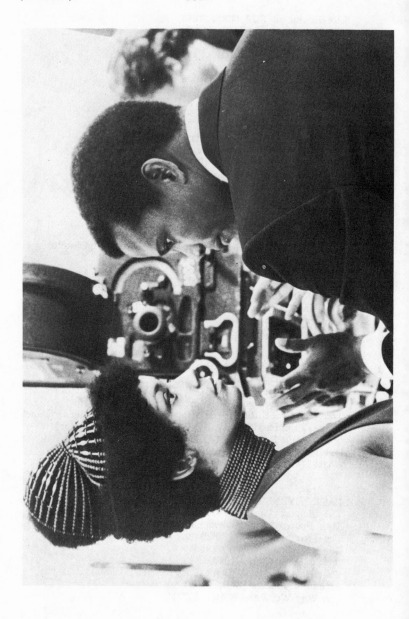

Roman Polanski (ca. 1968)

POLONSKY, ABRAHAM, b. 1910, New York City.
Force of Evil (MGM, 1948) (also co-script)
Tell Them Willie Boy Is Here (Univ., 1970) (also script)
Romance of a Horse Thief (AA, 1971)

PORTER, EDWIN STRATTON, b. 1869, Pittsburgh, Pa.; d. April
30, 1941
Tess of the D'Urbervilles (Par., 1913) (with J. Searle Dawley)
The Prisoner of Zenda (Par., 1913)
A Good Little Devil (Par., 1913)
In the Bishop's Carriage (Par., 1913) (with Hugh Ford)
Hearts Adrift (Par., 1913)
The Scales of Justice (Par., 1914)
A Woman's Triumph (Par., 1914)

Facing page: Esther Anderson with Sidney Poitier on the set of
A Warm December (National General, 1973).

The Crucible (Par., 1914) (with Hugh Ford)
Tess of the Storm Country (Par., 1914)
Such a Little Queen (Par., 1914) (with Hugh Ford)
The Dictator (Par., 1915)
The Eternal City (Par., 1915) (with Hugh Ford)
Sold (Par., 1915) (with Hugh Ford)
The White Pearl (Par., 1915)
Zaza (Par., 1915) (with Hugh Ford)
Jim the Penman (Par., 1915)
The Prince and the Pauper (Par., 1915) (with Hugh Ford)
Bella Donna (Par., 1915)
Lydia Gilmore (Par., 1916) (with Hugh Ford)

POST, TED, b. March 31, 1918, Brooklyn, N.Y.
The Legend of Tom Dooley (Col., 1959)
Hang 'Em High (UA, 1968)
Beneath the Planet of the Apes (20th, 1970)
Night Slaves (ABC-TV, 1970)
Dr. Cook's Garden (ABC-TV, 1971)
Yuma (ABC-TV, 1971)
Five Desperate Women (ABC-TV, 1971)
Do Not Fold, Spindle or Mutilate (ABC-TV, 1971)
The Bravos (ABC-TV, 1972)
Sandcastles (CBS-TV, 1972)
The Harrad Experiment (Cin., 1973)
Magnum Force (WB, 1973)

POTTER, H.C., b. Nov. 18, 1904, New York City.
Beloved Enemy (UA, 1936)
Wings Over Honolulu (Univ., 1937)
Romance in the Dark (Par., 1938)
The Shopworn Angel (MGM, 1938)
The Cowboy and the Lady (UA, 1938)
The Story of Vernon and Irene Castle (RKO, 1939)
Blackmail (MGM, 1939)
Congo Maisie (MGM, 1940)
Second Chorus (Par., 1940)
Hellzapoppin (Univ., 1941)
Mr. Lucky (RKO, 1943)
Victory Through Air Power (UA, 1943) (with Walt Disney)
The Farmer's Daughter (RKO, 1947)
A Likely Story (RKO, 1947)
Mr. Blandings Builds His Dream House (RKO, 1948)
The Time of Your Life (UA, 1948)
You Gotta Stay Happy (UA, 1948)
The Miniver Story (MGM, 1950)
Three for the Show (Col., 1955)
Top Secret Affair (WB, 1957)

POWELL, DICK (Richard Ewing Powell), b. Nov. 14, 1904, Mountain View, Ark.; d. Jan. 3, 1963.
   Split Second (RKO, 1953) (also producer)
   The Conqueror (RKO, 1956) (also producer)
   You Can't Run Away from It (Col., 1956) (also producer)
   The Enemy Below (20th, 1957) (also producer)
   The Hunters (20th, 1958) (also producer)

Stewart Granger (right) with Dick Powell on an MGM set (1952).

PREMINGER, OTTO, b. Dec. 5, 1906, Vienna.
   Die Grosse Liebe (German, 1931)
   Under Your Spell (20th, 1936)
   Danger--Love at Work (20th, 1937)
   Margin for Error (20th, 1943) (also script, actor)
   In the Meantime, Darling (20th, 1944) (also producer)
   Laura (20th, 1944) (also producer)
   A Royal Scandal (20th, 1945)
   Fallen Angel (20th, 1945) (also producer)
   Centennial Summer (20th, 1946)
   Forever Amber (20th, 1947) (replaced John M. Stahl)
   Daisy Kenyon (20th, 1947) (also producer)
   That Lady in Ermine (20th, 1948) (uncredited, with
    Ernst Lubitsch)

The Fan (20th, 1949) (also producer)
Whirlpool (20th, 1949) (also producer)
Where the Sidewalk Ends (20th, 1950) (also producer)
The 13th Letter (20th, 1951) (also producer)
Angel Face (RKO, 1952)
The Moon Is Blue (UA, 1953) (also co-producer)
Die Jungfrau Auf Dem Dach (German, 1954) (also producer,
    script)
River of No Return (20th, 1954)
Carmen Jones (20th, 1954) (also producer)
The Court Martial of Billy Mitchell (UA, 1955)
The Man With the Golden Arm (UA, 1955) (also producer)
Saint Joan (UA, 1957) (also producer)
Bonjour Tristesse (Col., 1958) (also producer)
Anatomy of a Murder (Col., 1959) (also producer)
Porgy and Bess (Col., 1959) (replaced Rouben Mamoulian)
Exodus (UA, 1960) (also producer
Advise and Consent (Col., 1962) (also producer)
The Cardinal (Col., 1963) (also producer)
In Harm's Way (Par., 1964) (also producer)
Bunny Lake Is Missing (Col., 1965) (also producer)
Hurry Sundown (Par., 1967) (also producer)
Skiddo (Par., 1968) (also producer)
Tell Me That You Love Me, Junie Moon (Par., 1970) (also
    producer)
Such Good Friends (Par., 1971) (also producer)

Q

QUINE, RICHARD, b. Nov. 12, 1920, Detroit.
    Leather Gloves (Col., 1948) (with William Asher) (also co-
        producer)
    Purple Heart Diary (Col., 1951)
    Sunny Side of the Street (Col., 1951)
    Sound Off (Col., 1952) (also co-script)
    Rainbow 'Round My Shoulder (Col., 1952) (also co-script)
    All Ashore (Col., 1953) (also co-script)
    Cruisin' Down the River (Col., 1953) (also co-story, co-script)
    Siren of Bagdad (Col., 1953)
    Pushover (Col., 1954)
    Drive a Crooked Road (Col., 1954)
    So This Is Paris (Col., 1954)
    My Sister Eileen (Col., 1955) (also co-script)
    The Solid Gold Cadillac (Col., 1956)
    Full of Life (Col., 1957)
    Operation Mad Ball (Col., 1957)
    Bell, Book and Candle (Col., 1958)

Facing page: Composer Thomas Z. Shepard (left), lyricist Robert
Brittan, and singer O.C. Smith with Otto Preminger discussing
Such Good Friends (Par., 1971).

It Happened to Jane (Col., 1959) (also producer)
Strangers When We Meet (Col., 1960) (also co-producer)
The World of Suzie Wong (Par., 1960)
The Notorious Landlady (Col., 1962)
Paris When It Sizzles (Par., 1964) (also co-producer)
Sex and the Single Girl (WB, 1964)
How to Murder Your Wife (WB, 1964)
Synanon (Col., 1965) (also producer)
Oh, Dad, Poor Dad, Mamma's Hung You in the Closet and I'm Feelin' So Sad (Par., 1967)
Hotel (WB, 1967)
The Moonshine War (MGM, 1970)

R

RAPPER, IRVING, b. 1898, London.
Shining Victory (WB, 1941)
One Foot in Heaven (WB, 1941) (replaced Anatole Litvak) (also co-producer)
The Gay Sisters (WB, 1942)
Now, Voyager (WB, 1942)
The Adventures of Mark Twain (WB, 1944)
Rhapsody in Blue (WB, 1945)
The Corn Is Green (WB, 1945)
Deception (WB, 1946)
The Voice of the Turtle (WB, 1947)
Anna Lucasta (Col., 1949)
The Glass Menagerie (WB, 1950)
Another Man's Poison (UA, 1952)
Forever Female (Par., 1953)
Bad for Each Other (Col., 1953)
Strange Intruder (AA, 1956)
The Brave One (RKO, 1956)
Marjorie Morningstar (WB, 1958)
The Miracle (WB, 1959)
Giuseppe Venduto Dai Fratelli (Italian, 1960) (with Luciano Ricci)
Ponzio Pilato (Italian, 1961)
The Christine Jorgensen Story (UA, 1970)

RATOFF, GREGORY, b. April 20, 1897, St. Petersburg, Russia; d. Dec. 14, 1960.
Sins of Man (20th, 1936) (with Otto Brower)
The Lancer Spy (20th, 1937)
Wife, Husband and Friend (20th, 1939)
Barricade (20th, 1939)
Rose of Washington Square (20th, 1939)
Hotel for Women (20th, 1939)
Day-Time Wife (20th, 1939)
Intermezzo (UA, 1939)
I Was an Adventuress (20th, 1940)

Public Deb No. 1 (20th, 1940)
Adam Had Four Sons (Col., 1941)
The Men in Her Life (Col., 1941) (also producer)
The Corsican Brothers (UA, 1941)
Two Yanks in Trinidad (Col., 1942)
Footlight Serenade (20th, 1942)
The Heat's On (Col., 1943)
Something to Shout About (Col., 1943) (also producer)
Song of Russia (MGM, 1944)
Irish Eyes Are Smiling (20th, 1944)
Where Do We Go from Here? (20th, 1945)
Paris Underground (UA, 1945)
Do You Love Me? (20th, 1946)
Carnival in Costa Rica (20th, 1947)
Moss Rose (20th, 1947)
Black Magic (UA, 1949)
That Dangerous Age [If This Be Sin] (British Lion, 1950) (also
   producer)
My Daughter Joy [Operation X] (British Lion, 1950) (also pro-
   ducer)
Taxi (20th, 1953)
Abdullah's Harem (20th, 1956) (also producer, actor)
Oscar Wilde (Four City, 1960)

RAWLINS, JOHN, b. June 9, 1902, Long Beach, Calif.
State Police (Univ., 1938)
Young Fugitives (Univ., 1938)
The Missing Guest (Univ., 1938)
Air Devils (Univ., 1938)
The Green Hornet Strikes Again* (Univ., 1940) (with Ford
   Beebe)
The Leather Pushers (Univ., 1940)
Junior G-Men* (Univ., 1940) (with Ford Beebe)
Six Lessons from Madame La Zonga (Univ., 1941)
A Dangerous Game (Univ., 1941)
Mr. Dynamite (Univ., 1941)
Sea Raiders* (Univ., 1941) (with Ford Beebe)
Mutiny in the Arctic (Univ., 1941)
A Dangerous Game (Univ., 1941)
Men of the Timberland (Univ., 1941)
Raiders of the Desert (Univ., 1941)
Unseen Enemy (Univ., 1942)
Bombay Clipper (Univ., 1942)
Overland Mail* (Univ., 1942) (with Ford Beebe)
Mississippi Gambler (Univ., 1942)
Torpedo Boat (Univ., 1942)
Sherlock Holmes and the Voice of Terror (Univ., 1942)
The Great Impersonation (Univ., 1942)
Arabian Nights (Univ., 1942)
Halfway to Shanghai (Univ., 1943)
We've Never Been Licked (Univ., 1943)
Ladies Courageous (Univ., 1944)

Sudan (Univ., 1945)
Strange Conquest (Univ., 1946)
Her Adventurous Night (Univ., 1946)
Dick Tracy's Dilemma (RKO, 1947)
Dick Tracy Meets Gruesome (RKO, 1947)
The Arizona Ranger (RKO, 1948)
Michael O'Halloran (Mon., 1948)
Massacre River (AA, 1949)
Boy from Indiana (Eagle Lion, 1950)
Rogue River (Eagle Lion, 1950)
Fort Defiance (UA, 1951)
Shark River (UA, 1953)
Lost Lagoon (UA, 1958)

RAY, NICHOLAS (Raymond Nicholas Kienzle), b. Aug. 7, 1911,
     La Crosse, Wisc.
They Live By Night (RKO, 1948) (also adaptation)
A Woman's Secret (RKO, 1949)
Knock On Any Door (Col., 1949)
In a Lonely Place (Col., 1950)
Born to Be Bad (RKO, 1950)
On Dangerous Ground (RKO, 1951)
Flying Leathernecks (RKO, 1951)
The Lusty Men (RKO, 1952)
Macao (RKO, 1952) (uncredited, with Josef von Sternberg)
Johnny Guitar (Rep., 1954) (also associate producer)
Run for Cover (Par., 1955)
Rebel Without a Cause (WB, 1955) (also story)
Hot Blood (Col., 1956)
Bigger Than Life (20th, 1956)
The True Story of Jesse James (20th, 1957)
Bitter Victory (Col., 1958) (also co-script)
Wind Across the Everglades (WB, 1958)
Party Girl (MGM, 1958)
The Savage Innocents (Par., 1960) (also script)
King of Kings (MGM, 1961)
Fifty-Five Days at Peking (AA, 1963)
The Doctor and the Devils (unfinished, 1965)
Wet Dreams (1973)

REED, JAY THEODORE, b. 1887, Cincinnati, O.; d. Feb. 24,
     1959.
The Nut (UA, 1921)
Lady Be Careful (Par., 1936)
Double or Nothing (Par., 1937)
Tropic Holiday (Par., 1938)
I'm from Missouri (Par., 1939)
What a Life (Par., 1939)
Those Were the Days (Par., 1940)
Life With Henry (Par., 1941)
Her First Beau (Par., 1941)

REED, LUTHER, b. July
14, 1888, Berlin, Wisc.;
d. Nov. 16, 1961.
The Ace of Cads (Par.,
1926)
New York (Par., 1927)
Evening Clothes (Par.,
1927)
The World at Her Feet
(Par., 1927)
Shanghai Bound (Par.,
1927)
Honeymoon Hate (Par.,
1927)
The Sawdust Paradise
(Par., 1928)
Rio Rita (RKO, 1929)
(also script)
Hit the Deck (RKO,
1930)(also adaptation)
Diana (RKO, 1930)(also
adaptation, 1930)
Convention Girl (First
Division, 1935)

REICHER, FRANK, b. Dec.
2, 1875, Munich, Ger-
many; d. Jan. 19, 1965.
The Case of Becky (Par.,
1915)
The Chorus Lady (Par.,
1915)
Mr. Grex of Monte Carlo
(Par., 1915)
The Secret Orchard
(Par., 1915)
The Secret Sin (Par.,
1915)
The Storm (Par., 1915)
Witchcraft (Par., 1916)
The Dupe (Par., 1916)
The Love Mask (Par.,
1916)
The Victory of Conscience
(Par., 1916)
For the Defense (Par., 1916)
Betty to the Rescue (Par., 1917)
The Black Wolf (Par., 1916)
Puddin' Head Wilson (Par., 1916)
Alien Souls (Par., 1916)
Castles for Two (Par., 1917)
Lost and Won (Par., 1917)
Sacrifice (Par., 1917)

James Stewart visiting Nicholas Ray,
on location for King of Kings (MGM,
1961).

Unconquered (Par., 1917)
The Inner Shrine (Par., 1917)
The Eternal Mother (Metro, 1917)
An American Widow (Metro, 1917)
The Trouble Buster (Par., 1917)
The Claim (Metro, 1918)
The Treasure of the Sea (Metro, 1918)
The Only Road (Metro, 1918)
Suspense (Screencraft, 1918)
The Prodigal Wife (Screencraft, 1918)
The Trap (Peerless-World, 1918)
The American Way (World, 1919)
The Battler (World, 1919)
The Black Circle (World, 1920)
Empty Arms (Photoplay Library, 1920)
Idle Hands (Pioneer, 1921)
Behind Masks (Par., 1921)
Out of the Depths (Pioneer, 1921)
Wise Husbands (Pioneer, 1921)

REINER, CARL, b. March 20, 1923, New York City.
Enter Laughing (Col., 1967) (also co-producer, co-script)
The Comic (Col., 1969) (also producer, script)
Where's Poppa? (UA, 1970)

REIS, IRVING, b. May 7, 1906, New York City; d. July 2, 1953.
One Crowded Night (RKO, 1940)
I'm Still Alive (RKO, 1940)
Footlight Fever (RKO, 1941)
The Gay Falcon (RKO, 1941)
A Date With the Falcon (RKO, 1941)
Week-End for Three (RKO, 1941)
The Falcon Takes Over (RKO, 1942)
The Big Street (RKO, 1942)
Crack-Up (RKO, 1946)
The Bachelor and the Bobby Soxer (RKO, 1947)
All My Sons (Univ., 1948)
Enchantment (RKO, 1948)
Roseanna McCoy (RKO, 1949)
Dancing in the Dark (20th, 1949)
Three Husbands (UA, 1950)
Of Men and Music (20th, 1950)
New Mexico (UA, 1951)
The Four Poster (Col., 1952)

RENOIR, JEAN, b. Sept. 15, 1894, Paris.
La Fille de l'Eau (French, 1924) (also producer, set designer)
Nana (French, 1926) (also producer, co-titles)
Marquita (French, 1927)
La Petite Marchande d'Allumettes (French, 1928) (with Jean

Tedesco) (also co-producer, script, adaptation)
Tire-au-Flanc (French, 1928) (also co-adaptation)
Le Bled (French, 1929)
Le Tournoi dans la Cité (French, 1928) (also adaptation)
On Purge Bébé (French, 1931) (also adaptation)
Le Chienne (French, 1931) (also co-script, co-adaptation)
La Nuit du Carrefour (French, 1932) (also script)
Boudu Sauvé des Eaux (French, 1932) (also co-script)
Chotard et Compagnie (French, 1933) (also co-script)
Madame Bovary (French, 1933) (also script)
Toni (French, 1934) (also co-adaptation)
Le Crime de M. Lange (French, 1935) (also co-script)
Une Partie de Campagne (French, 1936) (also script, actor)
Les Bas-Fonds (French, 1936) (also co-script)
La Vie Est à Nous (French, 1936) (with Jean-Paul le Chanois,
    Jacques Becker, Andre Zwoboda, Pierre Unik, Henry Car-
    tier-Bresson) (also co-producer, co-script, actor)
La Grande Illusion (French, 1937) (also co-script)
La Marseillaise (French, 1938) (also co-script)
La Bête Humaine (French, 1938) (also co-script, actor)
La Regle du Jeu (French, 1939) (also producer, co-script, ac-
    tor)
La Tosca (Italian, 1940) (with Carl Koch) (also co-script)
Swamp Water (20th, 1941)
This Land Is Mine (RKO, 1943) (also co-producer, co-script)
The Southerner (UA, 1945) (also script)
The Diary of a Chambermaid (UA, 1946) (also co-adaptation)
The Woman on the Beach (RKO, 1946) (also co-script)
The River (Indian, 1951) (also co-script)
La Carrozza d'Oro (Italian, 1952) (also co-adaptation)
French Can Can (French, 1955) (also script)
Elena et les Hommes [Paris Does Strange Things] (French,
    1956) (also co-adaptation, song lyrics)
Le Déjeuner sur l'Herbe (French, 1959) (also script)
Le Testament du Dr. Cordelier (French, 1959 (also script,
    narrator)
Le Caporal Epingle (French, 1962) (also co-script, dialog)
Le Petit Théâtre de Jean Renoir (French, 1971) (also script,
    narrator)

REYNOLDS, SHELDON, b. 1923, Philadelphia.
    Foreign Intrigue (UA, 1956) (also producer, script)
    Assignment to Kill (WB-7 Arts, 1969) (also script)

RITT, MARTIN, b. March 2, 1920, New York City.
    Edge of the City (MGM, 1957)
    No Down Payment (20th, 1957)
    The Long Hot Summer (20th, 1958)
    Black Orchid (Par., 1958)
    The Sound and the Fury (20th, 1959)
    Five Branded Women (Par., 1960)

Paris Blues (UA, 1961)
Hemingway's Adventures of a Young Man (20th, 1962)
Hud (Par., 1963) (also co-producer)
The Outrage (MGM, 1964)
The Spy Who Came in from the Cold (Par., 1965) (also pro-
    ducer)
Hombre (20th, 1967) (also producer)
The Brotherhood (Par., 1968)
The Molly Maguires (Par., 1970) (also producer)
The Great White Hope (20th, 1970)
Sounder (20th, 1972)
Pete 'N Tillie (Univ., 1972)

ROBERTS, STEPHEN, b. Nov. 23, 1895, Summerville, W.Va.;
    d. July 18, 1936.
Sky Bride (Par., 1932)
Lady and Gent (Par., 1932)
The Night of June 13, (Par., 1932)
If I Had a Million (Par., 1932) (with James Cruze, H. Bruce
    Humberstone, Ernst Lubitsch, William A. Seiter, Norman
    Taurog)
The Story of Temple Drake (Par., 1933)
One Sunday Afternoon (Par., 1933)
The Trumpet Blows (Par., 1933)
Romance in Manhattan (RKO, 1934)
Star of Midnight (RKO, 1935)
The Man Who Broke the Bank at Monte Carlo (20th, 1935)
The Lady Consents (RKO, 1936)
The Ex-Mrs. Bradford (RKO, 1936)

ROBERTSON, JOHN STUART, b. June 14, 1878, London, Ont.;
    d. Nov. 7, 1964.
Baby Mine (Goldwyn, 1917)
Intrigue (Vitagraph, 1917)
The Bottom of the Well (Vitagraph, 1917)
The Money Mill (Vitagraph, 1917)
The Menace (Vitagraph, 1918)
Girl of Today (Vitagraph, 1918)
The Make-Believe Wife (Par., 1918)
Come Out of the Kitchen (Par., 1919)
The Misleading Widow (Par., 1919)
Here Comes the Bride (Par., 1919)
Little Miss Hoover (Par., 1919)
The Test of Honor (Par., 1919)
Let's Elope (Par., 1919)
Erstwhile Susan (Realart, 1919)
Sadie Love (Par., 1919)
The Better Half (Select, 1919)
Dr. Jekyll and Mr. Hyde (Par., 1920)
Away Goes Prudence (Par., 1920)
A Dark Lantern (Realart, 1920)

39 East (Realart, 1920)
Footlights (Par., 1921)
The Magic Cup (Realart, 1921)
Sentimental Tommy (Par., 1921)
Love's Boomerang (Par., 1922)
The Spanish Jade (Par., 1922)
Tess of the Storm Country (UA, 1922)
The Bright Shawl (Associated FN, 1923)
The Fighting Blade (Associated FN, 1923)
Twenty-One (Associated FN, 1923)
Classmates (FN, 1924)
The Enchanted Cottage (FN, 1924)
New Toys (FN, 1925)
Shore Leave (FN, 1925)
Soul-Fire (FN, 1925)
Annie Laurie (MGM, 1927)
Captain Salvation (MG, 1927)
The Road to Romance (MGM, 1927)
Shanghai Lady (Univ., 1929)
The Single Standard (MGM, 1929)
Captain of the Guard (Univ., 1930) (with Paul Fejos)
Madonna of the Streets (Col., 1930)
Night Ride (Univ., 1930)
One Man's Journey (RKO, 1933)
Crime Doctor (RKO, 1934)
His Greatest Gamble (RKO, 1934)
Wednesday's Child (RKO, 1934)
Captain Hurricane (RKO, 1935)
Grand Old Girl (RKO, 1935)
Our Little Girl (Fox, 1935)

ROBSON, MARK, b. Dec. 4, 1913, Montreal, Canada.
The Seventh Victim (RKO, 1943)
The Ghost Ship (RKO, 1943)
Youths Run Wild (RKO, 1943)
Isle of the Dead (RKO, 1945)
Bedlam (RKO, 1946) (also co-script)
Champion (UA, 1949)
Home of the Brave (UA, 1949)
Roughshod (RKO, 1949)
My Foolish Heart (RKO, 1949)
Edge of Doom (RKO, 1950)
Bright Victory (Univ., 1951)
I Want You (RKO, 1951)
Return to Paradise (UA, 1953)
Hell Below Zero (Col., 1954)
Phffft (Col., 1954)
The Bridges of Toko-Ri (Par., 1955)
A Prize of Gold (Col., 1955)
Trial (MGM, 1955)
The Harder They Fall (Col., 1956)
The Little Hut (MGM, 1957) (also co-producer)

Peyton Place (20th, 1957)
The Inn of the Sixth Happiness (20th, 1958)
From the Terrace (20th, 1960) (also producer)
Nine Hours to Rama (20th, 1963) (also producer)
The Prize (MGM, 1963)
Von Ryan's Express (20th, 1964)
Lost Command (Col., 1966) (also producer)
Valley of the Dolls (20th, 1967)
Daddy's Gone A-Hunting (National General, 1969) (also producer)
Happy Birthday, Wanda June (Col., 1971)
Limbo (Univ., 1973)

ROGELL, ALBERT S., b. Aug. 1, 1901, Oklahoma City, Okla.
The Greatest Menace (Mayer, 1923) (also script)
The Mask of Lopez (FBO, 1924)
North of Nevada (FB, 1924)
The Dangerous Coward (FBO, 1924)
Galloping Gallagher (FBO, 1924)
The Fighting Sap (FBO, 1924)
The Silent Stranger (FBO, 1924)
Thundering Hoofs (FBO, 1924)
Lightning Romance (Rayart, 1924)
Geared to Go (Rayart, 1924)
Easy Money (Rayart, 1925)
The Circus Cyclone (Univ., 1925) (also story)
Crack O'Dawn (Rayart, 1925)
Cyclone Cavalier (Rayart, 1925)
Goat Getter (Rayart, 1925)
Super Speed (Rayart, 1925)
The Snob Buster (Rayart, 1925)
Youth's Gamble (Rayart, 1925)
The Fear Fighter (Rayart, 1925)
The Knockout Kid (Rayart, 1925)
Fighting Fate (Rayart, 1925)
The Patent Leather Pug (Rayart, 1926)
Men of the Night (Sterling, 1926)
Senor Daredevil (Associated FN, 1926)
The Man from the West (Univ., 1926)
The Wild Horse Stampede (Univ., 1926)
Red Hot Leather (Univ., 1926) (also story)
The Unknown Cavalier (Associated FN, 1926)
The Overland Stage (FN, 1927)
Grinning Guns (Univ., 1927)
Men of Daring (Univ., 1927)
The Devil's Saddle (FN, 1927)
The Fighting Three (Univ., 1927)
The Red Raiders (FN, 1927)
Rough and Ready (Univ., 1927)
Somewhere in Sonora (FN, 1927)
The Sunset Derby (FN, 1927)
The Western Rover (Univ., 1927)

The Western Whirlwind (Univ., 1927)
The Shepherd of the Hills (FN, 1928)
The Speed Champion (Rayart, 1928)
The Canyon of Adventure (FN, 1928)
The Upland Rider (FN, 1928)
The Glorious Trail (FN, 1928)
The Phantom City (FN, 1928)
The California Mail (FN, 1929)
Cheyenne (FN, 1929)
The Lone Wolf's Daughter (Col., 1929)
The Flying Marine (Col., 1929)
Painted Faces (Tiffany-Stahl, 1929)
Mamba (Tiffany, 1930)
Aloha (Tiffany, 1931)
Sweepstakes (RKO, 1931)
Tif Off (Pathé, 1931)
Suicide Fleet (Pathé, 1931)
Carnival Boat (RKO, 1932)
The Rider of Death Valley (Univ., 1932)
Air Hostess (Col., 1933)
Below the Sea (Col., 1933)
The Wrecker (Col., 1933)
East of Fifth Avenue (Col., 1933)
Fog (Col., 1934)
No More Women (Par., 1934)
Among the Missing (Col., 1934)
The Hell Cat (Col., 1934)
Name the Woman (Col., 1934)
Fugitive Lady (Col., 1934)
Unknown Woman (Col., 1935)
Atlantic Adventure (Col., 1935)
Escape from Devil's Island (Col., 1935)
You May Be Next (Col., 1936)
Roaming Lady (Col., 1936)
Grand Jury (RKO, 1936)
Murder in Greenwich Village (Col., 1937)
Start Cheering (Col., 1938)
The Lone Wolf in Paris (Col., 1938)
City Streets (Col., 1938)
The Last Warning (Col., 1938)
For Love or Money (Univ., 1939)
Hawaiian Nights (Univ., 1939)
Laugh It Off (Univ., 1939)
I Can't Give You Anything But Love, Baby (Univ., 1940)
Private Affairs (Univ., 1940)
Argentine Nights (Univ., 1940)
The Black Cat (Univ., 1941)
West Point Widow (Par., 1941)
Sailors on Leave (Rep., 1941)
Public Enemies (Rep., 1941)
Sleepytime Gal (Rep., 1942)
Jail House Blues (Univ., 1942)
Butch Minds the Baby (Univ., 1942)

True to the Army (Par., 1942)
Priorities on Parade (Par., 1942)
Youth on Parade (Rep., 1942)
Hit Parade of 1943 (Rep., 1943)
In Old Oklahoma (Rep., 1943)
Love, Honor and Goodbye (Rep., 1945) (also story)
Earl Carroll Sketchbook (Rep., 1946)
The Magnificent Rogue (Rep., 1946)
Heaven Only Knows (UA, 1947)
Northwest Stampede (Eagle Lion, 1948) (also producer)
Song of India (Col., 1949) (also producer)
The Admiral Was a Lady (UA, 1950)
Before I Wake [Shadow of Fear] (Grand National, 1955)
Men Against Speed (20th, 1958)

ROSEN, PHILIP E. (Phil Rosen), b. May 8, 1888, Marienburg,
     Russia; d. Oct. 22, 1951.
Beach Comber (Par., 1916)
The Road to Divorce (Univ., 1920)
The Path She Chose (Univ., 1920)
Are All Men Alike? (Metro, 1920)
The Little Fool (Metro, 1921) (with Bayard Veiller)
Extravagance (Metro, 1921)
The Lure of Youth (Metro, 1921)
The Young Rajah (Par., 1922)
Across the Continent (Par., 1922)
The Bonded Woman (Par., 1922)
Handle With Care (Associated Exhibitors, 1922)
The World's Champion (Par., 1922)
Abraham Lincoln (Associated FN, 1924)
Being Respectable (WB, 1924)
Lover's Lane (WF, 1924)
This Woman (WB, 1924)
The Bridge of Sighs (WB, 1925)
Heart of a Siren (FN, 1925)
Wandering Footsteps (Banner, 1925)
The White Monkey (FN, 1925)
The Adorable Deceiver (FBO, 1926)
The Exquisite Sinner (MGM, 1926)
Rose of the Tenements (FBO, 1926)
A Woman's Heart (Sterling, 1926)
Stolen Pleasures (Col., 1927)
California or Bust (FBO, 1927)
The Cancelled Debt (Sterling, 1927)
Closed Gates (Sterling, 1927)
The Cruel Truth (Sterling, 1927)
Heavon on Earth (MGM, 1927)
In the First Degree (Sterling, 1927)
Pretty Clothes (Sterling, 1927)
Salvation Love (FBO, 1927)
Stranded (Sterling, 1927)
Thumbs Down (Sterling, 1927)

The Woman Who Did Not Care (Lumas, 1927)
Burning Up Broadway (Sterling, 1928)
The Apache (Col., 1928)
Marry the Girl (Sterling, 1928)
Modern Mothers (Col., 1928)
Undressed (Sterling, 1928)
The Faker (Col., 1929)
The Peacock Fan (Chesterfield, 1929)
The Phantom in the House (Continental, 1929)
Extravagance (MGM, 1930)
Lotus Lady (Greiver, 1930)
The Rampant Age (Continental, 1930)
Second Honeymoon (Continental, 1930)
Worldly Goods (Continental, 1930)
Two-Gun Man (Tiffany, 1931)
Second Honeymoon (Continental, 1931)
El Codigo Penal [Spanish version of The Penal Code] (Col.,
   1931)
Branded Men (Tiffany, 1931)
The Pocatello Kid (Tiffany, 1931)
Alias, the Bad Man (Tiffany, 1931)
Arizona Terror (Tiffany, 1931)
Range Law (Tiffany, 1931)
A Man's Land (Allied, 1932)
Klondike (Mon., 1932)
The Vanishing Frontier (Par., 1932)
Texas Gun Fighter (Tiffany, 1932)
Whistlin' Dan (Tiffany, 1932)
Lena Rivers (Tiffany, 1932)
The Gay Buckaroo (Hollywood, 1932)
Self Defense (Mon., 1933)
Young Blood (Mon., 1933)
Hold the Press (Col., 1933)
The Phantom Broadcast (Mon., 1933)
Black Beauty (Mon., 1933)
Shadows of Sing Sing (Columbia, 1933)
Cheaters (Liberty, 1934)
Picture Brides (First Division, 1934)
Take the Stand (Liberty, 1934)
Dangerous Corner (RKO, 1934)
Woman in the Dark (RKO, 1934)
Little Men (Mascot, 1934)
Beggars in Ermine (Mon., 1934)
West of the Pecos (RKO, 1934)
Death Flies East (Col., 1935)
The Calling of Dan Matthews (Col., 1935)
Unwelcome Stranger (Col., 1935)
Born to Gamble (Rep., 1935)
Bridge of Sighs (Invincible, 1936)
Three of a Kind (Invincible, 1936)
Easy Money (Invincible, 1936)
It Couldn't Have Happened (Invincible, 1936)
Brilliant Marriage (Invincible, 1936)

Ellis Island (Invincible, 1936)
Missing Girls (Chesterfield, 1936)
Tango (Invincible, 1936)
The President's Mystery (Rep., 1936)
Jim Hanvey, Detective (Rep., 1937)
It Could Happen to You (Rep., 1937)
Youth on Parole (Rep., 1937)
Two Wise Maids (Rep., 1937)
Roaring Timber (Col., 1938)
The Marines Are Here (Mon., 1938)
Ex-Champ (Univ., 1939)
Missing Evidence (Univ., 1939)
Forgotten Girls (Rep., 1940)
Phantom of Chinatown (Mon., 1940)
Double Alibi (Univ., 1940)
Queen of the Yukon (Mon., 1940)
The Deadly Game (Mon., 1941)
Murder by Invitation (Mon., 1941)
Paper Bullets [Crime Inc.] (PRC, 1941)
I Killed That Man (PRC, 1941)
Spooks Run Wild (Mon., 1941)
The Man With Two Lives (Mon., 1942)
The Mystery of Marie Roget (Univ., 1942)
Prison Mutiny (Mon., 1943)
You Can't Beat the Law (Mon., 1943)
Charlie Chan in the Secret Service (Mon., 1944)
The Chinese Cat (Mon., 1944)
Return of the Ape Man (Mon., 1944)
Black Magic (Mon., 1944)
Captain Tugboat Annie (Rep., 1945)
The Jade Mask (Mon., 1945)
Army Wives (Mon., 1945)
The Scarlet Clue (Mon., 1945)
The Red Dragon (Mon., 1945)
In Old New Mexico (Mon., 1945)
The Cisco Kid in New Mexico (Mon., 1945)
Step By Step (Mon., 1946)
The Shadow Returns (Mon., 1946)
The Strange Mr. Gregory (Mon., 1946)
The Secret of St. Ives (Col., 1949)
Sins of the Fathers (Canadian Motion Picture Corp., 1949)
    (with Richard J. Jarvis)

ROSENBERG, STUART, b. 1928, New York City.
    Murder, Inc. (20th, 1960) (with Burt Balaban)
    Question Seven (De Rochemont, 1961)
    Fame Is the Name of the Game (NBC-TV, 1966)
    Asylum for a Spy (NBC-TV, 1967)
    Cool Hand Luke (WB-7 Arts, 1967)
    The April Fools (National General, 1969)
    WUSA (Par., 1970)
    Move (20th, 1970)

Pocket Money (National General, 1972)
The Laughing Policeman (20th, 1973) (also producer)

ROSSEN, ROBERT, b. May 16, 1908, New York City; d. Feb. 18,
   1966.
   Johnny O'Clock (Col., 1947) (also script)
   Body and Soul (UA, 1947)
   All the King's Men (Col., 1949) (also producer, script)
   The Brave Bulls (Col., 1951) (also producer)
   Mambo (Par., 1955 (also co-script)
   Alexander the Great (UA, 1956) (also producer, script)
   Island in the Sun (20th, 1957)
   They Came to Cordura (Col., 1959) (also co-script)
   The Hustler (20th, 1961) (also producer, co-script)
   Lilith (Col., 1964) (also producer, script)

ROSSON, RICHARD, b. 1894, New York City; d. May 31, 1953.
   Fine Manners (Par., 1926)
   Blonde or Brunette (Par., 1927)
   Ritzy (Par., 1927)
   Rolled Stockings (Par., 1927)
   Shootin' Irons (Par., 1927)
   The Wizard (Fox, 1927)
   Dead Man's Curve (FBO, 1928)
   The Escape (Fox, 1928)
   Road House (Fox, 1928) (with James Kevin McGuinness)
   The Very Idea (RKO, 1929) (with William LeBaron)
   West Point of the Air (MGM, 1935)
   Behind the Headlines (RKO, 1937)
   Hideaway (RKO, 1937)
   Corvette (Univ., 1943)

ROUSE, RUSSELL, b. 1916, New York City.
   The Well (UA, 1951) (with Leo Pokin) (also co-script)
   The Thief (UA, 1952) (also co-script)
   Wicked Woman (UA, 1953) (also co-script)
   New York Confidential (WB, 1955) (also co-script)
   The Fastest Gun Alive (MGM, 1956) (also co-script)
   House of Numbers (MGM, 1957) (also co-script)
   Thunder in the Sun (Par., 1959) (also co-script)
   A House Is Not a Home (Emb., 1964) (also co-script)
   The Oscar (Emb., 1966) (also co-script)
   The Caper of the Golden Bull (Emb., 1967)

ROWLAND, ROY, b. Dec. 31, 1910, New York City.
   Hollywood Party (MGM, 1934) (uncredited, with uncredited
      Richard Boleslewsky, Allan Dwan)
   A Stranger in Town (MGM, 1943)
   Lost Angel (MGM, 1943)

Our Vines Have Tender Grapes (MGM, 1945)
Boys Ranch (MGM, 1946)
Killer McCoy (MGM, 1947)
The Romance of Rosy Ridge (MGM, 1947)
Tenth Avenue Angel (MGM, 1948)
Scene of the Crime (MGM, 1949)
The Outriders (MGM, 1950)
Two Weeks With Love (MGM, 1950) (with choreographer Busby
  Berkeley)
Excuse My Dust (MGM, 1951)
Bugles in the Afternoon (WB, 1952)
The 5,000 Fingers of Dr. T. (Col., 1953)
Affair With a Stranger (RKO, 1953)
The Moonlighter (WB, 1953)
Witness to Murder (UA, 1954)
Rogue Cop (MGM, 1954)
Many Rivers to Cross (MGM, 1955)
Hit the Deck (MGM, 1955)
Meet Me in Las Vegas (MGM, 1956)
These Wilder Years (MGM, 1956)
Slander (MGM, 1956)
Gun Glory (MGM, 1957)
The Seven Hills of Rome (MGM, 1958)
The Girl Hunters (Colorama, 1963) (also co-script)
Gunfighters of the Casa Grande (MGM, 1965)
Sie Nannten Ihn Gringo (German-Italian, 1966)
The Sea Pirate (Par., 1967)

RUBEN, J. WALTER, b. Aug. 14, 1899, New York City; d. Sept.
  18, 1942.
Public Defender (RKO, 1931)
Secret Service (RKO, 1931)
Roadhouse Murder (RKO, 1932) (also co-script)
Phantom of Crestwood (RKO, 1932) (also co-story)
No Other Woman (RKO, 1933)
The Great Jasper (RKO, 1933)
No Marriage Ties (RKO, 1933)
Ace of Aces (RKO, 1933)
Man of Two Worlds (RKO, 1934)
Success at any Price (RKO, 1934)
Where Sinners Meet (Rep., 1934)
Java Head (First Division, 1935)
Public Hero Number One (MGM, 1935) (also co-story)
Riffraff (MGM, 1935)
Trouble for Two (MGM, 1936)
Old Hutch (MGM, 1936)
The Good Old Soak (MGM, 1937)
The Bad Man of Brimstone (MGM, 1938)

RUGGLES, WESLEY, b. June 11, 1889, Los Angeles, Calif.; d.
  Jan. 8, 1972.

Rosalind Russell with J. Walter Ruben on the set for <u>Trouble for Two</u> (MGM, 1936).

For France (Vitagraph, 1917)
The Blind Adventure (Vitagraph, 1918)
The Winchester Woman (Vitagraph, 1919)
Picadilly Jim (Select, 1920)
The Desperate Hero (Selznick, 1920)
Leopard Woman (Associated Producers, 1920)
Love (Associated Producers, 1920)
The Greater Claim (Metro, 1921)
Uncharted Seas (Metro, 1921)
Over the Wire (Metro, 1921)
Wild Honey (Univ., 1922)
If I Were Queen (FBO, 1922)
Slippery Magee (FN, 1923)
Mr. Billings Spends His Dime (Par., 1923)

The Remittance Woman (FBO, 1923)
The Heart Raider (Par., 1923)
The Age of Innocence (WB, 1924)
The Plastic Age (B.P. Schulberg, 1925)
Broadway Lady (FBO, 1925)
The Kick-Off (Excellent, 1926)
A Man of Quality (Excellent, 1926)
Beware of Widows (Univ., 1927)
Silk Stockings (Univ., 1927)
Fourflusher (Univ., 1928)
Finders Keepers (Univ., 1928)
Street Girl (RKO, 1929)
Scandal (Univ., 1929)
Girl Overboard (Univ., 1929)
Condemned (UA, 1929)
The Haunted Lady (Univ., 1929)
Honey (Par., 1930)
The Sea Bat (MGM, 1930)
Cimarron (RKO, 1931)
Are These Our Children? (RKO, 1931)
Roar of the Dragon (RKO, 1932)
No Man of Her Own (Par., 1932)
Monkey's Paw (RKO, 1933)
College Humor (Par., 1933)
I'm No Angel (Par., 1933)
Bolero (Par., 1934)
Shoot the Works (Par., 1934)
The Gilded Lily (Par., 1935)
Accent on Youth (Par., 1935)
The Bride Comes Home (Par., 1935) (also producer)
Valiant Is the Word for Carrie (Par., 1936) (also producer)
True Confession (Par., 1937)
I Met Him in Paris (Par., 1937) (also producer)
Sing, You Sinners (Par., 1938) (also producer)
Invitation to Happiness (Par., 1939) (also producer)
Too Many Husbands (Col., 1940) (also producer)
I Take This Woman (MGM, 1940) (replaced Josef von Sternberg,
   film completed by W.S. Van Dyke II)
Arizona (Col., 1940) (also producer)
You Belong to Me (Col., 1941) (also producer)
Somewhere I'll Find You (MGM, 1942)
Slightly Dangerous (MGM, 1943)
See Here, Private Hargrove (MGM, 1944)
London Town (Rank, 1946)

RYAN, FRANK, b. Oct. 18, 1907, Urbana, Ohio; d. Dec. 31, 1947.
   Call Out the Marines (RKO, 1942) (with William Hamilton)
   Hers to Hold (Univ., 1943)
   Can't Help Singing (Univ., 1944) (also script)
   Patrick the Great (Univ., 1945)
   So Goes My Love (Univ., 1946)

RYDELL, MARK, b. c. 1934.
  The Fox (WB-7 Arts, 1968)
  The Reivers (National General, 1969)
  The Cowboys (WB, 1972) (also producer)
  Cinderella Liberty (20th, 1973) (also producer)

S

SAGAL, BORIS, b. 1923, Dnepropetrovsk, Russia.
  The Crimebuster (MGM, 1961)
  Dime With a Halo (MGM, 1963)
  Twilight of Honor (MGM, 1963)
  Girl Happy (MGM, 1965)
  Made in Paris (MGM, 1966)
  The Helicopter Spies (MGM, 1968)
  Destiny of a Spy (NBC-TV, 1969)
  Night Gallery (NBC-TV, 1969) (with Stephen Spielberg, Barry
    Shear)
  U. M. C. [Operation Heartbeat] (CBS-TV, 1969)
  The 1,000 Plane Raid (UA, 1969)
  Hauser's Memory (NBC-TV, 1970)
  The Movie Murderer (NBC-TV, 1970)
  The Mosquito Squadron (UA, 1970)
  The Failing of Raymond (NBC-TV, 1971)
  The Harness (NBC-TV, 1971)
  The Omega Man (WB, 1972)
  Indict and Convict (ABC-TV, 1972)

ST. CLAIR, MALCOLM (Mal St. Clair), b. May 17, 1897, Los
    Angeles; d. June 1, 1952.
  George Washington, Jr. (WB, 1924)
  Find Your Man (WB, 1924)
  The Lighthouse By the Sea (WB, 1925)
  After Business Hours (Col., 1925)
  A Woman of the World (Par., 1925)
  On Thin Ice (WB, 1925)
  The Trouble With Wives (Par., 1925)
  Are Parents People? (UA, 1925)
  A Social Celebrity (Par., 1926) (also producer)
  The Show-Off (Par., 1926)
  The Grand Duchess and the Waiter (Par., 1926)
  The Popular Sin (Par., 1926)
  Good and Naughty (Par., 1926)
  Breakfast at Sunrise (FN, 1927)
  Knockout Reilly (Par., 1927) (also producer)
  Gentlemen Prefer Blondes (Par., 1928)
  Sporting Goods (Par., 1928)
  Beau Broadway (MGM, 1928)
  The Fleet's In (Par., 1928)
  Side Street (RKO, 1929) (also co-script)
  The Canary Murder Case (Par., 1929)

Night Parade (RKO, 1929)
Montana Moon (MGM, 1930)
Dangerous Nan McGrew (Par., 1930)
The Boudoir Diplomat (Univ., 1930)
Remote Control (MGM, 1930)
Goldie Gets Along (RKO, 1933)
Olsen's Big Moment (Fox, 1933)
Crack-Up (20th, 1936)
Time Out for Romance (20th, 1937)
Born Reckless (20th, 1937)
She Had to Eat (20th, 1937)
Dangerously Yours (20th, 1937)
A Trip to Paris (20th, 1938)
Safety in Numbers (20th, 1938)
Down on the Farm (20th, 1938)
Everybody's Baby (20th, 1938)
The Jones Family in Hollywood (20th, 1939)
The Jones Family in Quick Millions (20th, 1939)
Young as You Feel (20th, 1940)
Meet the Missus (RKO, 1940)
The Bashful Bachelor (RKO, 1941)
The Man in the Trunk (Par., 1942)
Over My Dead Body (Par., 1942)
Two Weeks to Live (Mon., 1943)
Swing Out the Blues (Col., 1943)
Jitterbugs (20th, 1943)
The Dancing Masters (20th, 1943)
The Big Noise (20th, 1944)
The Bullfighters (20th, 1945)
Arthur Takes Over (20th, 1948)
Fighting Back (20th, 1948)

ST. JACQUES, RAYMOND (James Arthur Johnson), b. c. 1932, Conn.
Book of Numbers (Avco Emb., 1973) (also producer, actor)

SALE, RICHARD, b. Dec. 17, 1911, New York City.
Spoilers of the North (Rep., 1947)
Campus Honeymoon (Rep., 1948) (also co-script)
A Ticket to Tomahawk (20th, 1950) (also co-story, co-script)
I'll Get By (20th, 1950) (also co-script)
Meet Me After the Show (20th, 1951) (also co-script)
Half Angel (20th, 1951)
Let's Make It Legal (20th, 1951)
My Wife's Best Friend (20th, 1952)
The Girl Next Door (20th, 1953)
Fire Over Africa (Col., 1954)
Gentlemen Marry Brunettes (UA, 1955) (also co-producer, co-script)
Abandon Ship! (Col., 1957) (also script)

SALKOW, SIDNEY, b. June 16, 1909, New York City.
Four Day's Wonder (Univ., 1937)
Girl Overboard (Univ., 1937)
Behind the Mike (Univ., 1937)
That's My Story (Univ., 1938)
Storm Over Bengal (Rep., 1938)
The Night Hawk (Rep., 1938)
Woman Doctor (Rep., 1939)
Fighting Thoroughbreds (Rep., 1939)
Streets of Missing Men (Rep., 1939)
Zero Hour (Rep., 1939)
She Married a Cop (Rep., 1939)
Flight at Midnight (Rep., 1939)
Cafe Hostess (Col., 1940)
The Lone Wolf Strikes (Col., 1940)
The Lone Wolf Meets a Lady (Col., 1940)
Girl from God's Country (Col., 1940)
The Lone Wolf Takes a Chance (Col., 1941)
Time Out for Rhythm (Col., 1941)
The Lone Wolf Keeps a Date (Col., 1941)
Tillie the Toiler (Col., 1941)
The Adventures of Martin Eden (Col., 1942)
Flight Lieutenant (Col., 1942)
City Without Men (Col., 1943)
Faithful in My Fashion (MGM, 1946)
Millie's Daughter (Col., 1947)
Bulldog Drummond at Bay (Col., 1947)
Sword of the Avenger (UA, 1948)
Fugitive Lady (Rep., 1951)
Scarlet Angel (Univ., 1952)
The Golden Hawk (Col., 1952)
The Pathfinder (Col., 1952)
Jack McCall, Desperado (Col., 1953)
Raiders of the Seven Seas (UA, 1953) (also producer, script)
Prince of Pirates (Col., 1953)
Sitting Bull (UA, 1954) (also co-script)
Robber's Roost (UA, 1955) (also co-script)
Shadow of the Eagle (UA, 1955)
Toughest Man Alive (AA, 1955)
Las Vegas Shakedown (AA, 1955)
Gun Brothers (UA, 1956)
The Long Rifle and the Tomahawk (ITC, 1956) (with Sam New-
field)
Gun Duel in Durango (UA, 1957)
The Iron Sheriff (UA, 1957)
Chicago Confidential (UA, 1957)
The Big Night (Par., 1960)
Twice Told Tales (UA, 1963)
Blood on the Arrow (AA, 1964)
Last Man on Earth (Associated Producers-Regina, 1964)
The Quick Gun (Col., 1964)
The Great Sioux Massacre (Col., 1965)
The Murder Game (20th, 1966)

SANDRICH, MARK, b. Oct. 26, 1900, New York City; d. March 5, 1945.

Runaway Girls (Col., 1928)
The Talk of Hollywood (Sono Art-World Wide, 1930) (also producer)
Melody Cruise (RKO, 1933) (also co-script)
Aggie Appleby, Maker of Men (RKO, 1933)
Hips, Hips, Hooray! (RKO, 1934)
Cockeyed Cavaliers (RKO, 1934)
The Gay Divorcee (RKO, 1934)
Top Hat (RKO, 1935)
Follow the Fleet (RKO, 1936)
A Woman Rebels (RKO, 1936)
Shall We Dance? (RKO, 1937)

Ginger Rogers and Mark Sandrich talk over Top Hat (RKO, 1935).

Carefree (RKO, 1938)
Man About Town (Par., 1939)
Buck Benny Rides Again (Par., 1940) (also producer)
Love Thy Neighbor (Par., 1940) (also producer)
Skylark (Par., 1941) (also producer)
Holiday Inn (Par., 1942) (also producer)
So Proudly We Hail (Par., 1943) (also producer)
Here Come the Waves (Par., 1944) (also producer)
I Love a Soldier (Par., 1944) (also producer)

SANTELL, ALFRED, b. Sept. 14, 1895, San Francisco.
Wildcat Jordan (Phil Goldstone, 1922)
Lights Out (FBO, 1923)
Fools in the Dark (FBO, 1924)
Empty Hearts (Banner, 1924)
The Man Who Played Square (Fox, 1924)
The Marriage Whirl (FN, 1925)
Parisian Nights (FBO, 1925)
Classified (FN, 1925)

Susan Hayward, Joseph Allen and Bob Burns with Alfred Santell (left) on <u>Our Leading Citizen</u> (Par., 1939).

Bluebeard's Seven Wives (FN, 1926)
Sweet Daddies (FN, 1926)
The Dancer of Paris (FN, 1926)
Subway Sadie (FN, 1926)
Just Another Blonde (FN, 1926)
Orchids and Ermine (FN, 1927)
The Patent Leather Kid (FN, 1927)
The Gorilla (FN, 1927)
The Little Shepherd of Kingdom Come (FN, 1928) (also producer)
Show Girl (FN, 1928)
Wheel of Chance (FN, 1928)
This Is Heaven (UA, 1929)
Twin Beds (FN, 1929)
Romance of the Rio Grande (Fox, 1929)
The Arizona Kid (Fox, 1930)
The Sea Wolf (Fox, 1930)
Body and Soul (Fox, 1931)
Daddy Long Legs (Fox, 1931)
Sob Sister (Fox, 1931)
Polly of the Circus (Fox, 1932)
Rebecca of Sunnybrook Farm (Fox, 1932)
Tess of the Storm Country (Fox, 1932)
Bondage (Fox, 1933)
The Right to Romance (RKO, 1933)
Life of Vergie Winters (RKO, 1934)
People Will Talk (Par., 1935)
A Feather in Her Hat (Col., 1935)
Winterset (RKO, 1936)
Internes Can't Take Money (Par., 1937)
Breakfast for Two (RKO, 1937)
Cocoanut Grove (Par., 1938)
Having Wonderful Time (RKO, 1938)
The Arkansas Traveler (Par., 1938)
Our Leading Citizen (Par., 1939)
Aloma of the South Seas (Par., 1941)
Beyond the Blue Horizon (Par., 1942)
Jack London (UA, 1943)
The Hairy Ape (UA, 1944)
Mexicana (Rep., 1945) (also producer)
That Brennan Girl (Rep., 1946) (also producer)

SANTLEY, JOSEPH (Joseph Mansfield), b. Jan. 10, 1890, Salt
        Lake City, Utah; d. Aug. 8, 1971.
The Cocoanuts (Par., 1929)
Swing High (Pathé, 1930) (also co-story)
The Loud Speaker (Mon., 1934)
Young and Beautiful (Mascot, 1934)
Million Dollar Baby (Mon., 1935)
Harmony Lane (Mascot, 1935) (also co-script)
Waterfront Lady (Rep., 1935)
Laughing Irish Eyes (Rep., 1936)

Dancing Feet (Rep., 1936)
Her Master's Voice (Par., 1936)
The Harvester (Rep., 1936)
We Went to College (MGM, 1936)
Walking on Air (RKO, 1936)
Smartest Girl in Town (RKO, 1936)
Meet the Missus (RKO, 1937)
There Goes the Groom (RKO, 1937)
She's Got Everything (RKO, 1938)
Blonde Cheat (RKO, 1938)
Always in Trouble (20th, 1938)
Swing, Sister, Swing (Univ., 1938)
The Spirit of Culver (Univ., 1939)
The Family Next Door (Univ., 1939)
Two Bright Boys (Univ., 1939)
Music in My Heart (Col., 1940)
Melody and Moonlight (Rep., 1940)
Melody Ranch (Rep., 1940)
Behind the News (Rep., 1940)
Sis Hopkins (Rep., 1941)
Dancing on a Dime (Par., 1941)
Rookies on Parade (Rep., 1941)
Puddin' Head (Rep., 1941)
Down Mexico Way (Rep., 1941)
Ice-Capades (Rep., 1941)
A Tragedy at Midnight (Rep., 1942)
Yokel Boy (Rep., 1942)
Remember Pearl Harbor (Rep., 1942)
Joan of Ozark (Rep., 1942)
Call of the Canyon (Rep., 1942)
Chatterbox (Rep., 1943)
Shantytown (Rep., 1943)
Thumbs Up (Rep., 1943)
Sleepy Lagoon (Rep., 1943)
Here Comes Elmer (Rep., 1943)
Goodnight, Sweetheart (Rep., 1944)
Rosie the Riveter (Rep., 1944)
Brazil (Rep., 1944)
Jamboree (Rep., 1944)
Three Little Sisters (Rep., 1944)
Earl Carroll Vanities (Rep., 1945)
Hitchhike to Happiness (Rep., 1945)
Shadow of a Woman (Rep., 1946)
Make Believe Ballroom (Col., 1949)
When You're Smiling (Col., 1950)

SARGENT, JOSEPH
Once Spy Too Many (MGM, 1966)
The Hell With Heroes (Univ., 1968)
The Forbin Project (Univ., 1970)
The Man (Par., 1972)
The Marcus-Nelson Murders (CBS-TV, 1972)

Sunshine (CBS-TV, 1973)
White Lightning (UA, 1973)

SAVILLE, VICTOR, b. 1897, Birmingham, Eng.
    The Arcadians (Gaumont-British, 1927) (also producer, script)
    The Glad Eye (Gaumont-British, 1927) (with Maurice Elvey)
        (also producer, script)
    Tesha (British International, 1928) (also producer, story,
        screenplay)
    Kitty (British International, 1929)
    Woman to Woman (Gainsborough-Tiffany Stahl, 1929) (also co-
        producer)
    The W Plan (Gaumont-British, 1930) (also producer)
    A Warm Corner (Gaumont-British, 1930) (also producer,
        script)
    The Sport of Kings (Gaumont-British, 1930) (also producer,
        script)
    Michael and Mary (Gaumont-British, 1931)
    Sunshine Susie (Gaumont-British, 1931)
    Hindle Wakes (Gaumont-British, 1932) (also script)
    The Faithful Heart (Gaumont-British, 1932)
    Love on Wheels (Gaumont-British, 1932)
    The Good Companions (Gaumont-British, 1933)
    Friday the Thirteenth (Gaumont-British, 1933)
    I Was a Spy (Gaumont-British, 1933)
    Evergreen (Gaumont-British, 1934)
    Evensong (Gaumont-British, 1934)
    The Iron Duke (Gaumont-British, 1935)
    The Love Affair of the Dictator (Topelitz, 1935)
    Me and Marlborough (Gaumont-British, 1935)
    First a Girl (Gaumont-British, 1936)
    It's Love Again (Gaumont-British, 1936)
    Dark Journey (London, 1937) (also producer)
    Storm in a Teacup (London, 1937) (with Ian Dalrymple) (also
        producer)
    South Riding (London, 1938) (also producer)
    Forever and a Day (RKO, 1943) (with Rene Clair, Edmund
        Goulding, Cedric Hardwicke, Frank Lloyd, Robert Stevenson,
        Herbert Wilcox) (also co-producer)
    Tonight and Every Night (Col., 1945) (also producer)
    The Green Years (MGM, 1946)
    Green Dolphin Street (MGM, 1947)
    If Winter Comes (MGM, 1947)
    Conspirator (MGM, 1949)
    Kim (MGM, 1950)
    Calling Bulldog Drummond (MGM, 1951)
    24 Hours of a Woman's Life [Affair in Monte Carlo] (Associ-
        ated British Pictures, 1952)
    The Long Wait (UA, 1954)
    The Silver Chalice (WB, 1955)

SCHAEFER, ARMAND L., b. Aug. 5, 1898, Tavistock, Ont., Canada.
   The Lightning Warrior* (Mascot, 1931)
   The Hurricane Express* (Mascot, 1932) (with J. P. McGowan)
   Cheyenne Cyclone (Kent, 1932)
   Sinister Hands (Kent, 1932)
   Wyoming Whirlwind (Capitol, 1932)
   Outlaw Justice (Majestic, 1933)
   Law and Lawless (Majestic, 1933)
   Fighting With Kit Carson* (Mascot, 1933) (with Colbert Clark)
   The Three Musketeers* (Mascot, 1933) (with Colbert Clark)
   Fighting Texans (Mon., 1933)
   Sagebrush Trail (Mon., 1933)
   Terror Trail (Univ., 1933)
   Sixteen Fathoms Deep (Mon., 1934)
   Burn 'Em Up Barnes* (Mascot, 1934) (with Colbert Clark)
   The Law of the Wild* (Mascot, 1934) (with B. Reeves Eason)
   The Lost Jungle* (Mascot, 1934) (with David Howard)
   The Miracle Rider* (Mascot, 1935) (with B. Reeves Eason)

SCHAFFNER, FRANKLIN J., b. May 30, 1920, Tokyo, Japan.
   A Summer World (1961--unfinished)
   The Stripper (20th, 1963)
   The Best Man (UA, 1964)
   The War Lord (Univ., 1965)
   The Double Man (WB-7 Arts, 1968)
   Planet of the Apes (20th, 1968)
   Patton (20th, 1970)
   Nicholas and Alexandra (Col., 1971) (also co-producer)
   Papillon (AA, 1973) (also co-producer)

SCHALTZBERG, JERRY
   Puzzle of a Downfall Child (Univ., 1970)
   Panic in Needle Park (20th, 1971)
   Scarecrow (WB, 1973)

SCHERTZINGER, VICTOR, b. April 8, 1889, Mahoney City, Pa.;
      d. Oct. 26, 1941.
   The Clodhopper (Triangle, 1917)
   The Millionaire Vagrant (Triangle, 1917)
   The Pinch Hitter (Triangle, 1917)
   Sudden Jim (Triangle, 1917)
   The Son of His Father (Par., 1917)
   His Mother's Boy (Par., 1918)
   The Hired Man (Par., 1918)
   The Family Skeleton (Ince-Triangle, 1918)
   Playing the Game (Par., 1918)
   His Own Home Town (Par., 1918)
   The Claws of the Hun (Par., 1918)
   A Nine O'Clock Town (Ince-Triangle, 1918)

String Beans (Par., 1918)
Hard Boiled (Par., 1919)
The Home Breaker (Par., 1919)
The Lady of Red Butte (Par., 1919)
Other Men's Wives (Par., 1919)
The Sheriff's Son (Par., 1919)
Quicksand (Par., 1918)
Upstairs (Goldwyn, 1919)
When Doctors Disagree (Goldwyn, 1919)
The Peace of Roaring River (Goldwyn, 1919)
The Jinx (Goldwyn, 1919)
Pinto (Goldwyn, 1920)
The Blooming Angel (Goldwyn, 1920)
The Slim Princess (Goldwyn, 1920)
Made in Heaven (Goldwyn, 1921)
What Happened to Rosa? (Goldwyn, 1921)
The Concert (Goldwyn, 1921)
Beating the Game (Goldwyn, 1921)
Mr. Barnes of New York (Goldwyn, 1922)
Head Over Heels (Goldwyn, 1922)
The Bootlegger's Daughter (Associated Exhibitors, 1922)
Scandalous Tongues (Associated Exhibitors, 1922)
The Kingdom Within (W.W. Hodkinson, 1922)
The Lonely Road (FN, 1923)
The Scarlet Lily (FN, 1923)
Refuge (FN, 1923)
Dollar Devils (W.W. Hodkinson, 1923)
The Man Next Door (Vitagraph, 1923)
Long Live the King (Metro, 1923)
The Man Life Passed By (Metro, 1923)
Chastity (FN, 1924)
Bread (Metro-Goldwyn, 1924)
A Boy of Flanders (Metro-Goldwyn, 1924)
Frivolous Sal (FN, 1925)
Man and Maid (Metro-Goldwyn, 1925)
The Wheel (Fox, 1925)
Thunder Mountain (Fox, 1925)
The Golden Strain (FN, 1925)
Siberia (Fox, 1926)
The Lily (Fox, 1926)
The Return of Peter Grimm (Fox, 1926)
Stage Madness (Fox, 1927)
The Secret Studio (Fox, 1927)
The Heart of Salome (Fox, 1927)
The Showdown (Par., 1928)
Forgotten Faces (Par., 1928) (also producer)
Manhattan Cocktail (Par., 1928)
Fashions in Love (Par., 1929) (also co-songs)
Redskin (Par., 1929)
The Wheel of Life (Par., 1929) (also song)
Nothing But the Truth (Par., 1929)
The Laughing Lady (Par., 1929) (also song)
Safety in Numbers (Par., 1930)

Heads Up (Par., 1930) (also co-song)
Paramount on Parade (Par., 1930) (with Dorothy Arzner, Otto
    Brower, Edmund Goulding, Victor Heerman, Edwin Knopf,
    Rowland V. Lee, Ernst Lubitsch, Lothar Mendes, A. Ed-
    ward Sutherland, Frank Tuttle)
Friends and Lovers (RKO, 1931)
The Woman Between (RKO, 1931)
Strange Justice (RKO, 1932)
Uptown New York (Sono Art-World Wide, 1932)
Cocktail Hour (Col., 1933)
The Constant Woman (World Wide, 1933)
My Woman (Col., 1933)
Beloved (Univ., 1934) (also theme song)
One Night of Love (Col., 1934) (also theme song)
Let's Live Tonight (Col., 1935) (also songs)
Love Me Forever (Col., 1935) (also story, theme song)
The Music Goes Round (Col., 1936)
Something to Sing About (GN, 1937) (also story, music)
The Mikado (Univ., 1939)
Road to Singapore (Par., 1940)
Rhythm on the River (Par., 1940)
The Road to Zanzibar (Par., 1941)
Kiss the Boys Goodbye (Par., 1941)
Birth of the Blues (Par., 1941)
The Fleet's In (Par., 1942)

SCHOEDSACK, ERNEST B. (Ernest Beaumont Schoedsack), b. June
    8, 1893, Council Bluffs, Iowa.
    Grass (Par., 1925) (with Merian C. Cooper, Marguerite Harri-
        son) (also co-producer, co-camera)
    Chang (Par., 1927) (with Merian C. Cooper) (also co-producer,
        camera)
    The Four Feathers (Par., 1929) (with Merian C. Cooper, Lo-
        thar Mendes) (also co-producer)
    Rango (Par., 1931) (also producer)
    The Most Dangerous Game (RKO, 1932) (with Irving Pichel) (al-
        so co-producer)
    King Kong (RKO, 1933) (with Merian C. Cooper) (also co-pro-
        ducer)
    Son of Kong (RKO, 1933)
    Blind Adventure (RKO, 1933)
    Long Lost Father (RKO, 1934)
    The Last Days of Pompeii (RKO, 1935)
    Trouble in Morocco (Col., 1937)
    Outlaws of the Orient (Col., 1937)
    Dr. Cyclops (Par., 1940)
    Mighty Joe Young (RKO, 1949)
    This Is Cinerama (Cin., 1952) (uncredited for prologue)

SCHUNZEL, RHEINHOLD, b. Nov. 7, 1886, Amburg, Austria;
    d. Sept. 11, 1954.

Das Mädchen aus der Acker Strasse (Part I) (German, 1919)
  (also actor)
Maria Magdalene (German, 1919) (also actor)
Katherina die Grosse (German, 1920) (also co-script, actor)
Der Marquis d'Or (German, 1920) (also for own production
  company, actor)
Der Graf von Cagliostro (German, 1920) (also for own produc-
  tion company, actor)
Geld auf der Strasse (Austrian, 1921) (also actor)
Der Roman eines Dienstrmädchens (Austrian, 1921) (also actor)
Bertrüger des Volkes (German, 1921) (also actor)
Der Pantoffelheld (Austrian, 1922) (also actor)
Die Drei Marien und der Herr von Marana (Austrian, 1922)
  (also actor)
Alles für Geld [Fortune's Fool] (German, 1923) (also actor)
Winstarke 9 [Die Geschichte Einer reichen Erbin] (German,
  1924)
Die Frau für 24 Stunden (German, 1925) (also co-script)
Hallo Caesar! (German, 1926) (also for own production com-
  pany, co-script, actor)
In der Heimat da Gibt's Ein wildersehn! (German, 1926) (with
  Leo Mittler) (also for own production company, actor)
ÜB'immer Treu und Redlichkeit (German, 1927) (also for own
  production company, co-script, actor)
Gustav Mond-Du Gehst so Stille (German, 1927) (also for own
  production company, actor)
Don Juan in der Mädchenschule (German, 1928) (also for own
  production company, actor)
Peter, der Matrose (German, 1929) (also for own production
  company, actor)
Phantome des Glücks [Der Mann In Fesseln] (German, 1929)
  (also story, script)
Liebe im Ring (German, 1930)
Der Kleine Seitensprung (German, 1931) (also co-script)
Ronny (German, 1931) (also co-script)
Das Schöne Abenteuer (German, 1932) (also co-script)
Wie Sag Ich's Meinem Mann (German, 1932)
Viktor und Viktoria (German, 1933) (also script)
Georges et Georgette [French version of Viktor und Viktoria]
  (French, 1933)
Saison in Kairo (German, 1933)
Die Tochter Ihrer Exzellenz (German, 1934)
A Jeune Fille d'une Nuit [French version of Die Tochter Ihrer
  Exzellenz] (German, 1934)
Die Englische Heirat (German, 1934)
Amphitryon [Aus den Wolken Kommt das Gluck] (German, 1935)
  (also script)
Les Dieux S'Amusent [French version of Amphitryon] (French,
  1935) (also script)
Donogoo Tonka (German, 1935) (also script)
Das Mädchen Irene (German, 1936) (also co-script)
Land der Liebe (German, 1937) (also co-script)
Rich Man--Poor Girl (MGM, 1938)

Ice Follies of 1939 (MGM, 1939)
Balalaika (MGM, 1939)
New Wine (UA, 1941)

SCHUSTER, HAROLD, b. Aug. 1, 1902, Cherokee, Iowa.
    Dinner at the Ritz (20th, 1937)
    Wings of the Morning (20th, 1937)
    Swing That Cheer (Univ., 1938)
    Exposed (Univ., 1938)
    One Hour to Live (Univ., 1939)
    Framed (Univ., 1940)
    Zanzibar (Univ., 1940)
    Ma, He's Making Eyes at Me (Univ., 1940)
    South to Karanga (Univ., 1940)
    Diamond Frontier (Univ., 1940)
    A Very Young Lady (20th, 1941)
    Small Town Deb (20th, 1941)
    On the Sunny Side (20th, 1942)
    The Postman Didn't Ring (20th, 1942)
    Girl Trouble (20th, 1942)
    My Friend Flicka (20th, 1943)
    Marine Raiders (RKO, 1944)
    Breakfast in Hollywood (UA, 1946)
    The Tender Years (20th, 1947)
    So Dear to My Heart (RKO, 1948)
    Kid Monk Baroni (Realart, 1952)
    Jack Slade (AA, 1953)
    Loophole (AA, 1954)
    Security Risk (AA, 1954)
    Port of Hell (AA, 1954)
    Finger Man (AA, 1955)
    The Return of Jack Slade (AA, 1955)
    Hidden Jungle (RKO, 1955)
    Dragoon Wells Massacre (AA, 1957)
    Courage of Black Beauty (20th, 1957)
    Portland Exposé (AA, 1957)

SEARS, FRED F., b. July 7, 1913, Boston; d. Dec. 1, 1957.
    Horsemen of the Sierra (Col., 1949)
    Desert Vigilante (Col., 1949)
    Across the Badlands (Col., 1950)
    Raiders of Tomahawk Creek (Col., 1950)
    Lightning Guns (Col., 1950)
    Prairie Roundup (Col., 1951)
    Riding the Outlaw Trail (Col., 1951)
    Snake River Desperadoes (Col., 1951)
    Bonanza Town (Col., 1951)
    Pecos River (Col., 1951)
    Target Hong Kong (Col., 1952)
    Smokey Canyon (Col., 1952)
    The Hawk of Wild River (Col., 1952)

Last Train from Bombay (Col., 1952)
The Kid from Broken Gun (Col., 1952)
The 49th Man (Col., 1953)
Mission Over Korea (Col., 1953)
Sky Commando (Col., 1953)
The Nebraskan (Col., 1953)
Ambush at Tomahawk Gap (Col., 1953)
El Alamein (Col., 1953)
Massacre Canyon (Col., 1954)
Overland Pacific (UA, 1954)
The Miami Story (Col., 1954)
The Outlaw Stallion (Col., 1954)
Cell 2455, Death Row (Col., 1955)
Wyoming Renegade (Col., 1955)
Chicago Syndicate (Col., 1955)
Apache Ambush (Col., 1955)
Teenage Crime Wave (Col., 1955)
Inside Detroit (Col., 1955)
Fury at Gunsight Pass (Col., 1955)
The Werewolf (Col., 1955)
Rock Around the Clock (Col., 1956)
Earth vs. the Flying Saucers (Col., 1956)
Miami Exposé (Col., 1956)
Cha-Cha-Cha Boom! (Col., 1956)
Rumble on the Docks (Col., 1956)
Don't Knock the Rock (Col., 1956)
Utah Blaine (Col., 1957)
The Giant Claw (Col., 1957)
Calypso Heat Wave (Col., 1957)
The Night the World Exploded (Col., 1957)
Escape from San Quentin (Col., 1957)
The World Was His Jury (Col., 1958)
Going Steady (Col., 1958)
Crash Landing (Col., 1958)
Badman's Country (Col., 1958)
Ghost of the China Sea (Col., 1958)

SEATON, GEORGE, b. April 17, 1911, South Bend, Ind.
Billy Rose's Diamond Horseshoe (20th, 1945) (also script)
Junior Miss (20th, 1945) (also script)
The Shocking Miss Pilgrim (20th, 1946) (also script)
Miracle on 34th Street (20th, 1947) (also script)
Apartment for Peggy (20th, 1948) (also script)
Chicken Every Sunday (20th, 1949) (also co-script)
The Big Lift (20th, 1950) (also story, script)
For Heaven's Sake (20th, 1950) (also script)
Anything Can Happen (Par., 1952) (also co-script)
Little Boy Lost (Par., 1953) (also script)
The Country Girl (Par., 1954) (also co-producer, script)
The Proud and the Profane (Par., 1956) (also co-story, script)
Teacher's Pet (Par., 1958)
The Pleasure of His Compan'y (Par., 1961)

The Counterfeit Traitor (Par., 1961)
The Hook (MGM, 1963)
36 Hours (MGM, 1964) (also script)
What's So Bad About Feeling Good? (Univ., 1968) (also producer, co-story, co-script)
Airport (Univ., 1970) (also script) (with uncredited Henry Hathaway)
Showdown (Univ., 1973) (also producer)

SEDGWICK, EDWARD, b. Nov. 7, 1892, Galveston, Tex.; d. May 7, 1953.
Fantomas* (Fox, 1920)
Live Wires (Fox, 1921) (also co-story)
Bar Nothin' (Fox, 1921)
The Rough Diamond (Fox, 1921) (also co-story, script)
The Bearcat (Univ., 1922)
Chasing the Moon (Fox, 1922) (also co-story)
Boomerang Justice (Russell, 1922)
Do and Dare (Fox, 1922) (also script)
The Flaming Hour (Univ., 1922)
The First Degree (Univ., 1923)
Single Handed (Univ., 1923) (also story)
The Gentleman from America (Univ., 1923)
Romance Land (Fox, 1923)
Dead Game (Univ., 1923) (also story, script)
Blinky (Univ., 1923) (also script)
Out of Luck (Univ., 1923) (also story)
The Ramblin' Kid (Univ., 1923)
Shootin' for Love (Univ., 1923)
The Thrill Chaser (Univ., 1923) (also co-story)
Hook and Ladder (Univ., 1924) (also co-story)
Broadway or Bust (Univ., 1924) (also co-story)
Ride for Your Life (Univ., 1924)
40-Horse Hawkins (Univ., 1924) (also co-story, co-script)
Hit and Run (Univ., 1924) (also co-story, co-script)
The Sawdust Trail (Univ., 1924)
The Ridin' Kid from Powder River (Univ., 1924)
The Hurricane Kid (Univ., 1925)
The Saddle Hawk (Univ., 1925) (also co-story, co-script)
Let 'Er Buck (Univ., 1925) (also co-story, co-script)
Spook Ranch (Univ.-Jewel, 1925) (also co-story)
Lorraine of the Lions (Univ.-Jewel, 1925)
The Phantom of the Opera (Univ.-Jewel, 1925) (with Rupert Julian)
Two-Fisted Jones (Univ., 1925)
Under Western Skies (Univ.-Jewel, 1926) (also story)
The Flaming Frontier (Univ.-Jewel, 1926) (also story)
The Runaway Express (Univ.-Jewel, 1926)
Tin Hats (MGM, 1926) (also story)
The Bugle Call (MGM, 1927)
Slide, Kelly, Slide (MGM, 1927)
Spring Fever (MGM, 1927)

West Point (MGM, 1927)
Circus Rookies (MGM, 1928) (also co-story)
The Cameraman (MGM, 1928)
Spite Marriage (MGM, 1929)
Doughboys (MGM, 1930)
De Frente Marchen [Spanish version of Doughboys] (MGM, 1930)
Free and Easy (MGM, 1930)
Estrellados [Spanish version of Free and Easy] (MGM, 1930)
Remote Control (MGM, 1930) (uncredited, with Malcolm St.
  Clair, Nick Grinde)
Parlor, Bedroom and Bath (MGM, 1931)
A Dangerous Affair (MGM, 1931)
Maker of Men (MGM, 1931)
The Passionate Plumber (MGM, 1932)
Speak Easily (MGM, 1932)
Horse Play (Univ., 1933)
What, No Beer? (MGM, 1933)
Saturday's Millions (Univ., 1933)
I'll Tell the World (Univ., 1934)
The Poor Rich (Univ., 1934)
Here Comes the Groom (Par., 1934)
Death on the Diamond (MGM, 1934)
Father Brown--Detective (Par., 1935)
Murder in the Fleet (MGM, 1935) (also story)
The Virginia Judge (Par., 1935)
Mister Cinderella (MGM, 1936)
Pick a Star (MGM, 1937)
Riding on Air (RKO, 1937)
Fit for a King (RKO, 1937)
The Gladiator (Col., 1938)
Burn 'Em Up O'Connor (MGM, 1939)
Beware Spooks! (Col., 1939)
So You Won't Talk (Col., 1940)
Air Raid Wardens (MGM, 1943)
A Southern Yankee (MGM, 1948)
Ma and Pa Kettle Back on the Farm (Univ., 1951)

SEGAL, ALEX, b. July 1, 1915, Brooklyn, N.Y.
Ransom (MGM, 1956)
All the Way Home (Par., 1963)
Joy in the Morning (MGM, 1965)
Harlow (Magna, 1965)
Decisions! Decisions! (NBC-TV, 1971) (also producer)

SEITER, WILLIAM A., b. Feb. 8, 1895, New York City; d. July
    26, 1964.
The Kentucky Colonel (W.W. Hodkinson, 1920)
Hearts and Masks (FBO, 1921)
Passing Thru (Par., 1921)
The Foolish Age (Robertson-Cole, 1921) (also co-script)
Eden and Return (Robertson-Cole, 1921)

Boy Crazy (Robertson-Cole, 1922)
Gay and Devilish (Robertson-Cole, 1922)
The Understudy (FBO, 1922)
Up and At 'Em (FBO, 1922) (also co-story)
When Love Comes (FBO, 1922)
The Beautiful and Damned (WB, 1922)
Bell Boy 13 (Associated FN, 1923)
Little Church Around the Corner (WB, 1923)
Daddies (WB, 1924)
The White Sin (FBO, 1924)
His Forgotten Wife (FBO, 1924)
Listen Lester (Principal, 1924) (also co-adaptation)
Helen's Babies (Principal, 1924)
The Family Secret (Univ.-Jewel, 1924)
The Fast Worker (Univ.-Jewel, 1924)
The Mad Whirl (Univ.-Jewel, 1925)
Dangerous Innocence (Univ.-Jewel, 1925)
The Teaser (Univ.-Jewel, 1925)
Where Was I? (Univ.-Jewel, 1925)
What Happened to Jones (Univ.-Jewel, 1926)
Skinner's Dress Suit (Univ.-Jewel, 1926)
Rolling Home (Univ., 1926)
Take It from Me (Univ.-Jewel, 1926)
The Cheerful Fraud (Univ., 1927) (also co-script)
The Small Bachelor (Univ.-Jewel, 1927)
Out All Night (Univ.-Jewel, 1927)
Thanks for the Buggy Ride (Univ.-Jewel, 1928)
Good Morning, Judge (Univ.-Jewel, 1928)
Happiness Ahead (FN, 1928)
Waterfront (FN, 1928)
Outcast (FN, 1928)
Synthetic Sin (FN, 1929)
Why Be Good? (FN, 1929)
Prisoners (FN, 1929)
Smiling Irish Eyes (FN, 1929)
Footlights and Fools (FN, 1929)
The Love Racket (FN, 1929)
Strictly Modern (FN, 1930)
The Flirting Widow (FN, 1930)
Back Pay (FN, 1930)
Going Wild (FN, 1930)
The Truth About Youth (FN, 1930)
Sunny (FN, 1930)
Big Business Girl (FN, 1931)
Kiss Me Again (FN, 1931)
Going Wild (WB, 1931)
Too Many Cooks (RKO, 1931)
Full of Notions (RKO, 1931)
Caught Plastered (RKO, 1931)
Peach O'Reno (RKO, 1931)
Way Back Home (RKO, 1932)
Girl Crazy (RKO, 1932)
Young Bride (RKO, 1932)

Is My Face Red? (RKO, 1932)
Hot Saturday (Par., 1932)
If I Had a Million (Par., 1932) (with James Cruze, H. Bruce
    Humberstone, Ernst Lubitsch, Stephen Roberts, Norman
    Taurog)
Hello Everybody! (Par., 1933)
Diplomaniacs (RKO, 1933)
Professional Sweetheart (RKO, 1933)
Chance at Heaven (RKO, 1933)
Rafter Romance (RKO, 1934)
Sons of the Desert (MGM, 1934)
Love Birds (Univ., 1934)
Sing and Like It (RKO, 1934)
We're Rich Again (RKO, 1934)
The Richest Girl in the World (RKO, 1934)
Roberta (RKO, 1935)
The Daring Young Man (Fox, 1935)
Orchids to You (Fox, 1935)
In Person (RKO, 1935)
If You Could Only Cook (Col., 1935)
The Moon's Our Home (Par., 1936)
The Case Against Mrs. Ames (Par., 1936)
Dimples (20th, 1936)
Stowaway (20th, 1936)
This Is My Affair (20th, 1937)
Life of the Party (RKO, 1937)
Life Begins in College (20th, 1937)
Sally, Irene and Mary (20th, 1938)
Three Blind Mice (20th, 1938)
Thanks for Everything (20th, 1938)
Room Service (RKO, 1938)
Susannah of the Mounties (20th, 1939)
Allegheny Uprising (RKO, 1939)
It's a Date (Univ., 1940)
Hired Wife (Univ., 1940)
Nice Girl? (Univ., 1941)
Appointment for Love (Univ., 1941)
Broadway (Univ., 1942)
You Were Never Lovelier (Col., 1942)
A Lady Takes a Chance (RKO, 1943)
Destroyer (Col., 1943)
Belle of the Yukon (RKO, 1944) (also producer)
Four Jills in a Jeep (20th, 1944)
It's a Pleasure (RKO, 1945)
That Night With You (Univ., 1945)
The Affairs of Susan (Par., 1945)
Little Giant (Univ., 1946)
Lover Come Back (Univ., 1946)
I'll Be Yours (Univ., 1947)
Up in Central Park (Univ., 1948)
One Touch of Venus (Univ., 1948)
Borderline (Univ., 1950) (also producer)
Dear Brat (Par., 1951)

The Lady Wants Mink (Rep., 1953) (also producer)
Champ for a Day (Rep., 1953) (also producer)
Make Haste to Live (Rep., 1954) (also co-producer)

SEITZ, GEORGE B. (George Brackett Seitz), b. Jan. 3, 1888,
    Boston; d. July 8, 1944.
The Exploits of Elaine* (Pathé, 1914) (with Louis Gasnier)
The New Exploits of Elaine* (Pathé, 1915) (also script)
The Romance of Elaine* (Pathé, 1915) (also script)
The Last of the Carnabys (Pathé, 1917)
The Hunting of the Hawk (Pathé, 1917)
New York Nights (Pathé, 1917)
The Fatal Ring* (Pathé, 1917)
The House of Hate* (Pathé, 1918)
Getaway Kate (Pathé, 1918)
The Honest Thief (Pathé, 1918)
The Lightning Raider (Pathé, 1919) (also script)
The Black Secret* (Pathé, 1919)
Bound and Gagged* (Pathé, 1919) (also actor)
Pirate Gold* (Pathé, 1920) (also actor)
Rogues and Romance (Pathé, 1921) (also producer, actor)
The Sky Ranger* (Pathé, 1921) (also actor)
Hurricane Hutch* (Pathé, 1921)
Go Get 'Em Hutch* (Pathé, 1922) (also producer)
Plunder* (Pathé, 1922-1923) (also co-script)
Speed* (Pathé, 1922-1923)
The Way of a Man* (Pathé, 1923-1924) (also script)
Leather Stocking* (Pathé, 1924)
The Fortieth Door* (Pathé, 1924)
Galloping Hoofs* (Pathé, 1924)
Into the Net* (Pathé, 1925)
Sunken Sailor* (Pathé, 1925) (also producer)
Wild Horse Mesa (Par., 1925)
The Vanishing American (Par., 1925)
Desert Gold (Par., 1926) (also producer)
Pals in Paradise (PDC, 1926)
The Last Frontier (PDC, 1926)
The Ice Flood (Univ., 1926) (also co-script)
Jim the Conqueror (PDC, 1927)
Great Mail Robbery (FBO, 1927)
The Blood Ship (Col., 1927)
The Tigress (Col., 1927)
Isle of Forgotten Women (Col., 1927)
The Warning (Col., 1928) (also script)
Ransom (Col., 1928) (also story)
Beware of Blondes (Col., 1928)
The Circus Kid (Col., 1928)
Court Martial (Col., 1928)
Blockade (RKO, 1928)
Hey Rube! (FBO, 1929)
Black Magic (Fox, 1929)
The Murder on the Roof (Col., 1930)

Guilty? (Col., 1930)
Midnight Mystery (RKO, 1930)
Danger Lights (RKO, 1930)
The Drums of Jeopardy (Tiffany, 1931)
The Lion and the Lamb (Col., 1931)
Arizona (Col., 1931)
Shanghaied Love (Col., 1931)
Night Beat (Action, 1931)
Sally of the Subway (Mayfair, 1931) (also story, script, dialog)
Docks of San Francisco (Mayfair, 1932)
Sin's Pay Day (Mayfair, 1932)
Widow in Scarlet (Mayfair, 1932)
Passport to Paradise (Mayfair, 1932) (also story/script)
Treason (Col., 1933)
The Thrill Hunter (Col., 1933)
The Woman in His Life (MGM, 1933)
Lazy River (MGM, 1934)
The Fighting Ranger (Col., 1934)
Shadow of Doubt (MGM, 1935)
Only Eight Hours (MGM, 1935)
Times Square Lady (MGM, 1935)
Calm Yourself (MGM, 1935)
Woman Wanted (MGM, 1935)
Kind Lady (MGM, 1935)
Exclusive Story (MGM, 1936)
The Three Wise Guys (MGM, 1936)
The Last of the Mohicans (UA, 1936)
Mad Holiday (MGM, 1936)
Under Cover of Night (MGM, 1937)
The Thirteenth Chair (MGM, 1937)
A Family Affair (MGM, 1937)
Mama Steps Out (MGM, 1937)
Between Two Women (MGM, 1937)
My Dear Miss Aldrich (MGM, 1937)
You're Only Young Once (MGM, 1938)
Judge Hardy's Children (MGM, 1938)
Yellow Jack (MGM, 1938)
Love Finds Andy Hardy (MGM, 1938)
Out West With the Hardys (MGM, 1938)
The Hardys Ride High (MGM, 1939)
6,000 Enemies (MGM, 1939)
Thunder Afloat (MGM, 1939)
Judge Hardy and Son (MGM, 1939)
Kit Carson (UA, 1940)
Andy Hardy Meets Debutante (MGM, 1940)
Sky Murder (MGM, 1940)
Gallant Sons (MGM, 1940)
Andy Hardy's Private Secretary (MGM, 1941)
Life Begins for Andy Hardy (MGM, 1941)
The Courtship of Andy Hardy (MGM, 1942)
A Yank on the Burma Road (MGM, 1942)
Pierre of the Plains (MGM, 1942)
Andy Hardy's Double Life (MGM, 1942)
Andy Hardy's Blonde Trouble (MGM, 1944)

SEKELY, STEVE (István Szekely), b. Feb. 25, 1889, Budapest.
Rhapsodie der Liebe (Austrian, 1929)
Die Grosse Sehnsucht (German, 1930)
Seitensprünge (German, 1930)
Hyppolita Lakaj [Hungarian version of Seitensprünge] (Hungarian,
    1931)
Er und Sein Diener (German, 1931)
Ein Steinreicher Mann (German, 1931)
Piri Mindent Tud [Piry Knows Everything] (Hungarian, 1932)
Repulö Arany (Hungarian, 1932)
Rouletabille Aviateur [French version of Repulö Arany] (French,
    1932)
Scandal in Budapest [Romance in Budapest] (Hungarian, 1933)
Rakoczy-Marsh (German Austrian, 1933)
Rakoczi Indulo [Hungarian version of Rakoczy-Marsh] (Hungari-
    an, 1933)
Iza Néni (Hungarian, 1934)
Ida Regénye (Hungarian, 1934)
Lila Akac [Wisteria] (Hungarian, 1934)
Buzavirag [Cornflower] (Hungarian, 1934)
Emmy (Hungarian, 1934)
Ball im Savoy [Ball at the Savoy] (Austrian-Hungarian, 1934)
Cimzett Ismeretlen (Hungarian, 1934)
Legy Jo Mindhalalig [Be True Until Death] (Hungarian, 1936)
Cafe Moszkva [Cafe Moscow] (Hungarian, 1936)
Szenzacio (Hungarian, 1936) (with Laszlo Vajda)
Naszut Felaron [Half-Price Honeymoon] (Hungarian, 1936) (also
    co-script)
Dunaparti Randevu [River Rendezvous] (Hungarian, 1936)
Lovagias Ügy [An Affair of Honor] (Hungarian, 1937)
Egy Lany Elindul [A Girl's Start] (Hungarian, 1937)
Két Fogoly [Two Prisoners] (Hungarian, 1937)
A 111-Es (Hungarian, 1937)
Pusztai Szel [Winds of the Puszta] (Hungarian, 1937)
Szerelemböl Nosültem [I've Married for Love] (Hungarian, 1937)
Segitség Örököltem! [Help! I've Inherited] (Hungarian, 1937)
A Noszty für Esete Toth Marival (European co-production,
    1938)
A Miracle on Main Street (Col., 1940)
Revenge of the Zombies (Mon., 1943)
Women in Bondage (Mon., 1943)
Behind Prison Walls (PRC, 1943)
Waterfront (PRC, 1944)
Lake Placid Serenade (Rep., 1944)
Lady in the Death House (PRC, 1944)
My Buddy (Rep., 1944)
The Fabulous Suzanne (Rep., 1947)
Hollow Triumph [The Scar] (Eagle Lion, 1948)
Blonde Savage (Eagle Lion, 1948)
Amazon Quest (Film Classics, 1949)
Stronghold (Lip., 1952)
Furia Roja [Spanish version of Stronghold] (Mexican, 1952)
L'Avventure di Cartouche (Italian, 1954) (with Gianni Vernuccio)

La Peccatrice del Deserto (Italian, 1955) (with Gianni Vernuc-
cio)
The Blue Camillia (1955)
Missing Scientists (D.V.K. Films, 1955)
The Day of the Triffids (AA, 1963)
The Girl Who Liked Purple Flowers (Hungarian, 1973)

SELANDER, LESLEY, b. May 26, 1900, Los Angeles.
Ride 'Em Cowboy (Univ., 1936)
Empty Saddles (Univ., 1936)
The Boss Rider of Gun Creek (Univ., 1936)
Sandflow (Univ., 1937)
Left Handed Law (Univ., 1937)
Smoke Tree Range (Univ., 1937)
The Barrier (Par., 1937)
Hopalong Rides Again (Par., 1937)
The Mysterious Rider (Par., 1938)
Partners of the Plains (Par., 1938)
Cassidy of Bar 20 (Par., 1938)
Heart of Arizona (Par., 1938)
Bar 20 Justice (Par., 1938)
Pride of the West (Par., 1938)
Sunset Trail (Par., 1938)
The Frontiersman (Par., 1938)
Heritage of the Desert (Par., 1939)
Silver on the Sage (Par., 1939)
The Renegade Trail (Par., 1939)
Range War (Par., 1939)
Santa Fe Marshal (Par., 1940)
Hidden Gold (Par., 1940)
Stagecoach War (Par., 1940)
Three Men from Texas (Par., 1940)
Knights of the Range (Par., 1940)
The Light of the Western Stars (Mayer-Burstyn, 1940)
Cherokee Strip (Par., 1940)
The Round-Up (Par., 1941)
Doomed Caravan (Par., 1941)
Pirates on Horseback (Par., 1941)
Wide Open Town (Par., 1941)
Riders of the Timberline (Par., 1941)
Stick to Your Guns (Par., 1941)
Thundering Hoofs (RKO, 1941)
The Undercover Man (UA, 1942)
Bandit Ranger (RKO, 1942)
Lost Canyon (UA, 1942)
Comrades (UA, 1943)
Border Patrol (UA, 1943)
Colt Comrades (UA, 1943)
Bar 20 (UA, 1943)
Riders of the Deadline (UA, 1943)
Buckskin Frontier (UA, 1943)
Lumberjack (UA, 1944)

Riders of the Deadline (Rep. , 1944)
Forty Thieves (UA, 1944)
Borderline Trail (Rep. , 1944)
Call of the Rockies (Rep. , 1944)
Stagecoach to Monterey (Rep. , 1944)
Cheyenne Wildcat (Rep. , 1944)
Firebrands of Arizona (Rep. , 1944)
Sheriff of Las Vegas (Rep. , 1944)
Sheriff of Sundown (Rep. , 1944)
The Great Stagecoach Robbery (Rep. ,. 1945)
Phantom of the Plains (Rep. , 1945)
Trail of Kit Carson (Rep. , 1945)
The Vampire's Ghost (Rep. , 1945)
Jungle Raiders* (Col. , 1945)
The Catman of Paris (Rep. , 1946)
Passkey to Danger (Rep. , 1946)
Traffic in Crime (Rep. , 1946)
Night Train to Memphis (Rep. , 1946)
Out California Way (Rep. , 1946)
The Last Frontier Uprising (Rep. , 1946)
The Red Stallion (Eagle Lion, 1947)
Saddle Pals (Rep. , 1947)
Robin Hood in Texas (Rep. , 1947)
The Pilgrim Lady (Rep. , 1947)
Blackmail (Rep. , 1947)
Strike It Rich (AA, 1948)
Guns of Hate (RKO, 1948)
Indian Agent (RKO, 1948)
Panhandle (AA, 1948)
Belle Starr's Daughter (20th, 1948)
Rustlers (RKO, 1949)
Stampede (AA, 1949)
Sky Dragon (Mon. , 1949)
Brothers in the Saddle (RKO, 1949)
The Mysterious Desperado (RKO, 1949)
Masked Raiders (RKO, 1949)
Riders of the Range (RKO, 1949)
Storm Over Wyoming (RKO, 1950)
Rider from Tucson (RKO, 1950)
Rio Grande Patrol (RKO, 1950)
Law of the Badlands (RKO, 1950)
Dakota Lil (20th, 1950)
Short Grass (AA, 1950)
The Kangaroo Kid (Eagle Lion, 1950)
Cavalry Scout (Mon. , 1951)
Flight to Mars (Mon. , 1951)
The Highwayman (AA, 1951)
I Was an American Spy (AA, 1951)
Saddle Legion (RKO, 1951)
Gunplay (RKO, 1951)
Pistol Harvest (RKO, 1951)
Overland Telegraph (RKO, 1951)
Trail Guide (RKO, 1952)

Road Agent (RKO, 1952)
Desert Passage (RKO, 1952)
Fort Osage (Mon. , 1952)
The Raiders (Univ. , 1952)
The Riding Kid (UA, 1952)
Battle Zone (AA, 1952)
Flat Top (AA, 1952)
Fighter Attack (AA, 1953)
The Royal African Rifles (AA, 1953)
Fort Algiers (UA, 1953)
Cow Country (AA, 1953)
War Paint (UA, 1953)
Fort Vengeance (UA, 1953)
Arrow in the Dust (AA, 1954)
The Yellow Tomahawk (AA, 1954)
Dragonfly Squadron (AA, 1954)
Return from the Sea (AA, 1954)
Desert Sands (!A, 1955)
Shotgun (AA, 1955)
Tall Man Riding (WB, 1955)
Fort Yuma (UA, 1955)
The Broken Star (UA, 1956)
Quincannon, Frontier Scout (UA, 1956)
The Wayward Girl (Rep. , 1957)
Tomahawk Trail (UA, 1957)
Revolt at Fort Laramie (UA, 1957)
Outlaw's Son (UA, 1957)
Taming Sutton's Gal (Rep. , 1957)
The Lone Ranger and the Lost City of Gold (UA, 1958)
War Party (20th, 1965)
Convict Stage (20th, 1965)
Fort Courageous (20th, 1965)
Town Tamer (Par. , 1965)
The Texican (Col. , 1966)
Fort Utah (Par. , 1967)
Arizona Bushwhackers (Par. , 1968)

SENNETT, MACK (Michael Sinnott), b. Jan. 17, 1880, Richmond,
    Canada; d. Nov. 5, 1960.
    The Good-Bye Kiss (FN, 1928) (also co-script)

SHAVELSON, MELVILLE, b. April 1, 1917, Brooklyn, N.Y.
    The Seven Little Foys (Par. , 1955) (also co-script)
    Beau James (Par. , 1957) (also co-script)
    Houseboat (Par. , 1958) (also co-script)
    The Five Pennies (Par. , 1959) (also co-script)
    It Started in Naples (Par. , 1960) (also co-script)
    On the Double (Par. , 1961) (also co-script)
    The Pigeon That Took Rome (Par. , 1962) (also producer, script)
    A New Kind of Love (Par. , 1963) (also producer, script)
    Cast a Giant Shadow (UA, 1966) (also co-producer, script)

Yours, Mine and Ours (UA, 1968) (also co-script)
The War Between Men and Women (National General, 1972)
   (also co-script)

SHEAR, BARRY, b. New York City.
   Wild in the Streets (AIP, 1968)
   The Todd Killings (National General, 1971) (also co-producer)
   Across 110th Street (UA, 1972) (also co-producer)
   The Deadly Trackers (WB, 1973)

SHERMAN, GEORGE, b. July 14, 1908, New York City.
   Wild Horse Rodeo (Rep., 1938)
   The Purple Vigilantes (Rep., 1938)
   Outlaws of Sonora (Rep., 1938)
   Riders of the Black Hills (Rep., 1938)
   Heroes of the Hills (Rep., 1938)
   Pals of the Saddle (Rep., 1938)
   Overland Stage Raiders (Rep., 1938)
   Rhythm of the Saddle (Rep., 1938)
   Santa Fe Stampede (Rep., 1938)
   Red River Range (Rep., 1938)
   Mexicali Rose (Rep., 1939)
   The Night Riders (Rep., 1939)
   Three Texas Steers (Rep., 1939)
   Wyoming Outlaw (Rep., 1939)
   Colorado Sunset (Rep., 1939)
   New Frontier [Frontier Uprising] (Rep., 1939)
   Cowboys from Texas (Rep., 1939)
   The Kansas Terrors (Rep., 1939)
   Rovin Tumbleweeds (Rep., 1939)
   South of the Border (Rep., 1939)
   Ghost Valley Raiders (Rep., 1940) (also associate producer)
   One Man's Law (Rep., 1940) (also associate producer)
   The Tulsa Kid (Rep., 1940) (also associate producer)
   Texas Terrors (Rep., 1940) (also associate producer)
   Covered Wagon Days (Rep., 1940) (also associate producer)
   Rocky Mountain Rangers (Rep., 1940) (also associate producer)
   Under Texas Skies (Rep., 1940) (also associate producer)
   The Trail Blazers (Rep., 1940) (also associate producer)
   Lone Star Raiders (Rep., 1940) (also associate producer)
   Frontier Vengeance (Rep., 1940) (associate producer only)
   Wyoming Wildcat (Rep., 1941) (also associate producer)
   The Phantom Cowboy (Rep., 1941) (also associate producer)
   Two Gun Sheriff (Rep., 1941) (also associate producer)
   Desert Bandit (Rep., 1941) (also associate producer)
   Kansas Cyclone (Rep., 1941) (also associate producer)
   Death Valley Outlaws (Rep., 1941) (also associate producer)
   A Missouri Outlaw (Rep., 1941) (also asociate producer)
   Citadel of Crime (Rep., 1941)
   The Apache Kid (Rep., 1941) (also associate producer)
   Arizona Terrors (Rep., 1942) (also associate producer)

Stagecoach Express (Rep., 1942) (also associate producer)
Jesse James Jr. (Rep., 1942) (also associate producer)
The Cyclone Kid (Rep., 1942) (also associate producer)
The Sombrero Kid (Rep., 1942) (also associate producer)
X Marks the Spot (Rep., 1942) (also associate producer)
London Blackout Murders (Rep., 1942)
The Purple V (Rep., 1943) (also associate producer)
The Mantrap (Rep., 1943) (also associate producer)
The West Side Kid (Rep., 1943)
Mystery Broadcast (Rep., 1943) (also associate producer)
The Lady and the Monster (Rep., 1944) (also associate producer)
Storm Over Lisbon (Rep., 1944) (also associate producer)
The Crime Doctor's Courage (Col., 1945)
The Gentleman Misbehaves (Col., 1946)
Renegades (Col., 1946)
Talk About a Lady (Col., 1946)
The Bandit of Sherwood Forest (Col., 1946) (with Henry Levin)
Personality Kid (Col., 1947)
Secrets of the Whistler (Col., 1947)
Last of the Redmen (Col., 1947)
Relentless (Col., 1948)
Black Bart (Univ., 1948)
River Lady (Univ., 1948)
Larceny (Univ., 1948)
Red Canyon (Univ., 1949)
Calamity Jane and Sam Bass (Univ., 1949) (also story)
Yes Sir That's My Baby (Univ., 1949)
Sword in the Desert (Univ., 1949)
Spy Hunt (Univ., 1950)
The Sleeping City (Univ., 1950)
Feudin', Fussin' and A-Fightin' (Univ., 1950)
Comanche Territory (Univ., 1950)
Tomahawk (Univ., 1951)
Target Unknown (Univ., 1951)
The Raging Tide (Univ., 1951)
The Golden Horde (Univ., 1951)
Steel Town (Univ., 1952)
Against All Flags (Univ., 1952)
The Battle at Apache Pass (Univ., 1952)
Back at the Front (Univ., 1952)
The Lone Hand (Univ., 1953)
War Arrow (Univ., 1953)
Veils of Bagdad (Univ., 1953)
Border River (Univ., 1954)
Dawn at Socorro (Univ., 1954)
Chief Crazy Horse (Univ., 1955)
Count Three and Pray (Univ., 1955)
The Treasure of Pancho Villa (Univ., 1955)
Comanche (UA, 1956)
Reprisal! (Col., 1956)
The Hard Man (Col., 1957)
The Last of the Fast Guns (Univ., 1958)

Ten Days to Tulara (UA, 1958) (also co-producer)
The Son of Robin Hood (20th, 1959) (also producer)
The Flying Fontaines (Col., 1959)
Hell Bent for Leather (Univ., 1960)
For the Love of Mike (20th, 1960) (also producer)
The Enemy General (Col., 1960)
The Wizard of Baghdad (20th, 1960)
The Fiercest Heart (20th, 1961) (also producer)
Panic Button (Gorton, 1964)
Murieta [Vendetta] (WB, 1965)
Daniel Boone, Trail Blazer (Univ., 1966)
Smoky (20th, 1966)
Snowjob (Cin., 1970)
Big Jake (WB, 1971)

SHERMAN, LOWELL, b. Oct. 11, 1885, San Francisco; d. Dec.
    28, 1934.
Lawful Larceny (RKO, 1930) (also actor)
The Pay Off (RKO, 1930) (also actor)
The Royal Bed (RKO, 1931) (also actor)
Bachelor Apartment (RKO, 1931) (also actor)
High Stakes (RKO, 1931) (also actor)
The Greeks Had a Word for Them (UA, 1932) (also actor)
False Faces (Sono Art-World Wide, 1932) (also producer, actor)
Ladies of the Jury (RKO, 1932)
She Done Him Wrong (Par., 1933)
Morning Glory (RKO, 1933)
Broadway Thru a Keyhole (UA, 1933)
Born to be Bad (UA, 1934)
Night Life of the Gods (Univ., 1935)
Becky Sharp (RKO, 1935) (died during production; film already
    shot scrapped, restarted with Rouben Mamoulian)

SHERMAN, VINCENT, b. July 16, 1906, Vienna, Ga.
The Return of Doctor X (WB, 1939)
Saturday's Children (WB, 1940)
The Man Who Talked Too Much (WB, 1940)
Flight from Destiny (WB, 1941)
Underground (WB, 1941)
All Through the Night (WB, 1942)
The Hard Way (WB, 1942)
Old Acquaintance (WB, 1943)
In Our Time (WB, 1944)
Mr. Skeffington (WB, 1945)
Pillow to Post (WB, 1945)
Nora Prentiss (WB, 1947)
The Unfaithful (WB, 1947)
The Adventures of Don Juan (WB, 1949)
The Hasty Heart (WB, 1949)
Backfire (WB, 1950)
The Damned Don't Cry (WB, 1950)

Harriet Craig (Col., 1950)
The Lone Star (MGM, 1951)
Goodby My Fancy (WB, 1951)
Affair in Trinidad (Col., 1952)
The Garment Jungle (Col., 1957) (with Robert Aldrich)
The Naked Earth (20th, 1958)
The Young Philadelphians (WB, 1959)
Ice Palace (WB, 1960)
A Fever in the Blood (WB, 1961)
The Second Time Around (20th, 1961)
Cervantes--The Young Rebel (1967--unreleased)

SHUMLIN, HERMAN, b. Dec. 6, 1896, Atwood, Colo.
Watch on the Rhine (WB, 1943)
Confidential Agent (WB, 1945)

SIDNEY, GEORGE, b. Oct. 14, 1916, New York City.
Free and Easy (MGM, 1941)
Pacific Rendezvous (MGM, 1942)
Pilot No. 5 (MGM, 1943)
Thousands Cheer (MGM, 1943)
Bathing Beauty (MGM, 1944)
Anchors Aweigh (MGM, 1945)
The Harvey Girls (MGM, 1946)
Holiday in Mexico (MGM, 1946)
Cass Timberlane (MGM, 1947)
The Three Musketeers (MGM, 1948)
The Red Danube (MGM, 1949) (also story)
Annie Get Your Gun (MGM, 1950)
Key to the City (MGM, 1950)
Show Boat (MGM, 1951)
Scaramouche (MGM, 1952)
Kiss Me, Kate (MGM, 1953)
Young Bess (MGM, 1953)
Jupiter's Darling (MGM, 1955)
The Eddie Duchin Story (Col., 1956)
Jeanne Eagles (Col., 1957) (also producer)
Pal Joey (Col., 1957)
Who Was That Lady? (Col., 1960)
Pepe (Col., 1960)
Bye Bye Birdie (Col., 1963)
A Ticklish Affair (MGM, 1963)
Viva Las Vegas (MGM, 1964) (also co-producer)
Who Has Seen the Wind? (ABC-TV, 1965) (also producer)
The Swinger (Par., 1966) (also producer)
Half a Sixpence (Par., 1968) (also co-producer)

SIEGEL, DONALD (Don), b. Oct. 26, 1912, Chicago.
The Verdict (WB, 1946)
Night Unto Night (WB, 1947)

Rita Hayworth studies script with George Sidney for Pal Joey (Col.,
1957).

The Big Steal (RKO, 1949)
Duel at Silver Creek (Univ., 1952)
No Time for Flowers (RKO, 1952)
Count the Hours (RKO, 1953)
China Venture (Col., 1953)
Riot in Cell Block 11 (AA, 1954)
Private Hell 36 (Filmmakers, 1954)
Annapolis Story (AA, 1955)
Invasion of the Body Snatchers (AA, 1956)
Crime in the Streets (AA, 1956)
Baby Face Nelson (UA, 1957)
Spanish Affair (Par., 1957)
The Lineup (Col., 1958)
The Gun Runners (UA, 1958)
Hound Dog Man (20th, 1959)
Edge of Eternity (Col., 1959) (also associate producer)
Flaming Star (20th, 1960)

Dolores Del Rio and producer David Weisbart (right) with Don Siegel off the set for <u>Flaming Star</u> (20th, 1960).

Hell Is for Heroes (Par., 1962)
The Killers (Univ., 1964) (also producer)
The Hanged Man (NBC-TV, 1964)
Stranger on the Run (NBC-TV, 1967)
Madigan (Univ., 1968)
Coogan's Bluff (Univ., 1968)
Death of a Gunfighter (Univ., 1969) (replaced Robert Totten)
Two Mules for Sister Sara (Univ., 1970)
The Beguiled (Univ., 1971) (also producer)
Dirty Harry (WB, 1971) (also producer)
Charley Verrick (Univ., 1973) (also producer)

SILVERSTEIN, ELLIOT, b. 1927, Boston.
Belle Sommers (Col., 1962)
Cat Ballou (Col., 1965)
The Happening (Col., 1967)
A Man Called Horse (National General, 1970)

SIMON, S. SYLVAN, b. March 9, 1910, Chicago; d. May 17, 1951.
A Girl With Ideas (Univ., 1937)
Prescription for Romance (Univ., 1937)
Nurse from Brooklyn (Univ., 1938)
The Crime of Dr. Hallet (Univ., 1938)
The Road to Reno (Univ., 1938)
Spring Madness (MGM, 1938)

Four Girls in White (MGM, 1939)
The Kid from Texas (MGM, 1939)
These Glamour Girls (MGM, 1939)
Dancing Coed (MGM, 1939)
Two Girls on Broadway (MGM, 1940)
Sporting Blood (MGM, 1940)
Dulcy (MGM, 1940)
Keeping Company (MGM, 1941)
Washington Melodrama (MGM, 1941)
Whispering in the Dark (MGM, 1941)
The Bugle Sounds (MGM, 1941)
Rio Rita (MGM, 1942)
Grand Central Murder (MGM, 1942)
Tish (MGM, 1942)
Whistling in Dixie (MGM, 1942)
Whistling in Brooklyn (MGM, 1943)
Salute to the Marines (MGM, 1943)
Song of the Open Road (UA, 1944)
Bud Abbott and Lou Costello in Hollywood (MGM, 1945)
Son of Lassie (MGM, 1945)
The Cockeyed Miracle (MGM, 1946)
The Thrill of Brazil (Col., 1946)
Bad Bascomb (MGM, 1946)
Her Husband's Affair (Col., 1947)
I Love Trouble (Col., 1947) (also producer)
The Fuller Brush Man (Col., 1948) (also producer)
For Those Who Dare (Col., 1949) (also producer)
Lust for Gold (Col., 1949) (also producer)

SINGER, ALEXANDR, b. 1932, New York City.
A Cold Wind in August (Aidart, 1961)
Psyche 59 (Col., 1964)
Love Has Many Faces (Col., 1965)

SIODMAK, CURT (Kurt Siodmak), b. Aug. 10, 1902, Dresden,
    Germany.
Bride of the Gorilla (Realart, 1951) (also script)
The Magnetic Monster (UA, 1953) (also co-script)
Curucu, Beast of the Amazon (Univ., 1956) (also script)
Love Slaves of the Amazon (Univ., 1957) (also producer,
    script)
The Devil's Messenger (Herts-Lion, 1962) (with Herbert L.
    Strock) (also co-script)
Ski Fever (AA, 1969) (also co-script)

SIODMAK, ROBERT, b. Aug. 8, 1900, Memphis; d. Mar. 10, 1973.
Menchen am Sonntag (German, 1929) (with Edgar G. Ulmer)
    (also story, co-script)
Abschied [So Sind die Menschen] (German, 1930)
Der Mann, der Seimen Morder Sucht (German, 1931)

Voruntersuchung (German, 1931)
Stürme der Leidenschaft [Tempest] (German, 1932)
Quick (German, 1932) (also French version, 1932)
Brennendes Geheimmis [The Burning Secret] (German, 1933)
Le Sexe Faible (French, 1934)
La Crise Est Finie [The Slump Is Over] (French, 1934)
La Vie Parisienne (French, 1936)
Mister Flow [Compliments of Mr. Flow] (French, 1936)
Cargaison Blanche [Woman Racket] (French, 1937)
Mollenard [Hatred] (French, 1938)
Ultimatum (French, 1938)
Pièges [Personal Column] (French, 1939)
West Point Widow (Par., 1941)
Fly By Night (Par., 1942)
The Night Before the Divorce (20th, 1942)
My Heart Belongs to Daddy (Par., 1942)
Someone to Remember (Rep., 1943)
Son of Dracula (Univ., 1943)
Cobra Woman (Univ., 1944)
Phantom Lady (Univ., 1944)
Christmas Holiday (Univ., 1944)
The Suspect (Univ., 1945)
Conflict (WB, 1945) (also co-story treatment)
The Strange Affair of Uncle Harry (Univ., 1945)
The Spiral Staircase (RKO, 1945)
The Killers (Univ., 1946)
The Dark Mirror (Univ., 1946)
Time Out of Mind (Univ., 1947)
Cry of the City (20th, 1948)
Criss Cross (Univ., 1949)
The Great Sinner (MGM, 1949)
The File on Thelma Jordan (Par., 1950)
Deported (Univ., 1950)
The Whistle at Eaton Falls (Col., 1951)
The Crimson Pirate (WB, 1952)
Le Grand Jeu [Flesh and Woman] (French, 1954)
Die Ratten (German, 1955)
Mein Vater, der Schauaspieler (German, 1956)
Nachts, Wenn der Teufel Kam [The Devil Strikes at Night]
    (German, 1957)
Dorothea Augermann (German, 1959)
The Rough and the Smooth [Portrait of a Sinner] (Renown, 1959)
Katya [Magnificent Sinner] (German, 1960)
L'Affaire Nina B (European co-production, 1961)
Der Schut (European co-production, 1964)
Der Schatz der Azteken (European co-production, 1965)
Die Pyramide des Sonnengottes (European co-production, 1965)
Custer of the West (Cin., 1967)
Der Kampf um Rom (German-Italian; released in two parts in
    1968 and 1969)

SIRK, DOUGLAS (Dietlef Sierck or Detelev Sierck), b. April 26,
    1900, Skagen, Denmark.
    April, April (German, 1935)
    Das Mädchen Vom Moorhof (German, 1935)
    Stützen der Gesellschaft (German, 1935)
    Das Hofkonzert (German, 1936) (also co-script)
    La Chanson du Souvenir (French, 1936
    Schlussakkord (German, 1936) (also script)
    La Habanera (German, 1937)
    Liebling der Matrosen (German, 1937) (also co-script)
    Zu Neuen Ufern (German, 1937) (also co-script)
    Hitler's Madman (MGM, 1943)
    Summer Storm (UA, 1944) (also co-script)
    A Scandal in Paris (UA, 1946)
    Lured (UA, 1947)
    Sleep, My Love (UA, 1948)
    Siren of Atlantis (UA, 1948) (uncredited, with Gregg Tallas)
    Shockproof (Col., 1949)
    Slightly French (Col., 1949)
    Mystery Submarine (Univ., 1950)
    The First Legion (UA, 1951) (also co-producer)
    Thunder on the Hill (Univ., 1951)
    The Lady Pays Off (Univ., 1951)
    Weekend With Father (Univ., 1951)
    No Room for the Groom (Univ., 1952)
    Has Anybody Seen My Gal? (Univ., 1952)
    Meet Me at the Fair (Univ., 1952)
    Take Me to Town (Univ., 1953)
    All I Desire (Univ., 1953)
    Taza, Son of Cochise (Univ., 1954)
    Magnificent Obsession (Univ., 1954)
    Sign of the Pagan (Univ., 1954)
    Captain Lightfoot (Univ., 1955)
    All That Heaven Allows (Univ., 1955)
    There's Always Tomorrow (Univ., 1956)
    Never Say Goodbye (Univ., 1956) (uncredited with Jerry Hopper)
    Written on the Wind (Univ., 1956)
    Battle Hymn (Univ., 1957)
    Interlude (Univ., 1957)
    The Tarnished Angels (Univ., 1957)
    A Time to Love and a Time to Die (Univ., 1958)
    Imitation of Life (Univ., 1959)

SJOSTROM, VICTOR (Victor Seastrom), b. Sept. 20, 1879, Arjang,
    Sweden; d. Jan. 3, 1960.
    Trägdgårdsmästaren (Swedish, 1912) (also actor)
    Ett Hemligt Giftermål (Swedish, 1912)
    En Sommarsaga (Swedish, 1912)
    Lady Marions Sommarflirt (Swedish, 1912) (also actor)
    Löjen och Tårar (Swedish, 1912)
    Aktenskapsbyrån (Swedish, 1913) (also script)
    Blodets Röst (Swedish, 1913) (also actor)

Ingeborg Holm (Swedish, 1913) (also script)
Livets Konflickter (Swedish, 1913) (also actor)
Halvblod (Swedish, 1913)
Miraklet (Swedish, 1913)
Dömen Icke (Swedish, 1914)
Prästen (Swedish, 1914)
Bra Flicka Reder Sig Själv (Swedish, 1914) (also script)
Gatans Barn (Swedish, 1914)
Högfjällets Dotter (Swedish, 1914) (also script, actor)
Hjärtan Som Mötas (Swedish, 1914)
Strejken (Sedish, 1914) (also co-script, actor)
Judaspengar (Swedish, 1915)
En av de Mänga (Swedish, 1915) (also script)
Sonad Skuld (Swedish, 1915) (also script)
Landschövdingens Döttrar (Swedish, 1915) (also script)
Havsgamarna (Swedish, 1915)
I Prövningens Stund (Swedish, 1916) (also script, actor)
Skepp Som Mötas (Swedish, 1916)
Hon Segrade (Swedish, 1916) (also script, actor)
Therese (Swedish, 1916) (also co-script)
Dödskyssen (Sedish, 1917) (also co-script, actor)
Terje Vigen (Swedish, 1917) (also actor)
Tösen från Stormyrtorpet (Swedish, 1917) (also co-script)
Berg-Ejvind och Hans Hustru (Swedish, 1918) (also co-script,
    actor)
Ingemarssönerna I & II (Swedish, 1919) (also script, actor)
Hans Nåds Testamente (Swedish, 1919) (also co-script)
Klostret i Sendomir (Swedish, 1920) (also script)
Karin Ingemarsdotter (Swedish, 1920) (also co-script, actor)
Mästerman (Swedish, 1920) (also actor)
Korkarlen (Swedish, 1921) (also script, actor)
Vem Dömer? (Swedish, 1922) (also co-script)
Det Omringade Huset (Swedish, 1922) (also co-script, actor)
Eld Ombord (Swedish, 1923) (also actor)
He Who Gets Slapped (Metro-Goldwyn, 1924) (also co-script)
    (as Victor Seastrom)
Name the Man (Metro-Goldwyn, 1924) (as Victor Seastrom)
Confessions of a Queen (Metro-Goldwyn, 1925) (as Victor Seas-
    trom)
Tower of Lies (Metro-Goldwyn, 1925) (as Victor Seastrom)
The Scarlet Letter (MGM, 1926) (as Victor Seastrom)
The Wind (MGM, 1928) (as Victor Seastrom)
The Divine Woman (MGM, 1928) (as Victor Seastrom)
Marks of the Devil (MGM, 1928) (as Victor Seastrom)
A Lady to Love (MGM, 1930)
Markurells I Wadköping (Swedish, 1930)
Väter und Söhne [German version of Markurells i Wadkopking]
    (Swedish, 1930)
Under the Red Robe (20th, 1937)

SLOMAN, EDWARD, b. July 19, 1887, London.
Philip Holden, Waster (American Mutual, 1916)

A Woman's Daring (American Mutual, 1916)
The Twinkler (American Mutual, 1916)
Lying Lips (American Mutual, 1916)
Pride and the Man (American Mutual, 1917)
My Fighting Gentleman (American Mutual, 1917)
The Frame-Up (American Mutual, 1917)
Sands of Sacrifice (American Mutual, 1917)
The Sea Master (American Mutual, 1917)
Snap Judgment (American Mutual, 1917)
New York Luck (American Mutual, 1917)
In Bad (American Mutual, 1918)
The Midnight Trail (American Mutual, 1918)
A Bit of Jade (American Mutual, 1918)
Social Briars (American Mutual, 1918)
The Ghost of Rosy Taylor (Mutual, 1918)
Fair Enough (Pathé, 1918)
Mantle of Charity (Pathé, 1918)
Money Isn't Everything (Pathé, 1918)
Molly of the Follies (Pathé, 1919)
Put Up Your Hands (Pathé, 1919)
Sandy Burke of the U-Bar-U (Goldwyn, 1919)
The Westerners (W.W. Hodkinson, 1919)
Slam Bang Jim (Pathé, 1920)
The Star Rover (Metro, 1920)
The Sagebrusher (W.W. Hodkinson, 1920)
Burning Daylight (Metro, 1920)
The Luck of Geraldine Laird (Robertson-Cole, 1920)
Blind Youth (National, 1920)
The Mutiny of the Elsinore (Metro, 1920)
The Marriage of William Ashe (Metro, 1921)
High Gear Jeffrey (American, 1921)
Quick Action (American, 1921)
The Other Woman (W.W. Hodkinson, 1921)
Pilgrims of the Night (Associated Producers, 1921) (also
    script)
The Ten Dollar Raise (Associated Producers, 1921)
Shattered Idols (Associated FN, 1922)
The Woman He Loved (American Releasing, 1922)
The Last Hour (Mastodon, 1923) (also presenter)
Backbone (Goldwyn, 1923)
The Eagle's Feather (Metro, 1923)
The Price of Pleasure (Univ.-Jewel, 1925)
Up the Ladder (Univ.-Jewel, 1925)
The Storm Breaker (Univ.-Jewel, 1925)
His People (Univ.-Jewel, 1925)
The Beautiful Cheat (Univ.-Jewel, 1926)
The Old Soak (Univ.-Jewel, 1926)
Butterflies in the Rain (Univ.-Jewel, 1926)
Surrender (Univ.-Jewel, 1927)
Alias the Deacon (Univ.-Jewel, 1928)
The Foreign Legion (Univ., 1928)
We Americans (Univ.-Jewel, 1928) (also continuity)
The Girl on the Barge (Univ.-Jewel, 1929)

The Lost Zeppelin (Tiffany, 1929)
Hell's Island (Col., 1930)
The Kibitzer (Par., 1930)
Puttin' on the Ritz (UA, 1930)
Soldiers and Women (Col., 1930)
Gun Smoke (Par., 1931)
The Conquering Horde (Par., 1931)
Murder By the Clock (Par., 1931)
Caught (Par., 1931)
His Woman (Par., 1931)
Wayward (Par., 1932)
There's Always Tomorrow (Univ., 1934)
A Dog of Flanders (RKO, 1935)

SMIGHT, JACK, b. March 9, 1926, Minneapolis, Minn.
I'd Rather Be Rich (Univ., 1964)
The Third Day (WB, 1965) (also producer)
Harper (WB, 1966)
Kaleidoscope (WB, 1966)
No Way to Treat a Lady (Par., 1968)
Strategy of Terror (NBC-TV, 1969)
The Secret War of Harry Frigg (Univ., 1968)
The Illustrated Man (WB-7 Arts, 1969)
The Traveling Executioner (MGM, 1970) (also producer)
Rabbit Run (WB, 1970)
The Longest Night (ABC-TV, 1972)
The Screaming Woman (ABC-TV, 1972)
Banacek (NBC-TV, 1972)
Dr. Frankenstein (NBC-TV, 1973)

SMITH, CLIFFORD S., b. Aug. 22, 1894, Lansing, Mich.; d.
    Sept. 17, 1937.
The Disciple (Triangle, 1915)
The Return of Draw Egan (Triangle, 1915)
The Patriot (Triangle, 1916) (with W.S. Hart)
Hell's Hinges (Triangle, 1916) (with Reginald Barker)
The Cold Deck (Triangle, 1917)
Truthful Tulliver (Triangle, 1917) (with W.S. Hart)
The Devil Dodger (Triangle, 1917)
One Shot Ross (Triangle, 1917)
The Medicine Man (Triangle, 1917)
The Learnin' of Jim Benton (Triangle, 1917)
The Boss of the Lazy "Y" (Triangle, 1917)
Law's Outlaw (Triangle, 1918)
Keith of the Border (Triangle, 1918)
A Faith Endurin' (Triangle, 1918)
Paying His Debt (Triangle, 1918)
Wolves of the Border (Triangle, 1918)
A Red-Hair Cupid (Triangle, 1918)
The Fly God (Triangle, 1918)
By Proxy (Triangle, 1918)

Cactus Crandall (Triangle, 1918)
The Pretender (Triangle, 1918)
Silent Rider (Triangle, 1918
Untamed (Triangle, 1918)
The She-Wolf (Frohman, 1919)
The Cyclone (Fox, 1920)
The Lone Hand (Alexander, 1920)
Three Gold Coins (Fox, 1920)
The Girl Who Dared (Selznick, 1920)
Vanishing Maid (Arrow, 1921)
Western Hearts (Associated Photoplays, 1921) (also for pro-
     duction company, story, continuity)
Crossing Trails (Associated Photoplays, 1921) (also for pro-
     duction company)
The Stranger in Canyon Valley (Arrow, 1921)
Daring Danger (American Releasing, 1922) (also producer)
My Dad (FBO, 1922) (also producer)
Scarred Hands (Madoc Sales, 1923) (also actor)
Wild Bill Hickok (Par., 1923)
The Back Trail (Univ., 1924)
Singer Jim McKee (Par., 1924)
Ridgeway of Montana (Univ., 1924)
The Western Wallop (Univ., 1924)
Fighting Fury (Univ., 1924)
Daring Chances (Univ., 1924)
Flying Hoops (Univ., 1925)
A Roaring Adventure (Univ., 1925)
The White Outlaw (Univ., 1925)
Ridin' Thunder (Univ., 1925)
Bustin' Thru (Univ., 1925)
The Red Rider (Univ., 1925)
The Call of Courage (Univ., 1925)
The Sign of the Cactus (Univ., 1925)
Don Daredevil (Univ., 1925)
The Arizona Sweepstakes (Univ.-Jewel, 1926)
Rustlers' Ranch (Univ., 1926)
Sky High Corral (Univ., 1926) (also script)
The Fighting Peacemaker (Univ., 1926)
The Phantom Bullet (Univ.-Jewel, 1926)
The Man in the Saddle (Univ.-Jewel, 1926)
The Ridin' Rascal (Univ., 1926)
The Set-Up (Univ., 1926)
The Scrappin' Kid (Univ., 1926)
The Terror (Univ., 1926)
A Six Shootin' Romance (Univ., 1926)
The Desert's Toll (MGM, 1926)
The Valley of Hell (Univ., 1927)
Spurs and Saddle (Univ., 1927)
Loco Luck (Univ., 1927)
Open Range (Par., 1927)
The Three Outcasts (Bell, 1929)
Ace Drummond* (Univ., 1936) (with Ford Beebe)
The Adventures of Frank Merriwell* (Univ., 1936)

Jungle Jim* (Univ., 1937) (with Ford Beebe)
Radio Patrol* (Univ., 1937) (with Ford Beebe)
Secret Agent X-9* (Univ., 1937) (with Ford Beebe)
Wild West Days* (Univ., 1937) (with Ford Beebe)

SPRINGSTEEN, R.G., b. Sept. 8, 1904, Tacoma, Wash.
Marshal of Laredo (Rep., 1945)
Colorado Pioneers (Rep., 1945)
Wagon Wheels Westward (Rep., 1945)
California Gold Rush (Rep., 1946)
Stagecoach to Denver (Rep., 1946)
Sheriff of Redwood Valley (Rep., 1946)
Home on the Range (Rep., 1946)
Sun Valley Cyclone (Rep., 1946)
Man from Rainbow Valley (Rep., 1946)
Conquest of Cheyenne (Rep., 1946)
Vigilantes of Boomtown (Rep., 1947)
Homesteaders of Paradise Valley (Rep., 1947)
Oregon Trail Scouts (Rep., 1947)
Rustlers of Devil's Canyon (Rep., 1947)
Marshal of Crippled Creek (Rep., 1947)
Along the Oregon Trail (Rep., 1947)
Under Colorado Skies (Rep., 1947)
Sundown at Santa Fe (Rep., 1948)
Renegades of Sonora (Rep., 1948)
Heart of Virginia (Rep., 1948)
The Main Street Kid (Rep., 1948)
Secret Service Investigator (Rep., 1948)
Son of God's Country (Rep., 1948)
Out of the Storm (Rep., 1948)
Flame of Youth (Rep., 1949)
The Red Menace (Rep., 1949)
Sheriff of Wichita (Rep., 1949)
Death Valley Gunfighters (Rep., 1949)
Hellfire (Rep., 1949)
Navajo Trail Raiders (Rep., 1949)
Singing Guns (Rep., 1950)
The Arizona Cowboy (Rep., 1950)
Hills of Oklahoma (Rep., 1950)
Covered Wagon Raid (Rep., 1950)
Harbor of Missing Men (Rep., 1950)
Frisco Tornado (Rep., 1950)
Belle of Old Mexico (Rep., 1950)
Honeychile (Rep., 1951)
Million Dollar Pursuit (Rep., 1951)
Street Bandits (Rep., 1951)
Oklahoma Annie (Rep., 1952)
Toughest Man in Arizona (Rep., 1952)
The Fabulous Senorita (Rep., 1952)
Gobs and Gals (Rep., 1952)
Tropical Heat Wave (Rep., 1952)
A Perilous Journey (Rep., 1953)

Geraldine (Rep. , 1954)
I Cover the Underworld (Rep. , 1955)
Cross Channel (Rep. , 1955)
Secret Venture (Rep. , 1955)
Double Jeopardy (Rep. , 1955)
When Gangland Strikes (Rep. , 1956)
Track the Man Down (Rep. , 1956)
Come Next Spring (Rep. , 1956)
Affair in Reno (Rep. , 1957)
Revolt in the Big House (AA, 1958).
Cole Younger, Gunfighter (AA, 1958)
Battle Flame (AA, 1959)
King of the Wild Stallions (AA, 1959)
Operation Eichmann (AA, 1961)
Showdown (Univ. , 1963)
He Rides Tall (Univ. , 1964)
Bullet for a Badman (Univ. , 1964)
Taggart (Univ. , 1964)
Black Spurs (Par. , 1965)
Apache Uprising (Par. , 1966)
Johnny Reno (Par. , 1966)
Waco (Par. , 1966)
Red Tomahawk (Par. , 1967)
Hostile Guns (Par. , 1967)
Tiger by the Tail (United Picture Corp. , 1968)

STAHL, JOHN M. , b. Jan. 21, 1886, New York City; d. Jan. 12,
    1950.
    Wives of Men (Pioneer, 1918) (also story, script)
    Suspicion (M. H. Hoffman, 1918)
    Her Code of Honor (Tribune-United, 1919)
    The Woman Under Oath (Tribune-United, 1919)
    Greather Than Love (American Cinema Association, 1919)
    Women Men Forget (United Pictures, 1920)
    The Woman in His House (Associated FN, 1920)
    Sowing the Wind (Associated FN, 1921)
    The Child Thou Gavest Me (Associated FN, 1921) (also pro-
        ducer)
    The Song of Life (Associated FN, 1922) (also producer)
    One Clear Call (Associated FN, 1922) (also producer)
    Suspicious Wives (State Rights, 1922)
    The Wanters (Associated FN, 1923) (also producer)
    The Dangerous Age (Associated FN, 1923) (also producer)
    Why Men Leave Home (FN, 1924)
    Husbands and Lovers (FN, 1924) (also producer)
    Fine Clothes (FN, 1925)
    Memory Lane (FN, 1926) (also producer, co-script)
    The Gay Deceiver (MGM, 1926)
    Lovers? (MGM, 1927) (also producer)
    In Old Kentucky (MGM, 1927) (also producer)
    A Lady Surrenders (Univ. , 1930)
    Seed (Univ. , 1931)

Irene Dunne and Charles Boyer (center) with John M. Stahl on the set for <u>When Tomorrow Comes</u> (Univ., 1939).

Strictly Dishonorable (Univ., 1931)
Back Street (Univ., 1932)
Only Yesterday (Univ., 1933)
Imitation of Life (Univ., 1934)
Magnificent Obsession (Univ., 1935)
Parnell (MGM, 1937)
Letter of Introduction (Univ., 1938) (also producer)
When Tomorrow Comes (Univ., 1939) (also producer)
Our Wife (Col., 1941)
The Immortal Sergeant (20th, 1942)
Holy Matrimony (20th, 1943)
The Eve of St. Mark (20th, 1944)
The Keys of the Kingdom (20th, 1944)
Leave Her to Heaven (20th, 1946)
Forever Amber (20th, 1947) (replaced by Otto Preminger)
The Foxes of Harrow (20th, 1947)
The Walls of Jericho (20th, 1948)
Father Was a Fullback (20th, 1949)
Oh, You Beautiful Doll (20th, 1949)

STANLAWS, PENRHYN (Penrhyn Stanley Adamson), b. March 19,
    1877, Dundee, Scotland; d. May 20, 1923.
  The Outside Woman (Realart, 1921)
  The House That Jazz Built (Realart, 1931)
  At the End of the World (Par., 1921)
  The Little Minister (Par., 1921)
  The Law and the Woman (Par., 1922)
  Over the Border (Par., 1922)•
  Pink Gods (Par., 1922)
  Singed Wings (Par., 1922)

STAUB, RALPH B., b. July 21, 1899, Chicago; d. Oct. 22, 1969.
  Sitting on the Moon (Rep., 1936)
  Join the Marines (Rep., 1937)
  The Affairs of Cappy Ricks (Rep., 1937)
  Navy Blues (Rep., 1937)
  The Mandarin Mystery (Rep., 1937)
  Meet the Boy Friend (Rep., 1937)
  Mama Runs Wild (Rep., 1937)
  Prairie Moon (Rep., 1938)
  Western Jamboree (Rep., 1938)
  Chip of the Flying U (Univ., 1940)
  Yukon Flight (Mon., 1940)
  Danger Ahead (Mon., 1940)
  The Heart of Show Business (Col., 1957) (also producer)

STEIN, PAUL L. (Paul Ludwig Stein), b. Feb. 4, 1893, Vienna;
    d. May, 1951.
  Der Teufel der Liebe (German, 1919) (also for own production
    company)
  Gewalt Gegen Recht (German, 1919) (also for own production
    company)
  Das Martyrium (German, 1920)
  Die Geschlossene Kette (German, 1920)
  Arme Violetta [The Red Peacock] (German, 1920)
  Der Schauspieler der Herzogin (German, 1920)
  Ehrenschuld (German, 1921)
  Das Opfer der Ellen Larsen (German, 1921)
  Stormflut des Lebens (German, 1921)
  Der Ewige Kampft (German, 1921)
  Es Leuchtet Meine Liebe (German, 1922)
  Nacht der Versuchung (German, 1922)
  Die Kette (Klirrt (German, 1923)
  Ler Löwe von Venedig (German, 1923)
  Ein Traum vom Glück (German, 1924)
  Ich Liebe Dich (German, 1924)
  Liebesfeuer (German, 1925)
  Die Insel der Träume [Eine Anstandige Frau] (German, 1925)
  Fünfuhrtee in der Ackerstrasse (German, 1926)
  My Official Wife (WB, 1926)

Don't Tell the Wife (WB, 1927)
The Climbers (WB, 1927)
The Forbidden Woman (Pathé, 1927)
Man-Made Woman (Pathé, 1928)
Ehre Deine Mutter (German, 1928)
Show Folks (Pathé, 1928)
Her Private Affair (Pathé, 1929)
The Office Scandal (Pathé, 1929)
This Thing Called Love (Pathé, 1929)
One Romantic Night (UA, 1930)
Sin Takes a Holiday (Pathé, 1930)
The Lottery Bride (UA, 1930)
Born to Love (Pathé, 1931)
A Woman Commands (RKO, 1932)
Lily Christine (Par., 1932)
Breach of Promise (Sono Art-World Wide, 1932)
The Song You Gave Me (Col., 1934)
Red Wagon (Wardour, 1934)
Blossom Time (Wardour, 1934)
Mimi (Wardour, 1935)
Heart's Desire (Wardour, 1935)
Faithful (Wardour, 1936)
Cafe Colette [Danger in Paradise] (Associated British Film Distributors, 1937)
Just Like a Woman (Associated British Picture Corp., 1937)
Black Limelight (Associated British Picture Corp., 1938)
Jane Steps Out (Associated British Picture Corp., 1938)
The Outsider (Associated British Picture Corp., 1939)
A Gentleman of Venture [It Happened to One Man] (RKO, 1940)
Poison Pen (Associated British Picture Corp., 1941)
The Saint Meets the Tiger (RKO, 1941)
Talk About Jacqueline (MGM, 1942)
Kiss the Bride Goodbye (Butcher, 1944) (also producer, story)
Waltz Time (British International, 1945)
Twilight Hour (British International, 1945)
The Lisbon Story (British International, 1946)
The Laughing Lady (British International, 1947)
Counterblast [So Died a Rat] (Pathé, 1948)
The Twenty Questions Murder Mystery (Grand National, 1950)

STEVENS, GEORGE, b. Dec. 18, 1904, Oakland, Calif.
Cohens and Kellys in Trouble (Univ., 1933)
Bachelor Bait (RKO, 1934)
Kentucky Kernels (RKO, 1934)
Laddie (RKO, 1935)
The Nitwits (RKO, 1935)
Alice Adams (RKO, 1935)
Annie Oakley (RKO, 1935)
Swing Time (RKO, 1936)
Quality Street (RKO, 1937)
A Damsel in Distress (RKO, 1937)
Vivacious Lady (RKO, 1938) (also producer)

Gunga Din (RKO, 1939) (also producer)
Vigil in the Night (RKO, 1940) (also producer)
Penny Serenade (Col., 1941) (also producer)
Woman of the Year (MGM, 1942)
The Talk of the Town (Col., 1942) (also producer)
The More the Merrier (Col., 1943) (also producer)
I Remember Mama (RKO, 1948) (also co-producer)
A Place in the Sun (Par., 1951) (also producer)
Something to Live For (Par., 1952) (also producer)
Shane (Par., 1953) (also producer)
Giant (WB, 1956) (also co-producer)
The Diary of Anne Frank (20th, 1959) (also producer)
The Greatest Story Ever Told (UA, 1965) (also producer, co-script)
The Only Game in Town (20th, 1970)

STEVENS, LESLIE, b. Feb. 3, 1924, Washington, D.C.
Private Property (Citation, 1960) (also co-producer, script)
Incubus (1961) (also script)
Hero's Island (UA, 1962) (also producer, script)
Della (Four Star, 1964)
I Love a Mystery (Univ., 1966) (also script)
Fanfare for a Death Scene (Four Star, 1967)

STEVENSON, ROBERT, b. March 31, 1905, Buxton, Eng.
Happily Ever After (Gaumont-British, 1932)
Falling for You (Woolf and Freedman Film Service, 1933)
Jack of All Trades (Gaumont-British, 1936)
Tudor Rose (Gaumont-British, 1936) (also script)
The Man Who Changed His Mind (Gaumont-British, 1936) (also script)
King Solomon's Mines (General Film Distributors, 1936)
Non-Stop New York (General Film Distributors, 1936)
Owd Bob (General Film Distributors, 1938)
The Ware Case (Associated British Film Distributors, 1939) (also script)
Young Man's Fancy (Associated British Film Distributors, 1939)
Return to Yesterday (Associated British Film Disbributors, 1939)
Tom Brown's Schooldays (RKO, 1940)
Back Street (Univ., 1941)
Joan of Paris (RKO, 1942)
Forever and a Day (RKO, 1943) (with Rene Clair, Edmund Goulding, Cedric Hardwicke, Frank Lloyd, Victor Saville, Herbert Wilcox)
Jane Eyre (20th, 1944) (also co-script)
Dishonored Lady (UA, 1947)
To the Ends of the Earth (RKO, 1948)
Woman on Pier 13 (RKO, 1949)
My Forbidden Past (RKO, 1950)
Walk Softly, Stranger (RKO, 1951)

The Las Vegas Story (RKO, 1952)
Old Yeller (BV, 1957)
Darby O'Gill and the Little People (BV, 1959)
Johnny Tremain (BV, 1957)
The Absent-Minded Professor (BV, 1960)
Kidnapped (BV, 1960)
In Search of the Castaways (BV, 1962)
Son of Flubber (BV, 1963)
The Misadventures of Merlin Jones (BV, 1964)
Mary Poppins (BV, 1964)
The Monkey's Uncle (BV, 1965)
That Darn Cat (BV, 1965)
The Gnome-Mobile (BV, 1967)
Blackbeard's Ghost (BV, 1968)
The Love Bug (BV, 1969)
My Dog, the Thief (NBC-TV, 1970)
Bedknobs and Broomsticks (BV, 1971)

STILLER, MAURITZ (Mosche [Mowscha] Stiller), b. July 17, 1883,
    Helsinki, Finland; d. Nov. 8, 1928.
Mor och Dotter (Swedish, 1912) (also script, actor)
De Svarta Maskerna (Swedish, 1912)
Den Tyranniske Fästmannen (Swedish, 1912) (also script, actor)
Vampyren (Swedish, 1912) (also script)
När Kärleken Dödar (Swedish, 1912)
Barnet (Swedish, 1912)
Livets Konflikter (Swedish, 1913) (also script)
Den Moderna Suffragetten (Swedish, 1913)
Bröderna (Swedish, 1913)
Gränsfolken (Swedish, 1913)
För Sin Kärleks Skull (Swedish, 1913)
Stormfågeln (Swedish, 1914)
Skottet (Swedish, 1914)
Det Röda Tornet (Swedish, 1914)
Dolken (Swedish, 1914)
När Konstnarer Älska (Swedish, 1914)
Lekkamratherna (Swedish, 1914)
Hans Hustrus Förflutna (Swedish, 1915)
Mästertjuven (Swedish, 1915)
Madame de Thebes (Swedish, 1915)
Hämnaren (Swedish, 1915)
Hans Bröllopsnatt (Swedish, 1915)
Lyckonalen (Swedish, 1916)
Kärlek och Journalistik (Swedish, 1916)
Vingarna (Swedish, 1916) (also script)
Balettprimadonnan (Swedish, 1916)
Thomas Graals Bästa Film (Swedish, 1917)
Alexander den Store (Swedish, 1917) (also script)
Thomas Graals Bästa Barn (Swedish, 1918) (also co-script)
Sangen om dem Eldröda Blomman (Swedish, 1919) (also co-
    script)
Herr Arnes Pengar (Swedish, 1919) (also co-script)

Fiskbyen (Swedish, 1920)
Erotikon (Swedish, 1921) (also co-script)
Johan (Swedish, 1921) (also co-script)
De Landsflyktige (Swedish, 1921) (also co-script)
Gunnar Hedes Saga (Swedish, 1923) (also script)
Gösta Berlings Saga (Swedish, 1924)
The Torrent (MGM, 1926) (uncredited, replaced by Monta Bell)
The Temptress (MGM, 1926) (uncredited, replaced by Fred
    Niblo)
Hotel Imperial (Par., 1927)
Barbed Wire (Par., 1927) (replaced by Rowland V. Lee)
The Woman on Trial (Par., 1927)
The Street of Sin (Par., 1928) (with uncredited Josef von Stern-
    berg)

STONE, ANDREW L., b. July 16, 1902, Oakland, Calif.
Sombras de Gloria (Sono Arts, 1930)
Hell's Headquarters (Capitol, 1932)
The Girl Said No (Grand National, 1937) (also producer, story)
Stolen Heaven (Par., 1938) (also producer)
Say It in French (Par., 1938) (also producer)
The Great Victor Herbert (Par., 1939) (also producer, co-
    script)

Andrew and Virginia Stone on the set for <u>Song of Norway</u> (Cin.,
1970).

There's Magic in Music (Par., 1941) (also producer, co-script)
Stormy Weather (20th, 1943)
Hi Diddle Diddle (RKO, 1943) (also producer)
Sensations of 1945 (UA, 1944) (also producer)
Bedside Manner (UA, 1945) (also producer
The Bachelor's Daughter (UA, 1946) (also producer, script)
Fun on a Weekend (UA, 1947) (also producer, script)
Highway 301 (WB, 1950) (also story, script)
Confidence Girl (UA, 1952) (also producer, story, script)
The Steel Trap (20th, 1952) (also story, script)
A Blueprint for Murder (20th, 1954) (also script)
The Night Holds Terror (MGM, 1955) (Also producer, script)
Julie (MGM, 1956) (also script)
Cry Terror! (MGM, 1957) (also co-producer, script)
The Decks Ran Red (MGM, 1957) (also co-producer, script)
The Last Voyage (MGM, 1960) (also co-producer, script)
Ring of Fire (MGM, 1961) (also co-producer, script)
The Password Is Courage (MGM, 1962) (also co-producer,
    script)
Never Put It in Writing (AA, 1963) (also script)
The Secret of My Success (MGM, 1965) (also script)
Song of Norway (Cin., 1970) (also co-producer, script)
The Great Waltz (MGM, 1973) (also producer, script)

STRAYER, FRANK R., b. Sept. 21, 1891, Altoona, Pa.; d. Feb.
    2, 1964.
Steppin' Out (Col., 1925)
An Enemy of Men (Col., 1925)
The Fate of a Flirt (Col., 1925)
The Lure of the Wild (Col., 1925)
Rose of the World (Col., 1925)
The Thrill Hunter (Col., 1926)
Sweet Rosie O'Grady (Col., 1926)
When the Wife's Away (Col., 1926)
The Bachelor's Baby (Col., 1927)
Rough House Rosie (Par., 1927)
Pleasure Before Business (Col., 1927)
Now We're in the Air (Par., 1927)
Partners in Crime (Par., 1928)
Just Married (Par., 1928)
Moran of the Marines (Par., 1928)
The Fall of Eve (Col., 1929)
Acquitted (Col., 1929)
Let's Go Places (Fox, 1930)
Borrowed Wives (Tiffany, 1930)
Caught Cheating (Tiffany, 1931)
Murder at Midnight (Tiffany, 1931)
Anybody's Blonde (Action, 1931)
Soul of the Slums (Action, 1931)
Dragnet Patrol (Mayfair, 1932)
The Monster Walks (Mayfair, 1932)
Behind Stone Walls (Mayfair, 1932)

Love in High Gear (Mayfair, 1932)
Gorilla Ship (Mayfair, 1932)
Dynamite Denny (Mayfair, 1932)
The Crusader (Mayfair, 1932)
Tangled Destinies (Mayfair, 1932)
Manhattan Tower (Remington, 1932)
Vampire Bat (Majestic, 1933)
By Appointment Only (Invincible, 1933)
Dance Girl Dance (Invincible, 1933)
El Rey de los Gitanos (Fox, 1933)
La Melodia Prohibida (Fox, 1933)
La Cruz y La Espada (Fox, 1933)
Las Fronteras del Amor (Fox, 1934)
In the Money (Chesterfield, 1934)
In Love With Life (Chesterfield, 1934)
Twin Husbands (Chesterfield, 1934)
Cross Streets (Chesterfield, 1934)
Fifteen Wives (Invincible, 1934)
Fugitive Road (Invincible, 1934)
One in a Million (Invincible, 1934)
Port of Lost Dreams (Chesterfield, 1935)
The Ghost Walks (Chesterfield, 1935)
Symphony of Living (Chesterfield, 1935)
Public Opinion (Chesterfield, 1935)
Death from a Distance (Invincible, 1935)
Society Fever (Chesterfield, 1935)
Murder at Glen Athol (Invincible, 1936)
Hitchhike to Heaven (Invincible, 1936)
Sea Spoilers (Univ., 1936)
Off to the Races (20th, 1937)
Laughing at Trouble (20th, 1937)
Big Business (20th, 1937)
Hot Water (20th, 1937)
Borrowing Trouble (20th, 1937)
Blondie (Col., 1938)
Blondie Meets the Boss (Col., 1939)
Blondie Brings Up Baby (Col., 1939)
Blondie Takes a Vacation (Col., 1939)
Blondie on a Budget (Col., 1940)
Blondie Has Servant Trouble (Col., 1940)
Blondie Plays Cupid (Col., 1940)
Blondie Goes Latin (Col., 1941)
Blondie in Society (Col., 1941)
Go West, Young Lady (Col., 1941)
Blondie Goes to College (Col., 1942)
Blondie's Blessed Event (Col., 1942)
The Daring Young Man (Col., 1943)
Footlight Glamour (Col., 1943) (also producer)
It's a Great Life (Col., 1943)
Senorita from the West (Univ., 1945)
Mama Loves Papa (RKO, 1945)
I Ring Doorbells (PRC, 1946)
Messenger of Peace (Astor, 1950)
The Sickle or the Cross (Astor, 1951)

STRICK, JOSEPH, b. 1923, Pittsburgh.
   The Big Break (1953) (also producer)
   The Savage Eye (Trans-Lux, 1959) (with Ben Maddow, Sidney
      Meyers) (also co-producer, co-script, co-editor)
   The Balcony (Emb., 1963) (also co-producer)
   Ulysses (Continental, 1967) (also co-producer, co-script)
   Justine (20th, 1968) (replaced by George Cukor)
   Tropic of Cancer (Par., 1969) (also producer, co-script)

STROCK, HERBERT L., b. Jan. 13, 1918, Boston.
   Storm over Tibet (Col., 1952)
   Gog (UA, 1954)
   Battle Taxi (UA, 1955)
   I Was a Teenage Frankenstein (AIP, 1957)
   Blood of Dracula (AIP, 1957)
   Rider on a Dead Horse (WB, 1962)
   The Devil's Messenger (Herts-Lion, 1962) (with Curt Siodmak)
   The Crawling Hand (AIP, 1964) (also co-script)

STURGES, JOHN (John Eliot Sturges), b. Jan. 3, 1910, Oak Park,
   Ill.
   The Man Who Dared (Col., 1946)
   Shadowed (Col., 1946)
   Thunderbolt (Mon., 1947) (with William Wyler)
   Alias Mr. Twilight (Col., 1947)
   For the Love of Rusty (Col., 1947)
   Keeper of the Bees (Col., 1947)
   The Best Man Wins (Col., 1948)
   The Sign of the Ram (Col., 1948)
   The Walking Hills (Col., 1949)
   Mystery Street (MGM, 1950)
   The Capture (RKO, 1950)
   The Magnificent Yankee (MGM, 1950)
   Right Cross (MGM, 1950)
   Kind Lady (MGM, 1951)
   It's a Big Country (MGM, 1951) (with Charles Vidor, Richard
      Thorpe, Don Hartman, Dan Weis, Clarence Brown, William
      Wellman)
   The People Against O'Hara (MGM, 1951)
   The Girl in White (MGM, 1952)
   Jeopardy (MGM, 1953)
   Fast Company (MGM, 1953)
   Escape from Fort Bravo (MGM, 1953)
   Underwater! (RKO, 1955)
   Bad Day at Black Rock (MGM, 1954)
   The Scarlet Coat (MGM, 1955)
   Backlash (Univ., 1956)
   Gunfight at the O.K. Corral (Par., 1957)
   The Old Man and the Sea (WB, 1958) (with Fred Zinneman and
      uncredited Henry King)
   The Law and Jake Wade (MGM, 1958)

Last Train from Gun Hill (Par., 1958)
Never So Few (MGM, 1959)
The Magnificent Seven (UA, 1960) (also producer)
By Love Possessed (UA, 1961)
Sergeants 3 (WB, 1962)
A Girl Named Tamiko (Par., 1962)
The Great Escape (UA, 1963) (also producer)
The Satan Bug (UA, 1965) (also producer)
The Hallelujah Trail (Col., 1965) (also producer)
Hour of the Gun (UA, 1967) (also producer)
Ice Station Zebra (MGM, 1968)
Marooned (Col., 1969)

STURGES, PRESTON, b. Aug. 29, 1898, Chicago; d. Aug. 6, 1959.

Veronica Lake with Preston Sturges (1941).

The Great McGinty (Par., 1940) (also script)
Christmas in July (Par., 1940) (also script)
The Lady Eve (Par., 1941) (also script)
Sullivan's Travels (Par., 1941) (also script)
The Palm Beach Story (Par., 1942) (also script)
The Miracle of Morgan's Creek (Par., 1944) (also script)
Hail the Conquering Hero (Par., 1944) (also script)
The Great Moment (Par., 1944) (also script)
The Sin of Harold Diddlebock [Mad Wednesday] (UA, 1947) (also script)
Unfaithfully Yours (20th, 1948) (also producer, script)
The Beautiful Blonde from Bashful Bend (20th, 1949) (also producer, script)
Vendetta (RKO, 1950) (uncredited, with Mel Ferrer and uncredited Stuart Heisler, Howard Hughes, Max Ophuls)
Les Carnets du Major Thompson (S. N. E. Gaumont, 1957) (also script)

SUTHERLAND, A. EDWARD, b. Jan. 5, 1895, London; d. Jan. 1, 1974.
Coming Through (Par., 1925)
Wild, Wild Susan (Par., 1925)
A Regular Fellow (Par., 1925)
Behind the Front (Par., 1926)
It's the Old Army Game (Par., 1926)
We're in the Navy Now (Par., 1926)
Love's Greatest Mistake (Par., 1927)
Fireman Save My Child (Par., 1927)
Figures Don't Lie (Par., 1928)
Tillie's Punctured Romance (Par., 1928)
The Baby Cyclone (Par., 1928)
What a Night! (Par., 1928)
Close Harmony (Par., 1929)
The Dance of Life (Par., 1929)
Fast Company (Par., 1929)
The Saturday Night Kid (Par., 1929)
Pointed Heels (Par., 1929)
Burning Up (Par., 1930)
Paramount on Parade (Par., 1930) (with Dorothy Arzner, Otto Brower, Edmund Goulding, Victor Heerman, Edwin H. Knopf, Rowland V. Lee, Ernst Lubitsch, Lothar Mendes, Victor Schertzinger, Frank Tuttle)
The Social Lion (Par., 1930)
The Sap from Syracuse (Par., 1930)
Gang Buster (Par., 1931)
June Moon (Par., 1931)
Up Pops the Devil (Par., 1931)
Palmy Days (UA, 1931) (with choreographer Busby Berkeley)
Sky Devils (UA, 1932)
Mr. Robinson Crusoe (UA, 1932)
Secrets of the French Police (RKO, 1932)
Murders in the Zoo (Par., 1933)

International House (Par., 1933)
Too Much Harmony (Par., 1933)
Mississippi (Par., 1935)
Diamond Jim (Univ., 1935)
Poppy (Par., 1936)
Champagne Waltz (Par., 1937)
Every Day's a Holiday (Par., 1937)
The Flying Deuces (UA, 1939)
The Boys from Syracuse (Univ., 1940)
Beyond Tomorrow (RKO, 1940)
One Night in the Tropics (Univ., 1940)
The Invisible Woman (Univ., 1941)
Nine Lives Are Not Enough (WB, 1941)
Steel Against the Sky (WB, 1941)
Sing Your Worries Away (RKO, 1942)
Army Surgeon (RKO, 1942)
The Navy Comes Through (RKO, 1942)
Dixie (Par., 1943)
Follow the Boys (Univ., 1944)
Secret Command (Col., 1944)
Having Wonderful Crime (RKO, 1945)
Abie's Irish Rose (UA, 1946)
Bermuda Affair (Col., 1956) (also co-script)

SWIFT, DAVID, b. 1919, Minneapolis, Minn.
Pollyanna (BV, 1960) (also script)
The Parent Trap (BV, 1961) (also script)
The Interns (Col., 1962) (also co-script)
Love Is a Ball (UA, 1963) (also co-script)
Under the Yum Yum Tree (Col., 1963) (also co-script)
Good Neighbor Sam (Col., 1964) (also producer, co-script)
How to Succeed in Business Without Really Trying (UA, 1967)
    (also producer, script)

T

TASHLIN, FRANK, b. Feb. 19, 1913, Weehawken, N.J.
The Lemon Drop Kid (Par., 1951) (uncredited, with Sidney
    Lanfield)
The First Time (Col., 1952) (also co-script)
Son of Paleface (Par., 1952) (also co-script)
Marry Me Again (RKO, 1953) (also script)
Susan Slept Here (RKO, 1954) (also uncredited co-script)
Artists and Models (Par., 1955) (also co-script)
The Lieutenant Wore Skirts (20th, 1955) (also co-script)
Hollywood or Bust (Par., 1956) (also uncredited co-script)
The Girl Can't Help It (20th, 1956) (also producer, co-script)
Will Success Spoil Rock Hunter? (20th, 1957) (also producer,
    script)
Rock-A-Bye Baby (Par., 1958) (also script)
The Geisha Boy (Par., 1958) (also script)

Say One for Me (20th, 1959) (also producer, uncredited co-
  script)
Cinderfella (Par., 1960) (also script)
Bachelor Flat (20th, 1961) (also co-script)
It's Only Money (Par., 1962) (also uncredited co-script)
The Man from the Diner's Club (Par., 1963)
Who's Minding the Store? (Par., 1963) (also co-script)
The Disorderly Orderly (Par., 1964) (also script)
The Alphabet Murders (MGM, 1966)
The Glass Bottom Boat (MGM, 1966)
Caprice (20th, 1967)
The Private Navy of Sgt. O'Farrell (UA, 1968) (also script)

TAUROG, NORMAN, b. Feb. 23, 1899, Chicago.
  The Farmer's Daughter (Fox, 1928)
  Lucky Boy (Tiffany, 1929) (with Charles C. Wilson)
  Sunny Skies (Tiffany, 1930)
  Hot Curves (Tiffany, 1930)
  Troopers Three (Tiffany, 1930) (with Reaves Eason)
  Follow the Leader (Par., 1930)
  Finn and Hattie (Par., 1930) (with Norman Z. McLeod)
  Skippy (Par., 1931)
  Newly Rich (Par., 1931)
  Huckleberry Finn (Par., 1931)
  Sooky (Par., 1931)
  Hold 'Em Jail (RKO, 1932)
  The Phantom President (Par., 1932)
  If I Had a Million (ep: "The Auto") (Par., 1932) (with James
    Cruze, H. Bruce Humberstone, Stephen Roberts, William A.
    Seiter, Ernst Lubitsch)
  A Bedtime Story (Par., 1933)
  The Way to Love (Par., 1933)
  We're Not Dressing (Par., 1934)
  Mrs. Wiggs of the Cabbage Patch (Par., 1934)
  College Rhythm (Par., 1934)
  The Big Broadcast of 1936 (Par., 1935)
  Strike Me Pink (Par., 1936)
  Reunion (20th, 1936)
  Rhythm on the Range (Par., 1936)
  You Can't Have Eveything (20th, 1937)
  Fifty Roads to Town (20th, 1937)
  Mad About Music (Univ., 1938)
  The Adventures of Tom Sawyer (New Trend Associates, 1938)
  Boys Town (MGM, 1938)
  The Girl Downstairs (MGM, 1939)
  Lucky Night (MGM, 1939)
  Broadway Melody of 1940 (MGM, 1940)
  Young Tom Edison (MGM, 1940)
  Little Nellie Kelly (MGM, 1940)
  Men of Boys' Town (MGM, 1941)
  Design for Scandal (MGM, 1941)
  A Yank at Eton (MGM, 1942)

Presenting Lily Mars (MGM, 1943)
Girl Crazy (MGM, 1943) (with choreographer Busby Berkeley)
The Hoodlum Saint (MGM, 1946)
The Beginning or the End (MGM, 1947)
The Bride Goes Wild (MGM, 1948)
Big City (MGM, 1948)
Words and Music (MGM, 1948)
That Midnight Kiss (MGM, 1949)
Please Believe Me (MGM, 1950)
The Toast of New Orleans (MGM, 1950)
Mrs. O'Malley and Mr. Malone (MGM, 1950)
Rich, Young and Pretty (MGM, 1951)
Room for One More (WB, 1952)
Jumping Jacks (Par., 1952)
The Stooge (Par., 1952)
The Stars Are Singing (Par., 1953)
The Caddy (Par., 1953)
Living It Up (Par., 1954)
You're Never Too Young (Par., 1955)
The Birds and the Bees (Par., 1956)
Pardners (Par., 1956)
Bundle of Joy (RKO, 1956)
The Fuzzy Pink Nightgown (UA, 1957)
Onionhead (WB, 1958)
Don't Give Up the Ship (Par., 1959)
Visit to a Small Planet (Par., 1960)
G.I. Blues (Par., 1960)
Blue Hawaii (Par., 1961)
All Hands on Deck (20th, 1961)
Girls! Girls! Girls! (Par., 1962)
It Happened at the World's Fair (Par., 1963)
Palm Springs Weekend (WB, 1963)
Tickle Me (AA, 1965)
Sergeant Deadhead, the Astronut (AIP, 1965)
Dr. Goldfoot and the Bikini Machine (AIP, 1965)
Spinout (MGM, 1966)
Double Trouble (MGM, 1967)
Speedway (MGM, 1968)
Live a Little, Love a Little (MGM, 1968)

TAYLOR, DON, b. Dec. 13, 1920, Freeport, Pa.
Everything's Ducky (Col., 1961)
Ride the Wild Surf (Col., 1964)
Jack of Diamonds (MGM, 1967)
The Five Man Army (MGM, 1970)
Escape from the Planet of Apes (20th, 1971)
Tom Sawyer (UA, 1973)

TAYLOR, RAY, b. New York City; d. Feb. 15, 1952.
Fighting With Buffalo Bill* (Univ., 1926)
Whispering Smith Rides* (Univ., 1927)

The Scarlet Arrow* (Univ., 1928)
The Vanishing Rider* (Univ., 1928)
The Avenging Shadow (Pathé, 1928)
Beauty and Bullets (Univ., 1928)
The Clean-Up Man (Univ., 1928)
The Crimson Canyon (Univ., 1928)
Greased Lightning (Univ., 1928)
Quick Triggers (Univ., 1928)
The Ace of Scotland Yard* (Univ., 1929) (with James W.
    Horne)
The Border Wildcat (Univ., 1929)
Come Across (Univ., 1929)
Eyes of the Underworld (Univ., 1929) (with Leigh Jason)
The Ridin' Demon (Univ., 1929)
A Final Reckoning* (Univ., 1929)
Pirate of Panama* (Univ., 1929)
The Jade Box* (Univ., 1930)
Battling With Buffalo Bill* (Univ., 1931)
Danger Island* (Univ., 1931)
Finger Prints* (Univ., 1931)
The One Way Trail (Col., 1931)
The Airmail Mystery* (Univ., 1932)
Heroes of the West* (Univ., 1932)
The Jungle Mystery* (Univ., 1932)
Clancy of the Mounted* (Univ., 1933)
Gordon of Ghost City* (Univ., 1933)
The Phantom of the Air* (Univ., 1933)
The Pirate Treasure* (Univ., 1934)
The Return of Chandu [The Magician] (Principal, 1934)
The Return of Chandu* (Principal, 1934)
The Fighting Trooper (Ambassador, 1934)
The Roaring West* (Univ., 1935)
Call of the Savage (Univ., 1935)
Tailspin Tommy and the Great Air Mystery* (Univ., 1935)
Outlawed Guns (Univ., 1935)
The Ivory-Handled Gun (Univ., 1935)
The Throwback (Univ., 1935)
Sunset of Power (Univ., 1936)
The Cowboy and the Kid (Univ., 1936)
Silver Spurs (Univ., 1936)
Tex Rides With the Boy Scouts (Grand National, 1936)
The Phantom Rider* (Univ., 1936)
Robinson Crusoe on Clipper Island* (Rep., 1936) (with Mack
    V. Wright)
The Three Mesquiteers (Rep., 1936)
The Vigilantes Are Coming* (Rep., 1936) (with Mack V.
    Wright)
Dick Tracy* (Rep., 1937) (with Alan James)
Drums of Destiny (Crescent, 1937)
The Painted Stallion* (Rep., 1937) (with William Witney)
Flaming Frontier* (Univ., 1937) (with Allen James)
Boss of Lonely Valley (Univ., 1937)
Sudden Bill Dorn (Univ., 1937)

Mystery of the Hooded Horseman (Grand National, 1937)
Hawaiian Buckaroo (20th, 1938)
The Spider's Web* (Univ., 1938) (with James W. Gorn)
Rawhide (20th, 1938)
Panamint's Bad Man (20th, 1938)
Frontier Town (Grand National, 1938)
Flying G-Men* (Col., 1939) (with James W. Horne)
Scouts to the Rescue* (Univ., 1939) (with Alan James)
Flash Gordon Conquers the Universe* (Univ., 1940) (with Ford
    Beebe)
The Green Hornet* (Univ., 1940) (with Ford Beebe)
Winners of the West* (Univ., 1940) (with Ford Beebe)
Bad Man from Red Butte (Univ., 1940)
Ragtime Cowboy Joe (Univ., 1940)
Law and Order (Univ., 1940)
Pony Post (Univ., 1940)
West of Carson City (Univ., 1940)
Riders of Pasco Basin (Univ., 1940)
Lucky Ralston (Univ., 1941)
Riders of Death Valley* (Univ., 1941) (with Ford Beebe)
Sky Raiders* (Univ., 1941) (with Ford Beebe)
Law of the Range (Univ., 1941)
Rawhide Rangers (Univ., 1941)
The Man from Montana (Univ., 1941)
Don Winslow of the Navy* (Univ., 1942) (with Ford Beebe)
Destination Unknown (Univ., 1942)
Gang Busters* (Univ., 1942) (with Noel Smith)
Junior G-Men of the Air* (Univ., 1942) (with Lewis D. Collins)
Treat 'Em Rough (Univ., 1942)
Mountain Justice (Univ., 1942)
Stagecoach Buckaroo (Univ., 1942)
Fighting Bill Fargo (Univ., 1942)
Cheyenne Roundup (Univ., 1943)
The Lone Star Trail (Univ., 1943)
Adventures of the Flying Cadets* (Univ., 1943) (with Lewis D.
    Collins)
The Adventures of Smilin' Jack* (Univ., 1943) (with Lewis D.
    Collins)
The Great Alaskan Mystery* (Univ., 1944) (with Lewis D. Col-
    lins)
The Boss of Boomtown (Univ., 1944)
Mystery of the River Boat* (Univ., 1944) (with Lewis D. Col-
    lins)
Raiders of Ghost City* (Univ., 1944) (with Lewis D. Collins)
Jungle Queen* (Univ., 1945) (with Lewis D. Collins)
The Master Key* (Univ., 1945) (with Lewis D. Collins)
The Royal Mounted Rides Again* (Univ., 1945) (with Lewis D.
    Collins)
Secret Agent X-9* (Univ., 1945) (with Lewis D. Collins)
The Daltons Ride Again (Univ., 1945)
Lost City of the Jungle* (Univ., 1946) (with Lewis D. Collins)
The Scarlet Horseman* (Univ., 1946) (with Lewis D. Collins)
The Michigan Kid (Univ., 1947)

The Vigilantes Return (Univ. , 1947)
Law of the Lash (PRC, 1947)
Pioneer Justice (PRC, 1947)
West to Glory (PRC, 1947)
Wild Country (PRC, 1947)
Stage to Mesa City (PRC, 1947)
Border Feud (PRC, 1947)
Black Hills (Eagle Lion, 1947)
Ghost Town Renegades (PRC, 1947)
Shadow Valley (Eagle Lion, 1947)
Range Beyond the Blue (PRC, 1947)
The Fighting Vigilantes (Eagle Lion, 1947)
The Return of Wildfire (Screen Guild, 1948)
Return of the Lash (Eagle Lion, 1948)
Mark of the Lash (Eagle Lion, 1948)
Cheyenne Takes Over (PRC, 1948)
Hidden Danger (Mon. , 1948)
The Hawk of Powder River (Eagle Lion, 1948)
Tornado Range (Eagle Lion, 1948)
The Tioga Kid (Eagle Lion, 1948)
The Westland Trail (Eagle Lion, 1948)
The Return of Wildfire (Screen Guild, 1948)
Check Your Guns (Eagle Lion, 1948)
Hidden Danger (Mon. , 1948)
Gunning for Justice (Mon. , 1948)
Crashing Thru (Screen Guild, 1949)
Outlaw Country (Screen Guild, 1949)
Shadows of the West (Mon. , 1949)
Dead Man's Gold (Screen Guild, 1949)
Frontier Revenge (Screen Guild, 1949)
Son of a Badman (Screen Guild, 1949)
Son of Billy the Kid (Screen Guild, 1949)
Gunning for Justice (Mon. , 1949)
Law of the West (Mon. , 1949)
West of El Dorado (Mon. , 1949)
Range Justice (Mon. , 1949)

TAYLOR, SAM, b. Aug. 13, 1895, New York City; d. March 6,
    1958.
    Safety Last (Pathé, 1923) (with Fred Newmeyer) (also co-
        script)
    Why Worry? (Pathé, 1923) (with Fred Newmeyer) (also script)
    Girl Shy (Pathé, 1924) (with Fred Newmeyer) (also co-script)
    Hot Water (Pathé, 1924) (with Fred Newmeyer) (also co-script)
    The Freshman (Pathé, 1925) (with Fred Newmeyer) (also co-
        script)
    For Heaven's Sake (Par. , 1926)
    Exit Smiling (MGM, 1926) (also co-script)
    My Best Girl (UA, 1927)
    Tempest (UA, 1928)
    The Woman Disputed (UA, 1928) (with Henry King)
    Coquette (UA, 1929) (also dialog)

Taming of the Shrew (UA, 1929) (also adaptation)
Du Barry, Woman of Passion (UA, 1930) (also adaptation)
Kiki (UA, 1931) (also script)
Skyline (Fox, 1931)
Ambassador Bill (Fox, 1931)
Devil's Lottery (Fox, 1932)
Out All Night (Univ., 1933)
The Cat's Paw (Fox, 1934)
Vagabond Lady (MGM, 1935) (also producer)

TAYLOR, WILLIAM DESMOND (William Cunningham Deane-Turner),
     b. April 26, 1877, Ireland; d. Feb. 2, 1922.
The Diamond from the Sky*
     (American, 1915) (with
     Jacques Jaccard)
The Last Chapter (Reliance,
     1915)
The High Hand (Reliance,
     1915)
The American Beauty (Par.,
     1916)
Ben Blair (Par., 1916)
Davy Crockett (Par., 1916)
He Fell in Love With His
     Wife (Par., 1916)
Her Father's Son (Par.,
     1916)
The House of Lies (Par.,
     1916)
Pasquale (Par., 1916)
The Parson of Panamint
     (Par., 1916)
The Redeeming Love (Par.,
     1916)
The Happiness of Three
     Women (Par., 1917)
The World Apart (Par.,
     1917)
The Varmint (Par., 1917)
Jack and Jill (Par., 1917)
Tom Sawyer (Par., 1917)
The Spirit of '17 (Par.,
     1918)

Huck and Tom (Par., 1918)   William Desmond Taylor (1922)
Up the Road With Sally
     (Selznick, 1918)
His Majesty Bunker Bean (Par., 1918)
Mile-A-Minute-Kendall (Par., 1918)
How Could You Jean? (Artclass, 1918)
Johanna Enlists (Artclass, 1918)
Captain Kidd, Jr. (Artclass, 1919)
Anne of Green Gables (Realart, 1919)

Judy of Rogue's Harbor (Realart, 1920)
Jenny Be Good (Realart, 1920)
Nurse Marjorie (Realart, 1920)
Huckleberry Finn (Par., 1920)
The Soul of Youth (Realart, 1920)
The Witching Hour (Par., 1921)
Sacred and Profane Love (Par., 1921)
Beyond (Par., 1921)
Wealth (Par., 1921)
Morals (Par., 1921)
The Green Temptation (Par., 1922)
The Top of New York (Par., 1922)

TETZLAFF, TED, b. June 3, 1903, Los Angeles.
World Premiere (Par., 1941)
Riff Raff (RKO, 1947)
Fighting Father Dunne (RKO, 1948)
The Window (RKO, 1949)
Johnny Allegro (Col., 1949)
A Dangerous Profession (RKO, 1949)
The White Tower (RKO, 1950)
Under the Gun (Univ., 1950)
Gambling House (RKO, 1950)
The Treasure of Lost Canyon (Univ., 1951)
Terror on a Train (MGM, 1953)
Son of Sinbad (RKO, 1955)
Seven Wonders of the World (Cin., 1956) (with Tay Garnett,
    Paul Mantz, Andrew Marton, Walter Thompson)
Young Land (Col., 1959)

TEWKSBURY, PETER, b. 1924.
Sunday in New York (MGM, 1963)
Emil and the Detectives (BV, 1964)
Doctor, You've Got to Be Kidding (MGM, 1967)
Stay Away Joe (MGM, 1968)
The Trouble With Girls (MGM, 1969)
Second Chance (ABC-TV, 1972)

THIELE, WILHELM (William Thiele), b. May 10, 1890, Vienna.
Fiat Lux (Austrian, 1923)
Carl Michael Ziehrers Märchen aus Alt-Wien (Austrian, 1923)
    (also co-script)
Franz Lehar (Austrian, 1923) (with Hans Torre)
Das Totenmahl auf Schloss Begalitza (German, 1923) (also
    script)
Die Selige Exzellenz (German, 1927) (with Adolf Edgar Licho)
    (also co-script)
Orient Express (German, 1927) (also script)
Der Anwalt des Herzens (German, 1927) (also co-script)
Die Dame mit der Maske (German, 1928)

Hurrah! Ich Liebe (German, 1928)
Adieu, Moscotte (German, 1929)
Liebeswalzer (German, 1930)
Valse d'Amour [French version of Liebeswaltzer] (German, 1930) (with Germaine Dulac)
Die Drei von der Tankstelle (German, 1930)
Le Chemin du Paradis [French version of Die Drei von der Tankstelle] (German, 1930) (with Max Vaucorbeil)
Die Privatsekrëtarin (German, 1930)
Dactylo [French version of Die Privatsekrëtarin] (German, 1930) (with Richard Pottier)
Der Ball (German, 1931)
Le Bal [French version of Der Ball] (German, 1931)
Madame Hat Ausgang (German, 1931) (also co-script)
L'Amoureuse Aventure [French version of Madame Hat Ausgang] (German, 1931)
Zwei Herzen und ein Schlag (German, 1932)
La Fille et le Garçon [French version of Zwei Herzen und ein Schlag] (German, 1932) (with Daven)
Mädchen zum Heiraten (German, 1932)
Marry Me [English version of Mädchen zum Heiraten] (German, 1932)
Waltz Time (Gaumont-British, 1932)
Grossfurstin Alexandra (Austrian, 1933)
Lottery Lover (Fox, 1935)
Don't Get Personal (Univ., 1936)
The Jungle Princess (Par., 1936)
London By Night (MGM, 1937)
Beg, Borrow or Steal (MGM, 1937)
Bad Little Angel (MGM, 1939)
Bridal Suite (MGM, 1939)
The Ghost Comes Home (MGM, 1940)
Tarzan's Triumph (RKO, 1943)
Tarzan's Desert Mystery (RKO, 1943)
The Madonna's Secret (Rep., 1946)
Der Letzte Fussgänger (German, 1960)
Sabine und die 100 Männer (German, 1960)

THOMPSON, J. LEE, b. 1914, Bristol, Eng.
Murder Without Crime (Associated British Picture Corp., 1950) (also story, script)
The Yellow Balloon (Associated British Picture Corp., 1952) (also script)
The Weak and the Wicked (Associated British Picture Corp., 1954) (also co-script)
For Better for Worse (Associated British Picture Corp., 1954) (also co-script)
As Long As They're Happy (General Film Distributors, 1955)
An Alligator Named Daisy (Rank, 1955)
Yield to the Night (Associated British Picture Corp., 1956)
The Good Companions (Associated British Picture Corp., 1957) (also co-producer)

Woman in a Dressing Gown (Associated British Picture Corp.,
1957) (also co-producer)
Ice Cold in Alex (Associated British Picture Corp., 1958) (also
co-script)
No Trees in the Street (Associated British Picture Corp., 1959)
(also for production company)
North West Frontier [Flame Over India] (Rank, 1959)
Tiger Bay (Continental, 1959)
Aim at the Stars (Col., 1960)
The Guns of Navarone (Col., 1961)
Cape Fear (Univ., 1962)
Taras Bulba (UA, 1962)
Kings of the Sun (UA, 1963)
What a Way to Go! (20th, 1964)
John Goldfarb, Please Come Home (20th, 1964)
Return from the Ashes (UA, 1965) (also producer)
Eye of the Devil (MGM, 1967)
Before Winter Comes (Col., 1968)
The Chairman (20th, 1969)
Mackenna's Gold (Col., 1969)
Brotherly Love (MGM, 1970)
Conquest of the Planet of the Apes (20th, 1972)
Battle of the Planet of the Apes (20th, 1973)

THORPE, RICHARD (Rollo Smolt Thorpe), b. Feb. 24, 1896,
Hutchinson, Kans.
Battling Buddy (Artclass, 1924)
Bringing Home the Bacon (Artclass, 1924)
Fast and Fearless (Action, 1924)
Hard Hittin' Hamilton (Action, 1924)
Rarin' to Go (Action, 1924)
Rip Roarin' Roberts (Artclass, 1924)
Rough Ridin' (Artclass, 1924) (also actor)
Thundering Romance (Artclass, 1924)
Walloping Wallace (Artclass, 1924)
The Desert Demon (Artclass, 1925)
Double Action Daniels (Artclass, 1925)
Fast Fightin' (Artclass, 1925)
Full Speed (Artclass, 1925)
Galloping On (Artclass, 1925)
Gold and Grit (Artclass, 1925)
On the Go (Artclass, 1925)
Quicker'n Lightnin' (Artclass, 1925)
Saddle Cyclone (Artclass, 1925)
A Streak of Luck (Artclass, 1925)
Tearin' Loose (Artclass, 1925)
Twin Triggers (Artclass, 1926)
Desert Demon (Artclass, 1926)
Double Dealing (Artclass, 1926)
The Bandit Buster (Associated Exhibitors, 1926) (also continuity)
The Bonanza Buckaroo (Associated Exhibitors, 1926)
College Days (Tiffany, 1926)

Coming An' Going (Artclass, 1926)
The Dangerous Dub (Associated Exhibitors, 1926)
Deuce High (Artclass, 1926)
Easy Going (Artclass, 1926)
The Fighting Cheat (Artclass, 1926)
Josselyn's Wife (Tiffany, 1926)
Rawhide (Associated Exhibitors, 1926)
Riding Rivals (Artclass, 1926)
Roaring Rider (Artclass, 1926)
Speedy Spurs (Artclass, 1926)
Trumpin' Trouble (Artclass, 1926)
Twisted Triggers (Associated Exhibitors, 1926)
Between Dangers (Pathé, 1927) (also continuity)
The Cyclone Cowboy (Pathé, 1927)
The Desert of the Lost (Pathé, 1927)
The First Night (Tiffany, 1927)
The Galloping Gobs (Pathé, 1927)
The Interferin' Gent (Pathé, 1927)
The Meddlin' Stranger (Pathé, 1927)
The Obligin' Buckaroo (Pathé, 1927)
Pals in Peril (Pathé, 1927)
Ride 'Em High (Pathé, 1927)
The Ridin' Rowdy (Pathé, 1927)
Roarin' Broncs (Pathe, 1927)
Skedaddle Gold (Pathé, 1927)
Soda Water Cowboy (Pathé, 1927)
Tearin' Into Trouble (Pathé, 1927)
White Pebbles (Pathé, 1927)
The Ballyhoo Buster (Pathé, 1928)
The Cowboy Cavalier (Pathé, 1928)
Desperate Courage (Pathé, 1928)
The Flying Buckaroo (Pathé, 1928)
Saddle Mates (Pathé, 1928)
The Valley of Hunted Men (Pathé, 1928)
The Vanishing West* (Mascot, 1928)
Vultures of the Sea* (Mascot, 1928)
The Bachelor Girl (Col., 1929)
King of the Kongo* (Mascot, 1929)
The Fatal Warning* (Mascot, 1929)
Border Romance (Tiffany, 1930)
The Dude Wrangler (Sono-Art World Wide, 1930)
The Thoroughbred (Tiffany, 1930)
Under Montana Skies (Tiffany, 1930)
The Utah Kid (Tiffany, 1930)
Wings of Adventure (Tiffany, 1930)
The Lone Defender* (Mascot, 1930)
The Lawless Woman (Chesterfield, 1931) (also co-script)
King of the Wild* (Mascot, 1931)
Lady from Nowhere (Chesterfield, 1931) (also editor)
Wild Horses (M.H. Hoffman, 1931) (with Sidney Algier)
Sky Spider (Action, 1931)
Grief Street (Chesterfield, 1931) (also editor)
Neck and Neck (Sono-Art World Wide, 1931)

The Devil Plays (Chesterfield, 1931) (also editor)
Cross Examination (Artclass, 1932)
Murder at Dawn (Big Four, 1932)
Forgotten Women (Mon., 1932)
Probation (Chesterfield, 1932)
Midnight Lady (Chesterfield, 1932)
Escapade (Invincible, 1932)
Forbidden Company (Invincible, 1932)
Beauty Parlor (Chesterfield, 1932)
The King Murder (Chesterfield, 1932)
The Thrill of Youth (Invincible, 1932)
Slightly Married (Chesterfield, 1932)
Women Won't Tell (Chesterfield, 1933)
Secrets of Wu Sin (Chesterfield, 1933) (also editor)
Love Is Dangerous (Chesterfield, 1933)
Forgotten (Invincible, 1933)
Strange People (Chesterfield, 1933)
I Have Lived (Chesterfield, 1933)
Notorious But Nice (Chesterfield, 1933)
A Man of Sentiment (Chesterfield, 1933)
Rainbow Over Broadway (Chesterfield, 1933)
Murder on the Campus (Chesterfield, 1934)
The Quitter (Chesterfield, 1934)
City Park (Chesterfield, 1934) (also editor)
Stolen Sweets (Chesterfield, 1934)
Green Eyes (Chesterfield, 1934)
Cheating Cheaters (Univ., 1934)
Secret of the Chateau (Univ., 1934)
Strange Wives (Univ., 1935)
Last of the Pagans (MGM, 1935)
The Voice of Bugle Ann (MGM, 1936)
Tarzan Escapes (MGM, 1936)
Dangerous Number (MGM, 1937)
Night Must Fall (MGM, 1937)
Double Wedding (MGM, 1937)
Love Is a Headache (MGM, 1938)
Man-Proof (MGM, 1938)
The First Hundred Years (MGM, 1938)
The Toy Wife (MGM, 1938)
The Crowd Roars (MGM, 1938)
Three Loves Has Nancy (MGM, 1938)
The Adventures of Huckleberry Finn (MGM, 1939)
Tarzan Finds a Son (MGM, 1939)
The Earl of Chicago (MGM, 1940)
20 Mule Team (MGM, 1940)
Wyoming (MGM, 1940)
The Bad Man (MGM, 1941)
Barnacle Bill (MGM, 1941)
Tarzan's Secret Treasure (MGM, 1941)
Joe Smith, American (MGM, 1942)
White Cargo (MGM, 1942)
Tarzan's New York Adventure (MGM, 1942)
Apache Trail (MGM, 1942)

Three Hearts for Julia (MGM, 1943)
Above Suspicion (MGM, 1943)
Cry Havoc (MGM, 1944)
Two Girls and a Sailor (MGM, 1944)
The Thin Man Goes Home (MGM, 1944)
Thrill of a Romance (MGM, 1945)
Her Highness and the Bellboy (MGM, 1945)
What Next, Corporal Hargrove? (MGM, 1945)
Fiesta (MGM, 1947)
This Time for Keeps (MGM, 1947)
A Date With Judy (MGM, 1948)
On an Island With You (MGM, 1948)
The Sun Comes Up (MGM, 1948)
Big Jack (MGM, 1949)
Challenge to Lassie (MGM, 1949)
Malaya (MGM, 1949)
The Black Hand (MGM, 1950)
Three Little Words (MGM, 1950)
Vengeance Valley (MGM, 1951)
The Great Caruso (MGM, 1951)
The Unknown Man (MGM, 1951)
It's a Big Country (MGM, 1951) (with Clarence Brown, Don
    Hartman, John Sturges, Charles Vidor, Don Weis, William
    Wellman)
Carbine Williams (MGM, 1952)
Ivanhoe (MGM, 1952)
The Prisoner of Zenda (MGM, 1952)
The Girl Who Had Everything (MGM, 1953)
All the Brothers Were Valiant (MGM, 1953)
Knights of the Round Table (MGM, 1953)
The Student Prince (MGM, 1954)
Athena (MGM, 1954)
The Prodigal (MGM, 1955)
Quentin Durward (MGM, 1955)
Ten Thousand Bedrooms (MGM, 1957)
Tip on a Dead Jockey (MGM, 1957)
Jailhouse Rock (MGM, 1957)
The House of the Seven Hawks (MGM, 1959)
Killers of Kilimanjaro (MGM, 1960)
The Tartars (MGM, 1960)
The Honeymoon Machine (MGM, 1961)
The Horizontal Lieutenant (MGM, 1962)
Follow the Boys (MGM, 1963)
Fun in Acapulco (Par., 1963)
The Golden Head (Cin., 1965)
The Truth About Spring (Univ., 1965)
That Funny Feeling (Univ., 1965)
The Scorpio Letters (ABC-TV, 1967)
The Last Challenge (MGM, 1967) (also producer)

TOPPER, BURT
    Hell Squad (AIP, 1958) (also producer, script)

War Hero (AIP, 1958) (also producer, script)
Tank Commandos (AIP, 1959) (also producer, script)
The Diary of a High School Bride (AIP, 1959) (also producer,
   co-script)
War Is Hell (AA, 1964) (also producer, script)
The Strangler (AA, 1964)
The Devil's 8 (AIP, 1968) (also producer)

TOURNEUR, JACQUES, b. Nov. 12, 1904, Paris.
   Tout Ça ne Vaut pas l'Amour (French, 1931)
   Pour Etre Aimé (French, 1933)
   Toto (French, 1933)
   Les Filles de la Concierge (French, 1934)
   They All Come Out (MGM, 1939)
   Nick Carter, Master Detective (MGM, 1939)
   Phantom Raiders (MGM, 1940)
   Doctors Don't Tell (Rep., 1941)
   Cat People (RKO, 1942)
   I Walked With a Zombie (RKO, 1943)
   The Leopard Man (RKO, 1943)
   Days of Glory (RKO, 1944)
   Experiment Perilous (RKO, 1944)
   Canyon Passage (Univ., 1946)
   Out of the Past (RKO, 1947)
   Berlin Express (RKO, 1948)
   Easy Living (RKO, 1949)
   Stars in My Crown (MGM, 1950)
   The Flame and the Arrow (WB, 1950)
   Circle of Danger (Eagle Lion, 1951)
   Anne of the Indies (20th, 1951)
   Way of a Gaucho (20th, 1952)
   Appointment in Honduras (RKO, 1953)
   Stranger on Horseback (AA, 1955)
   Wichita (AA, 1955)
   Great Day in the Morning (RKO, 1956)
   Nightfall (Col., 1956)
   Curse of the Demon (Col., 1958)
   The Fearmakers (UA, 1958)
   Timbuktu (UA, 1959)
   Frontier Ranger (MGM, 1959) (with George Waggner)
   Mission of Danger (MGM, 1959) (with George Waggner)
   Fury River (MGM, 1959) (with George Waggner)
   Savage Frontier (MGM, 1960)
   The Giant of Marathon (MGM, 1960)
   Mission of Danger (MGM, 1961)
   Fury River (MGM, 1961)
   A Comedy of Terrors (AIP, 1965)
   War Gods of the Deep (AIP, 1965)

TOURNEUR, MAURICE, b. Feb. 2, 1876, Paris; d. Aug. 4, 1961.
   The Man of the Hour (World, 1914)

Mother (World, 1914)
The Wishing Ring (World, 1914)
The Pit (World, 1914)
The Ivory Snuff Box (World, 1915)
The Cub (World, 1915)
Trilby (World, 1915)
The Irish Snuff Box (World, 1915)
A Butterfly on the Wheel (World, 1915)
Alias Jimmy Valentine (World, 1915)
The Closed Road (World, 1916)
The Pawn of Fate (World, 1916)
The Hand of Peril (Peerless-Brady-World, 1916)
The Rail Rider (Peerless-Brady-World, 1916)
The Velvet Paw (Peerless-Brady-World, 1917)
A Girl's Folly (Peerless-Brady-World, 1917)
The Poor Little Rich Girl (Artcraft, 1917)
The Pride of the Clan (Artcraft, 1917)
The Whip (Paragon, 1917)
Barbary Sheep (Artcraft, 1917)
A Doll's House (Artcraft, 1917)
The Undying Flame (Par., 1917)
The Law of the Land (Par., 1917)
Exile (Par., 1917)
The Rise of Jennie Cushing (Artcraft, 1917)
The Rose of the World (Artcraft, 1918)
The Blue Bird (Artcraft, 1918)
Sporting Life (Hiller & Wilk, 1918)
Woman (Hiller & Wilk, 1918)
Prunella (Par., 1919)
Victory (Par., 1919) (also producer)
The Broken Butterfly (Robertson-Cole, 1919)
The White Heather (Hiller & Wilk, 1919)
The Life Line (Par., 1919)
The County Fair (Guy Corswell Smith, 1920)
The Great Redeemer (Metro, 1920) (with Clarence Brown)
Treasure Island (Par., 1920)
The White Circle (Par., 1920) (also producer)
My Lady's Garter (Par., 1920)
The Last of the Mohicans (Associated Producers, 1920) (with
    Clarence Brown) (also producer)
Deep Waters (Par., 1920)
The Bait (Par., 1921)
The Foolish Matrons (Associated Producers, 1921)
Lorna Doone (Associated FN, 1923) (also producer, script)
The Christian (Goldwyn, 1923)
The Brass Bottle (Associated FN, 1923) (also producer)
Jealous Husbands (Associated FN, 1923) (also producer)
The Isle of Lost Ships (Associated FN, 1923) (also producer)
While Paris Sleeps (W.W. Hodkinson, 1923) (also producer)
The White Moth (FN, 1924) (also producer)
Torment (FN, 1924) (also producer)
Sporting Life (Univ., 1925)
Never the Twain Shall Meet (Metro-Goldwyn, 1925)

Clothes Make the Pirate (FN, 1925)
Aloma of the South Seas (Par., 1926) (also producer)
Old Loves and New (FN, 1926)
L'Equipage (French, 1927)
The Mysterious Island (MGM, 1929) (with Lucien Hubbard, Benjamin Christensen)
Das Schiff der Verlorenen Menschen (German, 1929) (also script)
Accusée, Levez-Vous (French. 1930)
Partir (French, 1930)
Maison De Danses (French, 1930)
Au Nom de la Loi (French, 1932)
Les Gaîtés de L'Escadron (French, 1932)
Les Deux Orphelines (French, 1933)
Le Voleur (French, 1933)
Justin de Marseille (French, 1935)
Koenigsmark (French, 1935)
Crimson Dynasty (French, 1936)
Samson (French, 1936)
Avec le Sourire (French, 1936)
Le Patriote (French, 1938)
Katia (French, 1938)
Péchés de Jeunesse (French, 1941)
Volpone (French, 1941)
Mam'zelle Bonaparte (French, 1941)
La Main du Diable (French, 1942)
La Val d'Enfer (French, 1943)
Cecile Est Morte (French, 1943)
Après l'Amour (French, 1947)
L'Impasse des deux Anges (French, 1948)

TUCKER, GEORGE LOANE, b. 1881, Chicago; d. June 21, 1921.
Traffic in Souls (Univ., 1913)
Behind the Scenes (Par., 1914)
The Middleman (London Films, 1914)
The Revenge of Mr. Thomas Atkins (London Films, 1914)
She Stoops to Conquer (London Films, 1914)
On His Majesty's Service (London Films, 1914)
Called Back (London Films, 1914)
The Fringe of War (London Films, 1914)
The Difficult Way (London Films, 1914)
Sons of Satan (London Films, 1915)
The Shulamite (London Films, 1914)
The Morals of Weybury (London Films, 1915)
The Game of Liberty (London Films, 1915)
The Prisoner of Zenda (London Films, 1915)
Rupert of Hentzau (London Films, 1915)
O-18 or A Message from the Sky (London Films, 1915) (with Frank Fowell)
The Man Without a Soul (London Films, 1916)
Arsene Lupin (London Films, 1916)
The Hypocrites [The Morals of Weybury] (London, 1916)

The Mother of Dartmoor (London Films, 1917)
A Mother's Influence (London Films, 1917)
A Man of His Word (General, 1917)
The Cinderella Man (Goldwyn, 1917)
The Man-Man (Tucker-Cosmofotofilm-Sherman, 1917)
The Mother (St. Regis, 1918)
Joan of Plattsburg (Goldwyn, 1918) (with William Humphreys)
Dodging a Million (Goldwyn, 1918)
Virtuous Wives (Associated FN, 1919)
The Miracle Man (Par., 1919)
Ladies Must Live (Par., 1921) (also adaptation)

TUTTLE, FRANK, b. Aug. 6, 1892, New York City; d. Jan. 6,
    1963.
The Cradle Buster (Par., 1922) (also script)
Second Fiddle (W.W. Hodkinson, 1923) (also co-script)
Youthful Cheaters (W.W. Hodkinson, 1923)
Puritan Passions (W.W. Hodkinson, 1923) (also co-script)
Grit (W.W. Hodkinson, 1924)
Dangerous Money (Par., 1924)
Miss Bluebeard (Par., 1925)
A Kiss in the Dark (Par., 1925)
The Manicure Girl (Par., 1925)
Lucky Devil (Par., 1925)
Lovers in Quarantine (Par., 1925)
The American Venus (Par., 1926)
The Untamed Lady (Par., 1926)
Kid Boots (Par., 1926)
Love 'Em and Leave 'Em (Par., 1926)
Blind Alleys (Par., 1927) (also producer)
The Spotlight (Par., 1927)
Time to Love (Par., 1927)
One Woman to Another (Par., 1927)
Something Always Happens (Par., 1928) (also story)
Easy Come, Easy Go (Par., 1928)
His Private Life (Par., 1928)
Love and Learn (Par., 1928)
Varsity (Par., 1928)
The Studio Murder Case (Par., 1929)
Marquis Preferred (Par., 1929)
The Greene Murder Case (Par., 1929)
Sweetie (Par., 1929)
Only the Brave (Par., 1930)
The Benson Murder Case (Par., 1930)
Paramount on Parade (Par., 1930) (with Dorothy Arzner, Otto
    Brower, Edmund Goulding, Victor Heerman, Edwin H.
    Knopf, Rowland V. Lee, Ernst Lubitsch, Lothar Mendes,
    Victor Schertzinger, A. Edward Sutherland)
True to the Navy (Par., 1930)
Men Are Like That (Par., 1930)
Love Among the Millionaires (Par., 1930)
Her Wedding Night (Par., 1930)

No Limit (Par. , 1931)
It Pays to Advertise (Par. , 1931)
This Reckless Age (Par. , 1932) (also co-script)
This Is the Night (Par. , 1932)
Big Broadcast (Par. , 1932)
Roman Scandals (UA, 1933) (with choreographer Busby Berke-
ley)
Ladies Should Listen (Par. , 1934)
Springtime for Henry (Par. , 1934) (also co-script)
Here Is My Heart (Par. , 1934)
All the King's Horses (Par. , 1935) (also co-script)
The Glass Key (Par. , 1935)
Two for Tonight (Par. , 1935)
College Holiday (Par. , 1936)
Waikiki Wedding (Par. , 1937)
Dr. Rhythm (Par. , 1938)
Charlie McCarthy, Detective (Univ. , 1939) (also producer)
I Stole a Million (Univ. , 1939)
Paris Honeymoon (Par. , 1939)
This Gun for Hire (Par. , 1942)
Lucky Jordan (Par. , 1942)
Hostages (Par. , 1943)
The Hour Before Dawn (Par. , 1944)
The Great John L (UA, 1945)
Don Juan Quilligan (20th, 1945)
Suspense (Mon. , 1946)
Swell Guy (Univ. , 1946)
Le Traque [Gunman in the Streets] (French, 1950)
The Magic Face (Col. , 1951)
Hell on Frisco Bay (WB, 1955)
A Cry in the Night (WB, 1956)
Island of Lost Women (WB, 1959)

U

ULMER, EDGAR G. (Edgar George Ulmer), b. Sept. 17, 1900,
Vienna; d. Sept. 30, 1972.
Menschen am Sonntag [People on Sunday] (German, 1929) (with
Robert Siodmak)
Damaged Lives (Weldon, 1933) (also co-story)
Mister Broadway (Broadway-Hollywood, 1933)
The Black Cat (Univ. , 1934) (also co-story, set designs)
Green Fields (Collective, 1937) (with Jacob Ben-Ami) (also pro-
ducer)
Cossacks in Exile (Avramenko Films, 1938)
The Singing Blacksmith (Collective, 1938)
Moon over Harlem (Meteor, 1939)
Fishke der Drume (German, 1939)
The Light Ahead (1939)
Natalka Poltavka (ca. 1939)
American Matchmaker (ca. 1940)
Tomorrow We Live (PRC, 1942)

Isle of Forgotten Sins (PRC, 1943) (also story)
Girls in Chains (PRC, 1943) (also story)
Jive Junction (PRC, 1943)
My Son, the Hero (PRC, 1943) (also co-script)
Bluebeard (PRC, 1944)
Detour (PRC, 1945)
Strange Illusion [Out of the Night] (PRC, 1945)
Club Havana (PRC, 1945)
The Wife of Monte Cristo (PRC, 1946) (also co-adaptation)
Her Sister's Secret (PRC, 1946)
The Strange Woman (UA, 1946)
Carnegie Hall (UA, 1947)
Ruthless (Eagle Lion, 1948)
The Pirates of Capri (Film Classics, 1949)
St. Benny the Dip (UA, 1951)
The Man from Planet X (UA, 1951)
Babes in Bagdad (UA, 1952)
The Naked Dawn (Univ., 1954)
Murder Is My Beat (AA, 1955)
Daughter of Dr. Jekyll (AA, 1957)
Hannibal (WB, 1960) (with Carlo Ludovico Bragaglia) (also pro-
    ducer)
L'Atalantide [Journey Beneath the Desert] (AIP, 1960) (with
    Guiseppe Masini, uncredited, Frank Borzage)
Beyond the Time Barrier (AIP, 1960)
The Amazing Transparent Man (AIP, 1961)
Helden Himmel und Holle [Settle Contro la Morte] [The Cavern]
    (German-Italian, 1964) (with Paolo Bianchini) (also producer)

V

VAN DYKE, W.S., II (Woodbridge Strong Van Dyke II), b. March
    26, 1889, San Diego, Cal.; d. Feb. 5, 1943.
The Land of Long Shadows (Essanay, 1917)
The Range Boss (Essanay, 1917)
Open Places (Essanay, 1917)
Men of the Desert (Essanay, 1917)
Gift o' Gab (Essanay, 1917)
The Lady of the Dugout (Jennings-Shipman, 1918)
The Hawk's Trail* (Burston, 1920)
Daredevil Jack* (Pathé, 1920)
Double Adventure* (Pathé, 1921)
The Avenging Arrow* (Pathé, 1921) (with William J. Bosman)
White Eagle* (Pathé, 1922) (with Fred Jackson)
According to Hoyle (Western, 1922)
The Boss of Camp 4 (Fox, 1922)
Forget-Me-Not (Metro, 1922)
The Little Girl Next Door (Blair-Coan, 1923)
The Destroying Angel (Associated Exhibitors, 1923)
The Miracle Makers (Associated Exhibitors, 1923)
Ruth of the Range* (Pathé, 1923) (uncredited, with Ernest
    Warde)

Nelson Eddy (left) and Jeanette MacDonald with W.S. Van Dyke II on a break from <u>I Married an Angel</u> (MGM, 1942).

You Are in Danger (Blair-Coan, 1923)
Loving Lies (Allied Producers & Distributors, 1924)
The Beautiful Sinner (Perfection, 1924)
Half-a-Dollar Bill (Metro, 1924)
Winner Take All (Fox, 1924)
The Battling Fool (C.B.C., 1924)
Barriers Burned Away (Associated Exhibitors, 1925)
Gold Heels (Fox, 1925)
Hearts and Spurs (Fox, 1925)
The Trail Rider (Fox, 1925)
The Ranger of the Big Pines (Fox, 1925)
The Timber Wolf (Fox, 1925)
The Desert's Price (Fox, 1925)
The Gentle Cyclone (Fox, 1926)
War Paint (MGM, 1926)
Winners of the Wilderness (MGM, 1927)
California (Arrow, 1927)
The Heart of the Yukon (Pathé, 1927)
Eyes of the Totem (Pathé, 1927)
Spoilers of the West (MGM, 1927)
Foreign Devils (MGM, 1928)
Wyoming (MGM, 1928) (also story)

Under the Black Eagle (MGM, 1928)
White Shadows in the South Seas (MGM, 1928) (with Robert
   Flaherty)
The Pagan (MGM, 1929)
Trader Horn (MGM, 1931)
Never the Twain Shall Meet (MGM, 1931)
Guilty Hands (MGM, 1931)
The Cuban Love Song (MGM, 1931)
Tarzan, the Ape Man (MGM, 1932)
Night Court (MGM, 1932)
Penthouse (MGM, 1933)
The Prizefighter and the Lady (MGM, 1933) (also producer)
Eskimo (MGM, 1933)
Manhattan Melodrama (MGM, 1934)
The Thin Man (MGM, 1934)
Forsaking All Others (MGM, 1934)
Laughing Boy (MGM, 1934)
Hide-Out (MGM, 1934)
Naughty Marietta (MGM, 1935)
I Live My Life (MGM, 1935)
Rose-Marie (MGM, 1936)
His Brother's Wife (MGM, 1936) (also co-producer)
San Francisco (MGM, 1936) (also co-producer)
The Devil Is a Sissy (MGM, 1936)
Love on the Run (MGM, 1936)
After the Thin Man (MGM, 1936)
Personal Property (MGM, 1937)
They Gave Him a Gun (MGM, 1937)
Rosalie (MGM, 1937)
Marie Antoinette (MGM, 1938)
Sweethearts (MGM, 1938)
Stand Up and Fight (MGM, 1939)
It's a Wonderful World (MGM, 1939)
Andy Hardy Gets Spring Fever (MGM, 1939)
Another Thin Man (MGM, 1939)
I Take This Woman (MGM, 1940) (started by Josef von Stern-
   berg, replaced by Frank Borzage, new version by Van Dyke)
Rage in Heaven (MGM, 1941)
The Feminine Touch (MGM, 1941)
Shadow of the Thin Man (MGM, 1941)
Dr. Kildare's Victory (MGM, 1941)
I Married an Angel (MGM, 1942)
Cairo (MGM, 1942)
Journey for Margaret (MGM, 1942)

VIDOR, CHARLES, b. July 27, 1900, Budapest; d. June 5, 1959.
   The Mask of Fu Manchu (MGM, 1932) (uncredited, with Charles
      Brabin)
   Sensation Hunters (Mon., 1934)
   Strangers All (RKO, 1935)
   Double Door (Par., 1934)
   The Arizonian (RKO, 1935)

His Family Tree (RKO, 1935)
Muss 'Em Up (RKO, 1936)
A Doctor's Diary (Par. , 1937)
The Great Gambini (Par. , 1937)
She's No Lady (Par. , 1937)
Blind Alley (Col. , 1939)
Romance of the Redwoods (Col. , 1939)
Those High Grey Walls (Col. , 1939)
My Son, My Son (Col. , 1940)
The Lady in Question (Col. , 1940)
New York Town (Par. , 1941)
Ladies in Retirement (Col. , 1941)
The Tuttles of Tahiti (RKO, 1942)
The Desperadoes (Col. , 1943)
Cover Girl (Col. , 1944)
Together Again (Col. , 1944)
A Song to Remember (Col. , 1945)
Over 21 (Col. , 1945)
Gilda (Col. , 1946)
The Guilt of Janet Ames (Col. , 1947)
The Loves of Carmen (Col. , 1948)
The Man from Colorado (Col. , 1948) (replaced by Henry Levin)
It's a Big Country (MGM, 1951) (with Richard Thorpe, John
    Sturges, Don Hartman, Don Weis, Clarence Brown, William
    Wellman)
Hans Christian Andersen (RKO, 1952)
Thunder in the East (Par. , 1953)
Rhapsody (MGM, 1954)
Love Me or Leave Me (MGM, 1955)
The Swan (MGM, 1956)
The Joker Is Wild (Par. , 1957)
A Farewell to Arms (20th, 1957) (replaced by John Huston)
Song Without End (Col. , 1960) (died during production, re-
    placed by George Cukor)

VIDOR, KING (King Wallis Vidor), b. Feb. 8, 1896, Galveston,
    Tex.
The Turn in the Road (Robertson-Cole, 1919) (also script)
Better Times (Brentwood-Mutual, 1919) (also script)
The Other Half (Exclusive International, 1919) (also script)
Poor Relations (Robertson-Cole, 1919) (also script)
The Jack-Knife Man (Associated FN, 1919) (also producer, co-
    script)
The Family Honor (Associated FN, 1920) (also producer)
Love Never Dies (Associated FN, 1921) (also producer)
The Sky Pilot (Associated FN, 1921) (also co-producer)
Woman, Wake Up (Associated Exhibitors, 1922) (also producer)
The Real Adventure (Associated Exhibitors, 1922) (also pro-
    ducer)
Dusk to Dawn (Associated Exhibitors, 1922) (also producer)
Wild Oranges (Goldwyn, 1922) (also script)
Conquering the Woman (Associated Exhibitors, 1923) (also pro-
    ducer)

King Vidor (ca. 1973)

Alice Adams (Associated Exhibitors, 1923) (also producer)
Peg o' My Heart (Metro, 1923)
The Woman of Bronze (Metro, 1923)
Three Wise Fools (Goldwyn, 1923) (also script)
Happiness (Metro, 1923)
His Hour (Metro-Goldwyn, 1924)
Wine of Youth (Metro-Goldwyn, 1924)
Wife of the Centaur (Metro-Goldwyn, 1924)
Proud Flesh (MGM, 1925) (also co-producer)
The Big Parade (MGM, 1925) (also producer)
La Boheme (MGM, 1926) (also producer)
Bardelys the Magnificent (MGM, 1926) (also producer)
The Crowd (MGM, 1928) (also producer, co-script)
Show People (MGM, 1928) (also co-producer)
The Patsy (MGM, 1928)
Hallelujah (MGM, 1929) (also producer, script)
Not So Dumb (MGM, 1930) (also co-producer)
Billy the Kid (MGM, 1930)

Street Scene (UA, 1931)
The Champ (MGM, 1931) (also producer)
Bird of Paradise (RKO, 1932)
Cynara (UA, 1932)
The Stranger's Return (MGM, 1933) (also producer)
Our Daily Bread (UA, 1934) (also producer)
The Wedding Night (Par., 1935)
So Red the Rose (Par., 1935)
The Texas Rangers (Par., 1936) (also producer, co-script)
Stella Dallas (UA, 1937)
The Citadel (MGM, 1938)
Northwest Passage (MGM, 1940)
Comrade X (MGM, 1940)
H. M. Pulham, Esq. (MGM, 1941) (also producer, co-script)
An American Romance (MGM, 1944) (also producer, story)
Duel in the Sun (Selznick Releasing, 1946) (with uncredited
    William Dieterle, William Cameron Menzies, Josef von
    Sternberg, Otto Brower, Sidney Franklin)
A Miracle Can Happen [On Our Merry Way] (UA, 1948) (with
    Leslie Fenton)
The Fountainhead (WB, 1949)
Beyond the Forest (WB, 1949)
Lightning Strikes Twice (WB, 1951)
Japanese War Bride (20th, 1952)
Ruby Gentry (20th, 1952) (also co-producer)
Man Without a Star (Univ., 1955)
War and Peace (Par., 1956) (also co-script)
Solomon and Sheba (UA, 1959) (also executive producer)

VIERTEL, BERTHOLD, b. June 28, 1885, Vienna; d. Sept. 25,
    1953.
Nora (German, 1923) (also co-script)
Die Perücke (German, 1924) (also script)
Die Abenteuer eines Zehnmarkscheines (German, 1926)
The One Woman Idea (Fox, 1929)
Seven Faces (Fox, 1929)
Man Trouble (Fox, 1930)
The Spy (Fox, 1931)
The Magnificent Lie (Par., 1931)
Die Heilige Flamme [German version of The Sacred Flame]
    (WB, 1931) (also co-script)
The Wiser Sex (Par., 1932)
The Man from Yesterday (Par., 1932)
Little Friend (Gaumont-British, 1934)
The Passing of the Third Floor Back (Gaumont-British, 1935)
Rhodes of Africa (Gaumont-British, 1936)

VIGNOLA, ROBERT G., b. Aug. 5, 1882, Italy; d. Oct. 25, 1953.
The Pretenders (Kalem, 1914)
Don Caesar de Bazan (Kalem, 1915)
The Luring Lights (Kalem, 1915)

The Vanderhoff Affair (Kalem, 1915)
The Black Crook (Kalem, 1916)
Audrey (Par., 1916)
The Evil Thereof (Par., 1916)
The Moment Before (Par., 1916)
The Reward of Patience (Par., 1916)
The Spider (Par., 1916)
The Velvet Paw (World, 1916)
Seventeen (Par., 1916)
Her Better Self (Par., 1917)
Great Expectations (Par., 1917)
The Fortunes of Fifi (Par., 1917)
The Love That Lives (Par., 1917)
The Hungry Heart (Par., 1917)
The Knife (Selig, 1917)
Double Crossed (Par., 1917)
Madame Jelousy (Par., 1918)
The Reason Why (Select, 1918)
His Official Fiancee (Par., 1918)
The Claw (Select, 1918)
The Girl Who Came Back (Par., 1918)
Experimental Marriage (Select, 1919)
The Home Town Girl (Par., 1919)
The Woman Next Door (Par., 1919)
You Never Saw Such a Girl (Par., 1919)
The Winning Girl (Par., 1919)
An Innocent Adventuress (Par., 1919)
Women's Weapons (Par., 1919)
Louisiana (Par., 1919)
The Heart of Youth (Par., 1919)
More Deadly Than the Male (Par., 1919)
The Third Kiss (Par., 1919)
The Thirteenth Commandment (Par., 1920)
The World and His Wife (Par., 1920)
The Passionate Pilgrim (Par., 1921)
Straight Is the Way (Par., 1921)
Enchantment (Par., 1921)
The Woman God Changed (Par., 1921)
Beauty's Worth (Par., 1922)
The Young Diana (Par., 1922) (with Albert Capellani)
When Knighthood Was in Flower (Par., 1922)
Adam and Eva (Par., 1923)
Yolanda (Metro-Goldwyn, 1924)
Married Flirts (Metro-Goldwyn, 1924)
Déclassé (FN, 1925)
The Way of a Girl (Metro-Goldwyn, 1925)
Fifth Avenue (PDC, 1926)
Cabaret (Par., 1927)
Tropic Madness (FBO, 1928)
The Red Sword (RKO, 1929)
Broken Dreams (Mon., 1934)
The Scarlet Letter (Majestic, 1934)
The Perfect Clue (Majestic, 1935)
The Girl from Scotland Yard (Rep., 1937)

VON STERNBERG, JOSEF (Joseph Stern), b. May 29, 1894, Vienna; d. Dec. 22, 1969.
  The Salvation Hunters (UA, 1925) (also producer, script)
  The Masked Bride (MGM, 1925) (uncredited, with Christy Cabanne)
  The Sea Gull [Woman of the Sea] (unreleased, 1926) (also script)
  The Exquisite Sinner (MGM, 1926) (also co-script)
  Children of Divorce (Par., 1927) (uncredited, with Frank Lloyd)
  Underworld (Par., 1927) (also script)
  The Last Command (Par., 1928)
  The Dragnet (Par., 1928)
  The Docks of New Orleans (Par., 1928)
  The Case of Lena Smith (Par., 1929)
  Der Blaue Engel [The Blue Angel] (UFA, 1930)
  Morocco (Par., 1930)
  Dishonored (Par., 1931)
  An American Tragedy (Par., 1931) (also co-script)
  Shanghai Express (Par., 1932) (also co-script)
  The Blonde Venus (Par., 1932) (also story)
  The Scarlet Empress (Par., 1934)
  The Devil Is a Woman (Par., 1935) (also camera)
  Crime and Punishment (Col., 1935)
  The King Steps Out (Col., 1936)
  I, Claudius (unfinished, 1937)
  I Take This Woman (MGM, 1938) (replaced by Frank Borzage, finished by W.S. Van Dyke II)
  Sergeant Madden (MGM, 1939)
  The Shanghai Gesture (UA, 1941) (also co-script)
  Duel in the Sun (Selznick Releasing, 1946) (uncredited, with King Vidor, and uncredited William Dieterle, William Cameron Menzies, Otto Brower, Sidney Franklin)
  Macao (RKO, 1952) (with uncredited Nicholas Ray)
  The Saga of Anathan (Japanese, 1953) (also producer, script, camera, narration)
  Jet Pilot (Univ., 1957) (with uncredited Howard Hughes)

VON STROHEIM, ERICH (Erich Oswald Stroheim), b. Sept. 22, 1885, Vienna; d. May 12, 1957.
  Blind Husbands (Univ., 1918) (also story, script, art director, actor)
  The Devil's Passkey (Univ., 1919) (also co-story, script, art director)
  Foolish Wives (Univ., 1921) (also story, script, co-art director, co-costumes, actor)
  Merry-Go-Round (Univ., 1923) (replaced by Rupert Julian) (also story, script, co-art director, co-costumes)
  Greed (Metro-Goldwyn, 1924) (also script, co-art director, co-costumes)
  The Wedding March (Par., 1928) (also co-script, co-art tor, co-costumes) (Part II released as [The Honey-

moon--Par., 1928) (co-script, co-art director, co-costumes)
Queen Kelly (UA, 1928) (also story-script) (revised version
supervised by Gloria Swanson, Edmund Goulding)
Walking Down Broadway (Fox, 1933-unreleased) (with uncredited Raoul Walsh) (also co-script) (revised by director Alfred
Werker for release as Hello Sister!--Fox, 1933)

VORHAUS, BERNARD, b. ca.1898, Germany.
On Thin Ice (Twickenham, 1933)
Money for Speed (UA, 1933) (also story)
Crime on the Hill (Wardour, 1933) (also co-script)
The Ghost Camera (Radio, 1934)
Night Club Queen (Real Art, 1934)
The Broken Melody (Associated Producers and Distributors,
1934)
Blind Justice (Real Art, 1934)
Ten Minute Alibi (British Lion-Transatlantic, 1935)
Street Song (Radio, 1935) (also co-story)
The Last Journey (Twickenham, 1935)
Dark World (Fox British, 1935)
Dusty Ermine (Wardour, 1936)
Cotton Queen (British Independent Exhibitors' Distributors,
1937)
A Smile in the Storm (Columbia, 1937) (with H. Sokol)
King of the Newsboys (Rep., 1938)
Tenth Avenue Kid (Rep., 1938)
Fisherman's Wharf (RKO, 1939)
Meet Dr. Christian (RKO, 1939)
Way Down South (RKO, 1939)
Courageous Dr. Christian (RKO, 1940)
Three Faces West (Rep., 1940)
Lady from Louisiana (Rep., 1941)
Angels With Broken Wings (Rep., 1941)
Hurricane Smith (Rep., 1941)
Mr. District Attorney in the Carter Case (Rep., 1941)
The Affairs of Jimmy Valentine (Rep., 1942)
Ice-Capades Revue (Rep., 1942)
Bury Me Dead (PRC, 1947)
Winter Wonderland (Rep., 1947)
The Spiritualist (Eagle Lion, 1948)
So Young, So Bad (UA, 1950) (also co-story, co-script)
Pardon My French (UA, 1951)
Fanciulle di Lusso (Italian, 1952)

W

WAGGNER, GEORGE (George Waggoner), b. Sept. 7, 1894, New
York City.
Black Bandit (Univ., 1938)
Honor of the West (Univ., 1939)

Mystery Plane (Mon., 1939)
Outlaw Express (Univ., 1939)
Wolf Call (Mon., 1939)
The Phantom Stage (Univ., 1939)
Stunt Pilot (Mon., 1939)
Drums of the Desert (Mon., 1940)
Man-Made Monster (Univ., 1941)
Horror Island (Univ., 1941)
South of Tahiti (Univ., 1941) (also associate producer)
The Wolf Man (Univ., 1941) (also associate producer)
The Climax (Univ., 1944) (also producer)
Frisco Sal (Univ., 1945) (also producer)
Shady Lady (Univ., 1945)
Tangier (Univ., 1946)
Gunfighters (Col., 1947)
The Fighting Kentuckian (Rep., 1949) (also script)
Operation Pacific (WB, 1951) (also script)
Pawnee (Rep., 1957) (also co-script)
Destination 60,000 (AA, 1957) (also script)
Frontier Ranger (MGM, 1959) (with Jacques Tourneur)
Mission of Danger (MGM, 1959) (with Jacques Tourneur)
Fury River (MGM, 1959) (with Jacques Tourneur)

WALKER, HAL, b. March 20, 1896, Ottumwa, Iowa; d. 1956.
Duffy's Tavern (Par., 1945)
Out of This World (Par., 1945)
The Stork Club (Par., 1945)
Road to Utopia (Par., 1946)
My Friend Irma Goes West (Par., 1950)
At War With the Army (Par., 1950)
That's My Boy (Par., 1951)
Sailor Beware (Par., 1951)
Road to Bali (Par., 1952)

WALKER, STUART, b. c.1890, Augusta, Ga.; d. March 13, 1941.
The Secret Call (Par., 1931)
The False Madonna (Par., 1932)
The Misleading Lady (Par., 1932)
Evenings for Sale (Par., 1932)
Tonight Is Ours (Par., 1933)
The Eagle and the Hawk (Par., 1933)
White Woman (Par., 1933)
Romance in the Rain (Univ., 1934)
Great Expectations (Univ., 1934)
The Mystery of Edwin Drood (Univ., 1935)
The Werewolf of London (Univ., 1935)
Manhattan Moon (Univ., 1935)
Her Excellency the Governor (Univ., 1935)

WALLACE, RICHARD, b. Aug. 26, 1894, Sacramento, Calif.; d.
       Nov. 3, 1951.
    Syncopating Sue (FN, 1926)
    McFadden's Flats (FN, 1927)
    The Poor Nut (FN, 1927)
    American Beauty (FN, 1927)
    A Texas Steer (FN, 1927)
    Lady Be Good (FN, 1928)
    The Butter and Egg Man (FN, 1928)
    The Shopworn Angel (Par., 1928)
    Innocents of Paris (Par., 1929)
    River of Romance (Par., 1929)
    Seven Days Leave (Par., 1930)
    Anybody's War (Par., 1930)
    The Right to Love (Par., 1930)
    Man of the World (Par., 1931)
    Kick In (Par., 1931)
    The Road to Reno (Par., 1931)
    Tomorrow and Tomorrow (Par., 1932)
    Thunder Below (Par., 1932)
    The Masquerader (UA, 1933)
    Eight Girls in a Boat (Par., 1934)
    The Little Minister (RKO, 1934)
    Wedding Present (Par., 1936)
    John Meade's Woman (Par., 1937)
    Blossoms on Broadway (Par., 1937)
    The Young in Heart (UA, 1938)
    The Under-Pup (Univ., 1939)
    Captain Caution (UA, 1940)
    A Girl, a Guy and a Gob (RKO, 1941)
    She Knew All the Answers (Col., 1941)
    Obliging Young Lady (RKO, 1941)
    The Wife Takes a Flyer (Col., 1942)
    A Night to Remember (Col., 1943)
    Bombardier (RKO, 1943)
    The Fallen Sparrow (RKO, 1943)
    My Kingdom for a Cook (Col., 1943)
    Bride By Mistake (RKO, 1944)
    It's in the Bag (UA, 1945)
    Kiss and Tell (Col., 1945)
    Because of Him (Univ., 1946)
    Framed (Col., 1947)
    Sinbad the Sailor (RKO, 1947)
    Tycoon (RKO, 1947)
    Let's Live a Little (Eagle Lion, 1948)
    Adventure in Baltimore (RKO, 1949)
    A Kiss for Corliss (UA, 1949)

WALSH, RAOUL, b. March 11, 1892, New York City.
    The Regeneration (Fox, 1915) (also producer, co-script)
    Carmen (Fox, 1915) (also producer, script)
    The Honor System (Fox, 1916)

Blue Blood and Red (Fox, 1916) (also producer, story, script)
The Serpent (Fox, 1916) (also producer, co-script)
The Conqueror (Fox, 1917)
Betrayed (Fox, 1917) (also producer, co-story, script)
This Is the Life (Fox, 1917) (also co-story, co-script)
The Pride of New York (Fox, 1917) (also story, script)
The Silent Lie (Fox, 1917)
The Innocent Sinner (Fox, 1917) (also script)
The Woman and the Law (Fox, 1918) (also script)
The Prussian Cur (Fox, 1918) (also story, script)
On the Jump (Fox, 1918) (also story, script)
Every Mother's Son (Fox, 1918) (also story, script)
I'll Say So (Fox, 1918)
Evangeline (Fox, 1919) (also producer, script)
The Strongest (Fox, 1919) (also script)
Should a Husband Forgive? (Fox, 1919) (also story, script)
From Now On (Fox, 1920) (also script)
The Deep Purple (Realart, 1920)
The Oath (Mayflower, 1921) (also producer, script)
Serenade (Associated FN, 1921) (also for production company)
Kindred of the Dust (Associated FN, 1922) (for production com-
   pany)
Lost and Found on a South Sea Island (Goldwyn, 1923)
The Thief of Bagdad (UA, 1924)
East of Suez (Par., 1925) (also producer)
The Spaniard (Par., 1925)
The Wanderer (Par., 1925) (also producer)
The Lucky Lady (Par., 1926) (also producer)
The Lady of the Harem (Par., 1926)
What Price Glory? (Fox, 1926)
The Monkey Talks (Fox, 1927) (also producer)
The Loves of Carmen (Fox, 1927)
Sadie Thompson (UA, 1928) (also script, actor)
The Red Dance (Fox, 1928) (also producer)
Me, Gangster (Fox, 1928) (also co-script)
Hot for Paris (Fox, 1929) (also story)
In Old Arizona (Fox, 1929) (with Irving Cummings)
The Cock-Eyed World (Fox, 1929) (also script)
The Big Trail (Fox, 1930)
The Man Who Came Back (Fox, 1931)
Women of All Nations (Fox, 1931)
The Yellow Ticket (Fox, 1931) (also producer)
Wild Girl (Fox, 1932)
Me and My Gal (Fox, 1932)
Hello Sister! (Fox, 1933) (uncredited with uncredited Erich von
   Stroheim who had together made the unreleased "Walking
   Down Broadway" from which this film was assembled)
Sailor's Luck (Fox, 1933)

Facing page: Franchot Tone (left), Joan Bennett, director Richard
Wallace, Cecil Cunningham, and Allyn Joslyn on the set of The
Wife Takes a Flyer (Col., 1942).

Raoul Walsh (ca. 1960)

The Bowery (UA, 1933)
Going Hollywood (MGM, 1933)
Under Pressure (Fox, 1935)
Baby-Face Harrigan (MGM, 1935)
Every Night at Eight (Par., 1935)
Klondike Annie (Par., 1936)
Big Brown Eyes (Par., 1936) (also co-script)
Spendthrift (Par., 1926) (also co-script)
O. H. M. S. (Gaumont-British, 1937)
Jump for Glory (Criterion, 1937)
Artists and Models (Par., 1937)
Hitting a New High (RKO, 1937)
College Swing (Par., 1938)
St. Louis Blues (Par., 1939)
The Roaring Twenties (WB, 1939)
Dark Command (Rep., 1940)
They Drive By Night (WB, 1940)
High Sierra (WB, 1941)
The Strawberry Blonde (WB, 1941)
Manpower (WB, 1941)

They Died With Their Boots On (WB, 1941)
Desperate Journey (WB, 1942)
Gentleman Jim (WB, 1942)
Background to Danger (WB, 1943)
Northern Pursuit (WB, 1943)
Uncertain Glory (WB, 1944)
Objective Burma (WB, 1945)
Salty O'Rourke (Par., 1945)
The Horn Blows at Midnight (WB, 1945)
The Man I Love (WB, 1946)
San Antonio (WB, 1946) (uncredited, with David Butler)
Pursued (WB, 1947)
Stallion Road (WB, 1947) (uncredited, with James V. Kern)
Cheyenne (WB, 1947)
Silver River (WB, 1948)
Fighter Squadron (WB, 1948)
One Sunday Afternoon (WB, 1948)
Colorado Territory (WB, 1949)
White Heat (WB, 1949)
Montana (WB, 1950) (uncredited, with Ray Enright)
Along the Great Divide (WB, 1951)
Captain Horatio Hornblower, (WB, 1951)
Distant Drums (WB, 1951)
The Enforcer (WB, 1951) (uncredited, with Bretaigne Windust)
Glory Alley (MGM, 1952)
The World in His Arms (Univ., 1952)
The Lawless Breed (Univ., 1952)
Blackbeard the Pirate (RKO, 1952)
She Devils (RKO, 1953)
A Lion Is in the Streets (WB, 1953)
Gun Fury (Col., 1953)
Saskatchewan (Univ., 1954)
Battle Cry (WB, 1955)
The Tall Men (20th, 1955)
The Revolt of Mamie Stover (20th, 1956)
The King and Four Queens (UA, 1956)
Band of Angels (WB, 1957)
The Naked and the Dead (RKO, 1958)
The Sheriff of Fractured Jaw (20th, 1958)
A Private's Affair (20th, 1959)
Esther and the King (20th, 1960) (also producer, co-script)
Marines, Let's Go (20th, 1961)
A Distant Trumpet (WB, 1964)

WALTERS, CHARLES, b. Nov. 17, 1913, Pasadena, Calif.
Good News (MGM, 1947)
Easter Parade (MGM, 1948)
The Barkleys of Broadway (MGM, 1949)
Summer Stock (MGM, 1950)
Three Guys Named Mike (MGM, 1951)
Texas Carnival (MGM, 1951)
The Belle of New York (MGM, 1952)

Lili (MGM, 1953) (also co-choreography)
Dangerous When Wet (MGM, 1953)
Torch Song (MGM, 1953) (also actor)
Easy to Love (MGM, 1953) (with Busby Berkeley)
The Glass Slipper (MGM, 1955)
The Tender Trap (MGM, 1955)
High Society (MGM, 1956)
Don't Go Near the Water (MGM, 1957)
Ask Any Girl (MGM, 1959)
Cimarron (MGM, 1960) (completed film for Anthony Mann)
Please Don't Eat the Daisies (MGM, 1960)
Two Loves (MGM, 1961)
Billy Rose's Jumbo (MGM, 1962) (with Busby Berkeley)
The Unsinkable Molly Brown (MGM, 1964)
Walk, Don't Run (Col., 1966)

WARHOL, ANDY, b. 1928, Pittsburgh.
Tarzan and Jane Regained Sort Of (Co-operative) (**, 1963)
Sleep (**, 1963)
Kiss (**, 1963)
Empire (**, 1964) (with John Palmer)
Henry Geldzahler (**, 1964)
Batman Dracula (**, 1964)
Soap Opera [The Lester Persky Story] (**, 1964)
Taylor Mead's Ass (**, 1964)
Suicide (**, 1965)
Screen Test One (**, 1965)
Screen Test Two (**, 1965)
The Life of Juanita Castro (**, 1965)
Drunk (**, 1965)
Horse (**, 1965)
Poor Little Rich Girl (**, 1965)
Vinyl (**, 1965)
Face (**, 1965)
Bitch (**, 1965)
Kitchen (**, 1965)
Afternoon (**, 1965)
Beauty Two (**, 1965)
Space (**, 1965)
Inner and Outer Space (**, 1965)
My Hustler (**, 1965)
Camp (**, 1965)
Paul Swan (**, 1965)
Hedy [Hedy the Shoplifter] (**, 1965)
The Closet (**, 1965)
More Milk, Evette [Lana Turner] (**, 1965)
Lupe (**, 1965)
Eating Too Fast (**, 1966)
The Velvet Underground and Nico (**, 1966)

**Film-Makers Co-Operative-Factory Release.

Chelsea Girls (**, 1966)
Four Stars (**, 1967)
Imitation of Christ (**, 1967)
I, a Man (**, 1967)
Bike Boy (**, 1967)
Lonesome Cowboys (**, 1968) (also producer, camera)
Blue Movie [Fuck] (**, 1968) (also producer, camera)
The Loves of Ondine (Andy Warhol, 1968) (also producer, camera)
Women in Revolt [Sex] (Andy Warhol, 1972)
L'Amour (Altura, 1973) (with Paul Morissey) (also co-script)

WAYNE, JOHN (Marion Michael Morrison), b. May 26, 1907, Winterset, Iowa.
The Alamo (UA, 1960) (also producer, actor)
The Green Berets (WB-7 Arts, 1968) (with Ray Kellogg, uncredited Mervyn LeRoy) (also actor)

WEBB, HARRY S.,
Coyote Fangs (Awyon, 1924) (also producer)
Ridin' West (Awyon, 1924) (also producer)
The Empty Saddle (Vitagraph, 1925)
The Mystery of Lost Ranch (Vitagraph, 1925) (with Tom Gibson)
Santa Fe Pete (Lariat, 1925)
Border Vengeance (Awyon, 1925) (also producer)
Cactus Trails (Awyon, 1925) (also producer)
Canyon Rustlers (Awyon, 1925) (also producer)
Desert Madness (Awyon, 1925) (also producer)
Double Fisted (Rayart, 1925) (also producer)
Silent Sheldon (Rayart, 1925) (also producer)
Starlight the Untamed (Rayart, 1925) (also producer)
The Man from Oklahoma (Rayart, 1926)
Starlight's Revenge (Rayart, 1926)
The Golden Stallion* (Mascot, 1927)
Heroes of the Wild* (Mascot, 1927)
Isle of Sunken Gold* (Mascot, 1927)
Dark Skies (Biltmore, 1929)
The Phantom of the North (Biltmore, 1929)
Untamed Justice (Biltmore, 1929)
Bar L Ranch (Big Four, 1930)
Beyond the Rio Grande (Big Four, 1939)
Ridin' Law (Big Four, 1930)
Phantom of the Desert (Syndicate, 1930) (also co-producer)
Westward Bound (Syndicate, 1930) (also co-producer)
West of Cheyenne (Syndicate, 1913)
Lone Trail (Syndicate, 1932) (with Forrest Sheldon)
Riot Squad (Mayfair, 1933)
Wolf Rides (Commodore, 1933)
Riding Thru (Steiner, 1934)
Tracy Rides (Steiner, 1934)

Fighting Hero (Steiner, 1934)
Unconquered Bandit (Steiner, 1935)

WEBB, JACK, b. April 2, 1920, Santa Monica, Calif.
Dragnet (WB, 1954) (also actor)
Pete Kelly's Blues (WB, 1955) (also actor)
The D.I. (WB, 1959) (also producer, actor)
--30-- (WB, 1959) (also producer, actor)
The Last Time I Saw Archie (AA, 1961) (also producer, actor)
Dragnet 1969 (NBC-TV, 1969) (also producer, actor)
The D.A.: Murder One (NBC-TV, 1969) (also producer)
O'Hara, U.S. Treasury: Operation Cobra (CBS-TV, 1971)
    (also producer)
Emergency! (NBC-TV, 1972) (also producer)

WEBER, LOIS (Mrs. Phillips Smalley), b. 1882, Pittsburgh; d.
    Nov. 13, 1939.
The Fool and His Money (Univ., 1914) (also actress)
The Merchant of Venice (Univ., 1914) (with Phillips Smalley)
    (also actress)
False Colors (Par., 1914) (also actress)
Hop, the Devil's Brew (Univ., 1915) (with Phillips Smalley)
    (also actress)
Sunshine Molly (Par., 1915) (also actress)
A Cigarette, That's All (Univ., 1915)
Scandal (Univ., 1915) (also actress)
Hypocrites (Bosworth, 1915) (with Phillips Smalley) (also script)
It's No Laughing Matter (Univ., 1915)
The Dumb Girl of Portici (Univ., 1916) (with Phillips Smalley)
Saving the Family Name (Univ., 1916) (also actress)
The People vs. John Doe (Univ., 1916) (also actress)
Idle Wives (Univ., 1916) (also actress)
Where Are My Children (Univ., 1916) (with Phillips Smalley)
The Flirt (Univ., 1916) (with Phillips Smalley)
The Price of a Good Time (Univ.-Jewel, 1917)
Even You and I (Peerless, 1917)
The Hand That Rocks the Cradle (Univ., 1917) (also producer,
    actress)
The Mysterious Mrs. Musslewhite (Univ., 1917)
For Husbands Only (Weber-North, 1918)
The Doctor and the Woman (Univ., 1918)
Borrowed Clothes (Univ., 1918)
Mary Regan (Associated FN, 1919)
A Midnight Romance (Associated FN, 1919)
When a Girl Loves (Univ., 1919)
Home (Univ., 1919)
Forbidden (Univ., 1919)
To Please One Woman (Par., 1920)
Too Wise Wives (Par., 1921) (also co-story, script)
What's Worthwhile? (Par., 1921) (also producer, script, for
    own production company)

The Blot (F.B. Warren, 1921) (also producer, script, for own production company)

What Do Men Want? (Wid Gunning, 1921) (also producer, script, for own production company)

A Chapter in Her Life (Univ.-Jewel, 1923) (also adaptation)

The Marriage Clause (Univ.-Jewel, 1926) (also adaptation)

Sensation Seekers (Univ.-Jewel, 1927) (also continuity)

The Angel of Broadway (Pathé, 1927)

White Heat (Pinnacle, 1934)

WEIS, DON, b. May 13, 1922, Milwaukee, Wisc.

Bannerline (MGM, 1951)

It's a Big Country (MGM, 1951) (with Charles Vidor, Richard Thorpe, John Sturges, Don Hartman, Clarence Brown, William Wellman)

Just This Once (MGM, 1952)

You for Me (MGM, 1952)

I Love Melvin (MGM, 1953)

Remains to Be Seen (MGM, 1953)

A Slight Case of Larceny (MGM, 1953)

The Affairs of Dobie Gillis (MGM, 1953)

Half a Hero (MGM, 1953)

The Adventures of Hajji Baba (20th, 1954)

Ride the High Iron (Col., 1956)

Mr. Pharaoh and His Cleopatra (1959--unreleased)

The Gene Krupa Story (Col., 1959)

Critic's Choice (WB, 1963)

Looking for Love (MGM, 1964)

Pajama Party (AIP, 1964)

Billie (UA, 1965) (also producer)

The Ghost in the Invisible Bikini (AIP, 1966)

The King's Pirate (Univ., 1967)

The Longest Hundred Miles (NBC-TV, 1967)

Did You Hear the One About the Traveling Saleslady? (Univ., 1968)

WELLES, ORSON, b. April 6, 1915, Kenosha, Wisc.

Citizen Kane (RKO, 1941) (also producer, story, co-script, actor)

The Magnificent Ambersons (RKO, 1942) (also producer, narrator)

It's All True (RKO, 1942--unfinished) (also producer)

Journey Into Fear (RKO, 1943) (uncredited, with Norman Foster) (also co-script, actor)

The Stranger (RKO, 1946) (also script, actor)

Macbeth (Rep., 1948) (also producer, script, actor)

The Lady from Shanghai (Col., 1948) (also producer, script, actor)

Othello (UA, 1952) (also producer, script, actor)

Confidential Report [Mr. Arkadin] (WB, 1955) (also producer, script, actor)

Orson Welles (ca. 1962)

Touch of Evil (Univ., 1958) (also script, actor)
Don Quixote (1959--unfinished) (also script)
The Trial (Gibraltar, 1963) (also script, actor)
Chimes at Midnight (Couner, 1966) (also script, actor)
The Immortal Story (Col., 1967) (also actor)

WELLMAN, WILLIAM A., b. Feb. 29, 1896, Brookline, Mass.
The Man Who Won (Fox, 1923)
Second Hand Love (Fox, 1923)
Big Dan (Fox, 1923)

Cupid's Fireman (Fox, 1923)
The Vagabond Trail (Fox, 1924)
Not a Drum Was Heard (Fox, 1924)
The Circus Cowboy (Fox, 1924)
When Husbands Flirt (Col., 1925)
The Boob (MGM, 1926)
The Cat's Pajamas (Par., 1926)
You Never Know Women (Par. 1926)
The Legion of the Condemned (Par., 1928)
Ladies of the Mob (Par., 1928)
Beggars of Life (Par., 1928)
Wings (Par., 1929)
Chinatown Nights (Par., 1929)
The Man I Love (Par., 1929)
Woman Trap (Par., 1929)
Dangerous Paradise (Par., 1930)
Young Eagles (Par., 1930)
Maybe It's Love (WB, 1930)
Other Men's Women (WB, 1931)
The Public Enemy (WB, 1931)
The Star Witness (WB, 1931)
Night Nurse (WB, 1931)
Safe in Hell (FN, 1931)
The Hatchet Man (FN, 1932)
Love Is a Racket (FN, 1932)
So Big (WB, 1932)
The Purchase Price (WB, 1932)
The Conquerors (RKO, 1932)
Frisco Jenny (FN, 1933)
Central Airport (FN, 1933)
Lilly Turner (FN, 1933)
Wild Boys of the Road (FN, 1933)
Heroes for Sale (FN, 1933)
Midnight Mary (MGM, 1933)
College Coach (WB, 1933)
Looking for Trouble (UA, 1934)
Stingaree (RKO, 1934)
The President Vanishes (Par., 1934)
Call of the Wild (UA, 1935)
Robin Hood of El Dorado (MGM, 1936) (also co-script)
Small Town Girl (MGM, 1936)
A Star Is Born (UA, 1937) (also co-story)
Nothing Sacred (UA, 1937)
Men With Wings (Par., 1938) (also producer)
Beau Geste (Par., 1939) (also producer)
The Light That Failed (Par., 1939) (also producer)
Reaching for the Sun (Par., 1941) (also producer)
Roxie Hart (20th, 1942)
The Great Man's Lady (Par., 1942) (also producer)
Thunder Birds (20th, 1942)
Lady of Burlesque (UA, 1943)
The Ox-Bow Incident (20th, 1943)
Buffalo Bill (20th, 1944)

William Wellman (1973)

This Man's Navy (MGM, 1945)
The Story of G. I. Joe (20th, 1945) (also producer)
Gallant Journey (Col., 1946) (also producer, co-script)
Magic Town (RKO, 1947)
The Iron Curtain (20th, 1948)
Yellow Sky (20th, 1948)
Battleground (MGM, 1949)
The Next Voice You Hear (MGM, 1950)
The Happy Years (MGM, 1950)
It's a Big Country (MGM, 1951) (with Charles Vidor, Richard
    Thorpe, John Sturges, Don Hartman, Don Weis, Clarence
    Brown)
Across the Wide Missouri (MGM, 1951)
Westward the Women (MGM, 1951)
My Man and I (MGM, 1952)
Island in the Sky (WB, 1953)
The High and the Mighty (WB, 1954)
Track of the Cat (WB, 1954)
Blood Alley (WB, 1955)
Goodbye, My Lady (WB, 1956)
Darby's Rangers (WB, 1958)
Lafayette Escadrille (WB, 1958) (also story)

WENDKOS, PAUL, b. Sept. 20, 1926, Philadelphia.
    The Burglar (Col., 1957)
    The Case Against Brooklyn (Col., 1958)
    Tarawa Beachhead (Col., 1958)
    Gidget (Col., 1959)
    Face of a Fugitive (Col., 1959)
    Battle of the Coral Sea (Col., 1959)
    Because They're Young (Col., 1960)
    Angel Baby (AA, 1961) (replaced Lazlo Benedek)
    Gidget Goes Hawaiian (Col., 1961)
    Temple of the Swinging Doll (20th, 1961)
    Gidget Goes to Rome (Col., 1963)
    Recoil (Lion, 1963)
    Johnny Tiger (Univ., 1966)
    Guns of the Magnificent Seven (UA, 1968)
    Attack on the Iron Coast (UA, 1968)
    Hawaii Five-O (CBS-TV, 1968)
    Hell Boats (UA, 1969)
    Fear No Evil (NBC-TV, 1969)
    Cannon for Cordoba (UA, 1970)
    Brotherhood of the Bell (CBS-TV, 1970)
    The Mephisto Waltz (20th, 1971)
    Travis Logan M. D. (CBS-TV, 1971)
    A Tattered Web (CBS-TV, 1971)
    A Little Game (ABC-TV, 1971)
    A Death of Innocence (CBS-TV, 1971)
    The Delphi Bureau (ABC-TV, 1972)
    Haunts of the Very Rich (ABC-TV, 1972)
    The Obsession (ABC-TV, 1972)

The Family Rico (CBS-TV, 1972)
Terror on the Beach (CBS-TV, 1973)
Honor Thy Father (ABC-TV, 1973)

WERKER, ALFRED LOUIS, b. Dec. 2, 1896, Deadwood, S.D.
Ridin' the Wind (Mon., 1925) (with Del Andrews)
The Pioneer Scout (Par., 1928) (with Lloyd Ingraham)
The Sunset Legion (Par., 1928) (with Lloyd Ingraham)
Kit Carson (Par., 1928)
Blue Skies (Fox, 1929)
Chasing Through Europe (Fox, 1929) (with David Butler)
Double Cross Roads (Fox, 1930)
Last of the Duanes (Fox, 1930)
Fair Warning (Fox, 1931)
Annabelle's Affair (Fox, 1931)
Heartbreak (Fox, 1931)
The Gay Caballero (Fox, 1932)
Bachelor's Affairs (Fox, 1932)
Rackety Rax (Fox, 1932)
It's Great to Be Alive (Fox, 1933)
Hello Sister! (Fox, 1933) (revise of Erich von Stroheim's un-
    released "Walking Down Broadway")
Advice to the Lovelorn (UA, 1933)
The House of Rothschild (UA, 1934)
You Belong to Me (Par., 1934)
Stolen Harmony (Par., 1935)
We Have Our Moments (Univ., 1937)
Wild and Woolly (20th, 1937)
Big Town Girl (20th, 1937)
City Girl (20th, 1937)
Kidnapped (20th, 1938)
Gateway (20th, 1938)
Up the River (20th, 1938)
It Could Happen to You (20th, 1939)
News Is Made at Night (20th, 1939)
The Adventures of Sherlock Holmes (20th, 1939)
The Reluctant Dragon (RKO, 1941)
Moon Over Her Shoulder (20th, 1941)
Whispering Ghosts (20th, 1942)
A-Hunting We Will Go (20th, 1942)
The Mad Martindales (20th, 1942)
My Pal Wolf (RKO, 1944)
Shock (20th, 1946)
Repeat Performance (Eagle Lion, 1947)
Pirates of Monterey (Univ., 1947)
He Walked By Night (Eagle Lion, 1948)
Lost Boundaries (Film Classics, 1949)
Sealed Cargo (RKO, 1951)
Walk East on Beacon (Col., 1952)
Devil's Canyon (RKO, 1953)
Three Hours to Kill (Col., 1954)
Canyon Crossroads (UA, 1955)

At Gunpoint (AA, 1955)
Rebel in Town (UA, 1956)
The Young Don't Cry (Col., 1957)

WEST, ROLAND, b. 1887, Cleveland, Ohio; d. March 31, 1952.
De Luxe Annie (Schenck-Select, 1918)
The Silver Lining (Metro, 1921) (also producer, script)
Nobody (Associated FN, 1921) (also producer, story, co-script)
The Unknown Purple (Truart, 1923) (also co-adaptation)
The Monster (Metro-Goldwyn, 1925)
The Bat (UA, 1926) (also producer, adaptation)
The Dove (UA, 1927) (also co-adaptation)
Alibi (UA, 1929) (also producer, co-script-titles-dialog)
Bat Whispers (UA, 1931) (also script)
Corsair (UA, 1931)

WHALE, JAMES, b. July 22, 1896, Dudley, Staffs, England; d.
        May 29, 1957.
Journey's End (Tiffany, 1930)
Waterloo Bridge (Univ., 1931)
Frankenstein (Univ., 1931)
The Old Dark House (Univ., 1932)
The Impatient Maiden (Univ., 1932)
The Invisible Man (Univ., 1933)
The Kiss Before the Mirror (Univ., 1933)
By Candlelight (Univ., 1933)
One More River (Univ., 1934)
The Bride of Frankenstein (Univ., 1935)
Remember Last Night? (Univ., 1935)
Show Boat (Univ., 1936)
The Road Back (Univ., 1937)
The Great Garrick (WB, 1937)
Sinners in Paradise (Univ., 1938)
Port of Seven Seas (MGM, 1938)
Under Suspicion (Univ., 1938)
The Man in the Iron Mask (Univ., 1939)
Green Hell (Univ., 1939)
They Dare Not Love (Col., 1941)
Hello Out There (Unfinished, 1949)

WILBUR, CRANE, b. Nov. 17, 1889, Athens, N.Y.
Tomorrow's Children (Fox, 1934) (also script)
High School Girl (Fox, 1935)
The People's Enemy (RKO, 1935)
Yellow Cargo (Pacific, 1936) (also script)
We're in the Legion Now (Grand National, 1936)
Devil on Horseback (Grand National, 1936) (also story, script)
Navy Spy (Grand National, 1937) (also script)
The Patient in Room 18 (WB, 1938) (with Robert Connolly)
I Am Not Afraid (WB, 1939)

The Devil on Wheels (PRC, 1947)
Canon City [Canyon City] (Eagle Lion, 1948) (also script)
The Story of Molly X (Univ., 1949) (also script)
Outside the Wall (Univ., 1950) (also script)
Inside the Walls of Folsom Prison (WB, 1951) (also story, script)
The Bat (AA, 1959) (also adaptation, script)

WILCOX, FRED M., b. 1905, Tazewell, Va.; d. 1964.
Lassie Comes Home (MGM, 1943)
The Courage of Lassie (MGM, 1946)
Three Daring Daughters (MGM, 1948)
Hills of Home (MGM, 1948)
The Secret Garden (MGM, 1949)
Shadow in the Sky (MGM, 1951)
Code Two (MGM, 1953)
Tennessee Champ (MGM, 1954)
Forbidden Planet (MGM, 1956)
I Passed for White (AA, 1960) (also producer, script)

WILDE, CORNEL, b. Oct. 13, 1918, New York City.
Storm Fear (UA, 1956) (also as producer, actor)
The Devil's Hairpin (Par., 1957) (also as producer, co-script, actor)
Maracaibo (Par., 1958) (also as producer, actor)
The Sword of Lancelot [Lancelot and Guinevere] (Univ., 1963) (also as executive producer, actor)
The Naked Prey (Par., 1966) (also as producer, actor)
Beach Red (UA, 1967) (also as producer, actor)
No Blade of Grass (MGM, 1970) (also as producer)

WILDER, BILLY (Samuel Wilder), b. June 22, 1906, Vienna.
Mauvaise Graine (German, 1934) (with Alexander Esnay) (also story)
The Major and the Minor (Par., 1942) (also co-script)
Five Graves to Cairo (Par., 1943) (also co-script)
Double Indemnity (Par., 1944) (also co-script)
The Lost Weekend (Par., 1945) (also co-script)
The Emperor Waltz (Par., 1948) (also co-script)
A Foreign Affair (Par., 1948) (also co-script)
Sunset Boulevard (Par., 1950) (also co-script)
Ace in the Hole [The Big Carnival] (Par., 1951) (also producer, co-script)
Stalag 17 (Par., 1953) (also producer, co-script)
Sabrina (Par., 1954) (also producer, co-script)
The Seven Year Itch (20th, 1955) (also co-producer, co-script)
The Spirit of St. Louis (WB, 1957) (also co-script)
Love in the Afternoon (AA, 1957) (also co-script)
Witness for the Prosecution (UA, 1958) (also co-script)
Some Like It Hot (UA, 1959) (also producer, co-script)

Tony Curtis (left, with run in stocking) with Billy Wilder on the set of <u>Some Like It Hot</u> (UA, 1959).

The Apartment (UA, 1960) (also producer, co-script)
One, Two, Three (UA, 1961) (also producer, co-script)
Irma La Douce (UA, 1963) (also producer, co-script)
Kiss Me, Stupid (UA, 1964) (also producer, co-script)
The Fortune Cookie (UA, 1966) (also producer, co-script)
The Private Life of Sherlock Holmes (UA, 1970) (also producer, co-script)
Avanti! (UA, 1972) (also producer, co-script)

WILLIAMS, ELMO, b. April 30, 1913, Lone Wolf, Okla.
The Tall Texan (Rep., 1952) (also editor)
The Cowboy (Lip., 1954) (also editor)
Apache Warrior (20th, 1957)
Hell Ship Mutiny (Rep., 1957) (with Lee Sholem) (also editor)

WINDUST, BRETAIGNE, b. Jan. 20, 1906, Paris; d. March 18, 1960.
Winter Meeting (WB, 1948)
June Bride (WB, 1948)
Perfect Strangers (WB, 1950)
Pretty Baby (WB, 1950)
The Enforcer (WB, 1951) (with uncredited Raoul Walsh)
Face to Face (ep: "The Bride Comes to Yellow Sky") (RKO, 1952) (with John Brahm)
The Pied Piper of Hamelin (NBC-TV, 1957)

WISBAR, FRANK (Franz Wysbar), b. 1899, Tilsit, East Prussia; d. March 17, 1967.
Im Bann des Ulenspiegels (German, 1932)
Anna und Elisabeth (German, 1933) (also co-script)
Rivalen der Luft (German, 1934)
Hermine und die Sieben Aufrechten (German, 1935) (also co-script)
Die Werft zum Grauen Hecht (German, 1935) (also script)
Fährmann Maria (German, 1936) (also co-script)
Die Unbekannte (German, 1936) (also co-script)
Ball im Metropol (German, 1937) (also co-script)
Petermann Ist Dagegen (German, 1937) (also co-script)
Strangler of the Swamp (PRC, 1945) (also co-story, script)
Devil Bat's Daughter (PRC, 1946) (also co-producer, co-story)
Lighthouse (PRC, 1946)
Secrets of a Sorority Girl (PRC, 1946)
The Prairie (Screen Guild, 1947)
The Mozart Story (Screen Guild, 1948)
Haie und Kleine Fische (German, 1957)
Nasser Asphalt (German, 1958)
Hunde, Wollt Ihr Ewig Leben! [Battle Inferno] (German, 1959) (also co-script)
Nacht Fiel über Gotenhafen (German, 1959) (also co-script)
Fabrik der Offiziere (German, 1960)

Barbara (German, 1961)
Marcia o Crepa [Sprung in die Hölle] (Italian-German, 1962)
    (also co-script)
Durchbruch Lok 234 (German, 1963)

WISE, ROBERT, b. Sept. 10, 1914, Winchester, Ind.
    The Curse of the Cat People (RKO, 1944) (with Gunther von
        Fritsch)
    Mademoiselle Fifi (RKO, 1944)
    The Body Snatchers (RKO, 1945)
    A Game of Death (RKO, 1945)
    Criminal Court (RKO, 1946)
    Born to Kill (RKO, 1946)
    Blood on the Moon (RKO, 1948)
    Mystery in Mexico (RKO, 1948)
    The Set-Up (RKO, 1949)
    Three Secrets (WB, 1950)

Susan Hayward with Robert Wise discussing I Want to Live! (UA,
1958).

Two Flags West (20th, 1950)
The House on Telegraph Hill (20th, 1951)
The Day the Earth Stood Still (20th, 1951)
The Captive City (UA, 1952)
Something for the Birds (20th, 1952)
Destination Gobi (20th, 1953)
The Desert Rats (20th, 1953)
So Big (WB, 1953)
Executive Suite (MGM, 1954)
Helen of Troy (WB, 1955)
Tribute to a Bad Man (MGM, 1956)
Somebody Up There Likes Me (MGM, 1956)
This Could Be the Night (MGM, 1957)
Until They Sail (MGM, 1957)
Run Silent, Run Deep (UA, 1958)
I Want to Live! (UA, 1958)
Odds Against Tomorrow (UA, 1959) (also producer)
West Side Story (UA, 1961) (with Jerome Robbins) (also producer)
Two for the Seesaw (UA, 1962)
The Haunting (MGM, 1963 (also producer)
The Sound of Music (20th, 1964) (also producer)
The Sand Pebbles (20th, 1966) (also producer)
Star! (20th, 1968) (also producer)
The Andromeda Strain (Univ., 1971) (also producer)
Two People (Univ., 1973) (also producer)

WITNEY, WILLIAM, b. May 15, 1910, Lawton, Okla.
The Trigger Trio (Rep., 1937)
The Painted Stallion* (Rep., 1937) (with Ray Taylor)
S.O.S. Coast Guard* (Rep., 1937) (with Alan James)
Zorro Rides Again* (Rep., 1937) (with John English)
Dick Tracy Returns* (Rep., 1938) (with John English)
The Fighting Devil Dogs* (Rep., 1938) (with John English and Robert Beche)
Hawk of the Wilderness* (Rep., 1938) (with John English)
The Lone Ranger* (Rep., 1938) (with John English)
Daredevils of the Red Circle* (Rep., 1938) (with John English)
Dick Tracy's G-Men* (Rep., 1938) (with John English)
The Lone Ranger Rides Again* (Rep., 1938) (with John English)
Zorro's Fighting Legion* (Rep., 1939) (with John English)
Adventures of Red Ryder* (Rep., 1940) (with John English)
Drums of Fu Manchu* (Rep., 1940) (with John English)
Hi-Yo Silver (Rep., 1940) (with John English)
King of the Royal Mounted* (Rep., 1940) (with John English)
Heroes of the Saddle (Rep., 1940)
The Mysterious Dr. Satan* (Rep., 1940) (with John English)
Adventures of Captain Marvel* (Rep., 1940) (with John English)
Dick Tracy vs. Crime Inc.* (Rep., 1941) (with John English)
Jungle Girl* (Rep., 1941) (with John English)
King of the Texas Rangers* (Rep., 1941) (with John English)
Perils of Nyoka* (Rep., 1942) (with John English)

The Yukon Patrol (Rep., 1942) (with John English)
Spy Smasher* (Rep., 1942) (with John English)
Outlaws of Pine Ridge (Rep., 1942)
King of the Mounties* (Rep., 1942)
G-Men vs. The Black Dragon* (Rep., 1943)
The Crimson Ghost* (Rep., 1946) (with Fred C. Brannon)
Home in Oklahoma (Rep., 1946)
Roll on Texas Moon (Rep., 1946)
Helldorado (Rep., 1946)
Apache Rose (Rep., 1947)
Bells of San Angelo (Rep., 1947)
Springtime in the Sierras (Rep., 1947)
On the Spanish Trail (Rep., 1947)
The Gay Ranchero (Rep., 1948)
Under California Skies (Rep., 1948)
Eyes of Texas (Rep., 1948)
Night Time in Nevada (Rep., 1948)
Ghost Canyon Trail (Rep., 1948)
The Far Frontier (Rep., 1948)
Susanna Pass (Rep., 1949)
Down Dakota Way (Rep., 1949)
The Golden Stallion (Rep., 1949)
Bells of Coronado (Rep., 1950)
Twilight in the Sierras (Rep., 1950)
Trigger Jr. (Rep., 1950)
Sunset in the West (Rep., 1950)
North of the Great Divide (Rep., 1950)
Trail of Robin Hood (Rep., 1950)
Heart of the Rockies (Rep., 1951)
Spoilers of the Plains (Rep., 1951)
In Old Amarillo (Rep., 1951)
South of Caliente (Rep., 1951)
Pals of the Golden West (Rep., 1951)
Border Saddlemates (Rep., 1952)
South Pacific Trail (Rep., 1952)
The Last Musketeer (Rep., 1952)
Colorado Sundown (Rep., 1952)
The Fortune Hunter (Rep., 1952)
Old Oklahoma Plains (Rep., 1952)
The Wac from Walla Walla (Rep., 1952)
Old Overland Trail (Rep., 1953)
Down Laredo Way (Rep., 1953)
Iron Mountain Trail (Rep., 1953)
Shadows of Tombstone (Rep., 1953)
The Outcast (Rep., 1954)
Santa Fe Passage (Rep., 1955)
City of Shadows (Rep., 1955)
Headline Hunters (Rep., 1955)
The Fighting Chance (Rep., 1955)
A Strange Adventure (Rep., 1956)
Stranger at My Door (Rep., 1956)
Panama Sal (Rep., 1957)
Pale Arrow (Rep., 1957)

The Cool and the Crazy (AIP, 1958)
Juvenile Jungle (Rep., 1958)
Young and Wild (Rep., 1958)
The Bonnie Parker Story (AIP, 1958)
Valley of the Redwoods (20th, 1960)
The Secret of Purple Reef (20th, 1960)
The Cat Burglar (AA, 1961)
Master of the World (AIP, 1961)
The Long Rope (20th, 1961)
Apache Rifles (20th, 1964)
Arizona Raiders (Col., 1965)
The Girls on the Beach (Par., 1965)
I Colorados (Rep., 1967)
Forty Guns to Apache Pass (Col., 1967)
Ride the Wind (NBC-TV, 1967)
Tarzan's Jungle Rebellion (National General, 1970)
I Escaped from Devil's Island (UA, 1973)

WOOD, EDWARD D., JR.
Glen or Glenda? [I Led Two Lives] (Weiss Bros., 1953) (also
    producer, script)
Bride of the Monster (Banner, 1956) (also script)
Plan 9 from Outer Space (DCA, 1959) (also producer, script)
Night of the Ghouls (unreleased, 1959) (also producer, script)

WOOD, SAM, b. July 10, 1883, Philadelphia; d. Sept. 22, 1949.
Double Speed (Par., 1920)
Excuse My Dust (Par., 1920)
The Dancin' Fool (Par., 1920)
Sick-A-Bed (Par., 1920)
What's Your Hurry? (Par., 1920)
The City Sparrow (Par., 1920)
Her Beloved Villain (Realart, 1921)
Peck's Bad Boy (FN, 1921) (also adaptation)
Her First Elopement (Realart, 1921)
The Snob (Realart, 1921)
The Great Moment (Par., 1921)
Under the Lash (Par., 1921)
Don't Tell Everything (Par., 1921)
Her Husband's Trademark (Par., 1922)
Her Gilded Cage (Par., 1922)
The Impossible Mrs. Bellew (Par., 1922)
Beyond the Rocks (Par., 1922)
My American Wife (Par., 1923)
Prodigal Daughters (Par., 1923)
Bluebeard's Eighth Wife (Par., 1923)
His Children's Children (Par., 1923)
The Female (FN, 1924)
The Next Corner (Par., 1924)
Bluff (Par., 1924)
The Mine With the Iron Door (Principal, 1924)

The Re-Creation of Brian Kent (Principal, 1925)
Fascinating Youth (Par., 1926)
One Minute to Play (FBO, 1926)
Rookies (MGM, 1927)
A Racing Romeo (FBO, 1927)
The Fair Co-ed (MGM, 1927)
The Latest from Paris (MGM, 1928)
Telling the World (MGM, 1928)
It's a Great Life (MGM, 1929)
So This Is College (MGM, 1929)
The Girl Said No (MGM, 1930)
They Learned About Women (MGM, 1930) (with Jack Conway)
Sins of the Children (MGM, 1930)
Way for a Sailor (MGM, 1930)
Paid (MGM, 1930)
A Tailor-Made Man (MGM, 1931)
Man in Possession (MGM, 1931)
New Adventures of Get-Rich-Quick Wallingford (MGM, 1931)
Huddle (MGM, 1932)
Prosperity (MGM, 1932)
The Barbarian (MGM, 1933)
Hold Your Man (MGM, 1933)
Christopher Bean (MGM, 1933)
Stamboul Quest (MGM, 1934)
A Night at the Opera (MGM, 1935)
Let 'Em Have It (UA, 1935)
Whipsaw (MGM, 1936)
The Unguarded Hour (MGM, 1936)
A Day at the Races (MGM, 1937) (also producer)
Madame X (MGM, 1937)
Navy, Blue and Gold (MGM, 1937)
Lord Jeff (MGM, 1938)
Stablemates (MGM, 1938)
Goodbye, Mr. Chips (MGM, 1939)
Our Town (UA, 1940)
Raffles (UA, 1940)
Rangers of Fortune (Par., 1940)
Kitty Foyle (RKO, 1940)
The Devil and Miss Jones (RKO, 1941)
Kings Row (WB, 1942)
The Pride of the Yankees (RKO, 1942)
For Whom the Bell Tolls (Par., 1943) (also producer)
Casanova Brown (RKO, 1944)
Guest Wife (RKO, 1945)
Saratoga Trunk (Par., 1946)
Heartbeat (RKO, 1946)
Ivy (Univ., 1947)
The Stratton Story (MGM, 1949)
Command Decision (MGM, 1949)
Ambush (MGM, 1949)

WRIGHT, MACK V., b. 1895, Princeton, Ind.; d. 1963.
Haunted Gold (WB, 1932)
Somewhere in Sonora (WB, 1933)
Man from Monterey (WB, 1933)
Cappy Ricks Returns (Rep., 1935)
Robinson Crusoe on Clipper Island* (Rep., 1936) (with Ray
  Taylor)
The Vigilantes Are Coming* (Rep., 1936) (with Ray Taylor)
Winds of the Wasteland (Rep., 1936)
Comin' Round the Mountain (Rep., 1936)
The Singing Cowboy (Rep., 1936)
The Big Show (Rep., 1936)
Roarin' Lead (Rep., 1936) (with Sam Newfield)
Rootin' Tootin' Rhythm (Rep., 1937)
Hit the Saddle (Rep., 1937)
Riders of the Whistling Skull (Rep., 1937)
Range Defenders (Rep., 1937)
The Great Adventures of Wild Bill Hickock* (Col., 1938) (with
  Sam Nelson)
The Man from Tascosa [Wells Fargo Days] (WB, 1940)
The Sea Hound* (Col., 1942) (with Walter B. Eason)

WYLER, WILLIAM, b. July 1, 1902, Mulhouse, Alsace, France.
Lazy Lightning (Univ., 1926)
The Stolen Ranch (Univ., 1926)
Blazing Days (Univ., 1927)
Hard Fists (Univ., 1927)
Shooting Straight (Independent, 1927)
The Border Cavalier (Univ., 1927)
Straight Shootin' (Univ., 1927)
Thunder Riders (Univ., 1928)
Anybody Here Seen Kelly? (Univ., 1928)
The Shakedown (Univ., 1929)
The Love Trap (Univ., 1929)
Hell's Heroes (Univ., 1929)
The Storm (Univ., 1930)
A House Divided (Univ., 1932)
Tom Brown of Culver (Univ., 1932)
The Old Dark House (Univ., 1932) (uncredited, with James
  Whale)
Her First Mate (Univ., 1933)
Counsellor at Law (Univ., 1933)
Glamour (Univ., 1934)
The Good Fairy (Univ., 1935)
The Gay Deception (Col.., 1935)
These Three (UA, 1936)
Come and Get It! (UA, 1936) (with Howard Hawks)

Facing page: Tom Brown (left, facing), a makeup man, James
Stewart, Robert Young, and Florence Rice with Sam Wood (seated)
on the set for Navy Blue and Gold (MGM, 1937).

Dodsworth (UA, 1936)
Dead End (UA, 1937)
Jezebel (WB, 1938)
Wuthering Heights (UA, 1939)
The Westerner (UA, 1940)
The Letter (WB, 1940)
The Little Foxes (RKO, 1941)
Mrs. Miniver (MGM, 1942)
The Memphis Belle (Par., 1944) (also producer, script, co-camera)
The Fighting Lady (20th, 1944)
The Best Years of Our Lives (RKO, 1946)
Thunderbolt (Mon., 1947) (with John Sturges)
The Heiress (Par., 1949) (also producer)
Detective Story (Par., 1951)
Carrie (Par., 1952) (also producer)
Roman Holiday (Par., 1953) (also producer)
The Desperate Hours (Par., 1955) (also producer)
Friendly Persuasion (AA, 1956) (also producer)
The Big Country (UA, 1958) (also co-producer)
Ben-Hur (MGM, 1959)
The Children's Hour (UA, 1962) (also producer)
The Collector (Col., 1964)
How to Steal a Million (20th, 1966)
Funny Girl (Col., 1968)
The Liberation of L.B. Jones (Col., 1970)

Y

YARBROUGH, JEAN, b. Aug. 22, 1900, Marianna, Ark.
Rebellious Daughters (Progressive, 1938)
The Devil Bat (PRC, 1940)
Father Steps Out (Mon., 1941)
Caught in the Act (PRC, 1941)
City Limits (Mon., 1941)
The Gang's All Here (Mon., 1941)
Top Sergeant Mulligan (Mon., 1941)
South of Panama (PRC, 1941)
Let's Go Collegiate (Mon., 1941)
King of the Zombies (Mon., 1941)
Criminal Investigator (Mon., 1942)
Man from Headquarters (Mon., 1942)
Meet the Mob (Mon., 1942)
Lure of the Islands (Mon., 1942)
So's Your Aunt Emma (Mon., 1942)
Law of the Jungle (Mon., 1942)
She's in the Army (Mon., 1942)
Police Bullets (Mon., 1942)
Follow the Band (Univ., 1943)
Get Going (Univ., 1943)
Good Morning Judge (Univ., 1943)
Hi Ya Sailor (Univ., 1943) (also producer)

So's Your Uncle (Univ., 1943) (also producer)
In Society (Univ., 1944)
Moon over Las Vegas (Univ., 1944) (also producer)
South of Dixie (Univ., 1944)
Twilight on the Prairie (Univ., 1944)
Week-End Pass (Univ., 1944)
Here Come the Co-eds (Univ., 1945)
The Naughty Nineties (Univ., 1945)
On Stage Everybody (Univ., 1945)
Under Western Skies (Univ., 1945)
Cuban Pete (Univ., 1946)
House of Horrors (Univ., 1946)
Inside Job (Univ., 1946) (also producer)
She-Wolf of London (Univ., 1946)
The Brute Man (PRC, 1947)
The Challenge (20th, 1948)
Shed No Tears (Eagle Lion, 1948)
The Creeper (20th, 1948)
Triple Threat (Col., 1948)
Holiday in Havana (Mon., 1949)
The Mutineers (Mon., 1949)
Leave It to Henry (Mon., 1949)
Henry, the Rainmaker (Mon., 1949)
Master Minds (Mon., 1949)
Angels in Disguise (Mon., 1949)
Tall Timber (Mon., 1950)
Joe Palooka Meets Humphrey (Mon., 1950)
Joe Palooka in Humphrey Takes a Chance (Mon., 1950)
Triple Trouble (Mon., 1950)
Sideshow (Mon., 1950)
Square Dance Katy (Mon., 1950)
Father Makes Good (Mon., 1951)
Casa Manana (Mon., 1951)
According to Mrs. Hoyle (Mon., 1951)
Lost in Alaska (Univ., 1952)
Jack and the Beanstalk (Univ., 1952)
Night Freight (AA, 1954)
Crashing Las Vegas (AA, 1956)
Hot Shots (AA, 1956)
The Women of Pitcairn Island (20th, 1956)
Yaqui Drums (AA, 1956)
Footsteps in the Night (AA, 1957)
Saintly Sinners (UA, 1962)
Hillbillys in a Haunted House (Woolner Bros., 1967)
The Over-the-Hill Gang (ABC-TV, 1969)

YATES, PETER, b. 1929, Aldershot, Eng.
    Summer Holiday (Warner-Pathé, 1962)
    One Way Pendulum (Lopert, 1965)
    Robbery (Emb., 1967) (also co-script)
    Bullitt (WB-7 Arts, 1968)
    John and Mary (20th, 1969)

Murphy's War (MGM, 1971)
The Hot Rock (20th, 1972)
The Friends of Eddie Coyle (Par., 1973)

YORKIN, BUD (Alan "Bud" Yorkin), b. Feb. 22, 1926, Washington, Pa.
Come Blow Your Horn (Par., 1963) (also co-producer)
Never Too Late (WB, 1965)
Divorce American Style (Col., 1967)
Inspector Clouseau (UA, 1968)
Start the Revolution Without Me (WB, 1970) (also producer)
Cold Turkey (UA, 1971) (also executive producer)
The Thief Who Came to Dinner (WB, 1973) (also producer and for own co-production company)

YOUNG, HAROLD M., b. Nov. 13, 1897, Portland, Ore.
Too Many Millions (WB, 1934)
The Scarlet Pimpernel (UA, 1934)
Without Regret (Par., 1935)
Woman Trap (Par., 1936)
My American Wife (Par., 1936)
Let Them Live! (Univ., 1937)
52nd Street (UA, 1937)
Little Tough Guy (Univ., 1938)
The Storm (Univ., 1938)
Code of the Streets (Univ., 1939)
Newboys' Home (Univ., 1939)
The Forgotten Woman (Univ., 1939)
Sabotage (Univ., 1939)
Hero for a Day (Univ., 1939)
Dreaming Out Loud (RKO, 1940)
Bachelor Daddy (Univ., 1941)
Juke Box Jenny (Univ., 1942)
Rubber Racketeers (Mon., 1942)
The Mummy's Tomb (Univ., 1942)
There's One Born Every Minute (Univ., 1942)
Hi, Buddy (Univ., 1943)
Hi-Ya Chum (Univ., 1943)
I Escaped from the Gestapo (Mon., 1943)
Spy Train (Mon., 1943)
Machine Gun Mama (PRC, 1944)
The Frozen Ghost (Univ., 1945)
Jungle Captive (Univ., 1945)
I'll Remember April (Univ., 1945)
Song of the Sarong (Univ., 1945)
Citizen Saint (Clyde Elliott, 1947)

Facing page: Deborah Kerr and Peter Ustinov (right) with Fred Zinneman on the set for The Sundowners (WB, 1960).

Z

ZINNEMANN, FRED, b. April 29, 1907, Vienna.
Redes (Strand, 1934) (with Emilio Gomez Muriel)
Kid Glove Killer (MGM, 1942)
Eyes in the Night (MGM, 1942)
The Seventh Cross (MGM, 1944)
Little Mister Jim (MGM, 1946)
My Brother Talks to Horses (MGM, 1946)
The Search (MGM, 1948)
Act of Violence (MGM, 1948)
The Men (Col., 1950)
Teresa (MGM, 1951)
High Noon (UA, 1952)
The Member of the Wedding (Col., 1952)
From Here to Eternity (Col., 1953)
Oklahoma! (Magna, 1955)
A Hatful of Rain (20th, 1957)
The Old Man and the Sea (WB, 1958) (uncredited, with John
    Sturges and uncredited Henry King)
The Nun's Story (WB, 1959)
The Sundowners (WB, 1960)
Behold a Pale Horse (Col., 1963) (also producer)
Hawaii (UA, 1966) (replaced by George Roy Hill)
A Man for All Seasons (Col., 1967) (also producer)
The Day of the Jackal (Univ., 1973)

ZUGSMITH, ALBERT, b. April 24, 1910, Atlantic City, N.J.
Private Lives of Adam and Eve (Univ., 1960) (with Mickey
    Rooney) (also producer)
College Confidential (Univ., 1960) (also producer)
Sex Kittens Go to College (AA, 1960) (also producer, story)
Dondi (AA, 1961) (also co-producer, co-script)
Confessions of an Opium Eater (AA, 1962)
Dog Eat Dog (German, 1964)
Movie Star American Style, or LSD, I Hate You (Famous
    Players, 1966)
The Chinese Room (Famous Players, 1967) (also co-producer)
The Phantom Gunslinger [Grey Rider] (Famous Players, 1967)
The Very Friendly Neighbors [The Communal Marriage]
    (c. 1971)
The Outrageous Unbelievable Mechanical Love Machine (c. 1971)
Rapist (Famous Players, 1973) (also co-script)

ABOUT THE COMPILERS

JAMES ROBERT PARISH, New York-based freelance writer, was born near Boston on April 21, 1944. He attended the University of Pennsylvania and graduated as a Phi Beta Kappa with a degree in English. A graduate of the University of Pennsylvania Law School, he is a member of the New York Bar. As president of Entertainment Copyright Research Co., Inc. he headed a major researching facility for the film and television industries. Later he was a film interviewer-reviewer for Motion Picture Daily and Variety. He is the author of such books as The Fox Girls, The Paramount Pretties, The Great Movie Series, Actors' Television Credits (1950-1972), The RKO Gals, and Hollywood's Great Love Teams. He is co-author of The Cinema of Edward G. Robinson, The MGM Stock Company, and The Great Spy Pictures.

MICHAEL R. PITTS is the entertainment editor of the Anderson (Ind.) Daily Bulletin and holds a bachelor's degree in history and a master's degree in journalism from Ball State University. Formerly in public education, he has been published in numerous cinema journals, including Focus on Films, Films in Review, Filmograph, Film Fan Monthly, Classic Film Collector, and Cinefantastique. With Mr. Parish he has co-authored The Great Spy Pictures.

WILLIAM T. LEONARD, currently research director for the Free Library of Philadelphia Theatre Collection, has spent many years in theatrical and cinema research, contributing articles to several publications including Films in Review; has written reports for proposed Culture Centers including Lincoln Center for the Performing Arts and was one of the principal contributors of data for the American Film Institute's catalog volume, Feature Films: 1921-1930.

PIERRE GUINLE, born March 10, 1940 in Estagel in the Catalan-speaking part of the south of France, graduated from the Sorbonne with a degree in German. He is now a translator with the C.E.E. in Brussels. He is co-director of the French film magazine Presence du Cinema and has contributed researching data to many cinema journals in Europe and the United States.

NORMAN MILLER is employed by a New York City bank and has been a film buff all his life. He maintains a large private reference library of cinema materials from all over the world, providing a basis for his assistance to cinema scholars everywhere. Side interests in music, art, literature, and castles serve to highlight his film researching endeavors.

FLORENCE SOLOMON, born in New York, attended Hunter College and then joined Ligon Johnson's copyright research office. Later she was appointed director for research at Entertainment Copyright Research Co., Inc. and is currently a reference supervisor at A.S.C.A.P.'s Index Division. Ms. Solomon has collaborated on such works as The American Movies Reference Book, TV Movies, The Great Movie Series, and The George Raft File. She is the niece of the noted sculptor, the late Sir Jacob Epstein.